# SWEETNESS

# SWEETNESS

---

## THE ENIGMATIC LIFE OF
## WALTER PAYTON

---

# JEFF PEARLMAN

GOTHAM BOOKS

GOTHAM BOOKS
Published by Penguin Group (USA) Inc.
375 Hudson Street, New York, New York 10014, U.S.A.
Penguin Group (Canada), 90 Eglinton Avenue East, Suite 700, Toronto, Ontario M4P 2Y3, Canada
(a division of Pearson Penguin Canada Inc.) · Penguin Books Ltd, 80 Strand, London WC2R 0RL,
England · Penguin Ireland, 25 St Stephen's Green, Dublin 2, Ireland (a division of Penguin Books
Ltd) · Penguin Group (Australia), 250 Camberwell Road, Camberwell, Victoria 3124, Australia (a
division of Pearson Australia Group Pty Ltd) · Penguin Books India Pvt Ltd, 11 Community Centre,
Panchsheel Park, New Delhi—110 017, India · Penguin Group (NZ), 67 Apollo Drive, Rosedale,
Auckland 0632, New Zealand (a division of Pearson New Zealand Ltd) · Penguin Books (South
Africa) (Pty) Ltd, 24 Sturdee Avenue, Rosebank, Johannesburg 2196, South Africa

Penguin Books Ltd, Registered Offices: 80 Strand, London WC2R 0RL, England

Published by Gotham Books, a member of Penguin Group (USA) Inc.

First printing, October 2011
1   3   5   7   9   10   8   6   4   2

Gotham Books and the skyscraper logo are trademarks of Penguin Group (USA) Inc.

LIBRARY OF CONGRESS CATALOGING–IN–PUBLICATION DATA
Pearlman, Jeff.
Sweetness : the enigmatic life of Walter Payton / Jeff Pearlman.—1st ed.
p. cm.
Includes index.
ISBN 978-1-59240-653-1 (hardback)
1.  Payton, Walter, 1954–1999.    2.  Football players—United States—Biography.    I.  Title.
GV939.P39P43 2011
796.332092—dc22
[B]

2011011466

Printed in the United States of America
Set in Bembo with Serlio Display        •        Designed by Elke Sigal

# A NOTE ON SOURCING

The identifications of four sources are protected by pseudonyms through this book. They are: Lita Gonzalez, Nigel Smythe, Angelina Smythe, and Judy Choy.

As an author, this is not something I relish. However, the contributions of the individuals were deemed more valuable than the names themselves.

*To Cathy Lieberman*
*The embodiment of strength and compassion*

# CONTENTS

PROLOGUE                                                    *xiii*


## PART ONE
## COLUMBIA

CHAPTER 1       BUBBA                                        *3*
CHAPTER 2       LEARNING THE GAME                            *19*
CHAPTER 3       BLACK AND WHITE                              *29*
CHAPTER 4       THE EMERGENCE                                *38*
CHAPTER 5       RECRUITMENT                                  *54*


## PART TWO
## JACKSON

CHAPTER 6       JACKSON STATE                                *65*
CHAPTER 7       SOUL                                         *82*
CHAPTER 8       CONNIE                                       *95*
CHAPTER 9       HEISMAN HOPES                                *107*


## PART THREE
## CHICAGO

CHAPTER 10      GOING PRO                                    *123*
CHAPTER 11      BIRTH OF SWEETNESS                           *140*
CHAPTER 12      ZERO YARDS                                   *158*

CHAPTER 13    THE WAKE-UP CALL    *172*

CHAPTER 14    THE STRANGEST RUN    *186*

CHAPTER 15    DARKNESS    *207*

CHAPTER 16    THE UNBEARABLE BEARS    *223*

CHAPTER 17    A ROSE IN A DANDELION GARDEN    *244*

CHAPTER 18    POWER    *255*

CHAPTER 19    SHUFFLE    *280*

CHAPTER 20    SUPER LETDOWN    *304*

CHAPTER 21    AFTERMATH    *316*

# PART FOUR

## RETIREMENT

CHAPTER 22    NOW WHAT?    *341*

CHAPTER 23    A BOTTOMLESS VOID    *358*

CHAPTER 24    DEPRESSION    *376*

# PART FIVE

## FINAL

CHAPTER 25    SICK    *393*

CHAPTER 26    THE END    *409*

CHAPTER 27    LEGACY    *417*

CHAPTER 28    AFTERWORD    *424*

ACKNOWLEDGMENTS    *431*

NOTES    *437*

BIBLIOGRAPHY    *467*

INDEX    *471*

Most of life is a falling away.
A gradual surrender of the dream.
The reason sports provide such
dramatic material is that the climax
comes so early in a man's life,
the decline so swiftly.

—"The Athlete," author unknown

PROLOGUE

THE OLD MAN ANSWERED THE DOOR. I DIDN'T SHUDDER OR TAKE A STEP BACK or cringe or gasp or stammer. I simply looked him over, hunched and shriveled inside a fleece jacket, a blue taxi driver's cap pulled low atop his head.

I had been told ahead of time that Walter Payton's administrative assistant would likely greet me at his Hoffman Estates, Illinois, office on this arctic February morning in 1999, and while I didn't picture the person to be a senior citizen, it wasn't beyond the realm of possibilities that Payton—long known for his big heart and common-man sensibilities—would give a seventy-year-old the job.

"And who are you?" the man asked.

"Hi," I said. "I'm Jeff Pearlman with *Sports Illustrated.* I have an appointment."

"Uh . . . yeah," he said. "I suppose you do."

"Yes," I said. "I'm here to see . . ."

Then I stopped.

And gasped.

With a tilt of his head, I noticed something jarring: The old man's eyes were yellow. Not light yellow, either. It appeared as if all the white had been drained from the sclera, replaced by the bright hue of a YIELD sign. That wasn't all. Upon closer inspection, his cheeks were sunken, his shoulders coat-hanger thin, his forearms mere pencils.

He was not old. He was sick.

"Nice to see you," the man said, nodding wearily before extending a hand. "I'm Walter Payton."

. . .

That was the first time I met him.

That was the last time I met him.

We spoke for no more than thirty minutes. He sitting behind a desk, me—twenty-six years old and nervous as all hell—fiddling with my pen and notepad. A couple of days earlier, Payton had announced in a press conference that he was suffering from primary sclerosing cholangitis, a rare disease in which the ducts that drain bile from the liver become inflamed and blocked. It was flabbergasting news—not merely because, at age forty-five, Payton was still relatively young, but because he was the last person you would *ever* think this could happen to.

Forget that Payton was the NFL's all-time rushing leader, or that he is arguably the league's best-ever all-around football player, or that he missed but a single game over thirteen seasons. In the course of researching this book, I've heard five hundred different descriptions of Payton's unparalleled physicality—of the weights he lifted; of the linebackers he pulverized; of the cocksure muscleheads he arm-wrestled to submission; of the grip that, according to an old Bears fullback named John Skibinski, "took hold of you like a vise, until your hand turned blue and numb." My favorite analogy came from one Richard McMurrin, a building superintendent at the Chicago Bears' training complex in Lake Forest, Illinois, and a man not drawn toward exaggeration. "Walter," McMurrin told me, "was like a cannonball with skin stretched over it."

Although he had been retired for twelve years at the time we met, football players old and young still mythologized Payton's Hill—an incline that once stood near his house in Arlington Heights, Illinois. It was just sixty yards long but rose at an angle of 75 degrees, with loose dirt and small rocks and pebbles making footing treacherous. All off-season long, Payton would be sprinting the hill, up and down, up and down, up and down. "He'd invite some of the guys to work with him," said Vince Evans, a former Bears quarterback. "If you hadn't been to the hill before he'd look at you and laugh, because Walter would just climb up that like a bobcat. And you'd follow in his dust. I was a pretty good athlete, so the first time I said, 'This ain't nothing.' Well, halfway up I was sucking air. Once that one was over, he said we were going to do ten more. *Ten?* That was the real eye-opener to this guy's power."

So how the hell did this make sense, me fidgeting before a man who looked nothing like the five foot ten, 205-pound ball of iron from McMurrin's memories? According to the public statements of his doctors, Payton needed a liver transplant to survive beyond two years. That was, it turns out, incorrect. By the time we met, Payton's body was already ravaged by bile duct cancer—an awful byproduct of primary sclerosing cholangitis. His odds of survival? Infinitesimal.

I can only imagine what Payton must have been thinking, staring at a trembling *Sports Illustrated* reporter a mere four years removed from college. "I'm dying, and this is who you send?" He had that right. I was completely unqualified. I knew nothing about liver disease, little about suffering, and even less about death. In the entirety of my life, I had lost only two close relatives—both grandparents in their eighties.

"I'm dying, and this is who you send?"

The interview was mostly me looking down at a sheet of paper with a list of medical terms, reading a few words, then glancing Payton's way and saying, "So, uh . . . eh . . . are you in a lot of pain?" He was polite enough, under the circumstances, but surely as anxious to end things as I was. When my father inquired later that evening what it was like meeting a football player whose poster once graced my bedroom wall, I didn't hesitate. "Worst experience of my life." I sighed. "Like watching a superhero die."

. . .

More than a decade has passed since my visit to Hoffman Estates. In that span, I have gained a wife and two children. I've written four books, penned a slew of bylines, traveled a good chunk of the world. I have seen and lived and smelled and tasted and heard. It has been a mostly blissful ride, packed with enough highs to minimize the scattered lows.

Through the years, interviews have come and interviews have gone. I'll occasionally dig through the yellowed scrapbooks, stumbling upon stories I'd completely forgotten about. Ronnie Duquette, the sneaker collector from Oregon. A Mahopac High School football player named Mark Dessi. Theo Ratliff, gangly 76ers center. On and on.

Never, however, have I forgotten my thirty minutes with Walter Payton.

I can still see the brightness of his jaundiced eyes. I can still feel the frailty of his handshake. Most important, I can still hear his voice from that day—a strained-yet-high-pitched blur of words and phrases. Throughout this process, I have used that voice as a guide.

This is the first time I have written a biography of the deceased, and as other writers warned, the process is incomparable. One doesn't merely become obsessed with the subject. He chases it. Studies it. Craves it. Relentlessly obsesses over it. Dreams about it. Is haunted by it. Just two nights ago I was startled out of a deep sleep by yet another Walter Payton apparition. We were sitting in a vacant apartment. He was wearing a white T-shirt and shorts, with a rainbow-colored headband encircling his radiantly glistening Jheri curl. "Are you finding what you need?" he asked. "Do you get me yet?"

Then he vanished.

The truth is, Walter Payton has been extraordinarily hard to "get." By nearly all accounts he was a giving and compassionate man; one who took pleasure in randomly stopping awestruck Chicagoans on the street to ask how their day was going. His ex-teammates, dating all the way back to the segregated John J. Jefferson High School in Columbia, Mississippi, tell one story after another of a gleeful prankster setting off M-80s in the locker room and using an effeminate-sounding voice to prank call wives with lines like, "Just tell Matt that Pookie called, and our baby needs new shoes."

Yet Payton was also an emotional lockbox. He confided in precious few, and worked tirelessly to portray a certain happy-go-lucky image that belied his deep-seated emotional tumult. His cancer? Nobody's business. His marriage? Nobody's business. His post-NFL despondency that revealed itself in multiple cries for help (including several suicide threats)? Nobody's business. In 2005 his widow, Connie, and the couple's two children, Jarrett and Brittney, released a book, *Payton*, that was rife with inaccuracies—and the authors are three of the people who knew him best. Why, his own autobiography, *Never Die Easy*, is—by the estimates of his closest friends—40 percent fiction.

Just how enigmatic was Walter Payton? When he passed he was remembered at his own funeral for living forty-five productive, energetic years.

Unbeknownst to nearly everyone, he was forty-six.

He was a man whose life was cut tragically short, but who, in the words of Clyde Emrich, former Bears strength coach, "was given ninety years and . . . lived them all in [forty-six]." He trusted most everyone he met, and often paid for it. He never turned down a child's autograph request, and was unconditionally loved for it. His nickname, "Sweetness," was both perfect and misplaced.

"I lockered next to him for six or seven years," said Jay Hilgenberg, the longtime Bears center, "and I got to know him very well. We were friends, and I really loved the man."

Hilgenberg paused. He was sitting inside a golf clubhouse in Kenosha, Wisconsin. He rubbed a chin layered with gray stubble. A perplexed look flashed across his face.

"But do I understand Walter Payton?" he said. Another pause. "No, I don't. I'm not sure anyone does."

⊶⊷

# PART ONE

# COLUMBIA

## Tommy Davis,
### Columbia High School football coach

---

*We were playing Franklin County and we were undefeated and rolling along. That afternoon the visiting team arrived and one of our equipment managers found one of their scouting reports. He brought it in, gave it to me, and they had Walter Payton, number twenty-two, identified as "Billy Joe Badass Himself." I showed that to Walter privately. "Look what they're saying about you," I said. Well, he looked at that and he began to grit his teeth, and you could see the muscles tightening in his jaw. He handed it back to me without saying a word. We went out there and killed Franklin County, twenty-seven to zero, and he scored three touchdowns and kicked three extra points. You just didn't mess with Walter.*

## CHAPTER 1

# BUBBA

CHIP LOFTIN HAD A FESTIVE PARTY ON HIS FIFTH BIRTHDAY.

We know this because, on April 16, 1970, the editors of the *Columbian-Progress*—Columbia, Mississippi's weekly newspaper of record—deemed the affair important enough to warrant a front-page story. There's the headline, right below a black-and-white photograph of l'il Chip, smiling widely beneath an unruly mop of blond hair: CHIP LOFTIN HAS FESTIVE PARTY ON FIFTH BIRTHDAY.

The content of the article is nothing short of riveting. The party was thrown by Chip's mother, Mrs. B. G. Loftin, and was held from three thirty to five P.M. at the city park. "Chip and his friends enjoyed the playground," the piece read, "after which they assembled while he opened and displayed his birthday gifts." Chip's cake, baked by his mom and his aunt Shelby, depicted an automobile racetrack. Chocolate iced cupcakes, ice cream, and punch were also served, "from a picnic table covered with a birthday cloth."

Not that Chip's bash alone dominated the day's news. There were other fascinating front-page stories in the *Progress*; pressing orders of business like LAMPTON HOME LUNCHEON SETTING FOR MISS BERRY and MAY HOMEMAKERS HOLD APRIL MEET. Inside the fourteen-page paper, one could read about the wedding nuptials of Mr. and Mrs. Richard Hulon Davis; about a lovely party at the Fausts' house; about Columbia High School's scrappy baseball team; and a thrilling yard sale one town over.

Founded in 1882 with the merging of two other publications, the newspaper's name—*Progress*—had long dripped of cruel irony. Though in

1970 nearly 30 percent of Columbia's population was black, Lester Williams, the longtime editor and publisher, deemed the happenings of his city's minority denizens to be of little-to-no consequence. Forget covering the ongoing struggle of Mississippi's black population to garner equal footing— the *Progress* refused to acknowledge there *was a struggle*; that, sixteen years after *Brown v. Board of Education of Topeka* deemed separate-but-equal to be illegal, nearly everything in Columbia remained separate and strikingly unequal.

The fact that the owner of Columbia's lone roller rink, Royal Skating, denied blacks entrance? Not newsworthy. The fact that many of the town's physicians refused to see black patients? Not a story. The fact that the town's black high school, John J. Jefferson High, made due with tattered books and subpar materials and toilet seats that occasionally dangled off the rusted hinges? Hardly worthy for print. In the late 1960s, a black teacher named Fred Idom penned an unsolicited guest editorial for the *Progress* about the need for racial improvements within Columbia's schools. Not only did Williams refuse to run the article, he telephoned Roosevelt Otis, Idom's principal, to recommend he be disciplined. Were an outsider to visit Columbia and pick up most copies of the *Progress*, he would think the town was 100-percent white and as gosh-skippity-doo happy as a dimpled Chip Loftin at his fifth birthday celebration.

The truth was significantly more complicated.

Located in the heart of Marion County, Mississippi, a mere 112 miles north of New Orleans, Columbia (population: 7,500), was a town long ruled by expectations. *Met* expectations. If you were black, your house was situated on the north side of Church Street, in a section branded "The Quarters." If you were white, your house was located on the south side of Church Street. If you were black, at one time or another you likely worked at the Columbia Country Club, either caddying, cleaning, or cooking. If you were white, you likely played golf at the Columbia Country Club. If you were black, you did all of your food and household shopping at Jeanette's Grocery, a ragtag storefront on the corner of Owens Street. If you were white, you had the well-stocked, well-maintained Sunflower Food Store.

The unstated yet universally understood rule for the town's blacks was simple: Deal with it. Sure, there'd be the occasional "nigger" or "boy" references. And yes, the Marion County chapter of the Ku Klux Klan took a certain pleasure in lighting crosses in the nearby woods. But as long as one didn't complain, as long as one stayed on the right side of the street and walked with his eyes to the sidewalk and entered through the rear of a restaurant and enjoyed movies from up high in the balcony of the Marion Theatre, nobody from the white areas would pay you much mind.

So that's what Alyne Sibley did.

She was born on January 14, 1926, one of seven children raised on a farm in the rural outpost of Expose, Mississippi. In 1937, Marion County's Historical Society commissioned a detailed look at the region. The 187-page document spanned Columbia's founding in 1812 to its temporary status as the Mississippi state capital in 1821 to the rise of the Ku Klux Klan during the reconstruction period ("the best and most honorable men in the community"), and it spared few words in disparaging blacks. Wrote Maggie Byrd, a Columbia-based historian: "By nature and adaptability, the Negroes are best suited to agriculture. Negroes have done very little along the lines of industry in Marion County except in the field of lumbering. They are better suited to the weather conditions and hard labor than the White neighbor who by nature, by rearing and training is far more sensitive. As skilled workmen, even in the lumber trade Negroes have not proven satisfactory in the past."

Throughout her youth, Alyne was primarily responsible for helping her mother Luola pick cotton. At day's end her fingers would be bloody and raw from the repetition. Her real strength came in the kitchen. "The first meal I ever cooked, I was nine years old," said Alyne, whose long, thin fingers reminded people of sunflower stems. "My mother, she was sick and everybody else was in the field working. I said, 'Momma, I can cook.'" With her mother watching from a nearby seat, Alyne built a fire and prepared string beans, potatoes, corn bread, and fried chicken.

Alyne came to Columbia a decade later, and in 1947 she married Edward Charles Payton, a local laborer who, for reasons family members can't explain, went by Peter. ("In the South," said Eddie, his son, "everyone had a nickname. It's a form of respect.") The Columbia of today bears few distinctions from the hundreds of other desolate, midsize towns across America, what with a half-vacant business district and a landscape of drab gray buildings from long-ago eras. There are good parts and bad parts; corners where small plastic bags of cocaine are passed from dealer to buyer and corners where girls in pigtails and floral dresses sell lemonade for fifty cents per glass. There's a passable library and a handful of stately houses and a long-vacant movie theatre, Cinema II, with a marquee reading WELCOME HOME TROOPS in crooked black letters. At the Round Table restaurant over on Church Street, locals sit at a large revolving table and pass around heaping plates of fried chicken and collard greens. They talk about Jesus Christ and ninety-eight-degree summer days and the upcoming high school football season. Catch one of the city's old white residents in the right mood, and he'll quietly moan about things not being like they used to.

Once upon a time, Columbia was trumpeted across the state as the "City of Charm on the Pearl River." Though hardly a bustling metropolis along the lines of Jackson (the state capital located ninety miles north), it was a location that—thanks to a cozy spot along the east bank of the river—served as an early twentieth-century Mississippi boomtown. A never-ending parade of vessels made the ninety-mile trek along the Pearl River from the Gulf of Mexico to Columbia. Upon arriving, the crews took advantage of Columbia's restaurants, groceries, and appliance stores, then loaded their ships with lumber hauled from Mississippi's vast spans of wilderness (and cut in one of Columbia's handful of sawmills).

Columbia was a place where the camellias and azaleas were plentiful, where original colonial homes lined the streets of many of the fancier neighborhoods, where—thanks to the Gulf breezes—the summer days were mild and the nights surprisingly cool. Were one asked to predict a part of Mississippi that would thrive for years to come, he'd be hard pressed to pinpoint a better location than Columbia.

Alyne and Peter settled into a house on Short Owens Street—a small, white, ranch-styled home with two bedrooms, a den, and a tiny kitchen with beige tiled floors. All the neighbors were black, and a large handful of those were relatives. There was Aunt Helen, who was married to a preacher. There was Uncle Oliver—everyone called him Buck. There was another uncle, B. C., and a third, Uncle Clyde, who became a Muslim and changed his last name from Sibley to X. A cousin, Amos G. Payton, worked at the nearby church. Decades later, Paytons can still be found throughout Columbia's White Pages.

In the summer of 1951, Alyne gave birth for the first time, to a boy named Edward Charles. She and Peter had been trying to have a baby for years, but with little luck. "Back then we didn't have birth control," she said. "I was ready to have a baby, but nothing was happening." Shortly after Eddie's arrival, the family moved to a slightly larger home at 811 Bluff Road. "It was a perfect location," said Eddie. "It was right on the Pearl River, so you could walk outside and fish." Thirteen months later, Eddie's sister, Pamela, was born.

On July 25, 1953, the final child came along. He entered the world in the same way nearly all of Columbia's blacks joined society: on the floor of the house, pulled from his mother by a black midwife. He was named Walter—Walter Jerry Payton. But beginning in his first days, nobody called him that. He was simply "Chubby"—an ode to his robust cheeks and a belly dimensionally akin to a large loaf of sourdough bread. "There weren't many fat kids in the South, so he immediately stood out," said Eddie. "Walter had a chubby face and a chubby body, and you couldn't help but notice it. As he started to thin out a little, the nickname changed. Instead of 'Chubby,' we nicknamed him 'Bubba.' That one stuck."

In the South of the 1950s and '60s—and especially in the black South— children generally went by two names. Eddie wasn't Eddie—he was Edward Charles. Yet Walter Jerry was rarely Walter Jerry. He was "Bubba," and he was, from early on, the ultimate mama's boy. Wherever Alyne went, Bubba followed. He cried when she left him for a few moments, and wailed for her attention when Edward Charles—the more gregarious, more confident, more mischievous child—took a smack at his head or a slap to his behind. "Walter had his mother's personality," said Edna Foster, a family friend. "Real quiet, real soft-spoken, would do anything you asked."

If one had to be poor and black and a Mississippian in the late 1950s, he could do much worse than Bluff Road. Kids were everywhere, dashing barefoot through the neighborhood, fishing gaspergou and catfish along the muddy red banks of the Pearl, planning one adventure after the next. The Payton household was bordered by the river on one side and an enormous pickle processing plant on the other. To most adults, the factory was an eyesore—a gray slab of rank dreariness. Yet for the neighborhood children, it offered a maze of wonderment. Bubba and his playmates would dash among the salt barrels, trying to elude the night watchman. "If either he or your parents caught you running around the pickle plant," Payton once wrote, "you were in for it."

When Walter and his Bluff Road pals weren't weaving through dill stacks, they could often be found at the nearby slaughter pen, where truckloads of cattle and pigs arrived several times per day. To be a kid in Columbia at the time was to be regularly exposed to a certain brand of carnage. There was no squeamishness when it came to killing. Fathers and sons hunted and fished for meals. Mothers and daughters sliced and diced the meat. As soon as the boys heard even the faintest hint of a moo or an oink, they'd charge the pen and climb the iron-barred siding for a peek. The show was bloody, disgusting, and absolutely riveting. One by one, the cows stepped forward, and a man with a sledgehammer slammed them atop the skulls. The pigs received slightly more humane treatment—they were shot in the head with a .22 caliber rifle. Once, in an episode he would recall nearly twenty years later, an enraptured Walter saw a large Brahman bull take two sledgehammers and a .22 caliber shot to the head without falling. "I could watch them slaughter pigs and cows and bulls for hours," he wrote. "I'm convinced that none of those animals felt anything other than fear when they saw another animal go down."

For the boys and girls of Columbia's Quarters, segregation and bigotry failed to crush their youthful vigor. There was an innocent joy to their lives, one that transcended prejudice. They could run through the streets and play football in the fields and experience the same glee as their white counterparts on the other side of town. James Meredith, who in 1962 became the first black to attend the University of Mississippi, explained it perfectly when he said, "I can love Mississippi because of the beauty of the countryside and the old traditions of family affection, and for such small things as flowers bursting in spring, and the way you can see for miles from a ridge in the winter. Why should a Negro be forced to leave such things? Because of fear? No."

The Payton family moved for a third—and final—time in 1962, when Walter was nine, building a house with green siding at 1410 Hendricks Street. Peter, Alyne, and their boys—with the help of Martin Lenoir, Jefferson High's shop teacher—built the home themselves. "I told my children I was going to raise them the way my mother raised me," Alyne said. "They'd say, 'That's old fashioned.' I told them, 'That's OK, I'm going to do it anyway.' You don't change things because you won't know what you're doing."

The Payton house was the largest on the block. It also happened to be located directly behind John J. Jefferson High, giving the kids access to a limitless play space. Walter and Eddie were forced to share a small bedroom in the back of the house. "It was a plain room," said Eddie. "We had a bunk bed, with Walter on top and me on the bottom. There were no posters on the wall. Pretty simple."

In black Columbia, neighbors watched neighbors and everyone knew everyone. The houses were modest and the businesses limited. ("We didn't have shops on the black side of town," said Eddie. "We had joints. Clubs, barbershops, places like that.") The community pulled together to keep its children out of trouble and away from any of the white sections of town where potential conflict awaited. Doors were left unlocked, and friends could drop in unannounced. "Whenever I fried chicken, Walter would smell it, come on in, grab three pieces, and eat," said Earnestine Lewis, a neighbor. "He was a very nice, very mannerly little boy. Always 'Yes m'am, no m'am.'"

Both Alyne and Peter spent Mondays through Fridays working at Pioneer Recovery Systems, a plant where military-supply parachutes were stitched together and shipped off in bulk to the U.S. government. Their workdays were split—Peter, a custodian, usually clocked in before the morning-to-early afternoon shift, then returned home and Alyne, who did assembly line work, would take the four to eleven P.M. block. When she wasn't at the plant, Alyne held jobs in the houses of various white families, looking after their children, cleaning their laundry, mopping floors. On weekends, Peter made extra money by setting up a wood block on a corner of Owens Street and shining shoes for fifty cents a pair as blacks strolled to church. He also manned a five-acre garden on the outskirts of town, often bringing one of his sons along to operate the hand plow. ("We didn't have a mule," Walter once complained. "It was *hard* work.") Alyne, meanwhile, spent her Saturdays cooking pancakes at the Columbia Country Club, where whites ate and blacks labored. "She made the most delicious pancakes you've ever tasted," said Earnestine Lewis. "I used to tell her, 'Miss Alyne, you could be famous if you put those on the market.'" In later years Walter would bemoan growing up poor, but among Columbia's blacks the Paytons were comfortable. As the one in charge of family monies, Alyne religiously collected the weekly paychecks and deposited them in the local bank. The Paytons made few frivolous purchases, and worked as many hours as humanly possible.

One of the results, of course, was that both parents were permanently exhausted, with the slumped shoulders and baggy eyes to prove it. "We didn't have a babysitter," Alyne said. "They were always with me unless I was at choir or usher rehearsal [or work]. Then [my husband] would be home with them." Every Sunday morning, whether the children wanted to or not, Alyne dressed Edward Charles, Walter, and Pam in their most dapper outfits and walked them four blocks to the Owens Chapel Baptist Church, a nondescript redbrick building with a crucifix hanging above the entranceway. The pastor was Reverend Eli Payton, a distant cousin. Sunday school began at nine A.M., followed by services from ten thirty to one o'clock. The three children sang in the choir, and in the tradition of old-school black Southern Baptist ways, the services mixed hellfire preaching with transcendent singing. Alyne's children stood alongside their mother, Edward Charles occasionally looking away to stomp atop his brother's shiny brown loafers or elbow Walter's rib cage. When services ended, the family returned home for lunch, followed by the weekly two P.M. episode of *Tarzan* on channel 3. "When *Tarzan* was over," Walter once wrote, "the kids in the neighborhood burst from their houses, screen doors slamming, parents yelling, 'Quit slamming that door!' and all of us bellowing the Tarzan call." At five P.M. they'd return for evening services, which lasted another three hours.

Though she held no elected position or official post, Alyne was a central figure in Columbia's black community. She dispensed pearls of wisdom ("Never give your kids soda." "Rise early, sleep early, work hard."), advised her friends, helped whenever help was needed. When Archie Johnson, Walter's pal, describes Alyne as "remarkable," he echoes a sentiment shared by many. "Everyone loved Walter's mama," said Johnson. "One thing I remember is that she was really into making her home look nice. During the fall she'd drive out to the country, to a rural area called Hawthorne where some of her family lived. We'd ride up with her, and on the way she'd inevitably want to stop and get us to pick the cattails for her.

"Nothing about her life was haphazard. Everything was organized. She had a plan."

Alyne served as a church usher and was the leader, nurturer, and moral guide of the family. Peter, in turn, was the disciplinarian. Though only five foot five and maybe 140 pounds, with dark skin and unusually long fingers, Peter demanded respect from his children, both with his scowl and his belt. Docile in his day-to-day demeanor, Peter seemed to derive his greatest pleasure from meeting up with his closest friend, a neighbor named Brady Lewis, for a couple of hours in the backyard. There the two would lounge on a pair of lawn chairs, telling stories and polishing off a couple of dollar-fifty glass bottles of grape-flavored Mad Dog 20/20 until they were drunk. Because Columbia was a dry town, the two tried keeping their ritual a secret. But everyone knew. "Walter's dad was real quiet and agreeable," said Robert Virgil, who grew up with Walter and Eddie. "I remember his dad used to come to my house, and he'd help us kill a chicken or a hog. Then he'd drink his Mad Dog." Peter wasn't merely known by his first name. With the exception of his wife and kids, he was "Peter Payton" to everyone, in all circumstances. "Peter Payton didn't do no harm, and he wasn't a bad man, but we called him the town drunk, because he seemed to be drinking his Mad Dog all the time," said Earnestine Lewis. "No one ever bothered him because he never bothered nobody, but it was always the same thing—Peter Payton being drunk, Peter Payton stumbling around. Sometimes Miss Alyne would holler at him, make him come inside the house. He'd yell back, 'Oh, Alyne! Let me be!' But then he would always obey her. She wore the pants."

If Peter Payton's drinking created major problems, none of his kids seemed aware of it. If anything, the booze made him even more taciturn. Upon arriving home from wherever he might have been, Peter—voice as gentle as a pillow, if not a tad slurred—would review the day's events with his wife. They would share a bite to eat, watch some television. Then, if the two agreed that someone had behaved in an untoward manner, he calmly approached the offending child—rarely Pam, sometimes Walter, often Eddie—and said, simply, "Go out in the yard and get a switch." The soon-to-be victim would return with a thick stick (thin branches were unacceptable), then bend over, pants pulled down around the ankles.

When Peter Payton rolled up his shirtsleeves and grabbed the switch, it was all business. In the best-case scenario, a session lasted only four or five swings. Occasionally the stick snapped. "Then he'd go and get the belt," Eddie said. "It was leather, and it didn't break.

"Daddy was slick," Eddie continued. "We'd go to bed, and we'd think maybe a punishment wasn't coming. Then it'd be about eleven o'clock at night and you'd feel the blanket snatched from over you. You'd be in bed, curled up against a wall with nowhere to go."

It was an understood form of behavioral control at a time when black parents feared white reaction to unruliness among their offspring. Columbia's white population was, by Mississippi standards, mostly cordial toward the town's blacks. In August 1955, a fourteen-year-old boy named Emmett Till had been murdered in Money, Mississippi, for reportedly whistling at a white woman. In 1964, three political activists—one black, two Jewish—were lynched during a drive to Longdale, Mississippi. In Columbia, there was certainly intimidation and modest violence, but little more. If you were black, and you followed the societal script, you were largely left alone.

Alyne and Peter raised their children well, and took no chances. As the kids aged, their nonscholastic hours were filled with activities. Board games like Monopoly, Pokeno, and Chinese Checkers were rainy-day household staples.

Walter enjoyed two years as a Boy Scout—especially the camping outings along the Pearl River, when the boys would bring along their rifles and shoot water moccasins before leaping into the water. He took numerous fishing trips with his father and brother, spent several years developing into a credible schoolyard marbles player, and also had a brief passion for painting and spinning wood tops.

A brown upright piano stood in the corner of the den, and Eddie and Pam learned to play. Walter showed minimal interest in the instrument, opting instead for the drums. "He was a great drummer from a young age," said Eddie. "We didn't actually have a drum set in our house when he was very little, but he beat on anything you could make sound from. Books, tables, cans. Anything."

In the summertime, as other neighborhood kids ran from yard to yard seeking adventure, the Payton boys were put to work. Miss Alyne was not about to have her sons find trouble, so she made sure they were always occupied. An avid gardener, Alyne celebrated the end of each school year by having a local farmer deliver a mountain of dirt and dump it in the driveway. For the ensuing two months, Eddie and Walter were responsible for shoveling and pushing the topsoil over the entire yard, as well as applying fertilizer. Alyne's goal was to win the *Columbian-Progress'* Yard of the Week award (she eventually did). "It rains like you wouldn't believe during the summer in Mississippi, and the whole yard would get wet," Walter once said. "That caused the wheelbarrow to sink in the wet soil. We'd have to put boards throughout the yard and push the wheelbarrow to the end of them. I'd fill it, Eddie would pick it up and take it out and dump it, and Mama or Pam would spread it. At the time we thought it was good for the yard. We, or at least I, didn't know until much later that Mom had the topsoil delivered to keep us out of trouble in the summer. If you want my opinion, there was no reason to spread all that topsoil except to keep us occupied and around the house.

"[My mother is] probably the reason I'm so muscular. I was the one who did the shoveling. You can tell that by looking at my arms. [Eddie] pushed the wheelbarrow. You ought to see the muscles in his legs."

Though he gravitated toward his mother, much of Walter's demeanor came from his father. He was the rare child who was content to be left alone; who didn't need playmates or toys to keep him entertained. Often without company, Walter would dash through the woods, imagining himself as Robin Hood or Spider-Man or Zorro. "I rode pretend horses, swung on pretend vines, wore pretend outfits, shot pretend bandits," he wrote. "A woods could be anything I wanted it to be. I loved to climb trees . . . I liked to be up there, above everything, looking down, in control, having done the impossible, saved the kingdom, loved for the right, for justice and for truth."

Unlike his soft-spoken younger brother, Eddie always had a flock. His nickname was "Chief," appropriately coined because other kids followed his lead. If Eddie decided to hold an impromptu baseball game in the street, he was never alone. Walter often proved to be a perfect sidekick. When both boys were still young, one of their cousins, a pretty woman named Evelyn Carter, was dating Brady Lewis. If Eddie and Walter knew in advance the couple would be returning to Lewis' house, the brothers would tiptoe inside and hide behind his couch. "They'd listen to us talk," said Lewis, "and whenever I went to kiss Evelyn, they'd jump out and scare us."

When Eddie was twelve and his brother nine, the two boys snuck up the road to the home of Reverend LeRoy Hendricks, a local preacher. The house was surrounded by three towering plum tress. On most days, Eddie and Walter would look longingly at the plump fruit, hoping (never to avail) that a plum or two would somehow magically fall off a tree and fly into their arms. On this day, Eddie goaded Walter into crawling beneath the fence surrounding Hendricks' yard, grabbing as many pieces of fruit as possible, then running home. "Reverend Hendricks saw us," Eddie said. "But he only saw one of us, and he didn't know which one it was. So I had an idea." Eddie told Walter that, inevitably, their father would come home from work, hear the story, and select one of the boys for a beating. "Right when Daddy starts hitting one of us, the other has to walk in and confess," he said. "Daddy will think it's great we're telling the truth, and he'll let us both go!"

As soon as Peter arrived inside the house, Alyne informed him of what had transpired. He stared down both boys, then grabbed Walter by the collar and took him to a back room. Just as he drew back the switch, Walter wailed, "I did it Daddy! I did it! But Edward Charles was with me, too! He was right there!"

Both boys were pummeled. "That was the worst ass-whuppin' we ever got," Eddie said. "Both of us."

Not quite. Although Alyne spent most of her time either working, cooking, or gardening, her hobby was collecting old coins. Whenever Alyne stumbled upon a vintage piece of currency, she'd place it to the side and save it. "I had four to five hundred silver dimes," she once said. "And 'V' nickels." One day, little Walter figured out that his mother was stashing the loot in a closet by the staircase. "First he tries to pick the lock," Pam, his sister, recalled. "Then he just got a hammer and beat off the door." Walter filled up his pockets, taking—among other valuables—his mother's prized 1805 silver dollar. "That evening I lined everyone up," Alyne said. "I knowed who got the money. Who spent those dimes. But they had to tell me. My husband, he saw the whites in my eyes and without a word he went out and got a switch and started plaiting it. They were all sitting there looking pitiful. Pam and [Eddie] kept saying, 'Walter, why don't you tell Daddy you've got the money?' And Walter, he'd just sit there with a straight face and say, 'Why don't you tell Daddy you've got it?' "

Finally, after failing to elicit an admission, Peter Payton lined up his three children. He started with Walter, and unleashed a beating remarkable for its power and duration. "Before he was through Walter fessed up," Pam said. "So the others didn't have to get whipped."

Eddie and Walter took special delight in tormenting Pam, an easy target for the two boys. The brothers would wedge a bucket of water above her door, then wait for Pam to walk through and have it spill atop her head. In the middle of the night they scratched against her wall and made spooky sounds. "But the best thing we ever did," said Eddie, "is we put this sheet outside her window, then started shaking it back and forth like a ghost. She freaked out . . . probably didn't sleep for a month."

Years later, when Walter was asked how he developed his football skills, he thought back to the torturing of Pam. "When you have an angry sister chasing you with a broom and a wet dishrag," he said, "you pick up moves you never had before."

· · ·

In a typical sports narrative, Walter Payton should be a star athlete from the very beginning—the fastest, strongest, toughest, most hard-nosed fella on the black side of Columbia. He should be the can't-miss kid; the hero in the making, bestowed with an uncanny greatness perfectly suited for a future in the NFL or NBA or major leagues.

With Payton, there is little of that. He certainly wasn't uncoordinated. The speed was good, the strength above average. But in the fall of 1960, as he entered the first grade at the segregated John J. Jefferson High School,* Walter was merely one of thirty-two black faces in Mrs. Vonceal McLaurin's class. He was

---

* Oddly, though the school educated kindergarteners through seniors, it was formally named "John J. Jefferson High School."

on the short side, with closely cropped hair, noticeably dark skin, and wildly expressive eyes the size of his mother's homemade chocolate chip cookies. Two years earlier, Eddie had begun his schooling at Jefferson, and the staff of gym teachers had immediately recognized something special in the boy. Walter, by comparison, merely existed. Whereas Eddie ran with the power of a motorcycle, Walter glided along, content to be just one of the kids. Eddie carried himself as a champion. Walter did not. If he longed to excel in sports, it was a tightly kept secret. "We didn't have any great equipment or sandboxes at Jefferson, so the only games we played at recess were tag and different races," said Archie Johnson, Walter's classmate and friend. "Walter was good, don't get me wrong. But we all knew about Eddie and everything he could do. Walter didn't touch that."

Over on the white side of town, young boys were being introduced to the joy of organized sports. There was Pop Warner football and Little League baseball. On spring and summer evenings, parents and kids alike congregated at Columbia City Park, an oasis of manicured grass and neatly placed dirt where the echoing of cheers could be heard from far away. Participants were supplied with bright red and green and yellow and blue uniforms, with names like PANTHERS and TIGERS and REDS screen printed across the chests. Afterward, everyone would retreat to Cook's Dairy Delight on High School Avenue, where Lucille Cook (known to all as just "Miss Cook") served up her renowned dressed jumbo hamburgers and fresh-squeezed lemonade to the white boys and girls. Were the day especially hot, some might stroll to the town pool, cleaned daily and exclusively white.

Most black kids did not feel slighted, mainly because they knew no better. Cook's Dairy Delight? Little League? Did those things even exist? What the black side of town lacked in grassy knolls and new bats and mitts and helmets, it made up for in spirit. Instead of wallowing in self-pity over what they understood to be shoddy conditions, black teachers and coaches encouraged their kids to combine the resources at hand with the power of youthful imagination. Jefferson's playground was limited to a slide and the remnants of a wood swing. But running space was plentiful. "We didn't have any feeding systems," said Charles Boston, Jefferson's varsity football coach. "We didn't have junior high ball or Pop Warner—the white kids had all of that. In fact, we barely had enough equipment to field a high school team. What we did have was that when the bell rang at eight o'clock in the morning, and then two hours later again for recess, all the boys would end up in a football game."

"We all played football in the yard," said Edward Moses, Walter's childhood friend. "We used to go run in the woods, jump over ditches. We'd run straight down a row of corn in a cornfield, and when the corn was dry it'd really test your balance. If we were missing out on anything, I don't think we knew it."

In the spirit of his father, Walter remained mostly quiet during his first few years of school. Though occasionally mischievous, he mainly sat in class, capably doing his schoolwork and pining for recess. He wasn't one to sit up front, or raise his hand, or jump at the chance to show off his smarts. Nor was he one to fire spitballs at the blackboard. He was, in all senses of the word, ordinary. "Eddie loved school and he loved football," said Alyne. "Now Walter, he was different. He never let you know what he was interested in. He'd watch people, and then do whatever that person did better."

In 1963, when Walter was ten, a man named Ezekiel Graves spearheaded a movement to bring organized Little League to Columbia's black children. "Every year a couple of black families would come to the town's Little League sign-up day," recalled Colleen Crawley, a white contemporary of Walter's. "And they'd always be turned away." The local government denied Graves' request to have the games played at Columbia City Park, so he settled on a field outside the poorly maintained Duckworth Recreation Center. Walter was drafted by the team sponsored by Columbia Electric, a little store located downtown. The uniforms were green and white, and Walter wore No. 11 and played first base. His best friends were his teammates—Michael "Dobie" Woodson at second, Moses (who went by "Sugar Man") at shortstop, and Johnson in right field. The team played against other black Little Leagues in Marion County, and Walter fit right in. "I was OK in the field, but I couldn't hit the ball," said Johnson. "But Walter could hit the ball hard, and he was a good fielder. He looked athletic, even when we were young."

Because he was routinely compared to his faster, stronger, more developed and more gregarious older brother, classmates and teachers tended to overlook Walter's abilities. "Eddie was cocky, and Walter wasn't," said Robert Virgil. "Walter was soft-spoken, and Eddie had this incredible vocabulary, where he knew every word the teachers asked. It would be hard to have an older brother like that and not go unnoticed." Yet as he aged, going from elementary school to junior high, Walter's athleticism began to blossom. To start with, he was uncommonly strong, with a grip that drained the color from others' hands, and stumpy-yet-powerful legs that churned like a cement mixer. Walter never tinkered with weights (at black schools like Jefferson

High, the very idea of any sort of weight room was laughable), but he developed early—the muscles along his chest and forearms beginning to sprout at age twelve. "Walter got big, and we could no longer handle him physically," said Eli Payton, a classmate and distant cousin.* "It happened overnight."

During recess, Walter and his peers played outside the school. On Sundays, he and a gaggle of friends headed over to Westerfield Park for violent pickup games of tackle football. Walter insisted on playing quarterback, and he did so brilliantly. His arm was a cannon, his feet light and quick. Most impressive, he broke out a move previously unseen at Jefferson; an unstoppable little device where, when a tackler approached, Walter lifted one of his arms and forcefully jabbed the kid in the sternum. THUD! "That's the first time any of us saw the stiff-arm," said Woodson. "Thing was deadly."

"I look back at my style of playing football, and that evolved from my childhood because I loved the game of war," Walter once said. "When I held the football and somebody was going to take my football, I was going to hit them back first. I worked for that position and I wasn't giving it up or backing down. . . . I started then learning how to juke and spin and make me impossible to catch. That all came from my childhood. That is something that a coach did not instill in me, that particular style."

While Walter enjoyed sports, his apparent calling—one vigorously pushed by his parents—was music. For their middle child's seventh birthday, Alyne and Peter bought a drum set, then spent the ensuing years having their eardrums pulverized. What Jefferson High lacked in organized athletics, it made up for with a spirited music program that put the all-white Columbia High to shame. Beginning in sixth grade, Jefferson's students could audition for the school's dynamic marching band. Alongside Johnson, who mastered the trumpet, Walter tried out as a drummer/bongo player. Both made the cut. "It was thrilling," said Johnson. "The band gave us a way to travel and go places. The football team had a rigorous schedule, so the band did, too." Walter was eleven years old at the start of his sixth-grade year, and up until that point he'd rarely left the Marion County limits. Thanks to band, on September 11, 1964, he traveled via bus to Jackson, where the Jefferson High Green Wave faced the Jim Hill High School Tigers. Years later, Walter remembered little of the on-field action—the score, the stars, the uniform colors. What he could not forget, however, was the feeling of being there; of

---

* Not to be confused with Eli Payton the preacher, another cousin.

performing music before a large crowd; of seeing people stomp and clap and cheer. It was true love.

Though he never fully learned to read music, Walter could hear a song once or twice and immediately play it to perfection. Because Mississippi's black high schools were spread out across the state, the marching band made its way alongside the football team north and south, east and west. "We went to Biloxi, we went to Picayune," said Johnson. "We'd go to high-powered schools with great bands, and we'd show 'em how it's done."

By the time Walter entered the seventh grade, Eddie Payton was officially a local star. He was popular, funny, cocky, and good with the girls. Decked out in his band uniform, Walter Payton couldn't compete. He was merely a kid with a snare drum.

Then, one day, a man holding a whistle changed his life.

CHAPTER 2

# LEARNING THE GAME

HIS MEMORY IS FOGGY. UNDERSTANDABLY SO. IT HAS BEEN MORE THAN FORTY years since Charles Boston initially laid eyes on the thirteen-year-old boy with the tears streaming down his cheeks. In the decades that followed, kids have come and kids have gone. Many have graduated college, some have dropped out of high school. Most are alive. Too many are deceased. There are parents and grandparents, doctors and lawyers and garbagemen and street sweepers and drug dealers.

"Hard to keep track," Boston said. "Time flies."

This, however, the former head football coach at John J. Jefferson High School remembers. This, he will never forget.

"The first time I saw Walter Payton?" Boston said. "Well, it was pretty obvious he was no ordinary kid."

The year was 1966. Though it had been twelve long years since the United States Supreme Court had declared racially separate public schools to be unconstitutional, nobody in the state of Mississippi paid the ruling much mind. So Jefferson High School remained what it had always been—underfunded, lacking resources, and, to Columbia's vast white population, irrelevant.

Walter Payton was an eighth grader, known in small pockets of the school either for his drumming or, more likely, for his relation to Eddie Payton. The brothers were separated by three grades; by this time Eddie was a certifiable star and the talk of Jefferson High athletics. Unlike his demure sibling, Eddie had it all. He dated the prettiest girls, hung out with the coolest kids, walked with a can't-touch-this swagger. Though he was known to goof off and crack jokes in class, Eddie was largely given a free pass by teachers—a nod to his status.

In the summers, Eddie was signed by a couple of local black semipro baseball teams, the Columbia Jets and the Laurel Blue Sox, earning ten dollars a game in return for his line drives into the gaps and smooth glove at shortstop. He played varsity baseball and basketball at Jefferson, and excelled in both. "Truth is, in high school Eddie was faster than Walter and tougher than Walter," said Charles Virgil, a classmate. "He was only about five foot six, yet he could stand flatfooted directly under the basket, jump up, and dunk the ball." It was on the gridiron where Eddie Payton truly excelled, emerging as one of the state's best halfbacks. Just how good was Eddie? Columbia High's white players flocked to Gardner Stadium to see Payton in action. "We'd all go and sit in the northeast stands and just be blown away," said Steve Stewart, Columbia High's standout linebacker. "He was so much better than anything we had. Eddie Payton was the best football player I'd ever seen. He did things none of us could imagine."

And what of Walter? The head coach of Jefferson High School, Charles Boston, had been aware that somewhere within the building's confines his all-everything halfback had a younger brother. But it wasn't until an otherwise nondescript weekday afternoon that knowledge and reality collided. Boston, who also served as Jefferson's assistant principal, was sitting in his office, looking over some papers, when he was told that a junior high student was crying in the courtyard.

"Who is it?" he asked.

"Oh, just Eddie Payton's little brother."

Boston ran out to find Walter, all of five foot five, withering in pain on the ground. He had snapped his collarbone in a game of sandlot football, and his left arm now dangled like a fork on a string. "He's crying and crying and crying," said Boston. "So I picked him up, called his mother, and took him to Marion County General Hospital."

Throughout the long, gray hallways of Jefferson High School, everyone knew Charles Boston, and Charles Boston knew most everyone. Granted, he was the assistant principal, as well as the football coach. But it was more than that. In Boston, Jefferson's students found an advocate; a man who genuinely believed that, despite reason to think otherwise, young black boys and young black girls could emerge from a bitterly racist society to accomplish their goals. "Mr. Boston was the perfect example of the strong black male who was comfortable with himself because he never needed a white person to lean on," said Edward Moses, Walter's classmate and friend. "He didn't need a title, and he didn't need anyone to anoint him a leader. He led by nature. It was his gift." Born in the impoverished town of Laurel, Mississippi, in 1933, Boston was one of ten siblings in a family renowned for athletic excellence. An older brother, Peter, was perhaps the best wide receiver Laurel had ever produced. His little brother, Ralph, would go on to win a gold medal in the long jump at the 1960 Olympic Games in Rome. For one remarkable twelve-year stretch, there was always a Boston brother playing on the Oak Park High School varsity football team. "People accused the school of using the same guy for all those years," said Charles, who excelled in football and basketball. "We all punted, so that raised suspicions. But when Peter was in high school, he weighed a hundred eighty pounds. I was one-forty."

If Boston took one thing from his prep football experience, it was that brutal coaching methods—at the time a staple of black Southern football—were unnecessary. From the sidelines, Boston watched opposing coaches smack their players, punch their players, kick their players. Although Russell Frye, Oak Park's coach, occasionally laid his hands on others, he never touched Boston. "I told him I'd do the absolute best I could," he said, "but that I wasn't going to be abused." Boston was a good enough player for Frye to comply.

In 1959, following four years of football at Alcorn Agricultural and Mechanical College (later known as Alcorn State University), Boston was hired as a gym teacher/football coach by (tiny) Carver High School in (tiny) Bassfield, Mississippi. He was twenty-two years old, and he was greeted on his first day by a team with twenty-two players and seventeen ragtag uniforms. "We won three games that first year, and I was sure I'd be fired," Boston said. "I'd played on two championship teams in Laurel, and I was used to winning. But the people in Bassfield were so happy with me winning three games that they wanted to name me mayor." The following year, mighty John J. Jefferson High traveled eighteen miles to Bassfield to face Boston's team, which now only had seventeen active players. "Somehow we whipped them, nine to six," said Boston. "And everything changed."

In 1963, Jefferson High was led by a sports-crazed principal named W. S. MacLauren. Though the black schools could never match their white counterparts in scholarship winners or academic achievement or future college graduates, there was an unspoken goal of stepping ahead in athletics. Columbia High would, of course, never acknowledge Jefferson's on-field achievements. But Jefferson's staff and players *knew* they could be the better program. Hence, in the aftermath of the young coach from Bassfield showing up his team, MacLauren presented Boston, a married father of two, an offer he could not refuse: a four-hundred-dollar raise and the chance to continue teaching P.E.

Boston accepted—and the blacks of Columbia quickly turned against their new leader. The previous coach at Jefferson was Scott Jones, an ornery, unpleasant little man who wore a pair of spiked-toed shoes to practice in order to kick players who made boneheaded mistakes. Jones also kept a two-by-four piece of wood in hand, and never thought twice about slamming it into backsides. Such was what parents in the black communities expected of their leaders; a tougher-than-dirt approach to discipline. If your son came home from practice with black-and-blue welts across his arms and legs, well, he surely deserved it.

Boston never physically abused a player at Bassfield, and he would not do so at Jefferson. "I thought I was doing right," he said. "To get a guy in front of eight hundred people at a game and kick him . . . that has to be degrading." Boston won four games in his first season at Jefferson, and fared little better the next two. In the community, he was increasingly dismissed as a softie. But the players loved and respected him. Boston was the rare male authority figure who didn't do his talking with the backside of a hand. He drove his players home after practices and games, found them jobs in the community, and checked on their schoolwork. "When I played for Coach Boston I lived way north of Columbia, so on some days I wouldn't get home from school until ten or eleven at night," said Joe Owens, a former Jefferson lineman who went on to spend seven years in the NFL. "One day he showed up with a car—a 1954 Chevrolet Bel Air—and he let me keep it. I dropped off all the guys who lived in the rural areas, and we were all home by eight. He changed the whole way people thought about sports and attitudes toward players."

The following season, Jefferson's football team was graced by the arrival of the transcendent Eddie Payton, who teamed with a fullback named Ray Holmes to give the Green Wave one of the state's best backfields. With Eddie as the star, Jefferson won thirty-four games over four years. "Eddie changed a lot for us," said Boston. "He was the type of kid you hope for. Simply put, he was a ballplayer. He was short, but I used him at middle linebacker. I'd walk him up on that center's ear, and if you weren't ready Eddie would be all over you. And on offense, he was just unstoppable running the ball. I went from a dumb coach to a smart one overnight." Over time Boston developed an intimate relationship with the Payton family—he lived a few houses down on Hendricks Street, and gave Eddie a job playing alongside him on the Laurel Blue Sox (Boston was an accomplished semipro baseball player). On his daily walk to school, Boston would chat with Alyne and Peter. They embraced him as someone who had their sons' best interests at heart. "He was a good man," said Eddie. "He was very, very decent."

Walter, however, remained an enigma. He was attached to his mother—Boston could see that. And unlike Eddie, he didn't share absolutely every thought that floated through his cranium. "They were apples and oranges all the way down the line," said Moses, Walter's friend and classmate. "Eddie would find himself as the leader of any group he was a part of. Walter was much more laid-back—his leadership came from his gifts." Classmates told Boston that the boy was a secret prankster, but it was hard to see. The kid was so . . . *quiet.* On Jefferson's fields, he would run circles around the other boys, ducking, weaving, bobbing, slicing, juking, escaping. His moves were distinctly artistic and ethereal, so much so that a ridiculous rumor started about Walter Payton taking ballet classes after school.

And yet, as Walter Payton began his freshman year of high school in the fall of 1967, he showed little interest in organized football. He was a music guy; firmly entrenched as a drummer in both Jefferson's concert and marching bands. When asked about the gridiron, he mostly shrugged dismissively and noted, "That's Eddie's world. Not mine."

So what changed between his freshman and sophomore years? What pushed him toward organized football? In a word: Eddie. Or, to be more precise, Eddie's departure. Walter's older brother graduated from John J. Jefferson High in the spring of 1968, earning a prized football scholarship to Jackson State College, one of the best black schools in the nation. No longer, Walter believed, would he be measured against the Big Man on Campus. No longer would he have to meet the standards set by his sibling. "I followed an older brother who starred in my sport," said Boston. "And I can tell you one thing—it's thankless."

In the waning days of summer, 1968, Walter took part in organized football workouts for the first time. With the stifling Mississippi sun beating down on his shoulders, he trudged out to Jefferson High's practice field for the daily eleven A.M. gatherings. His shoulder pads were grayish and scuffed, likely hand-me-downs from Columbia High. There was a box of white jerseys in a large cardboard box, and each day the players would pick one randomly. Walter could be No. 2 one day, No. 23 the next. (Once the season started, he was assigned No. 22, which had belonged to Eddie. Whether he was happy about this or not, we'll never know. But he didn't complain.)

Out on the sandlots, the game had come easily to Walter—run fast, run hard, score. But now there were whistles blowing, coaches yelling, designated plays to follow. "The first time I got the ball in practice and heard all those footsteps coming, I panicked," he wrote in his 1978 autobiography. "I had visions of getting ground into the turf under the weight of a half-dozen huge upperclassmen towering over me, so I scooted to daylight and ran for my life." Walter, however, was running the wrong way. He scored for the opposing unit.

Boston stormed onto the field and lectured his new back. He demanded the play be run again. This time, Payton scooted through the wrong hole, where he was met by an oncoming linebacker. "I just stopped," he wrote, "in embarrassment." Despite the miscues, Boston had a soft spot for the green running back. Payton was physically gifted and eager to learn. He didn't talk trash, wasn't lazy, and never took a play off. "He was fun to have there," Boston said. "You liked being around him."

Even with a regal last name and an increasingly statuesque body, Walter was handed nothing. With Eddie's departure, Boston made it clear that the number-one halfback would be Everett Farr, a modestly talented senior with limited moves but an energetic approach. None of Walter's friends remember him complaining or being especially upset. Boston pulled him aside and assured him his day would come. In the meantime, he bided his time by starting at strong safety and checking in for Farr when the senior needed a breather.

In 1968 the Green Wave finished 7-3. Late in the season, in a game against Marion Central, Farr broke his foot, and Payton stepped into the starting lineup. His impact was minimal. According to memories, he scored four or five touchdowns and ran for anywhere between two hundred and four hundred yards. In his autobiography, Payton wrote of starting the first game of the season and being named to the league All-Star team. Neither recollection was real. "He was good," said Moses, who also played running back. "But we all had to learn the game."

Those in the know, however, couldn't contain their excitement. In Walter, Boston saw a bigger (Walter was five foot six as a junior, Eddie had been five foot four), stronger version of his brother. He was also significantly more versatile. Walter punted the ball beyond forty yards. He could kick twenty-five- to thirty-yard field goals. He tackled well, and was a knockdown defensive back. In his coach's mind, Payton had *It*—that certain undefined something that separates great from very good. "He was bursting with ability," Boston said. "If you knew football, you knew that much."

. . .

When Walter returned for his junior year at Jefferson, there was little ambiguity about the identification of the school's star athlete. Along with continuing his drumming in the concert band (he had given up marching band for football), Walter ran the hundred-yard dash for the track team, and played forward in basketball and shortstop in baseball.

Carrying the football, however, was Payton's gift. Boston favored the T-formation offense, and his junior class of players presented some titillating possibilities. The new quarterback was Archie Johnson, an honors student and future valedictorian who possessed a strong arm and quick feet. The left back was Moses, a small, spindly boy who happened to run like lightning. The right back was Michael Woodson, as quick as they came. And lining up directly behind Johnson, technically as the fullback, was Walter Payton.

"We were really frightening," said Johnson.

Just how good was Payton as a high school junior? On October 30, 1969, the *Columbian-Progress* actually ran his portrait above the following paragraph:

Walter Payton, a Junior [sic] at John Jefferson High School was chosen Player of the Week for his performance in the Travillion game. Payton . . . scored three touchdowns in the Greenwaves [sic] 46 to 0 victory over Travillion. He is the son of Mr. and Mrs. Edward Payton of 14010 [sic] Hendricks Street, Columbia.

The photograph, apparently taken in front of Jefferson High, shows a serious Payton. He is neither frowning nor smiling, but staring blankly into space, perhaps wondering whether this *Columbian-Progress* photo shoot is some sort of joke. In all his years at Jefferson, Eddie's picture had never appeared in the *Progress*.

For the first time ever, the whites in Columbia were talking about Jefferson High's football team. The innovative Jefferson offense combined blinding speed with sharp cuts, funky patterns, and innovative play calling. Payton and Moses even gave themselves their own nicknames—Payton was "Spider-Man," Moses "Sugar Man." The sobriquets stuck.

The two schools in town, the white and the black, usually played on back-to-back days at Gardner Stadium—Columbia High always first, Jefferson second, when the field was a mangled salad of dirt and grass chunks. As the season progressed, and talk of the Payton-Moses running tandem grew, an increasing number of fans either attended both games, or skipped out on Columbia High altogether.

Playing in something called the Tideland Conference, Jefferson's team traveled across Mississippi aboard a pair of beat-up old yellow school buses, complete with torn green seats and the inexplicable scent of dead elk. Boston always strove to schedule the hardest possible competition, which meant the Green Wave trekked an hour and a half to Laurel to face Oak Park High, and nearly two hours to Picayune for a date with George Washington Carver High. The travels were joyless, back-road jaunts to nowhere, with bus drivers always keeping an eye out for redneck cops looking to make an easy collar.

Jefferson went 8-2 Payton's junior year, routinely dismantling opponents. With a six-foot-six, 260-pound tackle named Bobby Price leading the way, Walter carried the football anywhere from eighteen to twenty-five times per game, emerging as Mississippi's best black halfback. Boston had been around long enough to know Payton was destined to be different. So he worked tirelessly with him. Payton was stronger than most linemen and faster than most defensive backs, but he initially lacked the ruggedness his coach had insisted upon. Boston drilled into his head the idea of attacking defensive players; of slamming into the tacklers before the tacklers slammed into him. He instructed Payton to use body parts as weapons—a sharp elbow to the chest, a pulverizing forearm to the chin.

Wrote Payton in his autobiography:

He taught me that when I could no longer successfully elude a tackler, I should let the man have a memory of the tackle as vivid as my own. In other words, why should I be the one who gets clobbered? As long as there are two of us in on the play, and I have been slowed by others to the point of where I can't break away from him, he ought to take half the blow. Then it won't hurt me so much. I enjoyed that. It made sense. . . . More and more often, the second time a guy came at me, he remembered that first shot he'd taken from me. If he hesitated or rolled into his tackle instead of driving into it, I had the upper hand. I'd ram right through him or over him, and suddenly it was the scared little running back scoring rather than the big brute executing a crushing tackle.

Because Columbia and Jefferson never played each other, the school's biggest rival was all-black Marion Central High, located three miles across town. Leading up to the meeting, Boston was more animated than usual. The Tigers were coached by Leslie Peters, a former Jefferson High star who was building an impressive program. "Here's the deal," Boston told his players the morning of the game. "If you score seventy points, I'll throw a barbecue for the entire team."

A barbecue? For everyone? Behind multiple Payton touchdowns and a big passing day from Johnson, the Green Wave jumped out to a 64–0 lead, but with less than two minutes remaining found themselves one score away from chicken-and-pork pay dirt. When a Jefferson defensive back named Herman Lee intercepted a Marion Central pass, the offense stormed back onto the field and took over ten yards away from the end zone. Michael "Dobie" Woodson, the fleet halfback/defensive back, was corralled from behind by Boston. "Dobie, you haven't scored yet, right?" he asked.

"No," Woodson replied. "Not yet."

"Well go out there and line up at quarterback and call a sneak," Boston said. "Get that seventy! Get it!"

Woodson jogged to the huddle and ordered Johnson to shift to receiver. He took the snap, cut left, and followed a guard. When he was but two yards from scoring, Woodson found himself bottled up. His legs were wrapped, and in front of him was a mass of prone bodies. "I had nowhere to go," he said. "But then I felt this push—this incredibly strong push." Woodson turned his head and saw Payton slamming into his back. "All thanks to Walter, I went over the pile and scored the seventieth point," Woodson said. "And the ribs were great."

With his mounting success and a bevy of hundred-yard games, Payton began to evolve from shy and soft-spoken to gregarious and engaging. He had always possessed a mischievous streak; always enjoyed yanking down someone's pants or prank calling a neighbor. Yet, outside of his tight comfort zone, Payton had been reluctant to show his inner child. Now, for the first time, that was changing. The bus trips were often long and miserable, but they provided Payton with a chance to play. He would sneak up behind Johnson and flick his ears. He would grab Woodson by the nose and yank his head. Most memorably, he would make music. With his helmet wedged between two legs, Payton whipped out his drumsticks and banged out one song after another. Teammates clapped and sang along, and Boston—a man raised with the idea that the two hours before a game was a sacred time meant for prayer and introspection—had no choice but to go along for the ride. If his superstar wanted to bang his helmet, who was the coach to say no?

The week after scoring seventy against Marion County, Jefferson traveled to nearby Hattiesburg to take on Travillion High. By this point, word had leaked out that the Green Wave was awfully good, and that Payton was even better. As their bus pulled up to the field, Jefferson's players and coaches found themselves surrounded by what looked to be the entire Travillion student body. The scowling faces and clenched fists were a classic attempt at pregame intimidation, at the time a regular part of the black high school football experience in Mississippi. If your team wasn't threatened with death, it meant your team wasn't especially good. "Came with the territory," said Woodson. "Nothing noteworthy about it." Led by Payton, the Green Wave filed off the bus. If Payton was even mildly scared by the surroundings, he wasn't letting on. He walked with his chest puffed out, guiding his teammates through the mob without saying a word. Behind another three Payton scores, Jefferson took a 35–0 halftime lead, and won 46–0. In the closing minutes, as the heat rose and the tempers flared, a mob of fans made threatening gestures toward Jefferson's sideline. "When the game is over," Boston told the players, "we're going to quickly walk to the bus as one group. Everyone stick together."

Jefferson escaped, and did so the following week, too, when a Bassfield High loyalist tossed a brick through the rear window of the Green Wave bus after another big win.

For Payton, nothing could ruin what he would long consider to be one of the most joyful stretches of his life. He had developed as an athlete, and also as a person. Everyone at Jefferson High knew that the strapping kid from Hendricks Street was the real deal. That, if football offered bright futures to those who played it well, he was destined for greatness.

And just then, when life was as smooth as could be, the steadfast town of Columbia, Mississippi, did the unthinkable.

It progressed.

CHAPTER 3

———— ⊶∞⊷ ————

# BLACK AND WHITE

THE ISSUE LINGERED.

That's probably the best way to explain what was going on throughout the state of Mississippi in regard to school desegregation in the late 1960s.

It lingered.

And lingered.

And lingered.

And lingered.

In 1954, the United States Supreme Court ruled that the concept of separate-but-equal public schools was no longer legal; that, in the aftermath of *Brown v. Board of Education of Topeka,* black children and white children would have to be educated in the same buildings, in the same rooms, by the same teachers. "Today I believe has been a great day for America and the Court," wrote Justice Harold H. Burton in a private letter to Chief Justice Earl Warren. "I cherish the privilege of sharing in this." Across the South, the ruling was not greeted with such magnanimity. In Virginia, Senator Harry Byrd Sr. organized the Massive Resistance movement, which committed itself to closing schools before integrating them. In Florida, the state legislature declared the decision null and void. And in Mississippi, a circuit court judge named Thomas Pickens Brady published a book, *Black Monday,* that called for the dissolution of the NAACP, the creation of a forty-ninth state for Negroes, and the abolition of public schools.

But the implementation of new laws doesn't occur overnight. In other words, Mississippi had time. One year after the *Brown* decision, the Court

reconvened to consider the practicality of immediate desegregation. In a ruling known as *Brown II*, the Court delegated the task of carrying out school
desegregation to district courts with an order that it occur "with deliberate
speed."

For all of the decisiveness of *Brown v. Board of Education of Topeka*, *Brown
II* was a comical ode to ambiguity. To liberal politicians and civil rights
advocates, "with deliberate speed" meant ASAP. Yet in states like Alabama
and Georgia and Mississippi, the Court's follow-up decree was accepted as a
rare and precious gift. "With deliberate speed" could mean tomorrow. It
could also mean next week, next month, next year . . . five years . . . ten
years . . . never.

Therefore in Columbia—as with the entire Magnolia State—lawmakers
hemmed and hawed and stalled as long as legally possible. A commonly utilized tool was something called Freedom of Choice, which allowed students
of all backgrounds to select the local school of their preference. Columbia
began the practice in the summer of 1967, informing all students who lived
within the town limits that they could decide—regardless of race—where
they wanted to go the following academic year. It was, of course, a gimmick.
White government and school officials knew darn well that no Caucasians
would opt to attend the black schools and that few—if any—blacks would
risk the physical and emotional abuse of transitioning to a white school.

In the fall of 1967, an eighth grader named Delores Dukes became the
first black student to attend Columbia Junior High. Her parents had been
approached during the summer by a local civil rights leader named Ida Grouper, who was looking for someone strong enough to break a barrier. Grouper
knew Delores' mother, Lucille, was passionate about the civil rights movement, and that she had three daughters attending Jefferson. When Grouper
asked whether she would be willing to sacrifice one of her girls for the cause,
Lucille volunteered her youngest.

"But, Mom," whined Delores, "why me and not Jean or Dorothy?"

A devout Southern Baptist who never cursed, Lucille looked down
toward her daughter and said, matter of factly, "Because you don't take no
shit."

For Dukes, the transition proved brutal. She recalled the September
day when the superintendent of schools welcomed her to Columbia Junior
High by walloping her across the legs with a fan belt. ("To discourage me
from going to school," she said.) When Dukes punched the man in the

face, she was temporarily expelled. "My father (Willie Dukes) brought his gun to school the next day and told him, 'If you ever hit my daughter again, I will blow your brains out,'" she said. Delores was reinstated, but her first few weeks proved nightmarish. Teachers refused to call on her. Classmates tagged her "nigger" and "coon." The KKK telephoned her house, threatening to shoot her. "There's this whole narrative of white Columbians accepting and embracing blacks," she said. "Maybe some did, but that's not the way I remember it."

In the next couple of years, a small handful of black students joined Delores in the white schools, only to be met with similar hostilities. Eli Payton, Walter's distant cousin, jumped from Jefferson to Columbia Junior High as an eighth grader, hoping his warm disposition would carry him through. "Didn't work that way," he said. "I got in a lot of fights. There was one guy, a kid named Mike Garrett, who would call me every name in the book and tell me I couldn't sit in certain seats. There were teachers who thought you were stupid and didn't expect answers from you. And there were other teachers who wouldn't even speak to you."

Brenda Ellis, Eli's older sister, also made the move. With the siblings' shift to the white schools came threats and crank calls. Their father, John Payton, had worked alongside whites for much of his life. "He could always do things other blacks weren't allowed to," said Brenda. "But when we started going to the white schools, some of those same white friends stopped talking to him. They said, 'You need to call me Mister now.'"

With its April 10, 1969, staff editorial, titled "Race Differences," the *Columbian-Progress* hit back at those pushing for full scholastic integration. Written by Lester Williams, the newspaper's editor, the piece called for blacks and whites to accept and embrace their differences—beginning with the fact that blacks are clearly dumber: "Too many are afraid to admit citizens are obviously not equal in abilities or talents, that races have differences too. But those inequalities are normal and desirable. In fact, it would be tragic if we were all equal, wanted the same things and had the same talents and preferences."

Surprisingly, many of Columbia's black residents shared the local paper's opposition stance. While there was empathy for the individual plights of students like Delores, Eli, and Brenda, there was also a general belief that, when it came to integration, why rock the boat? To the blacks of Columbia, Jefferson was a perfectly fine school; the stores on their side of town were plenty suitable; their having to enter through the rear of most buildings was a mild inconvenience; the separate water fountains at the JCPenney was no real problem. So why damage the relatively peaceful relations between races?

For the most part, Walter Payton's parents, Peter and Alyne, concurred with this philosophical outlook. Although they certainly weren't thrilled with some aspects of second-class citizenship, it was a matter-of-fact way of life. As far as they were concerned, Eddie had received an excellent education at Jefferson, sans the social pressures that would come with integration. "There's this belief that blacks were outraged about life," said Eddie. "Not true. We were comfortable. Maybe we were naïve—I don't know. But we were, factually, comfortable and at peace."

Having waited long enough for Southern schools to comply with the Supreme Court's 1954 ruling, the government finally took definitive action. On November 19, 1969—two and a half months into Walter Payton's junior year at Jefferson High School—the United States Court of Appeals for the Fifth Circuit ruled that Columbia and Marion County schools had to be fully integrated by year's end. In a blistering editorial, Thurman Sensing, a columnist for the *Progress* and executive vice president of the Southern States Industrial Council, echoed the sentiment of many whites when he wrote, "How can it be just to compel a student to attend a particular school in order to meet a fixed racial formula? The final say-so on a child's education should belong to parents, not some bureaucrat whose mind is full of socialist notions regarding the way people's lives should be managed."

To men like Sensing and Williams, forced integration was a disaster waiting to happen. At the very least, the men believed there would be hundreds upon hundreds of picketers and nonstop violence. More likely, there would be anarchy.

· · ·

It started with the toilets.

During the two-week Christmas break, Columbia's white parents and black parents were asked to offer their insights into the town's new schooling setup. Beginning on January 5, 1970, the school system would, at long last, become fully integrated. Columbia High School would house black and white high school students, while Jefferson High would become the middle schools for both races.

Before the plan kicked in, however, a handful of white parents made a demand: Every one of Jefferson High School's toilet seat covers needed to be replaced. "That's how screwed up the thinking was," said Tommy Barber, a white student at Columbia High. "Like white people didn't mess up toilet seats, too."

"It was interesting," adds Fred Idom, a black teacher who transferred from Jefferson High to Columbia High. "When the schools were separate, whites insisted everything was equal and that we needed to stop our complaining. But as soon as the ruling came down, they renovated Jefferson and fixed it up so it would be ready for the whites."

The first physical act of integration took place on December 27, 1969, when four remaining members of Jefferson High's varsity basketball team— including Walter—and seven remaining members of Columbia High's varsity basketball team congregated in the Columbia High gymnasium to become one. The meeting occurred on an otherwise forgettable Saturday morning, and was—for lack of a better word—awkward. The whites mingled on one side of the gymnasium, the blacks on the other side. Ned Eades, Columbia High's coach, forced all the boys to shake hands. They did so, but haltingly. A former minor league baseball player, Eades was—by Mississippi standards—open-minded about integration. If the black players could help win some games, he was all for it.

The sounds that day were familiar ones—sneakers squeaking against a wood floor, dribbling reverberating off the walls—but the faces were not. Walter Payton, all of sixteen years old, was the only black kid some of the whites had heard of; a football supernova whose name was increasingly recognizable within the town's borders. "When Coach pulled us together to tell us the blacks would be joining us to integrate, we were all very skeptical," recalled Don Bourne, a white member of the basketball team. "I was a starter at forward, and my biggest fear wasn't having to play with blacks—it was losing my position."

Much has been written about Walter Payton's role in Columbia's integration, and how his skills as a football player broke down certain barriers. What goes overlooked, however, are those early days on the court. An undisciplined ball hog lacking range and court savvy, Payton was hardly the best of the four blacks to come over from Jefferson (that honor belonged to the unforgettably named Myjelious Mingo, a six-foot-six center who owned the post). But his value as a disarming presence was invaluable. By the completion of that first meeting, Payton was cracking on white teammates he'd never before met and black teammates he'd known forever. "He was smiling

the whole time—just a warm guy at a difficult moment," said Roger Mal-
latte, a white basketball player. "If he was uncomfortable being there with
us, it never showed. I think most of us left that first day feeling much more
comfortable about what was happening. If all the black guys were like Walter
Payton, we'd be OK."

Nine days later, on the morning of January 5, 1970, the town's blacks
and whites woke up to a new world. The sun officially rose at 7:03 A.M. The
temperature would reach a high of fifty-seven degrees, with a slight breeze
from the north and nary a cloud in the sky. Whether people liked it or not,
beginning on that Monday, Columbia High School was an integrated facility of learning.

Based upon a handful of highly publicized integration standoffs—most
famously James Meredith trying to enroll in the University of Mississippi in
1961 and Governor George Wallace blocking entrance to the University of
Alabama in 1963—many Columbia residents feared/expected the worst. "You
have to understand that within the previous seven years, we had a president
assassinated, Martin Luther King was assassinated, Bobby Kennedy was
assassinated, and George Wallace was shot," said Colleen Crawley, a white
Columbia High student. "People were still reeling. And right on the heels of
that, we're integrating." Though Marion County's branch of the KKK
wasn't as loud as it once had been, there was always the threat of revitaliza-
tion. More worrisome was the looming presence of Columbia Academy, a
nearby private school that had been founded three years earlier when the
inevitability of desegregation forced many white citizens into a state of
panic. As soon as the Fifth Circuit Court of Appeals announced its ruling,
the phone at Columbia Academy began to ring nonstop. "It was a white
flight school in every sense of the term," said Thomas H. Blakeney, Columbia Academy's headmaster at the time. "People were motivated by the fear of
such cultural change. I knew some black people before desegregation, but
only in limited settings. To go from that to completely desegregated schools
was a huge upheaval." Blakeney hardly exaggerates. Pre-desegregation,
Columbia Academy had an enrollment of fifty-three students. By the completion of the 1970 academic year, that total had swelled to a hundred and
fifty—all white. "Looking back, the school was a big mistake," said Blakeney. "Clearly it was. But people—myself included—weren't as enlightened
as they are today. I guess we were sheltered."

Columbia High School's doors opened at eight A.M. In black and white houses across the town, the apprehension was palpable. Black parents feared white violence. White parents feared the worst: savage black boys trying to impregnate their precious white daughters, brutish black girls lacking couth, mediocre black teachers dispensing flawed knowledge. "Exposure," said Pat Bullock, whose son Lee was a white student at Columbia High. "Many of the whites in our town didn't want their kids exposed. When I was growing up, my parents threatened to disown me if I invited a black person to our house for a party."

"There were a lot of rumors about how the blacks acted," said Diane Weems, a white student whose parents forced her to transfer to Columbia Academy. "Stabbings and knives and things like that."

Anticipating hostilities, members of the local and national media camped out in front of the white, concrete brick, two-story building. *Newsweek* sent a reporter, as did the *Associated Press*, the Jackson *Clarion-Ledger*, and all three networks. A bushel of television cameras stood at attention, waiting for . . . something.

Here was something: Eight teenagers, all white, paraded back and forth along the sidewalk, armed with signs reading HELL NO, WE WON'T GO and GIVE OUR SCHOOLS BACK and BIRDS OF A FEATHER FLOCK TOGETHER. They marched for approximately forty-five minutes, and were largely ignored. "They looked ridiculous," said Archie Johnson, Walter's friend. "You almost felt sorry for them."

Once inside, the students were ushered into the auditorium, where Johnson, Jefferson High's student body president, and Barber, Columbia High's student body president, sat side by side on the stage. They took turns speaking to the students—590 in all; 180 black. "If everybody could just see everybody else as a human being," Barber said, "it might just turn out all right. Be a big surprise to everybody."

Barber's words were greeted with a loud cheer. Then Johnson stepped to the microphone and flashed a peace sign. "There is no conflict between old and new," he said. "It is a conflict between false and true. We can become a lighthouse in Marion County. Let it be said we, the students of our community, are trying to improve our conditions."

· · ·

The transition went well, though there were missteps. Columbia High's administration completed the 1970 academic year by having blacks and whites situated in separate classrooms. Furthermore, with so many white students bolting for Columbia Academy, the school district didn't need to retain all its teachers. Eighteen holdovers—all from Jefferson, all black—were fired. Backed by the NAACP, the dismissed staffers sued. "The court mandated that we all be offered our positions back, but we were badly manipulated," said Idom, one of the dismissed. "Let's say you were a principal before the lawsuit. Well, you'd be brought back as an assistant principal. Let's say you were a head coach of some team. They'd bring you back, but to be an assistant. It was unconscionable."

As they passed each other in the hallways, whites and blacks struggled to communicate. It had been one thing to initially accept integration—the students knew it wasn't their decision to make, and to fight back made little sense. Now, however, a cloud of hostility loomed. Black students couldn't help but notice that Columbia High's facilities—the ones they had been told were equal to Jefferson's—were fancy and clean. An immaculate science laboratory. Textbooks without eight or nine names scribbled on a weathered inside cover. There were angry glares and harsh words. "After we integrated, a bunch of students of both races were in a room and a teacher said, 'Are there any questions people from one race want to ask the other race?'" recalled Michael Woodson, Walter's friend. "This little white girl raises her hand and says, 'Is it true black people have tails?'"

Laughter ensued, but the general mood was one of great distrust. In the cafeteria, the students segregated themselves. One would never sit at the table of the opposite race. "I got suspended three or four times that first semester for fighting the blacks," said Wayne Phillips, a white student. "I was prejudiced. I called people 'nigger' and thought nothing of it. And I wasn't the only one."

So what inspired students of both races to let their guards down? The clichéd answer has long been "sports"—the ability of blacks and whites to come together on a field of play. Yet the simplicity of that reply demeans what actually occurred. From the depths of a student body uncomfortable with itself, a small handful of leaders emerged. Johnson and Barber, the class presidents, were two. But the most important—the most *influential*—was Walter Payton.

Whether you were black or white, the best athlete in school would almost certainly approach you with an extended hand or a high five or a pat on the shoulder. It was the Alyne in him—the need to please all comers, no matter the circumstances. Walter had no illusions that he could bring the school together. No, his goal was significantly simpler than that—to be righteous. Of all the white students at Columbia High, Phillips was one of the most vile. He started fights with blacks, called them names, condemned them to hell. Payton targeted him as a potential ally. Shortly after integration began, Phillips found himself in a fight with a black football player. A large handful of black students jumped in. Phillips said some of them had crowbars. Payton dashed toward the scrum and pulled people off. "Don't start with Wayne!" Payton yelled. "He's OK! He's OK!" The fight ended.

"He came up to me one day and said, 'Wayne, if any of my black friends mess with you, you tell me,'" recalled Phillips. "I couldn't believe it. So I said to him, 'Walt, if any of the white guys mess with you, you tell me.' I ran with the bad guys, and he had no reason to want to befriend me. But he did. He befriended many of us. It wouldn't be a lie to say he changed our perspectives.

"He really did."

CHAPTER 4

# THE EMERGENCE

From North Carolina to Florida, from Louisiana to Georgia, from Kentucky to Mississippi, there is a universal language of the South, and it is football. People enjoy basketball and respect baseball. But what takes place between the hash marks of a football field determines the true worth of an individual, of a school, of a community.

In most towns below the Mason-Dixon Line a quarterback reigns over a valedictorian; a halfback with 4.4 speed is far superior to a math whiz with a 4.0 GPA. If a high school graduates 99 percent of its students, the achievement is acknowledged. If a high school wins a state football title, the achievement is immortalized. "People have their heroes," said Richard Howarth, the former mayor of Oxford, Mississippi. "Down here, they're predominantly football players." While the early days of Columbia's integration went as smoothly as anyone could have hoped, nothing would be declared an official success until April 3, 1970, when Wildcat spring football practice was scheduled to begin.

If the Columbia school board had envisioned using its high school football program as a gateway to racial tranquility, it had a perplexing way of showing it. For the past five years, the Wildcats had been coached by Jerry Wilkerson, a fierce sideline presence who punished his players by whipping them with a thick rope that dangled from a loop in his belt. "Wilkerson would run us to death," said Gerald Haddox, Columbia High's quarterback in 1969, "and dare you to ask for a drink of water." With the coming of desegregation, the set-in-his-ways Wilkerson was dismissed.

In a fair world, Wilkerson's replacement would have been a no-brainer.

Charles Boston had coached Jefferson for seven years with startling success. As the Columbia High program often floundered under Wilkerson, struggling to crack .500 in the mediocre South Little Dixie Conference, Boston's Green Wave routinely contended for the Tideland Conference title. Even though it was significantly more difficult for black high school players to receive scholarships than white ones, Boston sent one player after another into the collegiate ranks. Three even landed in the NFL.

Instead of considering Boston for the job, however, Hugh Dickens, Columbia's new superintendent of schools, decreed that Wilkerson's replacement must have a master's degree. The stipulation ruled out 99 percent of Mississippi's black coaches—most of whom had to overcome merciless layers of racism merely to receive an undergraduate diploma. "I obviously knew I could handle the position and do very well," said Boston. "But the times were difficult. People felt as if we had to take all these baby steps."

Boston's former Jefferson High players were outraged, as were many of the town's black residents. Even Payton, the ultimate unifying presence, was taken aback. This was his hero. His role model. Sure, times were fragile. But if Charles Boston couldn't earn a head-coaching position, what hope did the rest of the black community have? "It was such a joke," said Fred Idom, a black teacher. "He was as qualified as anyone could possibly be."

Boston's initial instinct was to express his anger. Then he thought about his father, Peter Boston. "When I was a boy he farmed on a little place owned by a white lady," he said. "I don't think she ever charged my daddy a penny worth of rent. We had to keep the weeds, and we grew things we could eat. I never saw Daddy have trouble with anybody of another race, and that made an impact on me. There was good in the world, and it was important to try and find it. So I chose to ignore the bad and look for the positive. It was all I could do to survive."

On April 27, 1970, Columbia High announced the hiring of Tommy Davis as the school's new head football coach. A sturdy thirty-six-year-old white man with short brown hair, narrow shoulders, and no visible neck, Davis had spent the past six years coaching eighty miles away in Heidelberg, Mississippi. ("I don't think I'd ever even been to Columbia," he said. "Maybe I passed through once.") As much as anyone, Davis grasped the delicateness of integration and sports. He departed Heidelberg not because of any nomadic stirrings, but because, with the coming of desegregation, nearly all of his players left to enroll in the nearby private school. "It was about an eighty percent black school district," he said, "and I was losing every one of my returning guys."

Upon accepting the Columbia job, Davis was told that, in order to win over the black players, he would be wise to reach out to Boston. The two met in early May, each man uncertain what to make of the other. Davis knew a handful of blacks, but he had never directly worked with one. Boston knew a handful of whites, but he had never directly worked with one. "I was a father of three kids and I wanted the extra income from coaching," said Boston. "But I did have some pride. I told him I'm a sideline guy, and I'm not going to go sit in some press box."

Davis named Boston the receivers' coach, and unofficially, his liaison to the black players. It was badly needed. Because of the backlash to integration, Columbia's roster was decimated, what with a mere seventeen players skeptically returning to the team. An additional twenty blacks signed on, meaning the Wildcats had a total of thirty-seven warm bodies. "I wanted to stay and play quarterback," said Haddox, who departed for Columbia Academy. "But a lot of our parents didn't want us on the same team as the black kids."

As was the case in basketball, an air of caution choked the football team's first integrated workouts. With Haddox's departure, the leading contender for the quarterback job was Archie Johnson—Jefferson's black signal caller. "Before practice began," said Johnson, "I was told by some of the adult blacks that under no terms was I to allow anyone to change my position." Many of Columbia's returnees couldn't fathom such an idea. Meanwhile, the team's best defensive lineman was Steve Stewart—a white boy and the top holdover tackler for Columbia High. "Those first practices, I thought we were going to kill each other," said Kim Fink, the Wildcats' backup quarterback. "We played so hard, trying to prove our manhood and our worth. We did all we could to get our pads off and throw punches. We wanted to just destroy the other guys. We saw them as threats and as encroachers.

"But I'll say this," said Fink. "One kid stood out, and you knew—whether you supported integration or didn't—that we had a chance to be pretty darn good."

That kid was Walter Payton.

He was, beginning with that initial workout, different. Stronger. Quicker. More powerful. A five-foot-eight, 193-pound block of dynamite. Oh, Johnson could wiggle out of the pocket and throw a tight spiral downfield. And Edward Moses, aka "Sugar Man," was as fast as anyone had ever seen. And Stewart pulverized opposing ball carriers. "We had a bunch of excellent athletes," said Stewart. "But Walter was on a new level. My first impression of Walter was, 'Holy cow—this kid literally has no fat on him!' With his shirt off, his body was like a Greek god. I asked him that first day if he lifted weights, and he said he didn't. I couldn't believe it. I just couldn't believe it. He was a statue."

Before that first practice, some of Columbia's white players were under the illusion that Sherman Green, the Wildcats' leading rusher from the previous season, would keep his job. Green was a tough kid who grinded out yards. By the time practice ended, however, it was clear Payton and Green resided on different levels. "Sherman was a big, strong white guy," said Eli Payton, a black defensive back. "Well, one day Sherman spit on Walter. I don't know if it was an accident or on purpose, but Walter screamed, 'Shit man, look what you did!' and slapped him. Just slapped him across the face. That was the only incident between the two, but it set a tone. Walter wasn't going to take anything from anyone."

In one of the first postintegration drills, Rickey Joe Graves, a hard-hitting white linebacker, knew Payton would be coming straight toward him. The play was designed as such—halfback takes the handoff, bursts directly through the hole and toward the middle of the field. Graves, itching to prove himself to the blacks, licked his chops. "I got to the spot right when he did," said Graves, "and I thought to myself, 'I'm gonna lay it on this guy.'" Graves' feet left the ground and his arms reached out, only to have Payton's knees explode into the bottom of his chin. "Walter was gone," said Graves. "He made believers out of everyone."

· · ·

Walter's senior year of high school began on September 7, 1970. Now that Columbia High was officially integrated, there were no more picketers or threats of defection to Columbia Academy. For the first time, the black and white students were mixed into one classroom. Any past physical divisions were over.

It was a new era in the town's race relations, and to the chagrin of many white parents, their children seemed to like it. In the aftermath of all the warnings and hysterics, the black kids were, by and large (gasp!) nice. They weren't tail-dragging mutants, out to bring down the genteel Southern society whites had strived to create. They were respectful and decent and shockingly friendly.

Oh, and they could play football.

Not all of them, obviously. But as the Wildcats prepared for their September 4th opener against Prentiss High at Gardner Stadium, there was a renewed sense of optimism. It had been years since Columbia High brought much suspense to the gridiron. Under Wilkerson, the Wildcats generally wound up as a solid-yet-predictable team, bogged down with a dull offense and so-so overall talent. Now, thanks to desegregation, one couldn't deny a refreshing energy throughout the town. The fascination was genuine: How would this play out?

Located twenty-five miles to the north of Columbia, Prentiss' Bulldogs had dominated the Wildcats, winning twenty-one straight games against their conference rivals. Like Columbia, the school was in the midst of full-fledge integration, and also like Columbia, the process had gone relatively smoothly. "It was easy," said Larry Fike, the Bulldogs' star halfback/linebacker. "We were about fifty percent white, fifty percent black, and I don't remember any fights at all." If anything, Prentiss' white players utilized their new teammates as informants to the ways of opposing blacks. "All week leading up to the game, we kept hearing, 'Watch out, they have this stud running back,'" said Fike. "But when you're seventeen or eighteen years old, you think you're a stud, too. So we went over there believing Walter was just another good running back who we'd easily stop."

The opening game of the season began at seven thirty P.M., on a warm Mississippi night perfect for September football. With the sun setting over the stadium, the sky was an orange-pink canvas. The scent of popcorn filled the air. The squeals of young children running beneath the stands provided a familiar soundtrack. A sellout crowd of nineteen hundred spectators paid three dollars per ticket, there as much for the curious spectacle as for the sport itself. Those who couldn't attend gathered by their radios, listening to the game on WCJU, Columbia's AM station. Davis was the new coach, and he brought with him a pro set offense. Johnson was the quarterback, with Payton and Moses starting in the backfield. Lining up split to the right was Lee Bullock, a white—and deaf—wideout who learned to read Johnson's lips as he called the plays. "It was a wonderful moment," said Graves. "We had had the offensive linemen to be a good team, but we lacked running backs and a quarterback. At Jefferson, their linemen were OK, but they had great skill position players. You merged us together, and it was beautiful."

Along the sideline Columbia High's seven cheerleaders—all white, with green skirts and white pom-poms—kicked their legs and shouted their encouragement. In a small section of the bleachers, black and white members of the school's integrated marching band sat side by side.

As is often the case, the game failed to meet the hype. At least early on.

Through one and a half quarters of play, neither team scored. The Prentiss defense, geared up to stop Columbia's one-two rushing tandem of Payton and Moses, stuffed the line of scrimmage with eight men, daring the Wildcats to pass. The Bulldogs, meanwhile, mustered little offense of their own. "You could see that Columbia had talent," said Butch Nobles, Prentiss' center and linebacker. "We were waiting for something to happen, hoping like heck it wouldn't."

Late in the second quarter, with no score and the crowd quiet, the Wildcats took over at their own thirty-yard line. From the sideline, Davis called 22 Sweep Right—a pitch to Payton. The play had already been run four or five times for little gain, but Davis felt Prentiss was about to break. Columbia's offensive line—four whites, one black—was bigger and faster than the Prentiss defense. They just needed to create a hole. Johnson took the snap from Quin Breland, his center, pivoted his hips, and gently tossed the ball to No. 22, his longtime friend and classmate. Payton tiptoed a couple of steps behind his right tackle, then—*whoosh!*—burst outside. "He was coming right toward me, and I remember thinking, 'Here I go! I've got him!'" recalled Fike. "I go to make my tackle, I man up, and I'm grabbing nothing but air. So I start giving chase, thinking I'll certainly chase him down, because I'm a very fast runner. Well, he pulls away from me. *He pulls away!*" Payton dashed down the field untouched, a green-and-white blur of power and speed. By the time he reached the Bulldogs' twenty-yard line, Payton spun around, raised the football above his head, and waved to the defenders. He jogged into the end zone backward.

It was an act of unheard-of cockiness; an act that, in ordinary Mississippi circumstances, would have resulted in whites branding him an "uppity nigger." A mere fifteen years earlier Emmett Till was murdered in Money, Mississippi, for reportedly whistling at a white woman. And now, 190 miles to the south, here was Walter Payton, taunting his white pursuers.

In one corner of the stands, a handful of college football coaches watched in disbelief. In attendance were assistants from Ole Miss and Mississippi State, as well as Barney Poole, an assistant coach at the nearby University of Southern Mississippi. As soon as Payton held the ball aloft, the men began complaining aloud. One was more vocal than the others. "Can you believe the nerve of this kid?" said Bob Hill, an assistant coach at Jackson State College, Mississippi's largest historically black school. "To have that little respect for an opponent is inexcusable. I would never sign someone like that." Hill, of course, wanted Payton in the worst possible way. "I hoped the other coaches would buy my bluff," he said. "They tended to think in packs."

Poole, a former all-American end at Ole Miss who played professionally for six seasons, was visibly disgusted. Upon returning to his school's Hattiesburg campus, Poole filed a scouting report that read: "Tremendous athlete, but we don't need a smart-alecky nigger on our team."

Payton was far from "smart-alecky." He was humble and soft-spoken, but he had been taught to play sports with emotion and flavor. Throughout black high schools in the South, mild trash talking was not merely accepted, but encouraged. So was taunting. Midway through the season Boston had to explain to Davis that the way some of the black players behaved on the bus rides to road games—talking and laughing and busting chops—was nothing to get upset over. "He didn't understand," said Boston. "I said, 'Tommy, they'll be ready. Just let them be.'"

Columbia led Prentiss 7–0 at halftime, but with the exception of Payton's long run the team looked out of sorts. At the beginning of the third quarter, Payton struck again. On a second down and ten from the Columbia twelve-yard line, Johnson grabbed the snap, spun hard, and presented the ball to his charging fullback, who ran straight toward Keith Brenson, the Bulldogs' 240-pound nose tackle, cut left, and burst into the guts of the defense. The second Bulldog to have a shot at the tackle was Nobles. "I was playing strong side linebacker, and I was supposed to key on Walter," said Nobles. "On the bright side, I can honestly say he didn't run over me. But that's only because he didn't need to—he was so fast, I never came close to catching him. He left me in the dust." It was Walter's second touchdown of the game. Remarkably, the play had been mishandled—Walter was supposed to head outside, not stay behind the center and guards. No matter.

The Bulldogs scored late to make the final score 14–6, and when the final gun was fired the noise in the stadium was deafening. White fans and black fans, forever separated by societal rules, cheered together. Afterward, few in Columbia were discussing the snapping of the twenty-one-game losing streak, or Davis' new offense, or the play of the poised black quarterback.

"Walter was the story," said Forrest Dantin, a white lineman. "He was beyond belief."

.  .  .

If you listen to many of Columbia's white denizens, this is the point when peace and understanding commenced. *Thanks to Walter Payton's athletic brilliance,* the narrative goes, *whites and blacks merged as one, bound together over the beautiful game of football and the Wildcats' newfound success. For the first time ever, they cheered together, laughed together, cried together. All because of high school football. All because of Walter Payton.*

"Walter came along and started setting all these records," said Hugh Dickens, the superintendent of Columbia schools. "And suddenly whites found themselves applauding the blacks. That made the black community feel proud because it was finally getting recognition, and it made the white community feel proud, too. Our success in football resulted in our success as a whole."

Is this true? Much depends on who's asked. On the one hand, Columbia's whites were now infatuated with Walter Payton—slapping him high fives, shaking his hand, singing his praises, and bragging about "our" star. When he drove to school in his green Chevrolet pickup truck, people—black and white—honked and waved. The change of heart was remarkable, if not sadly predictable. The *Progress,* a newspaper that, for its first eighty-eight years refused to cover seemingly any event involving blacks, started hailing the senior back as a gridiron savior and claiming him as one of Columbia's own.

Yet the majority of the town's blacks surely saw through the façade. Now that the school was integrated, it cancelled all of the previously held dances and the senior play for the 1970–71 academic year. Just a few months earlier Columbia extemporaneously closed its town pool after an increasing number of blacks began to use it. "That shows what some thought of us," said Michael Woodson, a black player. "We were second-class." Walter Payton had been a marvelous kid long before integration. He was polite, intelligent, well-spoken, engaging. "After they saw Walter could run the football," said Eli Payton, "everyone was *yee-haw!* and happy." This was hardly a phenomenon unique to Columbia. As towns throughout the South experienced the positive athletic impacts of their new black stars, white Mississippians even came up with a phrase—"*Give the ball to LeRoy*"—to surmise their philosophy. As long as the black boy could play football, he was perfectly welcome. "White Mississippians said it all the time, thinking they were being funny," said Charles Martin, a civil rights expert and the author of *Benching Jim Crow.* "'LeRoy' was a term, like darkie, like coon, like nigger. Only it had a little less sting."

Thanks largely to Payton's heroics, the integrated Wildcats were the kings of Columbia. They followed the opener with a 20–0 victory over Hazelhurst that included the most spectacular touchdown of Payton's high school career. "It was a long [run], and I was hit three or four times," he wrote in his autobiography. "The first guy that hit me nearly knocked me over. I spun around and put my hand out to keep from going down, but when I recovered my balance and straightened up I ran over another guy who tripped me up. As I started to fall forward a defender grabbed me from behind, which was just enough to keep me from falling. When I shook loose of him, I was gone." (Recalled Emmett Smith, Hazelhurst's head coach: "We spent our entire week working out a way to stop Walter Payton, and on Friday we learned we couldn't stop Walter Payton.")

After that victory, Columbia traveled 126 miles northwest to Vicksburg to face Warren Central High, which had beaten the Wildcats 39–0 a year earlier. The Vikings were coached by Dewey Partridge, a star receiver at Ole Miss in the late 1950s. In the week leading up to the game, Partridge devised a plan to shut down Columbia's rushing attack. He took offensive lineman Archie Anderson and lined him up on the defensive line, across from the tight end. As Warren Central's strongest player, Anderson's job was to lock up the tight end, thus allowing a linebacker to go unobstructed after Payton. "From the standpoint of getting me and the tight end on each other, it worked," said Anderson. "But it was a failure, because you were asking the linebacker to tackle Walter Payton one-on-one. And that was impossible."

"At one point they threw a screen to Walter, and I thought I was about to pick it off," said David Chaney, a Warren Central defensive end. "Then— snap! Out of nowhere, he jumped up, caught the ball and took off. I'd never seen anyone move like that. Never." Payton scored three touchdowns and ran for 123 yards in the 32–0 win.

"We were just kicking ass and taking names," said Johnson, the quarterback. "Greatness came very easily for that team."

· · ·

The Columbia High Wildcats beat Mendenhall 16–6 to improve to 4-0, then downed Crystal Springs 34–21 to post the first 5-0 mark in school history.

Leading up to the clash at Gardner Stadium, Crystal Springs coach Leon Canoy managed to get his hands on a few rolls of Columbia film. He couldn't believe what he was witnessing. Davis and Boston had designed four special plays just for Payton. Two, Spider Left and Spider Right, were screen passes into the flat that, with proper blocking, were seemingly impossible to stop. Two others, Alcorn Left and Alcorn Right, were misdirections that gave Payton the option of running or throwing. Also unstoppable. "Back then the taping would be done off of a little ol' tripod, and the tapes would start up close, then go wide," said Canoy. "You'd watch Walter, and the image would always switch to a wide shot because he'd wind up running away from everyone. He'd almost be out of the picture by the end of the plays." High school running backs generally fall into one of two categories. They are either gnat-like slashers, à la Moses, or straight-ahead bowling balls. Payton was both. He ran hard on every play, never stopped churning his arms and pumping his knees. His stiff-arm, developed on the sandlots of Jefferson, could paralyze opposing defenders, and his hips rarely locked into one position. "I began to see that once in a great while you can use getting hit to keep your balance," Payton wrote. "It's all a matter of reflexes and coordination and eyes and hands and feet." In other words, opponents were helpless. They might stop him once. Twice. Three times. But inevitably, he'd break a run.

Like the other men faced with shutting down Columbia High's high-powered offense, Canoy devised a plan: His linebackers would cheat toward the line, hoping to make contact before the play developed. They would grab Payton's legs, drag him down, and force Johnson to throw the ball.

"Didn't work," Canoy said.

Payton, Moses, and Johnson teamed to rush for more than two hundred yards. "They were incredible," said Jimmie Stovall, Crystal Springs' cornerback. "I'll never forget my one big play against Walter. He came around that corner and I hit him and he hit me. We both went down. I mean, it was a heck of a collision. He came back one play later and scored. I came back a bunch of plays later and was never the same. Forty years later, my shoulder still hurts."

If older white fans were thrilled by Columbia High's football prowess, they had mixed feelings over the social implications. Until Payton's senior year, young blacks and young whites were almost completely separate. Unless you were a black child whose mother served as a nanny for white families, odds are you lacked interactions with the opposite race. Now, however, blacks like Payton, Johnson, and Moses were genuine heroes on the Columbia High campus. They walked the halls with heads held high and chests puffed out. They wore their jerseys the days of games, and sported snazzy green-and-white football jackets with their nicknames ("Spider-Man" for Payton, "Sugar Man" for Moses) embroidered atop the chest. The initial skepticisms of white teammates eroded quickly. Most of the athletes—black and white—were deliberately grouped together in physical education class, and a bond developed. "Those guys on that team wouldn't let other people talk badly about their teammates—black or white," said Dantin. "Not because of race, but because that's your teammate."

On the bus rides back from road games, one of the black players—often Payton—would break out a transistor radio and blast the music. The songs were almost always Motown—Marvin Gaye, The Four Tops, Martha Reeves and the Vandellas—and the crooning grew louder throughout the ride. As gifted a dancer as he was a runner, Payton stood, arms waving, rear shaking. "It sounds like a scene from a movie," said Dantin. "But the black kids would start singing The Temptations, and we'd all join in. All of us. Those trips became like Temptation greatest hits sing-alongs. It was so incredibly fun."

In preintegration Columbia, decades of Jefferson football players either partied in someone's backyard or, occasionally, at Pete Walker's Place, a black club, that featured a three-songs-for-a-quarter jukebox and Pete's special brand of bootleg. But the world was changing. Accompanying Columbia's football players on the bus trips to away games was the school's all-white fleet of cheerleaders. In the past, a black kid in Columbia wouldn't dare glance longingly toward a white girl. "Integration," said Woodson, "completely mixed that notion up."

Throughout his early high school days, Walter had dated a black girl named Jill Brewer. Notably pretty, with big brown eyes and high cheeks, Jill attended nearby Marion Central High, and was two years Walter's junior. She wasn't his first girlfriend. ("Walter was a popular guy, and he'd dated some girls," Brewer said. "But he was my first boyfriend.") They had met in 1967, at a semipro football game being played at Gardner Stadium. She was shy and guarded. He was also shy, but a bit more bubbly. "Apparently I gave him my number," she said. "We grew to be very close." The two met up at various school functions, at sporting events, at parties. Brewer's mother ran a small recreation center known as the Shop, and together they played pool and ate ice cream. Because Brewer lived nine miles outside of Columbia on Highway 43, the couple struggled to see each other every week. "But," she said, "I really liked him. Walter was such a sweet boy. If I had a daughter I'd want her to have a boyfriend who treats her with the respect he gave me."

By the time Columbia desegregated its schools, Walter and Jill were no longer a pair. "When we broke up, he said I was breaking his heart," said Brewer. "I told him it was just puppy love. From then on, whenever I'd see him, he'd greet me the same way—'Hey, Puppy Love!'"

Payton's first intimate moment with a white girl came in the fall of his senior year. Walter and Kim Fink, the white backup quarterback, discussed the idea of setting each other up with girls from the opposite race. "We were both kind of progressives," said Fink. "I had friends who would have had nothing to do with African-American girls. But not me. I was excited."

One night, with his parents perched in front of the television, Fink snuck out of the house with a six-pack of Falstaff Beer and picked up Walter. They headed for a spot known as the Duck Pond, an undeveloped subdivision on the outskirts of town where kids went to make out. The girls met them there— Walter's was blond, with blue eyes; Fink's had brown hair, with brown eyes and dark skin. "We just fooled around and stuff—nothing big," said Fink. "But we had to meet far away for it to happen. You couldn't get caught doing that stuff back then."

Which made Walter's life increasingly difficult. Because in that marvelous fall of 1970, he developed a crush on a beautiful cheerleader with peach-toned skin who sat in front of him in biology class. Her name was Colleen Crawley, though friends called her "Tweet" for her thin, birdlike legs. She was, like Walter, a senior, with long brown cascading hair, doe eyes, and an easygoing manner that had half the senior boys smitten. Unlike some of her peers, Colleen was open to the idea of having black friends. Her mother, Patricia, had been born and raised in New York City; a Queens girl who came to Mississippi by way of marrying an air force enlistee from the Magnolia State. Colleen was seven when her family relocated, but she maintained her open-mindedness. "My mom wasn't a sheltered person," said Colleen. "She worked for a social organization that got a lot of federal grant money to help race relations. Part of her job was going to black homes, then writing proposals. She'd come back and tell us, 'You wouldn't believe how these people are living. You just wouldn't believe it.'" Because of Patricia's overt empathy, the Crawfords found themselves on the receiving end of threatening calls from the KKK. "Mom heard the phrase 'nigger lover' quite a bit," said Donna Williams, Colleen's sister. "But she was tough."

Colleen never aspired to become a cheerleader, but when Diane Weems, the captain of the Columbia High team, transferred to Columbia Academy, her friends talked her into filling the vacancy. She knew little of pom-poms or touchdowns, but took an immediate liking to the fast kid in the No. 22 jersey. On bus rides, Walter was funny and respectful. He was the type of boy who surrendered his seat for the girls, and waited patiently for others to exit the vehicle before doing so himself. "Something about Walter stood out, and not just football," said Crawley. "I think it's that he was just very nice." There were three senior cheerleaders in 1970—Colleen, Sandra Height, and Dawn Givens—and each one paired up with a black senior star. Height bonded with Johnson, the quarterback. Givens took to Moses, the fleet half-back. And Colleen Crawley often found herself alongside Walter Payton.

They became close—the cheerleader who thought of Payton as a friend; the running back who thought of Crawley as a love interest. The two sat next to each other on the bus, smiled in the hallways, waved from afar. On more than one occasion Walter carried her books home from school, a quaint act that surely caught the ire of her neighbors on North Park Avenue. "He'd see me walking and he'd get his friends to drop him off so he could walk me to my house," she said. "I invited Walter over every now and then if my parents were out and I was babysitting. He came to my home once or twice with some of the other black guys. I remember that some of the kids would bring a six-pack of beer and we'd play records. But Walter never drank."

Walter clearly believed he and Crawley were an item. Or at least a potential item. He bragged to his friends about her, and was smitten by her beauty. "Oh, he had a thing for Colleen," said Woodson. "He wanted to date her badly."

On more than one occasion during his senior year, Payton bragged to his friends and teammates that he was close to bedding Crawley. One time, as he told it, he knocked on the front door to Colleen's house, and heard her voice call, "Come in, Walter! It's open!" Upon entering, he spotted her on the bed, naked, waiting for him. "So I ran all the way home," Walter would say, laughing. "I couldn't get caught with a white girl in her house. They'd kill me." Because boys are boys and tall tales of sexual conquest seem to be a requisite part of the male adolescent experience, Walter can probably be excused that the story was pure fiction.

"I liked Walter a lot—*as a person*," Colleen said. "But there is no way we could have dated back then. Forget that I had two boyfriends my senior year, and that I was Junior Miss for the city and I was editor of the school paper and involved in community theatre. The problem was the times. In 1970, you could not be white and openly date a black person, or vice versa. It just wasn't allowed.

"But he was very special," she added. "And the thing I think a lot of people noticed about him was he never fully looked up. He would look down and glance up occasionally with his big bright eyes. He was very humble.

There were other people better looking than he was, but it was his personality. He'd look at you and you had to feel good."

Even without Crawley as a girlfriend, Walter and his friends found plenty of ways to entertain themselves. Buried within Payton's quiet exterior lurked a daredevil. With the exception of running the football, Payton's true love might have been the motorized scooter his parents had once bought him as a birthday present. When the days were long and dull, Walter revved up the red scooter and drove to the nearby town of Harmony, where the rolling, unpaved streets looped and curved like giant pretzels. At the time, the posted speed limit was 40 mph—which Payton promptly ignored. "He would kick it up to sixty miles per hour . . . seventy miles per hour," said Woodson. "Boy drove like a maniac." One day, while coming around a sharp turn, Walter skidded across the road before barreling through a barbed wire fence and into a pen of cows. "He wasn't hurt," said Woodson, "but only because of luck."

Payton took pleasure in waiting for his father to fall asleep on the couch, then boosting his truck and driving into the night. It was a beat-up jalopy with a five-speed engine, and to take off one had to push the vehicle down the street, pop the clutch, and jump in. "Sometimes we'd get back to Walter's house and his dad would be awake," said Moses. "Boy, would he give Walter an earful. 'Stop stealing my truck!' But by this age he was too big to get hit. So we'd just laugh it off."

. . .

Thanks in large part to Payton, Columbia High won its first seven games, and talk of an undefeated season and South Little Dixie Conference title heated up. On October 24, the Wildcats traveled fifty miles north to Magee, Mississippi, to take on the archrival Magee High Trojans in what many presumed would be an easy win.

One year earlier, Columbia sans Payton shocked Magee, at the time the conference's top team, 14–3. Now, even though the Wildcats were bigger, stronger, and faster, they found themselves facing a daunting opponent: the officials. Payton carried the ball twenty-three times that evening, and according to Danny Davis, a Columbia High senior who was covering the game for the student newspaper, the *Hi-Lites*, nearly all of his long runs were called back. "It was some of the worst officiating I've ever seen," said Davis. "Payton couldn't touch the ball without a whistle being blown." Throughout the season, Tommy Davis and Boston had wondered when (not *if*) the referees would penalize their team for having multiple stars with dark skin. It was a common phenomenon in the first year of integrated ball—all-white crews singling out black players in key moments.

Here, on Magee's field, injustice reigned. On the first play of the game, Johnson faked a handoff to Payton, dropped back, and threw a majestic forty-yard spiral to Moses, who caught the ball and cruised toward the end zone. On Columbia's sideline players were leaping up and down when—flag. "They called Sugar Man offside," said Woodson. "A terrible, terrible call." McGee jumped out to a 10–0 lead, and despite a miraculous ten-yard Payton touchdown run late in the fourth quarter ("I swear to God, he carried the entire Magee team into the end zone," said Danny Davis), the Wildcats failed to come back. They lost, 17–8, and for the entirety of the one-hour bus ride home after the game, Payton sat alone, head in hands, sobbing.

The Wildcats went on to finish 8-2, an extraordinary run for the first integrated team in school history. Payton scored at least one touchdown in every game, and was named all-conference and all-state. "The whole season showed people that blacks and whites belonged together, side by side," said Dantin. "It was an enormous success by all standards."

He paused.

"But," Dantin adds, "it would have been sweeter had we won every game."

. . .

With the pressure of football now behind him, Payton reveled in his remaining days at Columbia High. He attended biweekly meetings of the Future Homemakers of America, which were overflowing with coeds learning how to boil eggs and iron shirts. Merely an average student throughout high school, usually bringing home report cards with Bs and a few Cs, at Columbia High Walter developed a genuine interest in assisting the mentally impaired.

A young teacher named Mike Callahan started a Columbia High branch of the Youth Association for Retarded Children. He roamed the halls looking for volunteers, and among the dozen or so students he roped in was an engaging football star with a free sixth period. "We'd meet once per week during school and figure out ways to help," said Becky Sinclair, a freshman Walter's senior year. "We were small, but the people involved were sincerely interested in doing good. It was a lot of tutoring and assisting those who needed help."

Walter wasn't merely a jock looking to snag credit or up his Q-rating. On Saturday mornings Payton joined Callahan, Sinclair, and Co. on trips to the Ellisville State School, one of Mississippi's six state-funded residential mental retardation facilities. Once there Walter would chat with the kids, or play drums, or tell stories of his football adventures. "He was such a caring person," said Sinclair. "He'd sit with a child on the ground and talk with him forever. Just the two of them."

In the late spring of 1971, Columbia High's branch of the Youth Association for Retarded Children took a bus to the state conference, 260 miles to the north in Tupelo. Upon arriving, Walter, Sinclair, Edward Moses, and three or four other white students walked to a nearby hamburger restaurant for lunch. They were denied service. "It never dawned on us," said Sinclair. "But even when you were going somewhere to do good, you couldn't always escape the racism of the time."

Walter spent the spring competing in both baseball and track—sprinting from one practice field to another as the demands of his coaches dictated. "I was never that fond of the game," he once wrote of baseball. "But we had a good time."

Track and field was another story. If Payton's achievements on the gridiron were extraordinary, then his long jump accomplishments are, to quote Boston, "absolutely unbelievable." Because Columbia High's facilities did not include a track, Boston, the head coach (here was one job a black man was deemed capable of holding), dragged Payton out to the football field, where he'd run and leap, run and leap, run and leap. "I'll never forget Walter trying the long jump for the first time in practice," said Tom Watts, a teammate. "He ran down the runway, took off over the pit, and landed in the bushes behind the pit. It was like watching a superhero fly through the air. Except Walter didn't have a cape."

Making his track and field debut at the Hazelhurst Relays in April 1971, Payton set a meet record with a jump of 20'7"—then proceeded to win nine consecutive dual meets. He broke the Columbia High mark with a 22'11¼" leap, and later took the state championship by soaring 22'3". "He would jump out of the pit," said Billy Mason, a teammate. "That's not an exaggeration—Walter literally left the pit. And you wanna know the funniest thing about that?

"To Walter, it was no big deal. Just another day in the life."

CHAPTER 5

# RECRUITMENT

The article dominated the December 17, 1970, front page of the *Columbian-Progress*. Atop the fold, fifty-point bold headline, two columns wide:

## WILDCATS SIGNED BY STATE SCHOOLS

Five Columbia High School Wildcats have signed football scholarships with Mississippi schools.

Coach Tommy Davis, head coach at Columbia High School, and Coach Charles Boston, commended them for an outstanding year with the Wildcats and wished them successful seasons with their schools in the coming college years.

Not only were the boys commended for being good athletes but for fine academic records and team and school spirit which builds schools of character, the coaches noted.

The five Wildcats signed with three schools, one with the University of Southern Mississippi, two with Jackson State College and two with Mississippi Valley State College.

Signing with the University of Southern Mississippi was Steve Stewart, son of Mr. and Mrs. Ben Stewart. While visiting in Columbia last week, Coach Barney Poole of USM said he was extremely proud that Steve had decided "to cast his lot with us." Stewart, a 6'2" end weighing 190 pounds, played mostly defensive end but also played some offense, doing a good job at both.

Edward "Sugar Man" Moses, five foot seven and 150 pounds, played halfback. He is the son of Mrs. Laura Moses and the late Willie Moses. He signed with Jackson State College.

Another Jackson State signee was Walter "Spider Man" Payton, son of Mr. and Mrs. Edward Payton. He stands six feet tall, weighs 193 and played fullback.

Alvin L Benson, director of public relations at Jackson State, said he was extremely glad to see the two Wildcats come to Jackson State, as both were outstanding Wildcats. Then, in his call to the *Columbian-Progress*, he voiced what must be the sentiments of many Mississippi coaches when he said, "They'll be playing with us instead of coming back to plague us with an out-of-state team."

Because the year was 1970 and the ten schools of the Southeastern Conference were still dragging their feet when it came to recruiting black athletes (the legendary Bear Bryant signed Alabama's first black player in 1971, and Ole Miss waited until 1972), Southern stalwarts like Walter Payton—an all-state running back whose size-speed combination made him an undeniable Division I talent—went largely ignored in their home regions. The few SEC- or Mississippi-based schools that might have considered Payton were turned off by his antics from the Prentiss game, when he held the ball aloft and jogged backward into the end zone. "When I was talking to Southern Miss, the recruiter asked me if I would like to have Walter as a college teammate," said Stewart. "I told him, 'Heck yeah!' But the man refused to get over him holding that ball in the air. They had one of the best running backs in the country completely available, and they ignored him. Holding that ball up became Walter's signature."

With Columbia High, a small school in an oft-overlooked portion of the state, very few colleges actually knew of Payton. The members of the historically black Southwestern Athletic Conference (SWAC) sent scouts, but only one NCAA Division I program went after Walter Payton.

"We had him," said Vince Gibson, the head coach of Kansas State University. "Walter Payton was going to be a KSU Wildcat. It was a done deal."

Indeed, before the *Columbian-Progress* announced his intention to attend Jackson State, Payton was being strongly pursued by a rising power from the Big Eight. In the fall of 1970, a Kansas State assistant coach named Frank Falks received a list of Southern prospects from some of the more obscure high schools. "I had never heard of Walter Payton," said Falks, a former all-American linebacker at Parsons College. "Didn't know the name, didn't know the statistics. But we needed a running back, so I went down to Columbia to watch him."

Every so often, a college recruiter stumbles upon a gem who—for one reason or another—falls through the clutches of rival schools. It doesn't take much to recognize when it's happening. The town has one gas station, a dive bar, and a hole-in-the-wall restaurant. Traffic lights are scarce, as, for that matter, is traffic. You're the only person with a notepad at a game, and when the kid runs or throws, nary a camera flash bursts.

That was Falks' experience at Columbia High. As the Wildcats' No. 22 dashed up and down the field, no other recruiters could be found. Falks was all alone. "Once you saw him, there was no question he'd be great," said Falks. "No question whatsoever."

Falks approached Payton after the game, then returned to his house on Hendricks Street to meet with Alyne and Peter. He sat down at the kitchen table, sipped a cool glass of iced tea, and made his pitch. It was a strong one: *Come to Kansas State, you'll receive a great education and you'll play against the absolute best. Come to Kansas State, and maybe—just maybe—you'll have a shot at going professional.* In November 1970, Walter flew to Manhattan, Kansas—a place he had never before heard of—to make an official recruiting visit. Boasting 13,847 students, the sprawling campus of trees and paths and brick buildings was twice as large as Payton's hometown. He was given a tour of the athletic dormitories, of the student center, of the new KSU Stadium, with its thirty thousand seats. He watched with wide-eyed wonderment as sexy coeds passed, and found himself imagining life in this wondrous—if glacial—new place nearly nine hundred miles from home.

Over the following months Falks followed up with repeated phone calls, as did Gibson. "A talent like his could have taken us to a new level," said Falks of a team that went 6-5 in 1970. "Walter alone was probably good for three or four more wins a season."

Yet at the same time Kansas State was giving Payton the hard sell, so was Jackson State and its new head coach, Bob Hill. A former star running back at the school, Hill spent eight years as a line coach and offensive coordinator before being hired in December 1970 to take over his beleaguered alma mater. Having scouted Walter Payton in Columbia High's season opener against Prentiss, Hill knew of the youngster's unparalleled talents. "Oh man, he was something," said Hill. "You saw him play one time and it was clear he was the real goods."

Unlike Gibson, Hill possessed an ace up his sleeve. During Walter's senior season in high school, one of Jackson State's standouts was a junior running back by the name of Payton—*Eddie Payton*. In a forgettable 1970 campaign that saw the Tigers go 3-7, Eddie Payton ran for 339 yards and four touchdowns. Hill, a renowned hard-ass who lavished praise upon few, lavished praise upon Eddie, and assured him even better times should he woo his little brother to the Mississippi state capital. "So Eddie promised me Walter would be coming," said Hill. "I said, 'Eddie, do I have your word on it?' and he said I did. I said, 'You're telling me for your father?' and Eddie said, 'Yes, I am.' I took that to mean Walter would be playing for us."

Eddie, though, wasn't Walter's father. He wasn't Walter's mother, either. He was his older brother, and an antagonizing one at that. Although Walter loved and admired his sibling and attended as many Jackson State games as possible, he also found him to be occasionally deceptive, misleading, and condescending. "I didn't let them fight," Alyne once said, "but I do think Walter sort of resented the older boy. Eddie would say, 'Let me show you how to do this,' and Walter would say, 'No, I don't want to know.'" Ever since Walter took up football as a sophomore at Jefferson, he had sought Eddie's approval. It was hard to come by. Eddie was outgoing and gregarious; the life of any party and a beloved piece of the Jackson State campus. But he was (and, some forty years later, remains) insecure to a fault. From afar, he heard of Walter's phenomenal output at Jefferson and Columbia, and a part of Eddie—according to those who know him well—felt forgotten. It's one thing for a standout to be replaced by another standout. Happens all the time. But to be eclipsed by a sibling? Later on, when both men were playing in the NFL, Eddie was asked what it's like to have a brother as a star. "I don't know," he replied. "Why don't you ask Walter."

"There's a lot of jealousy there, and there has been for a long time," said one of Eddie's close friends. "Eddie loved Walter very much. But, like any older brother would, he had a hard time handling Walter's success. It gnawed at him."

Eddie's antagonism made Walter apprehensive about attending Jackson State. When, in December 1970, the older brother pressed the younger brother to accept a scholarship to the college, Walter agreed. Yet it was far from sealed. Charles Boston, Payton's head coach at Jefferson High and the assistant at Columbia, let it be known that, for the right opportunity from the right school, the running back was still on the market. Apparently word got around. That spring a portly defensive assistant from Florida State University was traveling through Mississippi when Boston got ahold of him. "He said to me, 'Coach, we got a guy here who didn't get signed by any of the college teams but I think he's a really good player. Do you have any scholarships left?'" recalled the Seminole coach—a man named Bill Parcells. "I said 'Yeah, we got one but I don't think we'll use it. We'll probably keep it.'" Boston was determined that Parcells see Payton, so he had Walter take part in a spring practice with the upcoming varsity team. Parcells attended. "The kid's about five foot nine, one-seventy, and he's a running back," Parcells recalled. "And he runs pretty good, but I look at [Boston] and say, 'Coach, we've got six backs better than him at Florida State, plus he's a little too small.'"

Walter's future came down to two schools. *Wildcats? Tigers?* When Jackson State signed Moses to a scholarship, it wasn't because the college collected five-foot-seven scatbacks. "Truthfully, we gave that to the little guy because we craved Walter," said Hill. "That's how you recruit." Kansas State took an equally direct approach, promising all sorts of greatness and glory. "We wanted him terribly," said R. C. Slocum, at the time a Wildcat assistant. "You don't get those type of players every day." Despite his differences with Eddie, Walter was intrigued by the idea of playing in the same backfield as his brother. But he thought Kansas State—with games against national powers like Nebraska and Oklahoma—offered an amazing opportunity. There was, however, the winters of Manhattan, Kansas. There was, however, the tyrannical rule of Hill, who, according to Eddie, ran a football team like a military platoon. "Bob Hill was the black Bear Bryant," said Moses. "Walter didn't like what he heard about Bob Hill's style. He was brutal and raw."

Finally, in the late spring of 1971, Walter made up his mind, signing a national letter of intent to attend Kansas State.* A few weeks later, in early June, Payton returned to Manhattan for a summer recruiting party at the

---

* In *Never Die Easy*, the autobiography Walter wrote with *Sports Illustrated*'s Don Yaeger shortly before his death, it is said that he debated between Jackson State and the University of Kansas. The same point is made in *Payton*, a biography released by Walter's family. Both texts are incorrect. "We never recruited him," said Don Fambrough, the University of Kansas football coach at the time. "And believe me—if we'd recruited Walter Payton, that's something I would remember."

breathtaking Turtle Creek Reservoir. With twenty-five of his fellow incoming freshmen on hand, Payton partook in waterskiing and swimming and gorged on hotdogs and hamburgers grilled by the coaching staff. "He was a really handsome, clean-cut, articulate kid," said Slocum. "When he came to the cookout, we knew he would play for us. It was exciting."

With that, Kansas State's coaches made a program-defining error: They relaxed. When Payton returned to Columbia, he took up an offer from Eddie to move into a Jackson State dorm room for the remainder of the summer. Moses came along as well, and Hill encouraged both players to enroll in summer school classes. He also set Payton up with a go-only-if-you're-very-bored job working in a nearby gymnasium. "Coach Hill wanted his hands on Walter," said Moses. "But Walter was turned off by it all."

Payton took two classes that summer, and made regular trips from Jackson to Columbia. With each passing day his feelings of dislike toward Hill grew. He failed to understand the coach's demeanor. Not an hour went by without Hill checking in on Payton, gauging his happiness, urging him to embrace Jackson State's campus for all its splendor. Finally, enough was enough. The pressure was too much. On one of their trips home together, Payton and Moses took a drive to Pearl River Junior College in Poplarville, Mississippi. The school had gained fame for producing Willie Heidelburg, a running back who had recently become the first black to sign with the University of Southern Mississippi. "We all knew about Willie, and what he'd done," said Moses. "So we got in Walter's mother's car, unbeknownst to his mom, his dad, Eddie, and Coach Hill. And we looked into getting a tryout."

Payton and Moses tracked down John Russell, Pearl River's head coach, and requested an on-the-spot audition. According to Moses, Russell asked whether they brought along equipment. "We didn't," said Moses. "And he wouldn't loan us any to try out in." Flabbergasted, they shuffled off, never to return.

The two teammates begrudgingly headed back to Jackson for the remainder of the summer, and on one of the final days Hill agreed to chauffeur Payton home to Columbia. He was still hoping Walter would become a Tiger. "Walter wanted to drive my car, so I let him," Hill recalled of his brand new red-and-white Cadillac. "Man, if I hadn't been recruiting him . . . I mean, he was just a crazy driver. Speeding like an insane person. But I didn't say anything, I just found myself praying all the way that he didn't hit a tree or a car or some person crossing the street.

"When we finally got there his mom fixed dinner for us. He wanted to go around and see some girl. So, fine, he left, and he stayed out a long time. And I was just content because his mom had cooked these peas, and oh, man, I loved peas. And chocolate cake. And oh, man, her biscuits. So I'm content— I ain't worried about what time he'd get back. But his father was upset—*how can he keep this man's car like that?* He was mad. It was rude, but he could have kept the car. Anyway, I wasn't worried about it. I'm saying to myself, 'I know I've got him, because his old man isn't gonna stand for no mess.' Even though Kansas State was still trying to get him. So when he got back, Walter said, 'Coach Hill, you go on back to Jackson, and I promise you I'll be there in the morning.' I'm all smiling. I've got me a piece of cake, I've got myself a running back. Because I didn't have to worry no more about Kansas State or anyone else."

But Payton had signed his letter of intent with the Wildcats which, from Gibson's perspective, was written in blood. The university sent Payton his one-way plane ticket to the Midwest. He was scheduled to leave on a Tuesday afternoon from, of all places, Jackson, and would arrive that evening in Manhattan. His dorm room was ready. His purple-and-white practice jersey hung from a locker. His name and number—PAYTON 22—was printed in black marker atop white athletic tape. No matter what Eddie Payton or Bob Hill were saying, Walter steeled himself to fly off to Kansas. He packed his bags, cleaned out his childhood bedroom, hugged his mother and sister, shook his father's hand, and departed Columbia for the Jackson Airport.

With one itsy bitsy stop.

Because he arrived in Jackson more than five hours before his flight was scheduled to depart, Payton paid a final visit to his brother. He showed up just in time for the start of one of the Tigers' practices. "The campus was as beautiful as I remembered it," Payton wrote in his autobiography. "When Coach Hill saw me, he called me over to talk."

The two sat down and watched the players run through their drills.

"Have you decided where you're going?" Hill—ever persistent—asked.

"I think so," Payton replied.

"Well," said Hill, "I just hope it's a place that puts as much emphasis on education as it does football, like we do here. You know, Jackson State has a lot to offer, and I'm talking about a lot more than football. You have to get your education, because nobody plays football all his life."

Hill paused before continuing. "I can show you on paper," he said, "that ninety-eight percent of the guys that play football here get their college degrees."

Payton was no dummy. He knew Hill was pulling out all the stops. After a summer in Jackson, Payton was close with many of the Tiger players. He knew his way around the campus, felt comfortable in the environs, had his brother to lean on.

Though Hill's speech hadn't fully swayed him, it did cause Payton to skip his flight to Manhattan. The Kansas State coaches had arranged for Walter to take a bus from Manhattan Regional Airport to campus. They waited for two hours—no word. "I finally called someone from Mississippi to ask where Walter was," said Gibson. "They told me he was going to Jackson State. I said, 'Jackson State? He signed with us.'"

Payton had yet to actually make the official decision, but he was close. He went back to Columbia the next day, accompanied by his brother and Hill. With the two looming over him, pressuring him to dump Kansas State and sign with the Tigers, Walter fled the house and took a long drive. Upon returning, he sat down with his mother. "Mama," he said, "I have no idea what to do."

Alyne Payton—strong-willed, tough, focused—had never liked the idea of her youngest son going all the way to Kansas. "If you can't make up your mind where you want to go to school, I'll make it up for you," she said. "You're going to Jackson State."

That was that. *Almost.* The administrators at Kansas State were furious. In their minds, Walter Payton had been kidnapped. Everything Hill had done—allowing Walter to attend summer school, lining up a job, driving him home—was part of an elaborate scheme. When it came to the ethics of college football, Hill was no Mother Teresa. He bought recruits meals and clothing, hid them from opposing programs, and made promises he couldn't keep. According to numerous players, he reveled in paying for various achievements (a punt return for a touchdown netted ten dollars) and in setting bounties upon opposing stars. ("He once offered us fifty dollars to knock [Grambling quarterback] Doug Williams out of a game," said Vernon Perry, a Tigers safety. "I actually did it, and Bob paid up.") John Peoples, Jackson State's president, recalled Hill telling him, "I can get Walter Payton, but you have to let me do what I have to do."

"I said, 'That's fine—just don't do anything illegal," said Peoples. "Don't do anything wrong."

After Payton *finally* signed a letter to attend Jackson State, Peoples received a call from James McCain, Kansas State's president. A rugged former lieutenant commander in the navy, McCain was infuriated. "Dr. Peoples, I'm planning on reporting you to the NCAA."

"Reporting me?" Peoples asked. "For what?"

"For kidnapping," McCain replied. "You kidnapped Walter Payton."

"I don't know what you mean," Peoples said. "But I do know that Walter Payton has not enrolled with you. So how can someone be kidnapped if he's not enrolled?"

McCain seethed. Peoples was right—though Payton had signed the letter, he'd never enrolled in Kansas State. At the time, that was enough for an athlete to go wherever he preferred. "I'm going to call the NCAA about this," McCain said. "You'll hear back from me soon."

It was the last time the two ever spoke.

Walter Payton was coming to Jackson State.

PART TWO

# JACKSON

### W. C. Gorden,
### Assistant Football Coach, Jackson State

---

*We had running backs at Jackson State who were bigger than Walter, who were stronger than Walter. But as I learned, fifty percent of talent is height, is weight, is strength, and is speed. The other fifty percent—the most important fifty percent—is that the youngster has to want to be a superb football player. And Walter had that compelling desire to lift weights, to condition himself, to run a riverbank up and down, to run the stadium steps. After practice he'd go eat dinner, then come back to the gym. He didn't play the game for the crowd appeal or the attention. He played for the love.*

CHAPTER 6

# JACKSON STATE

THROUGHOUT HIS BLISSFULLY PLACID BOYHOOD, WALTER PAYTON WAS NEVER one to make trouble or start a fight. Oh, maybe he and his pals would steal a couple of melons from a field, or perhaps he'd drive thirty miles above the speed limit in his daddy's truck. But when it came to conflict, and especially conflict over civil rights and desegregation, Walter was nowhere to be found. When, in April 1968, Martin Luther King Jr. was assassinated in Memphis, the blacks of Columbia held a march from Jefferson High School to City Hall. Not only did Walter refuse to participate, he didn't even attend as an observer.

At Jackson State, however, Walter encountered an entirely new perspective on race. Although he had spent much of his summer living on the Jackson campus, with the arrival of the 4,800-member student body for the start of the fall semester came an eye-opening education on what it was to be black, proud, *and* vocal. In his hometown, Walter had watched and learned from his elders, who survived by shuffling past whites with eyes lowered and mouths shut. If one addressed a white person, it was always with a deferential "sir" or "ma'am." The ideas of black pride and black power weren't ideas at all.

Now, however, at a school where 98 percent of the student body was black, all Walter Payton had to do was pick up a copy of the *Blue and White Flash*, Jackson State's monthly student newspaper, to understand how his world—and *the* world—was changing. "Before it's too late, you had better start thinking for yourself," wrote Jonathan Grant in a November 1971 editorial titled "Awaken Black Youths." "Our fore-fathers [sic] were treated cruel, treated like animals, sold like cattle, drug up and down the streets, hung by the neck from an oak tree, tarred and feathered, and burned at the stake. Will you awaken, or will you let this kind of thing perpetuate continuously? Are you an animal or a human being? Are you a first class citizen, or a second class citizen?"

Grant's piece ran alongside another column, "A Black Man's Hope," that began with the sentence, "I am a man of a darker color. My oppressor will not let me go any further."

"We were all about making a statement," said Coolidge Anderson, an editor at the *Flash*. "I wanted to be a revolutionary in the movement. We didn't hate whites, but we hated what segregation had done."

Less than a year and a half before Walter's official enrollment, the Jackson State campus was home to great tragedy. On May 14, 1970, Phillip Gibbs, a twenty-year-old Jackson State student, and James Green, a seventeen-year-old senior at nearby Jim Hill High School, were shot and killed by state police during an on-campus protest over race relations. The altercation began when police mistook the sound of a dropped glass bottle for the unloading of a round. "They opened fire on the girls' dormitory," said Milton Webb, a Jackson State freshman at the time. "Students were in front of the dorm, innocently standing there, and the police started shooting away."

"When you're shot at by the police and state troopers for thirty seconds with automatic rifles, you don't think about much except surviving," said Eddie Payton, who witnessed the event. "I was out there bullshitting with some other football players, and when we saw the state troopers come we just turned to get back to our dorm. By the time we reached the dorm the whole sky was lit up from gunfire."

Despite repeated assertions from law enforcement that race had nothing to do with the killings, most of Jackson State's students and faculty found the explanation implausible. Even fifteen months later, as Walter and his fellow freshmen arrived, the pain from that day had yet to subside. "You don't get over something of that magnitude," said John Peoples, the college president. "Not in a month, not in a year, maybe not ever."

Were Walter Payton compelled, he could have walked over to the Alexander Residence Center to run his finger over a bullet hole. He could have followed the lead of the small band of students who changed their last names to X. He could have grown out his Afro, penned angry editorials for the

*Blue and White Flash*, marched across campus in one of the ongoing protests over the mistreatment of blacks throughout the state of Mississippi.

Any such acts, however, would have been out of character. Because Walter Payton, eighteen years old and as nice and agreeable a kid as one could find, was attending college in Jackson for three simple reasons: to play football, meet girls, and receive a quality education.

In that order.

. . .

Had Walter Payton been a member of the Kansas State student body, he would have found himself on one of the nation's more beatific campuses, surrounded by grass and trees and dignified brick buildings with a Harvard-esque feel.

Jackson State was no Kansas State. Located on the western side of Mississippi's capital, a mere five-minute drive from downtown, the 125-acre campus was your prototypical city school, an uninspired gray and pewter in color, with patches of green tossed in amongst concrete bleakness. A road, J. R. Lynch Street, divided the campus in half, providing students with the steady hum of cars and trucks passing through. Though far from the ugliest college in America, Jackson State's physical beauty (as well as the funding it received from the state) paled in comparison to Mississippi's prominent white schools: Ole Miss, Mississippi State, and Southern Miss.

The football facilities were no better. The team's locker room was located inside a decrepit converted army barracks that had been built during World War II. The floor was rotting wood, the walls decaying drywall.

Not that Walter particularly cared. Jackson State quickly felt like home, especially when he was assigned to share quarters with his brother, Eddie, and his best friend from Columbia, Edward "Sugar Man" Moses, also a freshman running back. The three were placed in a second-floor room in Sampson Hall, the school's football dormitory. There was one regular bed and a bunk, two small bedrooms with a common area, and a bathroom located down the hall. As a star senior with the Tigers, Eddie possessed enough sway to have his own room or, at most, one upper-class roommate. "But I wanted to show Walter the ropes and take care of him," Eddie said. "He was my little brother, and this was going to be a new experience for him."

Despite lingering sibling resentment, Eddie made Walter's early collegiate adjustment significantly easier. He talked to him about which classes to take, where to hang out, who to trust, and who not to trust. Their mother, Alyne, made regular drives up to see her boys, and when the season started she would arrive Saturday mornings with fresh-baked treats. (In Eddie and Walter's years at the school, Alyne never missed a home game.) "I was feeling right at home," Walter once wrote. "Eddie was a great kid with just the right personality for a football player—maybe better than mine. He was the type who believed he could do anything if he really tried." Though far from a wallflower, Walter couldn't compete with his brother's social ease. He watched in amazement as Eddie lingered in front of Sampson Hall, heckling people as they passed. "If he saw a carload of girls to flirt with," Walter wrote, "he'd walk right out there and hold up traffic for half a block to talk with them." Eddie also introduced Walter to the large oak tree positioned approximately three feet from the window in their room. When Hill imposed curfews, often stationing himself at the Sampson Hall front entrance (Hill was fond of a cologne appropriately named "Trouble," and players could smell him as they snuck back in), Eddie, Walter, and Sugar Man would grab ahold of the tree, use its branches to scale down the trunk, and indulge in a night on the town at Nita's or the Doll's House or one of the other clubs on Lynch Street. "We'd go out to dinner, go out to the park, get some girls, and do some making out. Then we could come back in and go up," Eddie said. "Security would never stop us because of who we were, but then one day Coach Hill found out what we were up to."

"And," Eddie said, "he immediately had all the branches removed from the tree."

In Columbia, a young black man always had to watch what he said, and who he said it to. But here, on the all-black campus, Walter felt at ease. The vast majority of his teammates hailed from identical small-town backgrounds—poor and black, forced to gaze downward when whites passed, praised by whites only for their athletic gifts. They knew what it was to be called "nigger" and "coon," and they could relax in the knowledge that, in college, nobody uttered such things.

Walter's social adjustment to college was smooth, and the first few days were filled with the euphoric giddiness of a new adventure. Yet the freedoms that came with life away from home were mere mirages.

Soon Walter would get to know a force of nature known as Bob Hill.

· · ·

He was born in 1935 on an eight-acre farm in Tippo, Mississippi, a nondescript rural town with dirt roads and dirt driveways and dirt aspirations for the black kids who filled its streets. Robert Hill loved sports as a boy, but had little reason to think they'd take him anywhere beyond the bathroom sink where his grandma, Lillie Vance, patched up his bloody knees and elbows. Besides, most of his time was devoted to picking cotton in the family fields—his all-but-guaranteed future occupation. "I could pick three hundred pounds of cotton easily, and people admired that," said Hill, who was born out of wedlock and raised by Lillie. "We didn't have a school bus, and barely had a school. We had schools in churches in different areas, but you only went until eighth grade. Then, if you wanted to go to high school, you moved in with a relative or friend who had one nearby. Otherwise, you started your long life as a worker."

Come September 1949, young Bob, age fourteen, followed the annual late-summer routine of plucking thick white clumps of cotton. He was one of hundreds of Tippo blacks working the field; one of hundreds of Tippo blacks who loathed the bleakness of the task but knew no alternative. "I didn't particularly mind picking the cotton," he said, "but the chopping it, and picking the grass out, and spacing it—just terrible. You had to make sure you didn't cut too much of it down, and if you did you might get a whuppin'." That October, in what would become a life-altering decision, his grandma Lillie insisted he move to nearby Charleston to live with his other grandmother, Janie Hill, and attend Tallahatchie Agricultural High School, an all-black facility that guided its students toward blue-collar careers. "Boy, was I ever happy," he said. "When we started picking cotton the weather was good and the cotton was opening. But it began raining mid-October, and I guess my grandma figured enough was enough—let's get this kid doing something more meaningful."

Bigger, stronger, and rougher than most of his peers, Bob immediately caught the eye of Joe Allen, the school's principal and head football coach. Until that point, he had never seen a football. "They insisted I come out for the team, so I did," he said. "They gave me a jersey, and I finally figured out how to put the jersey on. Then I jogged out to practice with my helmet on. Everyone started laughing and teasing, because I had the helmet on backward."

Hill struggled to learn the game, and caught his fair share of beatings from Allen, an impatient man who kicked and punched those who failed to execute. The following year a new coach, David Alford, held the job, and moved Hill from wide receiver to running back. He immediately took to the position. "It was the contact," he said. "I grew up on a farm, herding the cows, working with the cattle, riding horses, and I liked physical activity." Hill's grandmothers, however, feared for his life, and demanded "Junior" (as they called him) drop sports to focus on schoolwork. "I had to slip out and play," he said. "My aunt Bessie was a schoolteacher, and she came up for one of the games. The other team kicked off, and I was back receiving. And I got the kickoff. It was an old dusty field. I got tackled by five or six people, and the dust is all over my face. She ran out on the field screaming, 'Junior! Junior! Junior! Come on! You see why I don't want you to play!' She didn't know anything about the game, because she lived out in rural parts and we didn't know anything about football. All the guys laughed."

His family acquiesced, and by his senior year Bob was one of the best fullbacks around, a punishing ball carrier who lowered his sizeable head, squared his broad shoulders, and demolished opposing defenders. He was the type of kid Mississippi's black schools—Jackson State, Alcorn College, and Mississippi Vocational College (later to be known as Mississippi Valley State)—craved, yet he was a football ghost. "Nobody came to see me," he said. "Ever." Thankfully, a Tallahatchie Agricultural High teacher named Sally Williams had attended Jackson State, and knew the college's head coach and athletic director, T. B. Ellis. She called and raved about Hill's size and aggressiveness. "No promises," Ellis told her, "but I'll give the boy a look."

The year was 1952, and as soon as Hill learned of the opportunity, he packed a duffle bag and told his grandmothers not to expect him for dinner. Any dinner. Ever again. "I was through with the cotton fields," he said. "I left home and decided that I'd either make the team at Jackson State or join the army." He caught the three-hour bus ride south to Jackson, knowing nothing about Jackson State or T. B. Ellis or the college game. Ellis took one look at the boy, with his muscular forearms and powerful legs, and thought of Jack Spinks, the six-foot, 235-pound Alcorn fullback who had recently become the first black ballplayer from Mississippi to be drafted into the NFL. Then he watched him run. Hill was raw, but bursting with promise. After a week of tryouts, Ellis tacked a piece of paper with the final roster onto a board in the athletic dormitory. Hill could barely look. This was his life—"it was either football, the army, or cotton," he said. "And I didn't want the army or cotton." When he finally worked up the nerve and spotted his name, in small black lettering seven or eight down from the top, he let out a euphoric roar.

Hill's four years as a student-athlete at Jackson State go down as the best of his life. He was inserted into the starting lineup midway through his freshman season by Ellis, who ran the T-formation and sought size for his power running attack. When John Merritt took over as head coach the following year, he leaned on Hill even more, turning him into a primary ball carrier. A studious player who could absorb large quantities of information, Hill studied his coaches' mannerisms and styles. Both Ellis and Merritt were oft-angry leaders who mentally and physically intimidated their legions, and Hill fed off of it. The worse the punishment, the madder he became. The madder he became, the better he played.

Upon graduating from Jackson State in 1956, Hill was drafted in the twentieth round by the Baltimore Colts. He was with the organization for one year, never appearing in a game but paying close attention to Weeb Ewbank, the third-year head coach who would go on to a Hall of Fame career. Hill spent the following season with the Toronto Argonauts of the Canadian Football League before suffering a career-ending right leg injury. "I didn't want to stop playing at twenty-four years old, but I had no choice," he said. "Physically, it was over for me. I couldn't run like I used to."

Hill heard the cotton fields of Tippo whispering his name; chanting for him to come back home and take his rightful place among the relatives and friends who were fulfilling their natural destinies. This call would serve as a driving force for years. "We all have motivations," he said. "Mine was not going back."

Hill worked for one year as an assistant to LeRoy Smith at Mississippi Vocational College, then moved to Magee, Mississippi, to serve as the head coach at the all-black Magee High School. He took over a team that had existed for only one season, with a roster of roughly twenty kids, almost all of whom picked cotton in the wee morning hours, worked at the local poultry farm catching chickens in the evening, and practiced from seven to nine at night. The coaches of larger schools giddily added Magee to their schedules, eager to pick up the certain victory.

Combining the fierce discipline of Ellis and Merritt with the on-field ingenuity of Ewbank, Hill led his team to an 8-2 mark, earning a reputation as a local football savant. Nearly all of the opposing teams ran the T-offense Hill knew from high school and college; Magee operated the wide-open pro set utilized by Johnny Unitas and the Baltimore Colts. Nearly all of the opposing teams ran a traditional 4-3 defense; Magee went with a 5-3 setup, blitzing on nearly every down. "Oh, man, it was a lot of fun," Hill said. "I'd have receivers spread out all over the field, and our quarterback, Earnest James, could throw with anyone. There were no scouting reports back then, and we'd surprise everyone."

After two years Hill moved on to Rowan High in Hattiesburg. Over

two seasons his teams went 22-0, winning back-to-back state championships. Hill's greatest tool was fear, along with a willingness to skirt a rule or
two in the name of victory. One of his stars, a flanker named Eugene Bournes,
had played for him at Magee, a forty-seven-mile drive from Rowan. "I
brought him with me to Rowan," Hill said, "and, wink-wink, adopted him
as my son. He lived with me. Man, could he play."

Hill's successes didn't go unnoticed in the black college ranks. In 1963
Merritt left Jackson State to coach at Tennessee State, and the school wanted
to bring in a handful of young assistants to help the new head coach, Edward
"Ox" Clemons. Four coaches in their twenties and thirties were added, including the twenty-eight-year-old Hill as the offensive coordinator. When Clemons fell ill after one season, he was replaced by Rod Paige, Hill's college
roommate and a man who, thirty-seven years later, would be appointed the
nation's secretary of education by President George W. Bush. "Bob was my
assistant, and he was unlike any coach I've ever seen," said Paige. "He understood the power of fear. As a player, you didn't want to disappoint him,
because the wrath of God would come down upon your head."

Hill served under Paige for four years, and the two worked well together.
Perhaps Hill's greatest coup came in the fall of 1967, when he drove to Columbia, Mississippi, one Friday night on a tip about a fullback named Ray Holmes.
Hill wasn't impressed by the kid, but couldn't take his eyes off a little halfback
with blinding quickness. Hill especially liked the bowlegged way the boy
stood—Ellis had long ago taught him that bowlegged athletes possessed better
balance. Once he returned to campus, Hill told Paige about Eddie Payton.
"This Eddie Payton is the man," he said. "This is who we want."

When Paige heard he was five foot eight, 170 pounds, he laughed. "No,"
he said dismissively. "Too small."

Hill was undeterred. Having also been employed as Jackson State's (relatively disinterested) baseball coach, he was gifted with a handful of "baseball"
scholarships he could use however he saw fit. Though Eddie was by no means
a scholarship-worthy baseball player, he hit the ball hard enough where the
case could be made (he participated in two practices with the baseball team,
never appearing in a game). He signed with Jackson State, and a euphoric Hill
bounced into Paige's office to deliver the news. "Paige was really mad," Hill
said. "But by the second day of practice he was sold on Eddie."

When Paige departed Jackson State after the 1968 season and the school
named another assistant, Ulysses "U. S." McPherson, as his replacement, Hill

seethed. He was smarter than McPherson, a harder worker than McPherson, and a better all-around coach than McPherson—and most everyone knew it. Hill spent two unhappy years as an assistant on the staff, then quit to solely coach baseball.

McPherson was fired after the disastrous 3-7 1970 season, but a frustrated Hill held little hope of being hired. He wearily approached John Peoples, the school's president, and expressed his interest. "Doc," Hill said, "I can bring you a winning football program. I know I can." Peoples conferred with Ellis, the athletic director, who supported Hill. Yet at the same time the president and AD were hemming and hawing, Hill accepted a job as an assistant football coach at North Carolina Central. When word got out that Hill was leaving, Peoples pounced. "Stay here," he told Hill, "and you've got your dream gig."

He agreed to the job in December 1970, with a whopping five-thousand-dollar annual salary and an office the size of a dwarf's coffin. Hill and his wife, Yvonne, were ecstatic.

The returning players, however, realized that hell had no fury like Robert Hill. As an assistant coach, Hill's power had been limited. He could scream and berate and intimidate, but come day's end it was up to the comparatively mellow McPherson to enforce discipline. Such was no longer the case.

Walter Payton knew of Hill's hotheaded reputation, and because of it had mixed feelings about coming to Jackson State. During recruiting, however, Hill had offered Walter one glowing compliment after another. "Bob Hill was an absolute con artist," said Doug Shanks, Jackson's former city commissioner and a diehard Tigers booster. "Those kids didn't go to school. They practiced eight, ten hours every day. But Hill knew how to deal with them, and somehow make them feel special."

In the weeks leading up to his debut as a college head coach, Hill was, by all accounts, a lunatic. "As soon as he hit the football field for practice, it was clear he was crazy—stone crazy," said Matthew Norman, a sophomore defensive back. "He was very do or die. He would foam at the mouth, drool from the mouth, growl. Off the field, Bob was a normal man. But the football field was his sacred ground. He was all about blood." The players bestowed upon Hill the nickname "Thirst"—for bloodthirsty.

The first two weeks of September were brutally hot, with temperatures reaching the mid-nineties with oppressive humidity. Hill denied his players water throughout the ceaseless twice-a-day workouts. Replenishment, he believed, was for the soft, and Jackson State would be as hard as steel.

"Players were falling down, dying from the heat," recalled Joe Bingham, an offensive guard, "and he'd kick them while screaming, 'Die! Die! Die!' He'd say, 'If you die, I'll roll you over with the sled.'"

It took Hill mere days to establish himself as a cruel, unforgiving taskmaster. "If someone did something wrong, Bob would tell him he was going to break his plate," recalled Norman. "Which meant he was going to take your meal card from you, and you could no longer eat on campus." It also took Hill mere days to develop a further appreciation for his freshman back. Eddie Payton was the team's top returning rusher, having totaled 339 yards in 1970. He was fast, quick, tough, resilient. Walter, though, was better.

"Eddie was real good, but we're talking about different types," said Curtis Jones, a defensive back. "Eddie was good between the tackles, but Walter was good between the tackles and outside the tackles. Eddie could catch but Walter could catch better." Eddie had earned the nickname of "Monk" for his monkey-like dexterity, and before long teammates were calling Walter "L'il Monk." On one of the first days of full-roster workouts, a sophomore fullback named Tom Holloway was casually standing a few yards off of the goal line, fielding kickoffs in shorts and a T-shirt. As a ball approached, Holloway extended his arms, reached out his hands, then—*whoosh!* Out of nowhere, a blur bumped into Holloway, grabbed the ball, and ran. "I said, 'Who the hell is this guy?'" said Holloway. Payton jogged back toward Holloway, guffawing loudly. "I just wanted to see if I could catch it," he said. "My name's Walter—Walter Payton." Holloway wasn't amused. "OK, Walter Payton," he replied. "But freshmen don't do that."

"From day one he stood out," said Rodney Phillips, a Tiger quarterback. "He was in the best shape of anyone on the team. In practice, Walter was just running all over the place. The determination and desire was remarkable. And man, the things he could do! He could run the ball, obviously. But he could also pass the ball, kick the ball, catch the ball."

When he recruited Payton, Hill knew the youngster possessed skills as a runner and receiver. But here he was in practice, blowing everyone away. "The goal of the linemen was to bench press three hundred pounds," said Bingham. "Walter was the one little guy who could lift with us. It was amazing." Walter could be found throwing fifty-yard spirals and booting straight-toe thirty-five-yard field goals. If nothing else, Hill had a potential solution to his program's longstanding place-kicking problems. Lee Triplett remained the starting kicker, but his leash was a short one. "Walter had a leg as strong as any I'd seen," Hill said. "It's easier naming things Walter can't do than things he can."

One thing Walter couldn't do was keep his number. Payton had grown attached to No. 22, the digits he had worn throughout his three high school seasons. There was just one problem: In high school, Walter was given No. 22 by Charles Boston because the number had previously been worn by Eddie. Now, at Jackson State, Eddie was the featured back, and by no means interested in being numerically charitable.

Walter's second-favorite number was thirty-four, one he had never worn, but one that somehow caught his fancy. At the time, the number was owned by Holloway, the redshirt sophomore fullback from Chicago. "I had no real attachment to thirty-four, so when Walter asked for it I handed it over and took number forty-one," Holloway said. "I have a picture on my mantle of me wearing number thirty-four. Everyone who comes in says, 'You have Walter Payton's number?' And I say, 'No, Walter Payton has mine.'"

On Jackson State's football team, tradition dictated that freshmen did much watching and little playing. They were primarily present to absorb Hill's ritual beatings, and if they did so without crying or quitting, they might—*might*—contribute as sophomores. Walter Payton, however, was different. Though only eighteen years old and naïve to weight training, Payton's physique was unlike any other Tiger player. "Big calves, nice frame, small waist, legs like fire hydrants," said Willie Barnes, the team's trainer. "A total rock." He had the longest arms anyone had ever seen—ones that dangled from shoulders to below the knees. "They went on forever, and they looked like Popeye's arms," said Al Harris, a future NFL teammate. "He stuck his arms out into my chest, and I could barely grab his shoulder pads." There was also an air of maturity to the kid; a confidence that most nervous freshmen lacked. Hill and W. C. Gorden, the defensive coordinator, nearly came to blows arguing whether the freshman should begin his career as a running back or defensive back. "He had the skills for both," said Gorden. "He would have been a phenomenal safety." When Hill announced the roster of those who would dress, two Paytons were listed. Hill warned Walter not to become cocky or comfortable. "The bus works," Hill told him, "whether you're on it or not."

While Tiger players and coaches were excited for the new season, the community showed little interest. After years of losing, the student body had become increasingly ambivalent. The city of Jackson was even more so. In its special college football preview section, *The Jackson Daily News*, Jackson State's hometown paper, gave significantly more ink to the programs at Ole Miss, Mississippi State, Southern Miss, Millsaps College, Delta State, Alcorn State, as well as several of the nation's top teams, including Ohio State and Southern California. The paper finally got around to the Tigers on the bottom of the twenty-seventh page, devoting a whopping 198 words to a piece titled "J-State Seeks Improvement."

> Jackson State's Mighty Tigers will need a complete turnaround in 1971 or the term "Mighty" may be replaced with "Meek." . . . A new head coach with a penchant for winning and a veteran quarterback [Sylvester Collins] who led the Southwest Athletic Conference in total offense in 1970 are the keys to the Tigers hopes.

The Tigers opened their 1971 season by traveling to Prairie View, Texas, for a September 18 afternoon game against perennially subpar Prairie View A & M. Hill's plan was in place—his well-conditioned team would pummel the Panthers with brutal physicality. He envisioned a final score of 30–0. Maybe even 40–0. "We were better in all areas," he said. "No contest."

Yet in a matchup as dull as it was sloppy, Prairie View slogged its way to a 13–12 win, the difference courtesy of Triplett's missed extra point early in the first quarter. On the bright side, the defense played well, and Eddie Payton ran for two touchdowns. On the down side, Walter Payton showed why freshmen were freshmen.

In anticipation of the opening kickoff, Walter stood alongside a fellow back named James Marshall. As the ball came closer, Walter moved up, hesitated, backed away, slammed into Marshall, stumbled, then let it bounce three or four times before jumping atop it on the seven-yard line and being flattened by a mound of Prairie View tacklers. As he trotted toward the sideline, he did his best to avoid Hill. To no avail. "Walter, what the hell were you thinking!" Hill barked. "Sit your ass on the bench, and don't let me see you again!" It was the last time Walter touched the ball that afternoon.

· · ·

The aftermath of the Prairie View loss was not pretty. If Jackson State's players thought they had it hard in the lead-up to the opener, they learned quickly that Hill's devotion to punishment knew few boundaries. The Tigers had two long weeks before their second game, a trip to Frankfort, Kentucky, to play lightly regarded Kentucky State, and Hill was determined to weed out the weak links. He looked over his roster and knew the talent was legitimate— along with the Payton siblings, ten others, including senior flanker Jerome Barkum and freshman linebacker Robert Brazile, would go on to play in the NFL. But under McPherson the work ethic had been underwhelming; the accountability nonexistent. Losses were greeted with dismissive shrugs, and players could often be found partying later in the evening. "No longer," said Hill. "I wouldn't accept that."

The coach had three favorite methods of punishment. First, there were the rocks. Hill would chew out a player, pick up a small rock, scream, "See this rock? Go find it!" then chuck it over a fence into a pack of weeds. Whether it took two minutes or two hours, the guilty party had to return with the exact rock. Second, there were the down-ups. "He'd stand there like a military drill instructor, screaming 'Down! Up! Down! Up!'" said Douglas Baker, a sopho- more center. "You'd jump onto your stomach, jump up, run in place, then jump back down over and over again." The worst, however, was rolling. Were Hill really angry, he'd order players to line up on a goal line, lie down, and roll a hundred yards to the opposite goal line. "It doesn't sound especially bad, but it was torture," said Porter Taylor, a reserve quarterback. "You'd vomit, and it'd make you sick that evening and well into the next morning. There was nothing I wanted to hear less than, 'Roll the field.'"

Several Tigers quit instead of dealing with the coach's brutality. They were either upperclassmen who had grown comfortable with McPherson or naïve freshmen unaware that they had signed up for the Green Berets. Ear- nest Wiley, a highly recruited defensive end from Mississippi, left the team after a month, when Hill ordered him *not* to marry his girlfriend. "I decided my life was more important than football," Wiley said. "So I got married and quit."

"Some guy passed out on the field, and throw-up was coming out of his mouth," recalled Lafayette Nelson, a tight end who transferred to Lane Col- lege. "Bob Hill screamed for someone to get him off the field, and they picked him up and towed him off. I knew I needed to get out of there."

Although Walter Payton didn't fully escape disciplinary action in the wake of his poor debut at Prairie View, Hill thought it wiser to develop the kid than break him down. "I always told my players the same thing," he said. "'There ain't no such thing as treating y'all alike. I'm gonna be fair with all of y'all—but not alike.'" Walter had received solid tutoring in high school under Boston and Tommy Davis, but he was still green. Jackson State's offense utilized the quick pitch, which baffled Walter to no end. Jackson State's offense counted on a back reading his blockers. Again, Walter had no idea. "He had competitive speed," said Eddie Payton. "But not blinding speed. And when he arrived, he had no real grasp how to use it."

Beginning that week, and lasting throughout their time together, Hill took Walter under his wing with the vision of creating a team-carrying superstar. "The first thing he needed to learn was how to block," said Hill. "Walter never really had to do it before." At nights, when most of the other players were watching TV or studying, Hill dragged Payton to Jackson State's gymnasium, where he hung a tackling dummy from a steel beam. "He'd pound that thing over and over until he was sore and the dummy was even sorer," Hill said. "If you were going to play in my backfield, you had to be able to do more than just misdirect an oncoming tackler. You had to destroy him."

Hill's second priority was changing the way Walter ran. Though larger and stronger than his older brother, Walter tended to take handoffs and immediately break for the outside. This worked in high school, when he was faster than the majority of cornerbacks and safeties. But here, in college, it infuriated Hill. He wanted his ball carriers to emulate Alan Ameche, the legendary Colts fullback who had impressed him during his brief stay with Baltimore in 1956. "I put Walter at the top of the I-formation behind a fullback, but he wouldn't go up in the hole," Hill said. "He hated contact."

Hill had an idea. He stopped a practice and called for Willie Swinning, the team's trainer. With Walter within earshot, Hill handed Swinning a satchel and bellowed, "Bring this to the brick pile over there and fill it with three or four bricks!" When no one was looking, Swinning placed four footballs—not bricks—into the bag.

Hill positioned himself near the out-of-bounds line and resumed practice. He called for a drill involving a handoff. Sylvester Collins, the quarterback, gave the ball to Payton, who—as always—started to drift outside. Hill charged forward, wildly swinging the bag toward Payton's head. "Back inside!" Hill screamed. "Get your ass back inside!" The play was called again. And again. And again. "It took him a couple of times with me swinging that bag of bricks," said Hill, "but he finally started charging into the hole. That's how he began running inside."

Back in Columbia, Boston had advised Walter to run with raised knees—to lift them as high as possible in a chopping motion. Hill, the old workhorse back, hated the style. Great running backs, he told Payton, run with long strides and extended legs. They make it as hard as possible for opposing defenders to drag them down. "If you're running with your knees high, they're gonna be close to your body," he said. "And if your knees are close to your body, a tackler can grab everything at once.

"If you want to be explosive, the best thing to do is run with long strides. The longer your strides, the faster you go. We're gonna open holes for you, but if you have short, choppy steps somebody will grab you around the legs and trip you up. I want you to stick your legs out, and if someone tries grabbing them, keep extending . . . keep pumping. I know you're from the country. You know when the cows come out to the pasture and eat all the green corn? Then you come out to get them and if you're running they start shitting over everything and the shit is flying everywhere? Well, that's how I want you to run. I want to see shit flying."

As a boy, Walter Payton had never milked a cow, chased a cow, or watched a cow eat green corn. Nonetheless, he grasped what his coach was saying— run hard.

. . .

If the botched kickoff return against Prairie View taught Hill anything, it was that perhaps he was asking too much, too soon of Walter. In the 42–33 win over Kentucky State, Payton dressed and played, but only occasionally spelling his brother or John Ealy, another back.

Next up for the Tigers was their home opener against Bishop College at Mississippi Veterans Memorial Stadium. Located five miles from campus in downtown Jackson, Memorial was considered a football jewel. Beginning with its grand opening in December 1950, the stadium—oval in shape, with dueling cement stands reaching high into the sky—served as home to many of the great contests in Mississippi football history. The place officially held forty-six thousand spectators (though an extra fourteen thousand could be crammed in), and the state's two Division I football powerhouses, Ole Miss and Mississippi State, regularly scheduled games there. "When you walked into Memorial and the stadium was filled with fans, it was something else," said Curtis Jones, a Jackson State defensive back. "You felt like a king."

Coming off of a win, the Tigers entered the game filled with optimism. The Blue Tigers of Bishop College, on the other hand, were a mess. A Division II school from Dallas that offered only a handful of half-scholarships, Bishop's coach was Dwight Fisher, a man in his mid-sixties whose antiquated offensive and defensive schemes dated back to the 1930s. Fisher's roster was comprised of nonprospects and castoffs. From 1971 to 1975, the offense scored ten total touchdowns. "Our players were mostly guys who couldn't make it anywhere else," said Herman Jordan, Bishop's quarterback. "We had a nice campus, but no facilities and no staff. A couple of days before home games, all the players would be out there lining the field."

So certain was Hill his team would dominate that, for the start of the game, he sent the freshman Payton back to return the kickoff. Standing toward the right hash mark, his white jersey bright and unblemished, he caught the ball on the twenty-five-yard line, turned left, dashed past a gaggle of flailing tacklers, and was finally brought down thirty-three yards later, at Bishop's forty-second. Three plays later, Collins connected for a touchdown with Barkum, the senior flanker who would go on to a twelve-year career with the New York Jets, and the Tigers were on their way.

The Blue Tigers were listless and inept, falling behind 14–0 before the completion of the first quarter. With the game already in hand, Hill began the second quarter by inserting Walter into the backfield, alternating him with his older brother in the first-ever Payton-Payton rotation. "You didn't want to tackle one," said Hill. "And you didn't want to tackle the other."

Walter Payton's first collegiate touchdown came on first and goal from the two, when he took the handoff from Collins, bent his knees, sprung high into the air, and dove over the top of the line of scrimmage and into the end zone.

Near the end of the half, Eddie Payton ruined a Jackson State scoring opportunity by fumbling on Bishop's two-yard line. Though the Tigers ended the half with a 21–0 lead, Hill was incensed. As his team returned to the field after the break, Walter was told he would carry the load. "It was the right time to test him out," said Hill. "We weren't going to lose that game even if he struggled."

After holding Bishop to three and out, Jackson State's offense received the ball and casually marched down the field. On first and ten from Bishop's twenty-five, Collins spun to his left and pitched the ball to Walter. The freshman charged behind Emanuel Zanders, his six-foot-one, 255-pound left guard, cut outside, and dashed down the field, untouched and all alone. If the 40–7 win belonged to Barkum, who caught five passes for ninety-nine yards and scored three touchdowns, the breakout performer was Walter Payton, whose 143 rushing yards on eighteen carries introduced the city of Jackson to its newest star.

"That day was when I knew Walter would one day play in the NFL," said Brazile. "When you watched him run with the ball in that game, it was clear he was special."

.   .   .

Without drastically changing Eddie's role, Hill increasingly turned toward Walter. The two backs substituted for each other, slapping hands as one entered and the other exited. By late in the season they were splitting time until, before the game at Mississippi Valley State on November 20, Hill decided he would finally go with the all-Payton starting backfield. "It just made sense," said Hill. "They both ran hard, they both blocked well, and they both were lethal catching screens out of the backfield. In practice I would pit them against each other as motivation, but they didn't need it. They were motivated without me."

The game took place on a bright and windy afternoon in Itta Bena, Mississippi, and if spectators believed they were witnessing some sort of sports sibling history, little was discussed. "Nobody gave it much thought," said Eddie. "Even we didn't. We both felt we were good enough to start together, so it was something we'd expected. When you expect something, it's not shocking or overly memorable." On the Devils' dirt-and-rock-coated field, Jackson State won 17–7, with Eddie running for his tenth touchdown of the season to take hold of the SWAC scoring lead. Walter's longest run was a twenty-yard burst up the middle on the second play of the game. He also kicked a seventeen-yard field goal and two extra points. Had Ole Miss or Mississippi State started brothers at running back, the media crush would have been overwhelming. The *Clarion-Ledger* marked the Payton pairing by not even mentioning it in the following day's paper, and misspelling Payton (as "Peyton") five different times.

"It was never surprising," said Eddie. "Just really pathetic."

The Tigers won their final two games of the season, finishing with a 9-1-1 record (mere percentage points behind Grambling for the conference title) and sealing Hill's anointment as the SWAC Coach of the Year. Eddie led the team with 799 rushing yards, and Walter followed with 651 more. He also kicked three field goals and thirteen extra points.

"Walter spent his first year showing us how good he could be," said Hill, "and the next three years turning into a legend."

CHAPTER 7

SOUL

THERE ARE NICE BELTS AND THERE ARE UGLY BELTS. AND AT JACKSON STATE College, there was Mary Jones' extra-special belt.

The bullet one.

Yes, you read that correctly. Somewhere within Mississippi's capital city in the early 1970s, there was an eighteen-year-old female student from Tunica, Mississippi, with short straight hair, brown eyes, long legs, an engaging personality, and a belt featuring the bullets of an M16 assault rifle.

Jones purchased the accessory at a vintage clothing store in Oklahoma during a field trip several years earlier, when she served as a majorette in the Rosa Fort High School marching band. "To be honest, the bullets were replicas," said Jones. "But they looked real, and the belt was neat—brown, with these gold bullets covering it. As soon as I saw it, I knew I had to buy it."

Jones arrived on Jackson State's campus in May 1972. Fresh off of high school graduation, she enrolled in summer school and asked Earl Dishman, a pal from back home, to drive her to campus. "He had my clothes in his car, and he dropped me off and said he'd be back in a few hours," Jones recalled. "Well, Earl had some friends on the other side of Jackson and he decided to stay with them. I didn't see him for a week."

Jones found herself stuck in wardrobe purgatory. She had a dorm room to live in and cafeteria food to eat, but no spare clothing. "So every day for my first entire week on campus I wore the same thing—the same jumpsuit, the same bullet belt," she said. "People started looking at me and saying, 'Hey, Bullet!' They never called me Mary again. Always Bullet."

Before long, Mary "Bullet" Jones became famous at Jackson State for two things: her ubiquitous belt and her out-of-this-galaxy dancing skills.

Beginning when she was a little girl, Bullet emulated her mother, Mary Francis Jones, as she boogied around the house, arms waving, rump shaking. By the time she reached Jackson State, Bullet was as dazzling a dance-floor practitioner as many had ever seen. "Boy, could she groove," said Coolidge Anderson, editor of the *Blue and White Flash*. "Weren't many people on campus who worked it like Bullet did."

Well, there was one. If Bullet was Jackson State's Ginger Rogers, its Fred Astaire was Walter Payton. Throughout a freshman year noteworthy for gridiron excellence, Payton generated equally rave reviews for his improvisational dance talents. Wherever one looked, he could find Walter dancing. Inside classrooms. Within the corridors of Sampson Hall. Standing in line for lunch. On the bus rides to away games. "He danced just like Rerun from *What's Happening!!*" said Jackie Slater, an offensive lineman who went on to a twenty-year NFL career. "The moves were crazy and wild and extremely athletic."

"There was a porch in front of our field house, and as we were getting ready to play the football games Walter would stand there and dance, dance, dance, dance," said Porter Taylor, a quarterback. "Coach Hill would walk by, take a look at Walter moving all around and say, 'OK, we're ready.'"

At the start of his sophomore year of college, Payton's primary goal was to lead the Tigers to the SWAC title. With Eddie having graduated and playing professionally in Canada, Walter knew Jackson State's hopes rested largely on his shoulders. He spent much of the summer in Jackson on the banks of the Pearl River, running through its quicksand-like terrain and envisioning glorious Saturday afternoons inside Memorial Stadium. "If you have to come under control to make a cut, the pursuit will catch you," Payton once said of running along the river. "In the sand, you have to move one leg before the other is planted. It makes all your muscles work. Sometimes when I'm done even my neck will be aching."

Because Hill was college football's Richard Nixon when it came to adhering to rules, he had his entire team spend the majority of the summer at Jackson State, violating multiple NCAA regulations by practicing up to three times per day.

Yet unbeknownst to the Tigers coach, the sly back wasn't merely pondering pigskin. Like nearly all Jackson State students, Walter was a rabid fan of *24 Karat Black Gold*, a half-hour television program that aired every Saturday morning on Jackson's NBC affiliate, channel 3.

The program's concept was simple and, in the age of *American Bandstand* and *Soul Train*, unoriginal: Invite a large number of local black high school and college students to a television studio and have them dance to the latest hits. "That was it," said Lee King, *24 Karat Black Gold*'s creator and a one-time radio engineer for James Brown. "Our show was eighty percent dancing, and the other twenty percent was videos and appearances by regional and national artists. It worked so well because it was an outlet for African-Americans in Mississippi. Their ambitions were at a low level because they didn't have a lot of recreational things to do in the area. So when our show came out, it was their *Bandstand*."

Without telling Hill (who would have certainly objected), on a Tuesday evening in early September 1972, Walter and a couple of friends drove to the WLBT studio on South Jefferson Street, where auditions were being held for the new season. The line stretched down the block and around the corner—hundreds of young blacks in search of stardom. "We had to introduce ourselves, say what college we attended, what our major was," said Jones. "Then we formed a *Soul Train* line and danced. If we were good, they invited us back the following week. There was no salary, but we didn't care. It wasn't about that."

"I was from Augusta, Georgia, so I had no idea who Walter was," said King. "But he auditioned with this freestyle dance that was crazy and different. He had a great way of carrying himself, too. He radiated something unique."

The tapings took place on the first Monday of every month—four episodes shot in one exhausting evening. Though he often walked onto the dance floor straight from football practice, muscles aching and knees throbbing, as soon as the TV cameras rolled and the sounds of Earth, Wind & Fire or the Jackson 5 blared across the room, Walter came to life. His wardrobe was, even for the times, outrageous—bright purple cutoff shirts, baggy velvet pants, tight jeans, some sort of fedora-esque hat. The popular dance style of the time was called "Pop 'n' Lock," a precursor to break dancing that incorporated fluid and wavy isolated movements with tight robotic illusions. His go-to move was the Centipede, slinking to the floor and moving his body in wavelike motions. "Oh, he was an excellent dancer," said Jones. "Walter used to inject a lot of the techniques they did in football . . . some of the calisthenics and exercises. He was really flexible with his body; more so than the rest of us."

Because the Tiger football program was still finding itself, Payton the running back had yet to establish himself as a household name in Jackson. Payton the dancer, on the other hand, was huge. "The show aired every week, so people became familiar with us," said Jones. "Throughout the fall and spring, we turned into celebrities. Kids would yell out when we drove by and people would stop and ask about the dances. It was thrilling."

Like many who met Payton, King developed affection for the boy. He was goofy and quirky and always messing around with someone. At the time King owned a beautiful white Cadillac, and Walter said he'd like to repay him for the dancing opportunity by taking the vehicle to the car wash. King accepted the offer on multiple occasions, never giving much thought to the fact that his car would be gone for three hours a pop. "When I scolded him about it taking too long, Walter would give me some story about the vacuum not working," said King. "Well, one day someone took me to where Walter was supposed to be cleaning, and I caught him with a bunch of females in the car."

Midway through the academic year, King announced that *24 Karat Black Gold* was affiliating itself with the first-ever *Soul Train* National Championship Dance-Off. Throughout the country, each state would host its own competition, with the winning couples flying to Los Angeles to appear on *Soul Train* and vie for the title of America's Best Dancers. At the time, Payton and Jones were teamed on *Black Gold* with fairly mediocre partners. "So Walter came up to me one day and said, 'How about entering the *Soul Train* contest together?'" Jones said. "'I really think we can win this thing if we team up.'" For the next three weeks the two met in a second-floor room of Jackson State's student union building and danced until their toes blistered. "We had forty-fives and LPs, and we practiced for endless hours," Jones said. "We expected to win."

The first round of the competition was held at the College Park Auditorium on Lynch Street. Hundreds of couples took to the floor as the judges cruised the room, tapping out those who didn't make the cut. Along with forty-nine other couples, Walter and Mary survived the first week, then lasted again as the total was reduced to twenty-five, and then again to a mere ten. The championship round was held on a Sunday, ten couples dancing for the right to appear on one of black America's most popular television programs. "I'd never left Mississippi in my life," said Jones. "I'd never even been on an airplane. So the possibility was breathtaking."

The ten couples were pared down to five, then three. Walter gazed at Mary. Mary gazed at Walter. They locked eyes, knowing to ignore the judges and just move. Finally, the music stopped. The couple looked around, and nobody was left. "I was overcome with joy, and so was Walter," said Jones. "To be chosen to represent the entire state of Mississippi! What an honor!"

By the time Walter and Mary flew to Los Angeles, it was the summer of 1973. The local radio station, WOKJ, presented both students with plane tickets and five hundred dollars in spending money. ("Five hundred dollars!" laughs Jones. "I couldn't believe it.") They stayed at the Hyatt in Los Angeles, and were given tours of Hollywood and Beverly Hills. Upon arriving at *Soul Train*'s studio, they met Don Cornelius, the famed deep-voiced host and producer.

The show was taped the night after they arrived. Couples from across the nation danced away, until fifty were whittled down to thirty, and thirty were whittled down to fifteen, and fifteen were whittled down to two. The victors would be gifted two brand-new olive green Dodge Chargers—"and we really wanted those cars," Jones said.

Walter wore jeans with wide legs, a cutoff shirt that revealed his muscular stomach, and Gene Simmons–esque platform heels. Atop his head was an apple cap, a style staple for black men in the early 1970s. He and Mary danced as well as they ever had. So, unfortunately, did the couple from Louisiana. "Mississippi and Louisiana were the last two standing," said Jones. "They were just a little bit better than we were."

Walter and Mary left empty-handed.

"But the story of dancing with Walter," said Mary, "has lasted me a lifetime."

.   .   .

If Walter Payton tiptoed cautiously toward his freshman year of college, he barged in, shoulder first, as a sophomore.

Though he had enjoyed playing alongside his older brother in the Tigers backfield, Walter was his own man, in need of neither guidance nor sibling-provided protection. "At first I was glad to room with people I knew, but it was almost too much after a while," he wrote in his autobiography of living with Eddie and Edward Moses as a freshman. "I began to wish that I'd roomed with strangers."

With a year of school—and football—under his belt, Walter was more relaxed and confident. His roommates were now Rodney Phillips and Rickey Young, two young Tiger stars who shared Payton's on-campus notoriety and were thrilled to have access to his deluxe stereo system with a *real* remote control. "He had powerful amps," said Matthew Norman, a teammate, "and he'd try to knock the walls down with music." Walter strolled campus with a smile glued to his face, exchanging high fives with teammates, offering causal nods to pretty women. He liked to fish with linebacker Robert Brazile in a nearby reservoir and stay up late gabbing with his pals in a common area of the residence hall. In his hands he often carried a wood slingshot, and when the spirit moved him he would pick up a rock and pluck unsuspecting pigeons. "Not to be mean," said Taylor, the Tigers quarterback. "Just Walter being a big kid."

Without Eddie, Walter could be himself without worrying about someone hovering over his shoulder. There was the dancing on *Black Gold*. There were the trips to the Penguin Restaurant, a little place just off of campus where, for a dollar fifty, Walter would buy two hot dogs, slather them in coleslaw and the Penguin's special sauce, gobble them down, and sprint back to the dorm before Hill could catch him.

There were the women.

Back during his freshman orientation, Walter had been standing in a courtyard when he took notice of a pretty coed named Lorna Jones. A local girl who graduated from Jackson's Wingfield High, Lorna was immediately taken with Payton's kind eyes and humble disposition. "He wasn't all that handsome, but he was very nice and very intelligent, even though he didn't think of himself as smart," said Jones. "He also had a shyness to him that was quite endearing."

Unlike Walter, Lorna lived at home with her parents, both educators, both unflinchingly strict. Her mother, M. V. Manning Jones, refused to allow Lorna to stay out late or, heaven forbid, sleep elsewhere. Kissing boys was against the law. When Walter visited, the two could not be together in a room behind a closed door. "I had my own den, and we'd sit there, but we were never really alone," said Lorna. "My dad would walk back and forth, back and forth." Despite their mistrust of all members of the opposite sex, M. V. and Lawrence Jones liked their daughter's boyfriend. He was polite and friendly, and came over frequently to help cook shrimp and stir chili. When he once needed to attend a certain award presentation, the Joneses even took Walter to JCPenney to buy a pair of shoes.

During Christmas break toward the end of 1971, Walter brought Lorna to Columbia to meet his parents. Because her family was so forbidding, Lorna was allowed to go only as long as her best friend, Patrice Turner, came along, and under the order that they return by evening's end. In the shadow of the Payton Christmas tree, with Patrice hovering nearby, Walter handed Lorna a small box. Inside was a promise ring with, in her words, "an itty, itty, itty, bitty diamond."

"That was a big thing," said Lorna. "Back then you gave promise rings as a token of a serious relationship. We had real feelings for one another. I loved him."

Walter majored in history as a freshman, compiling twenty-eight credits and earning a GPA between 2.0 and 2.5. He had spent endless hours studying alongside Lorna, who was passionate about her major, special education. During many of their conversations, Walter thought back to his days mentoring disabled children at Columbia High, as well as playing alongside a deaf high school teammate named Lee Bullock. He would end up switching his major to audiology, a branch of science that studies hearing, balance, and related disorders. He was, almost certainly, the nation's only top-flight football player to focus on such a field. "He really cared about people," Lorna said. "Studying with him and talking with him about special ed were great moments. We shared a bond."

As sophomores, however, the dynamic shifted. With Eddie's departure, Walter was thrust into the role of football (and dance) superstar, fawned upon by fellow students, handed one Division II honor after another. The anonymity of his freshman year had vanished, and with his newfound celebrity, said Lorna, came a sizeable ego. "That first year I never had to worry about other girls," said Lorna. "But sophomore year—he turned into a dog. A lot of girls were throwing themselves at Walter, wanting to get with a star, and he didn't put up much of a fight." On multiple occasions, Walter left Lorna waiting at her doorstep. The two would plan a study night—he never showed. They'd schedule an evening at the movies—no Walter. She heard the rumors of one girl this night, another girl that night. "We went from being exclusive and serious to having this kind of off-again, on-again thing where he would show up, not show up, be nice, be moody," Lorna said. "I loved him, but I didn't love how he always treated me."

·  ·  ·

Unlike Walter's freshman season, the Tigers entered 1972 with high expectations. When a team finishes 9-1-1, as Jackson State did, people crave more of the same. The Tigers were returning twenty-three lettermen, and in Payton and fullbacks Young and Phillips, Hill boasted three standout sophomore backs.

The Tigers opened at home against Prairie View on September 16, and the six thousand or so fans who braved a cold rain witnessed one of the uglier games in school history. Jackson State won 16–13 over a vastly inferior opponent, but there was nothing pretty in the performance. "I was trying to explain to Coach Hill during the game why we were struggling with their 4-3 defense," said Charles Brady, a Tigers defensive tackle. "Coach punched me in the belly and told me to shut up." With Hill rampaging up and down the sideline and Payton held to under fifty total yards, the afternoon felt like a disaster. When the game ended Hill entered the locker room, grabbed his clipboard, marched toward Payton and Young, and slammed both of them over the heads.

"Next week we have Lane!" he screamed. "You better play better! You better play fucking better!"

. . .

Odell Tate carried a gun.

If there's one thing you need to know about Lane College's dysfunctional football program in the fall of 1972, it's that the man in charge packed heat. When Tate was hired by the tiny, historically black Jackson, Tennessee–based college prior to the season, it was with the idea that the longtime high school coach would instill a sense of pride and discipline.

To the members of Lane's executive board, that meant teaching the virtues of hard work and commitment and punctuality and intensity.

To Tate, it apparently meant violent craziness.

"The gun was a .25 automatic," recalled Cameron Franklin, a Lane offensive guard. "He would bring it to practice every day and keep it in his back pocket. One week we were practicing, and somebody had egged and toilet-papered his car. He thought the players did it, so he started waving the gun at us, screaming, 'If I catch who did this to my car, I'll pop 'em!'"

Combined with a coach's madness, the team's lack of overall talent (the Dragons played in the mediocre SIAC (Southern Intercollegiate Athletic Conference) spelled doom. Lane was playing at Jackson State for the second time in school history, a matchup that had nothing to do with gridiron glory and everything to do with finances. With an enrollment of merely thirteen hundred students and a budget that paled in comparison to other schools its size, Lane was always on the lookout for ways to score an extra buck. Hill's

Tigers, meanwhile, needed a sure-shot victory or two before facing Grambling, Alcorn, and the other heavyweights of the SWAC. As was common practice, Jackson State agreed to pay Lane a couple of thousand dollars to come to Memorial Stadium.

In anticipation of the game, Tate worked his players to death. "Coach was determined we needed to be in tip-top shape when we played them," said Wilkins Raybon, a Lane linebacker. "So that week he ran us and ran us good. He thought he was getting us in top condition, but really he was wearing us down. By the time the game started, we were exhausted."

Tate warned his players that the Tigers had a running back—"That number thirty-four!"—who wouldn't succumb to mere arm tackles. What he didn't know was Payton featured a new weapon that, through the course of his career, would serve as the ultimate equalizer. Midway through the summer, Hill had asked Walter if he was interested in accompanying him on a recruiting trip to Birmingham, Alabama (Hill enjoyed taking his players for long rides). The two settled into the coach's Cadillac, and as he drove Hill told the story of how he broke loose in his days as a runner at Jackson State. "When I played here, we used to get rolls of athletic tape that came in these big cardboard boxes," Hill said. "Well, one day a trainer threw out one of the boxes, so I grabbed it, cut it right down the middle, and taped it around my arm. Then I put my jersey over it so nobody would know." As Hill remembered it, he lined up in the backfield, took a handoff, and started down the sideline. "When a defensive back came up, I just walloped him in the head with the cardboard—POP! It worked like magic, and I didn't feel pain. From that day on, every time someone tried to tackle me I'd cock my elbow and hit him with a forearm. That became my calling card."

Hill wasn't endorsing the procedure, just regaling in yesteryear. The next time Walter came to practice, however, he was wearing a knee pad over his arm. Hill asked Willie Barnes, the team's trainer, what was going on. "I don't want my guys having nothing on their arms," he said. "Did you give him that?" To which Barnes replied, "Yes, but Walter said you told him he could wear it." Hill laughed, then pulled all the running backs aside. "I have a rule," he said. "Nothing can be on your arms." Hill paused. "But Walter is different."

From that day forward, Payton's forearm served as a cement block. He raised it, then slammed it down upon an opponent's head. He used it like a club and gnashed it into an oncoming tackler's jaw. Whereas defenders once only had to worry about Walter's speed and toughness, they now had to concern themselves with assault and battery. Thanks to the forearm, Walter would never play victim again. "After games his elbow would be the size of a grapefruit," said Vernon Perry, the Jackson State safety. "They'd drain the blood out of it every week."

The Dragons had no idea what they were in for. "They walked into the cafeteria a few hours before the game talking all sorts of junk about what they were going to do to us," said Milton Webb, Jackson State's middle linebacker. "We just laughed and said, 'OK, we'll see. We'll see.'"

Fearing the Jackson State running game, Tate shifted his best player, Larry "Sleepy" Harris, from cornerback to safety, hoping he could charge the line and bottle up some of the inevitable holes. For the initial few minutes it worked—the Tigers failed to score on their first possession.

The tide quickly turned. With 7:16 remaining in the first quarter, Payton, lined up in the I-formation behind Young, took the handoff from quarterback Jimmy Lewis and charged straight ahead, six yards into the end zone. A handful of maroon-and-blue-clad Dragon players were sprawled across the field. "Rickey Young blocked one of our guys so hard, he knocked his front teeth out," said Franklin. "Man, those guys were bad dudes."

The Tigers scored on their next possession, with Lewis hitting receiver Allen Richardson for a forty-one-yard touchdown strike. Payton ran in the extra point, then reached the end zone again moments later on an eight-yard scamper that included no fewer than three forearms smashing into the heads of would-be tacklers. As the teams jogged into their respective locker rooms for the halftime break, the scoreboard reading 35–0, Jackson State's players barked wildly at the Dragons. "They should have stopped the game," said Harris. "Every time I looked up I saw number thirty-four running toward me. He was a beast. You could not arm tackle him. It was impossible."

For Lane, the second half was even worse. Tate stubbornly refused to switch from a 4-3 defense to a six-man defensive line, so Hill continued to run the ball. Payton scored four more times, including a weaving twenty-seven yarder late in the fourth quarter to cap the 72–0 romp. Lane's defenders were so physically decimated by Payton's stiff-arms and elbow blasts that, in the final minutes, Tate replaced them with offensive players. "I touched Walter one time all game," said Raybon, "and it was when he was in the end zone. We were disgraced."

Payton's totals for the day proved the best in Jackson State history: 279

yards rushing, a SWAC-record seven touchdowns. "To tell you the truth, I blew that one," said Hill. "I had once scored seven touchdowns when I played at Jackson State, and I never wanted anyone to touch that record. So I don't know what I was thinking."

As Payton walked off the field after the final gun, Lane's players approached him one by one, hands extended, pride battered. Though they had received a hellacious beating, most knew they had witnessed something special.

"I didn't leave the field until they cut off the scoreboard," said Bobby McKiver, a Lane linebacker. "I just sat there, shocked that we let one man kill us like that. Finally, our team doctor came out to get me. He said, 'Bobby, the sun will rise again.'"

"Doc," McKiver replied, "it seems pretty damn dark to me."

. . .

As word of Walter's accomplishment spread slowly across the country, the general reaction was ho-hum. Wasn't there always some Division II halfback or Division III quarterback putting up astronomical numbers against a high school–caliber defense nobody had ever heard of?

Within a week, however, more than ten NFL scouts arrived on the Jackson State campus to attend Tigers practices. Hill held some vague form of the same conversation on multiple occasions:

> **Scout:** So is this Payton kid for real?
> **Hill:** He's the best pure runner I've ever seen.
> **Scout:** What's he like off the field?
> **Hill:** He's quiet and polite and never causes any trouble. Before practices he gathers all the other running backs and leads them in prayer. That's Walter.
> **Scout:** Do you think he'll do well in the pros?
> **Hill:** One day, he'll own the pros.

The Hill-Payton relationship was a quirky one. With on-field excellence, the player felt increasingly comfortable messing with the coach. Mimicking him behind his back. Mimicking him to his face. Jokingly telling teammates to ignore the old man. Even taking his car when the keys were left dangling from the ignition. Hill was superstitious, and Walter delighted in finding stray black cats and placing them in his office. (In one bizarre moment, a Jackson State player tied a noose around a black cat's neck and hung it from the rearview mirror of Hill's car. Hill never drove the vehicle again.)

In case anyone thought Hill might have mellowed after his first season, they were quickly reminded otherwise. When a center named Willis Sweeney botched a snap during special teams drills, Hill stopped practice. "Take your shit off right now!" he screamed. Sweeney paused. His coach wasn't serious . . . was he? "Take your shit off now! I'm not fucking around!" Surrounded by teammates, Sweeney removed his helmet, his jersey, his shoulder pads, and his shoes. "Now be the fuck out of the dorm by tomorrow! You'll never play for this team again!"

With Payton, however, Hill was different. He liked how on Sunday mornings, come rain or shine, Walter would wake up at eight to attend services at the nearby church. He liked how, before every game, he pulled aside all the other Tiger running backs and embraced them in tight hugs. Walter tried his first beer as a sophomore at a dorm party, drank the whole thing, and vomited profusely. "I'm never doing that again," he told a defensive back named Curtis Jones. (Recalled Milton Webb, a middle linebacker: "When the season ended Walter would come down to the clubs with us. We'd all gather at the Tiger Lounge and drink beer. Walter would come, sit, engage for a few minutes—but never drink. Never.")

Mainly, Hill liked how, suddenly, Jackson State was a hot ticket. A sell-out crowd arrived at Memorial Stadium the following Saturday to watch the Tigers come back from a fourteen-point deficit to beat Kentucky State 28–14. Though far from one of Payton's most memorable games, players remembered it for Hill's halftime histrionics. The coach stormed into the locker room, screamed, "Where's that black motherfucker?" spotted Payton and once again slammed him over the head with a clipboard. Then, for a reason nobody ever understood, Hill ordered all his players to shave. In a shocking moment of defiance, John Tate, a six-foot-two, 230-pound linebacker, refused. Hill grabbed him around the neck and ordered Willie Barnes, the trainer, to bring a razor. "Either you shave, motherfucker!" Hill said, "or I'll do it for you!" Tate shaved, and Hill celebrated by kicking a wide receiver named Earnest Richardson in the testicles. "A couple of days later we decided we were going to boycott Coach," said Charles Brady, a defensive tackle. "That shit lasted fifteen minutes. We knew we were too good to ruin a season."

The Tigers improved to 4-0 with a 35–10 road dismantling of Bishop

College, then beat Southern for a fifth-straight victory. Jackson State was now ranked fifth in the latest NCAA Division II poll—the highest spot for a SWAC school. Payton was the team's brightest star. "Walter was like a Frank Sinatra," said Roscoe Word, the Jackson State receiver. "God blessed him to sing, he blessed Walter to play football. His ability was a gift from God, but you couldn't hurt him, he always gave one hundred percent and he was never an asshole. He didn't ask for preferential treatment or act like a star. He ate in the dining room just like everybody else."

Hill's greatest fear—that the offense was becoming too reliant on one player—came to fruition midway through the Bishop game, when Payton absorbed a helmet to the left knee and hobbled off the field with a ligament strain. He would miss three ensuing contests—two of which, with Rickey Young doing most of the ball carrying, Jackson State lost. "We weren't as good as I thought we'd be," said Hill. "We lacked something, especially when Walter wasn't in there. We just weren't a complete team."

Despite the shortcomings, the Tigers benefited from a down year for the SWAC. On November 23, they beat Alcorn State 28–14 to clinch a tie with Grambling for the conference championship. Because he was limited to eight games, Payton's numbers seem merely good, not great—he ran for 781 yards and, with sixteen touchdowns and twenty-one extra points, led the SWAC in scoring. But thanks to the performance against Lane, plus the mounting buzz from scouts, the legend of Walter Payton was growing.

"Beginning that season," said Hill, "when people talked Jackson State football, they talked about Walter. And when they talked about Walter, they talked about the next great superstar."

CHAPTER 8

CONNIE

WALTER PAYTON HAD A LONG MEMORY.

If you did something wonderful for him, he rarely forgot. If you did something terrible to him, he rarely forgot, either. Like many athletes of his ilk, Payton used such mental dexterity to his advantage. When an opposing player took a cheap shot, Walter would store the image in his head. A month could pass, a year could pass, five years could pass. Inevitably, payback would come with a forearm to the chin or a stiff-arm to the sternum. Words rarely followed. Walter Payton wasn't one to gloat. Just deliver.

In the summer leading up to his junior year at Jackson State, Walter—as was required by Bob Hill—remained on campus for practice. He worked out at the field house and held down a show-up-and-do-little maintenance job at a nearby park that was arranged for him by Doug Shanks, Jackson's city commissioner. In the course of those weeks, lingering on a mostly empty campus, the stifling Mississippi heat beating down upon him, Walter found himself trying to win back the affections of Lorna Jones, his on-again, off-again girlfriend.

Tired of her beau's philandering, Lorna had mostly washed her hands of Walter. She reunited with an old high school flame and moved on with her life. Yet Payton remained undeterred. He knew Lorna still wore the promise ring he had once given her, which led him to believe hope remained. "He made a strong push, and we did actually get back together," Lorna said. "But there was a big obstacle standing in the way—my mother."

As the wife of an unfaithful husband, M. V. Manning Jones bristled at the idea of Lorna and Walter reconnecting. She knew how he had treated her daughter, and demanded Lorna have nothing to do with him. Walter was no longer allowed to call or visit. "He came one time to my house to have it out with my mother," she said. "Two hardheaded individuals going at it." As Lorna waited in the den, M. V. and Walter met in the kitchen. After ten minutes of threats and accusations ("My mom told him he needed to apologize to me for the way he treated me," Lorna said. "He refused."), Walter stormed from the room, uttered, "I'm gone," and left the house. "Good riddance," M. V. told her daughter. "He's not good enough for you."

For the next few months, Walter and Lorna engaged in a covert romance. The two held hands, kissed on the steps outside Sampson Hall, cruised down to Lynch Street for hamburgers and Cokes. They tiptoed around Jackson, careful not to run into Lorna's parents or any of her parents' friends.

"[The mother] thought Walter wasn't good enough for her girl," said Bob Hill. "Here's Walter—he's got no trouble at all. He's a top football player, a dedicated student, a nice, nice kid—and she refused to let her daughter near him. I thought it was shameful."

Until his final moments of life, Walter never forgot the slight. As far as he was concerned, he was the innocent victim of a mother gone crazy. It irked and offended him. Mostly, it *drove* him. Walter was jolted by the racism of his hometown and the successes of his older brother and the intensity of his head coach. But were there a singular moment that infuriated him to the point of motivation, it was a mother telling her child, "Walter Payton isn't good enough for you."

"He would talk about it often," said Ginny Quirk, Walter's executive assistant for the final fourteen years of his life. "The way that made him feel, and how it pushed him to make something of himself."

Divorced from his first wife, Yvonne, in 1973 Hill was dating Betty Ballette, a New Orleans resident who flew up to Jackson on weekends. One day, while driving through campus, Hill spotted his star running back hiding behind a large oak tree, trying to track down Lorna. "I stepped on the brakes and I said, 'Walter, let me introduce you to somebody,'" recalled Hill. "He was heartbroken over his girl, but he was also open to the idea." Doing his best Yente the matchmaker, the coach gave Payton the phone number for Betty's niece, a high school senior in New Orleans named Connie Norwood. Hill had met Connie on his trips to Betty's house, and immediately liked her. A soft-spoken cheerleader with light cocoa skin and almond-shaped eyes, Connie was a complete package—funny, studious, sharp. She was even a standout dancer, appearing regularly on a weekly New Orleans dance show, *The Walt Boatner Hour.* "Call her," Hill told Walter. "She's expecting to hear from you."

Because he had no telephone in his dorm room, Walter snuck into a Jackson State guidance counselor's office and dialed Connie's number. She had been told by her aunt that a college boy would be contacting her, but never believed it. He was in Mississippi, she was 190 miles away in the Crescent City. What was the point? "I was very surprised to hear Walter's distinctive, high-pitched voice on the other end," Connie once wrote. "We talked for hours [that first night]."

Shortly thereafter, Connie flew to Jackson for a visit. Hill picked her up at the airport and brought her to his house. Hanging from a living room wall were photographs of some of the great players he'd coached at Jackson State—Jerome Barkum, Leon Gray, Rodney Phillips, Walter. As Connie looked the images up and down, Hill said, "Which one of those young men do you think is Walter?" Connie zeroed in on one particular picture. The young man was black, with unkempt eyebrows, a wide nose, a miniature Afro, and pimples dotting much of his forehead. The curled-lip expression on his face suggested he had just whiffed sour milk. "Oh, boy," she thought to herself, "please don't let it be that one."

Bingo.

"OK," Connie said to Hill, taking a second glance. "Maybe he's not *that* bad."

Their first date came a day later, a stroll to nearby Lynch Street. Walter was awkward—far from what she had expected of a sports star. He glanced toward the ground a lot and struggled to make decent conversation. When he did talk, it was about Lorna and her intrusive mother. He jabbered on incessantly about the girl, until Connie wondered why she had bothered. "We spent that evening just kind of talking about her and that whole situation," Connie said. "I ended the weekend thinking, 'He's a nice guy, he's here, I'm going back home. That's it, and I just hope he gets back together with his girlfriend.'"

To Hill's dismay, in the following weeks Walter did not mention Connie again. He continued to mope over Lorna, desperate to make things work. In Hill's mind, this wasn't the way a real man behaved. To whine over a woman's affection? The last thing Hill wanted was a halfback more concerned with a broken heart than the pigskin. "This was *my man*," said Hill. "I helped a lot of my players with their girlfriends. These were my guys."

In an act that violated approximately ten million NCAA regulations, in the spring of 1974, Hill dug into his personal account and paid for Payton to fly back to New Orleans and spend a weekend with Connie, her parents, and her three brothers. What if Walter refused to go? Not an option. He was going. "I called after two days to see how it was, and to check what time he'd be getting back here," said Hill. "Betty was supposed to put Walter on the plane the next day, but he refused to go. He stayed the whole week. Betty told me he was sleeping on the stairway—he fell in love that quickly."

Connie recalled things differently. She has said that Walter was guarded and lacking in manners. "When it was dinnertime, he wouldn't eat with my family at the table," she said. "When everybody was through with dinner, he would want me to then go with him and get something to eat. It was like he was too shy to eat with everybody else. My mother just didn't understand that."

Yet something about Walter Payton caught Connie's fancy. He was sensitive, which was a rare trait among the men she knew. His bashfulness, while annoying, was also endearing. There appeared to be no phony machismo to the boy. No strut or bombast or arrogance. He only discussed football when asked, and never bragged about his own achievements. If anything, he appeared prouder of his dance moves than his off-tackle moves.

With Hill's blessing, Connie and Walter kept in close contact. They spoke every week on the phone, and she visited Jackson State on multiple occasions. Eventually, Walter broke up with Lorna. "He did it in a very cowardly way," Jones said. "He had his brother's girlfriend tell me he didn't want to date me anymore and that he had another girl. I couldn't believe it. It broke my heart."

As Connie's senior year at Alcee Fortier High School came to a close, Hill desperately wanted her to attend Jackson State to keep his prized player happy. "I couldn't have my players worried about love," Hill said. "I had several players fall in love and I kicked them off the team because it messed them up. But I liked Connie and Walter together. The combination worked." After checking with Walter, Hill said he marched into the office of John Peoples, Jackson State's president, and insisted Connie Norwood be awarded a full four-year scholarship to the school. "All she had to do was walk up and give her name," he said. "I told [Peoples] I needed that scholarship. Walter had to be happy. He *had* to be." (When asked, Peoples said he had "no recollection, one way or the other, of being involved with this.")

One year later, Connie was a Jackson State student.

And Walter Payton was happy.

. . .

Though Bob Hill could be a sentimental sort, he was first and foremost an obsessive winner. Loyalty was loyalty, but it only extended so far. As great as Payton had been over the course of his freshman and sophomore seasons, Hill would never turn down the opportunity to bring in another elite ball carrier.

That's why, in the late summer weeks of 1973, Walter was dismayed to find that the incoming freshman class included a halfback with superior speed; a halfback the legendary Red Smith would later call "a greyhound with muscles." As a product of Greenville High School in Greenville, Mississippi, Wilbert Montgomery faced the same barriers Payton had two years earlier—despite eye-opening statistics and abilities to rival any player in the South, the state's white universities refused to pursue him. Hill, however, was smitten. "Man, I loved that kid," he said. "[While I was recruiting him] I took him to a local sporting goods store where I had a credit and I said, 'Get anything you want—get clothes, get shoes, get anything.' Wilbert bought about three pairs of pants and a pair of shoes, and I thought, 'That's all he gets? What a kid! What a terrific kid!'"

In his first week of practice with the Tigers, Montgomery exceeded all expectations. He ran hard and he ran fast. Montgomery only lacked one component vital to Jackson State. "Toughness," said Matthew Norman, a defensive back. "He passed out on the field one day from the heat. He just couldn't handle it."

"We were going through drills," recalled Jackie Slater, the star offensive lineman, "and Wilbert was just a freshman, asking out loud, 'Do I really want to go through this?'"

Payton, on the other hand, was as determined a player as most Tigers had ever seen. Much of his free time was spent at Memorial Stadium, running the mountainous steps until he could barely breathe. He would deliberately show up around noon, when the facility was empty and the moist air could be sliced like a piece of sponge cake. If the stadium was being used, he'd either run miles through the streets of downtown Jackson ("We'd jog to the movies, to the zoo, to get something to eat," said Robert Brazile. "Walter just loved to jog.") or retreat to a nearby high school. "You could look out the window in the women's dorm at certain parts of the day and you'd see Walter working out by himself in the insane heat," said Jo Ann Durham, a Jackson State student who briefly dated Walter. "Nobody else could hang with him."

"His training was unparalleled," said Vernon Perry, Jackson State's safety. "He'd take me to the Pearl River and we'd run through the sand in our football cleats. *In our football cleats!* Who would even think to do that?"

Certainly not Montgomery. Hill was familiar with the new kid's shortcomings, but figured he could beat toughness into him. Hill was also made aware that Abilene Christian, a small NAIA school in central Texas, had desperately craved his services and wasn't giving up easily. According to Hill, Jackson was home to a wealthy Abilene booster with a private jet who had been snooping around campus, whispering sweet nothings to Montgomery. During one weekend in late August, Hill had to depart to Memphis for a meeting. Before leaving, Hill ordered assistant coach Sylvester Collins, a former Tigers quarterback, to babysit Montgomery. "Don't let him out of your sight," Hill said. "Wherever you go, he goes. Wherever he goes, you go." Collins brought Montgomery to his home, but absentmindedly left him alone for an hour. During that time, the Abilene booster knocked on the door and told Montgomery his escape to paradise awaited. They returned to Montgomery's Jackson State dorm room, packed his stuff, and flew off to Texas. "He snuck out because he couldn't take it," said Ricky Taylor, the Tigers quarterback. "But the guy couldn't carry Walter's water. I don't care what anyone said."

A mere three months later, Montgomery ran for 146 yards, caught nine passes for 74 yards and scored six touchdowns in Abilene's win over Stephen F. Austin. He would lead the NAIA in scoring, and go on to a Pro Bowl career with the Philadelphia Eagles, rushing for 6,789 yards and scoring fifty-seven touchdowns. Had he remained at Jackson State, one can argue the Tigers would have boasted the finest running back tandem in the history of college football.

"I would have started Walter and Wilbert together," Hill said. "Almost certainly. Then he left. That's how recruiting was back then. It was dog-eat-dog. Abilene ate my dog."

· · ·

By the time Jackson State kicked off its 1973 season with a September 8 visit to the University of Nebraska at Omaha, NFL scouts and executives were increasingly aware that the nation's most talented collegiate halfback played for the Tigers. So, for that matter, was Jackson State's rapidly expanding fan base. Just two years earlier most of the people who attended games at Memorial Stadium came to see the Sonic Boom of the South, the college's extraordinary marching band. Now Payton was a marquee attraction. Blacks from across the state of Mississippi showed up to catch the action. The university's sports information director, Sam Jefferson, began referring to the facility as "Payton Place," and Tiger games rivaled those of Ole Miss and Mississippi State for fan-generated electricity. On the day of the season's biggest games, sixty thousand spectators packed the stadium.

Ever since he first stole Payton from Kansas State, Hill had dreams of molding himself the perfect running back. Now, that vision was coming to fruition. At the start of the season, Hill implored Payton to refuse to run out of bounds. "Never die easy," he told him. "If you're going to die anyway, die hard." Specifically, Hill meant that, 99 percent of the time, a defensive player was going to slam into a running back whether he was angling toward the sideline or charging straight ahead. "You're red meat," he told Payton, "and they're hungry." Hill had always been impressed with Payton's stiff-arm, which he brought to Jackson State via Columbia High School. But he wanted his star to use it more often, and with even greater viciousness. Hill aspired for defensive backs to see Payton coming and wince. "When I was playing at Jackson State there was a game against Kentucky State, and on fourth and five I broke a tackle and stepped out of bounds, because I thought I had the first," said Hill. "Well, I didn't. I decided from then on that I'd never go out of bounds by choice. So I'd tell Walter, 'Don't be a coward. Initiate the contact. If they're dumb enough to try and tackle you up high, break out the bone and throw it.' "

The Tigers traveled to Omaha for the opener, where Coach Al Caniglia and the Maverick players had little idea what they were in store for. "Our scouting report mentioned Walter Payton," said Ted Sledge, an Omaha defensive tackle. "But we didn't know very much." The weather was in Nebraska-Omaha's favor. Following three straight days of torrential rain, Rosenblatt Stadium's surface was a platter of mud soufflé. Yet despite the sludge, and despite Omaha stuffing the line with six players, Payton broke loose, carrying the ball seventeen times for 120 yards and a touchdown, kicking a twenty-five-yard field goal and an extra point, and catching four passes for 72 yards. Jackson State won handily, 17–0.

Afterward, in an appalling act of poor sportsmanship, a gaggle of Jackson State's players (not including Payton) surrounded the Mavericks' bus and began shaking it, chanting, "Bring on the Big Red! Bring on the Big Red!"— a reference to the University of Nebraska's powerful Cornhuskers. "They were good," said Jim Sledge, Ted's brother and a Mavericks defensive tackle who had transferred from the University of Nebraska, "but they would have been killed by the Huskers."

In the immediate aftermath of the Omaha victory, Mississippi Governor Bill Waller held a press conference to praise Payton and Jackson State. "This team," he said, "is deserving of the full attention and support of all state officials and the people of Mississippi."

A couple of days later William Winter, Mississippi's lieutenant governor, visited a Tigers practice and told the assembled media (well, one reporter) that, "the potential for good public relations for Mississippi from the Jackson State team had never been fully realized. We've had such a good thing out here for years, and the only people who have really noticed have been the pros."

Such was the draw of Walter Payton. He was a lock for a hundred yards per game, no matter the defense, no matter the game plan. When a team like Mississippi Valley State dedicated itself to stuffing the interior, Payton swept outside, using his speed and quickness to run for 151 yards in a 26–22 victory. When a team like Bishop College, the Tigers' week five opponent, assigned a linebacker to shadow Payton wherever he went, Rickey Young, Jackson State's six-foot-two, 180-pound fullback, made a mockery of the strategy, bulldozing said player into the turf.

In fact, it was Payton's otherworldly performance against Bishop that had Jefferson and the school's small public relations staff believing they could, come senior year, mount a credible Heisman Trophy campaign.

Like Lane one season earlier, Bishop was a nondescript NAIA Division II black college with a handful of scholarships and little business standing toe to toe with Jackson State. They entered the game 1-3, with lopsided losses to three schools—Langston University (49–13), Ouachita Baptist (40–19), and Northwestern State (28–7)—the Tigers would have crushed. "Bishop was pretty much always terrible," said Curtis Jones, a Tigers defensive back. "There was a tradition—we'd beat up on them and eventually they'd quit." Located in a residential neighborhood on Dallas' south side, Bishop stood as an afterthought on the college football landscape. "We had a wonderful choir and a wonderful band," said Robert Roberts, a Bishop receiver. "Most people came to Bishop to train to become Baptist preachers, not football players."

The Bishop-Jackson State matchup was the first part of a Memorial Stadium doubleheader, featuring Kentucky and Mississippi State in the nightcap. Many whites were accidentally exposed to Payton and Co. as they entered the stadium early to hunker down for the featured game. This would prove to be a most serendipitous find.

On Jackson State's first offensive play of the afternoon, from its own forty-five-yard line, quarterback Jimmy Lewis tossed the ball to Payton for a sweep around the left end. Bishop's best player was a defensive back named Bobby Brooks, who would go on to play three seasons with the New York Giants. In the previous few days, Brooks had grown tired of hearing Bishop's coaches rave about Payton. "Every week the coaches told us the story of some receiver . . . some quarterback . . . some running back who's supposed to be so great and amazing," Brooks said. "Then I'd go on the field and think, 'Man, this guy is nothing.'"

Brooks assumed Payton couldn't possibly be as dominant as word had it. "Well, Walter's running this sweep right toward my way, and I go to hit him," Brooks said. "I wrap up both legs and I fall to the ground making the tackle, and I look up to see how he fell. Well, I notice he's not down. He's doing a show pony leg kick all the way down the field. That's the first tackle I ever missed in a game. Ever. I was so pissed, so angry, that I got up, and just as he's about to step into the end zone, I caught him and gave him one of those clothesline hooks that I stole from Deacon Jones. He scored, and we got into a fight because it wasn't an especially nice thing to do."

Against all odds and logic, Bishop stormed back to take a 9–7 lead into the second quarter, and the Blue Tigers began to consider the possibilities of a shocking upset.

Instead, they were destroyed.

"Those guys from Mississippi were wood-hauling, deep-sea-fishing-with-their-bare-hands monsters," said Roberts. "They were Roman gladiators."

Though Payton put up better numbers in his sophomore-year effort against Lane, those who watched—and played—in the Bishop game considered it the most magnificent showing of his first three college seasons. He started off the second quarter with a forty-six-yard dash through the heart of the defense, then caught a seventeen-yard touchdown pass from Lewis before running for another one-yard touchdown run. His white uniform, bright and unblemished before the game, was bright and unblemished afterward, too. "It was like he was a ghost," said Jackie Robertson, Bishop's standout defensive end. "We'd go back to the huddle and talk about stopping him, and we couldn't. We were hitting him, but it was like he was going right through you. Three or four times I knew I had a perfect tackle on him, and when I made the tackle I put my head down, locked my arms at the wrists, and took the guy down. Only he wasn't there. He vanished."

Decades later, Robertson remains haunted—and mystified—by one particular play, when Payton came around end on a sweep and was met head-on by the lineman. "I locked him up, felt him, had my eyes closed when we hit the ground, felt him fall below me," he said. "I even said to him, 'Now I've got you!' The next thing I hear is the crowd screaming, and Walter Payton's crossing the goal line."

By the time the clock hit 0:00, Jackson State led 60–12, and Payton's stat line read 162 yards on only thirteen carries. "You couldn't just hit him," said Rhiny Williams, a Bishop defensive tackle. "If you wanted to bring Walter Payton down, you had to pulverize him. And it never happened."

In the aftermath of the game, Bishop's players shuffled onto their bus for the seven-hour drive back to Dallas. Robertson's mother, Nerciel Young, had attended the game, and she gave her son a large box of peanuts to share with his teammates. As he walked toward his seat, Robertson shouted, "Anyone here want some nuts?"

Williams perked up. "Are they roasted," he asked, "or boiled?"

Edmund Peters, Bishop's defensive coordinator, went off. "Peanuts?" he screamed. "Is this some sort of joke? Walter Payton just ran over your asses and you're talking about peanuts? You must be fucking kidding me!"

The players burst into laughter.

.  .  .

As the wins mounted and the hundred-yard rushing games piled up, Walter Payton's legend grew. Against Mississippi Valley State, Hill called a halfback dive—*from the Devils' five-yard line.* "Walter jumped up, flew five yards through the air, and landed in the end zone," said Brazile, the standout linebacker. "Nobody could believe it. But that's not crazy—it's Walter." Against Kentucky State, Payton literally carried five defenders on his back for seven yards. "He was one man," said Oscar Downs, Kentucky State's kicker, "but he played like ten." So revered was the junior halfback that, a couple of days before the biggest game of the year, a clash with Grambling State, he was presented with a key to Jackson by the city council. Around campus, women became increasingly flirtatious, inviting him to parties, lingering outside his dormitory, hoping for a shot with the gridiron star. "He would practice signing his name over and over," said Matthew Norman, a Tigers defensive back. "Because he knew, one day, he'd be signing a lot of autographs and big checks."

When he wasn't on the field Payton was almost always in his room, laughing with teammates and taking some of the younger players under his wing. "Coach Hill had a nine P.M. curfew for freshmen, so we didn't have much to do at night," said Herman Burrell, a freshman linebacker from Mobile, Alabama. "Our entertainment was Walter Payton. Other upper classmen would leave. But he'd sit with us freshmen, and he'd dance in the foyer while we sat and clapped. Walter was special with the freshmen. He made us feel important."

An opportunity to further buttress his legend came on October 20, when Grambling arrived in Jackson for a matchup so highly anticipated that the *Clarion-Ledger* actually placed a preview story on the front page of the sports section. Coached by a legend-in-the-making named Eddie Robinson, Grambling was the pride of the SWAC—a nationally known program that even rednecks and racists seemed to admire for its ability to churn out professional players. Grambling had defeated Jackson State in four of the teams' five previous meetings, and Hill was fed up. During practices that week he beat on his players with a torturous cruelty excessive for a man known for torturous cruelty.

By the time the Grambling game began, Hill's men were exhausted and emaciated from a week of nonstop down-ups and wind sprints in the ninety-degree heat. Jackson State was thought to be the better ball club, what with Payton leading the SWAC with 690 rushing yards and Jimmy Lewis pacing the league in most passing categories. The defenses were both strong (Grambling ranked number one in the SWAC, Jackson State was number two), the coaches both admired. The teams sported identical 5-1 general records, as well as 3-1 marks in the SWAC.

Yet even though Waller officially proclaimed October 20 to be (to Payton's great embarrassment) "Walter Payton and Tiger Day," an exhausted Jackson State had no chance. A boisterous sixty thousand fan–crowd poured into Memorial Stadium for the clash, expecting Payton and Co. to run all over Robinson's 4-3 defense. But Jackson State's offensive line was tired, sluggish, and unable to move Grambling's two star defensive ends, Ezil Bibbs and Gary "Big Hands" Johnson. The result was a dispiriting 19–12 setback—in the words of the *Claron-Ledger*'s Steve Burtt, "a sloppy, penalty-plagued game" that crushed Hill's hopes of an outright SWAC title.

For those football fans who lavished praise upon the Michigans and Nebraskas while dismissing Grambling and Jackson State as nonentities,

Payton's stat line called into question his ability to compete at the highest level. He ran fifteen times for a pedestrian seventy-nine yards and was outgained by twenty-five yards by someone from Grambling named Rodney Tureaud. Yet to Robinson and his players, Payton conducted himself masterfully. The Tigers played two quarterbacks, Jimmy Lewis and Porter Taylor, neither of whom fared well. The line was beaten off the ball all night, and Young uncharacteristically missed a series of blocks. That Payton gained seventy-nine yards wasn't a disappointment, but a miracle. "Payton is fantastic," Robinson said afterward. "He can beat you if you give him the slightest chance."

"His legs kept moving, and moving, and moving—he never gave up," said Bibbs. "I tackled him one time and it took me ten yards to bring him down. He had such strong legs. If you tried to tackle him up high you would never bring him down. I never saw one person bring him down. When you looked in his eyes, you saw that there was no fear. You could hit him, give him your best hit—heck, we had three all-Americans on that line with me. We'd hit him, drop him in the backfield, taunt him. He'd jump right back, look right at us like, 'You didn't hit me hard enough.' Some of those hits were brutal. But he didn't fear it."

· · ·

When the season came to its end, Jackson State found itself a disappointing 9-2, again tied for the SWAC crown. Payton was heartbroken, and wondered aloud whether he could have done more to help the Tigers. Sure, he ran for 1,322 yards, scored a school record twenty-four touchdowns, kicked one field goal and thirteen extra points. Sure, he caught fifteen passes for 188 yards. Sure, he blocked like an offensive tackle. "He wanted to win like I wanted to win," said Hill. "His drive was real."

Some of the pain was lessened on December 19, when Payton was selected to the 1971 Black College All-American Football Team and anointed its Offensive Player of the Year. The sponsoring companies, Chevrolet and the Mutual Black Radio Network, flew Payton to New York City (or, to a kid whose only previous airplane trip was to Manhattan, Kansas, "the other Manhattan") and put him up at the New York Hilton, just a few blocks from Times Square. Having rarely left the state of Mississippi, Payton was wide-eyed and speechless.

"I'll tell you one thing," he said to Eddie Bishop, a Southern University defensive back, "I'm never going to live in a big city like this. I couldn't survive more than a day."

CHAPTER 9

HEISMAN HOPES

THEY ARRIVED AT APPROXIMATELY THE SAME TIME—ONE, A MARVELOUS
SIGHT for Walter Payton's lonely eyes; the other, an alluring bronze mistress he
aspired to woo.

One was Connie Norwood.

The other was the Heisman Trophy.

Thanks to Bob Hill's generous offer of a full scholarship, in the fall of
1974 Norwood officially enrolled as a freshman at the newly minted Jackson
State University (the school was no longer merely a college). Walter's girlfriend would settle easily into campus life—she made a handful of close
acquaintances and became a member of the Jaycettes, the school's halftime
female pep squad. "Everyone called her 'Mrs. Thing,'" said Robert Brazile,
the Tigers' standout linebacker. "Because Connie referred to everyone as
'Mr. Thing.'" She was energetic, engaging, and hard not to like. Yet if Connie thought life alongside Jackson State's BMOC would be without its complications, she was badly mistaken.

To begin with, at a time when students were embracing black pride and
racial self-discovery, many of the school's coeds were less than enamored by
the football superstar—with pigmentation as dark as charcoal—dating a light-
skinned girl like Connie. "He was the school stud," said Rogelio Solis, a
friend and editor of the student newspaper. "The local high school girls would
always come up to his car and slip him their numbers. One time he was giving me a ride, telling me about the situation. I said, 'How bad can it be?' Walter opened his glove compartment, and scraps of paper came pouring out."

While she was, indeed, black, Walter's choice of Connie stirred something in Jackson State's females. Black women were embracing their heritage—wearing Afrocentric garb, letting their hair grow naturally, anxious to revel in their beauty and to show men that black—deep, dark, rich blackness—was beautiful and worthy of love.

Yet Payton, like many of his football teammates, wasn't interested. Whether it was some sort of societal conditioning or based upon his roots in segregated rural Columbia, he possessed a strong physical attraction to white and light-skinned women. It began with Colleen Crawley in high school, and continued throughout his life. "Walter made that very clear," said Mary "Bullet" Jones, his *Soul Train* dance partner and a person with extremely dark skin. "After we met he told me, 'You're the only dark-skinned girl that I'd ever think of being with, because I much prefer light skin.'"

Connie felt the eyes of others bearing down upon her and wondered what she could do to be more accepted. "Most of the time, I thought, 'You can have him. He's a moody person,'" she once said. But, of course, she didn't want other women to have *him*. Yes, Walter was moody. If a game went poorly, he brooded for hours. If he didn't like the number of carries he was receiving, he whined and complained. And yet, Walter was funny. And charming. And extremely well put together. While other Tigers roamed the world in sweatpants and T-shirts, Walter was straight out of GQ. "His jeans were always pressed, his shirt was always fitted so you could see his muscles," said Brazile. "His shoes were always freshly shined and sparkling white."

As a senior, Walter was perfectly at ease. Having spent his summers taking classes in Jackson, he actually completed his undergraduate course work in three years, and began the 1974–75 academic campaign taking masters-level classes in special education. In other words, his was a relaxed existence.

Armed with a rainbow-hued customized Ford van with a shag rug interior (with help from his parents, he bought the vehicle after his junior year), Payton fancied himself a cartoon character brought to life. He developed unusual behaviors that, were he not the star running back, probably wouldn't have flown. Explained simply, Payton liked to test people; to see how far he could take a gag until those around him exploded. When unsuspecting friends and teammates were focused elsewhere, he approached from behind and bit them on the shoulder—*hard*. "I would walk into the office with my back turned, and instead of saying hello, Walter would slip behind me, grab me, and scare me to death," said Edith Guston, a secretary in the Jackson

State football office. "He was playful like that." Were Walter waiting at a red traffic light, he'd turn toward a nearby pedestrian and scream as loud as possible. "Just to scare the guy," said Vernon Perry, Jackson State's safety. "Gave Walter a good laugh." Several of the Jackson State players were locals, and Payton enjoyed visiting their boyhood homes, sitting on the porch, and firing his rifle at squirrels, dogs, and mailboxes.

For kicks, in the lead-up to Halloween Walter and teammates Perry and Brazile purchased a hideous rubber mask from the nearby five-and-ten store. They proceeded to ride around town in Walter's van, taking turns scaring people. "It was a blast," said Perry. "We'd pull up next to a car, and Walter or Robert would put it on and they'd make little kids cry." On Halloween night Payton donned the mask and tiptoed toward a parked automobile. Inside, a Jackson State player was making out with his girlfriend. Payton, Perry, and Brazile surrounded the car while shaking it and screaming. The teammate, completely naked, jumped out and ran, leaving his girlfriend behind. "That's how bad that mask was," Perry said. "Walter was a hoot."

Though more serious and studious than Walter, Connie embraced the comfort that came with knowing he was by her side, as well as the status befitting a football star's girlfriend. Before long she was known all over campus—the Jaycette with the athletic hero. Even to those who resented Connie's presence, she and Walter were Jackson State's star couple. "Oh, Connie was beautiful," said Douglas Baker, a Tigers center. "You didn't get to be a Jaycette unless you were statuesque and gorgeous and could dance. She had all of that."

Connie, however, was hardly the only object of Walter's affection. Throughout the later portion of Payton's junior year, Jackson State's staff began toying with the idea of mounting a campaign to land Payton the Heisman Trophy. The Tigers were loaded with talented players and, specifically, talented running backs. Along with Payton and Rickey Young, Hill's backfield included Joe Lowery, aka "The Rubber Ball," a bruising, undersized tailback who would later attend training camp with the Denver Broncos, and John Ealy, a speedy senior from Baton Rouge, Louisiana.

"We had a lot of stars to choose from," said Hill. "But the newspapers barely covered us and we had almost no budget to speak of. So one day I got the team together and said, 'Look, what we need to do is get more people coming to the games so we can increase our funds. To do that, we need a star.'" Hill cited John Wayne, at the time starring in *The Train Robbers*, and Telly Savalas, TV's beloved *Kojak*. "Here's Walter," Hill told his men. "He's got all the potential. We can take him and promote him and put him up for the Heisman. He has an outside chance because of our budget and who we play, but he has a legitimate chance because he's that good. But before we do this, I need to know that you guys won't be angry or resentful. I need to know that our team will stick together, even when we're putting an individual out front."

Hill left the room, leaving his sixty-six players alone to discuss the issue. When he returned, Brazile stood up. "Coach," he said, "if it's good for the program, it's good for us."

The campaign had never gained much traction when Walter was a junior, but now it caught a wave. One day Doug Shanks, the Jackson city commissioner and Tigers loyalist, came to one of Payton's summer workouts accompanied by Alan Nations, a local journalist who had worked on political campaigns. Shanks pulled Payton aside, introduced him to Nations and said, "Walter, Alan here is going to try and get you some publicity for the Heisman." Payton nodded, and Nations, in the name of small talk, asked, "Walter, are you married?"

"No," Payton replied. "Do I need to be?"

"He was serious," said Shanks. "Walter would have found a way to get hitched in the name of winning that trophy."

Though he failed to propose to Connie, Walter did take one peculiar step. When asked by members of the media for his age, Payton said "twenty" instead of "twenty-one." On those occasions when he needed to supply his birthday, he wrote July 25, 1954—*not July 25, 1953*. For some peculiar reason, Payton seemed to believe the award's voters would view him more favorably as a younger man. Back in the 1970s, when collegiate athletics weren't close to being the billion-dollar business that they are today, such details could be easily overlooked. If Walter Payton said he was twenty, Sam Jefferson believed he was twenty. The deception stuck. For the remainder of his life, Payton would be listed as being one year younger than he actually was.

The real Heisman run began on July 6, 1974, when subscribers of *The Sporting News*, at the time one of the nation's leading sports weeklies, turned to Dick Young's regular column, "Young Ideas," and read the following: "Long range, long-shot prediction: Walter Payton, Jackson State running back, will be the first man from a black college to win the Heisman Trophy, six months hence."

Shortly thereafter the *Associated Press* sent a story across its wires titled, "Payton a 'Heisman' Hopeful."

The Payton-for-the-Heisman drive, possibly a virtue of its unusualness on behalf of a small college player as well as a recognition of Payton's accomplishments, already has drawn some national note.

Newspapers from New York, Miami, and other cities have already called, and the university is pushing publicity with great vigor.

Payton, whose ego appears to have remained of modest proportions despite the publicity boomlet, shyly explains that his teammates inspired the campaign.

"We had several players at the time that were just as good or better than I am, but the positions they played would have made it harder to publicize them, so they voted to push me."

As well connected as anyone in the city of Jackson, Hill asked Marvin Hogan, the head of a local nonprofit agency called Friends of Children, to use the office's printing machines to mass-produce signs and bumper stickers reading WHY NOT PAYTON FOR HEISMAN TROPHY? Sam Jefferson, Jackson State's sports information director, shipped the material to newspapers, magazines, and television stations across the country, along with a crude two-page synopsis that included the sentence, "He doesn't smoke, drink, or frequent the so called 'Hep Parties.'" Before long, newspapers like *The New York Times* and *Newsday* were referring to Payton and his Heisman ambitions. Ironically, with the exception of Payton himself, no one at Jackson State believed he had a real shot.

"We were fully aware it wouldn't happen," said Jefferson. "We harbored no illusions, and while I won't say it was impossible, it was improbable. You can't be a small school on a shoestring budget and expect to mount a real campaign against the big guys."

Payton, however, now had a new motivation. Throughout the first three years of his collegiate career, Payton ran with power and determination. But he never ran with a grudge. To Hill's dismay, Payton would barrel over defensive players, then extend his hand after the whistle to help them up. He was a gentleman in shoulder pads.

With the Heisman hype, Hill no longer had to worry. Payton heard the talk—via TV, via magazines, via newspapers—that while he was a promising back, he paled in comparison to the nation's two supposedly elite ball carriers, Archie Griffin of Ohio State and Anthony Davis of Southern Cal. "There's no comparison," Payton told a reporter from *The Atlanta Constitution* in a rare moment of public boastfulness. "I'm better than they are, and I know it." Payton was particularly galled by the attention afforded Griffin, a junior from Columbus, Ohio, who stayed home to play for the Buckeyes.

"What Walter really needs is exposure," Frank Bannister, Jr., a commentator for the Mutual Black Network and, at the time, the only black Heisman voter, told Jackson State's student paper. "Not enough people have seen Walter, but we're trying to work on that. If the committee is in a mood sympathetic to the small colleges and black colleges then Walter just might slip in. He has the records, the ability, the character, he's worked with handicapped kids, he's a good student, and he's been a team leader. He should win it."

In *Sports Illustrated*'s highly anticipated College Football Preview issue, Payton's name appeared on page 82, a passing reference within a single essay devoted to the nation's small colleges. Griffin's visage, meanwhile, was plastered across the cover, a football tucked beneath his right elbow, running the ball toward presumptive glory. "I can't say I knew a whole lot about Walter," said Griffin. "I'd heard his name, but Jackson State wasn't on TV, so I didn't get a chance to see him. It's a shame, because he obviously deserved the attention."

Beginning with the *Sports Illustrated* slight, Payton became obsessed with Griffin. Ohio State's star was five foot nine, 185 pounds—roughly the same height as Payton, but fifteen pounds lighter. He ran a 4.6 forty, a tenth of a second slower than Payton's 4.5 time (Jefferson often cited Payton's 4.4 speed—which was as legitimate as his supposed six-foot-one stature). Griffin seemed to have great vision and strong hands, but whenever Ohio State was on national television (a common occurrence), Payton watched, his veins bulging with each word of praise from an announcer. "Look at this garbage!" Payton would yell. "The holes they're opening for him are enormous. I'd run circles around this guy."*

"It was a controlled rage," said Rodney Phillips, Payton's roommate and teammate. "Archie was getting all that publicity, and Walter couldn't. But he knew he was the better football player. We all did."

Payton's goal was to show it to the world and have the finest season in college football history. Though the resentment certainly fueled him, it was naïve. In actuality, the so-called doubters didn't exist, because few

---

* Payton's take on Griffin would prove prophetic. Selected by Cincinnati in the first round of the 1976 NFL draft, Griffin lasted seven years, never gaining more than 688 yards in a season. "Archie and Walter were actually very similar people," said Tom Klaban, Ohio State's kicker and, in 1976, an invitee to Bears camp. "Both polite, modest, soft-spoken gentlemen."

people who mattered took Walter Payton's efforts seriously enough to even be termed doubters. (Noted Jefferson at the time: "Lots of newspapers around the nation don't even print our scores, much less give details of the games.") Payton was a true Heisman candidate, in the same way Lyndon LaRouche runs for president every four years. He could accumulate ten thousand yards and five hundred touchdowns in 1974, and the feats would still be largely dismissed as low level. To most Heisman voters, SWAC statistics were meaningless.

"Walter felt he needed to go above and beyond in order to get the due he was deserved," Hill said. "He probably needed to be perfect. As did our team."

The Tigers fielded a preposterously talented club in 1974, with thirty-eight returning lettermen and a fully intact offensive line. Rickey Young would emerge as an elite fullback, and quarterback Jimmy Lewis was often mentioned (incorrectly, it turned out) as a professional prospect. With Brazile and Tate at linebacker, the defense was fierce. Twelve members of the team eventually played in the NFL—more than both supposedly superior in-state schools, Mississippi State and Ole Miss.

The spotlight, however, was on Walter Payton. In practices, defensive players could unload on quarterbacks, on receivers, on linemen. "But if you touched Walter, Coach Hill would hit you with a wood board," said Perry. Or worse. A Bishop wide receiver named Joe Pierce recalled watching a Jackson State morning practice the day before the game. "A linebacker hit Walter and made him fall down," said Pierce. "There was a collective gasp, and the coach walked over to a tree, ripped off a branch, ordered the linebacker to bend over, and then hit him across the butt several times."

Jackson State won two of its first three games, with Hill giving the ball to his star halfback in every possible scenario. After opening the season with a heartbreaking 10–6 loss to Morgan State in a benefit game at Veterans Stadium in Philadelphia (Payton returned a kickoff eighty-one yards, but fumbled near the goal line on the potentially game-winning drive), the Tigers kicked off their home schedule by destroying Prairie View at Memorial Stadium, 67–7. Payton ran for two short touchdowns and threw a thirty-six-yard spiral to Jeremiah Tillman for a third. They followed with a 25–6 homecoming triumph against Mississippi Valley, with Payton contributing two touchdowns, a field goal, two extra points, and a two-point conversion.

Payton's numbers were terrific, but Hill wanted more. The coach believed that in order for Jackson State to become a nationally known program, Payton needed to appear Jim Brown–like in his splendor. A bunch of hundred-yard rushing games wouldn't cut it. Neither would a handful of touchdowns and field goals. He couldn't merely be a good running back at a SWAC school of limited note. "We wanted to open eyes to Walter," he said. "To let everyone in the country see that this was no ordinary football player."

Enter Nebraska-Omaha.

One year earlier, Hill's team had opened its season by flying to the Midwest and crushing the Division II Mavericks, 17–0. Now, as part of a home-and-home agreement, UNO would be coming to Jackson for an October 5 meeting—the rare predominantly white college willing to trek to Memorial Stadium and face the Tigers. This was, for Payton and Jackson State, the perfect storm. "The way we saw it, those teams had an opportunity to play a so-called nigger school," said Charles Brady, a Jackson State defensive tackle. "And we wanted to punish them."

In 1973, the Mavericks were a solid football team coached by the engaging Al Caniglia. They finished the year 7-2-1, and hope abounded. On a February evening in 1974, however, Caniglia returned home after a day of meetings, collapsed from a massive heart attack, and died. He was fifty-two. "Al was a great man," said Bill Daenhauer, the team's defensive coordinator. "He took care of you, and always made sure everything was going well for those around him. He wanted you to succeed." With his death less than two months before the start of spring practices, the school acted quickly to find a replacement. Don Leahy, Nebraska-Omaha's athletic director, hired C. T. Hewgley, a standout offensive and defensive tackle at the University of Wyoming from 1948 to 1950 who, in 1973, coached his alma mater's offensive line.

A tank driver with the 45th Infantry Division in Europe during World War II (as well as an infantry company commander in Korea), Hewgley used his first meeting with the Maverick players to let them know long hair—a staple under the liberal-minded Caniglia—was no longer tolerated. "We had a quarterbacks session once, and he took us to his house to show us a jar of the 'Gook ears'—his words—that he brought back [from Korea]," said John Bowenkamp, a UNO quarterback. "We were eighteen, nineteen, Vietnam was winding down and most of us were against the war. The ears didn't go over so well."

Neither did Hewgley's football philosophies. Befitting an ex–drill sergeant, the new coach used the preseason to run his players into the ground, often implementing three-a-day practices with no water. "I was two hundred and thirty-eight pounds the year before he arrived," said Ted Sledge, a star defensive tackle. "After some of the games my senior year I weighed one-ninety-eight. You can't play the line like that. Not possible." Under Caniglia, the Mavericks relied on star halfback Saul Ravenell, a third-team all-American in 1973, by operating the I-formation. "We switched to the wishbone when Hewgley took the job, only we didn't have fast quarterbacks," said Ravenell. "The whole thing was a disaster. A bunch of guys quit. Others didn't play very hard. When you have a coach like C. T. Hewgley, the motivation is hard to come by."

The Mavericks arrived in Mississippi on the afternoon of October 4 and spent the night at the Ramada Inn, a short drive from Memorial Stadium. On the evening of the game (scheduled to begin at eight P.M.), the team took a bus to the stadium, only to be greeted by hundreds of Jackson State diehards. "We went there and everyone was black," said Ravenell. "The fans, the cheerleaders, the players. We were mainly white, and our players had never been in that sort of setting. I'm black, so I wasn't affected. But they were intimidated. Normally our team would be all pumped up before a game. This time, nothing was said. We were surrounded by tens of thousands of black faces, and we were afraid."

"We had no chance," said Daenhauer. "None."

The Mavericks won the opening toss and elected to receive. Their offense took over on the twenty-nine-yard line, and Bowenkamp, a Kansas State transfer starting in place of the injured John Smolsky, jogged onto the field. Hewgley called for a swing pass to Ravenell out of the backfield. Bowenkamp took the snap and rolled right. With Ravenell covered by Tate, the quarterback tucked the ball and turned upfield. POP! He was clocked by Brazile, a six-foot-four, 240-pound linebacker who would later be nicknamed "Dr. Doom" during a fabulous ten-year NFL career. Bowenkamp crumpled to the ground before Brazile's hand grabbed his shoulder pads and jerked him upward. "White boy," Brazile growled, "don't you *ever* run this way again."

The Mavericks punted, and moments later Young scored on a twenty-yard romp through the middle of UNO's defense, kicking off an offensive explosion unparalleled in the history of Memorial Stadium. The Tigers led 48–0 at halftime, with Hill having decided early on that the day would be devoted to Payton and his Heisman hype. The highlight film—black-and-white and grainy—serves as an ode to a great runner at his absolute greatest.

"My best safety was a kid named Mike McDermott—a real tough guy from Colorado," said Daenhauer. "Walter broke through the line one time, and Mike hit him squarely in the chest . . . just unloaded on him. Walter ran right through him like he wasn't even there. I'd never seen that before."

"There was one play when Walter Payton was running, and he was going to my right down the sidelines," said Jim Sledge, a defensive tackle (and Ted Sledge's sibling). "My brother was going full steam at him, and he stiff-armed him right in the chest, knocked him back, and scooted another fifty yards."

The Tigers won 75–0, the most lopsided game in college football that season. Payton carried the ball eighteen times for 183 yards and six touchdowns. Afterward, UNO's players expected to receive a stern browbeating from their coach. "There's nothing I can really tell you after a game like that," Hewgley said, his voice near a whisper. "We got our butts handed to us by a superhero."

Four days later, the *Associated Press* named its National College Back of the Week. According to an *AP* article, among those considered for the award were Andrew Johnson of the Citadel, Joe Washington of Oklahoma, Walt Snickenberger of Princeton, and Billy Waddy of Colorado.

The winner was chosen by unanimous consent: Archie Griffin.

"Walter," said Hill, "never got his due. Never."

. . .

Indeed, overlooked in the aftermath of the 75–0 rout was a monumental achievement: With the six touchdowns against Omaha, Payton scored his 410th career point, breaking the NCAA record. So lightly regarded was Jackson State and the SWAC by the national media that John Husar of the *Chicago Tribune* dismissively wrote toward the end of his weekly column that Payton "*apparently* has broken the record—*his school claims.*" The old mark, set by Dale Mills of Northeast Missouri, had stood for fifteen years. "The record meant a lot to me," said Mills. "Because it showed what you can accomplish with drive and hard work. But I wasn't disappointed when Payton broke it, because he seemed to be that type of player."

Mills and Payton actually shared some uncanny commonalities. Payton was from Columbia, Mississippi, Mills from Columbia, Missouri. Payton was a five-foot-ten halfback, Mills was a five-foot-ten halfback. Payton followed his older brother Eddie to Jackson State, Mills followed his older brother Bill to Northeast Missouri. Payton started playing as a freshman. Mills started playing as a freshman.

"It's all very odd," said Mills, now seventy and a retired high school science teacher. "I actually met Walter once in the Kansas City International Airport. It was 1988 or '89, and my son saw Walter and brought me over to introduce us. I said, 'Walter, you broke my scoring record.' I don't think it meant too much to him, but he was very gracious about it."

· · ·

Through late October Payton continued to believe he had a shot at the Heisman. Inside the Jackson State locker room, coaches and teammates insisted the honor was within reach—a dangling carrot that consumed the running back's attention. "If they are going to go by ability and stats," he told the *Blue and White Flash*, "they will have no other choice."

Was he deliberately fooling himself? Sort of. Payton certainly knew that while he was wallowing in SWAC obscurity, Griffin was in the midst of a phenomenal streak of exceeding one hundred rushing yards in thirty-one straight games. Yet, in his mind, stranger things had happened. What if Griffin and Anthony Davis got hurt? Or slumped? What if Jackson State won the rest of their games, and Payton ran for more than two hundred yards in all of them? Then, surely, he'd receive his due. Or, at the very least, be strongly considered.

The Tigers followed the Omaha bloodbath by walloping Bishop in Dallas, 36–10 (Payton ran for 144 yards and three touchdowns), then traveled to Baton Rouge, Louisiana, for a Homecoming Day face-off with Southern University, a SWAC rival. Like most of the league's teams, Southern could not match Jackson State's talent in a position-by-position comparison. They were thin in most of the skill areas, and ran a wishbone offense that was as simple as it was ineffective.

The Jaguars entered the game 4-1, and Charlie Bates, the team's cagey coach, based his entire defensive game plan around stopping Payton. "Let them throw, let other guys run the ball, let them kick field goals," he told his players. "But if you let Walter Payton get space, he'll run all over us. Choke him at the line, we win."

For teams like Omaha and Bishop, the strategy would have been pointless. Payton was faster, stronger, and tougher than the opposition, and his line opened gaping holes on nearly every play. If a defensive end or linebacker didn't get to him, he was gone. Southern, however, featured a defense with three lighting-quick linebackers and a bruising front four. "You had to have three or four people watching him at all times," said Harry Gunner, the Jaguar defensive coordinator. "Back in those days, if you did an extensive job scouting Jackson State, you knew they gave away certain formations and plays. Our guys were great at following directions. So we told them, 'Here's the play that's probably coming—don't let Payton get loose.'"

In one of the most exciting—and controversial—games in SWAC history, Payton took a rare beating. His uniform was caked in dirt, his chest stung from a cornucopia of crushing blows. The fans at Mumford Stadium relentlessly taunted him, cursing his name and mocking his Heisman efforts. Two years earlier the Tigers had ruined Southern's homecoming with a last-second win, and the memory in Baton Rouge was raw. Entering the fourth quarter, the Tigers trailed 21–13, but marched down the field and had the ball at Southern's four-yard line. On first and goal, Payton took the handoff and barreled over Armond Brown, the team's star linebacker, and into the end zone. "It was crushing, because we were determined not to lose," said Brown. "Not in front of our own fans."

With the score now 21–19, Hill kept his offense on the field, electing to tie the game with a two-point conversion. Lining up at the three-yard line, quarterback Jimmy Lewis pitched the ball to Payton, who was drifting left. Payton lowered his head, charged forward, and ran into a pair of Southern defenders at the goal line. He lunged forward, the upper half of his body clearly falling into the end zone. Several Jackson State players raised their hands, celebrating yet another Payton achievement. The crowd booed. Whistles were blown. Bates, the Southern coach, began thinking about the upcoming kickoff return.

Not so fast.

The five officials gathered in a small huddle, talked for another minute or two. Finally, a decree was issued. The ball had never crossed the goal line. No score. "The ref told me Walter's knees had hit the ground first," said Hill. "I couldn't believe it. There was no way he didn't score. No possible way."

Payton grabbed the football and slammed it toward the turf in disgust. He ripped his helmet off his head and threw it aside. "No way!" he screamed. "No way in hell!"

The Jaguars held on for the 21–19 triumph, a crushing blow for Jackson

State and for Payton. Though he ran for 113 yards and a touchdown against one of the nation's best defenses, all was lost. In his mind, the defeat killed the Heisman hopes.

Upon returning to Jackson, Hill inspected all available photographs from the game. One in particular showed Payton stretched far across the goal line. He sent the picture to various media outposts, hoping to keep the Payton flame alight. The only news outlet to run the photograph was Jackson State's own *Blue and White Flash*, which blew it up and placed it beneath a headline reading YOU BE THE REFEREE.

The game marked the last time Hill ever had Payton charge through the defense on a goal line play. Blessed with powerful legs and Bob Beamon–esque leaping ability, Payton would be better served going over—not through—packed-in opponents. "From that point on, we began a drill in practice," said Hill. "I'd have all the linebackers hold hands, and Walter would have to fly over them without being pulled down.

"That's how he learned to soar."

. . .

With the loss to Southern, Walter Payton's senior season was pretty much shot. The Tigers fell again, to Grambling, the following week, and then Payton shocked the coaching staff by sitting out a game against Bethune-Cookman with a mild knee injury (he was used solely as a kicker). The Tigers won their season finale with an emotional 19–13 win at Alcorn State, and Payton's collegiate career was complete. After his final game, Payton, along with Connie and a couple of Tiger players, purchased two six-packs of Colt 45 Malt Liquor.

"I'm telling you, I chugalugged the first tall, cold can before Rickey (Young) had the car started again," Payton wrote. "I guzzled the second, third, and fourth on the way, and I finished the fifth as we got out of the car. It hadn't quite hit me as we walked in the door, but as I popped the top on number six and began sipping, I became so drunk I could hardly see."

Connie, who never drank, was infuriated. "You ought to be ashamed of yourself, Walter Payton," she lectured. "You're just getting what you deserve."

She was right. Payton spent the remainder of the night hunched over a toilet.

With Jackson State's season over, the NFL's personnel gurus continued to flock to campus to conduct workouts. Their praise was universal. As Tom

Siler noted in his weekly *Sporting News* column: "Pro scouts, judging from my research, would prefer Payton to Griffin. He's twenty pounds heavier [this was a tremendous exaggeration on the part of Jackson State's coaches, who listed Payton as a six-foot-one, 215-pound bruiser with 4.3 speed]. Payton, the scouts say, is a great runner." The Dallas Cowboys, owners of the second pick in the upcoming draft, were so wowed by Payton that they actually sent Hill a buffet of weight equipment to fill a sparse exercise room in Sampson Hall and make a good impression. The Atlanta Falcons came multiple times. So did the Colts. And the Dolphins. And the Bears. And the Raiders. Scouts loved the way Payton ran and caught and blocked, and they especially appreciated how, after scoring a touchdown, he took the ball and casually handed it to an official. "He always acted like he'd done it before, and he'd do it again," said Bernard Fernandez, who covered Jackson State for the *Clarion-Ledger.* "He was no ordinary kid." Ken Herock, an Oakland scout, had heard stories of Jackson State's freak of nature, but wanted to see for himself. "He was an NFL back, that much was obvious," said Herock. "I scouted Archie Griffin at Ohio State, and I wasn't sold. He was too small, and not that quick. But Walter had all the tools you looked for. And the most impressive part was his makeup. He'd sit down and watch the tapes with you and break them down. There was nothing not to like."

For Heisman voters, it mattered not. Though Payton rushed for 1,029 yards, and tallied nineteen touchdowns, one field goal, and six extra points for the 7-3 Tigers, he was a nonfactor. As predicted, on December 3, 1973, New York's Downtown Athletic Club announced that Griffin, the Ohio State junior, had won the Heisman Trophy in decisive fashion. Having rushed for 1,695 yards and twelve touchdowns, he was an overwhelming—and easy—choice.

Walter Payton placed fourteenth.

PART THREE

# CHICAGO

### Larry Ely,
### Chicago Bears linebacker, 1975

*I came to the Bears from my first NFL team, the Cincinnati Bengals. One of the coaches there in the spring of 1974 was Bill Walsh. I ran into him somewhere after I'd signed with the Bears, and I told him about going to Chicago and trying to win a spot. He said, "You've got a real treat coming." I said, "What?" He said, "You guys have a rookie running back named Walter Payton, and he'll end up being the best who ever played the game."*

*That was before Walter ever took a single NFL handoff.*

CHAPTER 10

GOING PRO

WALTER PAYTON WAS WEARING A PURSE.

Back in the fall of 1974, such an accessory was, inexplicably, en vogue for young Southern men of color. So that's what the greatest football player in the history of Jackson State University had slung over his shoulder: A black leather handbag, dangling from a thin strap.

As did Robert Brazile and Rickey Young, his two Tiger teammates. The three men, all either twenty-one or twenty-two, all nervously twitching, stood alongside a wall in the nondescript Hattiesburg law office, saying nothing, staring toward the ground. Decked out in fancy new suits and shiny dress shoes, the players felt awkward and out of place. As star collegiate athletes, Payton, Brazile, and Young were used to the casualness of university life, as well as the dirt and grass of a hundred-yard field.

But not to this.

They were brought here on this late-November day by Bob Hill, who, when he wasn't terrifying his players, took it upon himself to safeguard their futures. Back in his days as a high school coach, Hill had been introduced to Paul H. Holmes, a local white attorney known to everyone as, simply, Bud. The two struck up a friendship, fostered primarily upon Holmes' unorthodox approach to race relations. Instead of tiptoeing around issues of black-white, Holmes attacked race with the tactfulness of a jackhammer. "Y'all are a helluva lot better off than we are," he told blacks on more than one occasion. "Your ancestors knew somebody wanted you and paid good money. My ancestor was probably sent here out from some prison. My people came out of prison, yours were selected. We all came here under difficult conditions. So why be mad?"

Hill liked Holmes. Liked his honesty, liked his vulgarity, liked his passion for football. Mostly, he liked that he was one of the few white attorneys in Mississippi willing to extend a helping hand toward young blacks. In 1969, when Hill was still the backfield coach at Jackson State, one of his former high school players, a kid named Verlin Bourne, had gotten in some legal trouble. He called Bud. "I don't know if you'd take a black client," said Hill. "But I know this kid, and . . ."

Holmes stopped him midsentence.

"Hell, why wouldn't I?" he said. "Bring the nigger up here and lemme meet him."

Hill laughed. Such was Bud being Bud.

Now, five years later, Hill and Holmes were at it again. The NFL Draft was scheduled for January 28, 1975, and according to the many scouts who had visited Jackson State's campus, all three players were guaranteed to be selected—Payton and Brazile within the first dozen or so picks. The problem, however, came with representation. While various Southern attorneys and agents scoured the campuses of Ole Miss, Mississippi State, and Southern Miss, few—actually, none—trekked out to Jackson State. It's not that the Tigers lacked talent. Everyone knew Hill's program was a buffet of NFL prospects. No, this was about reputation. The white Mississippi agent who represented black players was known as a sellout to his race. College coaches wanted nothing to do with you. Prospects were told to ignore your phone calls. "Truthfully," said Holmes, "I didn't give a shit. If you could play, you could play."

That's why Hill and his players were here, in Holmes' office, seeking out representation. The five men spoke for roughly twenty-five minutes, with the coach and agent doing 99 percent of the talking. Holmes would look up at Payton and Brazile and Young, their eyes wide, their lips pursed. He felt as if he understood what it was to be them—young and black and Southern born. That's why, as the meeting closed and silence choked the room, he turned to Hill and spoke loudly.

"Coach," Holmes said, "I just don't think I can represent these boys."

Hill was stunned. "Really," he said. "What's the matter?"

"Well," said Holmes, "they seem like perfectly nice niggers. But look at those purses. I've never, ever represented any little queers before."

With that, the players burst into laughter. Holmes shook their hands and promised honesty and respect. "All I ask of you is to be good citizens, look people in the eyes, and carry yourself with dignity," he said. "If you can do that, we can work together."

Walter Payton nodded. He had no idea what he was getting himself into.

. . .

Born on October 29, 1932, Bud Holmes was raised in the shadow of D.W. Holmes, his larger-than-life father. A onetime captain of the Ole Miss baseball team, D.W. played several years as a semipro pitcher before earning his law degree from Ole Miss. In 1948, at age fifty-seven, D.W. was elected mayor of Hattiesburg—a progressive, forward-thinking Democrat who planned on adding blacks to the city's police force (a radical idea at the time) and refused to cower at social progress. While growing up in Lake, Mississippi, D.W.'s closest lifelong friend was a black man named Lawyer Cox. "Lawyer was like Daddy's brother," said Bud Holmes. "It wasn't that Daddy always thought he had to do right by blacks. He just thought people should be fair. If that meant giving people equal rights and respect, then that's what it was."

Two years after his election, D.W. was traveling through the nearby town of Collins, Mississippi, when he was hit head-on by a drunk driver who had swerved into the wrong lane. He died on impact.

Eighteen years old and a senior at Hattiesburg High, young Bud Holmes was met by a harsh reality. His father was dead—and real life wasn't easy. "We were never rich, but we were comfortable," he said. "Well, two days after Daddy died my car didn't have any gas, my dogs didn't have any food, and I had two dollars in my pocket. It was my wake-up call that the world wasn't going to show me much pity."

Bud took a job in the bookstore at the University of Southern Mississippi, working with athletes who needed academic assistance. He enrolled at the school, and befriended a professional baseball player from West Point, Mississippi, named Bubba Phillips. Working his way through Detroit's minor league system, Phillips, a Southern Miss grad, needed someone local to watch his automobile while he attended spring training in Lakeland, Florida. Holmes was happy to oblige. "That alone made me a big man on campus," he said. "Hell, I was driving Bubba Phillips' car. You couldn't get much bigger than that." Holmes graduated in December 1953 with a degree in history, then spent two years in the army before attaining his law degree from Ole Miss in June 1958.

Holmes began practicing law locally, and also worked on a handful of political campaigns. His true passion, however, was assisting the Southern Miss athletic department. Oftentimes alongside Phillips, he combed the state looking for high school gridiron stars worthy of playing for the Golden Eagles. The Southern Miss brass came to trust Holmes, who compensated for his lack of athleticism (he was a high school cheerleader) with a keen eye for talent and a confident swagger that sold his alma mater to dozens of youngsters. Holmes also put his legal knowledge to use, representing Southern Miss athletes in various minor skirmishes.

Before long Holmes was an established part of the Southern Miss family. In 1969, he was asked by the school to negotiate a deal with the New Orleans Saints, a four-year-old NFL franchise, to relocate its training camp from Bowling Green, Ohio, to the Southern Miss campus. Two years later, the team was in Hattiesburg. "I succeeded, and that helped my reputation a great deal," he said. "It made a statement."

Shortly thereafter, Ray Guy, Southern Miss' all-American punter, approached Holmes about representing him in the 1973 NFL Draft. Guy remains the only punter in NFL history to be selected in the first round. A year later another Southern Miss player, defensive end Fred Cook, asked Holmes to be his agent. Cook was taken in the second round. "I didn't do anything special," Holmes said. "But I was honest and up-front with those boys. They appreciated that."

From the very beginning, he had a different perspective on race. With his father's commitment to decency, Bud was never one to condemn blacks, or demand segregation, or openly fear the coming of *Brown v. Board of Education of Topeka*. As far as Bud was concerned, to deny someone a piece of the pie based solely on skin color was sinful. When D.W. died, Bud's first call was to Lawyer Cox.

And yet, his take is complicated. As far as Holmes was concerned, blacks were blacks and whites were whites, and the societal divide was—to a certain degree—a key to harmonic living. "I grew up in a town where, at most, you had one or two murders per year," he said. "Nobody had a lock on their door. If a black man didn't support his family, the black community had a group of preachers and hardworking men called a spirit group. And they'd visit him and say, 'Listen, if you don't take care of your family, we'll take action.'

"Well, today there's killing, there's dope, there's fighting over the welfare checks. I don't mean to say we necessarily should go back to a segregated society. But when you had segregation, you let the blacks come forward and control their people. And they did. There are a lot of negatives to the problems integration brought. A lot of older blacks would say that if they could do it over again, they'd take it back. There were black movie theaters, black banks, black funeral homes. The blacks took great pride in themselves. And if a kid screwed up at school, the black teacher would call home and say, 'I wore him out.' Then the parent would wear the child out, too. Today they learn all you have to say is, 'That white teacher called me a nigger.' And the teacher gets in trouble. So they learn all they have to do is holler 'Racism! Racism!' And the school system went to shit. People try to run and hide from that, but it's the truth of the matter."

Dating back to his youth, Holmes has tossed around the word" nigger" with the casualness of a throw pillow. From his viewpoint, it isn't stated with contempt, merely as a word that's no less inappropriate than "apple" or "hello." A nigger can be a nice black or a jerk black, a successful one or an utter failure, male or female, young or old. In the heart of rural Mississippi, Holmes is beloved by many blacks as an honest, straightforward purveyor of truth. "There aren't many people I'd trust with my life," said Eddie Payton. "But Bud is one of them. His word is his bond."

Walter Payton didn't initially know what to think. He trusted Hill, and Hill trusted Holmes. Yet as two big showcases for the nation's elite college seniors, the East-West Shrine Game and the Senior Bowl, approached, Payton wasn't certain his best strategy would be to hire a local agent with a limited number of NFL clients. On December 24, he and Brazile flew to California to participate in the East-West Shrine Game at Stanford Stadium. The players spent five days in Palo Alto, practicing, mingling with peers, conducting interviews, meeting with scouts, and being wooed by agents. "The only time I ever saw Walter cry was that Christmas morning," said Brazile. "Truth is, we both were crying, because it was the first Christmas for either of us without our families. I saw a different side of Walter, and he saw a different side of me." The East-West flew in players from across the nation. The big names were Steve Bartkowski, the University of California quarterback (widely presumed to be the number one pick in the upcoming draft), and Maryland defensive lineman Randy White. Payton was a curiosity. "People probably wanted to know how he would hang with bigger, tougher, more prominent players," said Holmes. "Back then Jackson State was discarded, if people even heard of it at all."

One person well aware of Payton's potential was Mike Hickey, at the time a scout with the New England Patriots. Hickey had made two trips to Jackson State during the season, and he urged his franchise to find a way to add the running back. "He was a kid who excelled in every category," said Hickey. "Besides his obvious ability, Walter had a maturity that was well beyond the SWAC or anywhere else. A lot of guys from small schools come up with chips on their shoulders, and it's not a good thing. But Walter was calm and easygoing, and he got along with everyone. If you didn't like him as a scout, you had no business being in the profession."

On one of the days leading up to the East-West game, Hickey was chatting with Payton and Brazile inside their hotel room at the Hyatt. The phone rang every ten minutes or so, one agent after another offering his services. "This phone is killing us," Brazile said. "It's so annoying." The next time it rang, Hickey picked up. Howard Slusher, sports' most powerful agent, was on the other end—probably the tenth time he'd called in three days. "He thought I was Brazile, so he started giving me the big pitch," Hickey said. "I cut him off and said, 'Man, I don't want you.'" Both players laughed, and Payton had an idea. Hickey was a nice guy in his early twenties with a laid-back attitude and significantly deeper NFL ties than Holmes. "Hey Mike," he said, "would you consider representing us? You seem to understand us, and you get along with us real well."

Hickey was flattered. He called home later that night, briefly debating the idea with his wife, Kathy. Red Hickey, Mike's father, had been a well-known NFL player and coach and was now working as a scout with the Dallas Cowboys. That was the life Mike most wanted to emulate—finding players, not negotiating on their behalves. "Plus, I had a wife and two little girls in Foxborough, Massachusetts," he said, "and I thought I would be cutting off my career if I left the Patriots."

Payton (as well as Brazile) wound up sticking with Holmes, whose advice to his newest client in the lead-up to the collegiate bowl games was simple: *Show that you belong on this level. Prove the doubters wrong.*

Playing for an East squad led by legendary Michigan coach Bo Schembechler, Payton rushed for forty-nine yards on sixteen carries, unspectacular numbers that impressed absolutely everybody. Dave Pear, a highly touted defensive lineman from Washington, long recalled trying to tackle the mysterious Division II running back. "Never heard of him," said Pear, who went on to a six-year NFL career. "Then he hit me and I never forgot him. The guy was an absolute horse. He refused to fall down. Just flat-out refused."

Though the scouts in attendance marveled at his performance, Payton was crestfallen. He was outrushed by two other players (LSU's Brad Davis and Arizona's Jim Upchurch), and worried that his stock had plunged. "Walter could be very insecure about himself," said Holmes. "He was confident, but only to a certain point."

Two weeks later, Payton drove to Mobile, Alabama, to play in his second—and last—pre-Draft All-Star event, the heavily watched, heavily hyped Senior Bowl. Because organizers of the game had mistakenly scheduled it for the same day as the Honolulu-based Hula Bowl, they had to woo players with thousand-dollar payouts. It would be Payton's first professional check.

Payton had approached the East-West contest cautiously. Not this one. "He actually had an entourage around him leading up to the game," said Jim Germany, a running back from New Mexico State, "and the entourage was all the black college players hanging all over him. They knew how good Walter was, and they gravitated toward him."

"The first time I noticed Walter was on picture day," said Emmett Lee Edwards, a wide receiver from Kansas. "We were all standing together for photos, and everyone was trying to show who they were. I looked over at Walter, and something about him was just different. I came from Kansas, so I'd seen running backs like Gale Sayers and John Riggins. But I knew immediately Walter was in a different category. He looked like a guy who'd gained a lot of yards. You could see it. I went back and told Delvin Williams, my roommate, 'This Payton guy has something to him. I don't know what it is—he just does.'"

Entering the week of the game, Mark Mullaney, a defensive lineman from Colorado State, had never seen or heard of Walter Payton. One day, after the North and South teams finished their practices, Mullaney was the last person to exit the locker room. He heard a curious noise from the stadium, and wandered over. There, all alone, was Payton, running the stairs and, afterward, standing in the end zone, jumping straight up and hanging from the goalpost. "He could actually grab it with ease," said Mullaney, who went on to a twelve-year career with the Minnesota Vikings. "It was astonishing. Everyone else was long gone, probably eating dinner. And here's this kid, by himself, working out." Shortly thereafter, Mullaney received a call from his father, Ed, who worked as a player agent. "He asked me if there was anybody down there who particularly impressed me," said Mullaney. "I told him about Walter Payton from Jackson State. And I'll never forget his reaction. He said, 'Walter who?'"

"I was the captain of the team, and our coach said I could call my own plays, but that I had to give this Jackson State kid his fair share of carries," said Bob Avellini, a quarterback from Maryland. "I had no idea who he was. On the first day of practice I turned to hand the ball to him and he was so quick, I barely got it to him. Then I watched him run—*oh my God!*"

Three days before the January 11, 1975, contest, Payton told the assembled media that he planned on cruising off in the brand-new Dodge Charger awarded to the game's MVP. "I didn't have a good game in the East-West," he said, "and I want to show everybody what kind of back I am." The cockiness hardly came naturally to Payton, who rarely uttered so much as a peep on the football field. But he believed he *needed* attention to secure his future. "We just didn't know," said Brazile. "Everything was a mystery to us."

In a dull 17–17 tie, Payton led all rushers with seventy-three yards on thirteen carries. He returned two kickoffs for forty-two yards, caught two passes and punted three times for a forty-one-yard average. On the first play of the game, he was stopped for a loss by Dave Wasick, a defensive lineman from San Jose State. "I hit him, and he jumped up real quick," said Wasick. "So I jumped up real quick, too. I thought we were gonna fight, but he just ran back to the huddle. Later on I asked him why he got up like that. He said, 'When you play in the SWAC, if you don't get up quickly they'll gouge your eyes out.'"

Though the MVP award went to Bartkowski (likely because writers decided on the winner before the completion of the game—the South team tied the score on a field goal with twenty-five seconds remaining), a point had been made. "Walter was the best guy in the draft," said Hill. "And it was obvious."

· · ·

Well, maybe not obvious. At least not to everybody.

Shortly before the January 28–29, 1975, NFL Draft, the Atlanta Falcons sent offensive lineman George Kunz (as well as the number three overall pick) to Baltimore for the right to select Bartkowski, the golden-haired quarterback out of Cal. At six foot four and 212 pounds, Bartkowski was the model big-statured, big-armed pocket passer. As a senior he had thrown for

2,580 yards and twelve touchdowns, and his breathtaking spirals evoked comparisons to a young Roman Gabriel. During one practice, Bartkowski had supposedly launched a ball an unfathomable 103 yards. "I am strictly a thrower," he said. "I drop back and turn the ball loose."

After the Falcons made their pick, Bartkowski was flown from California to Manhattan to meet the press. Payton, for his part, followed the goings-on from his room inside Jackson State's Sampson Hall, sitting alongside Brazile and hoping for an early telephone call. Because the draft was not yet televised or broadcast, players were forced to wait for a team to contact them with the good news. Payton knew the Falcons were going to go with a quarterback, and that was fine with him. For all its hype as a growing Southern metropolis, Atlanta was too close to Mississippi for Walter's tastes. One year earlier, leading into his junior season, Payton had actually been drafted by the Birmingham Americans of the fledgling World Football League (the league selected underclassmen). Even had he desired to turn pro at the time, there was no way in hell Walter Payton was going to kick off his career a mere 240 miles away from Jackson. Where was the adventure in that?

No, Payton wanted to go somewhere different. Somewhere snazzy. Which is why he had hoped and prayed that the Dallas Cowboys, holders of the draft's second overall selection, would take him.

Coming off of an 8-6 season, Dallas was a model NFL franchise. The team was blessed with a cornerstone quarterback in Roger Staubach, a dazzling wide receiver in Drew Pearson, and the game's best young offensive line.

Gil Brandt, the team's vice president of player personnel, visited Jackson State multiple times, and he considered Payton to be a can't-miss ballplayer. So, for that matter, did the Cowboys' receivers coach, a thirty-five-year-old former tight end named Mike Ditka. "I remember the debate of whether we draft Walter or Randy White," said Ditka. "And I can remember we always had a staff meeting and talked about those things and [head coach Tom Landry] kind of took a vote and all the offensive coaches for sure voted for Walter, and of course, the defensive coaches voted for Randy."

Though Landry's background was in offense, the legendary head coach thought his team needed to plug a hole in the defensive line. Plus, Dallas would be investing a great deal of money in the selection, and wanted the player to last. "What really swayed our mind was that, at the time, [Buffalo's] O. J. Simpson and [Pittsburgh's] Rocky Bleier were the only two running backs to start in the league for over five years," said Brandt. "But even know-ing that, it was the only time in the history of our drafts that within an hour of the pick we were still trying to decide who to take. It simply came down to longevity—we thought Randy would last longer than Walter. So we got Randy White."

With the third pick, the Baltimore Colts selected Ken Huff, a six-foot-four, 252-pound offensive guard out of the University of North Carolina. Like Payton, Huff didn't see it coming. In college he had been an all-American who bench-pressed in excess of five hundred pounds and pro-jected into an excellent NFL prospect. "Without question, the best offensive lineman in this year's draft," raved Joe Thomas, the Colts GM (who bypassed Dennis Harrah and Doug France, two future All-Pro linemen). But he was far from a franchise changer. "I was floored," Huff said. "I thought I'd go in the first couple of rounds, but I had no idea and no expectations. I was going out that morning to grab breakfast with my girlfriend when my agent called to tell me I'd been drafted. I said, 'Really? Are you sure?'"

The fourth selection belonged to Chicago, an organization Payton equated with the bubonic plague. In 1975 the NFL was comprised of twenty-six franchises, and none held less intrigue for Payton than the Bears. To begin with, the team was bad. They had finished last in the NFC Central in 1974 with a 4-10 mark, and hadn't posted a winning record since 1967. Secondly, while Payton had never been to the Windy City, he imagined its denizens plowing through ten feet of snow and enduring tundralike temperatures. Yes, he wanted to leave Mississippi. But not for the North Pole.

Doug Shanks, Jackson's city commissioner and a diehard Jackson State supporter, visited Payton and Brazile during the early stages of the draft. He was standing in the doorway when Hill telephoned the room. Walter's col-lege coach had received a call from Jim Finks, Chicago's general manager. "Walter," Hill said. "Congratulations! You were chosen fourth in the first round by the Chicago Bears!"

Shanks has never forgotten what he witnessed. "Walter was crying like a baby, absolutely devastated," Shanks said. "He had dreams of playing for the Dallas Cowboys, not the Bears. That was the last thing he wanted." Twenty minutes later, the phone rang again. The Houston Oilers, selecting sixth, plucked Brazile. The linebacker was euphoric. The running back was crushed. He, too, wanted to go to Houston. Or Dallas. Or Miami, San Diego, San Francisco.

Anywhere but Chicago.

Under the strict order of Holmes, Payton put on a happy face for the press. When Ponto Downing of the *Clarion-Ledger* arrived at Sampson Hall, Payton and Brazile borrowed a pair of Suzuki motor scooters and gleefully cruised campus, accepting congratulatory hugs from friends and classmates.

Wrote Downing in the next day's paper, beneath the headline J-STATE PAIR "BUZZING" AFTER HEARING DRAFT NEWS:

Making like a black Butch and Sundance, the pair cavorted on their bikes about the J-State campus and the downtown area, stopping occasionally to greet well-wishers and recite their feelings. "Chicago will be in the Super Bowl," exclaimed Payton while a more subdued Brazile stated, "If Houston has a first team, I'll be on it."

Perhaps the zany antics of the touted twosome could be attributed to the unseasonably warm weather Tuesday and the hint of spring in the air but more likely it could be construed as one last fling. An attempt, for the moment, to shove aside the idea that fun and games were over, for as the draft most certainly means sudden fortune, it is also the realization to the end of collegiate careers. . . . Payton, who expresses a desire to go to New York, said Chicago was his second choice and joked, "They'll love me in Chicago!"

Just how elated was Payton? More than two hours after he was selected, Tom Siler of *The Sporting News* called Alyne, Walter's mother, to get her reaction. "I didn't know about it," she said. "Walter hasn't called me, but I guess he will later in the day."

Unlike their number one pick, the Bears were giddy. As soon as the Colts took Huff, a roar emerged from the team's draft room at the La Salle Hotel in downtown Chicago. "We've been sweating it out all night," Jack Pardee, the team's new coach, told the *Chicago Tribune*. "What happened is what we were hoping for." Ever since Gale Sayers retired after the 1971 season, the team had been desperately seeking a running back to carry the offense. In 1974, Chicago's leading rusher was Ken Grandberry, an eighth-round draft pick out of Washington State who gained 475 yards and scored two touchdowns.

The Bears had recently fired Abe Gibron, their head coach for three seasons, and replaced him with Pardee, a former All-Pro linebacker. Within a few days of being hired, Pardee met with Finks, the general manager, and Jim Parmer, a scout. The new coach had played collegiately at Texas A&M, and was partial to his state's brand of steel-jawed, hardnosed football. His first instinct was to focus on Don Hardeman, a powerful runner from Texas A&I. Parmer, however, was adamant about Payton. "We can't make a mistake on this kid," he told Pardee and Finks. "He's too good to pass up." Bill Tobin, a newly hired scout with the club, had visited Jackson State twice while working for the Green Bay Packers. He was equally enthusiastic. Payton from the stands was a blur. Payton up close was even better. Strong. Fast. Rugged. Powerful. Exceptionally large thighs. Elbows the size of bread boxes. And his fingers—long and thick like ripe plantains. "He could put a baseball in the palm of his hand," said Bob Bowser, a longtime football executive, "and his fingers would touch."

"He was easy to find on film," Tobin said. "The small-school question was 'Could he handle the big lights?'"

Pardee remained unconvinced until he traveled to Mobile for the Senior Bowl. Sitting along the sidelines during practices, Pardee couldn't believe what he was watching. The little back from Jackson State was slamming into bigger, stronger, more powerful defensive players from Division I schools and causing serious damage. "You didn't have to be any type of high-powered sleuth to see that the kid had some talent," said Pardee. "Talk about a thoroughbred. He had great body control, great eye-hand coordination, great ability to change direction. I was sold."

. . .

Bud Holmes, however, wasn't sold.

He wasn't sold on Payton as a person, and he wasn't sold on Payton as a client. Midway through the *Clarion-Ledger* story from the day of the draft, Payton was quoted as saying, "I still do not have an agent." Holmes was taken aback. Hadn't Payton said to him, "You're my agent," several days earlier? Hadn't they shook hands?

Over the course of the next few days, Holmes never heard from Payton. Then, on a late Friday evening, the phone rang. It was Walter. "Bud, I'm confused," he said in a panic. "I'm at the airport and I have to go up to Chicago for a press conference, and I don't know what to do."

Holmes was furious. "OK, Walter, do you have something to write with?" he said.

"Yeah," Payton said. "I've got a pen."

"Here's what you do," Holmes said. "You get on an airplane and you fly to Chicago. As soon as you get off the plane, go to a phone booth."

"OK," Payton said. "Got it."

"Good," Holmes said. "Now, in that phone booth they'll have the newest Yellow Pages. Open the book and look under 'Attorneys.' It's spelled A-T-T-O-R-N-E-Y-S. Got it?"

"Yeah," said Payton. "I got it."

"Great," Holmes said. "Get yourself one, because you're gonna need a crazy son of a bitch to represent you. I don't fool with crazy bastards like you."

Payton stuttered and stammered. Holmes didn't. "I ain't heard a word from you, and I do not beg," he said. "To hell with your flight. If you're not here in my office at ten o'clock tomorrow morning—and I don't mean ten-oh-one—you can get someone else to represent you. Because I'm not putting up with this bullshit."

Never mind that the Bears had planned an entire trip in his honor—Payton left the airport in Jackson. "The team sent me to pick him up at the terminal in Chicago," said Pat McCaskey, a public relations assistant with the team and the grandson of George Halas, the Bears' owner. "I waited and waited at the gate. No Walter." The following morning, Holmes arrived at his Hattiesburg-based office at seven o'clock, and found Payton standing by the entrance. Holmes brushed past him without saying a word. His secretary rang him moments later. "Walter Payton is here," she said. "He said he has an appointment."

"He does," Holmes replied. "But it's at ten. Tell him to come back then."

When Payton returned, Holmes gave him one of the great tongue-lashings of his young life. "Walter," he said, "we can start over or we can just put an end to this thing. If you can't communicate better than that, we have no future together, because I don't put up with bullshit. And what you did to me was pure bullshit."

Payton apologized, and promised Holmes he was done acting like a juvenile. "You're my agent," he said. "I trust you. You tell me what to do, I'll do it."

Holmes nodded. The problem was, he wasn't quite sure what his client should do. Payton had already skipped his introductory press conference, a transgression that left Finks, Pardee, and the legendary Halas furious. Two days later, Payton was still missing in action. Under Holmes' directive, he returned none of the Bears' calls, leaving the organization to look hapless and, to a certain degree, pathetic. It was all part of a plan: Halas had publicly called the Bears' draft "our team's best in a decade," which served to excite a habitually disappointed fan base. In other words, the Bears had to hammer out a contract with Payton. They *absolutely had to.* When a Jackson-based NBC reporter tracked down Payton, the running back followed Holmes' script to a tee. "There are other leagues, and I have to give them consideration, too," he said. "I've already been contacted by the Canadian Football League. If an offer comes up that I can't resist, that's part of life, because I'm in it not only for the love of the game but for the money."

Was Payton genuinely interested in moving to Canada? "Not a chance," said Holmes. "It was all a ploy."

On February 2, a full five days following the draft, Payton arrived in Chicago, but not as the Bears had hoped. After ignoring dozens of calls and Western Union telegrams from the team, Holmes was contacted by Brent Musburger, at the time an up-and-coming sports reporter for the local CBS affiliate. The station asked Holmes if he'd be willing to bring his client to Chicago for a one-on-one sit-down interview. "We'll send a plane for both of you," Musburger said. "Then put you on the air."

Holmes liked it. Payton liked it. Here was a way to set the agenda; to let the people of Chicago know that Walter Payton wanted to be a Bear, but the organization wasn't making an effort to sign him (a complete lie—how could an offer be made if Holmes refused to pick up the telephone?). "It was a good strategy for them," said Musburger. "At the time the Bears were thought of as a very cheap operation. The best thing Walter could do was make it sound like he was itching to come play here." The agent and the football player boarded the turboprop jet at Jackson's airport, and en route worked out a devilish plan. Told by Bob Hill that his new client owned a perverse sense of humor, Holmes thought it'd be fun to introduce themselves to the Windy City as a couple of small-town bumpkins. "Walter and I made up this big scenario," Holmes said. "I was gonna be an ignorant lawyer, and Walter was going be an even more ignorant, dumb black who just barely got out of the fields and could barely read and write. Walter was all for it."

The plane landed at Meigs Field. It was a typical winter day in Chicago, with fierce winds blowing off of Lake Michigan and several feet of snow covering the ground. By design, Payton was the last person to exit the aircraft.

He stuck his head out the door, crinkled his nose, and screamed, "Uh-uh, no way. I ain't playing in this mess. What is that stuff? Is that cotton?"

"No Walter," Holmes said. "That's snow."

"Snow!" said Payton. "Well, I ain't ever seen that before."

"Boy," bellowed Holmes, "get your ass off that airplane!"

"Uh-uh," Payton replied. "I ain't stepping into that mess. Mama told me I could come back to the house if I don't like it here. I wanna to go on back home now, Mista Bud."

Payton finally made his way from the plane to an airport hangar, where the interview would be conducted. Upon meeting Musburger, Payton repeatedly referred to him as "Mista Mooseburger."

"Walter was cutting up, using 'nigger' every other word, just watching the shock cross people's faces," said Holmes. "They must have thought this guy from the woods of Mississippi was some idiot. He'd say, 'Mister Bud, I just want to be a good little nigger and do what you tell me to do.' "

Roughly five minutes before Musburger was scheduled to conduct the live interview, he asked Payton to cease using any "ethnic words."

**Payton:** "Mista Mooseburger, what's an ethnic word?"

**Musburger:** "Well, you keep using that word."

**Payton:** "What word is that?"

**Musburger:** "The word that describes black people in a negative light."

**Payton:** "I don't understand, Mista Mooseburger."

**Musburger:** "Walter, you can't say 'nigger' on TV."

**Payton:** "Oh, Mista Mooseburger, don't you worry. I'm a good little nigger, Mista Mooseburger, I promise. Tell him, Mista Bud. Tell Mista Mooseburger that I'm a good little nigger!"

With no time left, Musburger took a deep breath, stared into the camera, and began the segment. A handful of Jackson State highlights flashed across the screen, and Musburger opened by asking Payton—who calmly sipped from a glass of orange juice—how he felt about being drafted by the Bears.

"I'll tell you, Brent, nothing thrills me more than the very idea of being able to play for a franchise as storied and legendary as the Chicago . . ."

"The interview was fantastic," said Holmes, who later received a plaque from Payton that read HONORARY NIGGER. "And when it was over Brent came up to me laughing. He told me, 'Goddamn, Walter *is* a smart ass, isn't he?' "

. . .

The Bears were not happy. The interview was designed to make the organization look like a band of buffoons, and it worked. Later in the day, Finks called Holmes at his hotel. "Mr. Holmes," he said, "do you think it would be all right if I were to meet my number one draft pick? It seems everyone else has."

That night, Payton, Holmes, Finks, and Bill McGrane, an assistant to the general manager, met at a French restaurant in downtown Chicago. The two Mississippians had so enjoyed toying with Musburger that they kept the act going. Holmes wanted the Bears to believe they were dining with a backwoods agent and an even more backwoods football player. When the waiter passed out menus, Holmes noticed that one of the featured dishes was *pêcher le poisson*—fish. "Well look here, Walter!" he said. "They've got possum on the menu!"

"Mmmm!" yelped Payton. "I want me some of that there possum! I want it bad!"

"Walter," said Finks, "that's not possum. It's fish."

"Well, dang," Payton said. "I wanted a mess of that possum so bad!"

"Walter, they ain't got no grits, either," Holmes said. "Lord, I don't even see fried chicken or catfish."

When the waiter came to take an order, Payton looked up with confused eyes. "Do you have anything that's just kind of plain?" he said. "Like a piece of meat with nothin' on it?"

Throughout the meal, Holmes watched Finks' facial expressions morph from shocked to disgusted to dismayed to mystified. "At the start of dinner Jim Finks told us he hadn't had a drink in two or three years," said Holmes. "That night he had two double scotches."

Over the next few weeks, Holmes and Finks exchanged contract proposals, but the Bears were negotiating from a position of weakness. Their two top returning running backs, Grandberry and Carl Garrett, were marginal players, and as Holmes was speaking with Finks he was also being propositioned by Eugene Pullano, president of the Chicago Winds of the second-year World Football League.

A multimillionaire whose family made its fortunes in the insurance business, Pullano took Holmes and Payton to dinner and offered the world. Join the Winds, he said, and you'll make $150,000 annually, plus we'll pay for your apartment, buy you a new Cadillac, and sign Rickey Young to be your blocking back. The WFL had already lured several players away from the NFL, supplying it with much-needed early credibility. "This guy had a great big gold bear ring that had two ruby eyes," said Holmes. "Well, during dinner he took it off his finger and handed it to Walter. Just gave it to him."

Payton was tempted. The money was great, the perks even greater. But, come day's end, his dream wasn't to play with the Chicago Winds. (This proved to be a good thing. Averaging approximately three thousand fans per game and wallowing in debt, the Winds went 1-4 before folding midway through the season.) No, Walter Payton aspired to rule the NFL.

On June 3, 1975, four months after the draft, Payton and the Bears agreed on a three-year contract that paid $150,000 annually. Including a $126,000 signing bonus, it was the richest deal in franchise history. (Holmes wanted Payton to receive the highest signing bonus ever for a player from Mississippi. In 1971, the New Orleans Saints gave Ole Miss quarterback Archie Manning $125,000.) Payton wasted little time putting the money to good use, buying his dream car, a new gold Datsun 280ZX. Contacted by the *Tribune*'s Ed Stone, Holmes could barely contain his giddiness. "The major deciding factor was that it has been his life's ambition to play in the NFL," Holmes said. "Either offer would have made him financially secure, but one gave him the opportunity to play where he could break established records. He's got a history of breaking records wherever he goes."

At long last, Walter Payton was a Chicago Bear.

CHAPTER 11

# BIRTH OF SWEETNESS

IN THE DAYS AND WEEKS AFTER THE DRAFT, WALTER PAYTON HAD TO SWALLOW hard, put on his happiest face, and answer question after question about his new team. He talked of how, as a boy, he worshiped at the altar of Gale Sayers, the magical Chicago Bears halfback who, between the years of 1965 and 1968, was arguably the best player in the National Football League. "Gale Sayers has been my idol," he said. "I used to follow him, watch him when I could, and see what he did in the papers."

Payton was exaggerating about his admiration for Sayers; for a kid growing up in Columbia, Mississippi, in the 1960s, the Chicago Bears were all but invisible. The television in the Payton household was rarely on, and even if it was, Walter had little-to-no interest in following professional sports. He was an outdoor kid, best suited to running along trails and throwing balls and jumping through sprinklers.

In fact, were Payton better schooled on the recent history of the organization, perhaps he would have thought again and opted for Canada. Or the World Football League. Or a career in special education. Or joining a dance troop in Guam. With a 4-10 record, the Bears had finished last in the NFC Central in 1974, their sixth-straight losing mark. The team's offense ranked twenty-fifth in a twenty-six-team league, and an unforgivable seventeenth in defense (the franchise had built and protected its reputation on defensive dominance). With Sayers having retired in 1971 and Dick Butkus, the legendarily vicious linebacker, hanging up his uniform two seasons later, Chicago's roster was a starless collection of has-beens and never-will-bes. Their most noteworthy player was quarterback Bobby Douglass, a fabulous athlete with a cannon for a throwing arm, a club fighter's toughness, and no idea how to play the game. "We were as bad as football can get," said Bo Rather, a Bears receiver from 1974 to 1978. "We had a terrible offense, a terrible defense, and no running game to speak of. There was very little ability, and even Vince Lombardi wouldn't have made much of a difference."

Throughout the early 1970s, players who came to the Bears directly from Division I colleges were flabbergasted by the shoddy conditions and subpar attitudes. "It was terrible," said Wayne Wheeler, a wide receiver who had been drafted out of Alabama in the third round in 1974. "It was like going from college back to high school. I actually wrote [Alabama coach] Bear Bryant a letter asking for equipment, and he sent me brand-new gear because the stuff they gave us in Chicago was so poor. Not only was it used, it didn't even fit."

Since 1944, the Bears had based their training camp at St. Joseph's College in Rensselaer, Indiana, a decaying, bug-infested hellhole that, defensive line-man Gary Hrivnak recalled, "made us feel like we were in the army. We didn't have air-conditioned dorms or a weight room, and the fields were terrible." Once the season started, the conditions somehow worsened. The team held most of its practices at Soldier Field, its home stadium, which featured a rock-solid artificial turf surface that only hardened as the temperatures dropped. On the days Abe Gibron, the head coach, decided his team needed more space, he loaded the players on a couple of yellow school buses and drove them to nearby Grant Park. "That was the biggest joke," said Rich Coady, a Bears center from 1970 to 1975. "We'd get off the bus and they'd be throwing the winos off the patch of grass where we were going to work. There were no lines or goalposts, and for conditioning we'd be told to run up a big hill at the park that kids used for sledding. The older guys would run it once or twice, then lay on top and wait until everyone was done. The whole thing was a circus."

The ringleader was Gibron. A three-hundred-pound barrel of jelly, Chicago's coach had been a Pro Bowl offensive lineman with the Cleveland Browns. His gritty reputation endeared him to George Halas, the Bears founder and owner. Yet in his three seasons guiding the team, Gibron's claim to fame wasn't winning (his teams went 11-30-1), but eating and drinking. It was once said that if Helen of Troy had the face that launched a thousand ships, Abe Gibron had the face that lunched on a thousand shrimps. While most players were uninspired by his coaching acumen, the barrel-bellied, watermelon-headed Gibron dazzled all with his consumption skills. "He was the first person I knew," said Ernie Janet, a Bears offensive guard, "who could eat a hamburger in two bites."

"Abe and I would go to dinner, and he was known everywhere in Chicago because of how much he ate," said Bob Asher, a Bears tackle. "I remember going to Greektown with him, and every restaurant we'd pass a waiter would come out yelling, 'Abe, try this! Abe, try this!' He ate two full meals on the way to our meal."

For fans of comedy and characters, this was wonderful. For Halas and the Bears, however, Gibron's emergence as the face (and blubber) of a once-proud franchise was nothing short of a tragedy.

. . .

George Halas hadn't thought of becoming a legend.

The idea never entered his mind because, in 1920, football was a fringe endeavor, popular with a certain sect of society, but largely ignored. To become an iconic American figure in the sport was no more likely than becoming an iconic shoe salesman or dog walker. Baseball players and boxers were icons. Football players were circus freaks.

Halas was born on February 2, 1895, the son of a tailor from Pilsen, Bohemia, who immigrated to Chicago's West Side. George learned football first at Crane Tech High School, then under Coach Bob Zuppke at the University of Illinois, where he also lettered in baseball and basketball while earning a degree in civil engineering. In helping the Illini capture the 1918 Big Ten football title as a senior end, Halas recalled Zuppke once complaining that, "Just as a fellow begins to learn how to play football, he graduates from college and never plays again."

The words stuck with Halas, who graduated, then joined the navy and fought in World War I. He was initially stationed at a base in Great Lakes Naval Training Center, and bonded with the other recent college graduates (including two future professional stars, Paddy Driscoll and Jimmy Conzelman) who had played football at their respective universities. The soldiers formed their own team, and emerged as a national power. Because the war had decimated the rosters of collegiate programs, the 1919 Rose Bowl was played between the Great Lakes Navy and the Mare Island Marines. Halas' team won 17–0 (Halas still holds the Rose Bowl record for longest interception return without scoring—seventy-seven yards), and the military rewarded the victorious players by granting their releases.

Interestingly, Halas also excelled in baseball, and that same year he appeared in twelve games with the New York Yankees, playing right field and batting .091 with two hits and eight strikeouts in twenty-two at-bats. When the team sent him to the minors, Halas decided to focus on his first love.*

Though at the time pro football wasn't much of a game, Halas was intrigued by the possibilities. So, for that matter, was a man named A. E. Staley. As the president and owner of the A. E. Staley Corn Products Company of Decatur, Illinois, Staley thought it could be fun—and potentially profitable— to start his own semipro football team. He did so, and being a man of little ego, named the outfit the Decatur Staleys.

Staley hired Halas as his first coach, and in order to find opponents the team joined a new league that was being formed, the American Professional Football Association. The Staleys finished 10-1-2 in 1920, but with the American economy tanking, the team's operating costs exceeded gate receipts by fifteen thousand dollars. Following the season, Staley approached Halas with an offer he couldn't refuse. "I'm afraid we can't make a go of it here," he reportedly said. "But I think there is room for another professional team [along with the Cardinals] in Chicago. Take the team there and I will give you five thousand dollars if you keep the name of Staley because it will be a good advertisement for me."

Based out of Wrigley Field, the 1921 Chicago Staleys won nine games and the league title, but Halas wanted his franchise to forge an identity of its own.

The Chicago Bears were born.

So, for that matter, was the National Football League, the APFL's snappy new name beginning with the 1922 season. Until his death in 1983, Halas always remembered the first time he realized the NFL had a genuine shot. It came on the morning of January 30, 1922, when he picked up a copy of the *Chicago Herald and Examiner* and read the headline STAGG SAID BIG TEN CONFERENCE WILL BREAK PROFESSIONAL FOOTBALL MENACE.

The NFL was a menace? Really? "Terrific," said Halas. "Absolutely terrific."

---

* There has long been a myth that Halas was succeeded in right field by Babe Ruth. It was actually Sammy Vick who took over for Halas.

As the decades passed and the league grew from fringe to noticeable to headline-worthy to packed stadiums, the Bears—in the words of *Sports Illustrated*'s Frank Deford—became "the early history of the game itself."

Halas was Chicago's owner, coach, publicity director, and head ticket peddler. He also starred as a right end on both sides of the ball and was named to the league's all-pro squad throughout the 1920s. He invested everything he had (and more) in the team and league, constantly thinking up new ways of generating revenue. Halas opened a laundry, sold automobiles, dabbled in real estate. As Frank Graham wrote in the *New York Journal-American*, "he organized his players not only into a team but into a promotional outfit." On Saturday mornings, when Northwestern would host games at its Evanston campus, Halas had his players comb the stands, handing out flyers about the next day's Bear clash. Years later, when the Great Depression was in full bloom and the franchise was hemorrhaging money, Halas asked his mother to purchase five thousand dollars in stock to keep the Bears afloat.

In 1925 Halas had the vision to sign Red Grange, the legendary University of Illinois halfback, to a hundred-thousand-dollar contract, then trot the Bears out on a two-month, eighteen-game barnstorming tour, bringing a new level of visibility to the NFL. At the time, Grange was one of the sporting world's national treasures. If he deemed the NFL worthy of his services, fans would surely follow. They did—he debuted on Thanksgiving Day, and thirty-six thousand spectators jammed Wrigley Field to watch.

Halas ceased playing following the 1928 season, but he coached the team for four different spans into the late 1960s, winning a remarkable 324 games and bringing the T-formation offense to life. In 1933, Halas, along with Redskins owner George Preston Marshall, shattered the monotony of the NFL's lumbering run-run-run offensive approach by lobbying to make it legal to throw a pass from any point behind the line of scrimmage. He also added—among other things—daily practices, assistant coaches, press-box spotters, training camps, films, the first pro marching band, and first pro fight song ("Bear Down, Chicago Bears"). "Our game has assumed many of the characteristics of George himself," Pete Rozelle, the NFL commissioner, once said. "Wisdom and creativity, vitality and endurance and that singular trait of all athletes—competitiveness."

Halas was responsible for the careers of legends ranging from Sid Luckman, the Columbia quarterback who signed with the Bears in 1939, to

George Blanda to Bobby Layne to Sayers and Butkus and, ultimately, Payton. In 1963, the Bears went 11-1-2, capturing the NFL Western Conference championship and beating the New York Giants, 14–10, for its eighth title. Chicago's defense led the league in fewest rushing yards, fewest passing yards, and fewest total yards—only the third time such a feat had ever been accomplished.

And then, without much warning, the Chicago Bears collapsed. From 1964 through 1974, the franchise posted two winning records and zero playoff appearances. Their roster, once packed with standouts, was now a crypt for has-beens and busts. "A lot of progressive owners came along and passed Halas by," said David Israel, a *Tribune* columnist. "They operated in modern ways, and the Bears refused to change." The franchise relocated from Wrigley Field to Soldier Field in 1971, and while the move provided the team with a jump in capacity from forty thousand to fifty-five thousand, fans were running out of reasons to watch. A guaranteed sellout for decades, by the early 1970s the Bears were struggling to fill forty thousand seats.

Whereas once everything Halas touched had turned to gold, now he could do nothing right. The Bears mangled the draft, literally twice failing to make their first-round selections on time, and in 1970 losing a coin flip to the Steelers for the right to select a Louisiana Tech quarterback named Terry Bradshaw. Many speculated Halas, at sixty-eight, had lost the sharpness that once made him great. "George thought he was invincible and immortal," said Don Pierson, who covered the team for the *Chicago Tribune*. "He was well-meaning, but he'd lost some acuity." There were those who claimed that, with all his fame, Halas forgot what it took to be special. "The juices of humanity seem to have been squeezed from him," William Barry Furlong wrote in *The Sporting News*. "He smiles as though it hurts. He pats a man on the back stiffly, like uncooked spaghetti."

"[Halas]," wrote Furlong, "has all the warmth of broken bones."

By the time the Bears selected Payton, they were a forgettable second-tier club. As other teams were starting to construct top-of-the-line weight facilities, the Bears purchased a twelve-in-one exercise machine from Sears. "Guys used it," said Clyde Emrich, the team's strength coach, "to hang their coats." Vince Evans, a quarterback who joined the Bears in 1977 after four years at USC, says his college's whirlpools, "looked like a Jacuzzi at the Four Seasons," while Chicago's "were buckets." The Bears, wrote Jerry Green of *The Sporting News*, "had regressed to a desultory, slapstick organization." Or, as Coady once quipped when asked what it'd take for the team to contend against Minnesota and Green Bay: "A couple of key plane crashes."

What many failed to notice, however, was that things were beginning to change. In a shocking acknowledgment that his beloved organization was rudderless, on September 12, 1974, Halas hired Jim Finks, architect of the great Minnesota Vikings teams of the early '70s, to replace his son, George Halas, Jr., as general manager. For the first time in franchise history, a non-Halas was in charge. "I have the authority to hire or fire anybody in the organization," Finks said in his introductory press conference. "The Halases have agreed to turn over the full operation to me."

A quarterback with the Steelers from 1949 to 1955, Finks' claim to fame was once beating out an obscure rookie named Johnny Unitas for a roster spot. Upon retiring, Finks served as the backfield coach at Notre Dame for one and a half seasons, then was brought in as a chief scout and assistant coach by Calgary of the Canadian Football League. Within nine months he was the Stampeders' general manager, and in 1964 he was wooed by the Vikings to hold the same position. When, three years later, Coach Norm Van Brocklin quit Minnesota, Finks hired an unknown CFL castoff named Bud Grant. The move, initially lampooned, went down as a stroke of genius. Grant became one of the great coaches in NFL history, and Finks' reputation as a gridiron guru was sealed.

A fast-talking, chain-smoking hard-bargainer, Finks had a confident strut that masked a reputation for being honest and fair. His arrival was greeted gleefully in Chicago, a city fatigued by chronic losing. The headlines spoke for themselves—FINKS: HE'S A REAL BEAR (*Chicago Sun-Times*); NEW PAPA BEAR (*Chicago Tribune*); THE BEARS BEAR DOWN (*The Chicago Daily News*). On his first day, Finks promised every returning employee a fair shake, and he was true to his word. Instead of firing Gibron and his staff midway through a miserable four-win season, he waited until after the final game.

In Gibron's place, Finks hired Jack Pardee, a gritty Texan who had spent fifteen years as an NFL linebacker before coaching the Florida Blazers to the 1974 World Football League championship game. In the stoic, business-first Pardee, Finks brought Chicago a thirty-eight-year-old up-and-comer who looked to be the anti-Abe in every possible sense. "He has the temperament and disposition to be a successful coach in the NFL for years to come," Finks crowed, "and is the type of man who can lead the Bears back to where they belong."

"It was the first time in years that the Bears seemed to have a clue what they were doing," said Pierson. "And then they took the next step and drafted Walter Payton."

· · ·

Because these were the Bears, nothing was as simple as it seemed.

Normally, when a rookie comes to terms late with an organization, he reports to training camp and begins the arduous process of catching up. Payton, however, didn't have such an opportunity. On June 1, 1975, two days before Payton signed with the Bears, John McKay, USC's legendary coach, selected him to be on the fifty-four-man College All-Star football squad that would play the world-champion Pittsburgh Steelers in an August 1 exhibition at, coincidentally, Soldier Field.

At the time, the NFL considered the annual game to be a vital outreach tool, and any man chosen to play was required to do so. As a result, Payton would miss three full weeks of Bears' training camp to work with the All-Star team at Northwestern University.

On Wednesday, July 9, Payton arrived in Evanston, pulled his gold Datsun 280ZX up to the front of the swank Orrington Hotel and checked in. Though by now most everyone knew of his existence, there was still an element of mystique to small-school superstars. Among his fifty-three teammates were many of the biggest names in college football—the three men picked ahead of him in the draft (quarterback Steve Bartkowski, defensive tackle Randy White, and offensive guard Ken Huff), as well as marquee stars like USC quarterback Pat Haden, Ohio State defensive back Neal Colzie, and Penn State defensive lineman Mike Hartenstine (the Bears' second-round selection). Two Jackson State peers, linebackers Robert Brazile and John Tate, also took part.

While lip service was paid to beating Pittsburgh, most of the All-Stars came to Illinois anxious to party. Dave Wasick, a defensive lineman from San Jose State, arrived at the Orrington one day after Payton. Strolling through the lobby, he was greeted by the sight of Dennis Harrah, the Miami offensive tackle, lugging three cases of Budweiser toward the elevator. There was Russ Francis, the tight end from Hawaii, serenading a gaggle of young women with his guitar. "Every night was all-out craziness," Wasick said. "Randy White, Steve Bartkowski, Dennis Harrah, myself—we'd hit the town, stay out until three or four in the morning. One night we went to this bar, and these two enormous bouncers wouldn't let us in. Well, both of the bouncers ended up being punched out cold. It was wild."

The tone was set during the first official team meeting. With his fifty-four players sitting quietly, McKay strode to the front of the room and played a video from a practice session of the 1973 College All-Star team (the 1974 game had been cancelled because of an NFL players' strike). Instead of preparing for their matchup against the Miami Dolphins, the reel showed members of the team playing volleyball with a football, using one of the goalposts as a net.

"That was the last time this game took place, and there's no way we're doing things that way again," McKay said. A hushed silence blanketed the room. The coach smiled—"That's because this year we'll make sure to get you guys a real volleyball!" The players burst into laughter.

The initial practice was held on a Friday afternoon at Northwestern's Dyche Stadium. Bartkowski was one of the first to arrive, and he took the field early to warm up with Pat McInally, the wide receiver/punter from Harvard. While leisurely tossing the ball, Bartkowski spotted something that stopped his arm, midmotion. It was Walter Payton—and he was walking on his hands. "But not just a few feet," Bartkowski said. "Walter exited a field house on his hands, walked a hundred yards to the field on his hands, walked all the way around me to the far goalpost on his hands, and walked back on his hands. I'm talking about three hundred yards, easy."

Brazile and Tate had four years of freaky Payton athleticism under their belts. The other All-Stars did not. Payton leapfrogged coaches and dunked basketballs and tossed eighty-yard spirals. He stuck out his tongue and, somehow, turned it 180-degrees upside down. "He was a gymnast," said Louis Carter, a running back from Maryland. "He would bounce around, fall down, bounce right back up." Said Larry Burton, a Purdue wide receiver: "Walter was pulling out these handstands and backflips, and we were all like, 'What planet does this guy call home?'"

In an effort to impress his more famous teammates, Payton spent the first week of practices pulling out all the stops. He threw his forearm shiver at White and Wasick and every other defender naïve enough to step in his way. His stiff-arm froze defensive backs like Colzie and Texas A&M's Tim Gray. He held kicking contests with McInally, who went on to a Pro Bowl punting career with the Cincinnati Bengals, and launched bombs alongside Bartkowski and Haden. "Walter was always the last guy to leave practice," said McInally. "He would hang around and shag our kicks, and he'd run them all back forty yards at full speed."

"We couldn't wait to hit the bars and drink," said Jim Obradovich, USC's tight end. "Meanwhile, Walter would be working his ass off."

Midway through his three weeks at Evanston, a seemingly irrelevant life-altering moment took place. Known as "L'il Monk" at Jackson State, with the All-Stars Payton was referred to as either "Walter" or "Walt." One day, during an otherwise unremarkable practice, Payton was carrying the ball when he approached Colzie, the hard-hitting defensive back. Smiling ear to ear, Payton yelled, "Your sweetness is your weakness!" then stutter-stepped, lifted one leg high into the air, and burst down the field.

"What did Walter say to you?" Colzie was asked by teammates.

"Some nonsense," he replied, "about my sweetness being my weakness."

A nickname was born. From that point on, Payton was "Sweetness." After a lifetime of imperfect monikers that never quite worked, here was one that fit perfectly. The smiley, goofy, soft-spoken Payton was a sweet person. The cutting, dashing, swiveling Payton was a sweet runner. "We had a big blackboard in the middle of our locker room," said Ralph Ortega, a line-backer from the University of Florida. "Every single morning Walter would walk in and write SWEETNESS EQUALS WALTER PAYTON across the board. I thought, 'Who is this clown?'"

Two weeks into workouts, Payton was having the time of his life. McKay was the anti–Bob Hill, limiting practices to an hour and a half (and usually watching from the stands, a cigar wedged between his lips), refusing to enforce a curfew, and often returning to the hotel as intoxicated and red-eyed as his players. "My best times with Walter were racing through the streets of Chicago in his Datsun, him driving like a madman," said Richard Wood, a USC linebacker. "He was absolutely giddy."

Unfortunately, on the afternoon of July 19, the fun ended. While carrying the ball during practice, Payton tripped and fell to Dyche's artificial turf on his right elbow. A fiery pain shot through his arm. Within minutes, his elbow swelled to the size of a large grapefruit. By day's end, it looked like a coconut. "It was twice the size of what it should have been," said Kurt Schumacher, an Ohio State offensive lineman. "The thing was enormous."

McKay pulled Payton from further workouts and enlisted Allen Carter, his halfback at USC, as an emergency replacement. ("The joke was that McKay turned us into the USC All-Star team," said Walter White, a tight end from the University of Maryland. "Which he pretty much did.") The Bears sent Fred Caito, the club's longtime trainer, to Evanston to investigate the matter. Payton was suffering from bursitis of the elbow—his bursa, a fluid-filled sack that serves as a cushion between skin and bone, had become inflamed, and the elbow was infected. "I went to Walter's hotel and introduced myself, and told him we were going to see a doctor," recalled Caito. "Walter was a scared kid from Mississippi who didn't know what the hell he was doing in the big city." Caito brought Payton to his car, and the two began driving to the office of Dr. Ted Fox, the Bears' physician. Thirty-five years later, Caito still chuckles at what happened next. "We're in the car and his elbow is swelling and we have no idea what's going to happen," Caito said. "And Walter turned to me and said, 'Can you stop at that Baskin-Robbins down there?' I remember thinking, 'What? I don't have time for this.' But I agreed. So we went in, and then he didn't have any money. The kid was the highest-paid rookie in team history, and the first time we met he needed me to buy him an ice cream cone."

Fox examined Payton's elbow. He told him he'd have to sit out several days, and that he should wear special padding to prevent further impact. The doctor then reached for a long needle, with the intent of giving Payton a cortisone injection. Payton's face turned pale. Sweat poured down his forehead.

"I don't do needles," he told Fox.

"Well," said the doctor, "you do now."

The Steelers' All-Star game was played a week later, on a Friday night. More than fifty million viewers watched on ABC, and a near-capacity crowd of 54,562 fans (including the entire Bears roster) packed Soldier Field, anxious to see the Super Bowl champions, but also anxious to see their city's new featured halfback. Before kickoff, the public address announcer introduced each of the players as they jogged to midfield. The last one was Payton. *And now, the first pick of the Chicago Bears—Waaaaaalllllltttteeer Paaaaaayyyyton . . .*

"Soldier Field just lit up," said Fred O'Connor, the Bears' running backs coach. "And Walter jogged out, and he looked like the most magnificent athlete I had ever seen. I turned to Jack Pardee and said, 'I think I can coach this kid.'"

Chuck Noll, the stoic Steelers coach, assured the media his team was here to win, and he was correct. On the All-Stars' first offensive series of the game, Bartkowski hit McInally with a twenty-eight-yard touchdown pass.

As the Harvard receiver crossed the goal line, a Pittsburgh defender delivered a decidedly late blow, breaking McInally's left leg. "The guy was so embarrassed, he hit me after I scored," McInally said. "They had to carry me off on a stretcher."

The All-Stars actually led 14–7 at halftime, but played sloppily in the second half and lost, 21–14. With his elbow entombed in a white bundle, Payton paced the team with seven carries for a paltry sixteen yards. His primary goal—to prevent his elbow from exploding into a thousand pieces—was accomplished. "The whole three weeks was just a wonderful experience for Walter, for me, for all of us," said McInally. "We really bonded as a group of guys starting our careers at the same time."

On the day after the game, McInally found himself in Northwestern Hospital, his left leg immobilized, his spirits crushed over an injury that would wipe out his entire rookie year. He heard a knock on the door, and looked up to see a smiling Walter Payton. "He went out of his way to visit me," said McInally, who would play ten seasons. "I've never forgotten that." Payton even brought a card, which McInally continues to keep in one of his drawers. It reads: "Hang in there. You'll make it. But take the year off and eat."

. . .

Walter Payton arrived at the team's new Lake Forest, Illinois–based training camp with bells on. Literally. That's the sound many of the 1975 Chicago Bears associate with their first impression of the rookie running back from Jackson State—the jingling of bells.

Why did Walter Payton, a relatively humble young man, decide it'd be a good idea to introduce himself to teammates by tying a couple of small brass bells to his shoelaces, thereby broadcasting his attendance during drills with a jolly jingle? "I'm not sure," said Jerry Tagge, a journeyman quarterback. "Some of the veterans thought it was incredibly cocky. Personally, I found it sort of neat. If he ran for fifty yards, you would just listen to those bells ring—*ding a ling, ding a ling, ding a ling.* There was a real rhythm to it."

"I heard those bells and my first thought was, 'Who is this guy, and who does he think he is?'" said Witt Beckman, a rookie receiver out of Miami. "But then he ran, and nobody could touch him."

Not that Payton's NFL beginnings were purely sweet music. With his elbow still a mess, his participation in workouts was sporadic. He practiced one session, then missed the next three. He took one handoff, cut left, juked right, and burst fifty yards down the field. He took another handoff, absorbed a hit, and fell to the ground withering in pain. At one point Payton was sent to Illinois Masonic Hospital for further treatment, missing the exhibition opener against San Diego. When Pardee was asked about his young runner, he smiled and uttered the company line. "He's such a great guy," he told the *Chicago Tribune*. "He went out for a pass and the ball hit him in the arm. He couldn't fight the tears running down his cheek. But he was hurt."

For the Bears' new coach, the words tasted like soap. *A sensitive elbow? Are you kidding me?* Born April 19, 1936, in Exira, Iowa, Pardee was a person who, from a very early age, believed only in hard work and harder work—excuses be damned. He was milking cows on the family's farm at age five and digging holes for septic tanks at ten. By age fourteen Pardee was jackhammering in the oil fields of Christoval, Texas, a town of roughly five hundred people near San Angelo where his family had relocated. "To live I had to work," he once said. "Outside of football, the greatest pleasure I got was from working on our farm . . . working the tractor. I guess I'm just hyperactive, but I can't stand sitting around doing nothing for more than two days."

Pardee played his college football under Bear Bryant at Texas A&M. He will forever be identified as one of the "Junction Boys"—the thirty-five of one hundred players who survived Bryant's hellacious preseason training camp in Junction, Texas, when the temperatures reached 110 degrees and water was nowhere to be found. Pardee went on to spend fifteen years as an NFL linebacker with the Rams and Redskins, though his career—and life—came to a halt in 1964, when a mole removed from his right forearm was found to be melanoma. Told he could either die or have the arm amputated, Pardee chose option number three—an experimental eleven-and-a-half-hour operation in which his collarbone was broken and his body temperature drastically reduced. "I didn't think I'd die," he said. "I probably always had an indestructible attitude. Nothing was ever gonna happen to me. I'm not afraid of dying—it's not gonna happen."

If cancer was his greatest life challenge, Pardee's toughest football hurdle took place in 1974, when he was hired to coach the Florida Blazers of the fledgling World Football League. Though initially elated by the chance to guide a team, Pardee became disillusioned when, midway through the season, the players' checks began to bounce. "Somehow the owners who stopped paying everyone still had the services of a chartered jet," recalled

Bob Bowser, Pardee's special assistant with the Blazers and Bears. "The whole situation was laughable."

Despite every possible reason for his men to pack it in (No money. Games in Orlando's dilapidated Tangerine Bowl. Putrid facilities. A schedule that changed week to week. Minimal fans.), the Blazers kept playing, reaching the WFL title game before losing to Birmingham. When Jim Finks heard of the unpaid group of journeymen and their feisty coach, he knew who he wanted to replace Gibron on the Chicago sideline. "It was more of a gut feeling than anything else," Finks said. "We looked for something deeper."

Now, as Pardee arrived in Lake Forest each morning not knowing whether Payton would be on the field or in the trainer's room, he doubted the rookie's toughness and commitment.

But not his talent. Throughout his month in camp, Payton was the talk of the Bears. The hype began shortly before his arrival, when O'Connor, the new running backs coach, interrupted a team meeting one day to show a film clip of Payton at Jackson State. "I think it was done to inspire us," said Berl Simmons, a rookie kicker out of Texas Christian. "Walter must have run over or around all eleven defensive people, and we were just amazed. It was probably unusual for them to show that, but Walter was an unusual player."

On his first day of working out, Payton hung with the other running backs and receivers, fielding punts from Bob Parsons. When it was their turn, players waited for the balls, stepped to the left, stepped to the right, moved in, moved back—then made the catch. "Not Walter," said Jim Osborne, the veteran defensive lineman. "Bob kicked these beautiful punts, big spirals high into the sky, and when the ball finally came down Walter would catch them behind his back. I'd never seen anyone do that before."

In the NFL, great athletes are the norm. Everyone is either incredibly fast or exceptionally strong, so much so that the remarkable can often appear mundane. There was nothing mundane about Payton. "He had a gluteus that I've never seen on another person in my life," said Ken Valdiserri, the Bears' longtime media relations coordinator. "His ass was chiseled. It was the most unique thing I've ever seen. And if you walked into the locker room it was like, 'How can a guy have an ass like that?' The curvature and the depth and the definition of it."

"He was like an acrobat," said Tom Donchez, a backup running back. Ross Brupbacher, a Bears linebacker, called him, "A muscle." Don Rives, the ornery linebacker, said tackling Payton "was like tackling a barrel. I hit him as hard as I could in practice and he shed me like I was Little Bo Peep." Said Doug Plank, the team's twelfth-round pick from Ohio State: "At first I thought it weird that Walter was always flexing. Then it hit me—he's not flexing. He's made of rocks." Payton walked on his hands, flipped up, and landed in a split. He stood below a regulation basketball hoop, jumped up, and dunked with ease. "The punters were practicing one day, and he decided to give it a try," said Dave Gallagher, a defensive end. "He walked over, picked up a ball, punted it sixty yards, and walked away. No biggie."

"Genetically, he seemed to be just like a rubber ball," said Larry Ely, a linebacker. "When he got tackled, four . . . five . . . six people would have his legs, his neck, his arms, and he'd bounce back like a rubber ball to the huddle. How in the world did his ligaments and muscles take the pounding and bounce right back? You looked at him and wondered how any human being could be blessed with such a body."

"He took up golf one day with the Bears," said Bo Rather, a receiver. "He picked up an eight or nine iron and told us, 'See that light post out there? I'm gonna hit it.' The post must have been a hundred and twenty yards away, and Walter took the club, swung, and hit that post right down the middle. It was phenomenal. Whatever he did, he would be good at it."

Despite the mixed reaction to his shoelace bells, Payton was embraced by veterans and fellow rookies. He was assigned to share an apartment with Gary Hrivnak, a third-year defensive end out of Purdue who was surprised to find himself with a black roommate. "I don't know if they were trying to integrate the team more, but it was an eye-opener," said Hrivnak. "Walter was very quiet, but in a good way. He wasn't always talking about himself and everything he could do. He was unaffected by being a high pick and making good money." Hrivnak remembered Walter plastering a small section of wall with photographs of Connie, his college sweetheart. He also recalled the time he approached the room and heard the thump of soul music blaring from behind the door. "I walk in, and Walter had four or five African-American players inside and they're all dancing," Hrivnak said. "Well, he tried to drag this old white guy in the middle and teach me to dance. Everyone laughed—I was the butt of the joke. But it was OK, because Walter was just a nice, funny, lighthearted kid."

In the year 1975, a significant racial divide still existed in professional sports. White teammates hung with white teammates and black teammates

hung with black teammates. There was a lingering mistrust and a pronounced lack of understanding. Locker room card games were split among
racial lines. The tension over music was palpable—country and rock vs. R&B.
To many of the black Bears, their white teammates seemed stiff and judg-
mental. How could they possibly trust the Southerners from schools like
Alabama and Auburn and Ole Miss—the ones who seemed perpetually
uncomfortable in their presence?

A good number of the white Bears, meanwhile, didn't like what they
perceived to be the never-ending crowing and strutting of the blacks. They
found the players to be lazy, selfish, and heartless. All skill, no drive. "When
I got there we had a bunch of niggers," said Rives, a white linebacker from
1973 to 1978. "Great ability, but no work ethic. They were selfish twits, and
they wanted to blame everyone but themselves."

Just as he had done at Columbia High School five years earlier, Payton
somehow bridged the gap. Entering camp, Chicago's top two returning
running backs were Ken Grandberry, an unremarkable grinder who had led
the team with 475 rushing yards in 1974, and Carl Garrett, the cocky former
Pro Bowler. "Walter was different," said Rives. "His biggest attribute was
the fire in his gut, where he honestly believed nobody could stop him. I
loved that."

Payton didn't merely impress teammates—he wowed them. Steve Marcantonio, the team's fifteenth-round draft choice out of the University of
Miami, had never heard of Payton until they arrived together at camp. One
day all the players were required to partake in varied physical tests—bench
press, curls, push-ups, sprints. "I was a six-foot-six, two-hundred-and-one-
pound possession receiver going against all these great athletes," said Marcantonio. "I didn't stand much of a chance." The final activity was dips, where
a person stands between two parallel bars and lifts himself up and down as
many times as possible. "Back in college I used to finish every workout with
three sets of twenty dips, so I finally felt there was something I could excel
in," said Marcantonio. "We go through most of the testing, and sure enough
near the end I've smoked everybody. The second-best guy did thirty-seven,
and now it's me and Walter lined up next to each other. We're the final two."
Marcantonio put on his game face, took a deep breath, and completed fifty-
six straight dips—easily a personal record. "Everyone was so impressed," he
said. "I felt great." When Marcantonio finished, Payton—who had never
before lifted weights or attempted a dip—approached the bars. "He was just

this blur, up and down, up and down, up and down," said Marcantonio. "He gets to sixty-five and he looks over at me with this expression on his face like, 'Is this enough?' I just shrugged. He was too much."

Members of the Bears were blown away by their new star's physicality. Payton's legs looked like black pipes. His back was immense. He dead-lifted 625 pounds without a sweat. His hands, seemingly regular at quick glance, were thick and dense like slices of cheesecake. "You shook hands," said Jerry B. Jenkins, the coauthor of one of Payton's autobiographies, "and his wrapped all the way around yours."

Mark Nordquist, a veteran offensive lineman who had recently been traded to the Bears by the Eagles, spent the summer of 1975 working harder than ever. He lifted weights four or five times per week, and reported to Lake Forest with an extra thirty pounds of rock-solid muscle encasing his body. When it came time for the Bears to grade the players on the military press, Nordquist silenced the room by warming up with a handful of 250-pound lifts. "Then I put the pin at the bottom of the weight set to three hundred and ten pounds," he said, "and the room got even quieter, because nobody ever did that." After taking several deep breaths, Nordquist grunted loudly, pushed and lifted the weight. "I staggered away, breathing hard," he said. "Walter walks up, sits on the stool, and grabs the bar. I'm pointing at him, laughing, 'Watch this idiot rookie!' Well, Payton takes the bar and lifts it really fast—one, two, three times. Three times! He's five foot ten, two hundred and five pounds, I'm six foot four, two-sixty-five. The guys in the weight room screamed, 'There's a new sheriff in town! There's a new sheriff!' "

Despite some high moments, Payton's training camp was mostly misery. He missed the first four exhibition games because of the elbow infection, and when Parsons, the team's punter, suffered a twisted knee, Pardee considered having Payton take his place, just to keep him involved. While booting balls during a practice, however, Payton strained a muscle in his left leg, further stalling his progress. For the first time as Chicago's coach, Pardee lost his cool. "Jack was fed up with Walter always being hurt," said Richard Harris, a Bears defensive lineman. "He wanted to determine if Walter was a prima donna or a real player." With the entire roster sitting inside a classroom for a meeting, Pardee called Payton to the front and chewed him out. "If we knew you'd be the kind of guy you are," he said, "there's no way we would have wasted our number one pick on you!"

Finally, on September 6, Payton debuted at Miami's Orange Bowl against the Dolphins. As Don Pierson noted in that day's *Chicago Tribune*, Walter "has been practicing as if this were the Super Bowl. He has run every play at full speed and gets to the hole so fast he looks like he'd been catapulted out of a slingshot."

The game began at eight o'clock that night, and Payton was nervous. He paced the sidelines beforehand, muttering words of encouragement to himself while avoiding eye contact with teammates. The expectations of others were high, but the expectations for himself were even higher. Payton knew Chicago fans had been waiting to see what the kid from Jackson State could do. Was he the second coming of Gale Sayers, or merely another Ken Grandberry?

On that hot, muggy night, the answer came quickly. In yet another Bear defeat (Chicago lost 21–10), Payton was brilliant. He ran for sixty yards on twelve first-half carries, including bursts of sixteen and twelve yards. Payton had been scheduled to sit the remainder of the game, but after begging Pardee for extra work, he stayed in for much of the third and fourth quarters, gaining an additional thirty-four yards. "He was remarkable," said Waymond Bryant, a Bears linebacker. "The thing I remember is his cuts were so quick and so sharp, he made guys miss with ease. This guy was clearly better than anyone we had."

Payton played sparingly in the Bears' final exhibition game, a loss to the Oilers. In case there were any remaining doubts about the direction of the franchise, Finks and Pardee made clear the point: Garrett (who assured the media Payton would never take his job) was traded to the New York Jets for Mike Adamle, and Grandberry—the leading ground gainer from one season earlier—was cut, never again to appear in an NFL game.

"They told me not to worry, that I had a job locked up," Grandberry said. "Then they cut me. I was destroyed. It took my spirit away. Walter actually apologized to me for taking my job, and I said, 'You have nothing to be sorry about. You're terrific.'

"Years later my dad said to me, 'Yeah, you lost your job. But you lost it to Walter Payton. Who better to end your career?' "

Grandberry laughs.

"I hated to admit it, but Dad was right. Who better than Walter Payton?"

CHAPTER 12

# ZERO YARDS

AT THE START OF EACH NFL SEASON, BEFORE GAMES HAVE BEGUN AND INJURIES have occurred and expectations fail to meet reality, optimism is an organizational requirement. As the mindless blather goes, "Every team is 0-0" and "With a few breaks . . ." and "If everyone lives up to their potential . . ." It makes no difference whether your franchise is plagued by a roster of talent-less dopes, whether your coach is an alcoholic and your GM a heroin addict, whether you haven't won since Washington crossed the Delaware.

This, at long last, will be the year!

As the 1975 season opener approached, the city of Chicago felt like their Bears were on the rise. These were the new Bears. The young Bears. The better-than-before Bears. The potentially play-off-bound Bears who had languished in the depths of the NFC Central for far too long. Sixteen rookies made the opening-day roster. Ten starters from the disastrous '74 club were cut. In a piece titled "Bears are putting it all together," the *Tribune*'s Don Pierson welcomed in the season by noting that, "With a new attitude, a new general manager, new coach, new players, and a proven old formula, a new era of success cannot be avoided."

On the afternoon of Sunday, September 21, the new Chicago Bears debuted in front of a sellout crowd of 51,678 fans packed into Soldier Field. In the lead-up to the game, the *Tribune*'s Ed Stone wrote a glowing profile of Payton, hyping the rookie as the team's savior and including this dandy of a quote from the naïve newcomer: "Give me time, I'll give 'em a new Sayers."

In case any of the longtime holdovers thought things had changed, however, they were quickly reminded the Bears were the Bears. Two hours before kickoff, as the team was warming up on the field, a thick cast-iron sewage pipe exploded beneath the home concrete locker room, spreading a gusher of liquid waste. By the time the maintenance crew plugged the hole, six inches of brown sludge coated the floor. "It was a nightmare," said Bob Newton, an offensive lineman. "The whole room flooded, and we had to take all our gear across Soldier Field and dress on the visiting side."

"That was our greeting to Chicago in 1975," said Fred O'Connor, the backfield coach. "A foot of sewage."

It turned out to be the day's highlight. Though the Colts had finished 2-12 in 1974, their new coach, Ted Marchibroda, knew enough about Chicago's limited abilities to draw up a two-point defensive game plan:

- Let quarterback Bobby Douglass throw all day.
- Suffocate the rookie running back.

"That was it," said Joe Ehrmann, a Colts defensive tackle. "The entire goal was to stop Payton, who was supposed to be this stud, and have them have to pass."

"They were just a horrible team," added Tom MacLeod, a Baltimore linebacker. "The coaches told us, 'Watch out for the kid.' So we did."

The weather was pleasant, with temperatures in the mid-fifties and the majority of players wearing only pads and T-shirts below their jerseys. A raucous ovation greeted the Bears as they took the field for the opening kickoff. Payton was euphoric. It had been a long, injury-marred preseason, and he often questioned whether this day would actually come.

The Bears lost 35–7.

When P.A. announcer Chet Coppock said, "The Bears thank you for your attendance," deep into the fourth quarter, fans laughed. Even Baltimore took pity. Midway through the third quarter, Chicago defensive back Ted Vactor tore a calf muscle and could barely move. The only other available player, Nemiah Wilson, had already suffered an injury, so Vactor had to remain on the field. "I was lined up against [Colts receiver] Roger Carr," said Vactor. "And he refused to run past me. He could have scored every time had he wanted to. But we were already dead and buried." The day's lone standing ovation was bestowed upon Abe Gibron, the fired head coach who watched from the stands. Wrote the *Tribune*'s Don Pierson, in a game recap that read like Roger Ebert's *Ishtar* review: "The Bears offered no offense, no defense, and no expectations except the sewage. Pardee said he 'hasn't given up,' which is comforting since it was their first game. . . . The Bears look as remodeled as their Soldier Field home—new paint and new names on the outside, same old problems on the inside. No one knew why the sewers apparently backed up in the Bears' dressing room, any more than the Bears knew why the Colts, who really aren't that good, beat the hell out of them."

Payton's first carry of the day netted zero yards. His second carry of the day netted zero yards. His third carry went for three yards, but he lost ground on his next two attempts. Overall, Douglass handed Payton the football eight times, and he wound up with no yardage. When he exited the Bears' locker room, tearstains could be spotted on both of his cheeks.

"Zero yards for the number one pick?" he would later say. "I was so embarrassed. Like any rookie, I wanted to get to Chicago and prove I could play."

Truth is, Payton could play. His offensive line, however, was a mess. The six men blocking for him were an ode to NFL mediocrity. Center Dan Peiffer was the St. Louis Cardinals' fourteenth-round pick in 1973, and right tackle Jeff Sevy was a Bears' twelfth-round selection in '74. Left guard Noah Jackson had recently been signed from the Canadian league, and right guards Bob Newton and Mark Nordquist—who, oddly, alternated downs while running in plays from the sideline—were marginal veterans. The most star-crossed of the bunch was Lionel Antoine, the third overall pick in the 1972 Draft (one spot ahead of Ahmad Rashad, ten ahead of Franco Harris). Coming out of Southern Illinois, George Halas had likened Antoine to the great left tackles in NFL history. He was big (six foot six), he was strong, and he smoked a pack of cigarettes during most halftimes. A serious knee injury in 1972 downgraded him from line anchor to mediocrity, and he never came close to realizing his potential. "Lionel was a fairly OK player," said Ray Callahan, the team's offensive line coach. "Not much more."

Against the Colts, Payton would take a handoff, move half a step, then— nothing. The lanes were clogged. "They kept trying to run sweeps and we kept tackling him for a loss," said MacLeod. "He didn't have a chance. He could never get started."

Throughout the game, Payton jogged to the sidelines and caught an earful from O'Connor, his position coach. The fans, too, reigned boos upon him, the likes of which he had never before heard. Only afterward, when coaches and teammates studied film from the debacle, did they notice something startling: Payton had pieced together the most breathtakingly inept game anyone had ever witnessed.

"He ran for zero yards, but it was like I'd just watched someone gain a hundred and fifty," said Mike Adamle, Payton's backup. "He made a couple of moves in the backfield after he was trapped for losses just to get back to the line of scrimmage and I said, 'This guy's great.'"

"When the coaches said we were going to run a sweep right or left, Walter had to make every inch by himself," said Virg Carter, a backup quarterback. "Some of his runs to gain ten yards, he had to take on four or five guys on his own."

Many remained skeptical. After the final seconds had ticked off the clock and players from the two teams exchanged pleasantries, Ehrmann found himself jogging to the locker room alongside Stan White, Baltimore's outstanding outside linebacker.

"So much for the great Walter Payton," Ehrmann said. "That kid will never make it."

.   .   .

Stuck in a foreign city, plagued by a certain brand of Southern shyness, bewildered by the plummeting temperature, the twenty-two-year-old Payton had few people to turn to. Unlike the majority of his fellow rookies, who basked in their newfound independence, Payton hungered for structure and familiarity. He lived with his mother Alyne in a small one-bedroom apartment in Arlington Heights, a Chicago suburb. She cooked all of her son's favorites (in particular, biscuits and gravy), folded his laundry, and took his messages, but wasn't especially useful when it came to relieving him of his football-related anxieties. Eddie, his older brother, was off teaching high school P.E. in Memphis. They spoke via phone, but infrequently. Rickey Young, Payton's blocking back at Jackson State, was a rookie with the San Diego Chargers, busy trying to navigate his own way through the league. "There were many two A.M. phone calls," said Holmes. "Walter just needing to talk." Connie Norwood, Walter's girlfriend, was back at Jackson State, beginning her sophomore year. Her photograph sat atop his dresser, with each glance his mood growing increasingly forlorn. The two talked regularly (Payton only called from the Bears' headquarters, where players could use the phone free of charge), and Connie would come to Chicago for occasional visits. Marriage seemed to him like a wise idea. "You can move here to the city," he pleaded. "You'll love it." Connie knew better. She could wait.

Sometimes Payton would take his 280ZX and tear through the back roads, zipping past traffic lights and stop signs as the speedometer read 80 . . . 90 . . . 100 . . . 110. Other times he would lose himself in television—*Starsky & Hutch, Kojak, Happy Days*. Not one for the books, Payton's reading would come either via the *Chicago Tribune* or the Bible, which he opened each morning before driving off for practice or games.

Beginning with the preseason, many of Chicago's players met for beers and burgers every Monday night. Payton occasionally stopped in, but quietly, and only for ten to fifteen minutes. Never did anyone see alcohol touch his lips. When the regular season began, members of the Bears would congregate in Soldier Field's belowground parking lot after home games, then head out to the local bars and clubs. Payton almost never attended. "He didn't know what to expect, so he was kind of standoffish," said Bo Rather, a wide receiver. "Walter didn't speak to many people. He was extraordinarily uncomfortable."

The headaches first arrived during the exhibition season, then refused to leave. The pain was akin to a drill digging into his temples. Payton had never suffered from pressure-related anxiety while at Jackson State, probably because there wasn't much pressure. The Tigers were good, Payton was great, and winning came easily. Now the burden was overwhelming. "The headaches got really bad, to the point that he was missing practices," said Steve Schubert, a Bears wide receiver. "The skill he had was unbelievable, but that first year was a real struggle."

"Walter was very sensitive, and he put a lot of pressure on himself," said Peiffer. "Us not being a very good line surely exacerbated that."

Temporary relief came in the second week, when Chicago hosted the Philadelphia Eagles and, against a more-talented team, pulled out a 15–13 victory on a Bob Thomas field goal with eight seconds remaining. Payton, in the words of the *Tribune*'s Pierson, "[Shedded] his goat horns with uncanny brilliance," rushing for ninety-five yards and making several key catches from quarterback Gary Huff after Douglass was benched. "I recall that game very well," said John Bunting, an Eagles linebacker, "because afterward I remember thinking, 'I need to get out of this league, because some rookie just made a fool out of me.' Walter was young and raw, but he had a different speed, a different twitch, a different quick."

The victory, however fulfilling, proved to be a mirage. The 1975 Chicago Bears were bad, bordering on putrid, and if anyone held out hope of a play-off run, eight losses over the ensuing nine weeks shut those thoughts down. Having coached the Florida Blazers to the World Football League's World Bowl only a few months earlier, Pardee had a vision of success. This wasn't it. Consequently, Chicago's roster became a conveyor belt, with seemingly every available former Blazer coming in for a game or two, then being deemed substandard and shipped off to the scrap heap. Midway through the season, Chicago's offense featured an unheard-of seven new starters from the previous year. Payton was essentially playing for an expansion franchise. "You tried remembering names," said Richard Harris, a veteran defensive lineman. "But guys were in and out so quick, it wasn't always worth the effort."

"We realized we had to bite the bullet and rebuild the franchise one player at a time," said Pardee. "If you played for me in the past and you had some talent, I was giving you a look. Just take a number and line on up."

With the Lake Michigan winds becoming increasingly fierce and the losses piling up like mounds of icy snow, life with the team turned unbearable. The Bears traveled to Bloomington, Minnesota, and were pasted by the Vikings, 28–3 (Payton's postgame quote—"They weren't as good as I expected"—was greeted with dumbfounded silence by teammates), then visited Pontiac, Michigan, for what many of the players hoped could be a win over the mediocre Lions.

Instead, Detroit handed Chicago one of the most humiliating losses in the history of the franchise. Though the scoreboard read 27–7, Lion players mocked their rivals throughout. "That's the first time I've ever seen an opponent laugh at the other team," Pardee said afterward. "That's what they were doing out there. Laughing at us. We looked like a bunch of little boys playing grown men."

Payton accrued no yards for the second time in four weeks, and left midway through the game with a calf bruise. In the following morning's press conference, Pardee protected the rookie ("He played a good game. He blocked well.") and ripped the offensive line as a dysfunctional band of dolts. Unlike earlier in the season, however, when hope still existed and the mood remained upbeat, now fewer veterans were willing to hear such drivel. Payton and his little shoelace bells had been cute during camp, and talk of his inevitable greatness could be chalked up to giddy optimism. But now, when the games mattered, the kid wasn't performing. Did Franco Harris ever have the offensive line as a scapegoat in Pittsburgh? Did O. J. Simpson in Buffalo? Lydell Mitchell with the Colts? No, no, and no. So why wasn't Payton taking some of the blame and admitting he missed a lot of open holes?

Truth is, while Payton was liked from the beginning, many teammates found him perplexing and, as the season progressed, increasingly irksome. "He had this loud whistle that he'd do for no reason in the locker room," said Don Rives, a veteran linebacker. "I'd hear that and want to strangle him around the neck. But he was twenty-two. At that age, people are immature and stupid." Before the game in Detroit, Payton—who steadfastly attended team chapel services on Sunday mornings—asked all of the offensive line-men to join him in the shower of the visiting locker room. Bob Asher, a backup tackle, thought he wanted to review the Lions' defense. "Walter had us all join hands," Asher said, "and then he started praying—this really spiri-tual prayer that made everyone very uncomfortable."

Those who knew Payton well (his girlfriend, his mother, his brother) urged him to fight back the awkwardness and make a sincere effort to reach out toward teammates. But instead of endearing himself, Payton overcom-pensated and reverted to the mischievous kid from Columbia. He threw balled-up, damp, dirty practice socks at the heads of unsuspecting teammates (and whipped towels at bare rear ends and flicked ears with his drawn-back index finger). Before arriving for team meetings, he liked to stop at the neighborhood pet store, purchase a one-dollar mouse and, while Pardee was talking, let the rodent run free. Such was the way he behaved at Jackson State, and—because players at all collegiate levels ritually laugh at anything the star does—he thought he was being funny. Chicago, however, was a long way from Jackson. "Walter was starting to act like your annoying little brother or the middle kid who isn't getting enough attention," said Schubert. "He wanted to make sure you knew he was there."

"Walter was childish," said Bob Avellini, a rookie backup quarterback. "A nice guy, without a doubt, but childish. We'd be working out in shorts and he'd pull your shorts down. Maybe it's funny the first time. By the fifth time, it's not."

Equally agitating was Payton's mounting whininess. Back in training camp, when his elbow was swollen and throbbing, Payton ached to get onto the field. Now, in the midst of nonstop losing, the drive lessened. "He had some frustrating times," said Jim Osborne, the defensive lineman. "I under-stood. There were guys on the Bears who wouldn't have made my college team at Southern. It was that bad." Payton always seemed to have a complaint— his elbow was acting up, his hamstring was tight, his knee felt funny, he had a cold. He moped loudly, and with little restraint. "In that game against the

Lions, he came out and we looked him over," said Fred Caito, the team trainer. "When I told him I'd retape him and send him back out there, you could look at his face and sense his thinking—'I'm hurt and we're getting blown out. I don't want back in.'

"At that point I had real questions about Walter. He was supposed to be a good player, but he didn't have much of a desire to play. I even told him, 'Walter, everybody is hurt, everybody has something.' But he was a kid and he needed to grow up."

During one memorable practice, Payton was participating in a noncontact drill when he approached Earl Douthitt, a rookie cornerback out of Iowa, lowered his forearm, and slammed it into Douthitt's chin. Payton chuckled, but the defensive players stewed. On the next play, Payton again ran through the hole, where Douthitt was waiting. This time, he flattened Payton, sending him sprawling to the ground. "He gets up and he wants to fight me," said Douthitt. "He could dish it, but he couldn't take it. Typical whiner."

Payton's biggest gripe was with the play calling. Thanks to a lengthy history of preposterously terrible drafts, the Bears lacked anyone resembling a competent starting quarterback. Douglass had been mercifully released, Huff could not figure out NFL defenses (in six professional seasons, he would complete sixteen touchdown passes and fifty interceptions), and Avellini was raw and plodding (teammates nicknamed him "Slo-Mo Bob"). As a result, Chicago ran the ball with such regularity that defenses barely acknowledged the presence of wide receivers. Payton faced a never-ending string of eight-man fronts, and he came to dread the inevitable poundings.

On the day following the Detroit setback, Payton called Bud Holmes, his agent. "The coaching here is a joke!" he screamed. "Everything is so predictable! Pardee doesn't believe in throwing the ball! I can't take it!"

Holmes waited until his client was done venting. "Wait a minute," he said. "Hold on one second. I've got it right here."

"What do you have?" Payton asked.

"Your contract," Holmes replied. "Those sons of bitches! Those sons of bitches! I'm getting on the phone right now and I'm calling Jim Finks and we're gonna have it out!"

"What are you going to say?" Payton asked.

"Boy, they ain't paying you a damn to coach, and I'm sick of it," Holmes said. "All this damn coaching you want to do, and those sons of bitches ain't paying you a dime! Those sons of bitches are gonna pay you!"

"No," said Payton, "don't call."

"I'm going to!" countered Holmes.

"Don't," begged Payton. "Please don't."

Holmes paused, embracing his client's nervousness.

"Now listen here, you son of a bitch!" he said. "That coach wants to win more than you do because his job depends on it. Now you might disagree, but you do what he tells you. If he says you should stand on your head and bounce up and down, you go stand on your head and bounce."

"OK," Payton said. "I get it."

"And never call to complain about this again," Holmes said. "They pay you a lot of money to play football. Now shut the hell up and go play it!"

· · ·

For Chicago, the biggest matchup of a dismal season came on Sunday, October 19, when the Bears traveled to Pittsburgh to face the defending Super Bowl champions at Three Rivers Stadium.

Payton spent the week leading up to the game going through workouts with halfhearted intensity. When others ran, he jogged. When others jogged, he walked. One of the veteran Bears, a fullback named Cid Edwards, was in the final season of his career and beaten down by the losing. Throughout the week, Edwards was in Payton's ear, encouraging him to loaf. "Let the white boy take the carries," Edwards said of Mike Adamle, the backup halfback. "You've had a long season." Though now familiar enough with Pardee to know he was no cupcake (Said Carter: "In my two years of playing for Jack I think he smiled twice. And in both instances, he was really just squinting because the sun was in his eyes."), Payton figured his coach would understand that, on certain occasions, featured backs need to take it easy.

The Bears held their practices at Ferry Hall, an abandoned all-girls school near Lake Forest College. The offices and meeting centers were all converted classrooms and the locker room had been a science lab. While the facility was uninspiring by nearly all standards (Said Caito: "The guys from UCLA and USC would go there for the first time and shudder in disbelief."), it allowed players numerous inconspicuous spots to sneak off and smoke a cigarette or take a quick sip from a flask. So Payton hid. He stayed out of the way, lingered behind a corner, avoided Pardee's glare at all costs.

Upon arriving at practice Friday morning, Payton told O'Connor that his knee was hurting, and he needed a day off. The coach was incredulous— the Steelers featured a halfback, Rocky Bleier, whose right leg was filled with shrapnel from a grenade attack during Vietnam. A rookie with five games under his belt was asking out?

"There's an enormous difference between being hurt and being injured," said O'Connor. "Was Walter hurt? Sure. But he certainly wasn't hurt to the point that he couldn't participate."

As Payton watched from the sidelines, the Bears practiced with Adamle, a fifth-year halfback out of Northwestern, filling in. After the team retreated to the showers, Pardee called Payton into his office. "Walter," Pardee said, "we have a very strict rule here. You don't practice, you don't play. That's how it is, and it's written in stone. So you're out for Sunday. Mike's getting the start."

Payton nodded, left the room, sat down at his locker, and put his head-phones over his ears.

"What's wrong?" asked Roland Harper, the rookie fullback who used the neighboring locker.

"He won't let me play," Payton said. "I'm out."

"Walter pouted," said Harper. "He couldn't believe what Jack was doing to him."

Far from beloved, Bears players found Pardee to be unfriendly, unemotional, and when it came to the team's dull offense, unimaginative. "He put a bad taste in a lot of our mouths," said Wally Chambers, the defensive lineman. "We were used to Abe Gibron, the big teddy bear. There were no warm, fuzzy feelings toward Jack."

In this instance, however, the coach's decision was brilliant. Veterans applauded it. Though he approached every game hoping to win, Pardee realized that, whether his starting halfback was Payton or Adamle, the Bears were almost certainly not going to go on the road and beat the mighty Steelers. So why not make a statement?

"Long after I had played for Coach [Bear] Bryant at Texas A&M, I'd go to coaching seminars to hear him speak," said Pardee. "He used talk about disciplining players, and how if you're going to make a point you better do it with a good player, not the fourth-string tackle. Coach once sat Joe Namath for a game in college, and Namath never missed another one.

"Physically, Walter could have played against the Steelers. And I suppose I could have overlooked his faking the injury. But I saw it as an opportunity to make an important statement to everyone about what we expected."

That Sunday, Payton stood on the sideline in his uniform as the Bears battled the Steelers in what the *Tribune*'s Ed Stone rightly termed a "morbid" mismatch. Though it was hard watching his team slog through a 34–3 embarrassment, what upset Payton most was Adamle making his first NFL start.

As a white, undersized (five foot nine, 198 pounds) running back, Adamle had spent much of his five years in the NFL trying to prove he was worthy of more than special teams play. Yet in two seasons with the Chiefs, then another two with the Jets, he never exceeded 303 yards or two touchdowns. There was always a bigger name (Ed Podolak in Kansas City, John Riggins in New York) in front of him, as was now the case in Chicago. Yet at long last, thanks to Payton's phantom malady, Adamle was getting a shot. With dozens of family members and friends on hand, he gained 110 yards on seventeen carries, the best game for a Bears running back since Gale Sayers' retirement. Harper, a rookie also making his first NFL start, added eighty-six more.

Throughout the afternoon, Payton did and said the right things. He patted Adamle atop the helmet, applauded his effort, told him to wait for his blocks and steer clear of Jack Lambert, Pittsburgh's terrifying linebacker. Inside, he was devastated. "You could watch him sitting there and know he was upset," said Caito. "But that was the whole idea. He should have been upset. Great players are selfish. They want the ball."

Throughout his life, Payton bemoaned the afternoon in Pittsburgh. He told anyone within earshot that Jack Pardee had been wrong to keep him glued to the sidelines. "He liked saying, 'Bud, I could have played! I could have played!'" said Holmes. "And I liked saying, 'Walter, you fucked it up! You fucked it up!'"

Did the lesson stick?

In thirteen seasons, Payton never missed another game.

. . .

Decades before extensive broadcast coverage made the sport ubiquitous, there was something genuinely magical about ABC's *Monday Night Football*. The commentators—especially the cantankerous Howard Cosell—were national icons, and Pop Warner, high school, and college players dreamed of one day appearing on the telecast. From the first time he glanced over the Bears' 1975 schedule, Payton had anticipated breaking out on Monday night against the Vikings at Soldier Field. He imagined all his old friends glued to the television in Jackson State's Sampson Hall and back home in Columbia, Mississippi.

Instead, it turned into one of the worst nights of his life.

Because of his 110-yard performance against the world champion Steelers the previous week, Adamle got the start again. He opened the scoring with a fourteen-yard draw play for a touchdown. "I can't believe it's the Mike Adamle we were watching with the Jets," Cosell raved. "He's suddenly getting an opportunity with the Bears and proving he's a big-league runner." Payton was a backup for the first time since his freshman year in college, as well as the team's new kick returner. His special teams gig began well, as Payton fielded his first NFL kickoff and ran it back forty-three yards. Three plays later, however, Payton took a pitch from Huff, swept around the right corner, bolted down the field, twisted, ducked, swiveled—then fumbled when Minnesota's Terry Brown knocked the ball loose. "He was just making a great run," a disgusted Pardee said afterward. "In making the second effort he exposed the ball."

The Bears lost, 13–9.

Payton, who carried only ten times compared to Adamle's fourteen, was down. His NFL dreams had never involved working as a backup and returning kicks. "If they want me to run, I'll run," he told Joe Mooshil of the *Associated Press*. "If they want me to block, I'll block. If they want me to catch passes, I'll do that. And if they want to use me as a decoy, I'll be a decoy." The words were straight out of Bud Holmes' Guide to Media Talk: 101 and they were insincere. Payton wasn't in Chicago to block or return kicks (though he would lead the league with a 31.7 yard average on fourteen returns) or act as a decoy. He was a football player for one reason—to run the ball.

It was around this time—at his lowest point—that Payton needed a friend to confide in. He found one in Roland Harper. In the 1975 NFL Draft, teams selected a total of 442 players over seventeen rounds. Harper, an obscure fullback out of Louisiana Tech, was picked 420th—and only because Chicago had accidentally noticed him while scouting Charles McDaniel, the Bulldogs' star halfback. "Walter never felt he had to prove himself to the world," said Harper, a native of Shreveport, Louisiana. "But I did. I felt in my heart that I would play in the NFL, and that my blocking was good enough to take on any level of player."

Throughout training camp, Bears players and coaches went about the tasks at hand when—SMACK!—the unmistakable sound of pulverization caught their attention. "That was Roland doing his thing," said Tom Donchez, a reserve running back. "When he hit people, it stung." Payton and Harper shared myriad commonalities. Both were Southern blacks who took part in the integration of a high school (Harper's senior class at Captain Shreve High in Shreveport, Louisiana, was the first to include whites and blacks).

Both were driven to succeed and unwilling to accept failure. Both were raised by warm mothers and hard-driven fathers (Harper's dad, Eural, installed floors for banks and hospitals). Both played in the backfield. Both kept Bibles in their lockers and attended the team's weekly prayer meetings. Unlike Payton, however, Harper was universally beloved. He was talkative without being annoying and insightful without being arrogant. Teammates referred to him as "Preacher." The kid possessed an air of wisdom.

Before long the two backs were inseparable. They talked at length about God and about race and about football. Once, in an attempt to prank Fred O'Connor, the running backs coach, they swapped jerseys and showed up at a frigid practice wearing wool ski masks. The jig lasted for ten minutes, until O'Connor turned to Harper and said, "You might be wearing number thirty-four, but you're not Walter Payton."

"We became bookends," said Harper. "I understood what made him tick, what made him angry, what made him determined. He felt pressure to be the star, and if he didn't rush for one hundred yards he sometimes felt as if he was disappointing people. He was incredibly competitive, and if he didn't meet standards he wanted to hide."

With Harper at his side, Payton survived the rest of the horrible season, eventually returning to the starting lineup. But it wasn't fun. He hated the snow and dreaded the wind. Having spent 95 percent of his life in shorts and a T-shirt, Payton wondered aloud why people subjected themselves to Chicago's winters. At the time, Payton didn't know enough to embrace Chicago's greatness—the bountiful restaurants, the theatre district, the bustling nightlife, and nonstop action. He was a scared kid longing for simplicity.

Payton's spirits were hardly lifted by the junk that surrounded him. Chicago's quarterbacks combined to throw twenty-two interceptions in 1975 (with just nine touchdowns), and when asked to assess Payton, Pardee praised his running, his blocking, and—of all things—his ability "to pursue [interceptors] real well."

"Jack wasn't even trying to be funny," said Pierson. "We all cracked up—the Bears were so sad that a running back was being saluted for his skills as a tackler."

Payton saved his best game for his last, gaining more than three hundred total yards against the hapless New Orleans Saints at the Superdome. With his parents watching from the stands, Payton rushed for 134 yards on twenty-five carries, including a fifty-four-yard touchdown run. He returned two kicks for 104 yards. The Bears won 42–17, their fourth and final victory.

Payton's 679 rushing yards were the most for a Bear back since Sayers gained 1,032 in 1969, but the achievement provided little solace. Payton never wanted to go through a season like that again. He never wanted to be benched, and he never wanted to be considered an afterthought.

As soon as the Bears returned to Chicago, Payton packed up his apartment, loaded the Datsun, and headed back to Mississippi. He longed for warm weather and familiar smiles and some time away from the NFL grind. He spent his days fishing, napping, seeing old friends, and hanging out in old haunts.

Five months later, when he prepared to return to Chicago for summer training camp, Payton turned grumpy and dark. He dreaded going back. He asked Connie about moving with him to the Windy City—a proposition she found most unappealing. "If you want me to be there with you," she said, "then we need to be together the right way."

"So let me get this straight," he said. "If I don't marry you, you really aren't going to come to Chicago?"

Connie nodded.

A day later Walter presented Connie with a ring and assured her he would take care of the wedding arrangements. He called a pastor at Mount Cathray Baptist Church in Jackson and roped in two friends to serve as witnesses. Just how meaningful was July 7, 1976, the day they were to be wed? Connie forgot all about it. "I was out at the mall wandering around with some friends," she wrote. "I came home that evening with some shopping bags, only to find him sitting in my living room, pouting." With a furrowed brow, Walter glanced toward his future wife. "How dare you forget this day," he said. "First, you're going to make me marry you, and then you forget the day?"

"No, I'm ready," Connie said. "Let's go now."

The two headed for the church. No family members were invited or, for that matter, informed. The service was unremarkable. Afterward, Connie called her mother to explain. "You and Daddy work so hard every day, and to even give me the wedding you would feel I wanted would have been a financial burden," she said. "I don't want you to feel like this is something you have to do for me."

Oh, one more thing. Their daughter was dropping out of college to move to Chicago.

CHAPTER 13

THE WAKE-UP CALL

THE MESSAGE WAS FAR FROM SUBTLE. BUT, THEN AGAIN, NEITHER WERE JIM Finks and Jack Pardee, the two men responsible for turning around football's most woeful franchise.

On February 21, 1976, right around the time Walter Payton was fishing along the Pearl River, the Bears announced that the winner of the Brian Piccolo Award as the team's rookie of the year was—drum roll—Roland Harper.

*Roland Harper?*

From afar, it made little sense. Sure, Harper was a punishing blocker who started ten games and ran for 453 yards. But even when the holes didn't exist and defenses were stuffing the line with eight men, Payton was routinely spectacular. Many of his 679 yards materialized from nothingness, and his twisting, spinning dashes for daylight reminded one of a butterfly evading a net. "He could jump through the smallest hole," said Bob Avellini, the Bears quarterback. "And even if that hole became stuffed, he'd still find a way to get four yards. When Walter didn't gain yards, he still gained yards."

But as the Bears prepared for the 1976 season Finks and Pardee continued to question the halfback's drive, work ethic, and durability. Almost immediately after the players reported to Lake Forest—a college town twenty-five miles north of Chicago—for training camp in July, Payton began complaining of nausea and dizzy spells. On July 14, the third straight day of two-a-day workouts, he twice had to be helped off the field, much to the chagrin of his head coach. "I hope he's all right," Pardee told reporters. "I don't know what it is. He feels good and wants to go out and then he has dizziness and feels weak. He has a sinus condition which can affect the inner ear and cause nausea. But we're not going to work him out when he's sick."

Pardee, a man who survived Bear Bryant's ten-day summer football camp in Junction, Texas, as well as a near-death battle with cancer, wasn't going to be overly sympathetic to a hundred-thousand-dollar football player begging out because of dizziness. Even as Payton repeatedly complained, Pardee continued to deny his players water during workouts. "It was barbaric," said Wayne Rhodes, a rookie cornerback out of Alabama. "The heat was intense, we're doing two-a-days, and I'm having to suck the water out of my shirt. Everyone was dehydrated, and the coaches think they're building men. You're not building men. You're killing them."

When he managed to participate, Payton was exceptional. Having spent the off-season high-stepping through the sands along the Pearl River while completing work on his master's degree in special education at Jackson State, he reported to camp faster and stronger than the previous year. His rookie season had been an education in what to expect from NFL defenders, and Payton committed himself to running with an extra viciousness. "He was in the best condition I've ever seen anybody in," said Bo Rather, the wide receiver. "There was nothing extra on him. All lean muscle."

To Pardee, Payton was immature and unprepared; gifted, yet unwilling to put in the time to improve. As a man whose fifteen-year NFL career resulted in disjointed fingers and creaking bones, Pardee expected his minions to devote 100 percent of their on-field time to improving. They weren't here to joke or rest or goof off. They were here to follow orders and play football. Payton, however, was twenty-three years old and impossible to make sense of. Before games, as other players taped up or reviewed strategy, Payton habitually lay prone beneath a table, eyes closed, deep in some sort of zenlike trance. When he wasn't complaining of headaches or charging through defenses, Payton could be found in his rainbow-hued van, featuring an eight-track player and shag carpet. He went about his business quietly, which Pardee liked, but then, seemingly without warning, would pull these juvenile pranks that reminded everyone of his youth. Payton enjoyed sliding behind the Bears' switchboard and, in the highest of high-pitched voices, answering the phone as Louise, the female receptionist. He took to filling the socks of unsuspecting teammates with Swiss Miss hot cocoa powder and lathering their jockstraps with Ben-Gay (then giddily watching them scream in agony).

As one practice at Soldier Field came to an end, Payton was granted permission to leave a few minutes early in order to nurse a sore hamstring. "You could see these dark clouds over the horizon, and it started storming," said Ken Downing, a cornerback who spent four months on the taxi squad. "The entire team rushes for the locker room and Walter's locked all the doors. It's raining and lightning, and he's sitting in the hot tub, singing. They had to get a security guard to open the door." The players weren't laughing. "We were tired and cold," Downing said. "And a little confused as to why anyone would find that funny." (Years later Payton pulled a similarly obnoxious prank, blindly tossing a lit M-80 into a locker room filled with teammates. Amazingly, no one was hurt.)

The Bears opened the six-game exhibition season with a 15–14 win at Denver's Mile High Stadium, yet Payton missed most of the action after bruising his knee during warm-ups. He asked out of the next contest, too, a 27–16 triumph at Seattle, watching in street clothes from the sidelines. Fed up, Pardee announced after the game that Johnny Musso, the backup half-back who gained 176 yards against the Seahawks, might be the new starter. "You couldn't get a better game out of a back than that one," Pardee said. "If he keeps performing that way, I'm certainly not going to consider him a second stringer."

With that, Walter Payton miraculously rediscovered his health. The headaches and nausea disappeared. The knee no longer throbbed. When Finks slyly told the *Tribune* that "Durability is the test of greatness," Payton's ears burned. He ran for 122 yards and two touchdowns on thirty-one carries against the Colts, and added eighty-two more yards in a loss to the Cardinals. The following week at Tampa Bay, Payton rambled for ninety-one yards on a stiff right leg that caused him a slight limp. Asked by Pardee whether he should come out, Payton refused. "It was sore, and I'm still sore," he said afterward. "But I wanted to be in there."

Like many athletes at his skill level, Payton's primary motivator wasn't anger or love or a fiery speech from a coach. It was the insecurity that often accompanies greatness. Payton didn't mind missing a game or sitting out a practice. But the moment Pardee suggested someone might do it better, the running back perked up and stood at attention. When Mike Adamle ran through the Pittsburgh defense, Payton fumed. When Musso was named a potential starter, Payton bristled. "There was one game that we were leading big in the fourth quarter, so Walter was on the sideline," said Avellini, the quarterback. "His backup took off for some forty-yard gain, and everyone was clapping. But Walter was pissed. He turned to me and said, 'Those are *my* yards.'"

For the second straight year, the Bears entered the regular season hopeful. Avellini was a vast improvement at quarterback over the horrid Bobby Douglass and Gary Huff. The team used its first-round pick on an offensive tackle, all-American Dennis Lick of Wisconsin. Though there were no Dick Butkus types on defense, Wally Chambers was an All-Pro pass rusher, and linebacker Waymond Bryant was a splendid athlete. "We had sound talent," said Brian Baschnagel, a rookie receiver from Ohio State. "We weren't going to win the Super Bowl, but we weren't the worst team in the league, either.

"What it all came down to," said Baschnagel, "was Walter."

Conservative in every sense of the word, Pardee was of the mind that defenses won football games and offenses rested the defense. Nearly a decade before he became a proponent of the high-flying run 'n' shoot passing attack with the Houston Gamblers of the United States Football League, Pardee's ideal run-throw ratio was roughly 4:1. "The truth is, the running game was all we had," said Pardee. "If we were going to have any chance to win, it would be by protecting the ball, playing great defense, getting excellent field position, and controlling the clock. My goal as a coach was to find a way to win, and our best chance to win was to run."

The Bears opened the 1976 season against Detroit at Soldier Field. A year earlier, Payton debuted with one of the great thuds in team history, rushing for zero yards vs. Baltimore. Payton never let go of the humiliation from that afternoon—fans booing, Colt players taunting, coaches looking away in disgust.

Much like the Colts of '75, Detroit's roster was a mediocre collection of players coming off of a .500 season. Nevada oddsmakers listed the game as a toss-up, and they were right. The Lions were terrible. The Bears were terrible. The game was terrible. With the 54,125 spectators inside Soldier Field alternating boos with yawns, Chicago won 10–3.

Although Detroit stuffed the line on almost every down, Fred O'Connor, the team's backfield coach who called plays from the press box, refused to throw. He had Payton run twenty-five times, down after down after down. The scene was redundant: Avellini takes the snap. Avellini turns and hands to Payton. Payton slams into the defensive line after gaining little ground. With the exception of a fifty-eight-yard pass from Avellini to Greg Latta, the offense was a bore. Payton, who gained seventy yards, loved running the football, but he also loved an exciting, diverse, wide-open, play-to-win game plan.

Afterward, the embarrassed running back stormed off without speaking to the media.

He was as frustrated as ever.

. . .

Back in the mid-1970s, the NFL was a wasteland of chemical addictions. A large number of players smoked cigarettes and drank to excess. On the Bears, the drugs of choice were marijuana and cocaine.

"There was one offensive player in particular who had a serious coke problem," said one Bear. "Every night I would stand there and watch him blow his nose, and all these towels would be filled with blood. Sometimes I'd have to drive him places because he was so high. He wasn't alone."

Was Pardee aware of such goings-on? No. Was Finks? Probably not. But were you a member of the team, and were you interested in getting high, there were countless places to turn. Many of the players had their own personal dealers, and were more than willing to spread the word.

"Most of the guys on that team were smoking a whole lot of weed," said Ron Cuie, a running back selected in the fourteenth round of the '76 Draft. "There was a local bar near training camp, and all the guys would go there and get drunk and high. But not Walter. Never saw him."

"A lot of guys got hooked on drugs beginning with their time in the NFL," said Earl Douthitt, a former Bears defensive back. "That's what happened to me—cocaine abuse started when I got to the Bears. And man, was it hard to break."

Newly married and living with Connie in a small apartment in the Chicago suburb of Wheeling, Payton had nothing to do with the drug scene. Throughout his first twenty-three years of life, he'd drank fewer than ten beers total, and never took a hit from a joint. As for snorting lines of cocaine—not even a consideration.

Yet while Payton didn't use, the argument can be made that he was a direct victim of those who did. According to several players, drug use made the Bears a sloppy, oft-disinterested group of ballplayers that focused mildly on football excellence and intently on partying after the game. Whereas elite teams like the Steelers and Vikings played with methodical, robotic excellence, Chicago was messy. Blocks were missed. Routes were botched. Easy balls slipped through fingers. Wins were greeted happily, but losses were greeted indifferently. To

Walter at San Francisco's Candlestick Park before a game his rookie year. The young runner found life in the NFL to be harder than expected—especially surrounded by a mediocre collection of talent.

In the fall of 1970, Columbia High School fielded its first integrated varsity football team. Walter Payton, bottom row, third from right, was its star—and one of the key players in bringing the two races together.

Though he never aspired to play football as a youngster, by the time Walter reached Columbia High School, the game was his primary passion. He was handed No. 22 by Coach Charles Boston— the same number his older brother, Eddie, had worn.

PHOTO COURTESY OF JACKSON STATE UNIVERSITY

Walter's senior photo from the Columbia High School yearbook. Said a classmate: "The thing I think a lot of people noticed about him was he never fully looked up. He would look down and glance up occasionally with his big bright eyes. He was very humble."

PHOTO COURTESY OF COLUMBIA HIGH SCHOOL

During his freshman year at Jackson State, Walter, left, teamed with Eddie, his older brother, to form a dynamic backfield. The brothers roomed together, and Walter credited his sibling with making the adjustment easier.

On an Alumni Day scrimmage during his senior year at Jackson State, Payton ripped through the daunting Tigers' defense. "He was," said Vernon Hill, a teammate, "the most dynamic force I'd ever seen."

Walter turning up field during a game his junior year at Jackson State. Though Coach Bob Hill insisted his backs use two hands to carry the football, with Walter he often made exceptions.

Walter and Bob Hill (center), his head coach at Jackson State, mingle at an award ceremony. Though Payton was hardly a fan of Hill's brutal methods, the coach taught him more about running the football than anyone in his life.

"Walter had a different speed, a different twitch, a different quick," John Bunting, an Eagles linebacker, once marveled. He was right. A powerful runner, a devastating blocker, and marvelous as a pass catcher, Payton was the ultimate NFL weapon. Here against the Packers, he floats through the defense.

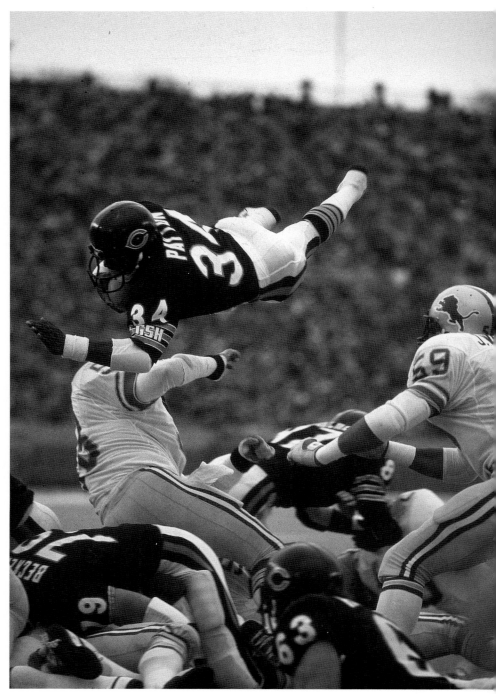

During his senior year at Jackson State, the Tigers failed to score a key touchdown against Southern when Walter charged toward the goal line, instead of soaring over it. His NFL career often served as an ode to the leap. Here, he skies over the Detroit Lions in a 1984 game at Soldier Field

Though never the biggest, fastest, or most imposing running back in the NFL, Payton's never-die-easy approach to carrying the football made him impossible to stop one-on-one. Here, it takes six members of the Los Angeles Rams' defense to do the job.

Walter breaks free for some of his record-setting 275 yards against the Vikings on November 20, 1977, at Soldier Field. Payton had been sick the entire week leading up to the game, and many inside the locker room assumed he wouldn't play. Instead, he had the finest individual game in league history.

Payton and quarterback Jim McMahon share a moment before a game. Rarely one to openly rip the organization, Payton was euphoric when, in 1982, the Bears finally drafted a top-flight quarterback. The gritty McMahon would help carry Chicago to the Super Bowl XX title.

Walter takes a break during training camp, circa 1986. Though very approachable, Payton could be shy, introverted, and guarded. He valued his privacy like few other athletic stars.

Walter and William Perry line up in the Bears' backfield on November 17, 1985, during Chicago's 44–0 drubbing of the Cowboys at Texas Stadium. Walter liked "The Refrigerator," personally, but was jealous of all the attention thrown his way.

watch a highlight film of the '76 Chicago Bears is to watch NFL football played not merely at its worst, but at its most inconsistent. "That," said Douthitt, "is what makes so much of what Walter did so incredible."

Payton was a man on an island, expected to deliver excellence, but lacking the necessary help to get him there. Except for Harper, the bruising fullback, Payton found few friends among his teammates. He laughed at their jokes and pulled colorful pranks and patted them on the rears in the aftermath of good plays, but for the most part the connection ended there. When Jerry Muckensturm, a Chicago linebacker, said, "I liked Walter, but I never felt like I got to know him," he spoke for the majority of teammates. Walter was trying to find his footing in the Windy City, but the going was slow.

Following the listless victory over Detroit, the Bears flew to San Francisco to face the 49ers, another mediocre team coming off of a 5-9 record. Because it was being played on the West Coast, and because the 49ers and the Bears both appeared to stink, and because the snoozer of week one had placed many Chicago fans in a catatonic state, the pregame buildup generated the buzz of a librarian convention. The contest lacked a single marquee name—Payton was still an unproven curiosity, and at the moment the Niners' best player was probably their kicker, Steve Mike-Mayer.

On the afternoon of September 19, 1976, everything changed.

With the skies clear, the Candlestick Park wind unusually still, and a crowd of 44,158 fans eagerly anticipating the home debut of head coach Monte Clark, Payton stepped onto the rocky brown-and-green field (still being used by baseball's San Francisco Giants) and pummeled the 49ers. Behind a mediocre offensive line, with a mediocre quarterback and a mediocre scheme, Payton ran for 148 yards and two touchdowns, the best game of his career. "He was incredible . . . just incredible," said Tommy Hart, a 49ers defensive end. "Before that game, the name Walter Payton meant very little to me. Afterward, I couldn't forget it."

Chicago received the opening kickoff, marched down the field, and scored on a twenty-yard Payton run that, more than thirty years later, Hart still struggled to comprehend. Immediately after taking the handoff, Payton was met head-on by Hart, San Francisco's six-foot-four, 245-pound Pro Bowler. Frozen behind the line of scrimmage, Payton's chest was smothered in Hart's jersey. The lineman began the process of bringing the back down when—hips twisting, knees rising—Payton somehow spun away and galloped for a big gain.

The remainder of the game was Payton ducking beneath tacklers, slashing through the secondary, eluding men double his size, and buckling the knees of Jimmy Johnson and Bruce Taylor, San Francisco's veteran defensive backs. On the 49ers sideline running back Delvin Williams, a future Pro Bowler, couldn't believe what he was witnessing. "The hardest thing to do is run when everyone knows you're getting the football," said Williams. "In those situations, you have to know where the flow is coming from and where the weakness of your blockers will be. You have to slow a bit, wait to make a move, then let it unfold. You use your ability and hope your teammates don't get in your way. It's extremely hard, yet Walter was out there doing it perfectly. And he was just a kid."

In the aftermath of the win, an incredulous pack of reporters listened as Payton pooh-poohed his performance. "I should have scored at least four touchdowns," he said. "And a hundred and forty-eight yards, that still wasn't good enough. A couple of times I got caught in the backfield and I shouldn't have."

Beginning at Jackson State, and throughout his years with Chicago, Payton habitually talked down his own efforts, bemoaning a yard left on the field or a phantom touchdown that should have been. The device was all Bob Hill: The less the hype, the lower the expectations. "I'd say part of that was an act," Avellini said. "Walter enjoyed being the star."

Now, in the heart of the '76 season, he suddenly was. Payton cleared 100 yards in three of the next four games, ripping through the Redskins for 104, then the Vikings for 141 and the Rams for 145. His weapon of choice was the stiff-arm, which Payton originally mastered on the sandlots of Columbia. When most running backs faced oncoming defenders, they lowered their heads and barreled ahead. With ever-increasing frequency, Payton opted to stick out his arm, jab an enemy in the face mask or sternum, and send him flailing. The highlight reels were now filled with the technique, one player after another dropping like a damp sandbag. "Other backs used stiff-arms, but Walter's recoiled, then exploded into you," said Frank Reed, a safety with the Atlanta Falcons "I mean, the dang thing stung. Once he hit you with that, it was KO." Don Wedge, an NFL official for twenty-four years, said Payton was the only offensive player to regularly reach out and grab for defenders' face masks. "It'd start as a stiff-arm and turn into a mugging," said Wedge. "It was, technically, a penalty, but it was so rare for an offensive player to do it that we never called it on Walter. He was ruthless."

Perhaps the most telling sign of Payton's greatness was that he was, in baseball lingo, tipping his pitches—giving the defense advance warning of what he was going to do. When a handoff was designed to head right, Payton's stance appeared normal. When a handoff was called for the left, however, Payton inadvertently lifted his right foot and tiptoed it forward seconds before the snap. "Other teams were well aware of it," said Johnny Roland, at the time an assistant coach with the Eagles. "You'd watch tape of the Bears and see the tendency. But even though we knew it, there wasn't much we could do. He could cut back so fast, so crisply, that he'd be gone quicker than you adjusted."

Though the Bears were barely average, winning three of their first four before dropping three straight, Payton emerged as the fresh young face of the NFL. In mid-October the *Los Angeles Times* sent Elizabeth Wheeler to write a lengthy profile, the first time a national publication took serious note. Shortly thereafter, *Sports Illustrated* requested a detailed file on Payton from Kevin Lamb, a writer for the *Chicago Daily News*. Lamb's words painted the narrative that Bud Holmes, Payton's attorney, wanted people to see. Holmes' PR advice to his client was simple: Say little, accentuate the positive, keep negative opinions to yourself. Hence, the bundle received by *SI*'s Eleanore Milosovic was a glowing ode to Walter. He liked the drums and listening to music, once interned briefly at Jackson's NBC affiliate, and was loved and respected by teammates. Wrote Lamb: "When Steve Schubert dropped a punt against Atlanta that set the Falcons up on the Bear fifteen in the fourth quarter of a scoreless tie, Payton was the first to talk to him on the sideline and console him. Last year a Lion player was running out-of-control toward a portable heater when Payton caught him."

Was Payton the only Bear to console Schubert? Hardly. Were there NFL players who actually would have allowed the Lion to barrel into a heater? Probably not. Did veterans find Payton's ongoing pranks obnoxious and irritating? Yes. But Chicago was a town crying for a hero, and Payton—handsome, talented, young—fit the suit.

With the mounting hoopla (Payton appeared on the cover of the November 22, 1976, *Sports Illustrated*, beneath the headline THE NFL'S NEW STARS), even *People* magazine joined the fray. Dennis Breo, a Chicago-based freelance writer, pitched the idea of a young, newly-married heartthrob who was tearing up the NFL—then was shocked when a lifestyle publication that rarely delved into sports actually bit. Breo spent ten days with Payton, and found himself neither liking nor hating the man. "Mostly, I was confused by him," Breo said. "He was shy and very secretive. Most of the time I was trying to interview him he was wearing his headphones, bobbing to music coming from his hi-fi stereo. I literally had to pull them off his head to ask a question."

At the time, one of the hot books in America was Erich von Daniken's *Chariots of the Gods?* which hypothesized that the technologies and religions of many ancient civilizations were supplied by space travelers. Though generally mocked, von Daniken's work had its supporters. Like Walter Payton. "Walter was a believer in it, which I found surprising," Breo said. "He believed in life on other planets, and that aliens had been here before us. He said it was something that intrigued him."

The story was published in the November 22, 1976, issue of *People*, and Payton—not one to express pleasure or scorn to the press—was livid. "The article is fine," he told Breo. "But what you guys did with that picture was just wrong."

*That picture* depicted Walter and Connie, fully clothed, rolling around on their bed.

"He was a private guy," said Breo, "and he didn't want people thinking of him that way."

What way is that?

"Good question," said Breo. "I guess the kind of guy who sleeps on a bed."

. . .

Long before the Hertz commercials. Long before *The Naked Gun*. Long before the *Monday Night Football* gig. Long before Nicole and Ronald, before the Ford Bronco, before the ill-fitting leather glove, before the acquittal heard around the world, before the thirty-three-year sentence for armed robbery.

Long before it all, O. J. Simpson was a football player. A fabulous, game-changing football player.

Heading into the 1976 season, there was Simpson, Buffalo's eighth-year halfback, and there was everyone else. The Juice had led the league with 1,817 rushing yards in 1975—his third crown in four seasons. The closest challenger, Pittsburgh's Franco Harris, trailed him by a whopping 571 yards. Though hardly the type to barrel over opposing tacklers, like Payton or the Redskins' John Riggins, Simpson's blinding speed made him a defense's nightmare. "When I was a rookie with the Patriots in 1975, we played O. J. at Buffalo," said Steve Schubert, a Bears wide receiver. "I swear, I saw the guy come into the line of scrimmage, then float out the other side without being touched. He was smooth like silk."

Drafted by the Bills out of USC with the first pick of the 1969 NFL Draft, Simpson walked with an air befitting a Hollywood star, not an upstate New York rookie. That's the way Simpson viewed himself—as a multifaceted entertainer whose gifts as an athlete could be used as a gateway into other high-profile worlds. Simpson wanted to be the center of attention. He craved the bright lights and glitter, and had recently filmed a cameo role for ABC's upcoming smash television hit, *Roots*. Among his close friends were Lee Marvin and Richard Burton.

"He was so much bigger than the team or the city of Buffalo," said Tom Donchez, a running back drafted in the fourth round by the Bills in 1975. "Buffalo was a whistle stop for him—a place to pick up a check. O. J. would hold court and have an expert opinion on anything, merely because he was O. J. That doesn't mean he wasn't liked by teammates, because he was. He was funny and engaging. But I think you took him with a grain of salt."

Simpson reveled in his place atop the NFL. With Jim Brown a decade retired and Gale Sayers five years gone, he reigned as the undisputable king of backs. It was with a skeptical eye and great cynicism, therefore, that Simpson began hearing about the kid from Jackson State trespassing on his terrain. When *Sports Illustrated* described Payton exploding "from his set like a grenade from an M79 launcher," Simpson dismissed the praise as excessive hyperbole. When O'Connor, Payton's backfield coach, said of his star, "God said he wanted a halfback, and he made Walter," Simpson chuckled. He never publicly mocked or questioned Payton, but within the sanctity of the Bills' locker room, Simpson scoffed. Hot backs came, hot backs went. Payton wouldn't last for long.

Just one problem: In the midst of one of his best seasons, Simpson couldn't shake free of Payton in the race for the NFL rushing title. As the Bills (who would finish 2-12) and the Bears (who would finish 7-7) slogged through forgettable campaigns, their featured stars went back and forth atop the leaderboard. Through the first six games, Payton held a seemingly insurmountable advantage—694 yards to 376 yards. Then Simpson went on a roll—tearing up the Jets and Patriots for a combined 276 yards in weeks seven and eight, and torching the hapless Lions for an NFL-record 273 yards in week twelve. Payton lost the rushing lead to Simpson on Thanksgiving Day, but regained it a week later with 110 yards against the Packers. On

December 6, the second-to-last week of the regular season, he carved up the first-year Seahawks for a career-best 183 yards. It was his seventh hundred-yard game, a new team record, and though the contest was played in Seattle's Kingdome, a nation was captivated.

Early in the game, a message scrawled across the video board informed the crowd that Simpson had just rushed for a seventy-five-yard touchdown against Miami. Seattle's 60,510 fans cheered wildly. At that point, Payton had gained a mere nine yards on five carries, and the Seahawk defense, featuring ex-Bear Richard Harris, was playing with uncharacteristic ferocity. Pride mattered to Seattle coach Jack Patera, and the last thing he wanted was for his club to offer an opposing player easy access to a rushing title.

Yet Payton had pride, too. Led by the loquacious Harris, Seattle's defensive players spent much of the first quarter barking inanities—"Not today! Not on our turf!"—that only served the infuriate Payton.

"You didn't want to motivate Walter," said Harper. "He fed off of that stuff."

By the time the half ended, Payton had run for 114 yards, but he was hurting. Spasms in his diaphragm were making it difficult to breathe, and a doctor and trainer helped him into the locker room. As the second half began, Payton was nowhere to be found. With the video board continuing to display Simpson's yardage (he gained 203 against Miami), however, Payton somehow regained his breath. Though the game was well in hand (the Bears won, 34–7), he carried nine times in the fourth quarter. Three runs nullified by penalties would have given him 227. Afterward, Pardee felt no need to hide the Bears's motives. "We weren't going to risk anything," he said. "But the line wants Walter to win the rushing title."

. . .

Entering the final week of the regular season, the NFL was filled with riveting story lines. Would the 12-1 Oakland Raiders fulfill their destiny and win the Super Bowl? Would the Tampa Bay Buccaneers, first-year laughingstocks, go 0-14? Could Colts quarterback Bert Jones finish strong enough to hold off Oakland quarterback Ken Stabler in the MVP race? (Answers: Yes, yes, and yes.)

All the news, however, paled in magnitude to the most fascinating rushing race in the fifty-six-year history of the league. With one game remaining, Payton led Simpson by a mere nine yards, 1,341 to 1,332.

Simpson-Payton carried the weight of a political election. People took sides—Payton was the upstart; the new kid. Not nearly as flashy as his rival, but gritty and determined. Simpson, on the other hand, was electric and explosive. He was the running back kids emulated in their backyards. Everyone wanted to be the Juice.

For their final game of the season, the 7-6 Bears would play host to the Denver Broncos, an 8-5 club with two things going for it: First, the Bronco players were comfortable enough in inclement weather so as not to flinch at stiff winds and twenty-three-degree temperatures. Second, Denver's Orange Crush defense excelled against the run, allowing a paltry 3.4 yards per carry, second best in the league. Payton was hardly helped by Soldier Field's cementlike turf, which only hardened with the winter cold. "There was actually a big hump in the middle of our field," said Bo Rather. "And the surface burned your knees and elbows, and that shit never healed. There was no worse place for a back."

Simpson, on the other hand, would be playing at Baltimore. The Colts had a lousy run defense, and Memorial Stadium offered a relatively cushy, well-maintained surface. Advantage: Juice.

With Soldier Field's scoreboard, in the words of the *Tribune*, "not equipped with the conveniences of the twentieth century," the Bears took the quasi-embarrassing, quasi-quaint step of hiring cheerleaders from nearby Warren Township High School to carry placards around the sidelines to update fans on Simpson vs. Payton. Despite the weather, which included 13 mph winds, Soldier Field was packed. Among those in attendance were Holmes, Bob Hill, and Alyne Payton, Walter's mother. The three flew up together from Mississippi on Holmes' private Learjet. Planning for a celebration, Alyne brought with her one of Walter's favorites—a raisin, pecan, and apple cake she had baked the day before.

Thanks to Baltimore's Sunday Blue Laws (a sporting event could not start before two o'clock Eastern Standard Time), both games were scheduled to kick off at one P.M. central time, meaning neither back would know in advance what he needed to shoot for. "There's no point in thinking about what's happening halfway across the country," Simpson said beforehand. "All I can do is concentrate on the Baltimore defense and hope that everything comes out well."

"I'm just going to go out there and play up to my ability," said Payton. "I'm not going to do anything different, I'm not going to go out there and make silly mistakes or take anything into my own hands, because I can't do it."

Because the Broncos had been eliminated from play-off contention, they could have understandably closed the season with limited interest. Instead, Denver's players took the field and attacked. Blessed with Randy Gradishar and Tom Jackson, two of the sport's best young linebackers, as well as an unblockable nose tackle named Rubin Carter, Denver's defense overwhelmed the Bears, clogging Payton's lanes and reducing Avellini, a subpar quarterback to begin with, to mud. He threw seventeen passes. He completed two.

The cheerleaders hired to flash placards had only bad news to report. In Baltimore, the Colts defense was playing dead, and Simpson accumulated seventy-five yards by halftime. "One of our guys was keeping up with Walter through a fan's radio on the sideline," Simpson said. "I had to keep telling him, 'Hey, cool it. We gotta play this game here.'" Payton, on the other hand, found himself smothered by a wall of orange and blue. Two yards. Three yards. One yard. Four yards. Midway through the third quarter, he picked up the phone and called O'Connor in the press box. "My teammates are more interested in me winning the rushing title than us winning the game," he said. "They're not focused. So do us all a favor and take me out." O'Connor refused. Avellini was a problem, the offensive line was a problem, the weather was a problem. Payton was not a problem. "He was the one thing we had going for us," O'Connor said.

Late into the third quarter, with his stat line reading forty-nine yards on thirteen carries, Payton took a handoff, cut to the right, and was sandwiched by Jackson, Gradishar, and safety Bill Thompson. Payton felt his right ankle tweak, and he crumpled to the ground in pain. It took Fred Caito, the Bears' trainer, less than a minute to diagnose a sprain. Payton's day was over.

As their lone superstar gingerly walked from the field, Chicago's fans let loose a long, powerful cheer. In the chilling silence that ensued, they watched Payton retreat to the bench, slump under a coat, place his head in his hands, and sob. Pardee strolled over to pat Payton on the back. "You have nothing to be ashamed of," he told him. "You're a champion." The man questioned for his toughness only four months earlier had stepped up. Never again would anyone ask about Walter Payton's drive.

The Bears lost, 28–14. Payton lost, 1,503 yards to 1,390 yards. (He did, however, surpass Gale Sayers' single-season team rushing record.) Though loathe to admit such an emotion at the time, Payton craved the rushing title. In his mind, Simpson was the galloping gazelle from Southern Cal and he was the small-town kid from Mississippi. It was David vs. Goliath, only with the wrong ending.

"It was, I guess, the low point of my career," he later said. "So much had been made of the fact that I had a chance to beat O. J. Simpson out for the rushing title. When I found myself lying there on the field and knew I had failed, it was like I didn't want to get back up . . . I'm a competitor. Being injured, not finishing the game, was eating inside of me. I didn't know how to cope."

That night, with the ankle still throbbing, Payton coped. He hosted his mother, agent, and college coach at his one-bedroom apartment. Together, the four, along with Connie, laughed and hugged and talked old times.

When the evening finally came to an end, an exhausted Walter Payton went to bed.

He didn't sleep a wink.

## CHAPTER 14

# THE STRANGEST RUN

HIS WORDS POSSESSED MEANING.

That's one of the intriguing parts of young Walter Payton. He talked quietly and infrequently enough for members of the Chicago media to often wonder whether the twenty-four-year-old ever spoke at all. Hence, when Payton opened his mouth and made a bold declaration, the sentiment wasn't to be taken lightly.

That's why, as occupants of the Bears administrative offices stared down the front sports page of the November 1, 1977, *Chicago Tribune*, their jaws dropped.

## PAYTON'S GOAL: QUIT IN 1 PIECE
### By Ed Stone

Walter Payton is concerned enough about the long-range physical toll on him that he plans to retire from pro football after three more seasons. . . . "There's just so much torment and brutality you can send your body through," he explained. "I want to get out of pro football with all of the physical ability I came in with."

Dating back to his early high school games, Payton refused to grant defenders the pleasure of bearing witness to his pain. Immediately after being hit, he jumped to his feet, patted the opposing player on the rear, and sprinted back toward the huddle. "I hated that," said Jeff Siemon, the Vikings' four-time Pro Bowl linebacker. "You'd stick him with a great shot, feel amazing about yourself . . . and then here's Walter, smiling and congratulating you."

Those who paid close attention to the Bears over Payton's first two seasons, however, knew the running back was taking a hellacious pounding. His arms and legs were often blue-and-purple canvases. His calves throbbed. "The yards he gained were all because of his talent," said Wally Chambers, Chicago's standout defensive lineman. "The line in front of him was never very good, so he had to make people miss. When he didn't, he got hit. *Hard*." Because of his spectacular 1976 campaign, which resulted in him being named *The Sporting News'* NFC Player of the Year, fans increasingly compared Payton with O. J. Simpson, his new rival. Yet there was a glaring difference: While Simpson ran behind an elite offensive line (right guard Joe DeLamielleure was a future Hall of Famer, left guard Reggie McKenzie an all-AFC selection), Payton's blockers were thoroughly mediocre. When asked, Payton spoke on behalf of their abilities, declaring guards Noah Jackson and Revie Sorey to be "Pro Bowl worthy" and capping touchdowns by allowing his linemen to handle the celebratory end zone spike. To confidants, however, Payton complained his bodyguards missed as often as they hit. "Walter never robbed anyone of his dignity," said Tom Hicks, a Chicago linebacker. "If guys blew blocks, he never threw the ball down or screamed or chewed someone out. Never. And he definitely could have."

Payton's Mondays, Tuesdays, Wednesdays, and Thursdays—an excruciating stretch during which he could barely move his arms and legs—were indictments of an offensive line that suffered through lengthy stretches of indifference and laziness. That the linemen received any notoriety at all was a testament to Payton's ability to make them appear competent. "Noah didn't have the mental stability to be great," said Mark Nordquist, a former Bears lineman. "And Revie had all the size and the speed, but no work ethic at all. He nicknamed himself Rock Hollywood and thought he was super. He wasn't." The days also spoke to the power of painkillers—which were used throughout the league. Payton robotically popped Darvons which, supplied by the team in sizeable locker-room buckets, were unhealthy, undocumented, and—from Payton's standpoint—indispensable. "I'd see him walk out of the locker room with jars of painkillers," said Bud Holmes, his agent. "And he'd eat them like they were a snack." During games, Payton approached the sideline and nodded toward Fred Caito, the team's trainer. There was no confusion over the intent. "If he got dinked on the field he'd go up to Freddie and say, 'Freddie, I need a Darvon,'" said Clyde Emrich, the Bears' former strength coach. "So Freddie would put one in Walter's hand and they'd keep walking by each other. Walter would take it without stopping. He didn't want people to know, because he knew if they knew he was hurt they'd go after him hard."

"Fred would have a handful of painkillers for Walter, and Walter would just pop them," said Don Pierson, the longtime *Tribune* beat writer. "He took so many pills. Fred would stand there, hand them to Walter, and Walter would eat them like mints."

When the medication alone didn't ease the pain, Payton lathered his arms and legs with dimethyl sulfoxide (DMSO), a mysterious nontoxic organic solvent used to treat horses. Though at the time few knew whether DMSO was healthy or harmful (more than thirty years later, the jury is still out), to Payton it felt like Ben-Gay, times a million. "It made your breath smell like garlic and your body just stink," said John Skibinski, who joined the Bears as a fullback in 1978. "But if you had a bruise, more times than not it made it disappear."

While the daily suffering was hardly embraced by Payton, it wasn't the reason he was considering an early retirement. No, that idea first entered his mind on a dark Chicago night in October, when an opposing player with crazed eyes and a rabid pit bull's sensibilities went on the attack.

Until that point, 1977 was shaping up to be the greatest year of Walter's young life. In March he met one of his heroes, Muhammad Ali, at a banquet, a moment that left him floating like a butterfly. Five months later, in another unforgettable encounter, the Bears played an exhibition game against the Cleveland Browns, whose kick returner and backup halfback was a five-foot-eight, 175-pound gnat from Jackson State named Eddie Payton. The older Payton brother had spent some time in the Canadian Football League, and was finally getting a shot to stick in the NFL. Walter outgained Eddie, thirty-four yards to twenty-one yards, hugged his sibling afterward, then noted to reporters, "I told you he was faster than me. Not better, but faster."

Best of all, for the first time in three years Jack Pardee seemed committed to a high-powered offense. During the off-season the team hired Sid Gillman, the revolutionary passing guru and former head coach of the San Diego Chargers, to liven things up as Chicago's offensive coordinator. No longer, it seemed, would the Bears run 80 percent of the time, or only line up two receivers and a tight end. Gillman promised four-wideout sets and Payton going deep along the sideline; wild slants and imaginative bombs. "He had a brilliant mind," said receiver Brian Baschnagel. "The football field was Sid's playground."

Though the Bears opened the season by losing two of their first three games, Pardee projected little panic. Payton had run well, but the overall adjustment to Gillman's ideas was awkward. "It takes time," Pardee said. "We'll get it right." On October 10, the 2-1 Los Angeles Rams came to Chicago. Playing quarterback was Joe Namath, now thirty-four years old and in his first season out of New York. The Rams had naïvely signed Broadway Joe as a free agent, hoping he could replicate the magic of his earlier days with the Jets. Namath, though, was a Xerox of his old self; painfully immobile and standing on a pair of knees held together by chewing gum and Scotch Tape. In planning for the game, Pardee and Brad Ecklund, Chicago's defensive line coach, drew up a strategy centered upon turning Namath into a piñata. The Bears were to hit Namath hard, often, and if need be, late.

In a game noteworthy for its sheer brutality, Chicago assaulted Namath, who—on those rare occasions he was able to cleanly get rid of the ball— watched his passes flutter pathetically into a driving rain and fierce wind. In the fourth quarter Waymond Bryant, the Chicago linebacker, was ejected after he knocked Namath out with an illegal tackle, thrusting the top of his helmet into Namath's Adam's apple. "The hit by Bryant was a cheap shot," said Dennis Harrah, the Rams' guard. "I didn't see it very well. But I knew it. I could feel it."

Having played in the SWAC, where coaches fought coaches and boun- ties were placed upon the heads of superstars, Payton was generally unflustered by the nastiness of professional football. Oftentimes, in fact, he embraced it. Early in the first quarter, while running a sweep, Payton was yanked out of bounds by Bill Simpson, a Rams defensive back who grabbed hold of his face mask and refused to let go. Payton, being Payton, popped up, said noth- ing, and jogged back to the huddle. Later on, following a third-quarter sweep by Roland Harper, Payton approached Simpson from behind and clipped him in the left knee with his shoulder pad. The hit was dirty, though Pay- ton's intent was merely to send a message, not actually hurt someone. "Walter," Simpson said, "what the hell are you doing?"

Payton shrugged off the question—what comes around goes around. But then the screaming began. And the threats. "I'm gonna fucking kill you,

Payton! You're a motherfucking dead man! Watch your back, motherfucker! Watch your back!"

The words emerged from the lips of one Isiah Robertson, Los Angeles' twenty-eight-year-old right outside linebacker. A 1971 first-round draft pick out of the SWAC's Southern University, Robertson wasted little time establishing himself as one of the league's best players, earning All-Pro honors as a rookie and being named the NFC Rookie of the Year. He was fast and ferocious, yet as the seasons passed, coaches and teammates began to question his stability. "Isiah was a very good player, but he was a pain in the ass," said Bob Pifferini, a Rams linebacker. "I can't think of too many nice things to say about him—he was so selfish, it was painful. He was our teammate, but if he and Walter came to blows, 99 percent of us would have rooted for Walter."

Robertson said he and Payton were friends dating back to college, which is unlikely, considering Payton was a senior at Columbia High when Robertson was a senior at Southern. He said he loved and respected Payton, and that the entire "motherfucking dead man" episode that night was blown out of proportion. The facts speak differently. Following the game, the *Tribune*'s Cooper Rollow approached Robertson's locker. He was quickly rewarded. "Wally Chambers is the poorest excuse for an All-Pro I ever saw," Robertson said. "If we ever meet again I intend to see that he gets his. The same thing goes for Walter Payton. He clipped Bill Simpson on one play. There was no excuse for it. If I ever get a chance I'm gonna end his career."[*]

For the first time anyone could remember, Payton was shaken beyond quick repair. He returned to the locker room after the game and paced back and forth, tears welling in both eyes. Here was the immature Mississippi kid struggling to deal with the reality of NFL brutality. He refused to speak to the press, dressed without showering, and left the stadium. He later confided in Harper that, were this the way professional football worked, he could do without. Cheap hits were one thing. Threatening an opponent's life was another. "This isn't for me," he said. "I don't play football to hurt people."

The following April, Robertson ran into Payton at the Grand Prix of Long Beach. When he extended his hand for a conciliatory shake, Payton turned away. "When I saw that response, I thought 'Is it my breath? Did I

---

[*] In a July 22, 1979, note to a peer, the *Tribune*'s Ron Sons recalled watching Robertson that night. "My definite impression," he wrote, "was that Robertson was riding a high stronger than Pepsi-Cola at the time. He may not remember what he said."

date your sister?'" Robertson said. "I yelled at him, 'If you're still upset over the fight your team caused, we'll have another fight right here.' It was bullshit."

Payton walked off, leaving Robertson in his dust.

. . .

As long as there are football fans in Chicago, there will be debates involving Walter Payton. Was he better than Jim Brown and Gale Sayers? Which was his best season? Can the Bears even possibly win without him?

The answer to one pressing question, however, has long been resolved. Namely, what was the most incredible run of Payton's career?

It came on November 13, 1977. Leading up to the game the Bears were, once again, floundering. Stubborn to a fault, Pardee tuned Gillman out, reverting to the predictable run-run-run philosophy that resulted in few points and a bored-to-death fan base. "If you were a receiver you were either a right receiver or a left receiver," said Baschnagel. "The only time you'd venture to the other side of the field was if you were in the slot. It was very, very archaic, and then they brought in Sid Gillman—and nothing changed."

"Shit, we'd watch film of Chicago's offense and laugh," said Dave Roller, a defensive tackle with the Packers. "It was junior high–level crap."

With the exception of Payton, whose 937 rushing yards through eight weeks led the NFL, little was going right. The Bears were coming off a 47–0 loss at Houston that Pardee called, "the worst thing I've ever been associated with in any form." The team's record dropped to 3-5.

Next up was a matchup with the Chiefs at Soldier Field. With two wins in its first eight games, Kansas City had stamped itself as a hapless ball club in the midst of a downward spiral. Throughout the early 1970s, the Chiefs were the pride of the AFC, a model organization built upon deep drafts and canny transactions. Unfortunately, like many franchises that enjoyed sustained success, Kansas City couldn't let go. With three thirty-two-year-old linebackers (Billy Andrews, Willie Lanier, and Jim Lynch), as well as thirty-four-year-old Emmitt Thomas at cornerback, its defense doubled as a home for aged, broken-down ballplayers. "We were hurting," said Andrews. "We couldn't stop anyone." Four opposing backs had already cleared a hundred yards, including Cleveland's Greg Pruitt's 153 two weeks earlier, and the word was out: Pound the Chiefs, they'll inevitably break.

With this in mind, quarterback Bob Avellini handed off to Payton again and again (by the end of the game Payton would carry a season-high thirty-three times). The runs were almost exclusively straight into the line, and while the Chiefs jumped out to a 17–0 halftime lead, Chicago's offensive players sensed the Kansas City defense wearing down. "We're going to keep running right at them," Pardee told his players at halftime. "They're about to break."

To start the second half, Chicago's offensive linemen held hands in the huddle, a symbolic gesture of unity for an occasionally fractured group. Though it went unreported in the press, Payton's blockers were hardly the tightest of friends. Noah Jackson, the 273-pound left guard known as "Buddha" for his sizeable gut, was regarded by teammates as lazy and selfish. For his part, Jackson thought left tackle Ted Albrecht, his neighbor on the line, had no business starting in the NFL. General contempt was also directed toward Revie Sorey, the right guard whose cockiness rarely matched his play. "Were we all having beers together?" said Dan Peiffer, a center. "Not often. But does that matter? Probably not."

Beginning in the second half against the Chiefs, however, the unit inexplicably clicked. Payton was running hard, and the linemen were blocking even harder. Jackson pancaked Lanier on a brutal Payton sweep, then Sorey drove Lynch into the ground with equal force.

And then came the greatest run of Payton's career.

Early in the third quarter, with the Bears still down by seventeen, Payton grabbed the ball from Avellini and swept right, where he was immediately met by Lanier and cornerback Tim Gray. Trapped, Payton spun around and retraced his steps back toward the middle of the field. The first to miss was Tom Howard, a rookie linebacker who grazed Payton with his right arm as the running back paused, skipped, then zoomed by. ("The idea of tackling Walter with one arm is crazy," said Avellini. "Couldn't be done.") Two Chiefs, Lynch and defensive end Whitney Paul, converged on Payton, who appeared momentarily trapped. His white shoes and blue jersey a blur, Payton turned upfield, extending away from the grasps of Lynch and Paul and into the waiting arms of Thomas. A future Hall of Famer who would retire with fifty-eight interceptions and a sterling reputation, Thomas did everything right. He squared his body, bent his knees, reached with both arms, and—BOOM! Payton trampled over him. "I threw two blocks on that play," said Robin Earl, the Bears' rookie fullback. "That's how long that play went on. I cut the defensive tackle and then I got up, saw Walter dancing around, and jumped on someone else's back."

Next up for Payton was Gary Barbaro, a second-year free safety. Like Thomas, Barbaro approached the situation perfectly. Empowered by a running start, he lowered his head and slammed into Payton. "Man, I exploded into him," said Barbaro, known throughout the NFL as a dangerous hitter. "I thought I knocked him off his feet, I hit him so hard. But I didn't wrap him up." Payton plowed into Barbaro and the safety dropped like a sack of bricks. "He actually stepped on me as he continued on," Barbaro said. "That's domination." Though he was momentarily slowed from nearly tripping over Barbaro's prone body, Payton outran Howard, who somehow returned to the play, and defensive tackle Willie Lee. By the time Payton was finally brought down, he had broken seven tackles and gained eighteen miraculous yards. A better run has never been caught on tape.

"If you look at the video I'm within three or four feet of him four times," said John Lohmeyer, a Chiefs defensive tackle. "I didn't give up, because it was well known that you couldn't get him down with ease, and he was an escape artist. I tried tackling him—we all did. But when I got near him, he'd already changed his mind and gone another direction."

Payton went on to score moments later, and added two more touchdowns while running for 192 yards in the Bears' 28–27 triumph.

Watching the highlights from his home in Los Angeles was Jim Brown, the NFL's all-time rushing king. Now forty-one years old and retired for twelve years, Brown had largely divorced himself from the sport. He tuned in sporadically, and only knew the names of a handful of players—Walter Payton not being one of them. "It was the first time I saw him," recalled Brown. "And I didn't know who he was and I saw him make this run. He fought for every inch. He must have twisted and knocked three or four guys over. Spun around, accelerated. And I said, 'Oh, my goodness—what kind of animal is this?' "

·   ·   ·

Seven days later, the Bears were scheduled to host the Minnesota Vikings at Soldier Field. Throughout the 1970s, the Vikings had dominated Chicago, beating them eight out of their last nine meetings while owning the rugged NFC Central. They were everything the Bears were not: balanced, well coached, disciplined, talented. Even without the services of Fran Tarkenton, their injured quarterback, the Minnesota offense was explosive, with the punishing running of halfback Chuck Foreman and a pair of dangerous receivers, Ahmad Rashad and Sammy White. Their defense, the famed Purple

People Eaters, was stacked. "We weren't in Minnesota's class," said receiver Brian Baschnagel. "But we wanted to be."

The days following the Kansas City game had been rough on Payton. Still learning how to handle Chicago's bitter winters, he came down with the flu, and was stuck in bed with a 104-degree temperature. Fed a steady diet of soup and tea by Connie, Walter made every effort to recover quickly. He tried practicing, but was largely useless. He tried attending practice as a spectator, but was even more useless. "We sent Walter home," Pardee said on Thursday. "I still hope he'll be ready to play on Sunday."

In normal circumstances, the Bears might have deactivated Payton. They were 4–5 and, despite the thrilling victory over the Chiefs, apparently going nowhere fast once again. Yet Vikings-Bears was more than a game. Finks, the Bears GM, had held the same position for ten years in Minnesota, and if there were one matchup that mattered to him, this was it. Finks wanted to show that his success with the Vikings was no fluke. Do something once, you might have gotten lucky. Do something twice, you're a proven commodity.

With a 6–3 record, the Vikings once again led the division. They were coached by Bud Grant, the icy legend Finks had hired in 1966. Five weeks earlier, the Vikings downed the Bears at home, 22–16. The game had gone into overtime, but that was considered to be a fluke. Asked now to assess the Bears, Grant had little positive to contribute publicly. "One more loss," he said coldly, "and they're out of the play-offs."

A couple of days before the game, Bob Holloway, the Minnesota defensive coordinator, told Bobby Bryant, a starting cornerback who specialized in pass coverage, that most of the playing time would go to the younger, stronger Nate Allen. "They wanted the focus to be on bringing down Walter," said Bryant. "We knew he was all they had." Moments before his club took the field, Grant warned of an imminent tornado. Dressed in their road whites with purple trim, the players quietly sat at their stalls. "The Bears as a team are not very good," he said. "You're better. But I hope you guys are prepared for this, because you're about to face one of the best football players I've ever seen play the game. He has raised the level and standard of play. And if you don't come up and meet him at that level, he will destroy you."

Even in the seconds leading up to his first carry, Payton felt queasy. He had prayed throughout the week for health, asking God and Jesus and anyone listening to bring power to his legs and speed to his feet. Instead, as he prepared for the noon kickoff, his body was besieged by hot and cold flashes. "When I left the dressing room," he later said, "I didn't think I could put on a Walter Payton performance."

It was a typical November day in Chicago—cold, brisk, unpleasant. Save for his ubiquitous white elbow pads, Payton wore nothing but a jersey to protect his upper body from the elements. Having blocked out Gillman and his pass–pass–pass game plans, Pardee's offensive strategy was simple: Payton. "We had three plays to run against Minnesota," said Fred O'Connor, the backfield coach. "One was a power run off tackle. One was an outside sweep to the strong side. And the last one was a run right down the middle, where we isolated on the middle linebacker."

The Bears began the game with the ball on their own twenty-six. On first down and ten, O'Connor signaled a play called Ride 38 Bob Odd 0— both guards, along with the tight end, pull, leading Payton around the corner. "My guy to block was Paul Krause, their safety," said Earl, the fullback. "We had a moat alongside the field, and I drove Paul so hard that I got under his pads and dumped him into the moat. I looked down at him and said, 'All day, Paul. All day.'" Payton gained twenty-nine yards, and the fans cheered in delight.

Avellini was Chicago's quarterback in name only. He waited for O'Connor to call a pass play, but to little avail. His line for the day: four completions, six attempts, thirty-three yards. "If your running back is gaining ten yards a clip," said Pardee, "why would you ever throw the football? We wanted to run to the left side of their defense, and the Vikings kept lining up perfectly. So we ran it down their throats."

By the time the first quarter was over, Payton had carried thirteen times for seventy-seven yards. He broke a hundred yards on his twenty-second carry, and by halftime was up to 144 yards on twenty-six attempts. As was the case against the Chiefs, Chicago's blockers—largely inspired by Payton's determination—were beating up the overwhelmed Vikings. ("We're the only line you'll see running forty yards downfield, looking for someone else to block," a giddy Sorey said afterward.) Yet the story was Payton. Though often credited for brute strength and a hawk's sense of vision, Payton's greatest gift might have been his balance. As other running backs spent their off-seasons lifting weights and sprinting down a rubberized track, much of Payton's time was devoted to either running through the muddy banks of the Pearl River or finding the sandiest dunes and clawing up their slopes. As far as he was concerned, the man who could bolt through mud and muck and sand without falling was the man who could take a hit and keep going. "His balance was unmatched," said Brent McClanahan, a Vikings running back. "There were so many times I would have fallen down if I were him. But he bounced off people like a rubber ball."

"I remember watching Walter from the sideline," said Bryant, the benched Viking cornerback. "All I could think was one thing—'I sure am glad I'm not out there.'"

Despite the awe-inspiring performance, Chicago was struggling to break through. Payton's one-yard touchdown run in the second quarter gave his team a 7–0 lead, and a thirty-seven-yard field goal from Bob Thomas with forty-three seconds remaining in the half made it 10–0. Having been reduced to a well-paid spectator, Gillman could be seen pacing the sideline, cursing audibly and casting dirty looks toward Pardee. Of all the events he had witnessed through his forty-six years in collegiate and professional football, nothing infuriated Gillman more than the day Payton tore up the Vikings. Where, he wondered, were the passes? The play-action fakes? The draw plays? The varied formations? "Someone told me Sid wanted to quit after that game, because any plays he called were changed to handoffs to Walter," said Terry Schmidt, a Bears cornerback. "Jack was old school, so we were old school. But it's a fair question—how does a guy run for that many yards and his team doesn't win big?"

At the end of the third quarter, the Bears led 10–7, and Payton was up to 192 yards on thirty-four carries. One year earlier O. J. Simpson had set the single-game rushing record with 273 yards against Detroit. Payton knew he was having one hell of a game, but there was no mention of Simpson's mark along Chicago's sideline. "It never came up," he said afterward. "I don't like people telling me stuff like that when the game's on the line."

With five minutes remaining, Payton needed sixty-three yards to top Simpson. Were this any other team operating any other offense, the cause would have been a lost one. But Pardee was unbending, Avellini untrusted, and Gillman uninvolved. The ball would be handed to Walter until his arms and legs fell to the ground. "When an opposing defense is told what is about to happen, they usually find a way to stop it," said John Hilton, the Bears' special teams coach. "But not that day. I found myself watching like a fan. All day he would fake like he was going to go out of bounds, then come back and knock someone in the keister."

With less than four minutes on the clock, Payton took a handoff from Avellini on the Bears' thirty-three, charged over right tackle, slashed right, and motored down the sideline. He stiff-armed two Vikings, ran over two more, and finally stepped out of bounds at the Minnesota nine. He was five yards away from tying the Juice. "We had to get it for him," said Don Rives, a Bears linebacker. "To be that close . . ."

After gaining three yards on a sweep around left end, Payton's fortieth and final carry of the day was another sweep, this time to the right. The run was unexceptional but also magical. Payton picked up four yards, good enough for 275.

The Bears held on to win, 10–7—"Ugly and beautiful," said Steve Schubert, a Bears receiver. "Ugly because we scored ten points with Walter running for 275. Beautiful because Walter was amazing."

Afterward, an exhausted Payton sat on his stool and took questions. His miniature Afro was tussled. His shoulders were slumped. Four hours earlier, he was unsure whether he was even going to play.

*Can you do it again?* he was asked.

"Nobody knows that far ahead," he said. "Nobody knows what can happen. Only God knows."

*Is a three-hundred-yard game possible?*

"I don't know. You have to call Him up."

When the pack cleared, *Sports Illustrated*'s John Underwood approached. "One question," he said. "How would *you* defend Walter Payton?"

For the first time all day, the running back seemed stumped.

"Well," he finally said, "the night before the game I'd kidnap him."

. . .

Following the wins against the Chiefs and Vikings, the Bears were 5-5 and, for the first time in more than a decade, a hot team.

Their star was even hotter.

Wrote Phil Elderkin of *The Christian Science Monitor*: "Nobody would ever confuse running back Walter Payton of the Chicago Bears with an expensive sports car, although he often corners as well. Actually, Payton is a mini-tank, almost as apt to run over people as he is to run around them. He has the torso of a Soviet weight lifter, but the legs of Secretariat."

Payton appeared on *The Today Show*. He was asked to take part in the wildly popular ABC television program *Superstars*, in which athletes from different sports compete against each other (it taped at season's end). He held a conference call with seventeen national writers and laughed as two Windy City newspapers—the *Chicago Tribune* and the *Chicago Sun-Times*—provided subscribers with free Walter Payton iron-ons. WORLD RUNS TO PAYTON, read a headline in the November 22 *Tribune*, and it was hardly an exaggeration. Wrote Pierson: "Payton's record rushing brought out a symphony Monday and he conducted it with a maturity that is growing off the field as well as on."

Was Payton still a juvenile pain in the ass? Yes—rolled-up socks continued to soar through the air and pants were regularly pulled down from behind. He ceaselessly mocked Robin Earl for his enormous rear end (Earl: "Walter would line up behind me and scream, 'I can't see! I can't see!'") and delighted in sneaking up on Len Walterscheid, a rookie defensive back, and strangling him with a deathly bear hug. During a trip to Tampa, Albrecht was convinced by veteran teammates to dump a bucket of ice water atop an unsuspecting Payton as he lounged by the pool. "Walter stood up, all wet, and screamed, 'OK, let the games begin!'" Hours later, when he returned to his room after dinner, Albrecht found his bed covered in ice. The next morning, Albrecht's shoulder pads were glued to a wood beam in the locker room.

The one Bear who seemed most irked by Payton was Avellini, the prickly quarterback who resented the excessive praise accrued by his teammate. Avellini, according to one of his offensive linemen, "thought he was better than everyone else. I don't know what he did in college at Maryland, but he thought he was God's gift to quarterbacking. The linemen—all of us—hated him." During a luncheon appearance at Chicago's Playboy Club, Avellini answered a guest's question by insisting he would throw more to Payton as soon as the halfback started running proper pass patterns. At practice the following day, Avellini spotted Joe Lapointe, the *Chicago Sun-Times* writer who used the quote. Avellini launched a pass that nearly slammed into the scribe's head. Walking by, an amused Payton picked up the ball, flipped it to Lapointe, and in his high-pitched cackle, said, "Here, fight back."

"Maybe Walter was annoying at times," said Doug Plank, the longtime safety. "But you had to love his spirit."

The kid whose effort and heart were once questioned by Pardee and Finks was suddenly the toughest Bear of them all. Less than twenty-four hours after his historic showing against the Vikings, Payton could be found at the team's Lake Forest practice facility, jogging back and forth through the chilling winds alongside his teammates. "He was running scout plays to get us ready for Detroit," said Pardee. "He has his head on straight."

With success and fame, Payton noticed teammates beginning to look his way for leadership. While he was hardly one to give a rousing pep talk, his dedication spoke volumes. Payton was usually the first on the field for practice and the last to leave the facility come day's end. He finished off every run with a forty-yard sprint, and could often be found in a dark corner, completing hundreds of push-ups and sit-ups.

Whereas others walked through the locker room in either sneakers or sandals, Payton wore shoes without heels or insoles. At practice. At home. On a trip to the movies. Driving his van. "He thought it built up leg strength," said Plank. "And if Walter thought something could help him, he'd be 100 percent dedicated to the idea. He was always pushing himself and challenging himself to get better. And if you see Walter Payton, a man gifted with so much talent, pushing himself, you want to push yourself, too."

Though the offensive linemen didn't always get along with one another, they came to love Payton. He offered regular credit and encouragement, and following the 1976 season bought each one a gold watch with the inscription THANKS FOR 1,000 YARDS. WALTER PAYTON.

Blocking for Payton was, in the words of Peiffer, "joyous . . . easy."

"Give him half a hole and he would hit it and be gone," Peiffer said. "If you did anything at all to block your guy, Walter was going to hit the hole and be past the line of scrimmage."

When he was scheduled to appear on national television, Payton showed up with his entire line in tow. "Talk to them," he told prospective interviewers. "They make me." While the sentiment was hogwash (if anyone was being "made," it was his mediocre linemen), it was from the heart. Late in the season, he was especially gleeful when Phyllis George, one of the cohosts of CBS's *NFL Today*, came to Lake Forest, ignored Payton, and focused an entire segment on his linemen.

"You need a nickname," George told the men.

"I think we'll be the Beehive," Sorey laughed, "because we protect the Sweetness."

The red-hot Bears traveled to Detroit to face the Lions on Thanksgiving Day, and Payton was held to twenty yards on seven carries in the first half. At the start of the third quarter, the words WALTER WHO? flashed across the Silverdome scoreboard. Payton's first handoff of the second half was a forty-three-yard burst around right end. By the time the game had ended, Payton's statistical line read 137 yards on twenty rushes (he also caught four balls for 107 yards), and Chicago won, 31–14. The Bears were now 6-5 and in the thick of the play-off race.

With three games left, Payton's 1,541 rushing yards left him 462 behind Simpson's single-season NFL record. In the time that had passed between the final week of the 1976 season and now, Payton's opinion of Simpson underwent a change. Though he harbored no animosity toward Buffalo's halfback, Payton wondered why, after the 275-yard showing, Simpson had neither called nor offered a public congratulatory word.

As a running back, Payton liked to think of himself as everything Simpson was not. The Juice was fast and sleek, but about as rugged as a Chanel handbag. He rarely ran through the guts of defenses; footage of Simpson confronting a linebacker or defensive lineman was rare. While Payton shunned the limelight, Simpson was the Reggie Jackson of football—were there a television camera within a hundred yards, he was the one speeding toward it, hair perfectly coiffed, teeth aglow.

"I was good friends with [49ers wide receiver] Dwight Clark," said Steve Fuller, who played quarterback for the Bears in the mid-1980s. "He told me that when O. J. was traded to San Francisco [in 1978] the team practiced on one field and O. J. practiced on the other, stretching on his own. The idea of Walter ever behaving like that was ludicrous."

When asked about Simpson's 2,003 yards, Payton hemmed and hawed and acted as if it were insignificant. But the record *was* significant—to him, to the offensive line, to the coaching staff. "If I don't catch any passes I feel worthless," said James Scott, the team's top wide receiver and a notoriously selfish player. "[But] I love Walter, and I'd like to see him break O. J.'s record. I'll do as much blocking as I can." Chicago won its next two games. With one Sunday remaining, the Bears were the talk of the NFL. Should he exceed 198 yards against the New York Giants, Payton would surpass Simpson. Were the Bears to travel to New Jersey and beat the 5-8 Giants, the team would qualify for the play-offs for the first time since 1963.

Football storylines have rarely been better.

· · ·

They woke up at the Sheraton in Hasbrouck Heights, New Jersey, on the morning of Sunday, December 18, and saw freezing rain.

Generally speaking, such weather didn't overwhelm the forty-three members of the Chicago Bears. When one signs a contract agreeing to make Soldier Field his home, he's well aware of the inclement conditions. "You never fully adjust, you just accept," said Waymond Bryant, the Bears linebacker. "When it was particularly snowy and cold, I used to try and think about a warm place. It worked until someone hit you and you fell across the snow."

In the course of one of the greatest individual seasons in National Football League annals, Walter Payton had run over, around, and through every conceivable obstacle. Frozen rain, though, was the most brutal opponent of all. Especially at Giants Stadium, which featured an unforgiving green Astroturf that made Soldier Field's cement slab feel like a bed of feathers. As soon as he spotted the rain outside his window, Payton knew hopes of eclipsing O. J. Simpson's 2,003 yards were diminished.

"There was no way I was going to run for 199 yards on that surface," he wrote, "so I could just forget about that. The sole concern now was to figure out how to beat the Giants in their own stadium on a terrible day."

The words come straight from Payton's 1978 autobiography, and while they read nicely, the sentiment is untrue. Dogged to the end, Payton wanted the record, and his linemen *really* wanted the record. "The Giants hadn't played by the rules," said Albrecht, the rookie left tackle. "They didn't sweep the field beforehand, which would have been the right thing to do. But before the game our locker room was very emotional. We needed to win. But we also needed to get Walter what we thought was his."

"All of our linemen felt very loyal to Walter, and they probably felt like that record was also *their* record," said Pardee. "But we got to the stadium and there was ten inches of snow on the field. We were a running team. We had a running philosophy. Our running back was the best in the NFL. But ten inches of snow is ten inches of snow."

When the Bears players stepped onto the field for warm-ups, they were shocked. To hell with running—it was hard enough to stand without falling. Ray Earley, the team's longtime equipment manager, had packed everyone's turf shoes for the trip, an enormous error in judgment. As the weather forecasters had predicted, this wasn't a field, so much as the East Rutherford municipal skating rink. "It was a joke," said Peiffer, the center. "The worst surface I've ever seen."

Shortly before kickoff, Bob Markus, a writer for the *Tribune*, called a friend who ran a sporting goods store in New Jersey. The man said he had a couple of dozen pairs of spiked shoes available, if the Bears so desired. Earley bolted the stadium, picked up the footwear, then rushed back. "It was kind of a leathery sneaker with a grip," said Jeff Davis, who was working the game for NBC. "They were better than nothing." By they time the shoes reached the locker room, however, it was halftime, and everything that could have gone wrong for the tennis shoe–clad Bears had gone wrong. The score was 3–3. Chicago fumbled the ball twice, while gaining a mere twenty-one yards on the ground. Half the players were suffering from frostbite, and Payton was shivering by his locker. Snot dripped from his nose. He was coughing. "It was miserable," said Joe Lapointe, who covered the game for the *Chicago Sun-Times*. "There were thirty-five thousand no-shows wisely missing a game nobody wanted to watch."

With the 5-8 Giants playing for pride and a paycheck ("Our organization was a complete mess," said Gordon Gravelle, an offensive tackle. "Dysfunctional inside and outside the locker room."), the host team's primary focus was keeping Payton's name out of the record book. New York excelled in few areas, but it boasted a stout run defense that ranked eighth in the league by allowing just 126.6 yards per game. "The only thing we did well was shut down running backs," said Clyde Powers, a New York defensive back. "We had Brad Van Pelt, who was a strong tackler, and Harry Carson was emerging. That gave us a chance against someone like Walter."

Both teams failed to score in the third quarter, but the Giants took a 6–3 lead early in the fourth when Joe Danelo kicked a nineteen-yard field goal. The Bears responded by marching down the field behind Avellini, whose twenty-six-yard pass to Scott set up Earl's four-yard touchdown run. Bob Thomas' extra point attempt was blocked, however, and Danelo's twenty-seven-yard field goal with thirty-eight seconds left in regulation tied things at nine.

The game was heading into overtime.

"There has never been a worse day to play football, so while I really, really wanted to win, I also really, really wanted the game to end so I could go inside," said Peiffer. "I remember on one play the Giants had an interception on us and I was cutting across field, completely uninvolved. The defensive tackle had an angle on me, and he hit me hard. I landed on my back and slid about ten feet across the ice. My shoulder pads acted as a scoop and loaded my jersey with ice. I looked at him and said, 'Goddamn, was that necessary?' He just laughed and laughed."

The Bears had gone fourteen years without reaching the postseason. Though Payton's chances of breaking Simpson's record had long ago evaporated, Chicago's players wanted to win and get the hell out of the cold and into the play-offs.

Early in the extra session, a handful of short Avellini passes set up a thirty-five-yard field goal attempt. Thomas jogged onto the field, stepped back, waited for the ball to be snapped, burst forward, swung back his right leg, and pushed it wide left. Two possessions later the ritual repeated itself, this time at the eleven-yard line. Thomas prepared to kick, the ball was snapped, and then bounced twice before being picked up by Avellini, who threw an incomplete pass to linebacker Doug Buffone. "I was getting worried there a little," Plank later said. "I was starting to wonder, 'How long can this keep going on?'"

The Bears mounted one last drive. With 1:22 remaining, they took over at New York's forty-five-yard line. Avellini hit tight end Greg Latta for one yard, then for eighteen yards down the middle of the field. The quarterback called for a time-out with forty-two seconds left and returned to the field facing first and ten at the Giant twenty-five. The few remaining fans stood on their feet and screamed as loud as possible. Avellini dropped back and, with linebacker Brian Kelley charging fast, spotted Payton in the right flat. The running back caught the ball, broke a tackle from free safety Larry Mallory, took off downfield, and was finally wrestled down at the eleven-yard line. The run was beautiful but maddening. It was vintage Payton, but his decision not to run out of bounds and stop the clock baffled Avellini. "It's such a macho thing, staying in bounds, and it was very poor thinking," Avellini said. "Now the clock is running. We were so screwed up, so poorly coached, that half the field goal unit was running onto the field while I'm planning on killing the clock with a play. None of this confusion would have happened had Walter run out of bounds."

With thirty-two seconds left and no time-outs remaining, Payton and the other offensive players jogged back off the field just as Thomas and the field goal unit sprinted to their marks. "Part of the field was covered with snow, another part was covered by cracked ice," said Thomas. "And beneath the cracked ice was freezing water." A spindly five-foot-ten, 178-pound Notre Dame grad, the kicker was something of an odd fit among teammates. An avid reader who, twenty-three years later, would become a justice on the Illinois Supreme Court, Thomas was a thinker. At times too much of a thinker.

Now Thomas was deep in his own psyche. This was a big kick. A *really* big kick. He looked up and spotted Don Rives, the team's ornery linebacker, barreling his way. "Thomas," Rives said, placing both hands around the kicker's neck. "You miss this, I'll chop your nuts off."*

Just in case the sentiment didn't resonate, punter Bob Parsons followed with some wisdom of his own. "[He] grabbed me by the shoulder pads and picked me up and said, 'If you don't make the kick, I'll break your neck,'" recalled Thomas. "So I said to him, 'You obviously weren't a psychology major at Penn State.'" Sitting in the stands, Thomas' mother, Anne, was too nervous to watch. She ran into the nearest bathroom and hid in a stall.

The snap from center Dan Neal was perfect, as was Avellini's hold. Thomas kicked the ball straight through the uprights, jumped into the air, and sprinted off the field. Anne was greeted in the bathroom by screams of "We won! We won! We won!" She assumed her son missed—until the reveler was identified as Jack Pardee's wife, Phyllis.

What if Thomas had shanked another one?

"I saw an exit sign to the left," he joked afterward. "I would have had them forward my mail to Asia."

Payton finished with forty-seven yards rushing, his second-lowest output of the season. It mattered not.

Chicago was going to the play-offs.

· · ·

Upon their return to Chicago at eight thirty Sunday night, the Bears were greeted at O'Hare Airport by more than three thousand fans, many of whom serenaded the players with "Mine eyes have seen the glory/Of the coming of the Bears . . ." A large number of revelers wore Bear jerseys. Others held signs, ranging in message from SUPER BOWL–BOUND BEARS to WALTER, KISS MY CHILD.

The Bears had no chance.

In eight days they would open the play-offs with a visit to Dallas, where the 12-2 Cowboys awaited. No matter how many Chicagoans told the players they could do it and no matter how starved the city was for a postseason victory, most of the Bears were well aware this was an unwinnable game. The Cowboys were the class of the NFL, blessed with an all-world

---

* Said Rives: "I like Bob, but he was a typical sissy kicker. I'm true to my word—if he misses the kick, he never has any kids."

quarterback named Roger Staubach, an all-world wide receiver named Drew Pearson, a wondrous rookie halfback named Tony Dorsett, and a defense featuring two of the game's elite linemen, Randy White and Ed "Too Tall" Jones. With the exception of Payton and perhaps Wally Chambers on the defensive line, an argument could be made that none of Chicago's players were good enough to start for Dallas. "It was a total mismatch," said Rives. "There was no way we could have won."

If a couple of Bears entertained even a slight hope of pulling off the shocker, it was squashed when the organization—long known for its thriftiness under George Halas—refused to fly the team to a warmer climate for a week of practice. Instead, Pardee's men were forced to work out in daily blizzards, with temperatures hovering in the low-teens. When the climate was absolutely unbearable (in Pardee's world, anything below five degrees), the team retreated to the Naval Station Great Lakes, which featured a handful of shoddy indoor dirt fields. "Here's how cheap the Bears are," said Earl, the fullback/tight end. "It's twenty-below zero here in Chicago and we have two feet of snow on the ground. Wouldn't you think the organization would fly us down to Dallas and find us a place to work out and prepare? But oh, no. They bus us to a barn about forty miles away, where we work out on a dirt floor. There are chickens and hogs and goats. We went to the barn because it was only thirty-five degrees in there, as opposed to the negative twenty it was outside. Every day after practice I had to take a towel and wipe away the snot bubbles. And they were black, because of all the dust from the barn. How do you properly prepare for the biggest game of your life inside a dirty, chicken-infested facility? You don't."

While most of his teammates were busy grousing about the shoddy conditions, Payton focused elsewhere. A couple of weeks earlier he had been told about the plight of Adrian Lister, a defensive end on the football team at nearby Wheaton Central High School. In a game against Glenbard South, Lister broke his neck, leaving him a quadriplegic. When Payton learned he was the boy's hero, he rushed to the intensive care unit at Central DuPage Hospital, sat by Adrian's bed, and spoke with him throughout visiting hour. Although the eighteen-year-old couldn't speak, he looked up as Payton repeatedly insisted that God's eyes were upon him. "If we athletes remember how lucky we really are, then we can't forget the thousands of Chicago people—including young ones like Adrian Lister—who are in hospitals or sick in their homes during this Christmas season," Payton told the *Tribune*.

"Some, like Adrian, will be in bed when Christmas is long gone. We athletes know how these people admire our talents. So we must give one hundred percent of ourselves in helping the less fortunate."

Even with the big Cowboy clash approaching, Payton was thinking about Adrian. He visited him again in the hospital, and set up the Adrian Fund to pay for the entirety of the rehabilitation costs.

On the morning of Monday, December 26, Doug Buffone, Chicago's veteran linebacker, addressed his teammates. "Look," he said, "I've got [the Cowboys] figured out. They're gonna have to put twelve men on the field if they hope to beat us." That afternoon, the Bears got hammered, 37–7, with Payton rushing for a mere sixty yards on nineteen carries. "We spanked the hell out of them," said Jay Saldi, a Dallas tight end. "All we focused on that entire week was shutting down Walter." While he was dispirited by the loss, Payton couldn't get Adrian out of his mind. The boy would never walk again. He was confined to a wheelchair, his life forever scarred by one unfortunate moment.

Losing to the Cowboys? Big deal.

CHAPTER 15

———— ∞∞∞ ————

# DARKNESS

THE DARKNESS OF THE WORST YEAR OF WALTER PAYTON'S LIFE ENDS HERE. IN
the town he will never again consider home. In the coroner's office he never
thought he'd visit. On a wood table covered with plastic film.

Here.

His father is dead—fifty-four years old, seemingly healthy as a thoroughbred one minute, cold and lifeless the next. When Bud Holmes called Walter to
tell him the news, he was greeted by silence. Long, painful, awkward silence.

"Walter, did you hear what I said?"

Silence.

"Walter . . ."

On the evening of Monday, December 11, 1978, Peter Payton was tending
to his five-acre farm on the outskirts of Columbia. "He called it his planta-
tion," said Holmes. "He grew tomatoes and peas and watermelons there, and
usually went after work to blow off some steam." While driving back home,
Peter stopped at the small grocery store, where he had been going for years. As
he entered the building, he blathered incoherently. "Pete, you better go home,"
one of the workers said. "You look like you've had a lot to drink."

"I haven't had anything," he replied.

Nobody believed him, because Peter Payton was a drunk. The smell of alcohol regularly reeked from his breath, and to spot him passed out on some bench
or in the front seat of his truck was hardly an uncommon occurrence. As the
father of two NFL players, Peter was a recognizable figure throughout Marion
County. When a recognizable figure attaches himself to the bottle, folks notice.

Peter exited the store and drove off. Moments later he crashed into an empty parked car at a gas station. When a couple of Marion County police officers arrived on the scene, they asked Peter to step out of his vehicle, then watched him stumble around, mumbling nonsense. When he refused to take a blood alcohol test, he was charged with driving under the influence of intoxicants and taken to the Marion County Jail. An officer allegedly tried contacting Alyne, but she was in Chicago with Walter. "You're going to spend the night here," Peter was told. "Sober up." He was placed in a single-person cell, with a concrete floor and an open toilet and a small bar of soap. The walls were made of cement.

Shortly before midnight, a handful of inmates screamed for help. Peter was having trouble breathing, and he needed medical assistance. Depending on who one asks, the guards either called for paramedics or ignored the pleas and attended to their business. Moments later, Peter collapsed. His breathing stopped; his gasps for breath silenced. An ambulance was finally summoned, but by the time it arrived Peter Payton was dead.

Walter couldn't believe it. Though never especially close to his father—who concealed his emotions and buried himself in his work—loss was loss, and this one stung. How would his mother cope all alone? What would she do?

Walter knew his dad drank too much, but there was no way he would be dumb enough to drive drunk. Peter Payton—a black man in the Deep South—had never before been arrested. Not once. So for his father to die in jail, all alone, was unbearable for Walter.

When he finally collected himself, Walter asked his agent to go to Columbia and deal with the situation on his behalf. Holmes drove the thirty-four miles from Hattiesburg, met with Robert Bourne, Columbia's mayor, and then headed for the jail, where he ran into Sergio Gonzalez, the Laurel, Mississippi–based doctor brought in to perform the autopsy. Having spent much of his life as a Mississippi power player, Holmes knew seemingly everyone, ranging from the most famous politicians to the mangiest streetwalkers. He asked Gonzalez whether he could sit in.

"Sure, Bud," the doctor replied. "I don't see why not."

Holmes has never forgotten the experience. Like everyone else, he assumed Peter had died of a heart attack. "I watched the whole damn thing, A to Z," Holmes said. "Because I didn't want any misunderstanding." Gonzalez began by making an incision from the left shoulder to the right shoulder to the base of the neck, then south to the base of the pubic bone. He removed the breastplate/sternum to expose the thoracic organs. "Next he takes Peter's heart out and he takes the lungs out, and he checks the lungs," Holmes said. "The lungs are very clear. Then he checks his liver, his kidneys, his stomach—nothing. At this point, the thing he knows he'll definitely find is a rupture in the heart, because it's the only logical conclusion. He gets his heart, he slices it, then he cuts the ventricles.

"Everything's right there, clear as a bell. No ruptures. I remember [Gonzalez] saying to me, 'If I didn't know any better I'd think this man is twenty-one years old, because every artery and every vein is perfect.'" There was one last place to look. Gonzalez retrieved an electric saw and cut off the top of Peter's skull. Gonzalez removed the dura, then sliced the jugular, carotid, and spinal cord, releasing the brain from the skull. "He didn't see anything at first, so he dug in deeper to get into the brain," said Holmes. "Well, there was a thing in there about the size of a big hen egg or turkey egg. He said, 'OK, let's see how long it's been bleeding.' He slices it, and it looks like a bunch of earthworms are hanging there. The brain is just in utter disrepair. [Gonzalez] looks at me and says, 'Well, we now know how he died.'"

Peter Payton wasn't intoxicated, and he hadn't suffered a heart attack. He passed from an intracranial berry aneurysm, a saclike outpouching in a cerebral blood vessel that ruptured and seeped blood into the cranium. Whereas the store clerks and police officers assumed Payton was merely under the influence, he was—in actuality—dying. According to Gonzalez's report, "the clot had been seeping blood into the brain for seventy-two hours and his motor reflexes were impaired." The pathologist's report said the condition would give the appearance that Payton was drunk.

Walter returned to Columbia with his mother, and the media couldn't resist. Paul Harvey, the nationally syndicated conservative radio commentator, told his listeners that Peter Payton had been intoxicated and unruly—and Walter became enraged. "He never forgot what Harvey said," said Ginny Quirk, who later worked for Payton. "That infuriated him." The story had everything to offer: death, race, intrigue. What were the odds of a Mississippi police department letting a black man die all alone *by accident*? There had to be wrongdoing. "I got a call for an interview from a Chicago TV station talking about a civil rights investigation," said Holmes. "I said, 'What civil rights investigation? If there was any wrongdoing, let's blast them. But let's not lose our sense over a whole lot of nothing.'"

Walter Payton refused to comment publicly on his father's passing.

Inside, however, he was livid. Brain aneurysm or no brain aneurysm, Peter Payton had died in jail. Though Columbia was the town where Walter was born and raised, any sentimental attachment was dead. From that point forward, he responded to inquiries about his place of origin by saying, "Jackson." Following his breakout 1976 season, Walter had visited the Columbia Country Club to play a round of golf. This was the spot where Eddie had caddied as a boy, and where, long ago, Alyne made her famed pancakes and hamburgers for the all-white membership. Having brought Columbia substantial fame, and having represented the town with dignity, Walter never imagined he wouldn't be allowed admittance.

He wasn't allowed admittance.

Now, two years later, there was this. One of Walter's close friends at the time was Ron Atlas, the owner of the Pool Hall and Cat House, a Chicago swimming pool store. Atlas was a licensed attorney, and Payton asked him to fly to Mississippi and help Holmes uncover the truth. "I couldn't go for some reason, but I remember the rage in Walter," Atlas said. "The first time I ever saw Walter cry was when his dad died, but then he became furious. He didn't have a whole lot of good to say about his hometown. He believed it was a racial thing, because he knew how Mississippi worked when it came to blacks.

"I really think the death of his father changed Walter," Atlas said. "Not racially, because he was as open-minded as they came. But he was a lot less trusting of people and their motives.

"A lot less trusting."*

.   .   .

The darkness of the worst year of Walter Payton's life begins here, eleven months before his father's death.

In Chicago. At the Bears' headquarters. On the afternoon of January 19, 1978.

Jack Pardee, the only professional coach Walter has ever known, and a man inclined to allow his back thirty carries per game, has resigned to take the same position with the Washington Redskins. The Bears, naturally, are taken aback. Pardee spoke of loyalty and trust and family, then left when a more ideal (and higher-paying) position came along. So what that Pardee

---

* As he grew older, Payton's stance softened. In an interview with ESPN's Roy Firestone in 1989, he said: "The reason it happened is it was a small town and people were not aware as to certain things . . . It wasn't a case of racism. It was just a small-town atmosphere. People didn't know what was wrong."

had spent the final two years of his playing career in the nation's capital? So what that coaching the Redskins was a dream job? The Bears were of one mind on the matter: good riddance. "No one cares that he's leaving, believe me," one player told the *Tribune*.

Added another: "I think we've gone about as far as this coaching staff can take us."

In the company of teammates, Payton nodded in agreement. If a coach didn't want to be in Chicago, the team would surely be better off without him. And yet, Payton was distraught. "I hate to see the guy leave," he told the *Tribune* while practicing at the Pro Bowl in Tampa. "He brought back a winning attitude to the team." Pardee had transformed him from a timid plebe to the recently named NFL Most Valuable Player. By benching him as a rookie, Pardee made Payton question his toughness. By running him repeatedly, Pardee taught Payton how to endure NFL punishment. By handing Payton the keys to the Bears offense, Pardee turned Payton into a star.

Pardee had been rugged and unsympathetic, but he also led an ordinary football team—one lacking a capable quarterback—to the play-offs for the first time in fourteen seasons. Maybe, just maybe, Chicago's players failed to recognize a great thing when they had one.

Over the twenty-eight days that followed, Jim Finks and his staff conducted an uncommonly secretive coaching search. Five candidates were brought to Chicago for interviews:

- John Ralston, former Denver Broncos head coach
- Ollie Spencer, Oakland Raiders offensive line coach
- Bill Walsh, Stanford University head coach*
- Don Coryell, former St. Louis Cardinals head coach
- Neill Armstrong, Minnesota Vikings defensive coordinator

Walsh would go down as, arguably, the greatest coach in NFL history. Coryell would go down as, arguably, the most influential offensive mind in NFL history.

The Bears hired the fifty-one-year-old Armstrong.

---

* When asked about the Bears not hiring Walsh, Mike Ditka said: "What happens if Bill comes to Chicago? I'll tell you this much—nobody would even know who I am, and I'd be tending bar in Dallas."

He was a good man. A friendly man. A qualified man who starred as an all-American end at Oklahoma A&M (later known as Oklahoma State) before spending five years with the Philadelphia Eagles and another three with the Winnipeg Blue Bombers of the CFL. Upon retiring as a player, Armstrong returned to Stillwater, Oklahoma, to serve as an assistant coach at his alma mater from 1955–61, then worked for the Houston Oilers in 1962 and '63. "I really came to love consulting with players and helping make them better," said Armstrong. "I thought to myself, 'Sooner or later, I'd sure like to be a head coach.'" In 1964 he was tabbed to guide the CFL's Edmonton Eskimos, and over six unremarkable seasons the team went 37-56-3. When the Vikings came searching for a defensive coordinator in 1969, he jumped at the opportunity.

Around the league, news of the Bears' hire was greeted with a pronounced yawn. Whereas Walsh was dynamic and Coryell inventive, Armstrong was a room-temperature bowl of vanilla pudding. "Neill was quiet, his gait was slow, he looked you in the eyes, and spoke with a calming voice," said Vince Evans, a Bears quarterback from 1977 to 1983. "He was just such a nice man. Maybe too nice."

"Neill Armstrong was anything but a hard-ass," said Mike Raines, a free agent in camp with the Bears in 1978. "He was the anti-hard-ass."

Like Finks, Armstrong was secretive and tight-lipped. When asked at his introductory press conference about Chicago's unimaginative play calling, the new coach shrugged. "I don't know what people consider dull about the Bears' offense," he said. "If it takes handing the ball to Payton thirty times a game to win, that's what we'll do."

With those words, an audible moan overtook the Windy City. More than thirty years later, Armstrong admits he was merely trying to be nice. "We needed a quarterback in the worst way, and we didn't have good enough wide receivers," he said. "But"—Armstrong laughed—"we did have one big piece."

He met Walter Payton for the first time a couple of days after the press conference, and the man who had once torched his Vikings defense for 275 yards didn't disappoint. Much to Finks' chagrin, Payton had spent the early days of his off-season competing in *Superstars*, the ABC program that pitted athletes from various sports against one another in random athletic events. On the final day of taping, Payton was running alongside water-skier Wayne Grimditch in the obstacle course when he approached a metal blocking sled.

"I was going so fast that when I hit [it] it flew up in the air," Payton said. "And when it came down it rocked back and caught me as I was going around it." The end result was a deep gash under his right knee that required eighteen stitches, left part of his leg feeling numb, and had the Bears up in arms.

Anxious to make a positive impression, Armstrong didn't broach the injury as he and Payton shook hands for the first time. The two were standing inside a room within Soldier Field's bowels. Payton, wearing jeans and a brown pair of cowboy boots, walked with a slight limp. Coach and player chatted aimlessly when Payton bent his knees, jumped straight up, and grabbed hold of a wood beam four feet above his head. As he dangled, Armstrong had a single thought: "Good God."

"A coach couldn't ask for a better present than Walter Payton," Armstrong said. "He loved to practice, he always went hard, he gave it everything he had, he was playful, he was gifted. There are people and there are special people. He was special."

Like most everyone who has ever met Armstrong, Payton took to his new coach. He would incessantly pester him about expanding his role, half-serious, half-joking.

"Coach, I wanna play defense."

"No, Walter."

"Coach, let me return kickoffs like I used to."

"No, Walter."

"Coach, if you ever need a punter . . ."

"No, Walter."

"On and on and on," said Armstrong. "If every member of that team were as eager as Walter, we'd have won the Super Bowl."

The Chicago Bears organization, though, left Payton puzzled. About to enter his fourth season, he looked around at the team's shoddy facilities and cringed. He saw how tight the organization was with money and sighed.* He watched from afar as Finks made one questionable move after another and genuinely wondered whether he was the only person scratching his head. A couple of weeks after Armstrong was hired, the Bears announced that their new offensive coordinator was Ken Meyer, the former San Francisco 49ers

---

* An interesting side-note: To augment his income, Payton signed an agreement with the Playboy Club to speak at a luncheon on the Monday afternoons following home games.

head coach not exactly known for innovative play calling. Were that not bad enough, entering the May 2, 1978, Draft the Bears lacked bullets, having sent their first-round selection to Cleveland for a past-his-prime quarterback named Mike Phipps (the Browns used the pick to take Alabama tight end Ozzie Newsome, who went on to a Hall of Fame career) and their second-round slot to San Francisco for a past-his-prime defensive lineman named Tommy Hart.

What frustrated Payton most, and what made him question his own future in Chicago, was Finks' approach toward renegotiating his expiring contract.

Entering the '78 season, Payton had one year remaining on a deal that would pay him approximately sixty-six thousand dollars in base salary, with thirty thousand dollars more potentially available via performance bonuses. According to a scathing March 13 *Tribune* article titled "How Bear Salaries Rate," Payton—the reigning NFL MVP, who rarely took a play off and who served as the centerpiece of an otherwise inept offense—not only earned less than stars like Buffalo's O. J. Simpson and Washington's John Riggins, but also Redskin halfback Mike Thomas (the Redskins' fifth-round pick in 1975, the same year Payton was drafted fourth overall). Wrote Don Pierson: "Compared with all players regardless of experience, twelve of twenty Bear starters received below-average pay."

Knowing the Bears' thriftiness was starting to wear thin on a city aching for football glory, Bud Holmes, Payton's agent, went on the offensive. To any reporter who asked, Holmes insisted that Payton would demand more than the $733,000 being made annually by Simpson, who had recently been traded by Buffalo to the 49ers. "I wish Walter were a free agent right now," Holmes told the *Tribune*. "That's the only way you know what he's worth. I want to end up with a contract that no one will ever raise a doubt in Walter's mind the fact he's appreciated."

As far as agents go, few were better than Holmes. He was loyal, available, attentive, demanding. This time, however, he went too far. Holmes assumed Chicago's fans would side with Payton, but at a time when America's economy was sagging and the national unemployment rate hovered at 7 percent, even the running back's greatest admirers cringed as the agent uttered nonsense like, "Walter's fans keep comparing him to O. J. They say, 'You're better than O. J. You broke O. J.'s record. Don't accept less than O. J. makes.'"

On July 19, Finks offered Payton a three-year contract paying $375,000 annually. The deal would make him football's second highest-paid player, far behind Simpson but ahead of such luminaries as quarterback Fran Tarkenton and running backs Riggins and Chuck Foreman.

Holmes said no.

Payton reported to Lake Forest for training camp, and while Armstrong was impressed with his work ethic, Payton's mind wasn't 100 percent on the game. On August 8 he told the assembled media that while he was no longer requesting Simpson money, he would play for no less than $513,000—70 percent of O. J.'s deal. He referred to Finks as a dictator, and questioned the team's commitment. For Chicago's largely blue-collar fan base, this sort of bluster was hard to take.

In the case of one legendary Bear, the words served as a final straw. While making an appearance at the Illinois State Fair, Gale Sayers, the Hall of Fame Bears running back who retired because of injury in 1971, was asked about the contract dispute. "There's a lot of things involved in contract negotiations, but I really feel Walter is making a mistake because it can happen anytime—a knee can go, he might have a bad year," Sayers said. "Anytime someone will give you $375,000 or $400,000 for being in the league three years, I think he's very foolish for not taking it."

In the way a young Mickey Mantle had once been shunned by a retired Joe DiMaggio, Sayers rarely had time—or kind words—for his heir apparent. "Walter and Gale had nothing in common," said Fred Caito, the team's trainer from 1972 to 1997. "They were opposite people and opposite running backs. I always said Gale Sayers could have played in a tuxedo, he was so smooth. Walter would have the tuxedo ripped and bloodied in two minutes." When he first arrived in Chicago, Payton craved Sayers' approval and guidance. Just as a groom longs for the blessing of his soon-to-be father-in-law, Payton wanted Sayers' nod. Instead, he received brief greetings and awkward silences; sly jabs and off-the-record criticisms. (In 1997, years after both men had retired, Sayers went out of his way to call Eric Dickerson the best running back of all time—even though Payton held nearly every important record.) To say the slights irked Payton is to delve into great understatement. They stung.

"Gale was jealous, and he never gave Walter credit," said Mike North, a longtime Chicago media personality who worked with both men. "It was a problem. As soon as Walter hit the scene, Gale became an afterthought. But if you ask Gale Sayers who was the greatest Bears running back of all time, alone, he'll tell you, 'Gale Sayers.' He was jealous of Walter. And Walter would say, 'I tried to befriend the guy. I don't know if he's bitter or what, but he had no interest in me.'"

Burdened by Sayers' criticism, as well as that of offensive guard Noah Jackson ("Walter's not running as well as he had," he said during training camp. "I know how Walter Payton can run. It's in his own mind."), Payton was residing in a hell of his own making. A part of him wished he had accepted the initial offer—just grabbed the loot and moved on with life. Now, however, it was too late, and the negative reviews were pouring in. "Somewhere along the way he became convinced that he should be the highest-paid player in football history," wrote David Israel in a *Tribune* column. "Walter is convinced that when he gets his freedom, and goes shopping someone is going to offer him that kind of money. He's crazy."

Finally, one day before the Bears' 1978 season opener against the Cardinals at Soldier Field, an agreement was reached. "Walter actually came into the room and said, 'They're offering me more than four hundred thousand dollars—what should I do?'" recalled Mike Raines, a free agent defensive end out of Alabama who roomed with Payton at Lake Forest. "I'd just played a season in the Canadian Football League making minimum wage. I told him he had to take it."

Payton signed three one-year contracts that would pay him $400,000 in 1978, $425,000 in 1979, and $450,000 in 1980. With incentive clauses that could add as much as $97,000 annually, Payton was now a $1.3 million man. As soon as the news was announced, Payton sat down with reporters, beaming from ear to ear. Even if it was not quite O. J. money, he was happy to be rich. He was even happier for the whole ordeal to be over.

· · ·

The call came to the Chicago Bears headquarters on the morning of Sunday, September 3, only seventy minutes before the opening-game kickoff against St. Louis. A receptionist picked up the telephone, held it to her ear, and heard this: "If Walter Payton plays today, I will shoot him."

The man identified himself as a member of the American White People's Party, an organization with the stated goal of "returning control of this continent to the Aryan peoples who originally conquered, populated, and created its culture and political institutions." He said that four party members armed with rifles and bombs were stationed inside Soldier Field, and that Payton, as well as any blacks sitting in the stands, would be gunned down.

The Bears front office faced a major decision. Finks learned of the threat and debated whether to say something. On the one hand, a person has the right to know about someone itching to assassinate him. On the other hand, the Chicago offense with a distracted Payton was barely an offense at all.

The information was kept quiet.

The Bears won 17–10, and Payton played brilliantly, running for 101 yards on twenty-six carries, catching three balls for twenty-two yards, and scoring a touchdown. Afterward, safety Doug Plank was euphoric. "No one can run an end like he can or add excitement and enthusiasm," he said. "Even when he lost six yards that time when he cut back and danced around, everyone was cheering. He transfers electricity to the team."

As Payton undressed by his locker, Stevie Wonder's *Greatest Hits* blaring from a small tape recorder, he was approached by Israel, the *Tribune* columnist. Midway through the game the media was told of the death threat. Israel asked Payton for a reaction.

"To what?" he said.

Israel explained, and Payton giggled. "When I go out on the field, I believe it's with Jesus Christ's help," he said. "If he said it's my time, it's my time. I can't do anything about it."

Upon further reflection, however, Payton was taken aback. Even though Finks made the decision to keep Payton out of the loop, the running back blamed Armstrong. Shouldn't someone have at least filled him in beforehand? Even if these guys were cranks, wasn't he owed a heads-up? Though never especially close with Pardee, Payton did trust him. The relationship with Armstrong, on the other hand, was off to a rocky start.

Chicago followed up the Cardinals triumph with wins over the 49ers and Lions, then dropped a nail-biter to the rival Vikings, 24–20. Throughout the city, fans were elated by a 3-1 start that had the Bears looking like contenders. Payton, however, was miserable, and needed to let everyone know how he felt. Through the first four games, Payton ran for 298 yards—164 less than the previous season. Usually jovial and upbeat around teammates, he now could regularly be found sitting alone at his locker, a pair of enormous black headphones blocking out the world. Like most of his peers, Payton gave constant lip service to the importance of winning. Football, he repeatedly said in good times, was a team game. "If the team wins, I'm happy." But now the team, led by a rugged defense, was winning, and he wasn't happy. To friends and family members, Payton whined about Armstrong's boring, predictable offense; about Avellini's limited ability at quarterback; about a line that seemed to take plays off and contribute to his pummeling. Following the Vikings defeat, Payton noticed a golfball-sized lump on his forearm that was filled with puss and blood. "Walter was poking it, and he looked like he wanted to throw up," said John Skibinski, a fullback. "His body was thrashed week after week."

Most of his complaints were valid, but the team was 3-1. "People at Walter's level of performance are often moody and guarded, and Walter was no exception," said Caito, the longtime Bears trainer. "There were times when you just left him alone and walked away."

"When Walter got all quiet, all bets were off the table," said Ted Albrecht. "It wouldn't last for long, but when it did, well, you stayed away. Far away."

This was the first time many teammates were exposed to their superstar's underbelly, and they didn't much care for it. Through his first three years in the league, hundreds of adjectives had been used to describe Payton, but never "selfish." He played hard, he played hurt, he stayed in games until the very end. Yet perhaps winning wasn't quite as singularly important to Payton as he'd initially let on. Even Harper, his blocker and best friend, was at a loss. "He wouldn't talk to anyone," Harper said. "He'd get in his own world, put those headphones over his ears, and ignore everything."

Never great with the media, Payton was now avoiding the press altogether. He would agree to interviews, then fail to show up. Or he'd respond to lengthy questions with dismissive one- or two-word answers. *Yes. No. Maybe. Don't care. No comment.* Pierson, thirty-four years old and the best of Bears beat writers, wasn't one to let an athlete walk all over him. In the September 29, 1978, *Tribune*, he teed off. "Payton is acting like a very hollow person these days," he wrote. "Writers and even some teammates are thinking of changing his nickname to 'Sourness.' Or at least to 'Sweet and Sour,' befitting his moodiness. Some wondered if he really did sign a new contract."

"Walter didn't like dealing with the press, and he let it show," said Pierson. "You had to ask him the same question three or four times before you got an answer, and it usually wasn't a good one. I think he took pride in being an opposite sort of guy—you ask him to do something, he takes the opposite route."

Had Pardee still been coach, Payton surely would have been called into the office for a talking-to. "Just so I get this straight, Walter," he'd likely say. "We're three-one, and you're moping. *Really?*" Armstrong, however, was no

Pardee. He wanted to win, but he wanted to win with happy players. "Neill had great credentials, but he was too nice," said Dan Neal, the Bears center. "Discipline fell off, because not as much was asked of us. Football coaches can't please everyone, and Neill probably tried too hard."

Chicago was the least-happy 3-1 club anyone had ever seen, and the outlook only worsened as the losses began to mount. Following the setback to the Vikings, the Bears dropped seven straight games, including humiliating showings against the lowly Buccaneers and Seahawks.

For Payton, there was a series of troubling incidents:

- In the days leading up to a matchup at Green Bay, Payton told a reporter from the *Milwaukee Journal* that the Packers were overrated and unworthy of their 4-1 record. Green Bay's Steve Luke, the starting strong safety, was incensed. "I made a point that week of shutting down Walter and shutting down their sweeps," said Luke. "Every player has one game from their career that sticks out. That's mine."

Though Payton ran for eighty-two yards on nineteen carries, he was merely an afterthought in the Packers' 24–14 victory. Luke, meanwhile, returned an interception sixty-three yards for a touchdown. Whenever he tackled Payton, he made sure to remind him of his words. "It became a matter of pride," Luke said afterward. "Pride is all-important."

- On October 10, two days after the Green Bay loss, police arrested Ronald Schons, a twenty-six-year-old Arlington Heights resident who had been making threatening calls to Payton and the Bears. Law enforcement officials nabbed Schons only after Payton noticed his car slowly circling his home.

Schons' initial threat came on October 1, when he called sportscaster Johnny Morris and said that unless he received one hundred thousand dollars, he would kill Payton. When the demand wasn't met, Schons telephoned the Chicago Park District's central switchboard and promised he would shoot Payton during the next game at Soldier Field.

Schons told police that he was a frustrated football player who had "applied with the Bears to become a member of the team."

- Following a 16–7 *Monday Night Football* loss at Denver, Payton was asked by Morris in an interview with WBBM-TV to assess Armstrong's coaching. "I kind of liked Jack Pardee's philosophy when he was here," Payton said. "He was the type of guy . . . he did everything and used every resource he had to win that particular game, even if it was overlooking running one extra player or using three plays more than the average, he did it. And that was the difference, I guess. Because when you get in a close situation, you put yourself where you stop thinking about your players. With Pardee, he was thinking about his players as well, but he was thinking about winning that game at the time at all costs."

Payton apologized a day later, but the mea culpa was unwarranted. His take on Armstrong was 100 percent correct.

- Back in 1978, two years before they became parents, Walter and Connie purchased a giant Airedale terrier. They named it Sweetness, and took the animal everywhere. Having always desired a pet of his own, Walter was enamored by Sweetness, who possessed the hulking stature of a medium-sized house.

Although the Bears had a strict no-pet policy inside their locker room in Lake Forest, who was going to tell Walter Payton that Sweetness wasn't welcome? On most mornings Payton strolled into the locker room accompanied by Sweetness. The dog snarled, Payton laughed. The dog jumped up on teammates, Payton laughed. The dog defecated on the carpet, Payton laughed. While a couple of Bears players liked Sweetness, the majority thought the dog would be better served elsewhere. Like in a casket.

"Why would anyone want a dog in a locker room?" said Bob Parsons, Chicago's punter. "Especially *that* dog."

Three days before the Denver game, Parsons was standing in front of his locker, lifting his shoulder pads over his head. A handful of players had been messing with Sweetness, taunting the dog with food, pulling his tail, barking wildly. "Well, the dog walks up from behind me, grabs my ass, and bites me right in the butt," said Parsons. "He broke skin. I mean, he literally punctured my skin. Boy, was I pissed off. What was Walter thinking? Why is your dog in there?"

Parsons' mood only darkened when Payton responded to the attack by laughing. "I get home that night and the phone rings," said Parsons. "I pick it up and it's someone barking like a dog. It was Walter.

"I wasn't amused."*

- The Bears traveled to Tampa Bay on October 22, only to be humiliated by the lowly Bucs, 33–19. Payton ran for a paltry thirty-four yards on fifteen carries, but most of the blame belonged to Armstrong and Meyer. Following the game, Dewey Selmon, a Tampa linebacker, said his team knew what was coming. "When Payton lines up at fullback, ninety-five percent of the time he's going to run," Selmon said. "It didn't work every time, but whenever he did that we put [linebacker Richard] Wood on him."

Although the offense had been predictable under Pardee, it had never been *this* predictable. "When I was up in the press box getting ready for the game, I'd write down the number twenty-five and put a circle around it," said Meyer. "That was my reminder that Walter needed to have the ball at least twenty-five times if we were to have any chance of winning."

Through the first eight games, the Bears had opened with a run 88 percent of the time, and started every possession with a run 82 percent of the time. They scored touchdowns or field goals on 40 percent of the series that began with passes, but only on 20 percent of the series that started with runs. "One statistic is indisputable," Pierson wrote. "The Bears have lost five in a row."

. . .

Walter Payton's father died on December 11. Five days later, in the name of pride and professionalism and whatever else one chooses to call it, Peter Payton's youngest son took the field, a member of a bad team playing a meaningless game to cap a nightmarish season.

The Bears beat the Washington Redskins 14–10, with Payton's forty-four-yard touchdown run on the first series setting the tone for a victorious day. His 1,395 yards for the year would rank second in the league, behind a

---

* One of the great tragedies of Payton's life took place a couple of years later, when he accidentally locked Sweetness out of the house on a cold winter day. The dog froze to death. "Walter," said Ron Atlas, his friend, "was crushed."

Houston Oiler rookie named Earl Campbell. Yet those who followed Chicago football knew numbers were meaningless. The 1978 season had been a disappointing one for Payton and a disappointing campaign for the 7-9 Bears.

Even the glow from the win extinguished quickly. With forty-eight seconds remaining in the game and the Bears' offense on the field, Roland Harper found himself eight yards short of one thousand rushing yards for the season. One month earlier the New York Giants were leading the Philadelphia Eagles, 17–12, with thirty-one seconds left. Instead of taking a knee, Giants quarterback Joe Pisarcik turned to hand off to fullback Larry Csonka. The ball was fumbled, and Eagles safety Herm Edwards picked it up and ran twenty-six yards for the game-winning score.

With that image fresh in his mind, Armstrong had quarterback Mike Phipps fall on the ball until the clock ran out. Harper spoke indifferently. ("Neill was a Christian, and I loved that about him," said Harper. "Did I want the thousand yards? Of course. But I was a team player first and foremost.") Payton, however, fumed. For all his greatness as a runner, Payton took immense pride in the crushing blocks he set to spring his dear friend. "Walter was actually a better blocker than runner," said Hank Kuhlmann, the running backs coach. "Without him, Roland isn't close to that many yards." In the history of the NFL, only two pairs of teammates had run for one thousand yards in a season. Now here they were, at the end of an insignificant game, and Armstrong couldn't even reward the team's most selfless, most beloved player with a couple of carries? Was this some sort of cruel joke?

"We were all pissed off after that," said Avellini. "There were plenty of times that season when Roland was supposed to get the ball on a trap play, but when we'd get to the line Walter would say, 'Do you mind if we switch— you block and I run?' I'd turn to Roland and ask if that was OK. And he never complained—never. He would switch. He was just a wonderful teammate. The perfect teammate. You'd do anything for him.

"Against Washington, everyone on the bench knew how close to one thousand yards Roland was, and if Neill didn't, well, shame on him."

Harper wound up with 992 yards and with that, the Bears' disastrous 1978 season came to an end.

Payton did his best to forget the whole year.

# CHAPTER 16

—⟨∞⟩—

# THE UNBEARABLE BEARS

WAY BACK IN JANUARY 1975, A COUPLE OF WEEKS BEFORE WALTER PAYTON was drafted by the Chicago Bears, Bud Holmes received a call from Charles Burch, the father of a member of the football team at Petal High School in Petal, Mississippi.

"Bud," Burch said, "I have a small favor to ask."

At the time, Holmes was best known as the agent of Ray Guy, the splendid Oakland Raiders punter who had starred at Southern Miss. Petal High was planning on holding a barbecue for its graduating seniors, and Burch wanted to know if Holmes—a big Petal High supporter who was hosting the event on his spacious lawn—could have Guy stop by and say a few words.

"Ray's busy," Holmes replied. "I'm sorry."

He was then asked if perhaps Bobby Collins, the soon-to-be-named head football coach at Southern Miss, was available. Holmes checked, to no avail.

"Bobby's busy, too," he said.

Was there anyone, Burch wondered, who might serve as a capable speaker?

"Well," said Holmes, "I have this one kid who's about to be drafted into the NFL. I can bring him."

"Great," said Burch. "We'll see you there."

Four days later, Walter Payton pulled up to Holmes' house, only to be greeted by two hundred or so high school seniors, all white, all dumbfounded by the sight of their black marquee guest. "So they're assembled, eating their hot dogs and hamburgers," Holmes said. "And Walter got up there and started talking, and he told a joke or two and they didn't laugh. And the more he talked, the more silent they were. I was like, 'Damn, these sons of bitches sitting here are being rude to Walter because he's black.' I was ready to run each and every one of them out of there. They come and eat my food at my place and they act like that? It was terrible."

Just when Holmes was about to snap, an amazing turn of events took place. Instead of cowering or slinking off, Payton talked smack. The Steelers and Vikings were scheduled to meet in the upcoming Super Bowl, and he was rooting for Pittsburgh. "One thing I know," Payton told the crowd, "is those Steelers are gonna rip apart the Vikes."

The kids started hooting.

"No?" Payton said. "You don't agree? Who here says Pittsburgh's gonna kick some ass?"

A bunch of hands went up.

"Well, who thinks the Vikings are gonna kill 'em?"

More hands.

"Within five minutes of him finishing that talk, those kids—all white— were shaking his hand, asking for his autograph," said Holmes. "I sat right there and said, 'I don't know how well this boy can run a football, but he has a unique charisma about him that you don't teach.' Just like you don't teach someone to run a football, you can't teach that skill of reading people. You might show them a little bit, but you can't teach it. I recognized right there that Walter had a certain gift from the Lord for communicating and reading people."

Over the ensuing four years, Holmes watched as his client blossomed socially. The same man who would be moody and shy and awkward and dismissive when placed in an undesirable setting (talking with the press, accepting criticism from a coach or teammate, being told by Connie what to do) morphed into a bolt of lightning when the spirit moved him. It was almost as if Payton were two different people—the one who brooded at the most insignificant slight vs. the one whose goal was to make everybody feel wanted. Charlie Waters, the standout safety for the Dallas Cowboys, never forgot meeting Payton for the first time at the 1976 Pro Bowl in New Orleans. "We're at practice, and nobody really knows each other that well so the conversations are sort of stilted," Waters said. "Well, after practice ended Walter wanted to play a game of touch football, so he rounded up a bunch of the athletes and we played touch. He was the Ernie Banks of football. All fun, all joy."

Following the 1978 season, Payton—momentarily interested in becoming a commodities broker—interned at Heinold Commodities, Inc., in Chicago. The company's employees expected a dumb, disinterested jock going through the motions. Instead, Payton was the life of the party—taking coworkers out for lunch; telling loud, rollicking stories; laughing uproariously. "He lit up many a room," said Holmes. "That was Walter."

When it comes to describing Payton's persona, the word "complicated" is frequently evoked. Jerry B. Jenkins, Payton's coauthor on his 1978 autobiography, recalled meeting Walter for the first time at the halfback's home. "He was wearing a skimpy pair of dark green Speedos," said Jenkins. "I thought he had just gotten out of the shower, but later I realized he did this kind of thing all the time just for shock value." A couple of weeks later, Jenkins scheduled to meet Walter for a prearranged interview. Nobody was home when Jenkins arrived at the house, and after sitting in the driveway for ninety minutes he left. That night, when he called the Payton household, Walter's mother answered the phone. "Walter feels bad about what happened," she said. "He wants you to come tomorrow at the same time."

When Jenkins knocked on the door the following day, Payton made amends. "He apologized," Jenkins said, "and as we were talking the phone rings. He picks it up and exaggerates the falsetto quality of his already high voice and said, 'Hello. No, this is his mother. May I take a message?' When he gets off the phone he winks at me and said, 'Sorry about yesterday. I forgot.'

"That," said Jenkins, "was just the way Walter was."

Though not officially diagnosed until later in his life, when Payton first learned of attention deficit hyperactivity disorder (ADHD) he knew he was one of the afflicted. Payton lacked the ability to sit still for more than a minute or two. His mind raced, his fingers twitched, his knees bounced. He could pace incessantly, and when he spoke his hands moved at 100 mph. He alternated between being a great listener and a terrible one. In 1977 Jenkins spent sixty hours interviewing Payton for the book. "While we talked he played pinball, prehistoric video games, watched TV, and painted his trophy room," said Jenkins. "I sat asking questions in the middle of the room while he painted one wall." Patience wasn't a virtue. He usually slept only two or three hours per night, and not by choice. "Were it possible," said Roland

Harper, "he wouldn't have slept at all. There was too much to do and too little time."

"He was fascinated by physical stimulus," said Ken Valdiserri, the Bears' longtime coordinator of media relations. "Anything that would just charge up a moment. A cherry bomb blowing up in front of people and seeing their reaction. He was stimulated by visual and flesh and emotional stimulus all at once."

Reporters hated dealing with him. None stated any dislike for Payton. They simply could not pin the man down. "He was as difficult to capture on paper as he was on the field," said Ron Rapoport, a *Sun-Times* columnist. "You never really felt as if you were getting to the bottom of him. The better he got, the more you wanted to know. The more you wanted to know, the more he kept you at a distance. The tough thing was that we weren't out to get the goods. We just wanted to know the guy and explain the guy. Here was this great player, and we had such great admiration for his abilities. We weren't there to hurt him, but to burnish the legacy.

"There was one game when Walter played brilliantly, and afterward he blew all the writers off. We were livid, because it wasn't the first time. Only later did we learn that he had promised an ill child some time, so he couldn't talk. And why the stupid son of a bitch didn't take us into his confidence and say, 'This is what I'm doing—give me a minute,' I'll never know. He was one enormous enigma."

Was Payton the dark cloud that brooded in the aftermath of insufficient carries, or was he the happy-go-lucky fool who tossed lit firecrackers at teammates' heads and skipped around training camp wearing a sombrero? Why did he seem to take so much pleasure in slapping guys so hard on the buttocks that, come the next morning, they'd be sitting atop a black-and-blue welt? Why were his hugs, literally, suffocating? Why did he relish sneaking up behind teammates and ripping the hairs from their calves? How did he seem so aloof one moment, then remember the name of your cousin the next? "He knew things about you that you didn't think he'd know," said Jimbo Covert, a Bears offensive lineman from the 1980s. "Something going on with your family. The names of your nephews. Little things that no other team-mate would get." Grasping Payton's behavior was like trying to take hold of a wet ferret. He could be the most sensitive person in the room, then turn around and say something that drew gasps and condemnation. Payton was prone to making inappropriate comments about teammates' sexuality that some found funny and others found disturbing. There were whispers around Chicago that he, himself, was gay—understandable scuttlebutt considering his off-putting behavior. "His nickname was Sweetness," said Arland Thompson, the team's fourth-round draft pick in 1980. "He pinched my ass so often I thought he was sweet on me."

"We were taking handoffs in a drill," said Dennis Runck, a free agent running back in 1982. "He slaps me on the ass and says, 'So, I hear you're gay.'"

"Walter didn't practice much during training camp, but he was always there during workouts in shoulder pads and shorts, encouraging people," said Mark Stevenson, who, in 1982, was invited to camp as a free-agent offensive lineman. "So we're going through offensive drills, and Walter's circling the huddle, yelling, 'Pull it! Pull it! Pull it!' He does this for two weeks, and nobody knows what he's talking about. Finally Kurt Becker, another lineman, says, 'Pull what, Walter?' And Walter screams, 'Pull my dick, motherfucker! Pull my dick!'"

"Were Walter alive today, he'd almost certainly have some sexual harassment suits thrown his way," said Duke Fergerson, a free agent wide receiver in camp with the team in 1982. "It's one thing to be playful and juvenile about discovering your sexuality. But Walter would almost be sexually intimidating to these rookies. He'd make passes at guys. He may have been kidding, but coming from someone of that status, it was very intimidating. It got to the point where I didn't want to dress around him. It was too uncomfortable."

Payton was steadfastly loyal (when the club cut a running back named Willie McClendon in 1983, Payton didn't speak to teammates for a week) and steadfastly confounding. He yelled. He whispered. He comforted. He mocked. "He'd meet you a couple of times and then give you a bear hug," said Covert. "Then he'd pinch you. Then he'd flick you in the ear. Then he'd pinch your ass. Then he'd pinch your neck. The he'd goose you. Rookies would come in and say, 'Is he gay?' No, Walter's not gay. He's just strange."

"Walter was kind of a nice guy, kind of a flaky guy," said Jon Morris, a backup center with the team in 1978. Morris joined the Bears for the final season of a fifteen-year career. He had been around some of the game's biggest names, from Jim Plunkett and Sam Cunningham with New England to Lem Barney and Doug English in Detroit. As far as superstars go, Morris said Payton was the daffiest. "He was distant and aloof, yet then he'd do some stupid high school and college frat stuff that made you want to strangle him. You'd take a shower and he'd turn all the lights off. He'd snap you in the rear with a towel. He was a pain in the ass, and yet he was also enjoyable. Few people were harder to figure than Walter."

Here's the odd part: As paradoxical as Payton could seem to those who stuck with the Bears, he was unusually gracious and outgoing toward players brought in with little chance of sticking. Some say this had to do more with Payton's insecurities than his large heart—a lightly regarded free agent from Bucknell or Delaware posed no threat to his job security. Others, however, maintain that he was simply good-guy Walter being good-guy Walter. Whatever the case, from the time Payton arrived in 1975 through his retirement in 1988, countless scrubs and C-listers raved about the star's treatment. They watched in awe as he gave the Lake Forest groundskeeper a break, hopped atop the mower, and cut the grass. They stood dumbfounded as *he* brought *them* cups of water. Whenever he made appearances on behalf of the Special Olympics, Payton would tap a third-string nobody on the shoulder and ask him to tag along.

"I was an undrafted free-agent quarterback from Northern Illinois who was invited to camp only to generate local interest," adds Pete Kraker, a 1979 free agent. "I wasn't going to make the team. But Walter introduced me to his wife, gave me his business card, checked in on me every day to see how I was doing. He had an extra quality about him."

"I was a good football player, but my real gift was being able to sing just like Michael Jackson," said Oliver Williams, a wide receiver and Chicago's twelfth-round pick out of Illinois in 1983. "Whenever he'd see me in camp Walter would yell, 'Michael Jackson—come on over here and sing to me, Michael Jackson!' He always wanted to hear 'Human Nature,' but he also liked 'Billie Jean.' I loved to sing anyway, but singing to Walter was an honor."

When Mickey Malham, a seventeenth-round draft choice out of Arkansas State, broke his arm during the 1977 preseason, Payton was the one who regularly bent down to tie his shoelaces. After Tommy Reamon, a former star halfback in the World Football League, was cut by the Bears, Payton promised to speak at the Tommy Reamon Football Camp in Christchurch, Virginia. (Reamon: "He came that summer and gave the kids a magical memory.") In 1982 Jim Schletzer was a free-agent punter out of Lee-McRae Junior College. This was his fifth training camp in five years, and he had never taken the field for live action. "I'm on the roster for a preseason *Monday Night*

*Football* game against the Chargers at Jack Murphy Stadium in San Diego," Schletzer said. "They brought along four other punters, and we were all supposed to rotate. Well, everyone else got in, and they passed over me. I'm standing on the sideline and Walter walks over and says, 'Why are they skipping you?' I shrugged—I didn't know. From that point on, Walter was bugging the coaches to give me a shot, telling them I deserved a chance to be out there.

"Well, in the fourth quarter—thanks entirely to Walter—they put me in. I got in the huddle, walked back a few yards, stood to punt—and just before the snap Mike Ditka called a time-out. I never punted. But how can I ever forget Water's level of compassion?"

Fans gravitated toward Payton, and he soaked in the affection. On road trips he would always find state police officers and trade Chicago Bears gear for one of their hats. Just for fun, he approached random people on the street, extended his hand and said, "Hi! I'm Walter—Walter Payton." During training camps he handed out large quantities of wristbands and gloves. He rarely (if ever) turned down autograph requests, even when fans interrupted a meal or private conversation. "He understood his celebrity," said Ron Atlas, his friend. "He got the responsibility that came along with it."

Beginning in 1977, at the conclusion of every season Payton appeared on behalf of Buick at the Chicago Auto Show. Standing on a platform alongside a Regal or LeSabre, he would sign one autograph after another until his hand cramped. The payoff was excellent—Payton earned a couple of hundred dollars for four or five hours of work, plus the new Buick of his choice. But his attendance genuinely was not about the money. Here, greeting *his* fans in *his* adopted city, Payton was in his element. Besides a signature and a quick word, nobody wanted anything of him. There was no pressure. No expectations. No hangers-on. As myriad C-list celebrities robotically went through the motions—sign, next, sign, next—Payton charmed away. He kissed grandmothers on the cheeks and wrapped Bear diehards in massive hugs. He looked people in the eye and gave each question serious consideration. When he signed a photograph, his name was usually accompanied by a Bible verse.

Yet, as Holmes notes, "there was a Dr. Jekyll and Mr. Hyde to Walter." Just in case flashy new automobiles weren't enough of a draw, all of the participating car companies hired a bevy of attractive young models to stand alongside the product. With rare exceptions, the women fit a familiar mold— early twenties in age, white skin, blond hair, large busts, blinding smiles.

Like Payton, they worked for hours, waving, grinning, pointing toward a motor or steering wheel.

At age twenty-five at the beginning of 1979, Payton remained awkward and goofy around members of the opposite sex. Even with Connie, now his wife of three years, conversation was generally stilted, and only went so far. Throughout his boyhood Walter's mother was responsible for cooking and cleaning and keeping things in order, and he expected Connie to fulfill a similar role. He didn't care what she thought about football or his contract or, frankly, much of anything. He spent his Saturday mornings soaking in cartoons—a ritual Connie failed to appreciate. (The one thing Payton never watched? Football. "For me to watch a football game at home," he said, "makes about as much sense as a secretary going home and spending her nights typing.") "Connie was very quiet, very sweet, very helpful," said Jenkins. "She seemed to adore Walter, though I did get the impression it was a typical pro jock marriage. Everything revolved around him and she was there to serve."

The couple now lived in a modest house in Arlington Heights, and while Walter apparently loved Connie (When asked to name his extravagances in a 1979 interview with the *Tribune*, he responded, "My wife."), he didn't seem especially interested in her. During his rookie season, when the two were apart, Walter desperately craved her company. But that was loneliness talking. In person, Walter and Connie formed a strange union. The things they had in common—dancing, Jackson State, Southern heritage, quirky humor (they attended the Bears' 1978 team Halloween party as the black Coneheads)—only extended so far. Connie struggled to adjust to Chicago ("[It] just seemed like this cold, faraway, miserable place with these little birdcage houses," she later said.), and they rarely took trips that weren't related to football. Conversational topics were limited. Social engagements were few. When they dined with couples, Walter's time would be fully devoted to the other male. There was little cuddling or hand-holding, and she struggled to grasp his unpredictable moodiness. Smiling, laughing Walter morphed into frowning, brooding Walter with a snap of the fingers. "Connie was real quiet and subdued, which Walter really wasn't unless he got in a funk," said Holmes. "She was not a real forceful person, and back then she was petrified of Walter. Not in a violent way, but in not wanting to get on his bad side. I never got any indication from Connie that she had any interest in going out and partying or drinking or cutting up behind his back. But the marriage was what it was. Connie was very tight with her first cousin Hazel [who was married to Rickey Young, Walter's former Jackson State teammate] and Cookie Brazile [the wife of Robert Brazile, another former JSU player]. I remember all three girls in the office one day and they were talking—'Honey, I'll tell you one thing. He can have all the hos he wants, as long as I get the money.' They all died laughing. But they knew what it was to be married to an athlete, and they surely accepted it."

Perhaps eventually. But in 1979, still in the early years of marriage, Connie didn't recognize the seeds being planted at the Buick events. Here, Walter Payton was king. The models hit on him with a jarring lack of subtlety. Female attendees slipped their phone numbers into his pocket. Walter wasn't quite sure how to respond, but celebrity clearly came with its perks.

Payton was known to talk up his love and commitment to Jesus Christ, and the temptations that came with NFL superstardom seemed to make him crave faith more than ever. Yet the little Bubba who attended Owens Chapel Baptist Church with his mother and siblings every Sunday was now all grown up. The concept of infidelity was nothing new—according to multiple family friends, Walter's father wasn't one to limit himself to his wife.

During training camp at Lake Forest College in 1978, Harper, the Bears fullback/chapel leader, brought Payton, quarterback Vince Evans, and defensive back Mike Spivey into a dorm room. He asked the men to hold hands and bow their heads, then led them in the Lord's Prayer. "We all rededicated ourselves to the Lord . . . being born again," said Spivey. "I am a born-again Christian, and in my opinion Walter exemplified a strong Christian man."

That's what Payton strove to be—a strong Christian man.

"I think Walter was an idealist, and he fought to hold on to those beliefs," said Holmes. "But the ideals got harder and harder to live up to."

．　．　．

It started with the athletic tape. Walter Payton would grab a roll and look it over. Once. Twice. Three times. There couldn't be any blemishes on the white surface. Not even a speck.

When the tape met his approval, Payton lifted his right cleat onto a stool, bending his knee ever so slightly. Using both hands, he pulled the tape as taut as possible, then began the slow, meticulous act of wrapping it around and around the footwear. Once the first shoe was done, he focused on the second.

The process, known throughout football as "spatting," was generally practiced by team trainers and equipment managers as a method of keeping shoes straight and in tip-top form. Yet Payton was particular. He also happened to be, hands down, the NFL's best spatter. "We were together at the 1978 Pro Bowl, and Walter was my personal spatter," said Ahmad Rashad, the Vikings receiver. "He could spat a shoe and there wouldn't even be a wrinkle. Not a single one. The great spatters are incredibly valued. Some trainers can do it, some can't. It's a thing of pride. Walter could do it on your shoe and it'd be just stellar."

Payton's devotion to the perfect spat reflected his devotion to brilliance. The reason he had trouble with, first, Jack Pardee and now, Neill Armstrong, wasn't because they were bad men or even particularly bad coaches. It was because neither one seemed to chase perfection. They desired to win, sure, but Payton rarely sensed any genuine life-or-death desperation from the organization. The Bears were as content prevailing 10–7 as they were 45–3. They took few on-field chances and even fewer off-the-field personnel risks. With the sixty-sixth pick of the third round of the 1979 NFL Draft, Finks tuned out the pleas of his scouts by ignoring a Notre Dame quarterback named Joe Montana in favor of running back Willie McClendon of Georgia. "Chicago's personnel guys will swear to you they went to work that day convinced the team would draft Montana," said Don Pierson. "Finks just didn't want to pull the trigger on that one. He believed in Bob Avellini, Vince Evans, and Mike Phipps." Other NFC teams—the Cowboys and Vikings in particular—went for the jugular. The Bears did not.

As far as wins and losses go, 1979 was a banner year for the Bears, who went 10-6 and reached the play-offs for just the second time in sixteen seasons. Yet Payton, by now in his fifth year, wasn't blinded by the mirage of a soft schedule and some lucky bounces (the Bears beat two two-win clubs, needed a desperation last-second play to overcome San Francisco, and defeated a Jets team lacking its star, wide receiver Wesley Walker). In what many considered to be the best sustained showing of his career, Payton rushed for 1,610 yards and fourteen touchdowns, and caught another thirty-one passes for 313 yards and two touchdowns. "Even that great year he had [1977]," linebacker Doug Buffone raved, "I don't think he was running like this."

With Harper, his invaluable fullback, out for the entire season with a knee injury, Payton was *still* unstoppable. He opened the year with 125 yards in a loss to Green Bay, and tore up the usually impenetrable Vikings for 182 yards a week later. He killed the Cowboys for 134 yards and, in a must-win regular season finale against the Cardinals, cruised for 157 yards and three touchdowns (Chicago dominated, 42–6, and Payton clinched his fourth-straight NFC rushing title).

Even with those magnificent showings, however, the Bears remained a bubble team that could not reach the next level. Now in his sixth year as the general manager, Finks still refused to draft or trade for a top-flight quarterback, believing he could always find some passable schlub for the position. When the Raiders offered Ken Stabler before the October 9 trading deadline, Finks barely picked up the phone. "We told [the Raiders] that we weren't interested," Finks said. "We felt like our quarterback situation was OK."

Payton was incredulous. OK? *OK?* Stabler was a four-time Pro Bowler who led the Raiders to victory in Super Bowl XI. The Bears, meanwhile, were continuing their maddening, never-ending tactic of sticking with one quarterback until that person messed up. Avellini, underwhelming in all phases, started the first three games before giving way to Evans, an athletic phenomenon whose balls went everywhere but straight. "Vince," said Tim Clifford, one of Evans' backups in later years, "was a quarterback who would have been better off playing linebacker." He lasted three starts as well, until Mike Phipps, thirty-two years old and in his tenth NFL season, took over. Together, the three men combined for fifteen touchdowns and sixteen interceptions. "We all got along well, because I think we bonded over the pathetic nature of our offense," said Avellini. "Me, Vince, and Mike were fighting for the job, and we had no receivers to speak of. San Diego gets rid of a wide receiver like John Jefferson [after the 1980 season], and instead of finding a way to get him, we get Golden Richards, the worst player I ever played with. That kind of thing brought us quarterbacks even closer. People blamed us, and probably with some good reason. But we weren't alone. The efforts to improve our team were pathetic."

Particularly depressing was the Bears' October 28 trip to San Francisco, where they faced a 49ers team coached by Bill Walsh, the man Finks failed to hire as head coach. Though he was burdened with a shabby roster filled with crumbs and leftovers, Walsh's revolutionary West Coast offense rolled up 455 total yards against the Bears. Steve DeBerg, a quarterback no more talented than any of Chicago's, passed for 348 yards and three touchdowns, and the Bears could only watch and dream. Though they won 28–27, it felt like a defeat. "To think of what we could have been doing under Walsh," said Avellini. "It was torturous."

By virtue of their 10-6 record, on December 23 the Bears traveled to Philadelphia to play in the NFC Wild Card game. Though the Eagles captured the NFC East title with an 11-5 mark, Chicago's players were confident. When asked about Harold Carmichael, Philadelphia's star receiver, defensive back Allan Ellis shrugged. "What about him?" he said. "The thing about Carmichael is you have the challenge of not forgetting the other receiver . . . I forgot his name."

"We have as good a chance to go to the Super Bowl," added Armstrong, "as any other team."

Known throughout the league as home to the most vile, most insidious fans, Veterans Stadium was a miserable place to play. The screams were loud, the taunts were tasteless, the artificial surface flimsy and unforgiving. Yet despite being three-point underdogs, the Bears came ready to play. Payton punched it in for two first-half touchdowns, and at halftime Armstrong's scrappy team held a 17–10 lead.

Early in the third quarter, on first and ten at their own fifteen, the Bears called for Z Crack 28. Phipps handed the ball to Payton, who—despite suffering from a painful pinched nerve in his shoulder—busted wide right, turned upfield and took off. He ran eighty-four yards to the Eagles' one before being pulled down by cornerback Herm Edwards. "That was the prettiest run I've ever seen," said Claude Humphrey, an Eagles defensive end. "I was on the field, and the way he ran after he broke into the secondary, he looked like a fine racehorse taking off into the open."

There was one problem. Seconds before the ball was snapped, receiver Brian Baschnagel moved. The left-to-right trot was legal to everyone in the stadium, but not referee Red Cashion, who threw a flag and penalized the Bears for illegal motion. "The official told me I was going toward the line when the ball was snapped," said Baschnagel. "I was confused and uncertain about what I'd done. The next training camp Dave McNally, the NFL's head of officials, came to talk to us about the rules. He walks into the room and said, 'Before anyone says anything, it was a bad call.'" Payton's eighty-four-yard scamper was voided. Momentum vanished. "From there," wrote the *Tribune*'s Bob Verdi, "the Bears slipped from great expectations into the Schuylkill River."

Chicago wound up punting—and losing, 27–17.

Following the game, the locker room was library quiet. Even though his gut told him the officials had erred, Baschnagel was devastated. The stereo-typical scrappy, slow, undersized (five foot eleven, 187 pounds) white receiver, Baschnagel stuck for ten years with the Bears primarily because of his atti-tude. "You wished all your players had his heart," said Armstrong. "He was like Walter in his devotion to hard work." Baschnagel's parents, Arthur and Dorothy, Philadelphia residents, had attended the game, as did his younger brother, Steve. The day meant everything to him. "I had my head down in my locker, hurting," he said. "And at that moment Doug Gerhart, our receiv-ers coach and someone I was very close with, told me in private he'd be leav-ing coaching to get into the family business. The combination of the loss, the penalty, and Doug's words got me glassy-eyed, and I started crying. Walter comes up, puts his arm around me, and he said, 'Brian, I know you feel terri-ble about that call.' And he consoled me and said, 'If everybody on the team had the attitude you have, we'd be going to the Super Bowl.'

"It was so classy. Walter had eighty-four yards taken away from him. He easily could have blamed me. Instead, he saw I was hurting and tried to make me feel better. I'll never forget that.

"Never."

. . .

The Philadelphia Eagles advanced to the Super Bowl.

The Chicago Bears went home.

Payton spoke optimistically of better days to come; of a franchise headed in the right direction. He was encouraged by some of the changes being made from within. In the summer of 1980 the team moved into Halas Hall, the $1.6-million meeting spot/dormitory/operations center located adjacent to Lake Forest College's Farwell Field. No longer were the Bears' facilities fourth-rate. No longer would players think of the team as a haven for cheap-skates.

Despite Finks' failure to land a quarterback of note, high-quality drafts were slowly beginning to yield results. "I don't like the word 'building,'" Finks said. "I just think we have the right people here to continue being a good football team." In 1979, the Bears used their two first-round picks on defensive players, a tackle out of Arkansas named Dan Hampton and a defen-sive end from Arizona State named Al Harris. The two became key con-tributors, and started for most of the ensuing decade.

The following year, Finks once again hit big in the first round, selecting an athletic linebacker from Louisville named Otis Wilson. Payton was ecstatic (the Bears' overall philosophy started with defense, and he was comfortable with that) until he learned that Finks spent a second-round selection on a fullback.

In taking Matt Suhey, a five-foot-eleven, 217-pound bowling ball out of Penn State, Chicago seemed to be giving up on Roland Harper, Payton's longtime blocking back who missed the entire 1979 season with a tear in the anterior cruciate ligament in his right knee.

Although not quite as tight as they had been as rookies, Payton and Harper remained close friends and devoted on-field comrades. Dave Williams did a serviceable job in Harper's stead, but Payton missed the crushing blocks that had been his pal's staple. As the Bears won ten games and advanced to the postseason, Harper watched from his couch, miserable and depressed. "I prayed," Harper said, explaining his recovery. "I prayed for His will to be done. If He gives you the strength, that's all you need."

Payton applauded Harper's efforts. He encouraged him and cheered for him and assumed normalcy would return in 1980.

Then, Suhey arrived.

Payton hated him immediately. "Walter assumed I was brought in to get rid of Roland," said Suhey. "He wasn't nice to me at all. He didn't talk to me and barely acknowledged me." Suhey long believed that Payton's negativity was solely about Harper. It was, however, more than that. For the first time, Payton was able to see the reality of his inevitable gridiron mortality. Harper had been one of the Bears' offensive captains for three seasons. He was quiet and respectful and universally beloved by coaches, players, and administrators. He played hard and worked out even harder.

What did it say about the Bears—about the NFL—that all the sacrifice and effort rendered Harper replaceable? One day, Payton realized, he would be replaceable, too.

Although Harper returned to start twelve games in 1980 (and limit Suhey to special teams duties), Payton was shaken by what Suhey's arrival signified. He was also shaken by the death of hope and optimism. Based upon their previous campaign, Chicago was the thinking man's pick to win the NFC Central and, just maybe, the Super Bowl. Yet the '80 Bears were once again dreadful, finishing 7-9 as an all-engulfing listlessness cloaked the offense. The discipline that Pardee once tried to instill had all but vanished. John Schulian, a columnist for the *Sun-Times*, recalled watching Evans and

Payton, standing ten feet apart along the sideline during practices, blistering the ball to one another. "It was begging Walter to break a finger or hand, and a person with real authority steps in and stops it," said Schulian. "But Neill didn't say anything because Walter was bigger than the team. It was a sad scene."

What irked Payton most was the offensive coaching staff's continued devotion to dull, outmoded football. On the other side of the ball, defensive coordinator Buddy Ryan had transformed his unit into a snarling, barking, growling pack of animals. "If I never face another defense like them, it'll be too soon," Cleveland quarterback Brian Sipe said. "They're terrific." The Bears defense ranked fourth in the league, and while the talents of players like Hampton, Wilson, and hard-hitting safeties Gary Fencik and Doug Plank were substantial, it was Ryan's attitude and gusto that fed the monster. "Buddy took the players he had and said, 'I'm gonna design a scheme for these players and make it work,'" said Plank. "And we fought for him. There were times he'd ask two safeties to be linebackers and we'd think, 'What are you doing?' But Buddy believed in us, so we believed in him. You wanted to win for him." Throughout the week, Ryan encouraged his players to punish those on the other side of the ball. Defensive linemen threw punches, cornerbacks taunted, linebackers gauged eyes and pulled hair. The result was a strained locker room, as well as a gaggle of black-and-blue offensive linemen and receivers. The only player defenders couldn't mess with was Payton. "That's because of how much respect and love I had for Walter," said Ryan. "I counted him as a defensive player, because if our quarterback threw an interception it'd almost always be Walter making the tackle. Also, I didn't want my guys hitting him because he was all we had. Without Walter, we wouldn't have scored a point."

On November 3, in a nationally televised *Monday Night Football* game in Cleveland, the offense hit a new low. With the Browns leading 3–0 early in the second quarter, Chicago marched down to the Cleveland twenty-three-yard line. Facing a third-and-eleven, Ken Meyer, the offensive coordinator, called a draw play to Payton. "A resoundingly innovative draw play," Bob Verdi wrote in the next morning's *Tribune*. "It put the Bears five yards closer to a field goal, which they missed. But that's not the point. Going for three points on third down, let alone fourth down, is the point."

Payton's frustration mounted with each loss. He complained to the media about the pounding he was taking (Payton often joked with John Skibinski, a white fullback, that "It's hard to see the bruises on a black guy."), and rightly wondered whether Chicago would ever field a Super Bowl–caliber club. By season's end, Payton had turned into the one thing he thought he would never become: a man after the money. As Bud Holmes reminded him on multiple occasions, winning wasn't the only way to win. According to his contract, Payton could earn an extra ten thousand dollars for clearing twelve hundred yards, five thousand dollars for fifteen hundred yards, seventy-five hundred dollars for two thousand yards and seventy-five hundred dollars for being involved in 70 percent of the Bears' offensive plays. On December 7, as Chicago cruised to a meaningless 61–7 home decimation of Green Bay, Payton kept on running. And running. And running. He scored his third touchdown to make the score 48–7, then defied Armstrong by returning to the game when the scoreboard read 55–7. "When you see guys like him coming back in with the score that lopsided, it kind of sticks in your mind," Estus Hood, a Packers cornerback, said afterward. "We'll remember it next time." By the time the final whistle blew, Payton had run for 130 yards on twenty-two carries, vaulting ahead of Detroit's Billy Sims and the Cardinals' Ottis Anderson into the NFC rushing lead. It was a rare happy moment in an otherwise dark run. "He wants that rushing title," guard Noah Jackson laughed afterward. "Probably means ten thousand dollars, and I get a piece of that rock, too."

Payton's 1,460 yards led the NFC.

. . .

Although 1980 had been a dispiriting year for Payton, it ended well. On December 26, Connie gave birth to the couple's first child, a boy named Jarrett Walter (he was named after a character from the television program, *The Big Valley*). "My son brought me tremendous joy and inspiration," Payton said. "I looked at him like he was going to be my hero someday."

When it came to nurturing and coddling a baby, Walter—like most male professional athletes of the era—knew little. Diaper changing was something a wife or nanny did. So was feeding. And pushing the stroller. And waking up in the middle of the night for a soothing moment in the rocking chair. Payton was elated to have a son, and when asked, he offered up all the right quotes. ("I want to give my child all the love I can.") But he wasn't a hands-on, heavily involved dad in the beginning.

One thing Payton felt compelled to do, though, was make certain Jarrett had a proper baptism. Which meant he first had to have a proper godfather.

Shortly after Jarrett's birth, Payton called Ron Atlas, his friend who owned the swimming pool store, and told him he was coming over for a visit. "Ron," Payton said, "I want you to be Jarrett's godfather. Are you up for that?"

"I'm honored," Atlas replied. "But you know I'm Jewish, right?"

"I don't care," Payton replied. "But just so you know, you have some real responsibilities."

"Like what?" Atlas asked.

"Like getting him baptized," Payton replied.

"Baptized," Atlas said. "I'm a Jew. What the hell am I gonna do about that?"

Payton shrugged. "Not my problem," he said. "Yours."

The next day, Atlas telephoned the offices of Rainbow PUSH, Jesse Jackson's religious and social development organization. He asked for the minister, and was shocked when he picked up the phone. "Reverend Jackson," Atlas said, "you don't know me and I don't know you, but I'm friends with Walter Payton and I have to get his son baptized. I'm Jewish, and I have no idea what I'm—"

Jackson interrupted. "Mr. Atlas," he said, "leave it all to me."

Two weeks later, Jarrett Payton was baptized by Jesse Jackson inside a ballroom at the Hilton in Arlington Heights. More than two hundred people attended the ceremony, and even Walter had to admit his friend did a heck of a job. "I was feeling great, because I'd pulled it off," Atlas said. "At the end of the night a stranger came up to me and said, 'Do you have the envelope for Reverend Jackson?'"

"What envelope?" Atlas asked.

"The one," he said, "with the money in it?"

"I gave five hundred dollars," said Atlas. "Well worth the price of admission."

.   .   .

Entering 1980, Payton genuinely believed the Bears had a chance of contending for the NFC title. Entering 1981, Payton knew the reality at hand: His team was horrible.

Worst of all, there was no escape. With the expiration of the third of the three one-year contracts he had signed in 1978, the NFL's top running back was, technically, a free agent, available for all twenty-eight teams to bid on. Yet free agency in the National Football League was merely a mirage. Not only did a player's last team have the right to match any offer, but widespread collusion among owners made said offers nonexistent (all teams were guaranteed $5.8 million annually via the NFL's television deal, thereby eliminating the need to spend on free agents to actually improve their teams). Here was Payton, twenty-eight years old, in his prime, and wildly popular, and no other teams requested meetings. "I talked to a lot of clubs, just social conversation," Holmes said. "No one ever acted seriously."

When Holmes told the *Tribune* Payton would demand one million dollars annually, George Halas, the team owner, laughed. "There's no way we're going to pay him that," he said—and he was correct. The Bears held all the cards.

Having been brought up with little money, the young Payton was generally disinterested in his own finances. He made a few investments, only checked his books every so often, trusted Holmes enough to assume the agent would do him right. Now, however, with the birth of Jarrett, his bank account became an understandably greater priority.

That's why, when the NFL's owners colluded against him, Payton turned his attention north, where the Montreal Alouettes of the Canadian Football League were plotting an invasion. Under the new ownership of a forty-three-year-old real estate magnate named Nelson Skalbania, the Alouettes were in the midst of an NFL raid that left the American league shuddering. Within a week's time, Skalbania had signed Vince Ferragamo, the star quarterback of the Los Angeles Rams, and James Scott, the moody-yet-skilled Bears receiver. Payton was the next—and biggest—target on his hit list. "I've offered Payton a contract," Skalbania said. "I shouldn't be saying this because, when you print it, the Chicago Bears are going to realize the situation and the price will go up. But I need a good running back."

Though Payton didn't want to leave the NFL, he couldn't ignore Montreal's offer, which was rumored to be around eight hundred thousand dollars annually. ("If Tokyo has a team," Payton said, "even they're a possibility.") Nor, for that matter, could the Bears, a franchise with a single star and a bleak future without him.

Payton and Holmes spoke at length about Montreal. Canada was, they both knew, a last resort. The fans were less rabid, the quality of play was merely OK, the United States' interest in the CFL was subzero. Eddie Payton, Walter's brother, had spent a season with Ottawa, and although he was one of the league's better players, in America it was as if he were invisible.

Most problematic was Skalbania—an unknown quantity with an iffy reputation. Holmes assumed he possessed the money, but he didn't know for sure. "Walter wanted to be a Bear," said Holmes. "And he wanted to stay a Bear."

Finally, on July 25, Payton and Chicago agreed to three one-year contracts worth close to seven hundred thousand dollars annually, plus incentives. Normally, a professional athlete would be giddy over becoming his sport's highest paid player. But not Payton. He signed because it was his only viable NFL option, and upon reporting to training camp refused to gush over the hiring of Ted Marchibroda as the new offensive coordinator or over Armstrong's insistence that the passing game was about to bloom. By now the happy-happy blather only irritated Payton. All one had to do was look around the locker room. Same quarterbacks, same receivers (minus Scott), a couple of young, inexperienced offensive linemen, and an attitude conducive to failure.

"I learned to be disillusioned that season," said Tim Clifford, a rookie quarterback who spent the year on injured reserve. "The intensity level in camp was incredible, and as soon as the season started half the players coasted. Those guys were on cruise control. It was embarrassing."

"The chemistry on that team was horrible," said one Bear, on the condition of anonymity. "We had some talented players like Walter and Doug Plank and Gary Fencik, but you knew very early on we were going to fail." Specifically, the player points to a coach who regularly arrived at practices smelling of alcohol, and an incident from training camp, when a high-profile member of the offense allegedly slept with a teammate's wife. "The guy who caught him beat the shit out of him," he said. "The locker room was split."

Though far from an A student at Jackson State, Payton was no idiot. This, he told anyone who'd listen, was not a good football team.

Chicago opened the 1981 season with a 16–9 loss to the Packers at Soldier Field (BEARS, PACKERS PLAY A YAWNER, read the *Tribune* headline), and followed with a 28–17 setback at San Francisco. In that game Payton—who in past seasons rarely coughed up the ball—fumbled twice, including one at the 49ers' one-yard line. The team finally won with a 28–17 thumping of lowly Tampa Bay in Week 3, but, after gaining a mere sixty-four yards on the ground, Payton lost it. He could accept losing (as a Bear, he had little choice) and he could accept bad games, but this was too much. The offensive line was borderline dysfunctional, opening dime-sized holes and failing to stay with its blocks. "The linemen were big, slow, and fat," said

Jack Deloplaine, a former Bears fullback. "When I was with Pittsburgh, all the linemen benched well over five hundred pounds. In Chicago, they weren't even close." When asked about his inability to gain a hundred yards through the first three games, Payton stepped out of character and pointed a finger at his blockers. "It got to the point where there wasn't any place to go," he said. "I attacked the defense. As a result of that, I had guys who were trying to tackle me lying on the ground. I broke my shoulder pads. Look at my [cracked] helmet." Teammates were shocked. If there was one guy who never blamed others, it was Payton. "Pay me eight hundred thousand dollars," responded an irritated Noah Jackson. "I'd take some shots. And I sure wouldn't be talking about my offensive line."

The following week, after gaining forty-five yards in a Monday night loss to the Rams, Payton was reminded of the time he presented his offensive linemen with gold watches. "This year," he said, "I'll give 'em pieces of my body."

None of Payton's body parts were absorbing greater abuse than his knees. At the conclusion of most games, he could be found on a training table, one knee covered with three or four ice bags, the other being drained of pus and fluid. The ritual was one Payton dreaded—he was terrified of needles, even when he knew an injection would ease his pain. "No teammate could question Walter's guts, because they saw him on that table, hurting," said Fred Caito, the Bears trainer. "I don't think anybody knows how he played week after week, because the abuse he absorbed would have killed bigger men."

It wasn't until the eighth week of the season that Payton cleared 100 yards in a game (107 in a 20–17 overtime victory against San Diego), but by then there was nothing left to salvage. At 2-6, Chicago was far out of the play-off race. With 537 yards, Payton was far out of the rushing race. The fans did not respond well. Jerry Kirshenbaum, the editor of *Sports Illustrated*'s Scorecard section, gave his Sign of the Year award to a Soldier Field spectator whose banner read CHICAGO HAS MORE DOG TEAMS THAN THE YUKON. After paying $58.40 for two tickets to the Bears' 24–7 loss to Washington on October 11 (Payton ran for five yards), James Tulley, a thirty-one-year-old school-supply salesman from Rockford, Illinois, filed a small-claims complaint against the organization for "misrepresenting itself as a professional football squad."

"We were the Bad News Bears," said Brian Cabral, a rookie linebacker. "At Soldier Field they actually put awnings and a tent over the tunnel we came in and out of to protect us from the beer and stuff the fans would throw on us and Neill."

Don Pierson, the spectacular *Tribune* beat writer, began receiving letters from readers demanding Armstrong replace Payton in the starting lineup with Willie McClendon, the third-year backup out of the University of Georgia. "I wanted to play," said McClendon. "I mean, I really wanted to play and I was frustrated on the bench. But anyone who thought Walter should sit was crazy. He was all we had."

Payton liked to tell people he didn't care what others thought, but the sentiment was false. Like most superstars, he longed to be admired and respected. Yet in the midst of a nightmare, admiration and respect were in limited supply. On his weekly radio show, Finks made a shocking decree. "Maybe Walter's best years are behind him," he said. "It would be foolish to think his best years are ahead of him. I don't think we have to feature him as much."

Payton was all alone. His line was terrible, his coach inept, his GM dismissive. Harper, his best friend, would start two games, the damage from three knee surgeries more pronounced than ever. Evans, the quarterback, threw the ball with J. R. Richard velocity and Steve Blass accuracy. "We had nothing—absolutely nothing," said Al Harris, the defensive lineman. "But Walter was about pride, and if you said he couldn't do it, he would find a way."

During a practice in mid-November, Payton became livid when Hank Kuhlmann, the Bears' gruff backfield coach, ripped him for a missed assignment, then told the halfback that he'd lost a step. Payton charged at the coach, throwing a wild punch that grazed his nose. Dumbfounded teammates separated the two. "Did we argue?" asks Kuhlmann. "Hell yeah, we argued. I was a taskmaster and he was a perfectionist. But I loved Walter."

For Payton and the Bears, the year couldn't end soon enough. They somehow beat Denver 35–24 in the season finale, then stripped off their uniforms as quickly as possible. "Before that game all of our cars were packed and ready to get out of town," Cabral said. "The last thing we wanted to do was savor that horrible year."

For the first time since his rookie year, Payton failed to make the Pro Bowl. His 1,222 rushing yards were the second lowest of his career. When asked, Hampton, the star defensive end, said he wouldn't put a broom to the Bears' offensive personnel—he'd break out a vacuum cleaner.

Before that could be done, however, an important decision needed to be made.

The Chicago Bears were about to be in the market for a new coach.

CHAPTER 17

A ROSE IN A DANDELION GARDEN

THE LETTER WAS COMPLETELY OUT OF LINE.

Mike Ditka has never admitted as much, but as one who lives according to a strict code of honor and righteousness, he almost certainly knows this to be true.

Midway through the 1981 season, when the Bears were once again embarrassing themselves, Ditka wrote to George Halas. At the time, the man known as "Iron Mike" was in his ninth year as an assistant with the Dallas Cowboys. Though he loved working for Coach Tom Landry and considered being a part of America's Team an incredible honor, from afar Ditka followed Chicago football with maddening frustration. He couldn't understand how one of the NFL's great franchises—one that had won eight league championships— was now the butt of jokes.

From 1961 to 1966, Ditka starred as the Bears' burly, rugged tight end, a hard-hat complement to the stylish Gale Sayers. He came to love the Windy City, from the brutal winters and unforgiving winds to the blue-collar fans braving negative-twenty-degree chills to catch a game. Hell, Ditka *was* Chicago.

So it was that one day, while sitting in his office at the Cowboys' lavish Valley Ranch facility, Ditka grabbed a pen and a sheet of paper and jotted down a short note to Halas, asking to be considered for Chicago's head coaching position should it become available.

If there is one ironclad rule that governs coaching searches in professional sports, it's that you never undercut a peer while he's holding a position. If you want to vie for a job, fine—just wait until it's vacant.

For Ditka, however, the opportunity to coach the Chicago Bears transcended all decorum. Once asked by *Sports Illustrated*'s Curry Kirkpatrick to name the most cherished accomplishment of his two decades in organized football, Ditka did not evoke winning a Super Bowl as a player or as an assistant coach or lasting twelve years as a tight end or appearing in five Pro Bowls. "I am proudest," Ditka said, "of being a Bear."

He was born on October 18, 1939, in Carnegie, Pennsylvania, the grandson of Ukrainian immigrants who changed the family name from Dyzcko (pronounced ditch-co in Polish) to Disco to, finally, the rugged-sounding Ditka (writer's note: imagine Mike Ditka as Mike Disco?). The oldest of four siblings, young Mike grew up in a government-subsidized housing project in Aliquippa, Pennsylvania, and inherited his famed work ethic from his father, Mike, Sr., a former marine who made ends meet as a steel and mill worker. "We played sports day and night," Ditka wrote in his autobiography. "In the spring, it was baseball until the sun went down. Football was the same way. Our fingers would crack and break open from playing basketball on the cold and wet court with a wet basketball. It didn't matter. That's all we had."

Like Walter Payton, Ditka was a late bloomer whose childhood was filled with church, mischief, and beatings. Once, as a third grader, he bought a pack of Luckies, marched out to the woods behind his house, took a puff or two, then tossed the cigarette to the ground. When his father returned home from work that night, he asked his wife, Charlotte, why the woods no longer existed.

"You'll have to ask our son," she said. "He burned them down."

The beating that followed was conducted with an old leather marine belt. It was the worst Mike Ditka ever received.

As a sophomore at Aliquippa High, Ditka stood five foot seven and 130 pounds. He tried out for the junior varsity football team as a defensive back, but was kicked off the practice field by coach Carl Aschman after absorbing one too many thumpings. He was ordered by the staff to prove his worth by cleaning the locker room latrines—an indefensibly cruel assignment that motivated the boy to come back stronger, faster, *meaner*. That summer he grew three inches and gained thirty-five pounds, then made the varsity as a middle linebacker. As a senior, Ditka—a muscular 185 pounds—emerged as one of the state's top players. "My whole life was based on beating the other guy, being better, being equal to, or just showing that I could be as good as anyone else," Ditka said. "I don't know if that's good or bad."

Ditka went on to the University of Pittsburgh, where he punted and played linebacker and tight end from 1958 to 1960. Were there more talented and polished players across the United States? Unquestionably. Was there a more driven one? No. Pitt's coaches stopped scrimmaging Ditka during the week, for fear that he would knock out teammates in the lead-up to a big game. "Pound for pound, Mike was as tough as any man I ever saw," said Jim Traficant, a Pitt quarterback who later went on to become a Democratic congressman from Ohio. "Tough and intense. He's the only visiting player I ever heard of who got a standing ovation at Notre Dame after rubbing a lot of Irish noses in the dirt."

Nicknamed "Pinhead" by teammates for his marine-styled crew cut, Ditka was respected for his soft hands (playing in an offense that rarely passed, he totaled forty-five receptions over three seasons) and feared for his Tasmanian Devil temper. When the Panthers trailed Michigan State at half-time during Ditka's senior year, a cornerback named Chuck Reinhold tried giving a spirited locker room pep talk. Ditka grabbed Reinhold and slammed him against a locker. "Whattaya mean, we'll get 'em?" he screamed. "You son of a bitch, if you hadn't missed that damn tackle we wouldn't be in this god-damned fix!" According to teammates, during another game Ditka punched out two Pitt players in the huddle. "You had to be a winner playing with Ditka," said Dick Mills, a teammate. "He would have it no other way."

Selected by the Bears in the first round of the 1961 Draft, Ditka emerged as Chicago's type of guy, winning the NFL Rookie of the Year award and, two seasons later, helping the team to the league title. He was all black-and-blue, with the crooked nose and blood-splattered jersey to prove it. In 1962, the editors of *Look* magazine searched for an NFL player who defined ruggedness. In a four-page photo essay titled "Pain Can't Stop a Pro," they focused on Ditka. "Football is a Spartan game," wrote Tim Cohane. "The big, quick, tough men who play it for a living carry on in action with painful injuries that would hospitalize the average man."

Ditka's time in Chicago was blissful—he caught 316 passes for 4,503 yards and thirty-four touchdowns and, along with Sayers and Dick Butkus, became a face and symbol of the franchise. Unlike many of his teammates, however, Ditka refused to cower at the sight of the legendary Halas. When, in 1967,

Ditka threatened to jump to the Houston Oilers of the American Football League, Halas dismissed him as a traitorous ingrate. Ditka responded with one of the great one-liners in the history of organized sports, accusing Halas of being so cheap "he throws nickels around as if they were manhole covers."

Ditka was promptly traded to Philadelphia, where he endured two seasons with the lowly Eagles before finishing his career with four solid years in Dallas. Upon retiring after the 1972 campaign, Ditka was hired by Landry. It was the oddest of coaching marriages. Landry was cool and detached. Ditka once famously picked up a table during a card game and threw it into a wall. "All four legs stuck," recalled Dan Reeves, a former Dallas player. "I said, 'Man, this guy hates to lose.' "

During a game between the Cowboys and Redskins early in his coaching career, Ditka stormed the field, itching to berate an official who called one too many penalties against Dallas.

"Are you a member of the Fellowship of Christian Athletes?" Ditka asked.

"No," replied the official.

"No?" Ditka said. "Well, fuck you! Fuck you! Fuck you!"

Ditka spent nine years alongside Landry, studying his every move. The Cowboys were brilliant—they drafted wisely, stressed discipline, discarded those players who shunned hard work.

The Chicago Bears under Neill Armstrong did none of these things.

That's why Ditka wrote the letter to Halas. Because, more than wanting to coach, he wanted to see the Bears return to their proper place atop the NFL.

On January 20, 1982, two weeks after Armstrong was dismissed, Halas held a press conference in his office. Calling himself a man of destiny and promising to bring Chicago "a winning football team, an interesting football team, and a football team that everybody is going to be proud of," the forty-two-year-old Ditka was named the tenth head coach in franchise history. His contract, a three-year deal that provided a hundred thousand dollars annually, made Ditka the NFL's lowest-paid coach. He didn't care—this was home.

Sitting alongside Ditka was a beaming Halas who, after allowing Finks to call the shots for more than seven years, had had enough. "Jim Finks will be in charge of all information on the draft," said Halas, eighty-six years old but still sharp and quick-tongued. "And that will be submitted to Mike and me, and we'll go over it." (His responsibilities gone, Finks resigned in August, 1983.)

Though Chicago's fans seemed to be thrilled with Ditka's return, the media was less enamored. Those few who remembered Ditka as a player couldn't imagine such a hot head surviving as a coach. In a blistering piece titled "Hiring Ditka Would Be Madness," the *Sun-Times'* John Schulian pointed out that "some of the people who have known Ditka best . . . wonder if there is a punch line to this joke."

So how did Walter Payton feel? In a word: indifferent. Having suffered through the hope and disappointment of two coaches, the Bears' brightest star knew better than to immediately buy into Ditka's bluster about toughness and heart. In fact, for the first time ever, Payton took off all of January. "It's been a tough year physically," he explained to the *Tribune*. Approaching his twenty-ninth birthday, Payton was beginning to increasingly ponder the wisdom of surrendering his body to a franchise that did little to protect it. "Why," he wondered aloud, "should I sacrifice so much for this team when this team doesn't sacrifice for me?"

Walter Payton demanded an answer.

He received three.

· First, on April 2, Ditka's Bears gathered as a team for the first time for a weekend mini-camp on the campus of Arizona State University in Tempe, Arizona. When Pardee held his initial meeting, he spoke of will and fight. When Armstrong held his initial meeting, he spoke of family and fun. When Ditka held his initial meeting, he warned the players to be afraid. *Be very afraid.*

"You were expected to be in the meeting room at seven o'clock that night," said Ted Albrecht, the veteran offensive lineman. "I check into the hotel, get down there early, start saying hi to everybody. Then Ditka walked in and the room got very quiet."

The coach stood before his new players, a Dallas Cowboys Super Bowl Ring adorning a finger on his left hand. He glared sternly toward Bob Fisher, a reserve tight end who was wearing sunglasses and a baseball cap while nibbling on the end of an unlit cigar. "Lemme make this clear," he scolded. "There'll be no hats, no sunglasses, and no tobacco in my meetings." Fisher, who would fail to make the team, felt two inches tall. Following the rant, Ditka asked the players to stand one by one and introduce themselves. Receiver James Scott, back after a disappointing year in the Canadian Football League, tiptoed into the room midway through and took a seat near the back. "Typical of Scottie," said Fred Caito, the trainer. "He thought he could do whatever the hell he wanted."

Not anymore.

"You!" Ditka yelled. "Who are you?"

Scott stood. "James Scott," he said. "Wide receiver."

"James Scott, wide receiver—get the fuck out," the coach snarled. "You're late, and I don't do late."

Scott froze, dumbfounded.

"James Scott, I'm not kidding," Ditka said. "Get. The. Fuck. Out." He called for Caito. "Fred, go grab one of those big garbage bags and empty James Scott's fucking locker out." Ditka and Scott stepped into the hallway, where the high-pitched screaming could be heard from miles away. After five minutes, Ditka returned. Scott did not. His possessions were, literally, tossed into the street. Two days later, with his tail between his legs, Scott apologized. "That was exactly the right message," said Caito. "That we were no longer going to put up with the bullshit."

Ditka stepped back to the front of the room and the meeting officially began. He ordered all the players to tell a teammate, "I love you." The commandment was met with awkward silence.

"Do it!" Ditka said.

*I love you . . . I love you . . . I love you . . . I love you . . .*

"This is a team, and a team is a family," Ditka said. "We stand up for one another, we fight for one another, we defend one another, we love one another." He proceeded to declare that the Chicago Bears were going to win the Super Bowl. "It's not my plan," he said. "It's my reality."

A couple of veterans scoffed. Ditka didn't stand for scoffing.

"Look at everyone around you," he yelled. "Really, look around."

He watched as players turned their heads left and right.

"OK," he said. "Eighty percent of you sons of bitches won't be here come September first. That's your warning."

Speech over.

• Second, on April 27 the Chicago Bears held the fifth overall pick in the NFL Draft. According to the *Tribune*, the team was strongly considering Walter Abercrombie, a record-setting halfback out of Baylor University. Payton couldn't believe it. The last thing the team needed was another running back.

As usual, he braced for inevitable disappointment—then watched with glee as the Bears took quarterback Jim McMahon from Brigham Young. When Finks was running the team, quarterbacks were all but ignored. Finks was no longer running the team. "Taking Jim," said Leslie Frazier, a defensive back, "was one of the most important decisions in turning the franchise around."

- Third, the Bears held a follow-up mini-camp at Lake Forest in May. It was supposed to be voluntary. According to league rules, it *had to be* voluntary. Wide receiver Rickey Watts, a player as lazy as Payton was driven, made a token one-day appearance before departing unannounced. He was the team's second-leading returning wide receiver, a player whose size-speed combination had been regularly praised by Armstrong.

"Clean out that fucker's locker," Ditka told Caito, the equipment manager. "He's done, too."

As ordered, Caito once again tossed all of Watts' possessions into a plastic garbage bag and placed it by a curb. When asked by the assembled media whether Watts' absence was excused, Ditka audibly snarled. "I don't know where he is," the coach said. "Wanna ask me if I care?"

"Do you care?" asked Kevin Lamb of the *Chicago Sun-Times*.

"Nope," said Ditka.

He genuinely didn't.

"Rickey Watts thought he was the greatest thing since sliced cheese," Ditka said. "And he was, talent-wise. But sometimes the gain of adding talent isn't worth what you lose. What you lose in the locker room isn't worth what you gain on the field."

Jack Childers, Watts' agent, called his client later that day, urging him to return to camp. Watts did, and Ditka begrudgingly granted him a second chance. "You're on a short fucking leash," Ditka said. "Very short."

Payton couldn't believe what he was seeing. It was as if Bob Hill, his coach at Jackson State, had been reincarnated into a stumpy white man with a Brillo Pad mustache and crooked fingers. Many of the older Bears came to detest Ditka, what with his militaristic ways and crazed snarl. For the coach's first morning workout, the players were told to dress in full pads. They began with a live, thirty-play eleven-on-eleven scrimmage and ended with ten forty-yard sprints. Noah Jackson, the overweight offensive lineman, turned to fans during a water break, sighed, and moaned, "See what y'all get for saying 'Good-bye Neill Armstrong?' "

Payton, however, loved it. Maybe, at long last, winning was a priority in Chicago.

· · ·

Or, maybe not.

Because Mike Ditka is a Bears icon, and because his team went on to eventually accomplish great things, people tend to forget that his first season as head coach was an unmitigated disaster.

Chicago kicked off its year with listless defeats to Detroit and New Orleans (Payton ran for forty-six total yards). Then a fifty-seven-day player strike threatened to wipe out the season. The impasse ended, but the bitter feelings did not. Payton, who lost nearly two hundred thousand dollars during the lockout, wondered aloud why the work stoppage even happened. Several Bears were furious over their star's hesitancy to support the union. "At first they were asking me if I would walk out and I said I'd have to get legal counseling," he said. "A lot of guys were disappointed with me then, but it was the only thing I could say. Now I look back on the agreement and the eight weeks I was out with them was a total waste for me."

Though Payton embraced Ditka's demands of excellence, the resumption of the season (seven more regular-season games would be played) reminded the Bears that, beneath his team-first verbiage, the running back possessed a selfish streak often obscured by statistics and smiles. For the bulk of his career, Payton had Ray Earley, the longtime equipment manager, keep him abreast of his rushing yardage totals during games. Payton would casually stroll past Earley, give him a look and hear, "You're at seventy-three," or "Eleven more and you've got a hundred."

"That was kept quiet," said Jay Hilgenberg, the offensive lineman. "But we knew."

Had Chicago been winning, perhaps Payton would have ignored any urges to again mope and whine aloud. But with the team limping toward a 3-6 record, he felt compelled to speak out.

"I don't know how long I can play here," Payton said. "I like it. I like Chicago. I've had no problem with management. I'm just disappointed. I'd rather not say why, but I'm going to call a press conference after the season and tell everything. I know what's wrong, I know why, but I can't say. At Jackson State, if we went 7-3 it was like a losing season. It's kind of hard to get here, where everyone is supposed to be professionals, and end up with the record we've got now.*

"I still like playing football. What are you going to write? How's this? 'A rose in a dandelion garden.'"

Through the first four weeks of the season, Payton had averaged only fourteen carries per game—by far the lowest of his career (from 1975 to 1981, he averaged twenty-one carries per game). While the number alone served as an indictment of Ed Hughes, the team's new offensive coordinator, it failed to convey the entire story. As opposed to his predecessors, Hughes, who knew Ditka from his time working as the backfield coach of the Cowboys, actually dedicated himself to establishing the pass. Even though he was but a raw rookie, McMahon was named the starter after the strike. Boasting a powerful arm, maneuverability in the pocket, and a feel for the position that Bob Avellini and Vince Evans (the two holdovers on the roster) lacked, McMahon's presence offered the Bears legitimate offensive possibilities. "We were able to employ Walter as a blocker, which he was phenomenal at," said Ted Plumb, the team's receivers coach. "We'd sit in meetings and Walter would take more pride in a great block than a great run." They could finally use Payton as a decoy and have opposing defenses bite. They could finally have Payton line up wide and not worry about the quarterback forgetting to look his way. They could finally throw deep.

Knowing how Payton had spent years stewing over his team's dud quarterbacks, Ditka assumed the back would be elated. He wasn't. "I feel like I've been on a free ride the last two weeks, getting paid for nothing," he said after carrying twelve times for sixty-seven yards in a Week 4 loss at Minnesota. "I thought you go with what's working."

Having played alongside Sayers and having coached Tony Dorsett in Dallas, Ditka knew an unhappy halfback was a relatively useless one. Upon reading Payton's words, he conferred with Hughes and insisted the Bears run more the following week, when they were scheduled to host the Patriots at Soldier Field.

The day began optimistically. Payton carried the ball on the first four

* Keeping with his oft-quirky ways, Payton never did hold the postseason press conference he had promised reporters.

offensive plays of the game, and the drive concluded when McMahon hit Ken Margerum for a seventeen-yard touchdown pass. From that point on, though, Payton—who missed a good chunk of the action with a leg injury—played a secondary role. He ran a mere thirteen times for seventy yards, and caught three more passes for twenty-four yards. The Bears, however, won big, 26–13, and afterward, euphoric teammates converged around McMahon, who passed for 192 yards and two touchdowns in the best showing of his early career.

One man sat alone at his locker, frowning.

Payton addressed the media, accusing New England linebacker Clayton Weishuhn of deliberately twisting his ankle at the end of a play. (Said Weishuhn: "That never happened. I was a rookie just happy to be starting. Do you think I'd deliberately hurt Walter Payton? No way.") He questioned the wisdom in giving him only thirteen chances and, off the record, ripped into Hughes.

> **Question:** Are you happy with the victory?
> **Answer:** "I'm happy we won," he said. "I'm always happy when we win."
> **Q:** Are you happier getting the ball more this week?
> **A:** Yeah, I guess I am. [Long pause.] But I'm still upset.
> **Q:** What are you upset about?
> **A:** When I hurt my ankle it was on a draw play. Either number fifty-three (Weishuhn) or number fifty-seven (linebacker Steve Nelson) rolled over on my ankle, and I think it was intentional.
> **Q:** That's why you're upset?
> **A:** I can't tell you. I'm a little disappointed. I'll tell you at the end of the year.

Wrote Steve Daley of the *Tribune* in a scathing column titled, "Walter's 'Problem' Has Bears on Run":

> Is there a conflict between Payton and the offense being designed by Ditka?
> "I'm not going near that one," an offensive starter said, lowering his voice. "No comment. That's a pretty touchy subject around here."
> . . . Payton wants the burden, needs the burden. He complains about his teammates from time to time in a broad, sweeping kind of

way, but what he wants from them is simply a little more effort. Work harder, the message seems to be, and I'll do the rest.

If there is a change coming to the Bears' offensive approach, a change that will be unwelcome to Payton, his method for dealing with it is a strange and private one. It is a kind of gamesmanship, a puzzle in which we are expected to guess the answer, whether Payton has an answer or not.

When he first accepted the Bears job, Ditka had been warned in private that Payton's image didn't always match reality. The toothy smile masked moodiness; the confident walk hid insecurity. "Walter went from energetic and peppy to dour and angry in a second," said Al Harris. "Like a light switch." Yet even with advance notice, Ditka was blindsided by his occasionally poor attitude. "If you spent enough time with Walter, you picked up that he wanted his vast modesty to be universally accepted," said Daley, a *Tribune* columnist from 1981 to '85. "But I remember talking to some players on how they worried about Walter, and how he never seemed fulfilled. He always seemed angry without usually whining about it, and he had a lot of resentment. He was resentful when McMahon came along and he wasn't sufficiently appreciated, and he was resentful when other Bears got the credit and he didn't. He was lionized and revered in Chicago, but it was never enough.

"Honestly I think Walter was unprepared for a team with other stars and a coach who was a star. He was the type of guy who said he was just part of the team, but who never fully believed it."

When told of Payton's harsh words after the Patriots win, Ditka—who had resisted taking any shots at his franchise player—could no longer hold back. "It's unfortunate," he said. "I can understand [the whining] if you play golf or tennis or billiards. You're one-on-one with the world. But we're a forty-nine-man sport."

The following day, Ditka called Payton at his home to clear the air.

"There's no problem at all," Ditka told the *Tribune* afterward. "Everything gets blown out of proportion."

Payton, who ended the shortened season ranked tenth in the NFL with 596 rushing yards, was asked for his take.

"No comment," he said.

CHAPTER 18

# POWER

IN THE SUMMER OF 1981, THE CHICAGO BEARS SIGNED A ROOKIE FREE AGENT
wide receiver by the name of Mike Pinckney. In two seasons at Northern
Illinois, Pinckney established himself as one of the better players in Huskies
history. As a senior he earned second team all-Mid-American Conference
honors by catching thirty passes for 392 yards and gaining another 563 yards
on kickoff and punt returns. Always on the lookout for a hidden gem, the
Bears gave the undrafted Pinckney a shot.

Although on the Northern Illinois campus Pinckney gained mild notoriety for his football exploits, his true claim to fame was a most peculiar one:
Mike Pinckney was a dead ringer for Walter Payton.

From the charcoal skin tone to the high cheekbones to the muscular
forearms, Pinckney looked as if he were the lead singer of a Sweetness tribute
band. "When I first got to camp with the Bears, fans were stopping me all
the time, yelling 'Walter! Walter! Walter!' and asking for autographs," said
Pinckney. "At first I corrected them, but after a while I'd just write 'WP 34.'
It made life easier."

Pinckney found the confusion funny, if not somewhat embarrassing.
Walter Payton was one of the great running backs of all time. Mike Pinckney was just trying to land a job. "I never even mentioned any of it to Walter," he said. "Too weird."

During camp, Pinckney's roommate was Tim Ehlebracht, a rookie wide
receiver from nearby North Central College. One night, the two players

took a drive to Naperville, where a handful of bars lined Chicago Avenue. Before settling upon a final destination, Ehlebracht hatched a plan. "Pinckney, let's do this," he said. "I'll introduce you as Walter and we'll see how far it can go."

Pinckney nodded, and as the teammates entered the first club Ehlebracht pulled aside the manager, a man he knew. "John, I'd like to introduce you to Walter Payton," he said, pointing toward Pinckney. "Walter wanted to get away from camp for a night. He'd appreciate it if you could keep it quiet that he's here."

Ehlebracht and Pinckney were guided to the club's roped-off VIP section. John showered the men with free drinks and food, but couldn't remain silent about the legendary running back's presence. "We sit down, and people are all over us, taking pictures, asking for autographs, pointing, shouting," said Pinckney. "Tim had introduced me to this beautiful girl as Walter Payton, and she was all over me. At one point the two of us walked to the dance floor, and all the people parted like the Red Sea. They wanted to see Walter Payton in the flesh."

After posing for a handful of pictures with the club's owners, Pinckney and his new lady friend drove to his room. "We start getting it on, and quickly our clothes are off," he said. "She's incredibly beautiful—Latin American, hot as a person can be. A ten out of ten. At one point the woman actually screams, 'I can't believe it! I'm getting laid by Walter Payton!'

"Well, it's five A.M. and I need to take her back to her car at the club. We're driving and she's asking me if my life is like this all the time—clubs and parties and women and all. I'm starting to feel guilty. How can I let this girl walk away thinking she got laid by Walter Payton? So before she gets out of the car I say, 'Listen, I have to tell you something important.'"

"What is it, Walter?" she replied.

"My name is not Walter Payton," he said.

"What are you talking about," she said. "Who are you?"

"Michael Pinckney."

"No, you're Walter Payton, the Chicago Bear. Walter Payton."

Pinckney opened up his wallet, removed his Maryland driver's license, and handed it to her.

Silence.

"You bastard!" she screamed. "You fucking bastard."

The woman stepped out of the vehicle and slammed the door.

"That's a true story," said Pinckney, who was cut before the season started. "One hundred percent true. The power of Walter Payton got me laid by the hottest girl I'd ever seen."

. . .

The power of Walter Payton is the power that accompanies athletic superstardom. It's the power fame has upon people. The power to eat for free whenever one chooses. The power to gain easy access to any club, any bar, any restaurant, any theatre. The power of Walter Payton makes people scream and squeal and leap and cry. It makes them crave access. Any access. A nod. An autograph. A handshake. One second. One hour. One night.

The Bears once traveled to London for an exhibition game. Payton anticipated a week of blissful anonymity. "Then we get out of a cab in London," said Shaun Gayle, a Chicago defensive back, "and he was mobbed."

"I once got Walter a Rolex that he wore all the time," said Ron Atlas, his friend. "Well, he lost it and he was devastated. I told him I'd find out if the watch was insured. I called the place where I bought the watch, and they in turn called Rolex. The thing wasn't insured, but two days later Rolex FedExed him a free watch. Just because he was Walter Payton."

When used in pursuit of righteousness, the power of Walter Payton was a beacon of blinding light. Throughout his career, Payton visited dozens of sick children in hospitals, hugged countless strangers, brightened more days than one could count. "He was an ambassador," said Matt Suhey, his longtime teammate. "Walter wore his celebrity and his notoriety with class and dignity. The NFL's Man of the Year Award is named after him, and it's very appropriate."

And yet, the power of Walter Payton could also be utilized in less altruistic ways. Fame inevitably warps and corrupts, and the celebrities able to resist its charms are few and far between.

Once upon a time, when Payton was a struggling Bears rookie trying to survive in a foreign city, he only had eyes for his future wife, Connie Norwood. They spoke nearly every day, often for hours at a time. Her photograph adorned his locker, and even as he watched veteran teammates treat their spouses like tattered rags, he refused to follow suit. Payton, alongside teammate/best friend Roland Harper, was a strict adherent to the teachings of the Bible, including the seventh commandment (Thou shall not commit adultery).

As the years passed and the power grew, however, Payton changed. In the spirit of the surface-deep '80s, his image became everything. Frugal in many areas (with automobiles obvious exceptions), Walter wouldn't think twice about dropping a couple of thousand dollars on a suit or two. He rarely (if ever) left home without his slacks neatly pressed and his shoes as shiny as new coins, and he could never have enough Rolex watches and gold bracelets (he was especially fond of a bracelet that spelled out P-A-Y-T-O-N in encrusted diamonds). His teeth were sparkling white, his skin unblemished, his mustache meticulously trimmed. "Dad was huge into fashion," recalled Brittney Payton, his daughter. "There was a men's store called Realta that was downtown. He would come at night and they'd open up for him. He loved to shop. He would sport his cowboy boots with jeans back in the day, or those big colorful sweaters, and he made it work."

Most important was the hair. If one looks back at photographs from Payton's first few years in Chicago, his miniature Afro was routinely messy and awkwardly skewed. It leaned right, it leaned left, it flopped to the front. Oftentimes, Payton merely covered his head with a state trooper's wide-brim model hat. Then, in the early '80s, he was approached by Willard Harrell, a running back for the St. Louis Cardinals who had a side business peddling a product called Curl Alive with Pro 39. "It was mainly a moisturizer for a black man's hair," said Harrell, Payton's teammate on the collegiate All-Star team in 1975. "It went on wet, it came off dry." In exchange for the usage of Payton's name on promotional material, Harrell gave the Bears' star an unlimited supply of Curl Alive with Pro 39.

Payton's Jheri curl emerged as one of *the* Jheri curls of the 1980s—moist yet not dripping; perky yet not over the top. "Dad messed up a couple of couches with his head," said Jarrett Payton, Walter's son. "He had that curl working."

"He did it beautifully," said Harrell with a laugh. "Walter's hair was the envy of black men nationwide."

They weren't the only ones to notice. The wallflower Walter Payton of years past had become a more confident, more social being. He stepped with an air of importance and no longer shielded himself from the world. Payton became especially comfortable around women who, in turn, became especially comfortable around him. "Walter walked through a lobby or a casino or wherever, and very quickly he'd have five or six or seven hotel room keys put in his pocket," said Bud Holmes, his agent. "Women sent him their photos. Naked pictures. Pictures in lingerie. He'd laugh about it, but that sort of temptation is not easy to ignore."

When Holmes negotiated a new contract with the Bears in 1981, one of the stipulations was that, on the road, Payton be granted his own suite. The reason was simple: He wanted a place to bring back his conquests. Although Payton continued to avoid regularly socializing with teammates, that didn't mean he failed to go out. From San Diego to Seattle, Detroit to Denver, Boston to Buffalo, Payton could often be found at the hot dance clubs, working the moves perfected on *24 Karat Black Gold* a decade earlier. Before long, Payton's personal black book featured a bevy of women in every city. Wherever the Chicago Bears traveled, Payton had females waiting for the signal to discreetly knock on his door at the Hyatt or Hilton or Marriott.

As Connie remained in Illinois caring for Jarrett, her husband was on the road, living *the life*. Those who knew him best say one of Payton's great gifts/ills was the ability to compartmentalize. When he was home in Arlington Heights, he could be the prototypical family man. When he was elsewhere, he could do whatever he pleased. To Walter, one behavior had nothing to do with the other. If Connie didn't know he was sleeping around, how could it possibly hurt her? As far as she was concerned, he sat in his hotel room watching TV and reading the Bible. That was her reality, and it was perfectly fine with Walter.

Not that such behavior was exclusive to road trips. Every February beginning in 1977, Walter spent a week working as a spokesman for Buick at the Chicago Auto Show. The gig was an excellent one, in that it afforded Payton a chance to casually interact with his fans. Buick set up a table, loaded it with pens and glossy photographs and had Payton sign away, talking up the virtues of Buick all the while. It was a good time for a superstar, but not necessarily an *innocent* good time. Payton always looked forward to the show, because he knew McCormick Place, the venue that hosted the event, would be overrun by young, up-and-coming models with dreams of celebrity.

Through the years, Payton's list of sexual conquests via the show was a long one. Many of the models returned year after year, and though Payton's reputation as a womanizer preceded him, his status and charm worked wonders. "I always felt bad for Connie, because Walter was as big a flirt as I'd ever seen," said Donna Vanderventer, who was employed as a secretary in the Bears' executive offices. "It was no different than Tiger Woods or Kobe Bryant. These guys go out and the girls are swooning, and unless they're strong, dedicated family men, it was all about feeding the ego. And women feed egos."

At the 1984 auto show, Payton found himself particularly smitten by a twenty-year-old model named Angelina Smythe. Breathtakingly beautiful, with wavy brown hair, olive-oil skin, and a perky figure, Angelina initially paid Payton no mind when the two met in an elevator. She had never watched a professional football game in her life, and was hardly impressed by his celebrity status.

"Angelina wasn't looking to meet someone," said a person familiar with the situation. "But Walter was a charmer. He would say things to draw a woman in. Not like, 'You're beautiful,' but something deeper psychologically.

"He had a big hole inside of him. He did it dishonorably. He used women—and especially younger women—for something he needed. And I'm not saying something merely physical. There was an emptiness in him. He sought out women to fill that hole. It was devilish."

At the time, Angelina attended church most Sundays and aspired to one day meet a nice man to marry. "She wasn't one to chase anybody," said the person who knew her. "But she was probably a little naïve."

Payton complimented Angelina and made her feel special. He was a sharp dresser, a fast talker, a suave mover. He had strong hands and powerful arms and wherever he went, people smiled and appeared to be moved. Everyone wanted his company, and he was giving it to her.

In the weeks that followed, Walter and Angelina engaged in a passionate affair. Sure, he was married. But it wasn't a *real* marriage, he told her. Just for show. He contacted her when Connie wasn't around, and Angelina excitedly took his calls. She was young, poor, and struggling. He was a bright light. "It was not a fling," Angelina said. "Otherwise the first time I met him it would have been done and over. I think Walter tried to be my friend as a way to get me closer to him, but not for the right reasons. I wanted to get to know him, but he was like a teenage boy—very, very immature. He asked if he could call me and I let him. But I knew he was married and I saw him with other women. It wasn't my best thinking, but I was young and naïve."

One morning in early May, Angelina telephoned Payton. Her voice was panicked. "I'm pregnant," she said.

Silence.

More silence.

A devout Christian, Angelina decided to keep the baby. Walter stopped calling. Stopped caring. The man who couldn't get enough of her now wanted nothing to do with her. Without saying a word to Connie (his wife didn't learn of Angelina until years later), he had an accountant work out a financial package that included a fifty-thousand-dollar trust and an agreement to pay child support through the child's twenty-first birthday. The terms of the deal: Leave Walter out of it, and never let the media catch wind.

When his son Nigel was born, on January 6, 1985, Walter was nowhere to be found. Angelina was all alone in a suburban Illinois hospital, bringing to life a child who would never get to know his biological father. She called Walter to tell him the news, and he didn't immediately respond. A couple of weeks later, Walter and Angelina met to sign financial documents. "He hopped out of the lawyer's office and seemed relieved it was over," Angelina said. "Nigel was a newborn and in the next room, but Walter said he couldn't see him . . . it would be too hard. I showed him pictures and he had a tear in his eye. Then he left and never looked back."

Two months later, on March 15, Connie gave birth to Brittney, the couple's second child. The arrival was all over the news, and images showed Walter gazing lovingly toward his little girl.

Before long, Payton would be named Chicago's Father of the Year by the Illinois Fatherhood Initiative.

He accepted the award.

. . .

How could he behave in such a way? How could a genuinely good guy (and Walter Payton *was*, in many ways, a genuinely good guy) ignore one child while lavishing affection upon two others?

"I can't explain it," said Ginny Quirk, Walter's longtime assistant and the vice president of Walter Payton, Inc. "I feel like, for many years, I knew Walter as well as anyone. I saw him at his best and at his worst. I saw him incredibly high and incredibly low. But how he could completely ignore his own child . . . I just don't have an answer."

There is, of course, an answer. Not a pretty one—but an answer nonetheless. Against logic and most theories of human emotion, Payton took all thoughts of Nigel and simply erased them. He removed the infant from his brain; literally ceased thinking about him. "Our office [in the 1990s] was in Schaumburg, a stone's throw away from where Nigel lived," said Kimm Tucker, the executive director of Payton's charitable foundation. "Walter couldn't face it. He could not. I told Walter that if he wanted to get right with God and if he wanted God to heal him, he'd have to do the right thing.

But in this area, he couldn't. He just put Nigel out of his mind." And if someone brought the boy up? Well, nobody brought the boy up because, save for four or five confidants, nobody knew he existed. From Connie to teammates to coaches to close friends, Nigel was a nonentity. One time Linda Conley, a close family friend, took Walter to see a palm reader on a lark. "She took his wrists and she said, 'I see three children—you have three children,'" said Conley. "Walter snatched his wrists back. That really got to him."

When Angelina contacted Walter's office to request money or supplies, she was never turned down. But Payton refused to take the call. An assistant handled everything. "Walter would see Angelina every once in a while, and he hated it," a friend said. "He never showed any interest in Nigel. That's the type of person he could be."

Payton loved women. But—and this includes Connie—they were disposable. Athletes often say that excelling at the highest level of sport takes an uncommon level of focus. If one finds a woman willing to accept certain conditions (as was the case with Connie), a relationship can work. It'll be one-sided and emotionally unfulfilling. But it will, in a strictly mechanical sense, *work*.

That's the way people speak of Walter and Connie's union. Initially, at Jackson State, the pairing was about love and companionship. But by the mid-1980s, the demise had begun. Yes, Walter's infidelity hardly helped. But the problem went beyond that. When the season was over, Walter rarely stuck around. A handful of pictures showed him changing diapers or holding a bottle, and for brief spells he was interested. But the images were largely staged; moments in time arranged by a photographer or magazine editor. "Was Walter an involved father?" said Bud Holmes. "No. Not really."

. . .

Payton devoted much of his away-from-the-field time to his two passions—fast vehicles and hunting. Both were pastimes Connie had zero interest in.

Through the years, Payton's garage and driveway served as headquarters to an endless showcase of pricey, high-performance cars, motorcycles, and mopeds. From Porsches (one featured the memorable vanity plate: IOUZIP) and BMWs to Testarossas and Lamborghinis, Payton was mesmerized by the sight of a fresh-off-the-assembly-line piece of metal. In 1976 he arrived at training camp in a new De Tomaso Pantera (with a mighty 351 Cleveland engine), the beginning of the obsession. "He drove a different car to the facility every day of the week," said Rick Moss, a defensive back in camp in

1980. "You'd wait anxiously to see what kind of fancy wheels Walter would be in."

"I took a lot of pride in my cars, and I had a lot of them," Payton said. "I had the Lamborghini . . . I had a Rolls-Royce, I had my Porsche, and then at any given time we had eight or nine vehicles in my family. I know it sounds crazy, but coming from where I grew up, I just always found cars, fast cars, a kind of 'I made it' statement."

The cars were not merely show-and-tell items. Payton made use of every ounce of performance in his vehicles. His CB handle was Mississippi Maniac, and it fit like a sock. When Payton, Doug Plank, and Len Walterscheid once made an appearance at a Kawasaki-sponsored event, they were gifted with motorcycles. Payton's teammates chose the (relatively) tame 750 LTD. Payton, velocity addict, went with the KZ 1100—"a genuine crotch rocket," said Walterscheid.

The stories of Payton's wild road antics are endless. "My second year in the league [1979] Walter and I had to go to a picture signing set up by the PR guys," said John Skibinski, a backup fullback. "We were in Lake Forest and we got out of practice at four fifty. It was snowing flakes the size of pancakes and we had to get to a dealership fifty miles away in a half-hour." Payton insisted the two take his new Porsche Carrera. Having never driven with Payton, Skibinski complied. "Before we get going Walter picks up a hamburger, some fries, and a milkshake," Skibinski said. "He's driving a stick in the snow, a hamburger in one hand, the shake in the other, picking up fries, going about a hundred miles per hour. I was shitting in my pants, thinking, 'If we die, my name will forever be immortalized in the headline SKIBINSKI AND PAYTON KILLED IN CAR WRECK. Well, we got there with two minutes to spare."

Hunting, meanwhile, relaxed Payton. In the basement of the home he had built in 1984, there was a state-of-the-art shooting range encased in soundproof glass. "He'd go down there and blast his rifles and semiautomatics," said Jeff Fisher, the Bears safety. "That was a weird peace for Walter." One year, as a present for his offensive linemen, Payton presented Remington 11-87 shotguns with the inscription THANKS FOR LEADING THE WAY engraved on the side. He spoke dreamingly to teammates of faraway trips to distant lands, where plump animals roamed free and hunting season commenced on New Year's Day and ended December 31. "He wanted to go to Alaska and chase down some grizzly bear," said Tim Clifford, a Bears quarterback and Payton's occasional hunting partner. "But he didn't want to use a gun, just a bow and arrow. I said, 'You know, Walter, I'm not going anywhere with only a bow against something that can outrun and out-climb me.'"

Payton, Harper, and other teammates used to take long treks into the woods, chasing down turkeys and squirrels and wild boars. Though their motto, "If it flies, it dies," might have been a tad crass, the sentiment was genuine. "It was like therapy for us," said Harper. "No worries, no other people—just the woods, the open air, and a lot of game."

Following the 1981 season, Payton, Harper, and Skibinski planned a five-day boar-hunting excursion to Crossville, Tennessee. Skibinski had spent considerable time with Payton in duck blinds and on lakes, and he relished the experiences. "The best moments I ever had with Walter were outdoors," he said. "We'd sit in a boat and not say crap for an hour. Then he'd say, 'That's enough. Let's get something to eat.'

"So we go on this trip to the backwoods of Tennessee, and we rented a Ford Bronco truck at the airport, but all they had was a Lincoln. Well, we get in the Lincoln and it's me, Walt, Roland, and one other guy—two whites, two blacks. Walter's driving through rural Tennessee down this gravel road, with a bunch of guns sticking out of the Lincoln, trying to find a place to hunt. We stop to have breakfast at this country dive, and there are some good ol' boys sitting there, listening to Hank Williams on the jukebox. Walt goes on over, deposits a quarter, and puts on Marvin Gaye. Every cap in that place turned to Walter, guns on hips. Then someone recognized him—'That's Walter Payton!' Once they figured that out it was like old home week, everyone asking for autographs and shaking his hand. And we had one helluva trip."

. . .

Although Payton's off-the-field behavior sometimes failed to match his gilded image, his football performance was as breathtaking as ever. Ditka followed up his disappointing rookie campaign with a marginally less dispiriting 8-8 record in 1983, but any scorn for the underwhelming coach was obscured by a developing news story that took hold of Chicago: the Chase.

As early as 1981, Walter Payton had been asked about the possibility of breaking Jim Brown's all-time NFL rushing mark. His 12,312 yards was, without question, the most revered number in the sport. In his nine-year career with the Cleveland Browns, Brown ran with a rage that left opponents awed. He is regarded by many to be the finest athletic specimen to ever wear an NFL uniform, and for years the idea of anyone touching his record seemed ludicrous. Payton agreed. "It's so far away, I can't even ponder it," he once said. "Jim Brown is in another league, as far as I'm concerned."

That was that, until Payton's '83 revival. Behind Johnny Roland, the trusted new running backs coach, and a revamped offensive line that included a pair of massive first-round picks at tackle (Keith Van Horne and Jimbo Covert), a dirt-eating right guard named Kurt Becker, and Jay Hilgenberg, a future great at center, Payton ran for 1,421 yards and six touchdowns. He also caught a career-high fifty-three passes for 607 yards and two touchdowns, and even threw for three touchdowns on six pass attempts. "At the beginning of the season I was very blunt with Walter," said Roland. "I told him that, despite all his God-given talents, people considered him to be a loser. 'You've never won a thing here,' I said. 'If you trust me and trust your line, you might be able to snap that streak.' It made sense to him and he had an incredible year."

Yet in a season that featured some noteworthy highs* and devastating lows,** many were secretly—and not so secretly—taken aback by Payton's newfound obsession with surpassing Brown.

When the television camera lights were on and the reporter notepads were out, Payton did his best to only talk team-team-team. All he wanted was for the Bears to win. If he ran for zero yards but the other fellas did well, he was happy. Whether he surpassed Brown or not was insignificant. *Blah, blah, blah.* It was utter nonsense. Having struggled to relate to his star throughout the miserable '82 season, Ditka committed himself to learning to read Payton. He studied the running back. Watched how he interacted with teammates and coaches. Gauged his wide-ranging moods. His conclusion: "If Walter got the ball, he was happy," said Ditka. "If he didn't get the ball, he wasn't so satisfied."

---

* He rushed for 161 yards and threw for seventy-seven yards against the Saints. "I never saw anything like Walter in that game," said Al Harris, the Bears linebacker. "There was a play where he was running toward our bench, and Walter wound up his arm like a bolo punch, and this defensive back for New Orleans [Dave Waymer], he hit this dude . . . you know how in a movie a boxer will wind up his whole arm like a propeller. Walter wound up his arm and threw a forearm. I was sitting on the bench and they were two yards from the sideline, and [Waymer] came flying through the air and landed by my feet. Remarkable!"

** Harper, his closest friend on the team, was finally cut; Halas, the man who drafted him, died at age eighty-eight.

Ditka never questioned Payton's earnestness, but the coach—for his many strengths—wasn't one to deeply psychoanalyze. Had he asked the right people, he would have been told Payton's commitment to the record superseded his commitment to winning. Which wasn't the worst thing, considering Payton's rushing success and the team's success usually went hand in hand.

But it could get awkward.

In the fifth game of the '83 season, the Bears were leading Denver by seventeen points with less than two minutes remaining—yet there was Payton, struggling with a nagging knee injury (he would have arthroscopic surgery on both knees after the season), still slamming into the line. When a reader wrote the *Tribune* a letter that called Payton's usage "idiotic," Don Pierson, the Bears beat writer, responded with a piece titled "Jim Brown the Reason Payton Ran." "He is in pursuit of Jim Brown's all-time rushing record," Pierson explained—as if that were enough.

"Walter wasn't a selfish guy," said Roland. "He was the consummate team player. But records meant something to him, and he went after them hard."

When the Bears were laughingstocks, Payton's stubborn refusal to run out of bounds earned him rave reviews. He was tough. He was rugged. He delivered hits before the hits were delivered to him. But while fans and journalists praised the approach, some teammates questioned the logic. Payton didn't merely refuse to run out of bounds at certain moments—he refused to run out of bounds, *period*. If Chicago needed to stop the clock, a handoff to Payton was an iffy proposition. He wanted yards. He needed yards. As Brown's mark loomed closer, the yards were all he thought of. "I loved Walter," said one teammate. "But he could be selfish in some very ugly ways."

Nobody grasped Payton better than the *Tribune*'s Pierson, one of the sport's great beat writers/B.S. detectors. In the aftermath of the Bears' 21–14 loss to the Los Angeles Rams on November 6, Payton—who cleared eleven thousand career yards that day—told the scribe that, "I'd rather turn back the eleven thousand for a win today." Pierson ran the quote, but only with the addendum, "Payton remarked *typically but not convincingly*" (emphasis added).

"Despite what Walter said, it was clearly obvious that surpassing Brown meant everything to him," said Pierson. "He liked to make no big deal of it, but it was enormous.

"He wanted that record."

. . .

For the men and women who composed the National Football League's media relations and corporate communications divisions, 1984 was going to be the year that sold itself.

With Jim Brown's record all but guaranteed to be broken, the action and intrigue needed no extra hype. Better yet, there were not one, but two, running backs fighting for the honor. Along with Payton, Pittsburgh halfback Franco Harris, a twelve-year veteran with four Super Bowl rings to his credit, was nearing the threshold. In fact, at the conclusion of 1983, Harris actually led Payton by 325 yards, 11,950 to 11,625.

Battle lines were drawn: Payton was flashy, Harris was pedestrian. Payton abused his body, Harris ran for the sidelines rather than absorb unnecessary abuse. Payton played for a perennial dog, Harris played for a perennial contender. "They were total opposites—both great, but very different," said Jerry Muckensturm, the longtime Chicago linebacker. "The biggest difference was approach. Franco avoided you, Walter looked to kill you."

The Payton-Harris showdown had all the makings of a classic sports battle; quite possibly the greatest one-on-one chase since Roger Maris and Mickey Mantle raced to surpass Babe Ruth's sixty home runs some twenty-three years earlier.

With one small problem: Walter Payton was a free agent.

Not that this had ever mattered before. NFL free agents could peddle their wares, call around, beg for a change of scenery. But, come day's end, owners and general managers knew it violated eight thousand different codes to make a bid on an opposing team's "property." Even as he was in his prime and running wild, Payton's independence in 1978 and '81 had generated zero interest.

Times, however, were changing. Beginning with its 1983 debut season, the United States Football League (USFL) had made clear its intent to directly confront Goliath, no holds barred. The most deafening salvo was fired on February 23, 1983, when Herschel Walker, the reigning Heisman Trophy winner from the University of Georgia, signed a three-year, $4.2 million deal to play with the New Jersey Generals. With that bombshell, NFL franchises found themselves scratching and clawing to retain their own. It was a fight not merely for quality players, but for legitimacy. The more stars to defect, the stronger the spring-based USFL became.

There was, of course, no bigger NFL star than Payton. Which was why, on January 10, 1984, the USFL's Chicago Blitz stunned the sporting world by presenting him with a three-year, six-million-dollar offer to become the highest-paid player in football history. "It's considerably more than [just six million dollars]," said Dr. James Hoffman, the Blitz owner. "The two million dollars is base salary. I guarantee that personally myself."

Payton, who made six hundred thousand dollars with the Bears in 1983, was flabbergasted. He never aspired to switch leagues. Truth be told, he never even *considered* the idea of switching leagues. But two million dollars a year to play football was set-for-life money. And having grown up poor in Columbia, Mississippi, set-for-life money was hard to ignore.

Michael McCaskey, the Bears' new president (and Halas' oldest grandchild), did his best to pretend the Blitz didn't exist. He pooh-poohed their bid, dismissing it to *The New York Times* as "making no business sense."

"We have a very good proposal to offer," he said. "It disturbs me that we are forced to make a business decision based on somebody else's poor business decision. The USFL is going to be like a soap bubble. It will grow and there will be nothing there, no fans or TV money."

Though McCaskey would be proven correct (the USFL folded after three spring seasons), it mattered not. Payton had long been irked by the Bears' thriftiness, and now another organization was willing to pay big. Throughout the '83 season, representatives of the USFL came to Soldier Field to watch Payton play, even sneaking down to the locker room after games and whispering sweet nothings in his ear. "I was a junior in high school, and my dad used to go to see Walter," said Ron Potocnik, Jr., whose late father was the Blitz GM. "I would always ask, 'Did you get him? Did you sign Walter? Did you?' They wanted him badly."

The Blitz pulled out every stop. They inked a handful of former Bears, including quarterback Vince Evans, one of Payton's close friends, and hired the well-regarded Marv Levy as head coach. They promised large crowds and tremendous hype and the opportunity to not merely carry a team, but a league. "Walter would have been the face of the USFL," said Evans. "No question."

Payton hemmed and hawed. He weighed pros and cons. He told Bud Holmes, his agent, to accept the USFL deal, then changed his mind. Then he changed it again. And yet again. The Blitz were blessed with an apparently deep-pocketed owner desperate to win. The Bears were in the NFL. The Blitz planned on running a high-flying, wide-open offense. The Bears were in the NFL. The Blitz had snazzy uniforms and gorgeous cheerleaders. The Bears were in the NFL. The Blitz were infatuated with Payton. The Bears were in the NFL.

"Walter thought about leaving, but I'm not sure he ever really believed it would happen," said Holmes. "The USFL had money, but it was a mystery. He wanted to go with a sure thing."

Never would Holmes perform more brilliantly than he did in the winter of 1984. He knew he was bargaining from a position of strength, and he wielded that power like an assault rifle. For years the Bears under Halas had specialized in undervaluing and demeaning players. Men would come to training camp requesting a ten-thousand-dollar raise and slink out with a slash in salary.

Now, thanks to the USFL, Holmes had the Bears where he wanted them. The resulting contract was unparalleled in the annals of American professional sports; one even Jerry Vainisi, the Bears' general manager (Jim Finks quit in August, 1983), tagged "brilliant." Payton's three-year deal called for little money up front, but a ten-million-dollar guaranteed annuity that would pay him (or, should he die before its completion, Connie) $240,000 a year for the next forty-four years. "It was the most complicated negotiation I've ever been involved in," said Vainisi. "We bought the annuity from New York Life for a couple of million dollars, so technically an insurance company was paying Walter his salary. It was Bud's idea, and he deserves a lot of credit. A lot of athletes think short-term. Walter and Bud did not."

And what of the Chicago Blitz? Led by the rushing of star halfback Larry Canada, Levy's team finished 5-13, playing before an average of seventy-five hundred fans at Soldier Field. The franchise folded at season's end.

"It would have been a shame for Walter to have jumped leagues," said Kevin Long, a former Blitz running back. "He belonged in the NFL. He belonged where the action was."

· · ·

The action was here.

On February 6, 1984, Walter Payton drove to downtown Chicago, entered the WBBM television studio, sat in a chair, had makeup applied to his face, grabbed a bite to eat, took a sip of water, walked onto a stage, and, for the first time ever, stood alongside Jim Brown and Franco Harris.

The occasion was an appearance on *The Phil Donahue Show*, at the time the reigning afternoon talk king, to discuss the record and its implications.

Impeccably dressed and mildly tempered, Payton watched, often with a bemused expression, as Brown and Harris sparred. The exchanges were weird, awkward, and demeaning for both men. According to Brown, Harris, at thirty-four, was a washed-up has-been who ran for the sidelines before taking a hit and who was hanging on solely to surpass the record. The legendary Steeler was, Brown declared, unworthy of the title NFL Rushing King. "Right now I could beat you, Franco, in a forty," said Brown, age forty-seven.

"I believe there are kids sixteen, seventeen, or eighteen who can beat me," Harris replied, "but I don't think Jim Brown can."

Through their nine years in the league together, Payton had come to like and respect Harris, a mild-mannered Penn State product who played hard and rarely complained. Harris was the anti–O. J. Simpson, in that— even as the Steelers ruled the '70s—he never courted publicity or sought out endorsement deals. "Nobody had anything bad to say about Franco," said John Brockington, a Packers fullback. "He was a gentleman."

Though significantly less talented than Payton, Harris was a skilled runner with deceptive speed and soft hands. His defining career moment— the unforgettable "immaculate reception" in a 1972 play-off game against Oakland—was hardly emblematic of his workmanlike approach. "I have a great deal of respect for Franco," Payton said. "I know him and his family, and on occasions we've spent a lot of time together."

Brown, on the other hand, was someone Payton wanted little to do with. While he spoke glowingly of the Hall of Famer in public, Payton failed to understand the bitterness that seemed to accompany Brown's words. *He* was the one, after all, who chose to retire in the prime of his career, at age twenty-nine; the one who walked away to become a movie star. Had Brown so desired, he probably could have run for twenty thousand yards, and none of this Payton-Harris hoopla would have ever existed.

Instead, there was a scowling Brown on the cover of the December 12, 1983, issue of *Sports Illustrated*, dressed in a Los Angeles Raiders jersey beneath the headline JIM BROWN: YOU SERIOUS? A COMEBACK AT 47? The threat, according to Brown, was a real one.

"Gaining a thousand yards in a fourteen-game season is like walking backwards," Brown told the *Tribune*'s Bob Greene. "Gaining a thousand yards in a sixteen-game season isn't even worth talking about. The standards today are lower, the conditions are easier, and the expectations are less.

"I may not come back," he added, "but I will if people don't admit to the fraud that's being perpetrated. . . . Who's to say a forty-seven-year-old can't do it? I'm not talking about being Jim Brown of 1965. I'm talking about being Jim Brown of 1984. If Franco Harris is gonna creep to my record, I might as well come back and creep, too."

Brown had mostly kind words for Payton, referring to him as a "gladiator." But Payton, to his credit, wasn't swayed. He found Brown to be an arrogant, dismissive, rude old man crying for a breadcrumb of attention. Were he to eventually own the mark, Payton promised himself he would never behave as Brown had.

· · ·

Although Payton had been burned by optimism before, 1984 seemed *different*. From the spectacular new contract to the dream home he and Connie were building in South Barrington (featuring a lake, a fishing pond, a miniature par-3 golf course, and the soundproof gun range in the basement) to the hype over Brown's record, Payton reported to training camp (now being held at the University of Wisconsin–Platteville—aptly described by Ted Plumb, the receivers coach, as "miles and miles of nothing but miles and miles") feeling euphoric.

Over the preceding few years Payton had spent his off-seasons working out in Chicago, sprinting up and down a hill that teammates describe as "dizzying" (Ted Albrecht), "vomit-inducing" (Jerry Doerger), and "so steep, you were kissing it while running up" (Dennis Gentry).

In the lead-up to 1984, however, Payton—fresh from arthroscopic surgery on both knees—returned to Jackson, Mississippi, where he stayed with his mother and ran through the sand hills and along the banks of the Pearl River while pulling a tire with a rope tied around his waist.* It was meant to be a time of rejuvenation; of returning to his youthful ways in search of an extra spark. "You have to have a goal, a challenge to motivate you," Payton said. "I've accomplished most of my goals, but you have to have something to motivate you more, to stimulate you to bigger heights."

If Payton needed motivation, all he had to do was look around the Chicago locker room, where the fruits of a series of wise drafts were beginning to pay off. "We wanted intelligent people," said Bill Tobin, who headed the

---

* "He invited me to come work out with him," recalled Billy Sims, Detroit's star halfback. "Oh, boy, did I make a mistake. He's running these crazy hills with thirty-pound weight packs on his back, and I just want to avoid throwing up."

team's personnel department. "We didn't care if Mike Singletary was too short or Jim McMahon had an eye problem. We looked for smarts, drive, heart." The pathetic offenses of Jack Pardee and Neill Armstrong were long gone, replaced by a cast of dynamic, talented characters and, in Ditka, a coach excited to utilize them. On defense, meanwhile, coordinator Buddy Ryan had built a ferocious unit about to take the NFL by storm.

In the waning days of the 1981 season, when Halas was preparing to fire Armstrong and his entire coaching staff, Singletary, the rookie middle linebacker, urged his fellow defensive players to send a note to the owner, begging him to keep Ryan. "[Defensive end] Alan Page wrote it, because he had a law degree," recalled Jim Osborne, a lineman and Payton's teammate for ten seasons. "We knew if they let Buddy go the defense would be set back another three or four years. We all signed the letter and sent it off, hoping for the best."

"When you write something like that, you never know how it will be perceived," added Page. "We could have been looking for work."

A couple of days later, Halas met with the entire defensive unit. Most of the men figured they were about to be fired. Instead, Halas praised them for their loyalty. He promised to retain Ryan. Consequently, when Ditka was hired, it was with one major condition—not only did the defensive coordinator have to stay, but he would have final say on that side of the ball. "I was fine with it," said Ditka. "But Buddy wanted to be the head coach, so he never accepted me. I was thrilled to have someone so talented on my staff. Whether we got along was irrelevant, as long as we could win together."

The two clashed. They were water vs. oil. Ali vs. Frazier. "The tension existed because they were very similar," said Al Harris. "They were both hamstrung, hardheaded men who were convinced they alone had the winning formula." The result of the Ditka-Ryan divide was a pair of units that genuinely loathed one another. During practices, Ryan instructed his players to hit, and hit at will. Ditka echoed the order to his offense. "Don't let them walk all over you!" Ditka would yell. "Fuck the defense!"

Although the Bears had failed to qualify for the play-offs in 1983, the team won five of its final six games to evoke genuine optimism. Even *Sports Illustrated*, which regularly dismissed the team, picked Chicago to win the NFC Central the next season.

"Sometimes a seed has to be planted," Singletary told *The Sporting News*. "I feel that, for the past two years, a seed has been planted. I feel it's grown and ready to reach its potential. Whatever growth it has, it has to be this year."

The Bears opened at home against Tampa Bay, and while the city was euphoric over an easy 34–14 triumph, Payton, who ran for sixty-one yards on sixteen carries, was back to brooding. In order to protect the thirty-year-old's knees, Ditka removed him when the Bears jumped out to a 27–7 lead early in the fourth quarter. It was a decision any head coach would have made, and no one on the Bears—even the backstabbing Ryan—found it objectionable.

As he walked toward the locker room afterward, Payton sulked, refusing to acknowledge the fans who called his name. Payton then blew off the media, speaking only to the hosts of the postgame TV show that paid him to appear.

A couple of days later, Payton attempted to explain his behavior, saying he was upset over not "playing my type of game." Ditka was incredulous. So were several teammates. "It was supposed to be all about winning," said Bob Avellini, the Bears' backup quarterback. "But sometimes it wasn't."

The poor mood didn't last. Payton ran for 179 yards in a Week 2 rout of Denver, during which he surpassed Brown's NFL record of 15,459 all-purpose yards. The following week he gained another 110 in a tight 9–7 triumph at Green Bay. (Afterward, some Packers were incensed over Chicago's dirty play. Said guard Greg Koch: "They're a bullshit team and a bullshit organization.")

"Walter was as good at that time as he'd been when he was younger," said Lynn Dickey, the Packers quarterback. "We made it our goal as a team to bust him up and destroy him with hard hits. But Walter just demoralized us. We couldn't stop him."

When Payton looked over the schedule before the start of the season, a September 23 trek to Seattle hardly jumped off the page. In the chase to overtake Brown, however, much had changed since the preseason. In a nod to the business-before-loyalty approach of the NFL, the Steelers had cut loose Harris in late August when he refused to agree to contract terms. The decision was a shocking one, considering Harris' proximity to the record, and the publicity-starved Seahawks eagerly picked him up.

As a result, a normally ho-hum matchup held genuine intrigue. Harris led Payton by thirty-four yards, and the Seahawks arranged a joint press conference for both men on the Saturday before the game. Payton, perhaps sensing Harris was on his last leg, arrived giddy, talkative, and gracious. He confessed the record meant a great deal, then used part of the session to lobby for a law in Illinois to require motorcyclists to wear helmets, noting that someone he knew had recently died.

Harris didn't show for the event.

Or, really, for the game.

Seattle won 38–9, but it was the duel-that-wasn't that generated the buzz. With 2:05 remaining in the first quarter, Payton took a pitch and scooted nine yards around right end. The run was unexceptional, but with it Payton trailed one less man. He outgained Harris for the game, 116 yards to 23 yards, and it became clear to most everyone that Seattle's veteran halfback was a dead man running.

Not that Harris agreed. "As far as I'm concerned, the race is on," he said. "It's up to me to see if I can make it a race. I think I can."

He couldn't.

The Seahawks released Harris six weeks later.

. . .

In the days following the Seattle defeat, all Payton could think about was Jim Brown. Save for their joint appearance on *Donahue*, the two legends had never spent any time together. In fact, Payton never even viewed footage of Brown running the ball until a week after Seattle, when he found himself watching a TV highlight film of the NFL's greatest running backs. "Jim Brown was big and strong and quick," Payton said afterward. "And he even made a one-handed catch. Hey, that's what football is all about."

The men were polar opposites. Although Brown was raised by a great-grandmother in an all-black community on St. Simons Island, Georgia, for the first eight years of his life, the remainder of his childhood was spent in Manhasset, New York. He was a five-sport star who went on to dominate in football and lacrosse at Syracuse University before entering the NFL for nine incredible seasons. "Jim Brown was the best who ever played," said Ross Fichtner, Brown's former teammate who later served as Chicago's secondary coach. "He's so far ahead of everyone else, it's not even funny. But Jim didn't have Walter's heart. Walter gave one hundred percent all the time, and sometimes teammates didn't think Jim was giving his all."

Unlike Payton, who rarely voted and *never* talked politics,* Brown dove headfirst into social causes. He spoke out forcefully about the plight of black

---

* Author's note: When I asked Jarrett Payton, Walter's son, whether his father had been a Democrat or a Republican, he shrugged. "Honestly," he said, "I don't know."

athletes and infuriated many by supporting Muhammad Ali when the boxer avoided serving in Vietnam. "Jim really stuck his neck out," said John Wooten, a former teammate. "There were a lot of people that hated Ali, and because Jim supported Ali they now hated Jim." Brown founded the Negro Industrial and Economic Union, a group that provided funding to hundreds of black-owned businesses, and condemned the bigotry that plagued America.

Having watched from afar as black athletes like Jackie Robinson and Joe Louis swallowed their tongues and accepted abuse from whites, Brown promised himself he would never follow suit. "My attitude was, in no way was I going to be that way," he said. "In no way did I ever feel that I would accept discrimination."

When asked about Payton's intelligence, friends focus on his ability to read people and gauge the mood of a room. "Walter's skill was in the power of observation," said Mark Alberts, a future business partner. "He could look over someone and perfectly understand him." Brown, on the other hand, was bright and worldly, quick with an opinion and well-versed in books and newspapers. He dared people to challenge his opinions, and cherished the look of befuddlement as he rattled off numbers and facts.

Brown retired from football at age twenty-nine to pursue a career in acting, and though the move saved his body from more abuse and provided him with a successful second career (Brown's film credits include *The Dirty Dozen, Three the Hard Way,* and *Mars Attacks!*), there was a part of the man that couldn't fully let go. He routinely expressed disdain—and disgust— toward the so-called "modern player," what with his fancy gear and thick pads and stuffed wallet. "My feeling is you're a sportsman or a capitalist," he told the *Tribune*'s Sam Smith. "I was a sportsman and played the game to win, not for records. We didn't stay in the game to set records. It was a question of dignity and true performance. Today, players want a million-dollar salary and won't play because their big toe is hurt."

When Payton ran over the Dallas Cowboys for 155 yards in a Week 5 loss, the anticipation of history was palpable. He needed a mere sixty-seven yards against the visiting Saints the following Sunday to finally become the NFL's rushing king.

In the days leading up to New Orleans, Payton was regularly prodded about Brown. It was predictable stuff—the media wanting sound bites about his admiration for the great hero. Payton, however, refused to comply. Yes, he was aware that Brown played in twelve- and fourteen-game seasons, and that he set his mark in fewer carries. But, to Payton, Brown was pathetic. When asked by Michael Janofsky of *The New York Times* whether he respected Brown, the answer was short and pointed. "Next question," he said. Would Brown be invited to the Saints game? "If he wants to come, that's fine with me," Payton said. "I have no control over that. It's up to the Bears' organization. We're trying to keep this as professional as possible. My job is to get the record; I'll leave the details to the organization."

In other words: No.

. . .

Though he was but twenty-six years old in 1984, Jeff Fisher was beginning to feel the wear and tear that is high-level football. A reserve safety and kick returner with the Bears, Fisher had played four years at USC, and now was in his fourth—and final—season in Chicago. Some teammates suffered sprained knees and ankles. Others seemed to be battling concussions by the week.

Fisher's feet chronically hurt.

One day, early in the '84 season, Fisher approached Ray Earley, the team's cantankerous equipment manager, and requested new insoles.

Instead of merely forking over the goods, Earley called Fisher a "damn pussy" and demanded he follow him to Payton's locker. Earley pulled out Walter's shoes. They were a battered pair of KangaROOS, with metal-tipped inch-long cleats.

"Stick your hand in!" Earley barked.

"What?" said Fisher.

"Stick your hand in! Stick the fucking thing in!"

Fisher did as he was told. "I actually scratched up my fingers, because Walter pulled the factory insole out of the shoe. He'd put one of those white thin baseball sanitary socks on, then put his foot in the shoe, so he could feel all seven cleats on the ground against his sole. In other words, when you put your hand in that shoe, you were feeling the nails from the screw beds normally covered by the insoles. He wanted to feel every nail.

"That," said Fisher, "was Walter."

Not only were Payton's feet rubbing up against metal, but his thigh pads—thin, ratty, smelly—were the same ones he first received as a sophomore at Jefferson High School. Payton liked the lightness. The flexibility. The fact that they felt like feathers atop his body. His game pants, meanwhile, were nothing but patches and frayed threading. He only gave them up after a tackler ripped out the seat. The antiquated equipment told a story that went beyond mere nostalgia. Walter Payton would do anything—absolutely anything—to gain an edge.

"That's why he became the all-time rushing king," said Fisher. "Maybe there were more talented players, and certainly there were bigger players. But Walter wanted it so badly. You could see it every practice, every game. His desire to succeed was unmatched."

Against the Cowboys, Payton had a large handful of family members and friends in attendance, just in case he broke the mark. Though falling short of 221 rushing yards can hardly be deemed an embarrassment, afterward Payton felt as if he'd let people down. Fans wanted the record. Teammates wanted the record. Coaches wanted the record. The pressure was immense.

"This is my week," he told friends in the days leading up to the Saints. "I have to get this over with."

In his typical hard-to-read ways, Payton longed for the attention, yet shunned the attention. He turned down very few interview requests in the lead-up to New Orleans, yet adamantly rejected the Bears' plans for a three-minute on-field ceremony that would include Connie, Jarrett, and his mother, Alyne. "Once it's over," he said, "just acknowledge it to the crowd and get on with the game. That's the key thing."

Of all the teams Payton could have faced with a record in the balance, the Saints were an ideal one. Though New Orleans boasted a 3-2 record and a fantastic young linebacker named Rickey Jackson, their defense was putrid against the run, allowing opposing offenses 149 rushing yards per game. Even better, the Saints players admired Payton. One of the team's consultants was Bob Hill, the former head coach at Jackson State ("I told the guys Walter stories all the time," Hill said), and the Saints and Bears held annual training camp scrimmages. "We formed a little bit of a bond from that," said Frank Wattelet, a New Orleans defensive back. "We all knew and loved Walter. He was a wonderful man." In other words, when the twelve o'clock game began, Payton wasn't staring down Green Bay or Minnesota. Saints players certainly didn't want Payton running all over them, but they weren't averse to being a part of football history.

Payton slept only a handful of minutes the night before, tossing and turning at the thought of not gaining the needed yardage. He knew he would inevitably set the record, but didn't want to do so with a meek tiptoe. "Walter ran with so much pride," said Suhey. "He never sought out the easy way."

With the Cubs scheduled to play San Diego in the nationally televised fifth game of the National League Championship Series, 12,000 of Soldier Field's 66,950 seats remained empty. Beneath a pewter-colored sky, the Bears stormed the field and jumped out to a 13–7 halftime lead. Payton accumulated sixty-four yards on fifteen carries, and needed only two more to own the mark. He was running intensely even for a player who *always* ran intensely. "On one play he hit me hard—really, really hard," said Jim Kovach, a Saints linebacker. "I remember looking up at his face mask and there was something hanging from it. It was my skin."

The record-breaking run came with 14:11 remaining in the third quarter, on a second-down-and-nine from the Bears' twenty-one-yard line. The play, Toss 28 Weak, was a simple one. Payton lined up behind Suhey in the I-formation, tiptoed four steps to his left, and received the pitch from McMahon. Covert, the left tackle, blocked down alongside tight end Emery Moorehead. Mark Bortz, the left guard, pulled while leading Suhey and Payton—who palmed the ball like a basketball in his right hand—into the hole. The only Saint with a shot of dropping Payton for a loss was linebacker Whitney Paul, who charged straight toward the play before being nudged inside by Bortz. Payton burst outside, took about ten rapid-fire steps up the field, and lunged powerfully into linebacker Dennis "Dirt" Winston. Paul, trailing the action, helped bring him down from behind. As soon as Payton landed, six yards from where the play began, CBS announcer Tim Ryan bellowed, "He's got it!" With the crowd standing and applauding, Payton— football in his left hand—leapt to his feet and extended his right arm to help Paul off the ground. Teammates and opponents rushed to offer hugs and handshakes and Jim Riebandt, the Soldier Field public address announcer, shouted, "Walter Payton has just set a new National Football League career rushing record!" Payton jogged to Saints coach Bum Phillips, shook his hand, and turned back toward Chicago's sideline, dodging a couple of TV cameramen who had slinked onto the turf. Payton held the ball aloft to even louder cheers, exchanged a leaping high-five with teammate Todd Bell, then found himself engulfed by dozens of Bears. "More than anything, it was surreal," said Pat Dunsmore, a Chicago tight end. "You realize it's a big moment, but you don't realize how big until you look back." With the fans chanting "Wal-ter! Wal-ter! Wal-ter!" Payton looked for someone with the Bears who could set aside the ball. He ended the festivities by shaking hands with Michael McCaskey, the team's president, but when Payton turned back to the field he found himself surrounded by photographers and cameramen. "Come on!" he squealed, shaking his arms in disgust. "Get off the field! Get off the field!"

On the New Orleans sideline, members of the Saints stood in wonderment. The moment was special. Not merely for one player or one team, but for football. For sports. "He was the epitome of what our game was all about," said Jimmy Rogers, a New Orleans running back. "It was an historic event, and we wanted him to be honored."

Payton returned to the huddle, waving to the fans one last time. He went on to gain 154 yards on thirty-two carries, as Chicago won handily, 20–7. Immediately after the final whistle blew, Payton was brought to the sideline, handed a pair of headphones, and placed on live television with Brent Musburger, host of *The NFL Today* and the man who, nine years earlier, flew the rookie running back to Chicago for his first televised interview.

"Walter," Musburger said, "you have been downplaying this record now for some time. But does it mean more to you personally now that you've accomplished it? Can you comment on what it means after you've surpassed it?"

With his hair wrapped in a white headband, Payton breathed deeply and deliberately. The crowd was still screaming. The air was moist and cold.

"Well, Bret . . ." he began—knowing good and well Musburger's first name was Brent.

Moments later, Payton accepted a call in a special tent from President Ronald Reagan, who was flying to Louisville on Air Force One. Upon being handed the phone, surrounded by dozens of people, he waited to hear the president's voice. With no one on the other end of the line, he cracked loudly, "Oh, the check is in the mail." The room broke up.

Even with 12,400 yards, Walter Payton remained a kid.

CHAPTER 19

SHUFFLE

In hindsight, knowing what we know now, it seems easy to assign *ah-ha!* moments to the Chicago Bears' inevitable greatness.

*Ah-ha!*—when the franchise hired Mike Ditka!

*Ah-ha!*—when the franchise drafted Jim McMahon!

*Ah-ha!*—when the franchise recorded "The Super Bowl Shuffle"!

*Ah-ha!*

Ask members of the team, however, and the dominance and splendor of the Bears can be dated to November 4, 1984, when the rough, tough, defending Super Bowl champion Los Angeles Raiders came to Chicago.

This was the game members of the Bears had been waiting for. Los Angeles was known as the franchise of renegades and misfits, bad-assess and outright terrors. Among the team's stars were Lyle Alzado, the steroid-loaded defensive end who had once boxed Muhammad Ali; Vann McElroy, the game's most ferocious safety; Matt Millen, the guided missile of a linebacker; and Howie Long, football's top pass rusher. The 7-2 Raiders snarled and barked and spewed nonstop trash, and if the antics themselves didn't intimidate, the unyielding physicality did. "We were a team of hitters," said McElroy. "We hit."

The Bears entered the game with a 6-3 record, but fans and opponents remained skeptical. In past years Chicago had gotten off to fast starts under Jack Pardee and Neill Armstrong, only to inevitably fall flat.

"It's like a boxer," Mike Ditka said. "You hit him in the nose enough times he's gonna respect you. The Raiders were always a physical football team, and that's what we talked about before the game. I said, 'We're going toe to toe with these guys. It's gonna be a heavyweight match, and we're gonna slug with them.'"

The day was perfect—fifty-one degrees, with minimal humidity. Payton ran for 111 yards and two touchdowns, and walked off the field with his head pounding, his knees throbbing, his fingers twisted and crooked. He didn't get the worst of it.

Chicago's 17–6 win was an ode to violence. Fights broke out following seemingly every other play. McMahon, the Bears gutsy quarterback, had to leave the game after lacerating his kidney. When he went to the bathroom and urinated blood, the team sent him to a hospital. "I could have died," McMahon said. "It was bleeding for two days. The doctor told me, 'Look, you're gonna die if we don't cut [the kidney] out.' I said, 'You can't cut it out. You cut it out and I'm finished. Just keep giving me morphine and leave me alone.' That's what he did." McMahon remained in the hospital for ten days. His season was over.

The Bears sacked Los Angeles' quarterbacks nine times—knocking starter Marc Wilson out of the game with hand and head injuries, then doing the same to David Humm by bruising his knee. "Our third-string quarterback was [veteran punter] Ray Guy, and we're standing there watching him about to pee on himself," said McElroy. "At halftime [Coach] Tom Flores is talking to Ray about possibly having to go in, and we're looking all over for a pack of cigarettes to give him to calm his nerves. Because he was freaking out."

A hobbled Wilson wound up returning to the game, but it mattered not. No Raiders quarterback was going to survive the Bears defense. "They were just sick," said McElroy. "Everyone was threatening everyone else, guys trying to kill each other. On that day, we had no shot."

Shelby Jordan, the Raiders' offensive tackle, slugged defensive end Richard Dent in the face and later accused him of excessive head slapping and throwing elbows into his nose. Late in the game, after Long was repeatedly cheap-shotted by right guard Kurt Becker, the Raider star screamed, "I'm going to get you in the parking lot after the game and beat you up in front of your family!" Becker laughed—but there was Long, after the players had dressed into street clothes, standing outside the Bears locker room, waiting for his nemesis. Becker never emerged.

Ditka and his coaches were elated. The Raiders bullied the NFL, and the Bears punched them in the mouth.

. . .

Without McMahon, the Bears—tough, fierce, hobbled—crawled through the remainder of the season, finishing 3-3 behind the mediocre quarterbacking of Steve Fuller and, briefly, Rusty Lisch and Greg Landry. That they held on to win the division is a big tribute to a swarming defense, and an even bigger tribute to the marvelous play of Walter Payton.

At age thirty-one, Payton was enjoying one of the best years of his career. He was named the NFL's Player of the Month for October, and although he struggled through a couple of poor games in November, it was primarily because defenses (no longer having to worry about McMahon) were back to stacking the line and daring Chicago to pass. On November 25, the Bears clinched their first-ever division title, beating the Vikings 34–3 behind Payton's 117 yards. As he walked off the Metrodome turf, the normally boisterous purple-clad crowd now silenced, Payton slowed to a saunter, soaking in in the moment. "I'm just going to enjoy it," he said. "It hasn't sunk in yet. It's strange."

Payton's season was remarkable—he ran for 1,684 yards and eleven touchdowns, earning his seventh trip to the Pro Bowl. What elevated it to phenomenal, however, was that—physically—he was no longer the same player he had once been. The lifespan of an NFL running back is, on average, 2.6 seasons, and with good reason. Through ten seasons, Payton had endured an ungodly number of hits. As contemporaries like Earl Campbell, Wilbert Montgomery, and Billy Sims began to slow down (or collapse completely), Payton somehow sucked up the pain and kept churning out yardage. Hardly a burner at age twenty-one, Payton at thirty-one possessed below-average speed and good, not great, maneuverability. The slashes and twists made famous from earlier days rarely took place anymore; the flamboyant runs decreasingly a part of the package. Johnny Roland, the running backs coach, sought to reduce Payton's load from sixty-five plays to between forty-five and fifty. The star refused. "It's almost like the speed didn't matter," said Keith Van Horne, a Bears offensive tackle. "Walter could cut back if he needed to, but he became a hole runner, which means he found the holes, rushed through them, and then attacked anyone in his way. He was so rugged, so tough, and so determined. That's why he lasted."

Through all the amazing performances Payton coaxed out of a declining body, one game stands out. It took place at Soldier Field on December 9, 1984, with the Bears hosting the Packers in an intense-yet-meaningless late-season matchup. Because of injuries to McMahon and Fuller, as well as the early-season release of Avellini, Chicago was forced to turn to Lisch, a devoutly religious twenty-seven-year-old best known as the man Joe Montana had once replaced as the starter at Notre Dame.

Lisch was an inconsequential player who opened eyes a week earlier when, in the midst of a game at San Diego, he responded to a Ditka browbeating by refusing to return to the game. "I asked Ed [Hughes, the offensive coordinator], 'Where's Lisch?'" Ditka said.

"He's not going back in," Hughes replied. "Said you can't talk to him like that."

Ditka approached the quarterback, who was sitting alone on the bench, arms crossed. "Please go back in the game," the coach said. "I didn't mean that stuff. You're a great kid." Lisch returned, the Bears lost, and the following Tuesday the quarterback brought the coach a gold crucifix.

Lisch started against the Packers, and evoked visions of Kim McQuilken's heyday. He completed ten of twenty-three passes and, in the words of the *Tribune*'s Bernie Lincicome, "If Rusty Lisch were the little Dutch boy with his finger in the dike, the coast of Holland would now begin somewhere around the middle of Westphalia." With the first half drawing to a close and a play-off birth wrapped up, Ditka made a quarterback change. He pulled Lisch and replaced him with the day's listed backup—Walter Payton.

*Walter Payton?*

Soldier Field erupted as the substitute—visibly calm, internally petrified—jogged into the huddle, kneeled, and called a play. "He took charge," said Jay Hilgenberg, the center. "One time he said, 'Screen left to Cal [running back Calvin Thomas] over there.' The rest of the time he had it all right." Payton took six snaps, all from the shotgun position. One of his passes fell incomplete. The other was intercepted by Green Bay's Tom Flynn. ("It was an innocuous play," recalled Flynn. "But I've always told people that I'm probably in the record books as the only person to intercept Walter Payton's pass from the quarterback position.") He ran four times for twenty-five yards. Later in the game, with Lisch back at quarterback, Payton took a handoff and threw a two-yard touchdown pass to Matt Suhey. He also rushed for 175 yards and a touchdown. Chicago lost 20–14, but it didn't matter.

"Walter did everything you could possibly do on a football field," said Lynn Dickey, Green Bay's backup quarterback that day. "I can't tell you how many times I'd hoped he'd get the flu before we played them."

. . .

The Bears entered the 1984 play-offs having lost two of their final three games and lacking a credible starting quarterback. Under pressure, Ditka came up with a plan for beating favored Washington, the two-time defending NFC champions, in the divisional game at RFK Stadium. "We were gonna ride Walter," he said, "and hope the defense took care of the rest."

In his first postseason appearance in five seasons, Payton dazzled. He ran for 104 yards on twenty-four carries, and early in the second quarter took the handoff from Fuller, rolled wide, and tossed a nineteen-yard touchdown pass to tight end Pat Dunsmore for a 10–3 lead. "Walter had a phenomenal arm—he could throw a ball fifty yards, easily," said Dunsmore. "He didn't have the best touch, but he got it right to me." Chicago's defense pummeled quarterback Joe Theismann and the Bears won, 23–19. Immediately afterward, as his teammates celebrated, Payton headed straight for the Washington locker room. Sprawled out on a training table was Ken Huff, the Redskins' right guard who had broken his right leg. Nine years earlier, Huff was drafted by Baltimore one spot ahead of Payton. "I hadn't seen Walter since 1975, and here he was, checking if I was OK," said Huff. "That just floored me."

Chicago's players celebrated loudly in the visiting locker room, but the festivities were short-lived. They would travel to San Francisco the following weekend to play the 49ers in the NFC title game.

The NFC West champions had just completed a 15-1 season, and opened the play-offs by demolishing the New York Giants, 21–10. In the week leading up to Bears vs. 49ers, Chicago's coaches and players strutted and crowed, bragged and boasted. The Bears were listed as nine-and-a-half-point underdogs, and Ditka loved it. "The German army couldn't beat us with nine and a half points," he growled.

"We're not going to lose the game," Payton said—and the words wound up hanging on the bulletin board in the 49ers locker room. "We know what we have to do to win at San Francisco," Ditka said—and the words wound up hanging on the bulletin board in the 49ers locker room.

**FINAL SCORE:**
**SAN FRANCISCO 23**
**CHICAGO 0**

The game was uglier than the outcome. Before 61,040 rabid fans at Candlestick Park, the 49ers sacked Fuller nine times and held Chicago to 186 total yards. "At halftime Ditka fired Ed Hughes," said Jay Saldi, the veteran tight end. "He was livid because we hadn't scored any points, and he screamed at Ed, 'Get the fuck out of the locker room!' Ed lit up a Marlboro and left." While Payton ran for a respectable ninety-two yards, few of his twenty-two carries held much significance. "What stood out," wrote Christine Brennan in *The Washington Post*, "was Walter Payton futilely churning toward the sideline, looking for yardage that didn't exist."

Ditka and his players could accept the domination. The 49ers were talented and experienced and widely believed to be chemically enhanced. "They beat the shit out of us," said Fred Caito, the Bears trainer. "And our offensive and defensive linemen said, 'These guys are 'roided up, and they're destroying us in the trenches. We can't compete with that.' I assure you many of our linemen started using after that game." What they could not accept—what they refused to accept—was the second-half sight of Guy McIntyre, a six-foot-three, 271-pound backup offensive lineman, lining up in the backfield alongside halfback Wendell Tyler. San Francisco coach Bill Walsh termed it his Angus offense—named for the Black Angus restaurant the steak-gorging McIntyre used to frequent. There was logic behind the move. The Bears had a hard-hitting free safety, Todd Bell, who was cheating toward the line and pummeling Tyler. McIntyre's blocking changed that.

The Bears, however, deemed his presence a slap in the face.

"It was brutal," said Jimbo Covert. "An ultimate sign of disrespect." Making matters worse, as the two teams walked off the field, members of the 49ers taunted the Bears. "Next time," one player said, "bring your offense."

Afterward, Payton sat at his locker, a look of disbelief crossing his face. He wanted to cry. He wanted to scream. He spoke haltingly, almost as if he were in a state of shock. "This is the worst ever," he said. "When you wait ten years for the chance, and you get this close, and get turned back, it's hard to deal with. It's the hardest thing I've ever had to deal with."

He was told that Ditka suggested a Super Bowl was within the organization's grasps for next year.

"Next year," said Payton, "is not promised to anyone."

•  •  •

On the morning of February 25, 1985, Walter Payton was scheduled to travel to New York to receive something called the Gordon Gin Black Athlete of the Year award. Once upon a time, such recognition (as well as the twenty-five thousand dollars in prize money and "hand-sculptured trophy by noted sculptor Ed Dwight!") would have meant something to Payton. Awards; medals; plaques; keys to Urbana, Illinois, or Mahopac, New York, or Thomasville, Georgia—those types of things carried weight with the young, eager-to-please athlete.

At age thirty-one, however, with the end of his career coming into focus, Payton was starting to think differently. Though he had been engaging and accommodating toward fans, throughout much of his career indifference often cloaked his behavior. "He was enigmatic," said Ron Atlas, his longtime friend. "He could be charming, but he wouldn't really go out of his way to help individual people." Because Bud Holmes, his agent, thought it important that every fan who took the time to write receive an autographed reply, a woman who could perfectly forge Payton's signature was hired to do the tireless work the football player had little interest in. "Walter knew how to please," Holmes said. "He brought flowers to secretaries, said nice things to people. But he could also be lazy and disinterested." When, following the 1979 season, Payton was hired by a not-for-profit agency in Indiana to speak to a group of children, he jumped at the opportunity—then forgot to show up. It wasn't a random oversight. "I sent the appearance fee money back to them and made Walter do it the next year for free," Holmes said. "I tried like heck to always keep that image up."

By the time his speed and elusiveness had begun to wane, Payton was keenly aware of the positive power of celebrity and the impact he had on people. Payton wasn't merely one to ask, "How's it going?"—he'd inquire about the family; the kids; the dogs; the farm. He wasn't merely a handshaker—he was a hugger. Of all the Bears, Payton was the one who knew the names of every ball boy and intern. "If you were the kid doing laundry in the equipment room, Walter made sure to get to talk with you," said Duke Tobin, who worked as a ball boy when his father, Bill, ran personnel. "Walter didn't just know the ball boys. He knew what they liked, where they went to school, who their parents were. He had this game he liked to play, where he'd grab one side of a football and you'd grab the other, and it'd be a tug-of-war. You couldn't possibly win, because his fingers were the longest I'd ever seen and he was as strong as an ox. But it was great fun."

Part of the overt warmth can probably be chalked up to Holmes relentlessly pounding home the point—*Folks want to be inspired. You inspire folks. Use that. Embrace that. Enjoy that.* But there was also a genuinely compassionate soft spot inside Payton. He liked seeing smiles and making a difference; liked knowing someone's day was completed by a few moments of shared space.

Payton politely called the Gordon Gin folks and told them he'd have to be late—"Something important has come up." That something important was T. J. Baker, a seven-year-old boy from Davenport, Iowa, who was fighting a malignant brain tumor. Baker's hero was Payton, and when the running back learned last minute that a fund-raiser was being held in Moline, Iowa (just over the Illinois state line), he committed to stopping by for a quick visit.

Payton stayed for four hours.

"We just chatted," he said. "I'd rather not say about what. Just being there, showing concern, caring, means more than what you talk about. It stays with you. You don't forget."

Payton never uttered another word about Baker. He didn't want to delve into details of his visit, because, frankly, it was nobody's business. A young child was dying. Wasn't that enough? "Walter could comfort people and love people and be there for people," said Holmes. "He had moments of amazing warmth."

Chicago's defensive line coach, Dale Haupt, had a teenage daughter, Helen, who baked Payton chocolate chip cookies before every home game for a stretch of five years. When Payton's son, Jarrett, was born, she made the baby a quilt—"just so Walter knew we were happy for him." Helen never expected anything in return. He was friendly and kind, and that was good enough. "So now I'm a freshman at Wake Forest and I'm home from school, and Walter calls," she said. "He wanted to see if I was home because he had something to give me. He drives to our house, and he hands me a beautiful gold bracelet. He stayed and we talked for the longest time. I think he just wanted me to know he appreciated the kindness through the years. A lot of athletes never thought like that. He did."

The Bears used their fourth-round pick in the 1985 NFL Draft to select Kevin Butler, a kicker from the University of Georgia. Bob Thomas, Payton's fellow rookie in 1975, had held the job for the majority of the decade, and the transaction did not bode well for his future. Still, when the team finally cut him on September 2, Thomas was despondent. Not wanting to bump into any teammates, he waited until nine fifteen A.M., when meetings began, to clean out his locker. "I was thinking how festive and lively the locker room usually was, and now it was perfectly quiet," said Thomas. "Well, I walk to my locker and Walter's sitting there, waiting for me." At Payton's behest, the two longtime friends walked outside the equipment room and rested on some old railroad irons. "For twenty minutes, he told me—a broken-down kicker—what it meant to play with me for ten years," Thomas said. "I was crying, and he buried my tears in his chest. I made some great kicks, I had some amazing memories, but that moment more than any other sticks out from my twelve-year career."

And yet, Payton's deep kindness was coupled with deep insecurity. Or, as Holmes said, "He could also be incredibly vapid and thin-skinned. It really depended on the day. Sometimes on the hour."

Indeed, two months after granting Baker a wish come true, Payton was in Chicago, pouting. According to a report in the *Tribune*, McMahon, the savvy-yet-brittle quarterback with all of three NFL seasons under his belt, was now the Bears' highest-paid player, earning $950,000 for the upcoming season. Payton, meanwhile, was a distant second at $685,000 (annuity not included).

The $265,000 contract disparity between McMahon and Payton made the running back's blood boil. So, for that matter, did the mounting dismissiveness he perceived to be coming from the press, the fans, and the Bears organization. "This is my eleventh year, and nobody takes me seriously," he moaned to *Sports Illustrated*. "You talk about the running backs that have been in the league, you ask, 'What about the running backs?' and the first names that pop into people's minds are Eric Dickerson, Tony Dorsett, Curt Warner, or Billy Sims, William Andrews, George Rogers. Every year, Payton's on the back burner.

"If you chart [the careers of other runners], you see peaks and valleys. Whereas my career, I like to think, has been like IBM or Xerox. I've been playing at the same level, and sometimes above, for at least nine years. I guess the people have come to expect that. Rain, sleet, snow, sprained ankle . . . or whatever, he's going to be there. Sometimes people tend to—not knowingly—they sometimes take things for granted. I guess I've been the Rodney Dangerfield of running backs.

"But it doesn't bother me. Rodney makes a lot of movies, drinks a lot of light beer."

Only it *did* bother him. While his rant concerned, in a literal sense, the NFL's other marquee running backs, the words had more to do with the

Chicago Bears. Entering the 1985 season Payton was, for the first time, not the team's sole focal point. There was McMahon, the hard-living, attention-seeking quarterback who talked smack and wore sunglasses indoors. There was Willie Gault, the speedy wide receiver who longed for a career in movies. There was Mike Singletary, the Butkus-esque middle linebacker, and his two high-flying cohorts, Wilber Marshall and Otis Wilson. And, of course, there was Ditka, the snarling head coach, and Buddy Ryan, the defensive coordinator who hated him. So loaded was the team that, shortly after reporting to training camp and soaking in all the talent, Butler called Cathy, his fiancée, and told her their wedding had to be moved from January 25, 1985—the day before the next Super Bowl. "We had so many weapons, and Walter wasn't the center of it anymore, even though he was so valuable," said Covert. "And while I'm sure he really enjoyed being part of all the winning, the other side of the coin was that it wasn't all about him. I think that was sometimes a little bit difficult for him. The other personalities came into play, and it wasn't that he was ever overshadowed, but he had competition."

With the cutting of Thomas, only defensive lineman Mike Hartenstine, receiver Brian Baschnagel, and safety Gary Fencik remained from the dark ages. Few of the modern Bears understood what made Payton go—the intensity, the need to prove people wrong, the insecurity. He was confused by the public gloating of younger athletes and turned off by what he perceived to be the constant cries for attention. It was one thing for the NFL's all-time rushing leader to crave the spotlight. It was another altogether for teammates who had accomplished precious little. "The challenges of being as recognized as he was and the face of sports for a city for many years would wear on anyone," said Shaun Gayle, the defensive back. "I'm sure it weighed on Walter, too."

What irked Payton most was the emergence of a rookie defensive lineman named William Perry. Drafted in the first round out of Clemson, "the Refrigerator" (as he was called) was immediately lambasted by Ryan, who labeled him too slow, too fat, too dumb to master Chicago's complex 46 Defense. Yet in an era when players rarely exceeded 300 pounds, the Fridge stood out. Gap-toothed and wobbly, he tipped the scales at 325 pounds, making him one of the league's largest players. He had a twenty-two-inch neck and a size fifty-eight coat. "I was born to be big," he told *Sports Illustrated*, "and I ain't disappointing nobody."

Upon seeing his new teammate at training camp for the first time, defensive lineman Dan Hampton nicknamed Perry "Biscuit"—as in, he was one biscuit short of 350 pounds. When Perry removed his T-shirt in front of other players, revealing mounds of Shamu-esque blubber, the moniker de jour changed to "Mud Slide."

"Funny thing is, Fridge was a great athlete," said Andy Frederick, an offensive tackle. "I saw him jump atop a thirty-six-inch table from the ground while holding weights in his hands and I saw him dunk a volleyball from below the rim."

It wasn't that Payton disliked his new teammate. Even for Ryan, who vehemently opposed the Bears selecting him (on his second practice with the team, Ryan called the Fridge "a wasted draft choice and a waste of money"), Perry was a big, loveable lug. No, what irked Payton was what the rookie symbolized.

Chicago won its first five games of the 1985 season, and the Bears were again legitimate Monsters of the Midway. Yet while triumphs over the division-rival Vikings (during which McMahon, suffering from a leg infection and fresh off of two days in traction for back problems, came off the bench in the third quarter to throw three remarkable touchdown passes—one made possible by a vicious block by Payton on a blitzing linebacker) and Buccaneers were satisfying, Ditka used a bright red Sharpie to mark October 13 on his calendar—the day the Bears were to face the 49ers at Candlestick Park.

Before the previous season's play-off loss, Ditka had never given much thought to San Francisco. It was a top-flight organization with one of the best coaches (Bill Walsh) and quarterbacks (Joe Montana) in the game, but the 49ers were hardly a heated rival. With that 23–0 slaughter, however, everything changed. Ditka didn't merely want to beat Walsh. He wanted to destroy and embarrass him.

Led by Payton's two touchdowns and 132 rushing yards, as well as a defense that sacked Montana seven times, the coach's wish came true. The Bears routed San Francisco, 26–10. "Unfortunately, when the 49ers beat us last year they didn't show much courtesy or dignity," Payton said. "They said negative things about our offense after shutting us out. We thought about that all during the off-season and the preseason."

Armed with a bad temper and a long memory, Ditka wasn't settling merely for a win. Here was a coach who, two years earlier, ordered his special team players to "get" Detroit kicker Eddie Murray, whom Ditka thought to be showboating. Here was a coach who once broke a bone in his hand by punching a steel locker after a loss. Now, in the waning minutes of the fourth quarter, with the game out of reach and the image of Guy McIntyre at fullback dancing through his cerebrum, Ditka made a lineup change. He inserted Perry, thus far only a defensive player, into the backfield, handing him the ball on the game's final two plays (Perry ran for four yards—one more than the 49ers' entire second-half total).

"Gives you a little food for thought on the goal line, doesn't he?" Ditka said afterward. "I mean, it's really something you've got to think about realistically. There's a chance that could happen."

In the following week's 23–7 whitewashing of Green Bay, Perry ran for a one-yard touchdown and was Payton's lead blocker on two more scores (Chris Cobbs of the *Los Angeles Times* described Perry's block of Packer linebacker George Cumby "as if [Cumby] were 225 pounds of prime rib").

With that, a pop culture phenomenon was born.

In the ensuing days Perry became the talk of a sports-obsessed nation. He was invited to be a guest on *Late Night with David Letterman* and, before long, also appeared on TV with Johnny Carson and Bob Hope. Perry signed a six-figure endorsement deal with McDonald's (Asked the *Los Angeles Times*: "Can McPerry be far behind?"), as well as smaller spokesperson agreements for companies that peddled bacon, thermal underwear, macaroni-and-cheese dinners, and paper towels. One Chicago TV station ran a Perry-related story every night for three straight weeks.

"The Fridge became an overnight rock star," said Greg Gershuny, the Bears' director of information services. "He could walk up to any restaurant and be ushered right into the place."

When asked, Payton said all the right things about Perry. But inside, he hurt. The kid had been with Chicago for half a year, and he was already earning pitchman deals Payton could only dream of. The same went for McMahon, a teammate Payton enjoyed and admired, but one who never worked especially hard and who also lived off of image more than reality. McMahon's initial reputation in Chicago—that of an unflappably cool cat—was born largely off of the mythology of sunglasses. Far from trying to make a fashion statement, though, McMahon wore shades at all times because, at age six, he accidentally speared his right eye with a fork, resulting in permanent ocular damage. Furthermore, McMahon's Mohawk haircut—one being emulated by hundreds of Chicago schoolchildren—came into existence only when Willie Gault attempted to salvage a self-service trim the quarterback had botched.

Yet the details didn't much matter for a public suddenly caught up in Chicago Bear fever. Well before Andre Agassi declared, "Image is everything" in his iconic Canon commercials, the Bears were bringing the slogan to life. Ten members of the team (including Ditka) had their own radio shows. Ditka was appearing in three television commercials, and the offensive linemen *(offensive linemen!)* were being featured in a Chevy advertising campaign. Perry and McMahon were both good, solid, above-average NFL players—who were suddenly anointed rock stars.

Payton, meanwhile, signed on to star in a spot for Diet Coke. One lousy spot. He did his best to adjust to his new place in the shadows. He kept his mouth shut, offered up boring canned quotes when asked and, on the field, peeled off an NFL record nine straight hundred-yard rushing games. Few people noticed.

Blessed with the NFL's best offensive line, Payton no longer had to create his own holes and hope for random openings. He had evolved, in a way that other top running backs never could. To the day his career ended, Earl Campbell wanted to barrel over people. To the day his career ended, Terry Metcalf wanted to juke and shake. Neither lasted long. Age and fatigue are a football player's two greatest opponents, and styles either change or die. Payton, a man always in touch with his body, realized quickness could not serve as a primary weapon. He finally had a top-flight school of blockers at his disposal, and he needed their help. "Later in his career Walter was the easiest running back in the world to block for," said Jay Hilgenberg, the All-Pro center. "If we had the six or seven hole called, that's where Walter was going to be, and he'd come with a lot of force."

It was a strange time to be Walter Payton. His out-of-wedlock son, Nigel, and in-wedlock daughter, Brittney, were born months apart. His team was hot and his Q-rating on the wane. He was piling up Pro Bowl–worthy numbers (he finished the season with 1,551 yards, the fourth-highest total of his career), yet wasn't the same back he once had been. He put on the happiest face possible, but came across to teammates as moodier and crankier than ever. "Walter was the personality of the team," said Butler, the kicker. "If Walter was loud and rambunctious that day, the pace of practice took off. But if things weren't going well, Walter would wear it on his forehead."

When he was the only story in town, it was easy to say, "I don't want the attention."

Now that the attention didn't exist, he wanted it.

· · ·

The song was a bad idea.

Walter Payton knew it was a bad idea because this sort of thing never works out in the end. Why didn't he talk trash? Because the minute you tell an opponent he stinks, he comes back and tackles you for a five-yard loss. Why didn't he brag and boast after a hundred-and-fifty-yard game? Because a thirty-yard game is inevitably around the corner. Payton knew what he wanted his image to be (and what Holmes had insisted it *should be*)—family man, happy, accessible, agreeable, kid friendly—and loudmouth braggart wasn't on the list.

That being said, really, what was he supposed to do on that mid-November day when Gault, the explosive wide receiver with stars in his eyes, told him that the rest of the high-profile Bears were planning on recording a rap song, and that proceeds would help feed the Chicago homeless? The title itself, "The Super Bowl Shuffle," symbolized everything Payton detested. Having had his hopes dashed time and time again, the last thing Payton wanted was for his cocky team to appear even cockier. He wasn't the only Bear to feel that way. "I disagreed strongly with it," said Covert. "Why would we want to tell people after nine or ten games that we were going to win the Super Bowl? I didn't want to get the shit kicked out of us in the play-offs."

Despite reservations, on the morning of November 23, Payton shuffled into a suburban Chicago recording studio, alongside Gault, Perry, McMahon, Singletary, and a handful of others. He didn't want to be there, but didn't want to be left out, either. How could the Chicago Bears do a song and not include Sweetness? How could Sweetness let others take all the glory?

Because he was the greatest of Bears, as well as a future Hall of Famer, Payton was selected to rap the tune's opening lyrics. The words were written by Dick Meyer, a slimy aspiring record producer who initially approached Gault with the "Shuffle" idea, and they were inane.

> *Well, they call me Sweetness,*
> *And I like to dance . . .*

Ever the *24 Karat Black Gold* star, Payton pulled it off without a hitch. "Walter was the best of the bunch, by far," said Darryl Krall, technical director of the "Shuffle" video. "He had that high Michael Jackson falsetto, and his sense of rhythm was perfect."

One day later the Bears destroyed the Falcons, 36–0, running their record to 12-0 and upping the team's confidence to an all-time high. Over the past three games, Chicago had outscored the opposition 104–3. With 102 yards, Payton was now leading the NFC and in pursuit of his second NFL rushing crown. "This team has not reached its peak," he said afterward. "We're capable of scoring sixty points. We don't know how good we are, and that's kind of scary."

"We aren't satisfied yet," added Singletary. "If you set your goals as being the best team of all time, the best players of all time, how can you be satisfied? People are waiting, expecting, for us to hit that slump. Will it be the Dallas game? No, maybe it will be the week after Dallas and the week before Miami. No, maybe it will be Miami.

"People are saying we've got to have that one day, that one game. But why? Why do we have to? If you keep trying to improve, every week, why does there have to be that one week? When will it happen? Maybe it won't happen."

On the day after the Atlanta triumph, a group of ten Bears posed for "The Super Bowl Shuffle" jacket cover. For roughly two hours, the men— clad in clean blue jerseys and white pants—stood inside a room, making wacky and tough and serious and goofy faces for a photographer named Paul Natkin and embracing the magic of a 12-0 roll. Payton, again, didn't feel right about the whole thing. The next game was a Monday night trip to Miami, where the 8-4 Dolphins awaited. Spearheaded by a twenty-four-year-old quarterback named Dan Marino and his two young, fleet wide receivers, Mark Clayton and Mark Duper (aka the Marks Brothers), Miami featured a group of offensive players who believed they could score on anyone in the league—Chicago included. "We are going to kick the Bears' butts," Duper said that week. "The Bears are in for the treat of their lives."

For Miami, there was added motivation in facing a team with an unblemished record. In NFL history, only one franchise, the 1972 Dolphins, had gone undefeated. Those Dolphins were coached by Don Shula, as were these Dolphins. There was a connection and a *need* to win. Throughout the week, members of that '72 group, including legendary figures like Nick Buoniconti, Larry Csonka, Jim Kiick, and Bob Kuechenberg, attended practices, pressuring the modern Dolphins to find a way.

The Bears, on the other hand, were surprisingly casual. When the chartered plane left Chicago, it had been fifteen degrees and snowy. When it set down in Miami, the temperature was seventy-five degrees, with a cloudless sky. The siren call of South Beach beckoned. "We didn't care about that

game," said Butler, the rookie kicker. "We weren't trying to go undefeated—
we were trying to win a title. So when we got to Miami all we were focused
on was having a good time. We all went out the night before the game, then
slept in as late as we could."

"Every time we had a game in Florida, some Bears fans were going,
too—and the Sunday night before that Miami game I think I saw just about
all of them out there somewhere," Steve McMichael, the veteran defensive
end, wrote in his book, *Tales from the Chicago Bears Sideline*. "I think we started
out at Hooters and it just denigrated from there."

As if the *Monday Night Football* matchup weren't hyped enough based
upon the presence of the undefeated Bears, the media labeled it as a battle of
the decades. A Miami radio station came up with a song about defrosting the
Refrigerator. A Miami TV reporter visited the city's zoo to interview a bear
and a dolphin. "Reporters fell from the sky like a seven-inch snow," Singletary wrote in his autobiography, *Calling the Shots*. "We were completely covered. They waited for us in our lockers and called our homes; the practice
field was staked out like the Democratic National Convention."

Immediately before kickoff, Chicago's players glanced across the field.
Lining Miami's sideline were all the old legends from '72, arms folded,
expressions stern. "It was like they were trying to put the voodoo on us," said
Ken Taylor, a rookie safety with the Bears. "They're standing there with their
legs kind of spread apart like Superman or something, and they got their big
arms folded like they are measuring us up. It was all just kind of weird."

With McMahon out for a third straight game with an injured right
shoulder, the start went to Fuller, who found himself confused by Miami's
defense and frustrated by his receivers' slippery fingers. Most shocking was
the sight of Ryan's defense, thought to be impenetrable, being shredded by
Marino, whose forty-eight touchdown passes one season earlier set an NFL
record. Back at the University of Pittsburgh, Marino had roomed with
Covert, the Bears' offensive tackle. A couple of days before the Dolphins
game, Ryan sauntered up to Covert and told him, "We're going to blitz your
asshole buddy this week and knock him on his ass."

"If you do," Covert replied, "he'll kill you."

Ryan ignored the warning. Marino, blessed with the league's quickest
release, killed him.

The Dolphins led 31–10 at halftime, and in the locker room Ditka
and Ryan—enemies on the sunniest of days—exchanged a couple of wildly

thrown punches before being separated. Ditka began screaming at Ryan early in the second quarter, wondering how much longer he was going to cover Nat Moore, Miami's speedy wide receiver, with a linebacker. Ryan colorfully advised the head coach to back off. "Ditka was right," said Dan Hampton. "He was basically saying, 'Hey Buddy, quit being an asshole and put a nickel back in there on Nat Moore.'"

All the while, Payton sat by his locker, boiling. Even though Miami ranked last in the league against the run, and even though Payton had cleared a hundred yards in a league-record seven straight games, Ditka didn't hand him the ball until late in the first quarter, with the Dolphins leading 10–7. For some reason, the Bears were leaning on Fuller, a castoff from Kansas City. "We have the number one running game in football, and Miami has the worst run defense," said Hampton. "So what does genius Ditka do? We throw the ball."

"I could have told you they would lose that game," said Holmes, Payton's agent. "Everyone on that team was all swelled up, cocky, and thinking they walked on water. Even with Walter, I could tell the fire wasn't there. They all wanted the stardom the Fridge was getting, and there was a ton of jealousy. You can't win with that hanging over a team."

Early in the fourth quarter, with the score 38–24, Fuller sprained his ankle and McMahon—who had begged Ditka to start the game—was inserted. He marched Chicago down the field, but threw a costly interception with 6:12 remaining to seal the Bears' fate. When Chicago regained possession, McMahon ignored the coaches and repeatedly handed the ball to Payton. Though it ranked about 12,471 on the night's storyline list, Payton was trying to break the consecutive hundred-yard rushing games mark he shared with O. J. Simpson and Earl Campbell.

"We're fourteen points down and Ditka sends in a pass play," McMahon said. "I said, 'Look, boys, we're down fourteen points. We're already in the play-offs. Let's get this man the yards he deserves.' Not one guy in the huddle had a problem with that. But Mike knew I didn't call the play he [ordered], so he starts yelling and screaming. I give the ball to Walter. They were only rushing three at this point, and he busts up for good yardage." With the veins on his neck bulging and his brown eyes about to explode from the sockets, Ditka called a time-out. When McMahon reached the sideline, the coach lit into him.

"Hey, Mike, you know they're dropping eight," McMahon replied. "Walter only needs about fifteen more yards for his record."

Ditka calmed down. "What?" he said.

"The record," McMahon replied. "His record."

Ditka had known nothing of it. "Yeah," he said, "we'll get him his record. But first we're going to do this play."

McMahon nodded as Ditka called for a pass to Dennis McKinnon. When he returned to the huddle, McMahon flashed a wide smile. "Boys," he said, "the shit is going to hit the fan, but we're going to run the ball again."

McMahon lined up behind center and looked toward Ditka, who knew he was being ignored. He threw his clipboard in the air and shrugged. Payton wound up with 121 yards on twenty-three carries, and while they were largely empty calories amassed at the end of a blowout, the running back was eternally grateful to his quarterback. From that moment on, McMahon could do no wrong.

. . .

Despite being annihilated before millions of spectators (the game was the most-viewed *Monday Night Football* telecast ever, with an astonishing 29.6 rating), most of the Bears remained undeterred. "Hey, we're human," Otis Wilson said afterward.

"This is not a catastrophe," added Singletary.

"Nobody's perfect," Ditka said. "And we proved it."

"A lot of guys were walking off of the field like, 'Finally, the pressure is off of us,'" said Covert. "When we got beat by Miami—I didn't want to lose, but it kind of lifted the pressure."

Win or lose, on Tuesday morning at eight the players were expected to meet at Park West, a well-known nightclub on Chicago's North Side, for the taping of "The Super Bowl Shuffle" video. Having assumed the Bears would demolish the Dolphins, Dick Meyer, the song's producer, booked the date two weeks in advance. He spoke to Gault via phone immediately after the loss, and was assured the Bears would still be there.

"Willie asked me if I'd be in it as we were flying back from Miami," said Hilgenberg. "I said, 'Hey, Willie, we just got killed on national TV. You think I'm gonna help you sing a song about the Super Bowl? No thank you. I don't want any part of that.'"

Though the Bears were a tight-knit group, there was something about Gault that rubbed many the wrong way. He was the prettiest guy on a rugged team; unwilling to throw a hard block or cross the middle of the field. "If I asked Willie to run an extra pattern it was as if I'd asked him to cut his nuts off," said Bob Avellini, the former quarterback. "He didn't want to play football. He wanted to make money." Early in his career Gault told the *Tribune* that, with a little work, he could make Payton a faster, better player. ("I could have gotten him from a four-point-six to a four-point-four forty," Gault said. "He had a hitch when he ran and wasted some motion.") The suggestion did not go over well.

Furthermore, Gault always seemed to be bragging. He dropped names incessantly (his friendship with Louis Farrakhan, the controversial Nation of Islam leader, won him little favor with white teammates), craved to be seen at the hottest clubs and biggest openings; wanted to be a celebrity first, a football player second. Teammates nicknamed him "Hollywood Gault," a sobriquet that was far from a compliment. When, three years later, he was dealt to the Raiders, teammates celebrated. "Willie Gault? When he was traded I knew we'd be a better team," McMahon said. "He always wanted to go out to the West Coast and be an actor. Well, for five years he was an actor playing a football player."

Payton tolerated Gault in the way one tolerates the annoying little brother who can't help himself. But when the receiver checked to make sure Payton would still be partaking in the video shoot, he received a stern look and a sterner lecture. "Are you kidding me?" Payton said. "After we just got our asses kicked like that? No way." McMahon also refused to attend, leaving a dumbfounded Meyer with two gaping holes. "We told them we weren't coming," McMahon said. "I guess they didn't believe us until we didn't show."

The airplane landed in Chicago at three thirty A.M. Less than five hours later twenty-two Bears showed up for the taping. Grumpiness morphed into embarrassment when they were informed of Payton's decision not to partake. If the greatest Bear thought it wrongheaded, what justification did the others have? "He was the guy we all looked up to," said Gayle. "We respected his judgment more than our own."

A couple of days later, when the sting of the Miami setback had lessened, Payton and McMahon filmed their scenes against a blue screen inside the racquetball court at Halas Hall and were spliced into the video. "It's a terrible piece of work," said Barbara Supeter, one of the video's executive producers. "We finished editing and filming on December 18, and on December 22 it was in stores. We didn't have any writers or choreographers to speak of. And yet, it became this phenomenon."

On the day before its release, Greg Gershuny, the Bears' director of information services, was sitting in his office when a member of the public relations staff came in with a tape of the "Shuffle." The two men listened, and when the song ended they sat in stunned silence. "We weren't sure whether to hide it or get it on the radio as soon as possible," said Gershuny. "It was confusing."

The "Shuffle" went on to become a smash hit—the single sold more than five hundred thousand copies, reached number forty-one on the Billboard charts and, against all logic, was nominated for a Grammy for best rhythm-and-blues performance by a group. Years later, Bears players have mixed feelings about the song. Thomas Sanders, the young running back, said some of the participants were promised large payments, then moaned as they were handed checks for six thousand dollars. "We got a whole lot less than we were told," he said. Many agreed to partake solely because of Gault's assurances that the proceeds would go to charity, yet only 50 percent wound up being donated to the Chicago Community Trust. "Willie said it'd be just like 'We Are the World,'" said Ted Plumb, Chicago's receivers coach. "His line was, 'If we're gonna feed the world, why not start with Chicago?'" Much of the rest of the money went into the pocket of Meyer, whose company, Red Label Records, was on life support. "I don't know what Dick promised anyone," said Supeter, "but I know people were pretty angry afterward."

When they learned that the charity was barely a charity, Chicago's players banned Meyer from their locker room and, for the most part, their lives. "The guy had the balls to come back and ask us to do 'The Super Bowl Shuffle II,'" said Gary Fencik, the veteran safety. "Singletary threw his gold record in the trash can. He threw it away and walked out."

. . .

The loss to the Dolphins proved to be an aberration, and Chicago wrapped up a marvelous regular season by winning its final three games against the Colts, Jets, and Lions. With a 15-1 record, the Bears were the NFC's top-seeded team. That earned them a week off, followed by a meeting with the NFC East champion New York Giants at Soldier Field.

Eight years earlier, when Payton prepared for his play-off debut against the Dallas Cowboys, Chicago's players were befuddled by their notoriously cheap organization's refusal to transport the team to a warm climate to practice. The Bears spent most of the ensuing week standing around in the sleet and snow, then traveled to Texas for a 37–7 decimation at the hands of America's Team.

Now, armed with genuine Super Bowl aspirations, on December 30, 1985, Chicago's front office sent its coaches and players to Suwanee, Georgia, to hold practices at the Atlanta Falcons' training complex. Along with moderate temperatures and agreeable conditions, Ditka liked the idea of keeping his team out of the spotlight. The music videos and magazine covers and endorsement deals were nice and dandy and swell, but the coach worried about his players losing their edge. In Chicago, no Bear—ranging from a superstar like Payton to a relative nobody like punter Maury Buford—could step from his house without being besieged. Women were everywhere. Meals were free. Drinks were plentiful. In Suwanee, home of the annual Old Town Holiday Festival and Caboose Lighting, the Bears were simply oversized goliaths preparing for a big game.

Though generally agreeable to allowing his men to be men (so to speak), Ditka preferred the players use the time in Suwanee to lay low and say little. On the day after his team's arrival into town, however, Payton sat down with a large handful of reporters and held a miniature State of Walter press conference. The topic was supposed to be the Giants. It wasn't.

"Dealing with the media has been a challenge for me," he said, spurred on by nothing in particular. "At times, I haven't been the best of people. I haven't been in the best of moods. I want to thank you people for putting up with me."

For a moment, a stunned silence overtook the setting. Through the eyes of Chicago's press corps, Payton had been a dizzying riddle to cover. He came. He went. He talked. He didn't talk. He made sense. He made no sense.

Payton wasn't quite done.

"I still feel I'm overlooked," Payton said. "Why? That's the sixty-four-million-dollar question."

With that, Payton rose and left, as the pack of journalists scratched their heads and wondered what had just happened. For Chicago newspaper veterans like the *Tribune*'s Don Pierson and Kevin Lamb of the *Sun-Times*, Payton's rare dose of honesty was refreshing. Yes, he was insecure. Yes, he wanted big numbers. Yes, he pouted if he didn't get enough carries. Yes, he resented the attention afforded others. Though Payton had rarely gone public with his feelings, none of this was a secret within the locker room. For the majority of Chicago's players, 1985 had been the culmination of a lifetime of hard work and dreams. For Payton, it was a mixed bag—the splendor of on-field success and a galvanized city; the disappointment of becoming (in his opinion) invisible.

To those not in the know, the words made no sense. Payton was supposed to be the ultimate team player, one who went his entire career without a single ill feeling or gripe. He stood as the NFL's Moses—a holy figure with nary a scar or wart. "Walter had a reputation," said Lamb, "that didn't quite meet the reality."

Three days later, in another group interview, Payton looked out at an even larger number of scribes and—to the organization's dismay—continued to plead his case. Payton desired more acclaim, "because inside this body beats a heart, and a brain functions. There are things that regardless of how strong or durable you are, you have to see or feel. Otherwise what you're doing has no value.

"You feel self-esteem, but if the people outside don't see it or don't appreciate it, next time . . . you're not going to be as motivated. It's like getting a banana split and you don't get the hot fudge sauce. There's something missing. [If you keep getting it that way] pretty soon you go up and just ask for ice cream and a banana."

Because Payton was a legend with an unblemished image, teammates always praised him to the press. *Walter is such a prankster. Walter is the leader. Walter is the pulse of our team.* In reality, most didn't know or understand him. Even the running back's closest confidants on the Bears—Suhey, Singletary, Gentry, and running backs Thomas Sanders and Calvin Thomas—could hardly be classified as extraordinarily close friends. They were comrades in battle; recipients of Payton's kind words and funny barbs; occasional dinner companions. But friends have some understanding of what the other person is feeling and thinking. No one genuinely grasped Payton. Especially the depths of his angst.

"At his core, Walter was incredibly insecure," said Holmes. "He would do things to draw attention, but only if it looked like he wasn't trying to draw attention. He might go to a banquet and if they were bringing out steak he'd say, 'I don't eat red meat.' And they'd ask what they could bring him and he'd ask for fish—then complain it wasn't cooked right. An hour later, he'd be sneaking to McDonald's for a Big Mac, begging me, 'Don't tell anybody! Don't tell!'

"We would go to Chicago Bulls games and he'd know exactly where the cameras were. You'd see him go up to the kids in the wheelchairs, and he'd go up, shake their hands, knowing the camera was on. Does that mean he didn't care? No. But he was aware of how it would be perceived, and that mattered immensely to him. On more than one occasion, Walter went to the airport without a ticket or reservation or nothing. He'd walk up to the American Airlines counter and say, 'I need a ticket to Las Vegas.' They'd be oversold, but they'd kick people off the plane and place him in first class. Walter loved that, even as he played humble."

Hence, while Payton's pouting about a lack of recognition puzzled teammates, it failed to entirely shock them. "Walter was Walter," said Sanders. "He answered to no man."

Heavily favored, the Bears dominated the Giants, 21–0, then prepared for a matchup with the Los Angeles Rams in the NFC Championship game. The team returned to Suwanee, and Payton again held court in front of the press. As opposed to the previous week, the running back found himself in a state of prolonged giddiness. He talked at length about the journey from Jackson State to the brink of a Super Bowl, and how the ritual beatings of years past brought immense appreciation. "For me, the Super Bowl would be the ultimate," he said. "It's all the work and effort and sacrifice to reach that plateau. It comes down to the desire to win the Super Bowl. It's like a writer who wants to win the Pulitzer Prize. He wants to be the best. The Super Bowl is it for us."

Now, at last, Payton was the story. If the Rams had any chance at winning (and, really, they didn't), it came in the form of Eric Dickerson, their splendid third-year halfback out of Southern Methodist. As a result, the media predictably pushed the Dickerson vs. Payton narrative. One was the young upstart trying to break through. The other was the grizzled veteran desperate to reach the biggest stage. One, Dickerson, ran upright, with blistering speed. The other, Payton, looked for holes and relied on strength and savvy. One, Dickerson, was known for petulance and lengthy contract holdouts. The other, Payton, was God's gift to football. Dave Anderson of *The New York Times* called the matchup a "throwback to the National Football League's primeval era when championships depended on such dinosaurs as Jim Thorpe and Red Grange, Ernie Nevers and Bronko Nagurski."

Just as Payton had once come along and supplanted O. J. Simpson as the league's best back, Dickerson was now trying to do the same to Payton. One season earlier, as the Bears flew to Los Angeles to play the Rams, Payton slid into the seat next to Leslie Frazier, a defensive back. "Do you think Dickerson is better than I am?" he asked.

"I was thinking to myself, 'Here's Walter, the greatest running back of all time, asking me whether someone was better than him,'" said Frazier. "What more do you need to understand about his pride?"

Payton had gotten to know Dickerson at the 1983 Pro Bowl, and he genuinely liked the kid. Dickerson was deferential and respectful, and credited Payton as an influence. That said, he also knew Dickerson, owner of 1,234 rushing yards during the regular season, was dead meat. Chicago's terrifying defense had spent the week thinking about bloodying the goggled running back—a California pretty boy if they'd ever seen one. They didn't care about Dieter Brock, the subpar quarterback, or his fleet of subpar receivers. Ryan told his minions the running back would fumble three times—"more if you hit him enough."

"Our entire goal was to shut Eric down," said Cliff Thrift, a Bears linebacker. "Our defense didn't just strive to control a player like Eric. We wanted to dominate him."

As was tradition, the Bears spent the night before the game at the McCormick Inn, a hotel in downtown Chicago. At six thirty A.M., Suhey heard a loud banging on his door. It was Payton. "He burst into the room and started jumping on the bed, biting me," Suhey said. "He was so hyper . . . he was even talking about going to the boat show. He was really wired. He was really anxious for this day to come."

With the crosswinds gusting around the stadium at 25 mph and a late snow sprinkling the field and 63,522 fans in a frenzy, the Bears punished Dickerson, holding him to forty-six yards on seventeen carries and forcing two fumbles. On his first carry of the game, Fencik nailed him for no gain. The tone was set. In pileups, Chicago's defenders twisted Dickerson's ankles and clawed at his eyes. When referees were looking elsewhere, they made his knees prime targets. It was, by far, the most vicious beating he would take in what became an eleven-year Hall of Fame career.

Technically, Payton was little better, running for a paltry thirty-two yards on eighteen attempts and catching seven passes for forty-eight yards. But his output mattered not. The Bears jumped out to a 10–0 halftime lead, scored again on a twenty-two-yard touchdown catch by Gault in the third quarter, then sealed it when Marshall picked up a fumble and rambled fifty-two yards into the end zone. With 4:26 left in the *first quarter*, the scoreboard flashed: THE BEARS WOULD LIKE TO THANK ALL OUR FANS FOR THEIR SUPPORT IN THE 1985 SEASON. The game was already over.

With two minutes remaining and the score 24–0, Glenn Miller's "In the Mood" blared from the Soldier Field speakers. Euphoric fans swayed their bodies back and forth, one enormous ocean of frigid glee. They chanted "Super Bowl! Super Bowl! Super Bowl!" When the game ended, the Bears players darted off the field, waving to the fans, twirling towels, laughing and smiling and shouting.

Payton took his own path. Gazing skyward, he sauntered slowly across the turf, helmet dangling from his right hand. Over the past decade, he had attended two Super Bowls as a guest, only to depart by halftime. This time, he would be going as a star.

## CHAPTER 20

# SUPER LETDOWN

IN THE VISITING TEAM'S LOCKER ROOM OF THE LOUISIANA SUPERDOME, THERE is a broom closet. It is small and dank and cluttered, with darkness' only foe a dangling hundred-watt lightbulb.

Ever since the stadium opened in 1975, football players big and small have used the closet for privacy and solitude. From prayer to euphoria to furor to despair, the room serves as a confessional booth at the Church of Battered Bodies (and Souls).

On the night of January 26, 1986, with his teammates whooping and hollering inches away, this is where one could find an outraged Walter Payton.

How did it come to this? How did the Bears' 46–10 walloping of the New England Patriots in Super Bowl XX end with an iconic NFL superstar wallowing in a pool of disgust and self-pity?

"To understand," said Bud Holmes, his agent, "you have to know Walter."

Beginning with the day following the NFC Championship game, Payton had been behaving, for lack of a better word, strangely. Of all forty-five members of Chicago's active roster, he had the greatest right to cherish the Super Bowl birth. He had been with the team longer than anyone; was witness to the lowest lows; was forever motivated by his 1975 debut, when the Colts held him to zero yards and the fans filed out in stunned resignation. "Walter knew what it was like to be a Bear when the Bears were a joke," said Steve Fuller, the quarterback. "This was his moment."

Unlike most of his teammates, Payton never allowed himself to be placed into a custom-fitted athletic cliché. As Mike Ditka and Jim McMahon

Whether he was having a good day or a terrible one, Payton was always tremendous with young fans. Here, during a training camp break in 1985, he shares some words with Garrick and Theresa Teckenburg.

When his career finally came to an end in a playoff loss to Washington on January 10, 1988, Payton refused to leave Soldier Field. As his teammates retreated to the locker room, he sat on the bench, helmet in hand, devastated. "I was just recapping some of the great moments," Payton said years later. "I didn't want to rush through it. Because if you stay there long enough these things will be etched in your heart and your soul."

On December 20, 1987, the Bears honored their all-time greatest player with the retiring of his uniform number at Walter Payton Day. According to Bud Holmes, his agent, Payton had no desire to retire, but was pushed out by an organization eager to move in a different direction.

Walter Payton's first business office was located in the rear of his restaurant, Studebaker's, in Schaumburg, Illinois. He used the small space for meetings. It was also the spot where, on April 13, 1988, Payton accidentally shot Elmer Hutson, the restaurant's 28-year-old manager, with a 9mm French-made Manurhin Pistolet.

To many who knew him, Payton was as impressive a prankster as he was a football player. Here, he takes a moment to mess with Ginny Quirk, his longtime assistant and confidant who later became the vice president of Walter Payton, Inc. "With Walter," said Quirk, "you could never rest."

Walter and his son, Jarrett, at Wrigley Field in 1986. Though Walter was once named the Illinois Fatherhood Initiative Chicago Father of the Year, he was an oft-absent parent who, through the end of his life, refused to meet his out-of-wedlock son.

Brittney and Connie Payton look on during a memorial service for Walter at Soldier Field on November 6, 1999. Though people assumed Walter and Connie had a happy marriage, they lived apart for most of the final decade of his life.

Behind his charming, good ol' boy Mississippi persona, Bud Holmes, here with Walter at a dinner, was a sharp and shrewd negotiator. He landed Walter a contract that still pays the family $240,000 annually.

Walter Payton spent many off-seasons making appearances for Buick at the Chicago Auto Show. The perks were hard to ignore—prestige, a free car, and an endless stream of women. During the 1984 event he commenced an affair with a 20-year-old model named Angelina. A year later, their son was born.

Because of a string of poor investments and business decisions, Payton was rarely able to relax after his retirement from football. Here, in 1995, he inspects the site for Walter Payton's Roundhouse, an enormous brewpub/restaurant in the Chicago suburb of Aurora. After Payton's death, his estate demanded his name be removed from the establishment.

Upon retiring from the NFL after the 1987 season, Payton's family assumed he'd take some time to rest and kick back. Hardly. A bored Payton quickly turned his focus toward automobile racing, joining Sports Car Club of America's Pro Sports 2000 series in the white No. 34 car. Said Tony Kester, his driving coach: "Walter's best attribute as a driver was his hand-eye coordination, which was off the charts. But a big problem was his strength. Walter was like Paul Bunyan, and Paul Bunyan would have had a lot of difficulty driving."

Though he initially became an assistant basketball coach at Hoffman Estates High School to fulfill court-ordered community service, Walter learned to love the school and the kids. He spent four years as a varsity assistant, and also coached JV. Said Bill Wandro, the varsity head coach: "He really related with the kids. He was genuine with them."

Walter throws out the first pitch on Opening Day at Wrigley Field on April 12, 1999. "Maybe I'll do this again next year when I nip this thing," he told Matt Suhey. He died less than seven months later.

Induction into the Pro Football Hall of Fame is supposed to be one of the highlights of a person's life. For Walter Payton, however, it turned into a nightmare. Instead of celebrating his career, Payton spent his four days in Canton, Ohio, worried about his wife and girlfriend somehow meeting. To his dismay, they did.

A shriveled, jaundiced Walter Payton at his office in Hoffman Estates, Illinois, in February, 1999. "He looked more and more like Sammy Davis Jr. every week," said Mike North, who hosted a radio show with Payton. "I don't say that humorously—he really did."

A young Walter Payton sits alone on the bench, waiting his turn. His early years with Chicago were rarely pretty, as Payton took routine beatings behind a soft offensive line. "It's hard to see the bruises on a black guy," he liked to joke.

and Mike Singletary spoke of the dreamlike glow that accompanied Super Bowl qualification, Payton seemed to sit back and cynically wonder whether this was as good as it got. He certainly would have preferred to be dancing a jig and floating on air, but to his great dismay, the spirit failed to move him. Having rushed for 275 yards in a game and having broken Jim Brown's record, Payton knew what it was to stand atop the football mountaintop. He already had tasted caviar and drank Dom Pérignon. When the fans exited Soldier Field and the aisles were swept and the lights were shut off after the Rams game, Payton was left with a sinking feeling that, after eleven years of playing for the ultimate team moment, it wasn't such a moment after all.

His ho-hum outlook was hardly helped by Chicago's opponent. Ever since the Monday Night loss to Miami in Week 13, Payton and most of his teammates were itching for a rematch with the Dolphins. When Don Shula's club reached the AFC Championship game, a Miami-Chicago Super Bowl seemed to be all but written in blood.

Somehow, though, the Patriots, an 11-5 wild card qualifier without a single household name on its roster, snuck into Miami and battered the Dolphins, 31-14. Instead of the media spending two weeks wondering whether Dan Marino could again carve up the Bears, the media would now spend two weeks wondering how badly Chicago's 46 Defense would decimate the Patriots' feeble offensive attack. New England already lost to the Bears, 20-7, in the second week of play, and was rightly listed as an early ten-point underdog. Weeks before kickoff, NFL Films had begun preparing a three-hundred-thousand-dollar production of the Bears' Super Bowl season. No New England video was in the works. "To be honest, we went into the Super Bowl knowing we were a better team, and that the Patriots couldn't win," said Cliff Thrift, the linebacker. "We were big, we were bad, and we were going to kick their butts. No mystery about it."

As was NFL policy, both organizations had two weeks to kill before the big game. Ditka gave his players three days off, and Chicago spent the rest of the first week working out at the University of Illinois' football field, which featured artificial turf and an enormous vinyl-coated polyester covering reminiscent of the Superdome. Some 175 journalists from across the globe attended the closed practices, desperate for newsworthy nuggets in an otherwise sports-dead time of year.

"What will it mean not to have the Honey Bears next season?" a reporter asked Steve McMichael of the soon-to-be-disbanded cheerleading squad.

"It sounds to me," the defensive lineman replied, "like you guys are running out of questions."

The Super Bowl beat took on significantly more liveliness on the night of Monday, January 20, when the Bears' chartered flight left arctic Chicago (temperature: thirteen degrees) and arrived at New Orleans International Airport (temperature: seventy-two degrees). "We got on the buses from the airport to our hotel, and a convertible full of girls pulled alongside us and started taking their tops off," said Tom Andrews, a Chicago center. "That was where it started."

Raymond Berry, New England's old-school coach, ran a tight ship. At the Hotel Intercontinental there were nightly curfews and meetings atop meetings. All players were expected to carry themselves in a manner befitting a professional football player. Ditka, on the other hand, demanded little—practice relatively hard, don't get arrested, and seize the day. Inside the New Orleans Hilton, where the Bears were based, the lobby bar was a magnet for action and the party never seemed to end. "Man, we had a great time," said Maury Buford, the punter. "I remember we flew down and Mike didn't put a curfew on us. Monday, Tuesday, Wednesday—we could do whatever we wanted for as long as we wanted. By Wednesday we were begging him for a curfew, because we were partied out."

"The Thursday practice before the Super Bowl was the worst," said Jimbo Covert. "We all went out Wednesday night. I had four or five beers before we left, and then we all went to Pat O'Brien's. I drank three hurricanes, and I felt like I'd blown the top of my head off. We were rock stars wherever we went. People even knew the offensive linemen."

The Bears overran Bourbon Street, drinking like sailors and boasting one sexual conquest after another. Having supplanted the Dallas Cowboys as the nation's most popular team, the Bears owned the city. By one player's estimation, for every New England fan there were five hundred people pulling for Chicago. "The Super Bowl was pretty much a home game for us," said Calvin Thomas, a Bears running back. "In the streets, all you saw was blue and orange."

As had been the case for much of the regular season, Payton took a backseat to Perry and McMahon. His saga was a fine one in the conventional sense (veteran finally makes it), but Super Bowl XX symbolized a new era. This was about immediate pleasure and neon-lit entertainment value. The game was being covered heavily by, of all outlets, MTV, a network that knew little of rushing yards and touchdowns but specialized in shock and imagery.

The talk of New Orleans was Perry's sizeable gut (How much gumbo could one man eat?) and McMahon's bruised buttocks (Why wasn't Hiroshi Shiriashi, his acupuncturist, allowed on the team plane?), which he gleefully flashed for a low-flying news helicopter soaring above Bears practice. "It was the craziest thing I've ever been a part of," said Kevin Butler, the rookie kicker. "Thank God they didn't have camera phones back then, because you can't imagine how over the top we were."

As McMahon made his way through the city with kinetic glee, Payton laid low. He ate primarily room service, and spent much of his time on his bed, watching TV. One evening, to the delight of teammates, he rented a couple of buses and had the Bears escorted to a seemingly abandoned club-house in the middle of Louisiana. From the kitchen emerged Justin Wilson, the famed Cajun chef, armed with vats of crawfish. "That was remarkable," said Greg Gershuny, the team's director of information services. "We ate like kings." With most of the players' wives not scheduled to arrive in New Orleans until a day or two before the game, there was ample opportunity to fool around—and many of the Bears did. Whether Payton took full advantage remains unknown. Two nights before the game, however, Payton called one of his friends in Chicago who had chartered a seventy-six-seat jet to New Orleans. "I need a spot on the plane," Payton said.

"You can't fly with us," the friend said. "You're already there."

"No," Payton replied. "There's someone I want you to bring to New Orleans for me. I need one seat."

"Under no circumstances could I turn him down," said the friend. "First, he got us about twenty tickets to the game. Second, we're good pals. Third, we were all caught up in Super Bowl hoopla, and much of the hoopla was about Walter. What was I to do?"

When Payton's "someone" arrived at the airport hangar, she was exactly what the friend expected—long legs, large chest, blond hair, short skirt. Her name was Jennifer, and she worked as a bartender. On that same day, Connie, having flown commercial, arrived in New Orleans with the two children. "I actually sat near Connie at the game," said the friend. "We all sat at the fifty-yard line, and I had to act as if nothing had happened."

Indeed, despite having fathered a child out of wedlock only one year earlier, Payton steadfastly pursued other women. It was around this time that he was diagnosed with genital herpes, a sexually transmitted disease that causes recurrent painful sores. Payton was initially shocked and dismayed by the

diagnosis, but rarely—if ever—found it necessary to inform future sexual partners of the viral infection.* "There was a certain pressure that came with being
idolized," said the friend. "Walter was away from home a lot, and he felt pulled.
He lived two lives—the loving husband and father in Chicago, and the slimy
womanizer on the road. Was he as bad as Tiger Woods? No. But it was a problem. People knew we were good friends, and they'd call and tell me, 'I saw
Walter out with so-and-so woman, and it wasn't Connie.' I didn't know what
to say. He was Walter Payton, the king of Chicago. I kept my mouth shut."

One person who didn't was Singletary, the Bears' All-Pro middle linebacker. Devoutly Christian and unafraid to show it, Singletary watched with
great disappointment as Payton regularly cheated on his wife. He obviously
knew athletes did such things, but expected more from someone of Payton's
character and esteem. "Mike finds out that despite Walter's stellar career and
reputation, he's catting around on the road," said a friend of Payton. "He had
a devoted wife, precious children, and yet he's being unfaithful." One afternoon during the 1985 season, while taking a team bus to the airport, Singletary slid into the vacant seat alongside Payton. "Man, you've got to clean up
your act," he said. "You've got a beautiful family and you claim to be a
Christian. You know better."

This was the first time someone had confronted him on his womanizing, and Payton was shocked. He turned toward the window, away from
Singletary, and pretended not to listen. In the reflection, Singletary saw tears
streaming down Payton's face.

Singletary had no idea what his friend was thinking. Through the end of
Payton's career, the two never spoke again.

· · ·

As a boy growing up in Corpus Christi, Texas, Raymond Berry learned the
sport of football at the knee of his father. A high school coach for thirty-five
years, Raymond, Sr. preached that, with the right mindset and preparation, a
poor team could beat a great one on any given day. "I listened to everything
he said, and I absorbed that message," said Berry. "No matter the odds, there
was always a way to accomplish your goals."

Berry's playing career personified this ethos. Though never especially

---

* Later in his life Payton also tested positive for Epstein-Barr virus, but never appeared to
suffer from any symptoms.

fast, he lasted thirteen years as a wide receiver with the Baltimore Colts, teaming with Johnny Unitas to win two NFL titles, play in six Pro Bowls and, in 1973, be inducted into the Pro Football Hall of Fame.

Now, at age fifty-two and in his first full year as New England's head coach, Berry thought back to his father's wisdom. "I knew the Chicago Bears were an incredible team," he said. "But I honestly felt we'd win the game. We just had to make sure we did several things right."

The game plan was relatively simple. On offense, the Patriots couldn't turn over the ball, and quarterback Tony Eason had to get his passes off within three seconds of receiving the snap. "We had a new offensive scheme that year, so we didn't do anything complex," said Berry. "Simplicity got us to the Super Bowl. Do the basic things well."

Berry handed all responsibilities for the other side of the ball to Rod Rust, the defensive coordinator. Fifty-seven years old and a well-regarded strategist, Rust was the anti–Buddy Ryan. He rarely bragged or boasted and never looked to undermine his head coach. "Buddy was too much of a self-promoter to me," said Rust. "Great at his job, but very cocky."

Like Berry, Rust watched tapes of the Bears and considered them beatable. If Chicago's defense was ferocious, its passing attack—ranked twentieth overall in the league—was merely average. McMahon was brittle; Willie Gault and Dennis McKinnon were OK receivers; and the tight end, Emery Moorehead, was a journeyman. "It was all about stopping the run," said Rust. "Payton was the first guy we wanted to defend. He was the linchpin to their offense. You stopped him, you stopped the Chicago Bears from scoring." New England's veterans took strange comfort in Chicago's cockiness. To them, the machismo reeked of insecurity—a nervousness over falling flat on the nation's biggest stage. The more the Bear players flapped their lips, the more the Patriots believed they were destined for an upset of Namath-ian proportions. "We had no doubt about winning," said Don Blackmon, a New England linebacker. "None."*

Payton had spent the morning of the game relaxing at the hotel, and arrived at the Superdome in chipper spirits. While eating his regular pre-

---

* Not everyone with New England was so confident. Said Les Steckel, the Patriots' quarterbacks and receivers coach: "I thought about calling the commissioner's office and asking if we could play with twelve guys of ours on the field. I'm not sure whether we would have won—but I definitely think we'd have had a shot with thirteen."

game meal of a bowl of Raisin Bran with the raisins meticulously picked out, he turned to Gault and said, "I feel great about this. We're gonna remember today forever."

As a Chicago captain, Payton was in charge of calling the coin toss. He walked out to midfield alongside Jimbo Covert, Shaun Gayle, Gary Fencik, and Mike Singletary and watched Bart Starr—one of seventeen former Super Bowl MVPs being honored—flip a silver dollar into the air.

Payton mumbled something, and as the coin landed tails he said, loudly, "Tails, I called!"

"You called heads," said Red Cashion, the referee.

"No," said Fencik. "He said tails."

The Patriots players began complaining. "Toss it again," said Steve Grogan, New England's backup quarterback.

Cashion laughed nervously. "He called tails," he said. "He is the winner, and it's [the Bears'] choice."

Chicago opted to receive, and Gault returned the opening kickoff eleven yards to the Chicago eighteen-yard line. On the game's first offensive play, McMahon tossed a pitch to Payton—"Who else!" said Dick Enberg, NBC's play-by-play announcer—who swerved left and gained seven yards. He popped up and trotted back to the huddle. The next call was another handoff, this time straight into the teeth of New England's defensive line. McMahon accepted the snap and gave the ball to a fast-approaching Payton, who took a step to his left and was immediately drilled by Garin Veris, the Patriots' six-foot-four, 255-pound defensive end. Veris' helmet dislodged the ball and Larry McGrew, a speedy linebacker, dove atop the loose object at the nineteen-yard line. New England was in business.

Payton, who fumbled six times during the regular season, had waited much of his life to play in a Super Bowl. He spent the night before the game tossing and turning in bed. TV on, TV off. Get up, get down. Light on, light off. A practitioner of positive visualization, he imagined himself slicing through New England's defense en route to 150 yards, three touchdowns, and the game's MVP trophy.

Instead, he fumbled.

Payton retreated to the sideline and spoke briefly with Matt Suhey, who implored him to shake off the blunder. Payton, however, was devastated. For two weeks, Chicago's defense barked loudly about pitching the first shutout in Super Bowl history. Now, as Tony Franklin's thirty-six-yard field goal soared through the uprights, the dream was dead.*

"My fondest memory of that game is the Patriots taking a 3–0 lead," said Gary Christenson, the Bears' ticket manager. "I was sitting next to the Patriots' ticket manager, and he had a grin from ear to ear. I thought to myself, 'Just wait, buddy. Just you wait.'"

For the remainder of the game, Payton was a nonfactor. The man who overcame prejudice and small-school bias and injury and shoddy offensive lines couldn't get the fumble out of his head. The mishap plagued him. Haunted him. He moped along the sideline, and though he was handed the ball twenty-two times, he ran for a meager sixty-one yards while failing to catch a single pass. Afterward, Chicago's players and coaches rationalized his poor performance by insisting New England obsessed over him, and that Payton's mere presence allowed McMahon to throw for 256 yards and run for two touchdowns. "The Patriots," said Gault, "were dead-set on holding Walter down."

Even with a cardboard Red Grange cutout starting in Payton's place, nothing could have stopped the Bears. Chicago was too fast, too strong, too intimidating. The Bears led 23–3 at halftime, then scored twenty-one unanswered points in the third quarter. By the time the game ended, the 46–10 victory stood as the greatest rout in Super Bowl history.

As the final minutes ticked away, Chicago players and coaches walked up and down the sidelines, hugging, laughing, embracing. This was the end result of a glorious season, and the Bears were committed to enjoying it. Mike Singletary hugged Otis Wilson and Wilber Marshall. McMahon and Gault, hardly the best of friends, exchanged a demonstrative high-five. Suhey wrapped his arm around Thomas, who wrapped his arm around Dennis Gentry.

And what of Walter Payton?

He pouted.

The fumble kicked off the funk. What catapulted it to a new level, however, was the fact that, as the Bears rolled up forty-six points, Payton was never granted entrance into the end zone. When Suhey ran for an eleven-yard touchdown late in the first quarter, Payton was the lead blocker. When

---

* Technically, some of the fault lies with McMahon. The handoff was designed to head toward the weak side of the defense, but the quarterback called the wrong formation. "Walter was furious with McMahon about that," said Bud Holmes. "He never said it to his face, but he blamed the fumble on him."

McMahon ran an option bootleg for a score early in the second quarter, Payton trailed him, waiting for a pitch that never arrived. When McMahon dove over the top from one yard out in the third quarter, Payton was sent wide right as a receiver.

With 3:22 remaining in the third quarter, Payton suffered the ultimate indignity. Chicago led 37–3, and again found itself positioned on New England's one-yard line. Ditka sent Perry into the game and lined him up alongside Payton in the backfield. When McMahon took the snap, he handed the ball to the Fridge, who trampled over McGrew into the end zone. As Perry leapt to his feet to spike the football, Blackmon reached out to his fallen teammate. "'Grew, you OK?" he asked.

"Damn," said McGrew. "I just made a highlight film for the next fifty years."

McGrew smiled. Even in defeat, he could laugh at the insanity of a 325-pound defensive tackle rushing for a Super Bowl touchdown. Payton, however, wasn't grinning. He returned to the sideline and took a seat on the bench. Early in the fourth quarter Jerry Vainisi, Chicago's general manager, noticed that Payton had yet to score. He rushed down to the field from the press box and reminded Ditka. "I know . . . I know," the coach responded. "We're trying to get him one."

It never happened.

"Those last two minutes of the game were agony for Walter," said Covert. "You could see it on his face—he just wanted out of there." When the final whistle sounded and the Chicago Bears were officially Super Bowl champions, Payton headed directly to the locker room. He entered, tore off his jersey, and slammed his shoulder pads to the floor.

"If you looked at Walter," said Ken Valdiserri, the team's director of media relations, "you would have thought we'd lost."

"For the ten years I had played with him, Walter claimed it didn't matter how many yards he got, how many touchdowns he scored—it was about winning," said Brian Baschnagel, the veteran receiver who, because of a season-ending knee injury, watched the game from above in the coaches' box. "That was the attitude I took, too. I didn't care how many passes I caught, as long as the Bears won. And I always felt Walter felt the exact same way. But when he reacted the way he did . . . it was the exact opposite of what he had claimed to be as an athlete."

As Chicago's players and coaches reached the locker room, Payton was nowhere to be found. Teammates wanted to congratulate him. Ditka wanted to tell him the Bears couldn't have done it without him. Members of the media, quickly stampeding into the room, wanted to know how it felt to finally fulfill a dream.

Valdiserri and Bill McGrane, the team's marketing director, were the first to reach Payton. His eyes were red, and tears streamed down his cheeks. "He didn't score and he didn't feel as if he'd contributed to the win," said Valdisseri. "I found it to be such an odd and awkward moment, because that's not what he represented throughout his career. I never knew him to bask in his statistics. At least that's not the way he made it seem. I thought it was a complete paradox."

Valdisseri and McGrane begged Payton to come out of the broom closet. "Walter," Valdisseri said, "how is it going to look if you don't talk? Here we just won the first Super Bowl for the Bears, and this should be the highest point of your career. Don't let your disappointment in your own performance bring down the moment."

Payton wasn't having it. "I ain't no damned monkey on a string," he snapped. "I don't have to jump up and smile just because TV wants me to."

He was livid at Ditka for ignoring him and livid at Perry and McMahon for hogging the spotlight and livid at himself for fumbling. *The highest point of his career?* Ha. It felt like 1975 all over again.

Around the time Valdiserri and McGrane were finishing with Payton, Bud Holmes entered the locker room. Ever since they first teamed up before the 1975 Draft, Holmes had paid special attention to his client's image. He knew of Payton's selfishness and insecurities (as well as his goodness and decency), and the last thing he wanted was for a nation of football fans to see it on display now, in the glow of victory.

Holmes stormed into the tiny closet, where he found Payton sitting on a box.

"What the hell is wrong you with?" Holmes screamed.

"You know what's wrong," Payton replied.

"Goddamn boy, one monkey does not stop the show," Holmes said. "The show's gotta go on. Look, Ditka was the one who didn't get you a touchdown. If the press wants to gut him for it, let it be their call. But if you go out there and do anything but brag on him for getting you to a Super Bowl and brag on him for letting you achieve so much, your reputation as a good guy is dead, and you'll be remembered as the selfish sack of shit who moped after a Super Bowl."

"But," Payton countered, "this isn't the way you treat a star."

"Bullshit," Holmes said. "Right now there are hundreds of reporters out there with sharp, sharp pencils waiting for you to blast him. Maybe they even agree with you. But if you blast him now, they'll come back in a few days and blast you even worse.

"So do me a favor and act like the happiest son of a bitch in the world. If I can find you a straw hat and a cane, you can come out and tap dance in front of everyone to prove it."

Payton asked Holmes for a couple of minutes to gather himself. When he finally emerged from the closet, he was shirtless, with a white towel dangling over his right shoulder. He was stopped by NBC's Bob Costas, who requested a live interview.

COSTAS: Walter, was there ever a time during your long career, when you were performing so brilliantly and your team was at a level beneath that, that you felt this dream would never come true?
PAYTON: Well, you try not to think about it. During the off-season when you see other people playing in the Super Bowl, you wonder and you say to yourself, 'Are you ever gonna get there and see what it feels like?' And it pushes you a little bit harder during that off-season to work to try to get there the following year. This team had their minds made up after losing to San Francisco last year that we were going to win the Super Bowl this year.
COSTAS: Can you describe the feeling for you personally?
PAYTON: Right now it really hasn't sunk in. I don't feel anything. It's one of those things where when you have it in your mind for so long what it would be like, and then after the actual event happens, it tends to take away from it. Right now I'm still a little bumped and bruised from the game. It really hasn't happened yet.

Standing to the side, Holmes was satisfied. Payton, however, remained petulant. Instead of making plans with teammates or family members, he retreated to the empty training room. "He and I left the Super Bowl together in a taxicab, after everyone was gone," said Fred Caito, the veteran trainer. "By the time we left the training room it was quiet and dark. He never even took a shower—just sulked." Upon reaching the hotel, Payton was greeted in the lobby by Lewis Pitzele, a Chicago-based music producer he had known via business dealings. Payton invited him to his room. "He started telling me why he wasn't going out, and then he started crying," said Pitzele. "I was answering the phone for him—ABC and CBS and *Good Morning America* were all calling the room, trying to book him for the next day. He didn't want to talk to anyone. We eventually went downstairs to the banquet, but he was crushed."

Many of Payton's teammates were perplexed and disappointed. Some were mad at the running back for his selfishness. Who cared about a touchdown in the Super Bowl? What difference did it make? "He felt like it would have been the crowning jewel on his career," said Covert. "But Walter didn't need a crowning jewel." Others were perplexed by Ditka slighting their beloved superstar. Maury Buford, the team's first-year punter, thought back to the preseason, when the coach embarrassed him during a Monday afternoon film session. "Ditka never could pronounce my name," said Buford. "In front of everyone he said, 'Murry, Morty, Marty . . . whatever the fuck your name is. You better get your shit together and stop shanking punts, or I'll have enough punters in here tomorrow to make your head spin.' I was crushed. Well, from behind me I feel a huge hand on my shoulder. It was Walter, and he whispers, 'Don't worry about that, Maury. Ditka pulls this shit all the fucking time.' That's who Walter was—someone who'd die for a teammate. He deserved a touchdown."

McMahon, the owner of two scores, kicked himself for not taking action into his own hands. "When they called the play for Perry," he said, "I should have just ignored it and given the ball to Walter." Jay Hilgenberg wondered how such an oversight could have happened. "We scored forty-six points—why couldn't Walter have scored at least once?" the center said. "In hindsight, there's no excuse."

Nobody felt worse than Ditka, who through the years came to love Payton as he had few other players. In the heat of the game, he simply failed to consider what a touchdown would have meant. "I would never do anything to hurt Walter," Ditka said. "As I've said repeatedly, I wouldn't want anyone else carrying the ball in any situation than him. Not Jim Brown, not Gale Sayers, no one. I scored a touchdown in a Super Bowl, and I wish I could take that and give it to him. Because the last thing I wanted to hear was, at his greatest career moment, Walter Payton feeling down.

"He was," said Ditka, "the best player I ever coached. And, in hindsight, he deserved better."

## CHAPTER 21

# AFTERMATH

WHEN A FRANCHISE PLAYER WINS A SUPER BOWL, THE WORLD BECOMES HIS oyster.

No, things didn't go as planned for Walter Payton in New Orleans. And no, he would not soon forget Mike Ditka failing to allow him to score a touchdown against the Patriots.

But if Bud Holmes had concerns that his client's petulance would leave a lasting—and damaging—impression on sports fans and corporate America, those fears were quickly put to rest. In the days and weeks following the big game, a smiling, giddy, reenergized Payton could be found everywhere. He was asked to attend a state dinner at the White House by President Ronald Reagan, America's foremost football fan (Brian Mulroney, Canada's prime minister, used the occasion to invite Payton to his home for some fishing). As always, he appeared at the annual Chicago Auto Show, signing autographs on behalf of Buick. Both the Cubs and White Sox requested he throw out the first ball at their home openers (he went with the Cubbies). He made the first public political statement of his life, using an NFL luncheon to expound on the strife in Libya (Payton: "It shows the uncertainty of what this world is heading for"). He participated in Hands Across America, a four-thousand-mile chain of hand-holders from New York to California, and was saluted by Jackson, Mississippi, with "Walter Payton Day" and a parade in his honor.

In one of the proudest moments of his career, Wheaties told Payton it wanted to place his image on the front of its cereal boxes—an honor bestowed on only four previous athletes (Bob Richards, Bruce Jenner, Mary Lou Retton, and Pete Rose). "To be on the box is sort of like a fairy tale that eventually came true," he said. "Because in the world we live in, it's a fantasy."

Payton's strangest post–Super Bowl endeavor came in the form of a rap single/video called "Rappin' Together," which he recorded with—of all people—William Perry as a follow-up to "The Super Bowl Shuffle." For some inexplicable reason, the idea sounded like a good one at the time: Take two football stars, hand them a sheet of lyrics written by four Evanston, Illinois, high school students, shove them in a recording studio, and let the magic happen. "There were two guys who knew I was a music promoter, and they said, 'Why don't you get Walter and the Fridge to do a rap together?'" said Lewis Pitzele, who became the song's co-executive producer. "I thought it was a wonderful idea." At the time, the genre was still considered fertile ground for goofball fluff (think Rodney Dangerfield's "Rappin' Rodney"). The words:

> *Together as a team we have a dream.*
> *Everyone will stand together.*
> *If we hold hands in this great land.*
> *We could make life a whole lot better.*
> *'Cause the people are the world we are the ones.*
> *Everyone should get involved.*
> *If we stand together and lock our hands.*
> *Our problems can be solved.*

Blessed with laughably bad lyrics and the inarticulate Perry, the "Rappin' Together" cassette single sold a couple of thousand copies before finding itself in Illinois' scattered bargain bins. "Walter was happy with the project," said Pitzele. "And if the space shuttle [*Challenger*] hadn't crashed the same week it was released, it would have been a huge hit.

"But," Pitzele said, "it wasn't."

. . .

Though Walter Payton felt as if he were finally getting his due, reality as a professional football player can be harsh.

On April 29, 1986, with the twenty-seventh selection of the first round of the NFL Draft, the Chicago Bears selected Neal Anderson out of the University of Florida.

Neal Anderson—the running back.

It was, of course, inevitable. At some point the Bears had to start grooming

Payton's successor, and Jerry Vainisi, the team's fourth-year general manager, rightly determined that the time was now. Despite all the praise and accolades coming Payton's way, he wasn't the same player he had been in years past. He was slower, more mechanical, less willing to deliver a hit. Still great, still tough, but no longer transcendent. "Walter had played eleven years, and even he knew we needed a running back," said Vainisi. "He was somewhat uncomfortable with it, especially because Neal was very good and chomping at the bit to play. Walter had a lot of pride."

So did Anderson. Florida's all-time rushing leader in yards, touchdowns, and attempts, the twenty-one-year-old Graceville, Florida, native was the first top pick of the Bears to ever miss his introductory press conference in the name of academics. "He's a scholar," an irked Mike Ditka said in explaining Anderson's absence to take two final exams. Anderson further annoyed the organization by holding out for most of training camp. When he finally signed a four-year, $1.3 million contract, Anderson reported to the Lake Forest complex and was ordered by the other running backs to fetch them doughnuts.

He steadfastly refused. As a freshman at Florida back in 1982, Anderson was told all first-year players were required to shave their heads. "It was a Gator tradition, but I wasn't having it," he said. "Some of the upperclassmen, these big linemen, broke into my room one night when I was sleeping. They had a pair of trimmers, and they decided they were going to hold me down and cut my hair. It didn't happen. I had a knife, and I made some threats. It didn't make me any friends, but I believe what I believe."

With the Bears, Anderson once again stood his ground. Jelly, cream, chocolate sprinkled—didn't matter. Neal Anderson would fetch no man a doughnut. "Even for Walter," he said. "I'm a stubborn person, and it's not my job to get you your morning sweet. It's my job to play football."

Throughout the season stories were written about the old Bear taking the new Bear under his wing; about Walter and Neal forming a potent one-two duo for a team that thrived upon running the ball. The whole bosom buddies narrative was fictionalized. "I don't think Neal ever bought into Walter," said Jay Hilgenberg, the veteran center. "He wanted to be his own guy." Payton eyed Anderson wearily, like a lion guarding his food. Anderson mostly stayed out of his way. "I can't say Walter embraced me, but he wasn't mean to me, either," Anderson said. "For a while the running backs didn't accept me, but over time it got better. Walter was friendly enough.

"I didn't come to Chicago to back Walter up and learn from him, as some thought I should have. No, I came to Chicago to play. To play tailback. That was my attitude. I think other people were more willing to learn from him and eventually hope to take over. That wasn't me."

Now thirty-three years old, with 14,860 career rushing yards, the assumption around the league was that the Bears would lessen Payton's load while gradually shifting the focus toward Anderson. Even Ditka, Payton's biggest supporter, said he wanted to "not get him beat up" with excessive usage. "I'm going to put him into situations probably a little differently than a year ago when I would have used him as a lead blocker," he said. "I don't think that's what I want him doing." Payton bristled at the suggestion.

Unlike Anderson, whose absence was generally ignored by teammates, Payton reported to training camp in Platteville, Wisconsin, with a bang— landing alongside one of the practice fields in a helicopter piloted by Gordon Ward of Chicago's Omni Flight. Payton paid eight hundred dollars for the one-hour, twenty-minute ride, and deemed the flight worth every cent. "Best entrance I've ever seen," said Henry Jackson, a rookie free agent linebacker. "It declared his importance." Payton further announced his presence (and status) by residing not in one of the drab dormitory rooms, but in the souped-up RV he parked adjacent to the facility. Equipped with a television, a kitchen, and all the frozen meat one could ever want, Payton's living unit was a camp hotspot. Technically, it was only supposed to serve as a place for Payton to relax. Factually, he lived there, and a ball boy was assigned to wake him each morning. "It was just like the trailer Clark Griswold had in *Vacation*," said Mike Tomczak, a backup quarterback. "Why sit in a dorm when you can bring five people into a mobile home and hang out and relax?"

If the 1985 season served as a confirmation of Payton's stature, 1986 was a final reminder. The Bears were, once again, great, going 14–2 and winning a third straight division title. But just as the brilliance of a classic movie cannot be recaptured in a sequel, an all-time legendary football team rarely lasts beyond one season.

Taken in and of themselves, Payton's numbers (1,333 rushing yards, eight touchdowns) alone told a dominant story, but the '86 Bears were a faded copy of the '85 edition. From the commercialism (McMahon plugged Taco Bell; Payton hawked Kentucky Fried Chicken; Gault endorsed his own clothing line; Perry promoted, well, everything) to the literary deals (Singletary, McMahon, and Ditka wrote books) to the increased club hopping and alcohol guzzling, Chicago lost its edge. The team was hungry, but not famished; angry, but not ferocious. Talk of a dynasty filled the newspapers and airwaves. Dynasties, though, start with a base level of unselfishness. "Everybody got greedy," said Fred Caito, the veteran trainer. "The players, the coach—everybody. It was a snowball rolling down a very steep hill. The money, the fame, the egos. It ate our team alive."

Buddy Ryan, the feisty defensive coordinator, departed to become head coach of the Philadelphia Eagles, and with him left the blood-thirst of the NFL's most dangerous defense. His replacement, Vince Tobin, was—in a stark departure from the cantankerous Ryan—a warm man who had served capably as the defensive coordinator of the USFL's Philadelphia/Baltimore Stars. With the Bears he immediately dismantled much of Ryan's 46 Defense, implementing the 4-3 alignment he knew and loved. "I told the guys that it wasn't me who took off, it was Buddy," said Tobin. "They could either work with me or decide not to and pull the team apart." Technically, Tobin succeeded—the '86 Bears again ranked first in the NFL in total defense, and allowed fewer passing yards and fewer yards per carry while posting only two fewer sacks than a year earlier. The defense even set an NFL record for fewest points allowed. Yet statistics fail to tell the whole story. Opposing quarterbacks who once quivered at the sight of Mike Singletary or Wilber Marshall no longer had fear in their eyes. Opposing running backs stopped bracing for hits seconds before impact. The unit's unpredictability was replaced with order. "Vince always comes out and says the defense was better under him, but it's just not true," said Jay Hilgenberg. "It was the attitude of our defense as an attacking defense that I think we lost. Buddy really brought that out. We weren't as terrifying. Those were mean guys, but they got a little more gentle."

Along with defensive coordinator, the other spot that damned the '86 Bears was quarterback. McMahon started four of Chicago's first six games, but his body was halfway to the morgue. He could barely move his right shoulder. "My arm was coming out of the socket," he said. "It was from an injury I first had in high school. I kept telling the doctor what was wrong. He said, 'That can't be happening. Do you know how painful that is?' I said, 'Yeah, I know. Happens every day.'" McMahon sat out the seventh game, which the Steve Fuller–led Bears lost at Minnesota, 23–7. At a team meeting the next day, Dan Hampton, the veteran defensive lineman, lit into McMahon. "I liked Jim and I still like Jim," Hampton said. "I think the combination of a lackadaisical approach to the game, the lackadaisical approach to being ready as a team, all those little things contributed."

With McMahon sidelined and team unity cracking apart, Chicago made a personnel decision that, in hindsight, crushed hopes of a repeat. Despite having a pair of backups on the roster (Fuller and Mike Tomczak), the Bears sent two draft picks to the Rams for the rights to Doug Flutie, the 1984 Heisman Trophy winner at Boston College. A five-foot-ten, 180-pound piano stool of a quarterback, Flutie had recently completed his rookie season with the New Jersey Generals of the now-defunct USFL. Immortalized for his last-second Hail Mary to upset the University of Miami as a senior, Flutie was a near-iconic sports figure.

Bears players decided they had no use for him.

Chicago was McMahon's team. And McMahon was a schoolyard bully. On the day after the trade, he showed up at practice sporting a red No. 22 jersey, the same one Flutie had worn in college and with the Generals. McMahon derisively referred to Flutie as "America's midget," and later mocked him while appearing on *The Tonight Show.* Teammates enthusiastically joined in.

"I was shocked we even considered taking him," Otis Wilson told the *Tribune.* "Nobody else picked him up, so why would we? Flutie has one play—that Hail Mary."

Asked how much he thought Flutie was worth to the Bears, Wilson shrugged. "How much change I got in my pocket?" he asked.

When Flutie entered the locker room for the first time, he felt the Lake Michigan chill. McMahon ignored him, as did most of the other players. "I was unwanted," he said, "and I knew it." Then Flutie was spotted by Payton. With the entire team watching, he walked up to the new quarterback, extended his hand, and said, "I'm Walter Payton—glad to have you here!" He directed Flutie to the entrance of the locker room, where a crude sign, made from copy paper and Magic Marker, hung from the door. NO PLAYERS UNDER 5'8" ALLOWED, it read. Payton grinned sheepishly. The handwriting was his.

"He ignored the whole McMahon thing and acted as a buffer for me," said Flutie. "There were only a handful of guys who went out of their way to make me feel comfortable, and Walter was one of them. He was such a wonderful man."

Seven weeks into his tenure with the Bears, Flutie finally made an impact. He replaced Tomczak in the second quarter of a game against Tampa Bay, hit Willie Gault for a fifty-two-yard gain on his first completion, and connected with Payton for a twenty-seven-yard touchdown on his second.

After exchanging hugs with jovial teammates, Payton took the ball and handed it to a fan. Later, when he was reminded that it had been Flutie's first NFL touchdown pass, Payton used the postgame press conference to ask that the ball be returned. "Walter being Walter, the fan actually brought it back," Flutie said. "He was beloved, and with great reason."

Unfortunately for the Bears, Flutie Fever failed to last. Ditka made the mistake of inviting his new quarterback to his house for Thanksgiving dinner, and the McMahon-led peanut gallery teed off. "It was Jim's insecurity, and it was wrong," Hilgenberg said. "Doug was a super guy, and he was exciting to have out there. He was the right guy to have starting. But we hurt ourselves by making it so hard on him."

On January 3, 1987, the Bears hosted the Redskins in a divisional playoff game at Soldier Field. With a league-best 14-2 record, Chicago remained the oddsmaker's favorites to return to the Super Bowl. It was not to be. Flutie completed only eleven of thirty-one passes and threw two interceptions. The Washington defense ganged up on Payton, holding him to thirty-eight yards on fourteen carries. With the Redskins leading 14–13 midway through the third quarter, the Bears pieced together a drive. Dennis Gentry returned the kickoff forty-eight yards to Washington's forty-two. Anderson swept eleven yards, then Calvin Thomas drove up the middle for thirteen more yards to the eighteen. "We were really coming off the ball there," said Covert.

On the ensuing play Payton was hit by Washington's Darryl Grant. He fumbled, and the Redskins recovered. Drive dead. Momentum gone. The Bears lost 27–13.

"I don't know what happened," Payton said. "You don't have to ask if I'm disappointed."

Afterward, a drained Payton sat by his locker and contemplated football mortality. He was thirty-three years old, and battered worse than ever. Every muscle hurt. Every joint ached. In the moments before the game, Caito, the team's trainer, had inserted a large needle beneath the nail on Payton's right big toe—yet another temporary remedy for the turf toe that ached with each step. Payton's forehead beaded with sweat. His hands shook. "He would grab my arm as the needle went into his skin," said Shaun Gayle, a defensive back. "The pain must have been excruciating." Though also burdened by a dislocated toe on the other foot that radiated anguish, Payton never used the maladies as excuses. "Instead of appearing like the old Walter Payton," Gary Pomerantz wrote in *The Washington Post*, "he just appeared old." The loss to Washington marked the seventh straight game in which he failed to crack a hundred yards. The fumble was his sixth in seven games. Across the league, word was out that Payton had lost much of what had made him extraordinary.

"My goal is sixteen hundred [yards] for next year," he said defiantly. "If Neal wants my job, if Thomas Sanders wants my job, if Matt [Suhey] wants my job, they'll have to be so good they're going to lead the league in everything and be the most valuable player because I'm going to work my butt off to attain that."

Little did Payton know, the Chicago Bears had a decidedly different plan.

· · ·

"There is no loyalty in sports," the man said. He was sitting at a bar, robotically downing one cup of coffee after another. "No loyalty. None. Zero."

Mike Ditka was on a roll. Twenty-three years had passed since Walter Payton prepared for his final season as a Chicago Bear, and the coach was still livid. "You're a commodity," he said. "You're paid, and when you can't produce, you're gone. There's no loyalty. And as the coach, I'm the one in the middle—if you're loyal, you're stuck. Because then you have to defend the reason you're loyal. And I mean, it's just the way it is. There's no loyalty."

Though time supposedly heals all wounds, it hasn't touched this one. Entering the 1987 season, Ditka—who took few marching orders—was given very specific ones by Michael McCaskey, the Bears' president: *If you want to continue to coach this team, you'll phase out Walter Payton and phase in Neal Anderson.*

Though often lampooned as one, Ditka is hardly a fool. He certainly recognized the signs of a fading star, and Payton was showing all sorts of them. Why, in the February 1 Pro Bowl in Honolulu, Payton fumbled yet again, this time with the NFC driving deep into AFC territory. Once upon a time he lost a handful of fumbles a season. Now he seemed to be losing one every game.

Despite this, Ditka still believed that Payton should, at worst, split carries with Anderson; that he remained a hard-nosed workhorse who could be counted on for one thousand yards and eight to ten touchdowns in 1987. "I had no intent of starting Neal over Walter," Ditka said. "It wasn't time yet."

That was the coach's opinion. The front office, however, had other ideas.

Shortly after the conclusion of the 1986 season, Bud Holmes received a call from McCaskey, who was blunt in his assessment of Payton's remaining value. "We're ready for Walter to come to the conclusion of his career," McCaskey said. "But we want to do it in the best way possible. We don't want to let Sweetness go, but we have other plans for the upcoming year."

Holmes wasn't shocked, merely disappointed. Payton's contract had expired, and he was looking for one final deal. Holmes knew his client believed he had another two or three quality seasons left in his body, and he wanted Payton—not the suits in Chicago's administrative suites—determining his own exit. And yet, Holmes, like Ditka, knew whereof he spoke. Approaching his thirty-fourth birthday, Payton had reached a point of diminishing returns. He couldn't cut like he used to. His pass routes lacked the crispness of previous years. Worst of all, he always seemed to be suffering. Throughout his career, Payton had taken tremendous pride in his toughness. Teammates loaded up on injections, and Payton refused to go anywhere near a needle. Teammates complained openly about *this* sprain, *that* bruise, *this* twist, *that* gash—and Payton kept quiet. Steroids were all over Chicago's locker room (said Fred Caito, the longtime trainer: "If we turned in guys for using steroids, half the team would be gone."), but Payton refused to touch them.

Now, however, he was regularly popping the painkiller Darvon, numbing his maladies as he also ignored the side-effect warnings. Doctors across the U.S. prescribed the drug—in moderation—as a painkiller, as well as for the treatment of diarrhea. In large doses, however, Darvon was believed by many watchdog groups to be a contributor to suicide. It resulted in shallow breathing, slow heartbeat, confusion, seizures, and jaundice. With alcohol, it caused—among other things—liver damage. The suggested dosage was one 65 mg tablet every four hours. Payton's intake far exceeded this.

Holmes didn't love the idea of a reduced Payton enduring the suffering of more hits, but he wanted his client to go out the right way. When McCaskey told the agent the organization might be forced to cut its greatest star, Holmes countered with an offer of his own. In mid-May, Payton and Holmes had flown to New York to meet with NFL commissioner Pete Rozelle about the possibility of becoming the league's first minority owner. Thanks to the efforts of Jesse Jackson, who was putting public pressure on Major League Baseball and the NFL to hire more minorities as managers, coaches, and front-office executives, Rozelle was intrigued by the idea of Payton one day heading an expansion outfit. "Rozelle said he would give Walter one of two things—the right to lead a team in Oakland or the right to do so in Phoenix," Holmes said. "We wanted Arizona, but there were already other people focused on that location. So I met with the Oakland people, and we had a deal tentatively worked out where Walter would come out there and they'd put up money, build a stadium, and hope for the best outcome."

A couple of days later, Holmes met with Walter and Connie at their home. He laid out all the possibilities, then asked, bluntly, "Walter, are you ready to move on, or do you want to keep playing until you no longer can?" Payton had spent the off-season hearing the whispers about his fate. The talk was embarrassing, agonizing, infuriating. In the way all great athletes *know* they can still play (even when they can't), Payton was certain the Bears needed him. "Alexander cried when there were no worlds left to conquer," Holmes told him. "You've already broken all these records. And if I can work it out where you now become the first black owner, should we go after it?"

Payton lived for football. For the locker room camaraderie. For the thrill of a long run down the sideline, of a crushing block, of a diving catch. Though he had always wanted to be thought of as more than merely a jock, he was—at heart—a jock. Football was his life.

"OK," he told Holmes. "One more season."

With that, Holmes telephoned McCaskey with a proposal. Walter desired a one-year, one-million-dollar deal (with an option for a second season, just in case Payton shocked the masses with a fifteen-hundred-yard output), along with a (seemingly temporary) position in Chicago's front office and a commitment from the team to immediately retire his No. 34 jersey.

"I'm sorry," said McCaskey. "We don't retire jerseys."

"Well, that's a deal breaker," said Holmes. "You'll have to cut Walter Payton."

Few negotiators could bluff like Holmes, whose Southern charm and perceived dopiness made for a lethal combination. Was he the model representative for a man trying to purchase his own franchise? Not particularly. Holmes had recently been disbarred by the Mississippi Bar Association after pleading guilty to misconduct before a federal grand jury. But Payton was justifiably loyal, and Holmes took pride in being the small-town Mississippi bumpkin who outwitted the big guns.

"We don't want to do that," McCaskey said.

"I know," said Holmes. "I want him to be able to say he quit to become an NFL owner. It's good for Walter, it's good for the Bears."

On July 28, 1987, at the Bears' Lake Forest facility, Payton announced that he would play one more season, then retire. "Nothing is final," he said. "But at this point that's what my thinking is. Unless something happens and Mr. McCaskey comes to me and says, 'Come back next year,' it looks like this will be the last one.

"Walter Payton never quits," he said. "I would say, 'Walter Payton has started in [a new] direction.' I feel I could play another three years and be productive. But the hardest thing for me to do is say, 'I know I can play; I want to play, but I'm going to stop.' It's something I feel I have to do."

Payton, surrounded by reporters, forced a smile.

He was miserable.

.   .   .

Monday and Tuesday were off days—"Recovery time," said Fred Caito.

Wednesday was a light day—"Walter would walk, loosen up, watch, go home," said Caito.

Thursday was a semi-busy day—"Walter would run ten plays or so," said Caito.

Friday and Saturday were more off days—"To get ready," said Caito.

Sunday was game day.

This is what many of the Bears recall of Walter Payton's final NFL training camp and season. As the other athletes were asked to sweat and grind and suffer through oft-brutal, oft-mind-numbing rituals, Payton was usually nowhere to be found. "Which was, of course, OK with everyone," said Frank Harris, a rookie free agent halfback out of North Carolina State. "He was Walter Payton. He had the right to do whatever he wanted." Throughout the bulk of his career, the Bears had tried to protect their star, limiting reps, resting him often, keeping hits to a minimum. In his heyday, Payton fought the approach. "During nine-on-seven inside drills he'd run every play," said Sanders. "If there were twenty drills to run, he'd want to do them all, because he sought perfection. He'd jump in, jump in, jump in, and the other backs would have to watch." Now, nearing the end, Payton was handled as a porcelain doll. If defensive players craved violence, they were welcome to tee off on Anderson or Sanders or any of the other runners. "I remember one offensive scheme, Walter came at me and I dropped my shoulder and turned to hit him," said Egypt Allen, a rookie defensive back. "Mike

Ditka blows the whistle, yells at me, and says, 'Don't you ever hit him again!' Walter started laughing. He still ran hard and he still looked for the collision. The team was worried about him, but he wasn't overly careful."

"If Walter was in a salty mood, he could run over you and you were powerless," said Doug Rothschild, a rookie free agent linebacker from Wheaton College. "You weren't allowed to lay a finger on him. Meanwhile he'd stiff-arm you in the face and laugh."

To Payton's chagrin, Ditka decided early on to name Anderson—not Suhey—the starting fullback. It was the coach's way of keeping his fading star in the lineup and, hopefully, happy. "Walter did not take that well," said Covert. "Mike wasn't ever going to sit Walter down, and at the end that's probably what he should have done. Walter didn't like sharing the backfield with Neal. He talked to me about it a couple of times. It wasn't pure jealousy. It was more of, 'I did this, this, and this, and I deserve more respect.' But his prime was over. Factually, it was."

Throughout his years in Chicago, one required only two hands to count the teammates Payton was especially tight with. In the early days, he spent considerable time with Roland Harper, Vince Evans, and James Scott. Later on, safety Todd Bell became a confidant—so much so that Payton was a groomsman in his wedding. Toward his final years, Payton and Suhey were inseparable. "Matt cherished and loved Walter, and Walter in return cherished and loved Matt," said Johnny Roland, the team's running backs coach. "Suhey was basically my coach on the field, and Walter just wanted to play. So when Matt talked, Walter listened. He trusted him to the death." The relationship often evoked comparisons to Gale Sayers and Brian Piccolo, Chicago's running back tandem from the late 1960s (their kinship was made famous in the aftermath of Piccolo's death from cancer with the release of *Brian's Song*, a 1971 ABC Movie of the Week). Like Sayers and Piccolo, one player was black, one was white. Like Sayers and Piccolo, one player was a flashy standout, one was gruff and workmanlike. Like Sayers and Piccolo, one player was a superstar, one was a supporting cast member. Seven years earlier, Payton had resented Suhey for being brought in as Roland Harper's replacement. Over time, however, a genuine bond formed. "My second year in the league we flew back from San Francisco after a tough loss and got in at one in the morning," said Suhey. "I was in my car getting ready to get something to eat, and he walked up and said, 'Where are you going?' I told him, and he said, 'I'm coming.' We went to a bar/restaurant called the Snuggery, and we had our first really good talk. We were from two different worlds, but we also related really well. That night was the beginning."

Now, near the end, Payton was furious. His dream was to have one last glorious season in the sun, with his good friend leading him through the hole. Instead, the speedy, modestly physical five-foot-eleven, 210-pound Anderson was forced into the role. "Neal was a good guy and a great player, and he deserved to play," said Suhey. "But he wasn't a fullback. Not naturally."

The Bears opened their season against the New York Giants at Soldier Field. Much was made of the Herculean matchup of the last two Super Bowl champions, which the *Tribune* called "the game of the year." For Chicago, the 34–19 rout was wonderful. Mike Tomczak, the team's starting quarterback, threw for 292 yards and two touchdowns and the defense compiled eight sacks, twice knocking quarterback Phil Simms out of the game. For Payton, though, the night was a disaster. He carried the ball eighteen times for forty-two yards, and caught three more balls for twelve yards. Excuses were made—the Giants were focusing on him; a sprained ankle suffered on a second-quarter sweep limited his mobility (Ditka: "A lot of guys wouldn't have kept playing."). Nothing stuck. As Payton struggled, Anderson soared. "Talk about hitting a hole," said Keith Van Horne, the offensive tackle. "Neal hit it and—*Whoosh!*—he was gone. I never blocked for anyone with his type of speed." Anderson ran for sixty-two yards on thirteen carries against New York, including a spectacular eight-yard burst past Lawrence Taylor, the Giants' immortal linebacker. "Lawrence Taylor hasn't been beaten to the corner by a fullback—ever," said Ditka. "But he was beaten by this kid." The praise sounded an awful lot like what coaches used to heap upon Walter Payton. The next day's *St. Petersburg Times* featured a story with the headline, END NEAR FOR PAYTON? *The Washington Post*'s Michael Wilbon chimed in with a stinging critique of Payton's showing:

> The Bears were so good in every way tonight that the almost incidental contributions of Walter Payton, 33, went almost unnoticed. The leading rusher in the history of the league, he looked every bit his age . . . [giving way to] Neal Anderson, whose all-around excellence suggests there is a new offensive hero in Chicago.

For Payton, the win provided predictably little solace. Neither did the following week's triumph, when Chicago slaughtered Tampa Bay, 20–3.

Though Payton scored two touchdowns (including his NFL-record 107th on a one-yard dive), he ran for a paltry twenty-four yards on fifteen carries and was pulled from the field on third downs. To make up for the lack of a genuine fullback, the Bears called an increased number of weak-side trap runs, where the tight end led. It wasn't to Payton's liking. Anderson, meanwhile, enjoyed the first hundred-yard game of his career, gaining 115 yards on sixteen carries. "They're keying on Walter," Ditka explained afterward with zero credibility. When the assembled media members tried speaking with Payton, he brushed past without saying a word or acknowledging congratulatory wishes for his tenth NFL record. "He was angry," a Bears spokesman said, "because he didn't think the press treated him well this week."

"You can tell he's upset," said Johnny Roland, the running backs coach. "Yeah, he's upset, because he's not being used to the best of his abilities. Walter is still a good player."

On the opening night of the 1986–87 NBA season, Julius Erving, the iconic Philadelphia 76er and a casual acquaintance of Payton's, announced that he would be retiring at the completion of his sixteenth year. He did so because, at age thirty-six, he recognized he was no longer capable of reaching a certain threshold, but wanted to give fans a chance to bid farewell. "Like the way John Havlicek did it," Erving said of the Boston Celtics star who retired in 1978. "He played a significant role his last season, even though he was not the star of the team. It was a good time to turn it over to other hands." Erving's final go-around was a thing of beauty—he received gifts and standing ovations at opposing arenas, and Philadelphia's normally acid-tongued fans gushed over his class. He never groused about playing time, or if Coach Matt Guokas called for Charles Barkley or David Wingate to take the final shot.

"I look at Walter's situation and I feel if anyone in football could do that, it's Walter," Erving said. "The whole season becomes a farewell tour and people appreciate seeing him for the last time instead of looking at what he's not doing on the field."

If Erving's final stand was an example of the perfect way to bow out, Payton's was an unmitigated disaster. On the day after the Tampa game, the NFL Players Association went on strike, demanding genuine free agency (where players would actually be free to switch teams once their contracts expired), improved pensions, and guaranteed contracts (at the time, only 4 percent of NFL contracts were guaranteed). For twenty-four days, Payton and his teammates stayed home as Gene Upshaw, executive director of the players association, accomplished, in Suhey's words, "nothing I can remember." Meanwhile, three games were played with replacements, as the Bears of Walter Payton, Reggie Phillips, and Mike Singletary morphed into the Bears of Sean Payton,* Eddie Phillips, and Mike Hohensee.

Many of the Bears mocked and ridiculed the replacements, but Payton wasn't one of them. Though he didn't cross the picket line, he refused to criticize those established veterans who did, or the so-called "scabs"—mostly unemployed nobodies living out a dream. Truth was, he stood to lose $62,500 for every missed game, and he thought the strike to be an enormous waste of time. "I had little to gain out of this strike personally, and a lot to lose," he said. "But the thing that kept me out the most is my teammates. Because I'm as useless as a car with no driver without my teammates." Except for two hunting excursions to Wisconsin and a trip to New York to appear as a veejay on MTV, Payton spent his weeks off bored and restless. He even, quizzically, started a band, the Chicago Six, composed of Hampton (bass), safety Dave Duerson (trombone and trumpet), and three members of the Chicago Blackhawks—Curt Fraser (guitar), Gary Nylund (guitar), and Troy Murray (tenor saxophone). Payton manned the drums, and while the group actually played a couple of local gigs, it didn't last long. "We weren't very good, but we were entertaining," said Fraser. "The whole thing was mostly for kicks, and to have the two teams bond."

The real Bears finally reported back to work on October 15, and Payton had high hopes for the return game at Tampa Bay ten days later. Instead, it was another downer. Though Chicago prevailed, 27–26, Payton was limited to thirty yards on six carries, and he fumbled yet again. Just how poorly did the day go? Before the game Payton agreed to meet Deana Reel, a seventeen-year-old from Asheville, North Carolina, who suffered from cystic fibrosis. Reel and her grandmother Helen were so inspired by Payton's example of overcoming the odds that they flew to Tampa to meet him. Payton hugged Deana and handed her an autographed football as the cameras flashed.

It was a hoax.

According to a report in *The Lakeland Ledger*, Deana had never heard of Walter Payton. Her grandmother put Deana up to it. "I don't really follow football," Deana later said. "I never knew any of the Bears by name. Just some guy named 'Fridge.'"

---

* Yes, *that* Sean Payton—the coach of the New Orleans Saints.

Following the game, Payton received a random call from Bill Cosby, who was at the peak of his fame as the star of *The Cosby Show*. "I know what's going on," he told Payton. "Don't let it get you down. You know whose picture is up in Theo's room. We didn't take it down."

· · ·

The Bears played nine more regular-season games, and except for fleeting flashes of brilliance, Payton's efforts were futile. He could still block relatively well, and did so valiantly on Anderson's behalf. ("He was an excellent pass blocker and an adequate run blocker," said Anderson. "In Walter's defense, he never had to run block much before.") But there was no denying that the old Sweetness was gone, never to return.

"Walter was over," said Caito. "He could still play, and he probably wanted to stick around, but it wasn't the same. His body was shot. He was bone on bone in some areas in his knees. He'd gained thousands of yards, but he'd taken a massive whuppin' and now he was paying for it."

"Walter couldn't get to the corner as well as he used to," said Al Harris, the veteran defensive end. "Neal was young and fast and he could catch the ball, and he needed to play. The hard thing with running backs is that, if you play long enough, you take all those licks and it destroys your body."

On November 14, Randy Minkoff of the United Press International (UPI) wrote a piece that appeared in hundreds of newspapers nationwide. It was a stinging 790-word critique of Payton's game. The take was harsh—and true.

There are ample examples of all-time great professional athletes staying around one year too long.

Athletes past their prime often tarnish their image by getting one extra campaign out of a body that should have called it quits earlier.

Willie Mays with the New York Mets, Bob Cousy with the Cincinnati Royals, and Franco Harris with the Seattle Seahawks come to mind as of late.

It's premature to put Walter Payton in that category—yet. But Payton, in his thirteenth and what he insists is his final NFL season, isn't going out the way many people would have liked.

The whole year was a disaster. The Bears were scheduled to play at San Francisco on a *Monday Night Football* game on December 14. During practice that Friday, a handful of offensive players decided to exact revenge on

Payton for the countless pranks he had pulled. Gentry, in particular, was itching for payback. A couple of years earlier, Payton had called his home on Thanksgiving, his voice disguised as a woman's. When Gentry's fiancée, Jaye, answered, Payton explained how his name was Gina, and he needed to speak with Dennis about "our baby."

"She was fixing dinner, basting the turkey, the stuffing, and the yams," Gentry said. "When I got home later in the day nothing was cooked. Nothing. I said, 'What the hell is going on?' She said, 'Who is this bitch so-and-so?' I said, 'What?' She said, 'Some woman called and said you're invited over to her house.' I was so furious at Walter. I couldn't wait to get him."

Now, with a gaggle of reporters watching, Sanders, Gentry, and a couple of others grabbed Payton from behind, pulled down his pants, and dragged him through the Lake Forest snow. What was supposed to be humorous turned strikingly sad—an aged star helplessly screaming and flailing away, his pants wrapped around his ankles, as onlookers cackled. A humiliated Payton stormed off without speaking. Said Sanders: "Let's just say it didn't go over well."

The ultimate embarrassment came three days later at Candlestick Park. Both teams boasted league-best 10-2 records, and both teams entered the clash talking lots of trash. With Anderson nursing a bruised shoulder, the focus of the offense was once again Payton, who started alongside Suhey, his old chum. Yet much like Muhammad Ali dying his hair and sucking in his gut, then being annihilated by Larry Holmes in 1980, Payton fooled no one. He lost a key fumble, rushed for only eighteen yards, and suffered a concussion after being nailed by defensive lineman Michael Carter. Chicago lost, 41–0.

"Walter took a step back from the other players on the team that year," said Sanders. "He was dealing with his football mortality, and it troubled him. One day he told me we needed to talk. I said, 'What is it?' Walter said, 'I just need to talk to someone.' He was struggling with the idea of separating from the game and being without the guys. It had been his life for thirteen years. He was feeling lost."

Six days after the 49ers contest, the Bears celebrated Walter Payton Day at Soldier Field. The NFL's all-time leading rusher used the occasion for his finest moment of the season.

Although the Bears would go on to lose to Seattle, 34–21, the fifteen minutes preceding kickoff were devoted to a glowing Payton. Mayor Eugene Sawyer presented him with the Chicago Medal of Merit; Virginia McCaskey, George Halas' daughter, handed Payton an oil portrait of himself; and

McCaskey begrudgingly announced No. 34 would be retired. Throughout the season, various teams had bestowed retirement gifts upon Payton—the Buccaneers gave him a plaque, the Packers a framed commemorative photograph, the Raiders a picture of George Blanda and a stereo. "I don't think he wanted that attention," said Bryan Wagner, the team's punter. "It embarrassed Walter." This, however, was a moment Payton cherished. "I never thought it would end this way," Payton told the crowd as he stood before a microphone near midfield, a cold wind appropriately blowing through the stadium. "I did it because it was fun. That's why I'm playing today. The toughest thing is to say good-bye to the ones you love"—he pointed toward the end zone, where his teammates were standing—"all those guys down there."

Payton went on to rush for seventy-nine yards. The day was his, and on the west side of Soldier Field two fans held a placard that read: SANTA: PLEASE SEND MORE WALTER PAYTONS. FIRST ONE WAS PERFECT. Afterward, Payton was asked by the *Tribune*'s Bob Verdi why he threw two footballs into the stands.

"That was just my way," he replied. "My way of saying thanks."

Wrote Verdi: "No, Walter. Thank you."

. . .

After enduring thirteen long, grueling NFL seasons, Payton deserved to have Hollywood's best writer come up with a proper ending. He deserved one last taste of glory. He deserved honor and pride. He deserved to run for two hundred yards in Super Bowl XXII, with the night capped by Payton leaping into the end zone for the winning score.

When asked for his ideal exit, Payton actually painted a similar scenario. "Three seconds left," he said. "We're on the twenty-yard line. We're down by a touchdown. I run the ball in for a touchdown. We end up winning the game and when I run into the end zone and throw the ball down, I just fly off."

If only.

On the morning of the biggest game of his life, Tommy Barnhardt woke up at the Conrad Hilton, took the elevator to the lobby, and joined his teammates for breakfast. In a couple of hours Chicago would host the Washington Redskins in a divisional play-off game at Soldier Field. Barnhardt, a rookie punter from the gumball-sized town of Salisbury, North Carolina, was terrified. "I glanced out the window and it was like thirty-five degrees below zero," he said. "I'd never punted in cold like that. I didn't know how." Brarnhardt loaded his plate with eggs and found a spot at a table occupied by Wagner, who was injured, and Payton. "So I go to get some ketchup, and when I come back to sprinkle salt on my eggs, the top of the salt container falls off and my eggs are covered with salt. I grabbed some pepper, and the same thing happens—pours everywhere. Walter starts cracking up, because he did it. Here's this huge game, and someone's fucking with me. I was annoyed, but it was Walter Payton. What could I say?"

Moments later, Payton joined Barnhardt in the elevator. The kid wore his stress like a suntan. "Look," Payton said, "I know you're nervous, but it's just wind. Kick it high and hard, and the wind will take it a mile. We have good enough people here to pick up the slack."

Barnhardt nodded appreciatively. "Walter really loosened me up," he said. "He saw how scared I was, and he wanted to help. It was genuinely decent of him."

Though the Bears had finished 11-4, Washington was the thinking man's pick to pull off the win. Chicago spent the week leading up to the game practicing on the campus of the University of Notre Dame. It was a huge mistake. In South Bend, Indiana, the bars are plentiful. The beer taps flow like Iguazu Falls. "We were in a college town and we partied hard the entire time," said Hilgenberg. "By the time Sunday came we were exhausted."

Though Chicago's defense ranked fourth overall in the league, it scared no one. "We haven't played [the 46 Defense] since the second game of the season," said Marshall, the veteran linebacker. "We have a new coaching staff. The attitude here was, 'Hey, we can trash that forty-six. We can win without that.'" Nobody feared coming to Chicago, or worried about Payton— expected to be the primary ball carrier with Anderson out with a knee injury—slicing up their linebackers. When, on his weekly radio show, Ditka predicted his team would reach the Super Bowl ("I think we'll win it all," he said. "Because we expect to win. We don't expect to lose to anybody."), the words were met with a collective yawn.

Payton prepared for the game by dodging most interview requests, knowing too well the first question would concern either his career-low 533 rushing yards or his fumble against Washington in the previous year's play-off loss. When he did talk, it was softly, with a jarring level of defeatism. "Sometimes I feel I'm the problem here," he said. "A lot of times, I don't even feel I belong here. These are feelings I never felt before. It's hard. A lot of times, I feel Matt [Suhey], Thomas [Sanders], and Calvin [Thomas] want to play more, and if I wasn't here, it seems everybody's wish would be granted. Sometimes I wish this year would hurry up and end, so these guys would get what they wanted."

Payton started the game alongside Suhey, with McMahon back at quarterback. All seemed right in the world, especially when Chicago jumped out to a 14–0 lead. Energized by a capacity crowd of 58,153, Payton, age thirty-four, looked like Payton, age twenty-four. He ran for seventy-four first-half yards—fifteen on his first carry, seven on the next play to set up the Bears' first touchdown. On the second scoring drive, he burst up the middle for fifteen yards on a third-and-ten draw, and gained seven on another draw. There was an inspired vigor to his step. The great Walter Payton had perhaps returned for one last play-off roll.

The Redskins, however, fought back, and held a 21–17 lead late in the fourth quarter. With 1:12 remaining in the game, the Bears received the football on their own thirty-four-yard line. Time was left for one last push. Yet after three plays netted a paltry two yards, Chicago faced a fourth-and-eight at the thirty-six. Forty-one seconds stood on the clock. McMahon dropped back, looked downfield. Willie Gault, the speedy receiver, was blanketed. So was Ron Morris, the rookie flanker from SMU. To his right, McMahon spotted a wide-open Payton. He caught the swing pass, turned up the field, and ran toward the right sideline. He saw the first-down marker, tantalizingly within reach, and aimed for it. As Barry Wilburn, a Redskins safety, approached, Payton reached out his left arm. Undeterred, Wilburn grabbed Payton by the back of his jersey while Brian Davis, a cornerback, closed in. Together, the two Redskins pushed Payton out of bounds . . .

One yard short.

He needed eight yards. He gained seven. The game was, for all intents, over. The two Redskins leapt in the air. Payton, for a moment, sat frozen. On the final play of his career, the running back who always popped up stayed down. The running back who never ran for the sideline found himself by the sideline. The running back who always seemed to gain the extra yard failed to gain the extra yard. It was as cruel a send-off as anyone could remember.

"All my life, I've wanted to be on the same field with Walter Payton, the legend," Davis, a twenty-four-year-old rookie, said afterward. "Just to touch him used to be a dream of mine. But Barry and I had him. I hated for it to end like that for Walter, but I said, 'We've got to go on.'"

Payton, who had run for eighty-five yards on eighteen carries, walked from one side of the field to the other, reached the bench, and plopped down. He sat there, motionless, while the Redskins ran out the clock. As players from both teams met for the customary postgame handshakes and hugs, Payton never moved. He remained on the bench, his face buried in his right palm, plumes of warm breath rising, chimneylike, from his face mask. "One more year, Walter!" a fan screamed. "You can do it!" A couple of minutes passed. A couple of more minutes. Factoring in the wind chill, the temperature was negative twenty-three degrees. His teammates were long gone. Payton sat. And sat. And sat. Tears streamed down his cheeks. His eyes were closed tight. "I was just recapping some of the great moments," Payton said years later. "I didn't want to rush through it. Because if you stay there long enough these things will be etched in your heart and your soul." What went through his mind? "Disappointment," he told ESPN's Roy Firestone. "Joy. Anxiety. Relief." The fans began to chant. "Wal-ter! Wal-ter! Wal-ter!" A handful of TV cameramen and newspaper reporters surrounded him, sapping the moment of its isolated beauty.

By the time Payton rose, nearly ten minutes had passed. He took a deep breath, gazed longingly into the stands, and walked off the field. Upon entering the locker room, Payton was met by stares and silence. A pack of reporters waited for Payton at his locker and Gary Haeger, the young equipment manager, parted them with his extended arms, clearing a path. Payton sat down, placed his right leg on an adjacent bench, and closed his eyes. He had yet to remove his helmet or the thermal gray gloves that covered his hands. Nary a question was asked.

Calvin Thomas, the reserve fullback, leaned in. "You all right?" he said.

"Just taking my time, taking it all off," Payton replied. "Just enjoying it, I guess."

"Hey Walter!" a photographer hollered.

"Thirteen years," Payton said with a whisper. "Thirteen damn years here and I'm still Walter, not Mr. Payton." He wore a blank expression. Was Payton kidding? Was he serious? Nobody seemed to know.

Dave Anderson, a *New York Times* columnist, described the scene that unfolded:

One by one, he tugged at the fingers of the gray thermal gloves and tossed them to [Haeger]. He lifted off his turf-scraped helmet, but left on a navy blue wool hood. He unbuckled his shoulder pads and pulled them over his black, curly hair. He sat down and tore the white tape off his shoes. He took off his knee pads and his striped uniform stockings, then he cut the tape off his right ankle and his left ankle. Now he reached inside his white uniform pants, yanked the thigh pads out and handed them to the equipment manager.

"Three years high school, four years college and thirteen seasons here," he said, "I've worn the same thigh pads."

He took off his wool hood, then he took off a blue sweatshirt and a white T-shirt. And wearing only his jockstrap, he walked to the shower room. When he returned with a smudge of soap near his left ear, Bill Gleason, a longtime Chicago sports columnist, was waiting at his locker. "You going to miss me?" Gleason joked.

"You going to miss me?" Payton asked.

"Absolutely," said Gleason, who waved at the swarm of notebooks and asked, "Are you going to miss this?"

"No, not too bad," Payton said, smiling. "But I'll miss you. What do you remember most?"

"How much fun you were," Gleason said.

"That's the main reason why I was playing," Payton said. "It was fun."

Sitting at his locker now, Payton put on knee-high black socks, gray jeans, a long-sleeved turquoise sports shirt and polished black cowboy boots. Quickly, he reached for a towel and wiped the boots. "Got to look the part," he said, smiling. Turning up the left sleeve of his shirt, he pulled a small bandage off his elbow, revealing a bloody scrape. He tossed the bandage onto the floor and walked to the trainer's room.

"I need another bandage," he said. "This one has too much Vaseline on it."

Payton retreated to a tent across from the locker room and answered a couple of questions. Yes, he was sad. No, he wouldn't reconsider retirement. Sure, he wished the game could have ended differently. "Overall, it's been a lot of fun," he said. "When you take away the fun, it's time to leave. That's why it's so hard to leave now. It's still fun. God's been very good to me. I'm truly blessed."

With those words, Payton called it a career. Bundled in a black cardigan sweater with a shawl collar, he walked alone into the frigid Chicago air.

What, at the age of thirty-four, would he do now?

The greatest running back in NFL history hadn't the slightest idea.

# PART FOUR

## RETIREMENT

*Tim Ehlebracht, Chicago Bears wide receiver,*
*1981 and 1982 training camps*

---

*I was cut by the Bears in 1982, and the only player I kept in any kind of touch with was Walter. Just casually, nothing regular. Well, in the early 1990s the daughter of one of my close friends got pancreatic cancer. Her name was Stephanie Motzer. We had a hundred-hole golf marathon to try to raise money and get her the best possible treatment. Along with the marathon we did an auction, and because I'd been with the Bears I was put in charge of getting stuff. I called Michael Jordan's PR firm and asked if we could get an autographed basketball. I told them it was so a nine-year-old girl could get treatment for cancer. They told me they get too many requests, so they don't give out balls to anyone. Then I called Walter's office and explained the whole situation—about the girl and her cancer and what had happened with Jordan. He told me I should give him a couple of days and he'd put something together. Two or three days later I went to his office. He had one of his jerseys autographed, he had signed photographs of all the current Bears, he had a baseball bat from Bo Jackson.*

*And he had a basketball autographed by Michael Jordan.*

CHAPTER 22

NOW WHAT?

FOR THE LAST THIRTEEN YEARS, WALTER PAYTON'S LIFE HAD BEEN A WELL-organized, well-patterned ode to the predictability and routine of the professional athlete. During seasons, the Chicago Bears made certain all his needs and wants were met. Travel plans—booked. Dinner reservations—done. Car pickup—scheduled. If he desired to read a newspaper, a copy of that day's *Tribune* or *Sun-Times* would be gently placed atop the chair before his locker. If he hungered for a hamburger and fries, a locker room kid would be sent to pick it up. If he craved a back rub, a massage therapist was at his beck and call.

Even in the off-season Payton's life was laid out for him. The family employed a live-in nanny, Luna Picart, a heavily accented Jamaican émigré who did 90 percent of the cooking, cleaning, and child rearing. Payton had an executive assistant, Ginny Quirk, who answered all his calls, filed all his papers, scheduled all his appointments. Bud Holmes pushed his client toward eventual ownership of an NFL team, handling most of the necessary filings and contacts. His accountant, Jerry Richman, made it so Payton rarely had to think about numbers. There has always been much talk of Payton's hands-on involvement in his charity, the Walter Payton Foundation. But, truth be told, Quirk and, later, Kimm Tucker, managed all of the day-to-day issues. Payton showed up when told, smiled when told, spoke on behalf of kiddies when told. He believed in the cause (helping care for low-income children), but rarely took the lead.

Now, because of the pampering, as an ex-football player Payton found himself burdened by a realization that had crippled thousands of ex-athletes before him: *I am bored out of my mind.*

"I had no idea how to fill my days," Payton said. "Prior to that, everything in my life was very regimental. Everything was, 'Walter, do this, Walter, do that.' There was not much in the way of me thinking. I was very much a creature of habit. I was the first to practice, I was the last to leave. I kind of thrived in an environment where I knew what was expected of me. Suddenly, I didn't know what to do . . . people have no idea what an adjustment that is."

Payton understood what it meant to be a celebrity, so he continued to play the role. In public, he laughed and smiled and waved and signed autographs. When strangers asked, he talked about how thrilled he was to be free of the burdens. "I'm not going to miss the pounding," he told ABC's Peter Jennings. "And the getting up at six and working out until dusk." The words were pure fantasy. He would miss it *desperately.* In a world occupied by mechanics and plumbers and flight attendants and lawyers, nobody wanted to hear a wealthy ex-football player whine about the sudden lack of purpose to his life. But that's what Payton was experiencing—a sudden lack of purpose. "He went from an abnormal existence as an athlete to a normal one," said Brittney Payton, his daughter. "How does anyone do that?"

In early February of 1988 Payton flew to Hawaii to preside over the opening coin toss at the Pro Bowl (he found his first taste as a has-been to be depressing, and didn't stay for the game), with a brief stop in San Diego to meet with Pete Rozelle, the NFL commissioner, about the possibility of one day owning an expansion franchise. He accepted a (largely nominal) position on the Bears' board of directors, was named winner of the World Book James Arneberg Award for outstanding service and was honored by Columbia High School with the retiring of his uniform number (still bitter over his father's death, he refused to attend the ceremony). It was all nice and dandy, but mind-numbingly dull. Once you've played in nine Pro Bowls, where's the thrill in being an attendee? Once you're honored 8,000 times, what's 8,001? Once you've had fifty thousand fans chanting your name . . . well, how does a person move beyond such a thing?

When, four years earlier, Walter and Connie built their dream home on five and a half acres in South Barrington, the idea was that it would serve as an oasis from the real world; that the shooting range in the basement and home theatre system and pool tables and lounge chairs and fishing pond would make 34 Mudhank Road (Walter created the house number himself) seem like a luxury address, not merely a house at the end of a street. Yet now that he had nothing to do and nowhere to do it, the home felt mostly like a prison. When he was there, Payton spent countless hours on the couch, thinking, wondering, hoping, napping. He would call people at all hours of the day and night, looking to chat, longing for ideas. Though he had just recently played his final game, a feeling of irrelevance came quickly. Off-season newspaper articles about the Bears no longer dealt with Payton. Sports radio mentioned him sporadically, if at all. When asked, Payton told people that he was still working out and staying in tip-top shape. Not true. When the final whistle blew, Payton's obsessive devotion to fitness died. He made regular pilgrimages to the nearby Bob Evans for bacon and eggs with a huge side helping of sausage. He gorged on Benihana whenever possible.

Once, while flying to an event, Payton sat next to a woman in first class who turned toward him and said, "Do I know you from somewhere?" Payton leaned close and said, "Actually, I'm one of the world's most famous male strippers. You've probably seen me perform." Payton rose, removed his jacket, and pretended to begin his routine. The woman was mortified until a boy approached and said, "Mr. Payton, can I have your autograph?"

She laughed uproariously. "Oh my God," the woman said, cackling. "That's the best trick anyone has ever played on me." An executive with Wendy's, she handed Payton a card that provided him a lifetime of free hamburgers. "Let's just say they knew him at the Wendy's drive-thru," said Tucker, who worked with Payton after his retirement as the executive director of his charitable foundation. "He loved those free burgers."

Walter Payton was a man who was recognized all over the country, yet he suddenly found himself very much alone. He kept in regular contact with none of his ex-teammates or coaches, and had long ago established a distant relationship with his older brother, Eddie. "When Eddie would call, a lot of the time Walter pretended he wasn't there," said Quirk. "He didn't have much to talk with his brother about. The bond was iffy."

While Walter and Connie remained married, it was a union solely in name and finances. "I started working for Walter in 1987," said Tucker. "I didn't even know he was married until probably a year later. I just thought Connie was the mother of his kids." Shortly after his retirement, Payton—a spokesperson for Inland Property, a real estate firm—was provided with a free fully furnished two-bedroom apartment on Chestnut Street in downtown

Chicago. He eventually split his time between there, a 3,500-square foot home he purchased in the Chicago suburb of West Dundee, Illinois, and the family house at 34 Mudhank (depending on when he wanted to be at the house with Jarrett, now seven, and Brittney, three). Husband and wife spoke when necessary, and Walter's dalliances were becoming common knowledge throughout Chicago. He confided in those he was close with that, when his children graduated high school, he would divorce Connie once and for all. "He didn't want the children to go through the rigors of a celebrity divorce," said Tucker. "He knew what the spotlight felt like when it was negative, and he hated the idea of Jarrett and Brittney experiencing any of that."

To those he trusted, Walter claimed he had never actually wanted to marry Connie; that the pressures of being young and alone had forced him to make a terrible mistake. He didn't necessarily hate her, but there was no love or, for that matter, like. There hadn't been for a long time. "Walter knew that if he left Connie all the work he'd done to his image would go by the wayside," said Ron Atlas, his longtime friend. "Connie was very well liked, and that was a problem. When they were a real couple, friends would always side with Connie when they argued, because she seemed like such a sweet person."

Of all the people he knew, Payton's closest confidant was, interestingly, Ginny Quirk. Irrepressibly upbeat and perky, the native Chicagoan was twenty-one years old and freshly dropped out of the University of Wisconsin–Stout when, in the late months of 1984, a headhunter sent her to interview for an executive assistant's job with "a high-profile businessman."

"I was told the person needed someone who could travel, someone who could take the ball and run with it, someone who could wear a lot of hats and handle a lot of assignments," said Quirk. "Until I walked in the door to interview with him, I had no idea the businessman was Walter Payton."

Upon being hired, it took Quirk approximately twenty seconds to understand the craziness of celebrity. Payton needed someone to organize his massive piles of fan mail ("I hired a slew of temps to knock it out and get a system in place."), to handle speaking engagements ("He made between ten thousand and twenty-five thousand dollars a talk, and was brilliant at it."), to oversee merchandising, and to make sure he never forgot or overlooked a request. Payton insisted on hiring a night owl, and Quirk soon learned why. He called her up to thirty times per day. At two in the morning. Again at three in the morning. Again at four in the morning. He asked her to check in on Holmes and Richman. He needed her to take care of something involving the children. He complained to her about Connie and confided in her about other women. Not for approval—just because, well, it seemed like she should know. When one saw Walter, one almost always saw Ginny. She was his shadow. Or, to be accurate, he was hers. "I talked to Walter more than any family member, more than any friend or boyfriend," she said. "Before cell phones were widespread he had this beeper that went off all the time. Then he had this big ol' Motorola cell phone, and he'd use it constantly. He was addicted to knowing if anything was going on—'Ginny, anybody call? Ginny, what you got? Ginny, tell me something.' He could drive me crazy. Really insane. But, at the same time, he became a family member. I loved him, and would have done anything for him."

The burden of loneliness and a dreadful marriage weren't Payton's only problems. As a player Payton had numbed his maladies with pills and liquids, usually supplied by the Bears. Now that he was retired, the self-medicating only intensified. Payton relied on Tylenol 3 and Vicodin, mixing the two drugs into cocktails he habitually ingested. In a particularly embarrassing episode, in 1988 Payton visited a handful of dental offices, complaining of severe tooth pain. He was supplied with different prescriptions for morphine, and hit up a handful of drugstores to have them filled. When one of the pharmacists noticed the activity, he contacted the authorities, who arrived at Payton's house and discussed the situation. Payton was merely issued a warning. "Walter was pounding his body with medication," said Holmes. "I wish I knew how bad it was, but at the time I really didn't."

Back when Payton drove his own RV to training camp, he used to load the rear of the vehicle with tanks of nitrous oxide, aka laughing gas. Used primarily in surgery and dentistry for its anesthetic and analgesic effects, Payton was provided with the chemical by a friend who dabbled in medical supplies. At nights and during breaks in the action, players snuck into Payton's trailer, loaded the nitrous oxide into balloons, then carried them around while taking hits. The goofy laughter could be heard throughout the training facility.

Now that he was retired, Payton turned to nitrous oxide more than ever. Large tanks filled up a corner of his garage, and he held a gas-stuffed balloon throughout portions of his days, taking joyous hits whenever the impulse struck. "I don't think Walter was addicted," said a friend. "But he sure liked it."

In need of some semblance of sanity, Payton decided the best he could do was throw himself into as many activities as possible, hoping one or two would fill the void. He took helicopter lessons. He bought more guns. He looked for antique automobiles. He dabbled in golf.

He ran a nightclub and shot a man in the leg.

Throughout his playing career, Payton—guided largely by Holmes and Richman—refused to simply allow his money to collect interest. He was an active investor, ranging from a twenty-six-acre shopping center to a seven-million-dollar, two-hundred-room hotel to 934 acres of undeveloped timberland in northern Mississippi to a Learjet that he and his partners rented out. A couple paid dividends—Payton and Holmes made a small fortune on the Lakeland Health Care Center, a nursing home in Lakeland, Florida. Most did not—Payton lost a large sum by investing in something called Heavy-rope, a weighted–jump rope, and he was one of several athletes to find themselves swindled by Miles Yanca, a ticket broker who was sentenced to eight years in prison for running a scheme that cost investors millions of dollars. "Walter didn't put a lot of real effort into being a businessman," said Quirk. "Bud tried to tell him that he needed to pay attention and manage his own stuff, but Walter didn't have the patience for meetings. He was really smart, and he could read people better than anyone I've ever met. But when it came to businesses, he trusted the judgment of others. Sometimes that works. Oftentimes it doesn't."

Payton had hoped to retire into a carefree life of fishing and hunting. Much of the money he had earned as a player, however, was gone, lost to bad investments and lavish purchases. He told those around him that he wanted to work. Truth was, he had no choice.

Of his many holdings, the one Payton enjoyed most was Studebaker's, a 1950s-themed nightclub and lounge located within a strip mall in the Chicago suburb of Schaumburg. Back in 1981, Holmes and a Houston, Texas–based businessman named Stuart Sargent teamed to open the first Studebaker's in Mobile, Alabama. A second, in Jackson, Mississippi, followed shortly thereafter, then three more in New Orleans, Baton Rouge, and Dallas. "Our goal was to have a nightclub for adults in their thirties and forties—one that wasn't dark and didn't come with an owner wearing a thick gold chain with a fake blonde on his arm," said Gene Gunn, an early investor. "We had done a lot of smaller Southern markets, and one day I asked Stuart whether he wanted to give it a go in some major northern cities. That's where Walter came in."

A Studebaker's opened in Chicago in 1983, and that same year the Schaumburg location came to life. Payton picked the strip mall, interviewed and hired most of the staff, used his name to bring instant credibility. Before long, the club was a line-around-the-block hotspot for mostly middle-aged revelers. People from throughout the region drove to 1251 East Golf Road to groove to Jerry Lee Lewis and Little Richard and watch the poodle-skirted waitresses perform choreographed dances atop the bar. At the same time the television sitcom *Cheers* was introducing America to a colorful gaggle of bar regulars, Studebaker's had its own clan of loyal customers who showed up nightly for the bountiful buffet and classic music. A genuine family atmosphere was cultivated, and Payton cherished it.

"That was really Walter's baby," said Quirk. "He opened a lot of other nightclubs over the next few years, but Studebaker's meant the most to him. He'd be in the deejay booth spinning records, in the kitchen waving to customers from the back, telling jokes to the employees. He was in his element."

Payton so loved being at Studebaker's that a cluttered, dingy, three-hundred-square-foot storeroom in the rear became his base of business operations. Upon retiring from the Bears, he spent increasingly long hours hunkered down in the cramped space. The nightclub's employees came to embrace Payton, who would hang out in the alley outside the rear entrance as they smoked cigarettes. Payton always seemed to have some sort of valuable handout—expensive cigars, five-hundred-dollar sunglasses—and he distributed the goods with great zest. "He was so empathetic to us," said Lana Layne, an employee. "There was no arrogance."

Lou Visconti, a disc jockey from 1984 to 1992, recalled telling Payton that, at six dollars an hour, he could no longer afford to spin records.

"Is that all we're paying you?" Payton asked.

"Yes," said Visconti. "I can't live on it."

"Come back tomorrow," Payton said. "I'll take care of it."

The next day, Visconti was informed that he would be making thirty-two thousand dollars annually, plus benefits. "Walter gave me my first salaried job," he said. "How many people can say the first raise they ever received was from Walter Payton?"

Layne began working at Studebaker's as a nineteen-year-old waitress in 1989. One morning, when her eight-year-old brother, Douglas, was off from school, she brought him to the bar. Before leaving home, she called and asked her boss whether he'd be willing to shake her brother's hand. "Of course," said Payton. "I'd be happy to."

"We get there, and Walter grabs Douglas, takes him into his office, and spends about two hours with him," said Layne. "He came away with a bunch of photographs and a football Walter signed. All he had to do to make Douglas' day was say hello. But he went so much further."

One of Payton's favorite employees was Elmer Hutson, a twenty-eight-year-old manager known to the entire Studebaker's staff as J. R. Based out of Miami, Hutson was asked by McFadden Ventures, Studebaker's parent company, to move to Illinois in 1987 and help manage the Schaumburg entity. Having never been to Chicago, he jumped at the opportunity.

On the afternoon of Wednesday, April 13, 1988, Hutson arrived early at the bar, to make certain his staff had cleaned ably the night before. While there, he engaged in a heated phone exchange with Mike McKenna, a representative from Coors Light. Fifteen minutes after hanging up, Hutson was summoned to see Payton. "I walk into his office, and he had a couch and two chairs up against the wall," said Hutson. "He was sitting on one chair and Mike McKenna—who came to complain about me—was in the other. I sat down on the arm of the couch, so the three of us were in a triangle. Walter had the phone to his ear, talking to Connie."

In his right hand, Payton was holding a 9mm French-made Manurhin Pistolet, which he had recently purchased for his collection. As he spoke with his wife, Payton repeatedly spun the gun, jokingly pointing it toward Hutson. "He twirled it a couple of times, then came back up with the gun and put it down again," Hutson said. "That's when it went off."

To the shock of the three men, a bullet exploded from the weapon and entered Hutson's left knee. It fragmented his kneecap, traveled nine inches up his thigh, took out approximately two inches of hamstring, and all of his cartilage. The bullet exited through the rear of the leg, leaving a three-inch hole.

Hutson fell to the floor and grasped his leg. "Was the gun loaded?" he screamed. Payton instinctively dropped the weapon. "Oh my God!" he said. "I almost aimed higher!"

"It felt like my entire leg was on fire," said Hutson. "It was the most excruciating pain I've ever experienced."

Payton immediately dialed 911, and followed with a call to his attorney. The bar's on-duty employees rushed to see what had happened. "Walter shot

J. R.!" somebody yelled. "Walter shot J. R.!" An ambulance rushed Hutson to Northwest Community Hospital in Arlington Heights, where a nurse asked him whether he had contacted his parents. "No," Hutson said, "I haven't."

"Well, you better do it now," she said. "Because the story's about to be released to the *Associated Press* wire."

Indeed, the next morning the news of the NFL's all-time leading rusher gunning down an employee had swept the nation. Hundreds of papers carried the story, and radio's talking heads wondered whether Payton would face charges. Payton visited the hospital and apologized profusely. When Hutson returned home ten days later, he was greeted by a new set of left-handed Wilson golf clubs, accompanied by a note from Payton. "I believe Walter was genuinely sorry," said Hutson. "He was a nice man who I really respected."

One year after the shooting, however, a limping, pain-stricken Hutson was let go by the club for what, he said, was no apparent reason. He later sued Studebaker's for failing to provide him with proper health coverage, and the business—to Hutson's shock/dismay—actually countersued. Though he doesn't directly blame Payton ("It's a chain," Hutson said. "He was just an investor."), Hutson lost much of the fondness he had for his old boss. "They actually made the argument that, knowing there was a loaded gun in the room, I should have taken precautions not to get shot," Hutson said. "It would almost be humorous, were my leg not in such bad shape."

Eventually, the two parties settled and Hudson received $209,000. He never heard from Walter Payton again.

·  ·  ·

Two months after shooting Hutson, Payton flew to New Jersey to attend the Mike Tyson–Michael Spinks heavyweight championship bout at the Atlantic City Convention Center. Though far from a diehard boxing fan, Payton was happy to trade in his status for some free tickets to the biggest bout of the year (albeit one that would last ninety-one seconds). For a man getting used to being out of the spotlight, the night proved a nice ego boost. Along with such luminaries as Sean Penn, Milton Berle, and George Steinbrenner, Payton was introduced to the crowd of 21,785, receiving a loud ovation when he stood and waved. He signed an endless stream of autographs, and posed for dozens of pictures.

In the months since his last NFL game, Payton had spent much of his time pursuing women *not* named Connie Payton. Though his tiny rear office at Studebaker's was a suitable place to conduct professional business (visitors marveled at the dozens of football helmets that lined the walls), it doubled as, in the words of Eamonn Cummins, "Walter's fuck pad." A bouncer first hired by the club in 1987, Cummins was in charge of determining who could—and couldn't—enter Studebaker's. He stood sentry at the front entrance, telephone by his side, and informed Payton of visitors. The majority of the club's female patrons were hardly Heather Locklear–esque. These were fanny-packers, not miniskirters; women with careers and, oftentimes, children, looking for a couple of hours of escape.

Payton, however, drew his own special genre. He would jump into the deejay booth during especially crowded nights, spin a couple of records, and emerge with fifteen phone numbers.

"So many females came by to see Walter," Cummins said. "He'd call me back to his office and say 'A woman is going to be here in ten minutes. I want you to get her and bring her right back.' They were always the same— bimbo-ish, big hair, always white, always kind of stupid. They were cheesy, mostly twenty-five–ish. I remember one Saturday night early in my career, a girl showed up at eight on a Saturday night. An hour or so later she left, and then another girl showed up. I went back there to bring her in and he was just laying on his couch, waiting and ready."

In Atlantic City, Payton's wandering eye zeroed in on a long-legged twenty-one-year-old flight attendant of Puerto Rican descent. She had brown eyes, bright teeth, wavy hair, and large breasts, and Payton made his move while both were waiting on a convention center line. Lita Gonzalez had never heard of Walter Payton, and certainly had no idea that he was a legendary football player. She could, however, tell that he was *somebody*. "He walked very confidently," Gonzalez said. "With an air of importance."

The two struck up a conversation, word about his wife never escaping Payton's mouth. As always, Payton was complimentary and smooth. Just as in football he used his hands to protect the pigskin, with women he used his hands to gently touch a shoulder, subtly brush back a stray hair. "He was very charming," said Gonzalez. The two went out to a club after the fight. The next morning Payton caught a flight back to Chicago and Gonzalez went to work for Continental Airlines. She assumed she would never hear from him again. Instead, he called incessantly. "When Walter wanted a girl, his approach was to call, call, call, call," said Quirk. "He would overwhelm people with contact. That's what he did with Lita. He made his interest clear."

Although Connie likely understood the nature of her marriage, she refused to let the public know. Thanks to her husband, her life was a comfortable one. She lived in a breathtaking home, employed a live-in nanny, shopped at the fanciest department stores, and dined out as she pleased. According to Holmes, Connie once approached him about possibly leaving Walter. "I told her the truth," he said. "'Connie, it's a helluva lot easier being Mrs. Walter Payton than the ex–Mrs. Walter Payton.'"

If Walter saw retirement as an opportunity to forge closer ties with his children, the steps he took were, at best, minimal. Though far from a disinterested father, he was, even without football, a largely absent one. No longer living at the home on 34 Mudhank, he checked in as often as he could, took them on trips every now and then, stopped by the house regularly. With Jarrett approaching his eighth birthday and Brittney having just turned three, retirement had provided Payton with an opportunity to finally become deeply involved in their day-to-day lives. Instead, Walter's wayward search for meaning and significance and excitement took him to a most quizzical place: the racetrack.

Even with the enjoyment he derived from Studebaker's and even with the nonstop flow of women entering and leaving his office, Payton was unable to uncover anything to match the adrenaline rush that came from slipping on his No. 34 jersey and running across Soldier Field. The buzz and jolt and euphoria had been addictive, as had the sense of comradery he shared with teammates. Now he was a man in need of a fix.

During one of his final seasons Payton had been introduced to Ove Olsson, owner of a race car shop, Olsson Engineering, in Lake Forest. Born and raised in Stockholm, Sweden, Olsson immediately admired Payton not for his celebrity status ("I had no idea who he was," he said), but for the silver Porsche 930 that he used as a primary vehicle. "I worked on his car early on, and we bonded," Olsson said. "We shared a passion for fast vehicles." As a kinship developed, Olsson became increasingly aware of Payton's dangerous driving habits. He would watch Payton clear 100 mph on his Kawasaki GPZ 750 and cringe. He would see him swerve left and right in the Porsche and gasp. He heard that Payton had been pulled over for driving 125 mph in a 35 mph speed zone (celebrity being celebrity, police let him off with a warning), and shook his head. Once, the driver of an adjacent vehicle became so incensed by Payton's recklessness that he rolled down a window and threw a large chain at the hood of the superstar's BMW. The sizeable indentation served as a warning sign to other cars: WATCH OUT. "He wasn't necessarily a bad driver," Olsson said. "He was just incredibly wild." One day, upon a chance meeting with Connie, Olsson pulled her aside and said, "I think it'd be a lot safer for Walter to drive on a track rather than the road."

Retired and in search of a spark, Payton took Olsson's words to heart. On April 16, he found himself behind the wheel of a Celica GT-S Liftback at the Toyota Grand Prix of Long Beach, a pro-celebrity event featuring such luminaries as Susan Ruttan and Brian Wimmer. The two-mile track wormed through the downtown streets of Long Beach, California, and Payton deemed the experience a barometer. Were he to do well and have fun, he'd take a stab at driving competitively in a semiprofessional circuit called the Sports Car Club of America's Pro Sports 2000 series. "For some reason Walter missed the test day before the race, and I was livid," said Olsson. "He was always too busy. There was always a phone to his ear, always a meeting to attend. Where was the commitment? But then he raced really well, and I think we both thought, 'Maybe this can work.'" Payton placed ninth, leapt from his car, and squealed with delight. He had slammed into a wall—*and loved it.* "I'm going to drive four or five, maybe six races in Formula 2000!" he said. "This was amazing!"

True to his word, Payton made the decision to compete regularly on the Sports Car tour. The races involved open cockpit vehicles featuring full bodywork. They were light (eleven hundred pounds on average; by comparison, NASCAR cars weigh three thousand pounds), with sophisticated suspensions, sway bars, and 2,000 cc, four-cylinder Ford engines. Because the cars were made from aluminum, it was a relatively safe form of racing. "If you hit something hard enough, aluminum crushes in gradually and absorbs energy," said Steve Knapp, a former driver who assisted Payton. "It was a soft car."

Those who observed Payton in his racing infancy recall a marginal talent who sabotaged his own improvement with the need to drive full throttle. Just as Walter Payton the running back knew no brake pedal, Walter Payton the driver knew no brake pedal, either. "He drove exactly like he played," said Knapp. "He cut very hard, he was really jerky, and he didn't know when to pull back."

"He wanted to run before he walked," said Tony Kester, his driving coach. "Walter's best attribute as a driver was his hand-eye coordination, which was off the charts. But a big problem was his strength. Walter was like Paul Bunyan, and Paul Bunyan would have had a lot of difficulty driving. Walter was so strong that he would push the brake pedal with too much force and lock the brakes. So we had to adjust the pedal to make it harder." If NASCAR and Formula One are auto racing's Major Leagues, the Sports 2000 series was *maybe* Class A. Most of the participants were part-time racers who worked nine-to-five jobs. Few fans attended, and those who did were either irrationally devoted to motor sports or uninspired by the day's selections at the local movie theatre. Experienced drivers viewed the series dismissively, as an entry-level endeavor and little more. For Payton, however, it served as a gateway to a higher caliber of competition as well as an adrenaline substitute for football.

His official debut took place on May 13, 1989, in the not-so-bustling Dallas suburb of Addison, Texas. For a man used to first-class accommodations and the most modern of equipment, this would seem to be an enormous comedown. The 1.57-mile track was built on the runways, perimeter roads, and streets of the dilapidated Addison Airport. There was minimal parking, zero concessions, and blistering heat that made the inside of a car feel like a microwave oven.

Payton and his crew arrived at the track approximately four hours before the one P.M. start. The enormous van that carried his car and equipment bore the insignia, PAYTON PLACE. Armed with a white Lola with No. 34 painted along the side, Payton nervously entered his vehicle and rolled toward the starting line. His heart was pounding, his breathing quickened. He last felt these sorts of jitters thirteen years earlier, when he lined up for his first NFL game.

Though he was but a rookie, Payton—ever the competitor—expected to win. Through the seventh of thirty-seven laps, he was running eleventh in a field of twenty-four, holding his own against tour veterans like Irv Hoerr and Darin Brassfield. Finally, on the eighth lap, inexperience kicked in. Payton's car skidded off the track and slammed into a tire wall, bringing *oohs* and *ahhs* from the scattered fans and audible cursing from the driver. "I was really running hot," Payton said afterward. "I was coming into turn six and suddenly there was oil on my visor. It must have been thrown up from the car in front of me. I reached up and tried to wipe it off my visor and shouldn't have done that. It smeared all over and I couldn't see anything. The next thing I knew I was off the track."

Because Payton was a first timer, his crew and the other racers took sympathy on his plight. Driving wasn't easy—especially for a rookie used to physically dominating in another arena. Yet as the season progressed and Payton traveled from venue to venue, the excuses became a regular part of his routine. His car wasn't good enough. His crew kept screwing up. The track was too slick. The steering wheel jammed. He crashed on multiple occasions, but the incidents were never—*never*—his fault. "His stubbornness was difficult," said Olsson, who traveled with Payton to seven races that first year. "He wasn't the best at taking responsibility for his own shortcomings." Truth was, Payton didn't train hard enough. There were businesses to run, appearances to make, women to see, his kids to visit. Racing came sixth or seventh on the priority list, which prevented him from rising from bad to mediocre.

Payton spent less than two years flailing around on the Sports 2000 circuit when, in 1990, an opportunity presented itself. Paul Newman, who, like Payton, had dabbled in the sport, was the co-owner of a team, Newman Sharp Racing, that participated in the highly competitive Trans-Am Series. Though Newman was obviously best known as an Academy Award winner, he was passionate about the track and, through eighteen years, had developed into a high-level driver.

As part of his team's sponsorship agreement with Oldsmobile, Newman was required to have a set number of celebrity participants. His big name had been Tom Cruise, but the actor dropped out to film three new projects. "Which made us all very happy, because Cruise was not merely a jerk, he was a jerk who couldn't drive for shit," said Barry Chappel, who handled Newman Sharp's sponsorship deals. "A bunch of guys who worked the different tracks had T-shirts made that said SCCA: SEE CRUISE CRASH AGAIN."

As opposed to the arrogant and inept Cruise, who once demolished five Nissan 300 cars in a single season, Payton was a refreshing breath of fresh air. Chappel traveled to Studebaker's to sell him on jumping from Sports 2000 to Trans-Am, and—against the advice of Olsson and Kester, who rightly insisted he was not ready—six days later Payton was in Atlanta, preparing to test for the team at the Road Atlanta track. He stayed in the Admiral Benbow Inn, a dump with moldy ceiling tiles and torn carpets that Newman, ever the bargain hunter, raved about.

Chappel and Newman flew via private plane to Atlanta to see him drive. It was only while they were thirty thousand feet above ground that the actor asked about the auditionee.

NOW WHAT? • 355

"Who is this guy we're gonna watch?" Newman said.

"Walter Payton," replied Chappel.

"Am I supposed to know that name?" Newman said.

Chappel was dumbfounded. "Paul, let me ask you a question," he said. "Where have you been for the last ten years?" He proceeded to pull out Payton's bio sheet, chock full o' NFL records.

"Holy shit!" Newman said. "He sounds perfect."

Wrote *Sports Illustrated* of Payton's foray into the Trans-Am circuit: "Anybody who thought Franco Harris ran out of bounds a lot should see Walter Payton drive a race car." He made his Trans-Am debut at the Road America track in Elkhart Lake, Wisconsin, in 1991, and quickly showed himself to be unprepared for the distance (usually one hundred miles), duration (more than an hour of straight driving), speed (200 mph), and power (750 horsepower). The cars were primarily Chevrolets, Dodges, and Fords, and they packed a punch.

He kicked off the 1992 season by placing twenty-first at Long Beach and twenty-seventh two weeks later at Detroit. "Walter's biggest problem was that he thought of himself as a professional driver, and he wasn't," said Bob Sharp, who co-owned the team with Newman. "In football, he was the complete package. In racing, he wasn't a pro. But he failed to realize that. He probably had ninety percent of what's needed to pull it off, but he needed a little more humility and a little more patience."

"He was better than Cruise, but he wasn't good," said Chappel. "His biggest problem was he couldn't keep the cars together. He crashed one, then he crashed another, then he crashed another. But Paul came to love him, because of the enthusiasm and energy he brought."

The first time Payton drove at famed Lime Rock Park in Lakeville, Connecticut, Newman rode shotgun to offer some pointers. Intimidated by the actor's presence, Payton accidentally spun the car. *Twice.* For the remainder of the trip Newman rode with his feet wedged against the dashboard, eyes "as big as silver dollars," Payton recalled with a laugh.

What Payton most loved about the racing world was the comradery among drivers. Back in Illinois, his life often felt bereft of meaning and purpose. He was lonely, sad, isolated. The track, however, offered substance. It was just like the Bears' locker room, what with Payton flicking ears and tying shoelaces together and embracing rivals in rib-crushing bear hugs (his track favorite was grabbing unsuspecting drivers by the wrists while walking by and having them helplessly drag along). Were the other drivers close, personal friends? No. But they were colleagues, and they served a very genuine purpose. "We were at a race in Sonoma, California, which was my home track," said Peter Musser, a veteran driver. "We were in a drivers meeting and he's got himself peeled up against a back wall. The head of the series is chewing us all out about reckless driving, just letting us have it. [Driver] Scott Sharp turns to Walter in the back and says, 'Walter, why don't you sit up here with the rest of us.' And in that high-pitched voice, Walter says, 'Nah, man, the brothers hang in the back.' The room just broke up laughing."

On the road Payton had nothing to hide and no preestablished image to live up to. He wasn't Sweetness, the larger-than-life Chicago icon. He was Walter, the mediocre driver and laid-back guy. Most of his peers didn't even know he was married.

"He ran with great-looking women," said Bobby Archer, a fellow racer. "That, I remember."

"Gorgeous women accompanied him," said Greg Pickett, another driver. "He was a magnet."

Payton never wore a wedding ring, and the woman by his side at most (but not all) events was Lita Gonzalez, the Continental flight attendant. Thanks to her job, Gonzalez had free access to the nation. On her off days she'd fly from her home in New Jersey and meet Payton at points ranging from Nevada to Dallas to Wisconsin. "She was there regularly," said Jim Derhaag, a competitor. "We all knew Lita and embraced her into our community."

On occasion, Payton also brought his children along. They enjoyed the excitement of the racetrack. The sounds of the engines. The speed. The euphoria. The colors. On August 20, 1993, Walter had eight-year-old Brittney accompany him to Elkhart Lake, Wisconsin, to watch a qualifying round at Road America. When Walter went off to drive he left his daughter in the company of the track officials. "We were on a golf cart," she said. "Me and a bunch of people I didn't know."

Strapped into his blue Ford Mustang Cobra (No. 34 painted across the hood), Payton lined up with the other drivers, taking off with the wave of a flag. It was an otherwise normal qualifying run—Payton hanging back, waiting to make some sort of move, preparing to transition from a straightaway to a curve. Running directly in front of Payton was Dick Danielson, a Hartford, Wisconsin, native with twenty-three years of racing to his credit.

As his Camaro steadied for the turn, Danielson shifted into fourth gear and lost all power.

"Walter is preparing to pass him, but it's like following a car on the freeway and the car in front of you stops," said Tom Gloy, owner of the Tom Gloy Racing Team. "Walter was pretty much helpless." Payton's Ford somehow eluded Danielson, but its front right tire nicked Danielson's left rear tire.

At 130 mph, tiny collisions mean big trouble. Payton's car swerved off to the side, hit the guardrail, somersaulted, flew thirty feet into the air, traveled a hundred feet, bounced four times, and finally, bounded off the guardrail and over a fence. "The fence!" said Jack Baldwin, a driver. "I'd never seen anyone clear that thing before." The final impact cut open the rear of the vehicle and sliced through a fuel cell. The car was engulfed by fire. Payton, knocked unconscious for a brief spell, regained his senses and leapt from the damage. "When I finally stopped I was looking upside down and there were flames," he said afterward. "All I could think of at that point was that I had to get out of there."

Riding in the golf cart, Brittney heard the call over the radio from Donald Sak, a driver who had witnessed the crash. "Get someone out here!" he screamed. "We have a terrible situation!" She was rushed to a tent situated alongside an ambulance. Her father was lying on the table, his eyes bloodshot from gasoline, bandages covering the burns on his neck. Jerry Clinton, a fellow driver, described Payton as resembling, "a big frog with his eyes bugged out." Brittney took one look and began to cry, which snapped Payton from his silence. "It's OK, Britt," he said. "It's OK. Daddy's fine. Daddy's fine."

"Oh, I was terrified," she said. "I thought my dad was Superman. I never saw him hurt, never saw him sick. I don't even remember him having a cold. Now here I was, without my mother or brother, and my father was on a stretcher. I can still remember the scent. The fuel or . . . whatever. The scent."

Walter and Brittney were taken to the nearby Valley View Medical Center, where he was treated and released that night. Back at the American Club Hotel, Payton walked around as if in a trance. He had survived some of the hardest hits known to the NFL—but nothing like this.

"That was pretty much the end of his racing career," Brittney said. "I don't think any of us were disappointed to see him give it up."

CHAPTER 23

# A BOTTOMLESS VOID

To the world, Walter Payton insisted he was done as a football player. He was a busy man. Auto racing. Motivational speaking. Trying to buy a team. He had moved on. He had stopped paying attention. He had no interest in a comeback. Not even a slight interest.

"Well," said Bud Holmes, Payton's longtime agent. "That's what people thought. Only it wasn't entirely true."

On the afternoon of September 24, 1989, a lightly regarded Miami Dolphins fullback named Tom Brown started the third game of his NFL career, against the New York Jets. Best known as Craig "Iron Head" Heyward's lead blocker at the University of Pittsburgh, Brown was a six-foot-one, 223-pound bulldozer who featured no quickness, no speed, no maneuverability. He was in the league for one reason—to slam into people and open holes. Yet for someone so powerful, Brown was irritatingly brittle. Since being selected by Miami in the seventh round of the 1987 Draft, he had endured the majority of his days on the physically-unable-to-perform list, battling an endless string of knee injuries. "I've spent more time with our trainers than their wives have the last two years," he said shortly before the 1989 opener. "It's been very frustrating."

Finally, though, Brown seemed to discover health. He had played well enough to wrestle the starting job away from veteran Ron Davenport, and was confidently knocking back Jets linebackers until an unbearable pain shot through Brown's right knee, and he fell to the ground at Joe Robbie Stadium. Once again, he tore a ligament. Once again, he was headed for the injury list.

The malady kicked off an unparalleled string of miserable luck for Miami running backs. Shortly after Brown went down, halfback Troy Stradford was lost for the season with cartilage and ligament damage to his right knee. Halfback Lorenzo Hampton followed by also tearing cartilage in his right knee, and fullback Marc Logan wound up on crutches with ligament damage in his left knee. Even halfback Sammie Smith, the rookie standout from Florida State, suffered an Achilles tendon bruise that left him hobbling.

Finally, with his team carrying but two healthy ball carriers (Davenport and Nuu Faaola), Dolphins coach Don Shula told the media he was preparing to hold an open casting call for available running backs. Among the first to be auditioned would be George Swarn, a twenty-five-year-old Miami of Ohio standout, and Kerry Goode, a Buccaneer reject who had played at the University of Alabama. This was hardly Eric Dickerson and Marcus Allen.

Having stopped following the day-to-day goings-on of the NFL, Holmes had no inkling of Miami's woes. So, when Payton called his home one evening, his high-pitched voice spitting out a hundred words a second, Holmes demanded his longtime client slow down and explain what in the world he was talking about.

"I want you to talk to Eddie Jones [Miami's vice president of administration] and tell him I'm interested," Payton said. "Tell him."

"Interested in what?" Holmes replied.

"Interested in playing for the Dolphins," he said. "They're not that far off from being a Super Bowl team. Tell him I'll come in and block, run—whatever they need."

Holmes was at a loss. Ever since Payton had retired at the conclusion of the '87 season, the two men worked tirelessly to make his post-football adjustment as smooth and seamless as possible. Though, years later, Payton blamed Holmes for encouraging him to hang up his uniform too early, the truth was he made the final decision on his own. "Nobody forced Walter to stop playing," Holmes rightly said. "It was his call."

Now, Payton was making the call to try a comeback. "Walter, here's what we'll do," Holmes said. "Sleep on this, and let's talk tomorrow morning. If you still want me to contact Eddie, I will."

The night came.

The morning arrived.

Holmes called Payton. "Well?" he said. "Are you still interested?"

"Interested in what?" the legend responded.

"In the Dolphins," Holmes said. "In returning to the league."

"Oh, that," said Payton. "Nah—forget it. I just got a little emotional. It's probably a bad idea"

Holmes was relieved.

"There's no way Miami would have taken Walter at age thirty-six," he said. "And if they did, it would have been a disaster. He was meant to retire a Chicago Bear, not a Dolphin. The way he went out was the right way."

. . .

At the same time Payton was thinking about Miami, he was also thinking about St. Louis. When he retired after the '87 season, the prime motivating factor was life after football likely including his becoming the first minority owner in league history. That's the way Holmes had phrased it—that while he would no longer enjoy the euphoria of crossing a goal line, Payton would know how it felt to become a legitimate trailblazer.

In the waning days of his career, Payton was told that the NFL badly wanted to return a team to St. Louis, which had been vacated when the Cardinals relocated to Arizona after the 1987 season. Not only was St. Louis the nation's eighteenth largest television market, and not only was it centrally located, and not only was it home to a good number of Fortune 500 companies, but it was a genuine sports hotbed. When Bill Bidwill, the Cardinals' owner, moved his franchise west, it wasn't because St. Louis was incapable of supporting football. No, he moved because the city—loathe to support a man considered to be miserly and not civic-minded—refused to fork over the two hundred million dollars necessary to build him a stadium.

Before Pete Rozelle, the NFL's legendary commissioner, retired in November 1989, he spoke with Payton on numerous occasions about St. Louis. It was, the commissioner believed, a perfect match: Here was a market in need of a team. Here was a league in need of diversity. Here was an iconic figure—beloved, intelligent, African-American—who had nobly represented the NFL and who excelled at bringing disparate people together. Plus, Chicago and St. Louis were separated by a mere three hundred miles. Though not exactly a local, Payton was close enough to travel back and forth with little hassle. "I always felt that Walter was one of the half-dozen real class players during my time in the league," Rozelle explained. "I have a great deal of respect for him. I think he would be a valued asset to any group."

Payton was interested, but skeptical. While he had earned a good amount of money throughout his thirteen-year career, he could hardly be classified as wealthy. His highest single-season salary was only one million dollars, and, thanks to a high number of dubious investments, he was not sitting on a major war chest. Payton had laid down hundreds of thousands of dollars into Studebaker's, as well as four other nightclubs, only later to learn that he had made a tremendous mistake. Those athletes who excelled financially at the conclusion of their careers did so not by relying on their finances, but their names. When an Arnold Palmer or Joe DiMaggio was approached about opening an establishment, they would listen as long as the endeavor did not involve forking over any dough. So while Payton was indeed titillated by the idea of calling an owner's box home, he wasn't willing to go broke in pursuit of it.

Which is where Jerry Clinton came in.

Raised in a housing project on the south side of St. Louis, Clinton was a former Golden Gloves boxer who, against all odds, worked his way up from lugging cases of beer to, in 1977, becoming the president of Grey Eagle Distributors, the Anheuser-Busch beer distributorship in St. Louis County. Clinton had initially purchased 5 percent equity in the company, then turned that into 50 percent and, eventually, 100 percent. Under his watch, Grey Eagle's market share went from 30 percent to 70 percent, and throughout St. Louis he became known as something of a financial Houdini. "Jerry was an incredibly successful businessman who came to represent our city in a lot of ways," said Walter Metcalfe, an attorney who represented Clinton and Grey Eagle for more than twenty years. "He had been very generous with local charities, and people loved him for that."

Unlike Bidwill, Clinton was civic-minded, and when he first caught wind that the NFL was looking to return to his city, he wanted in. "Jerry was a huge football fan," said Jim Otis, a friend and former Cardinals running back. "When he used to have the distributorship he'd come out to our practices and give all the players beers to crack open. I think he liked being around the game."

In the late 1980s, the main financial player in the expansion effort was Francis W. Murray, a Philadelphia-based entrepreneur who at one point had owned a minority share of the New England Patriots. Murray was the sort of man who people wanted to believe in, because the words that oozed from his mouth were usually appealing and complimentary. He made enticing promises, offered heaps of praise, spewed visions of grandeur that were ultimately more fantasy than reality. Growing up in Philly, he sold sodas and hot dogs at neighborhood bingo games to make money, and the stories he told about those days were uproarious and uplifting. When Fran Murray talked, people listened. "It was hard not to like Fran," said Clinton. "He was engaging." Rozelle approved of Murray's involvement, especially after his option to buy a controlling share of the Patriots from Billy Sullivan had failed to pan out.

Clinton was first introduced to Murray in 1987, and he was not impressed. They met in an office in Maryland Heights, Missouri, and Clinton was taken aback not by Murray's awkward mannerisms or braggart ways—but by his shoes. "He had on a blue pinstripe suit and brown shoes," Clinton recalled. "I thought that was very unusual. He was an excellent talker, an excellent motivator. I jokingly used to refer to him as Harold Hill, the Music Man."

For Clinton, an initial warning sign came when Murray—supposedly a multimillionaire—asked him for a three-million-dollar loan. Had he done some investigating, Clinton would have found that Murray had been successfully sued some twenty-two times for nonpayment of debts, stemming from, according to a St. Louis Post-Dispatch report, "the collapse of fast-food restaurants he owned in the 1970s." Furthermore, Murray had been sued eleven times by various local, state, and federal government branches on tax-related charges. His lone source of credibility with the NFL was his interest in the Patriots. The league had never properly delved into his credentials. Nor had Clinton. "I figured if my attorney brought Fran into my office," he said, "he'd been checked." On February 27, 1989, the two men announced the formation of the St. Louis NFL partnership. Murray owned 51 percent, Clinton 49 percent. "We're not asking anyone for anything," Murray said at the time—an odd declaration, considering he had just borrowed three million dollars.

This is what Walter Payton walked into.

Clinton approached him toward the latter months of 1989, when several NFL officials told the St. Louis folks that the bid would be enhanced with the running back's experience, image, and ethnicity. Payton had first outwardly expressed an interest in ownership in the summer of 1986, when he mentioned to The Washington Post that he would one day like to buy a team and move it to London. Now, three years later he had already met with groups attempting to expand into Oakland and North Carolina. Both efforts, though, had drawbacks—California was too far from Chicago and North Carolina was headed by Jerry Richardson, a wealthy restaurateur with little interest in sharing the load. Holmes insisted St. Louis was the best option, and Payton agreed.

There were, though, reservations. Like Payton, Clinton was heavily involved in motor sports, having also raced on the Sports 2000 and Trans-Am Series and sharing a close relationship with Paul Newman. Payton and Clinton were first introduced at a race in Long Beach, California, by Indy-driver Willy T. Ribbs, and became teammates, driving twin Mustang Cobras and at comparable skill levels. On the morning of the day Payton flipped his car at Road America, Clinton gave him a warning at the hotel. "This is a difficult track," he told Payton. "There are a myriad of things you have to look out for. Take four, five, or six laps at a slower speed so you can get a feel for the track."

Despite their shared history, however, Payton never felt especially at ease with Clinton (or Murray) as a business partner. They simply were not his preferred genre of people—loud, boastful, arrogant. He found Murray uncomfortably quirky and Clinton uncomfortably talkative. When Clinton entered a room, Payton noticed, the oxygen drained like helium from a punctured balloon. He talked and talked and talked and talked. As a racing cohort, that was fine. As a business partner—not so much. The last thing Payton desired was to join forces with a bunch of bigheaded executives with dreams of gridiron glory. Having grown up watching an aged George Halas, Payton was a fan of understated and reserved. Sure, Halas wasn't the ideal owner. But he knew his strengths, and his concern was winning, not PR. "Jerry was just kind of an ego guy," Payton once said. "A big name-dropper, a big egomaniac. Even though Jerry was not my type of guy, I always gave Jerry the limelight, always pushed it to him with the interviews. . . . Jerry wanted the prestige of being the team owner. I just wanted to get a team."

Payton ignored the warnings in his head and charged forward. He was, after all, being told that no money had to be put up and that his 10 percent share would be paid for out of the team's revenues. He was also promised to be the face of the franchise. When people thought St. Louis football, they'd think Walter Payton. "Walter wanted this to happen so badly, and he saw in St. Louis the best opportunity," said Ginny Quirk, his assistant and the vice president of Walter Payton, Inc. "Was there reason to be suspicious of some of the people involved? In hindsight, definitely yes. But when you're in the middle of something this big, and you see such a golden opportunity, you tend to hope for the best and overlook the little problems."

Payton was a wayward soul in search of meaning, and here—in NFL ownership—was meaning. He wanted to remain important and impactful. He wanted to have a voice that people would listen to. He heard about so-called NFL legends from past decades sitting behind a card table in ballroom C of the McCall, Idaho, Holiday Inn, signing autographed pictures for ten dollars a pop. *Attention ladies and gentlemen, now appearing alongside Tony Dow is . . .*

That *would not* be Walter Payton.

So, against his better judgment, Payton jumped headfirst into the St. Louis endeavor. He spent the next three years doing one of the things he did best—schmoozing. When Payton wasn't attending to his businesses in Chicago or racing cars at some far-off track, he could usually be found in St. Louis, talking football as the guest speaker at one rubber chicken dinner after another. The routine was mind-numbingly repetitive—Payton would stand up, introduce himself ("In case you don't know, I'm . . . "—laugher followed), talk for twenty-five minutes about the group's plan to bring football to St. Louis, field the most predictable questions known to man (*What did it feel like breaking Jim Brown's record?* "Amazing." *Were you mad at Mike Ditka for not letting you have a Super Bowl touchdown?* "Absolutely not."), then sign a hundred or so autographs before leaving. Payton knew that, at this point, his primary role was as a front man. There would be time later on to hire a head coach (Payton made it clear he wanted to bring in Johnny Roland, his running backs coach with Chicago) and evaluate players and man the draft and pick uniform colors and a team name. For now, he was supposed to put a face to the project while letting the experienced executives work their magic.

Despite mounting hostilities between Clinton and Murray, the group somehow convinced then–Missouri governor John Ashcroft to sign a financing bill for a new stadium/convention center. Shortly thereafter, bonds to finance the domed stadium sold out in less than three days. Clinton bragged that he had lined up "potential investors" to join the team but, in actuality, "investors" was "*an investor.*" Clinton asked more than a dozen local entrepreneurs for a modest quarter-million-dollar advance, and a mere one—Thomas Holley, president of a chain of discount stores—put in.

Clinton and Murray brandished Payton like a shield. He was the golden protector out front, charming the masses with his smile and his rollicking tales of gridiron glory. Payton's desire to be the first African-American owner was sincere, but there was something disconcertingly minstrel-like in the way he was utilized. Payton sang and danced and did a little shuffle, and his involvement in the behind-the-scenes dealings was limited. He shook hands, patted shoulders, told jokes, and believed he was making valuable inroads for the group. "The demographics are there, the proven product is there," he told Fred Mitchell of the *Chicago Tribune*. "Look at Anheuser-Busch and McDonnell Douglas. They are not there just for their own health. There is something in the city.

"We have someone who is from the area of St. Louis and knows the workings. And we have a guy who has been a minority owner in the NFL already. He knows football and he knows people and he has a pretty good track record in the NFL. We have all aspects covered."

In spite of Payton's efforts, though, many important public figures were concerned. Clinton was known throughout St. Louis, but his reputation was mixed. Some viewed him simply as a civic enthusiast with pure intentions. Others viewed him as a snake oil salesman. And Murray—well, he just seemed sort of crazy. "It would be like trusting a raccoon," Chris Kelly, an influential Missouri congressman, said of Clinton and Murray.

The St. Louis bid received a major boost in July 1990, when James Busch Orthwein, great-grandson of the founder of Anheuser-Busch and a man worth fifty-six million dollars, signed on. Of the three main financial players—Clinton, Murray, and Orthwein—Orthwein was Payton's preferred taste in partners. Gruff, gritty, and dignified, the sixty-nine-year-old yachtsman and rabid sport fisherman joined the team when Murray promised him 12 percent of the partnership in exchange for a sizeable loan. Though born into wealth, Orthwein was, in part, a self-made man. He helped build the St. Louis–based D'Arcy Advertising Co. into an international force, then later headed a private investment firm, Huntleigh Asset Partners. Unlike the other partners, Orthwein wasn't in this for glory. He simply saw a good financial opportunity, as well as the chance to aid his hometown. Yet as soon as he became part of the team, the problems began. Clinton was dismissive of Orthwein's involvement, complaining that the group needed neither his wisdom nor his deep pockets. This infuriated Payton, who was always mystified by the source of the group's hypothetical revenue. An NFL franchise would cost a hundred and forty million dollars. If Clinton was worth approximately twenty million dollars and Murray was seeking out loans and Payton was putting in nothing and investors weren't exactly lining up, who would be paying the bills?

In the summer of 1991, Murray—financially strapped, in debt to Orthwein for thirty million dollars, and facing further lawsuits from creditors— sold Orthwein his share in the Patriots and asked him to replace him as managing general partner of the St. Louis effort. Orthwein begrudgingly agreed, then told Clinton he needed to be the one making the final decisions. "With this amount of money I have to be in charge," he recalled saying to Clinton. "But I think we can work together."

This is when the bottom began to fall out. Clinton had spent too much time and too much money to surrender control. He didn't like Orthwein, didn't trust Orthwein, didn't want Orthwein involved in any manner. When Orthwein reminded Clinton of the so-called golden rule—*the person with the most money makes the rules*—Clinton lost it. In a meeting that took place six weeks before the NFL's expansion vote, Clinton told Orthwein that he was an unnecessary burden, and that he, Jerry Clinton, would approach the league by himself and make a solo pitch for ownership. "You know what?" Orthwein responded. "I'm going to give you the opportunity to find another partner, to find another money partner. OK? If you don't want me as a partner, and don't like what I have to bring to the table, then I'm going to give you the opportunity."

"Great!" Clinton yelled. "I want it! I'm gonna take it!"

Payton watched the exchange and said nothing. He later recalled it as the moment he first knew St. Louis was doomed. "I saw the whole thing crumbling right there," he said. "I just kind of sat there and said, 'Guys, I think we all have a common goal, which is to get this team.'"

On September 9, 1993, the partnership announced that Orthwein was stepping down, leaving Clinton in charge. "Frankly," Clinton said, "I think our current partnership structure is stronger as a result of these recent moves."

Payton was incensed. He called Clinton and chewed him out. "What the fuck are you thinking?" he screamed. "What did you just do to my dream? What the fuck did you just do?"

A flustered Clinton tried explaining his position, but to no avail. He went, hat in hand, to every wealthy person he knew, selling an opportunity nobody saw as an opportunity. A couple of weeks later, when it became clear he couldn't get the proper financing, Clinton shuffled aside so that E. Stanley Kroenke, a wealthy real estate developer from Columbia, Missouri, could step in, take the lead, and save the day. Kroenke told Payton that he was still wanted and needed, and the ex–running back offered his support. "I'm with you," he said. "If you can get this done, I'm with you." Payton's words hid his feelings: Hope was dead. He thrust most of the blame upon Clinton, whom he no longer spoke with. Not all that long ago, Clinton had paid nearly sixty thousand dollars of his own money to place a full-page advertisement in USA Today highlighting Payton's place among the St. Louis ownership group. Now the two were enemies. "I honestly think Walter was brainwashed by the other group," Clinton said. "I don't know how else to explain it."

On October 26, 1993, Kroenke, Payton, and company gathered at the Hyatt near Chicago's O'Hare Airport, where the NFL was holding its expansion meetings. Each city—St. Louis, Charlotte, Jacksonville, Baltimore, and Memphis—had its own suite, and the two NFL officials in charge of the expansion decision, Roger Goodell and Neil Austrian, went from room to room, listening to the pitches. The St. Louis presentation was, even with Payton's impassioned plea, a disaster. "You know what, guys, get this shit together," Goodell said. "This is ridiculous. You're there if you can cut the squabbling." The NFL announced that one of the teams would be given to Charlotte, but the decision on the other location wouldn't come until a month later.

In St. Louis, the news was greeted with mixed emotions. Maybe, just maybe, there was still a reason to believe.

There wasn't.

On November 30, Jacksonville, Florida—a city one-eighth the size of St. Louis, with the nation's fifty-fifth television market—was gifted with the second team. Payton knew the situation was looking grim, but he still couldn't believe it. *Jacksonville?* Just in case Payton's devastation wasn't raw enough, one of the partners in the Jacksonville bid was Deron Cherry, a longtime Kansas City Chiefs cornerback who, thanks in large part to the bumbling St. Louis crew, would beat out Payton to become the NFL's first African-American owner.

Cherry and Payton shared a friendship dating back to the 1983 Pro Bowl—Payton's sixth, Cherry's first. "One of the NFC's defensive backs warned me about Walter, that if you didn't tackle him early in a play he'd high-step all over you," said Cherry. "So they give him the football and he's high-stepping, and I came over and grabbed him around his neck, hog-tied him like one would a bull and brought him down. He got up and pushed me. I pushed him back. Then he looked me in the face and said, 'I like the way you play the game!'" The two kept in regular touch and years later, when Payton first joined the St. Louis group, Cherry ran into him at an event. "Shoot," Cherry said, "you're all but guaranteed a team. You guys have everything working for you."

Now, as the members of Jacksonville's expansion unit exchanged hugs inside the Hyatt, Cherry's joy was mixed with a modicum of guilt. This was supposed to be Walter Payton's moment. He worked for it. He deserved it. "He was the face of the NFL," Cherry said. "I remember how sad it was when he didn't get to score in the Super Bowl, and this was sort of the same way. He was denied something he clearly wanted very badly."

With nothing else to shoot for, a despondent Payton left the hotel and drove home. Four years of work for nothing.

He never felt more depressed. Or alone.

. . .

But wait. Go back. There was a bit of good news in 1993. Although Walter Payton would never fulfill his dream of owning an NFL franchise, on January 30 he became the twenty-third Chicago Bear to be voted into the Pro Football Hall of Fame. As his fellow inductees—Chargers quarterback Dan Fouts, Dolphins offensive guard Larry Little, and coaches Chuck Noll and Bill Walsh—greeted the news with equal parts glee and deference, Payton's take was odd. He called the honor "nice," but refused to display even a sliver of outward happiness. When informed of his induction, his reaction was unprecedented and perplexing. Journalists expecting the requisite *I'm-just-so-honored* response received little of the sort. Payton asked members of the local media whether the vote was unanimous, and brooded when told the tally (a panel of thirty-four pro football writers voted) was never revealed.

"I have mixed emotions," he said. "I want to make the Hall of Fame unanimously. I try to be the best I possibly can be. If I do something, I want to do it all the way. If I got in unanimously, it means I was recognized as the best at what I did. If I didn't get in unanimously, it means I wasn't the best by all people's standards. That would bother me." Here was the crowning moment of a football player's career, and he couldn't enjoy it.

One week later Payton, citing a general aversion to ceremony, called Pete Elliott, the Pro Football Hall of Fame director, to tell him he wouldn't be attending the formal introduction of the Hall's Class of 1993 at the Pro Bowl festivities in Honolulu. "He was very sincere," a baffled Elliott told the

*Chicago Tribune.* "He said it was a great honor, but he couldn't make it." In the thirty-year history of the Hall, this was the first time anyone could remember a living inductee skipping out on the introduction. (Around this same time, Payton also turned down an invitation to a dinner in Baltimore for the All-Time Black College Football Team. Of the twenty-two honorees, seventeen attended—including Deacon Jones and a former North Carolina A&T quarterback named Jesse Jackson.) A couple of days later Payton groused to the *Tribune* how hurt he was that, after news of his induction, so few former teammates called with warm wishes. "The only athlete who sent his congratulations was Michael Jordan," he said. "He sent a fruit basket and a card. Nobody else contacted me."

As the July 31, 1993, Hall of Fame induction ceremony approached, Payton struggled. Initially, the difficulty was in choosing a presenter. The first person to come to mind was Jim Finks, the former Bears general manager who used the fourth selection in the 1975 NFL Draft to pick an undersized running back from Jackson State. Payton actually asked Finks, who was honored by the request. When the sixty-five-year-old five-packs-a-day cigarette smoker was diagnosed with lung cancer, however, he had to decline. Bud Holmes, his longtime agent who was responsible for much of Payton's success, was next to be considered. Holmes quickly deferred. "Walter," he said, "nobody cares about me. Pick someone else. Pick a family member." Finally, after much deliberation, Payton settled on Jarrett, his charming, boisterous, twelve-year-old son. "Man, when Dad told me he wanted me to do that . . . I was nervous as a kid can be," said Jarrett. "My housekeeper, Miss Luna, helped me write the speech, and we went over it and over it in the kitchen. I wanted it to be perfect, because I knew how much this day meant to my dad."

Many of those who knew Payton relatively well were shocked by the anxiety he seemed to be experiencing in the lead-up to the ceremony. He was having trouble concentrating, and was short and curt with anyone who dared strike up a conversation. Normally jovial with fans and autograph seekers, Payton wanted no part of it. He demanded quiet and solitude. Some were under the impression that Jarrett's speech was burdening Payton; that his nervousness and apprehension had to do with a twelve-year-old standing before thousands of people and speaking glowingly of his father.

They had no idea.

Shortly after he learned of his acceptance into the Hall, Payton spoke with Lita Gonzalez, the New Jersey–based flight attendant who he was dating. "I'm coming to the ceremony," she said. "There's no way I'd miss it."

It had now been almost five years since she first met Walter, and Gonzalez's patience was wearing thin. Theirs was a relationship of extremes—either passionate romance or nonstop screaming and threats. Lita insisted they go to couple's therapy, and Walter begrudgingly agreed. "It was to pacify her," said Quirk. "Only a few visits." Lita demanded a commitment from Walter, and he finally made one, presenting her with a one-carat diamond "promise" ring that, he said, signified his love for her. Lita was momentarily placated, especially when he had her attend an increasing number of his races on the Trans-Am circuit. But just as the relationship seemed to be going well, something always interfered. Lita wanted to relocate to Chicago—Walter told her not to. Lita wanted Walter to finally divorce Connie and devote himself to her—Walter made one assurance after another, but never committed. Lita wanted Walter to take her to public events and have her on his arm—Walter couldn't. (He did, however, take Lita's father, Javier, to the 1988 Super Bowl in San Diego.) "It was a very hostile pairing," said Quirk. "I could never fully understand Lita's lack of common sense, because Walter made it clear through his actions that he wasn't going to commit fully to her. She gave herself to him, and he wouldn't give himself back."

"Honestly, I think Lita provided Walter with a motherly inner sanctum," Holmes said. "He could sit and talk to her and fantasize to her and he wouldn't get any resistance from Lita. Connie, on the other hand, always kept busy and had things to do besides listening to Walter ramble on. Lita was like a bottle to Walter's alcoholism. She provided what he needed. An ear."

In Payton's offices—first in the back of Studebaker's, then in complexes in Arlington Heights and, finally, Hoffman Estates—his fights with Gonzalez became the stuff of legend. Through the thin walls, he could be heard screaming, cursing, threatening over the phone. On countless occasions she returned the promise ring, swearing she was no longer interested. "Inevitably," said Quirk, "she would come back to him. She always came back." Walter told Lita she was his only love, and she believed him. Little did she know he was using the same line on countless others. "The number of women was dizzying," said Linda Conley, Walter's longtime friend and the kitchen manager at Studebaker's. "I loved Walter, but I'd always tell his girl-friends, 'He'll never be yours, so why waste your time?' He knew he was doing wrong, but it was a challenge to him: How many women could he land?

"My daughter Tyra was really into football, and she just adored Walter. Well, one day we walk into Studebaker's and there he was, kissing some blond girl. Tyra couldn't believe it. She was devastated. But that was Walter—you either accepted his behavior or you moved on."

At one point, Lita became so upset that she removed the promise ring from her finger, placed it in a FedEx package, and shipped it to Payton's office. Upon receiving the item, Payton brought it to his personal jeweler and had him replace the diamond with a replica. "He sent it back to her without say-ing a word," said Quirk. "They made up, of course, but he never brought it up. She probably still has that fake ring."

The last thing Payton needed was to have his Hall of Fame weekend complicated and compromised. But Lita, who rarely followed up on her demands of Walter, was following up on this one. She would be coming, dammit, and she expected to be treated as his girlfriend. "She was insisting she be seated in the front row," said Kimm Tucker, the executive director of Payton's charitable foundation. "We said, 'Lita, are you insane? We're mar-keting this man as a family-friendly spokesperson. His whole image is based around decency. You will ruin him.'" Although Walter hadn't lived at home for nearly five years, Connie was coming, too. She was, after all, his wife. She had stuck by him through the tough early years; had left the comforts of Mississippi for the Windy City; had endured his moods and his mischief; his intensity and his infidelity. To the press, she had never once uttered a foul word about her husband. As far as the world knew, he was committed, charming, dedicated Walter.

There was the image of a marriage to uphold, and Connie was not about to inspire stirrings of "Where was his wife?" should she not attend. It also so happened that her son would be giving the biggest speech of his life.

How could Connie Payton not be there?

A couple of weeks before the ceremony, Payton called Holmes at his home and—having just gotten off the phone with Gonzalez—said, "I'm ready. I want you to help me get a divorce from Connie."

"Walter," Holmes replied, "if you do this, it'll ruin your ass. Your whole image is built as this great, wholesome family guy. You leave Connie, that dies."

Said Holmes: "Honestly, I believe Walter knew what I would tell him, but he wanted an excuse to give to Lita as to why he wasn't leaving Connie. He was a real mess."

Walter didn't know what to do. He felt the ceiling crumbling and the walls caving in. There was no escape. After keeping Lita at bay for so long, how could he deny her a moment? After keeping Connie around for so long, how could he deny her a moment? "I can tell you that, without any question or doubt, his knowing both women were going to attend was first and foremost on his mind," said Quirk. "That was more of an issue to him than the event itself. What he feared most was coming to fruition. He had to face the music, and what a shit-ass time for that to happen. Talk about tainting a weekend. The induction into the Pro Football Hall of Fame is supposed to be the greatest moment in his life. And the truth is, it was probably the worst moment in his life."

Payton was scheduled to spend four days in Canton, Ohio, home to the Hall. He would arrive on Wednesday, July 28, and use the time to bask in the glow, appear at various functions, meet with the media. Before leaving Chicago, he placed Quirk in charge of what, eighteen years later, she still considers to be the most miserable professional experience she has ever endured: making sure Connie and Lita were never in the same place at the same time. "Lita certainly knew about Connie, but Connie at that point didn't have any idea about Lita," Quirk said. "I'm pretty sure she didn't board an airplane knowing that Walter's girlfriend would be there, too."

"Four full days. Four full days, and Lita and Connie were like two ships passing in the night. If Connie was scheduled to come late, I'd make sure Lita was there early. If Connie was coming early, Lita would be there late. I can't describe the horror of that trip. It was the worst thing ever."

Payton naïvely assumed Lita would be content sharing a room with him in the McKinley Grand Hotel, where the inductees stayed. Quirk had booked the reservation for Walter and Lita, and she also reserved a suite for Connie and the children. "I was told to make sure the rooms were as far apart as possible," said Quirk. "So that's what I did." Yet Lita was hardly placated. As far as she was concerned, this was to be her coming out weekend as Walter Payton's significant other. She brought a new dress. Had her hair and nails done. Lita dreamed of attending all the parties and functions; dreamed of being introduced by Walter to his family members, friends, and fellow inductees. "Lita had balls of steel in Canton," said Quirk. "She said, 'This is my time and I'm going to take a stand.'"

Walter had different ideas. As Fouts and Little and Noll and Walsh seized the moment by attending shindigs and accepting congratulatory wishes, Walter and Lita spent three days cooped up in the room. He only emerged every so often to make a required appearance. Occasionally he'd visit Jarrett and Brittney in their suite—but they were strictly prohibited from visiting his. Otherwise, he was MIA. He missed an important Thursday night function that left Hall officials fuming and earned the scorn of Bears legend Gale Sayers, who blasted his ho-hum attitude. Ray Nitschke, the Packer great, issued an impassioned plea to try and get Payton's attention. It didn't work. "Walter mostly hid," said Holmes. "The moment of a lifetime, and Walter's hiding out. After it was all done he called me and asked how he did. I told him the truth. I said, 'Walter, you did very well on stage, but I'm disappointed in you, the way you ignored your mama and your family and your kids. People don't do that. It's not fair.'"

On the morning of Saturday, July 31, Walter and Lita had a quiet breakfast in their hotel room before he, all alone, headed downstairs to the lobby of the McKinley Grand. From her room Quirk was on the phone, frantically finalizing the most awkward of seating arrangements. Because Walter and Connie were still assumed to be Walter and Connie, Quirk assigned her to the front row, alongside their children, Walter's mother, Alyne, his brother, Eddie, and his sister, Pamela. Lita, meanwhile, was situated one row back, two down from Quirk and alongside Susan Ward, a public relations specialist who was working with Payton. "Susan was the buffer," said Quirk. "I didn't want to sit next to Lita. She was causing too much drama."

Payton arrived at the front steps of the Hall shortly before the start of the event. He was visibly nervous and unfocused, and those few who were in the know had little doubt of the cause of his burden. Smooth and suave in public, Payton was terrified by the potential for center-stage embarrassment. Would Lita stand up and confront Connie? Would Lita storm off if he mentioned Connie in the speech? "Walter's ideal was to hide Lita," said Quirk. "But Lita wasn't having that."

At twelve fifty P.M., Jarrett rose to introduce Walter Payton into the Class of 1993. He felt his knees wobble and his hands quiver. This was a new level of pressure—thousands of eyes staring down upon him. His four-minute speech, however, was masterful. Nattily dressed in a beige blazer, white collared shirt, and colorful tie, Jarrett stood behind the podium and brought tears to his father's eyes. "This is an historic event that my dad, Walter, and the other members of the Payton family will treasure for the rest of our lives," he said in a high-pitched voice that cracked with adolescence. "My dad played thirteen seasons and missed only one game while breaking all the running back records. Not only is my dad an excellent athlete, he's a role model. He's my biggest role model and my best friend. I'm sure my sister will endorse this: We have a super dad."

When Jarrett finished, his father rose and consumed him in a hug. Walter Payton strode to the podium, tears streaming beneath his sunglasses and onto his cheeks. He was overwhelmed. By his child. By the event. By the subplots. He had devoted so much time to pooh-poohing and minimizing the moment, and now that the moment was at hand, he found himself being hit by a tidal wave.

"Thank you . . . thank you," he said as his voice broke and the applause died down. "You know, when I first got here, we made a wager who would be the first one to break down in tears and I was the first one to say that I wouldn't and I was the first one to say how strong I was and everything else. As it goes to show that a lot of times when you are amongst your peers such as these great athletes, you try to be something that you're not. And after hearing my son get up here and talk, I don't care if I lose the bet."

Payton proceeded to give an OK—not great—speech, packed with the requisite shout-outs to coaches like Charles Boston ("[He] took me under his wing and taught me the fundamentals of football.") and Bob Hill ("[He] showed me what hard work and determination would do if you put forth the effort.") and the standard acknowledgment that football is a team game, and *were it not for so-and-so and so-and-so I would certainly not be here today.*

With his girlfriend of five years sitting two rows away, and his wife of seventeen years sitting one row away, toward the end of his remarks Payton provided people with what they expected: "I want to stand up here and say that in this point of my life, that Jarrett, Brittney, and your mom, you guys will not have to worry about anything in your life no matter what the situation or how it ends. Because just as running up that hill and trying to catch runners such as Jim Brown and Gale Sayers motivated me to do more than I thought I possibly could do, you three will motivate me to make sure that your lives are happy and fulfilled."

The camera flashed to Connie, who nodded appreciatively. Lita, almost directly behind her, surely felt her heart sink. How many times had Walter told her that he couldn't stand his wife? That he desperately wanted to leave her, but there were just too many complications? "It was a weird choice of words," said Quirk. "But Walter had put on a show about his marriage for years. It came very naturally to him."

When the ceremony finally came to a close, Payton was able to take a deep sigh of relief. He had survived. It wasn't easy, but he had survived. With all eyes on his every move, he approached Connie for a hug and a kiss, then put his arms around his mother and his children. Lita, meanwhile, walked back to the hotel, alone. She plopped down onto a couch in the lobby, where she chatted with one of the few Payton acquaintances aware of her status. Holmes, meanwhile, returned to his room, still furious over the way Payton had ignored his family. After about forty-five minutes, his phone rang. It was Connie. "Bud," she said, "I was wondering if I could ask a favor of you?"

"Sure," Holmes replied.

"Well," said Connie, "I'd like you to introduce me to Lita."

Silence.

"Really?" said Holmes, who—along with most others—had no inkling Connie knew of Lita's existence. "Are you sure?"

"Yes," said Connie. "I am."

Moments later, Connie came to the McKinley Grand lobby and stood in front of a woman who was thirteen years her junior. "I introduced the two of them, and they sat and talked for quite a while," said Holmes. "They were friendly, chatty. There was no hair pulling. It was a very civil understanding." At one point, Connie looked Lita in the eyes and said, bluntly, "You can have him. He doesn't want me or the children."

By the time Payton arrived at the hotel, Connie and Lita had parted ways. He was shocked to learn of the meeting, but not entirely surprised. Canton was a small town, and the McKinley Grand wasn't so grand. If anything, Payton felt a quiet sense of relief. After tiptoeing around for four days, the truth had finally come out. And while Connie seemed to hate him for being a skirt-chasing dog and Lita seemed to hate him for the speech, it was almost time to pack up and return to Chicago.

## CHAPTER 24

# DEPRESSION

On an early morning in the fall of 1992, Bill Wandro, boys basket-ball coach at Hoffman Estates High School, was told there was a man in the hallway who was looking to volunteer his time.

"He's waiting to talk to you," a secretary said. "He wants to help."

How often had Wandro heard this one? At this upscale suburban high school of 1,995 students, every other father seemed to fancy himself the next John Wooden, itching to impart his (usually flawed) knowledge upon the fifteen boys who played for the Hawks. The profile was a familiar one: *middle-aged, bored, overly competitive, convinced he knew more than the head coach did.* Nonetheless, Wandro went to meet the aspiring coach. "So the guy starts talking to me and he says, 'I'd really like to lend a hand,'" said Wandro. "I asked if his son attended the school and he said no, but he loved basketball and understood the game. We're talking for two or three minutes before a kid comes up and says to him, 'Can I have your autograph?' He signs and I look at the name on this scrap of paper.

"'Holy cow,' I say. 'You're Walter Payton!'"

When Wandro asked why *the* Walter Payton would want to grace a mediocre suburban high school team with his presence, Payton explained that while football was his trademark, basketball was his love. The truth was a tad more complicated. Having been pulled over for speeding yet again (Payton was stopped for driving above the speed limit more than fifty times during his years in Chicago, yet almost always drove off with merely a warning), Payton was ordered by an unsympathetic judge to partake in six months of community service. Two weeks later, after undergoing a background check, Payton was introduced to Wandro's dumbfounded players as the newest volunteer assistant. Was this merely the case of a celebrity putting in his time? Hardly. "He came to every practice six days a week, two hours per day, plus every game," Wandro said. "He also coached the junior varsity team. He was a great coach—he really related with the kids. He was genuine with them." Payton encouraged the players to embrace wins with euphoric giddiness and take losses as experiences to learn from. He told stories of his Bears days, but never, it seemed, as bragging material. There was always a lesson. A moral. He convinced Wilson, a corporation he endorsed, to spring for new uniforms for both the varsity and JV squads—flashy royal blue-and-orange duds that, according to Wandro, "had our kids feeling like a million bucks."

Inside Hoffman Estate's gymnasium, Payton seemed to take pride in *not* behaving as a typical superstar athlete. When someone tossed a towel on the floor, he picked it up. When the janitors showed up to start sweeping, he grabbed a broom. Toward the end of every practice he and an assistant coach named Dan Davis engaged in spirited games of H-O-R-S-E. "We'd play two hundred thousand dollars a shot, and I got him down one-point-five million," Davis said. "One day he comes in and writes me a check for one-point-five million dollars. All the kids are going ape. I put the check in my pocket and we practice. When practice ends he comes up to me and says, 'Hey, Dan, don't forget about giving that check back.'"

Throughout the 1992–93 and 1993–94 seasons, Payton was heavily involved, plotting strategy, working the sidelines, staring down referees. He continued to participate the two ensuing years, but in a decreased capacity. There was personal business to attend to and a pair of kids to raise and the general business that is life.

In 1995–96, Wandro coached the Hawks to the Class AA state tournament in Peoria. Though Payton would only come to one or two practices a week, he was still a contributor. One day, shortly before the team was scheduled to depart for the big event, he arrived at the gymnasium and gave a rousing pep talk about commitment and trust and what it meant to be a champion. Wandro's players sat rapt throughout the fifteen-minute lecture, and as Payton neared the end he slipped off his Super Bowl ring and said, "If you don't believe you can do something, you won't ever get it done." With that, he handed the ring to one of the awestruck players, a senior center named Nick Abruzzo. "Nick, I want you to hold onto the ring for the weekend," Payton said. "I trust you, just like you need to trust one another."

As the members of the Hawks wandered off to the locker room, Wandro pulled Payton aside. "Walter, are you serious?" he asked. "I've coached these high school kids for years, and I wouldn't trust most of them with my CD player. You just gave one your Super Bowl ring."

Payton shrugged.

Later that night, Abruzzo hosted a pasta party for his teammates at his house. The players traded turns ogling the jewelry until it was time for everyone to leave. "OK," Abruzzo said, "who's got the ring?"

Silence.

"Seriously, guys, where's the ring?"

Silence.

"Fellas . . ."

"It vanished," said Abruzzo. "It just disappeared."

The Abruzzo family spent the night searching high and low for the treasured hardware. They dug through pillows, moved tables, emptied cabinets, shook canisters. Nothing. They called the local police department, whose officers questioned a handful of the players. Nothing.

Two days later, shortly before the team was scheduled to board a Peoria-bound bus, Abruzzo visited Payton at his office. With tears welling up in his eyes, he explained what had happened. A glum look crossed Payton's face. He was crushed—but refused to let it fully show. "You know, Nick, I've lost that ring a bunch of times myself," he said. "I once even left it in a hotel room and forgot about it. Don't worry, it'll turn up."

Burdened by the disappearance, Hoffman Estates lost its quarterfinal game to Westinghouse, 42–41. Upon returning to the office, Wandro swallowed hard, picked up the telephone, and called Payton.

"Walter," he said, "I feel just terrible about this. I don't know what to say."

Once again, Payton tried his best to play the incident down. Inside, however, he was heartbroken and his association with the Hoffman Estates basketball team would soon end. Through his remaining years, he remained convinced that one of the kids had swiped his jewelry, then lied about it. "It was never fully about the ring," said Davis. "I think Walter simply felt taken advantage of."

So what actually happened? On the night the ring went missing, some of the Hoffman Estates players were goofing around on a brown fake leather couch in the Abruzzos' basement. In the midst of the scrum, Payton's ring somehow slipped behind a cushion and into a pocket created by a torn swath of fabric.

Two years later the Abruzzos, moving to a new home, let it be known that they were discarding much of their old furniture. Phillip Hong, a graduating Hoffman Estates High senior who, as a linebacker for the Hawks, wore uniform No. 34 in honor of Walter Payton, claimed a worn brown couch that nobody else wanted. He brought it with him to Purdue University, and for the next three years the couch was a fixture in his various dwellings. "It came to college with me every year," Hong said. "From Chicago to West Lafayette, Indiana, from moving truck to moving truck."

One evening, in the midst of his junior year in the spring of 2001, Hong was sitting on the couch, watching TV. His red-and-tan Doberman pinscher, Bailey, was clawing into the underside of the couch, trying to retrieve a wedged-in chew toy. "Bailey was laying on his side digging with his front paw," said Hong. "In doing so, he ripped the lining out from under the couch." Hong dropped to his knees, stuck his arm beneath the couch, and wiggled his hand. He expected to grab a saliva-coated ball. Instead, Phillip Hong grasped Walter Payton's Super Bowl ring.

"You've got to be kidding me," he thought to himself. "You've got to be kidding."

A couple of days later, Hong was invited to Connie Payton's home, where he gladly handed over the lost jewelry. She gave him a framed photograph of her late husband, and took Hong to what once served as his hero's private office. "I got to sit in his chair," he said. "That blew my mind."

So euphoric in the moment was Hong that he failed to find it odd how Connie, Walter Payton's wife for twenty-three years, seemed to be completely unaware that the ring had ever gone missing.

· · ·

Though a misplaced Super Bowl ring hardly ruined Walter Payton's life, the symbolism of its fall through the cracks cannot be ignored.

Without a football career, without a racing career, without the potential ownership of an NFL franchise, Walter Payton often found himself suffocated by darkness. Oh, he wouldn't let on as such. He smiled and laughed and told jokes and pinched rear ends and tried his absolute best to come across as the life of the party. Inside, however, happiness eluded Payton in the same manner he had once eluded opposing linebackers.

Facing increased pressure from Lita Gonzalez to either commit or walk, in August 1994 Payton filed for divorce from Connie in the Circuit Court of Cook County, citing "irreconcilable differences" which "have caused the irretrievable breakdown of the marriage."

The truth was, Payton neither wanted nor needed a divorce—just a piece of paper to shut Gonzalez up by showing her that he was, indeed, trying. (Said Ginny Quirk: "Being married was inconsequential to Walter. He didn't deal much with Connie, but having her helped with his image.") Connie, however, did not take kindly to her husband's filing, and was especially livid when one of his attorneys leaked word of the potential split to the *Sun-Times*.

On November 29, 1994, Walter received a letter from Connie's lawyer, Joseph DuCanto, demanding twenty-five thousand dollars for her attorney fees and threatening to shatter his angelic reputation. DuCanto used the correspondence to make clear that, were the details of the "no-holds-barred confrontation" to go public, Payton's pristine image would likely find itself flushed down a toilet.

Walter read the letter, crumpled it up, and slammed his fist into his desk. He had provided Connie with everything she ever needed—and this was his reward? So what that he cheated on her for years. So what that he was an on-again, off-again father? So what? He was Walter Payton. *The* Walter Payton. If anyone was supposed to be making the threats, it was him. Not Connie.

Around this time, Payton actually began seeing yet another woman, a New York–based medical-supply saleswoman named Judy Choy, and encouraged her to move to Illinois so they could spend more time together. Though aware that Payton's marriage to Connie was a farce, Choy never knew about Gonzalez. "Judy's father was a private investigator, and he looked into Walter and found out a lot of stuff about him," said Linda Conley, a friend of Walter and Connie, as well as a former Studebaker's employee. "That was it. She was a strong woman, and she had pride." Months after being dumped, Payton hired his own private investigator to locate Judy, but to no avail. She had moved and disconnected her phone, and wanted nothing to do with him. Gonzalez, on the other hand, stuck around, hoping Walter could change. "It was a joke," Quirk said. "Walter was Walter. For good and for bad, there was no changing him."

He turned forty-three in 1996. By now, the stories had grown stale and tiresome. That first game against the Colts. The 275 yards against the Vikings. Battles against O. J. Simpson and Earl Campbell and Eric Dickerson. In the film *Everybody's All-American*, Gavin Grey, the faded football star played brilliantly by Dennis Quaid, bemoans life as an ex-athlete by wailing, "This shit is killing me. I feel like I'm just some old bullshitter. The more I tell these damn stories, the more I feel like I'm making it up. Like it never even happened to me." Payton was engulfed within a similarly hellish vortex, the numbing ritualistic mindlessness of former athletic greatness overwhelming any present and future potential. He was a fly stuck in amber—eternally No. 34 for the Chicago Bears, even when he wasn't No. 34 for the Chicago Bears. "I always wondered whether I did Walter a favor by helping him get so big," said Bud Holmes. "It's a fine line whether he would have been happier as a larger-than-life celebrity, or as a man back in Columbia, Mississippi, fathering ten or twelve illegitimate children, getting thrown in jail once a month, working some blue-collar job. If Elvis had it to do all over again, would he rather just drive a truck in Tupelo?"

Payton was the clichéd celebrity—surrounded by admirers, yet alone. "He called me many times at two, three in the morning, just wanting to talk," said Holmes. "There's a Norman Rockwell quote—'Pity the poor genius.' I pitied Walter." In his post-football years, many people insisted they were particularly close to Payton—Holmes, the agent; Mike Lanigan, his partner in Payton Power, a heavy-equipment company; Matt Suhey, his former fullback; John Gamauf, the vice president of Bridgestone/Firestone and partners with Walter on a racing team; Linda Conley, his employee at Studebaker's; Connie, his estranged wife.

While those individuals (with the exception of Connie) did, in fact, find themselves somewhere within the confines of Walter's miniscule inner circle, the two he confided in most were Ginny Quirk, his executive assistant, and Kimm Tucker, the executive director of the Walter Payton Foundation as well as his director of marketing. Walter Payton, Inc., was now located in suite 340 on the third floor of an office building in Hoffman Estates (Payton was given the space rent-free, in exchange for a couple of appearances on behalf of the landlord), and Payton was there nearly every day alongside the two women. They were, in many respects, his family. "I'll always remember a talk I had with [former Bears quarterback] Vince Evans when he called the office one day," said Quirk. "I asked him how he was doing, and he said, 'Ginny, it's kind of like being a Vietnam veteran. You go into combat and do things other people don't. Then you come out of it and you're supposed to be normal. And you're not. You work really hard at trying to adjust, but it's impossible. It's just impossible.'

"That," said Quirk, "is what Walter was experiencing."

Quirk and Tucker came to expect Payton's manic mood swings—giddy one second, despondent the next. He kept a tub of painkillers inside a desk drawer and popped them regularly. He ate greasy fast foods and gorged on fettuccine carbonara (his favorite dish) and dumped ten sugar packs into each cup of coffee and dunked pork rinds into hot sauce. Though a fast metabolism prevented Payton from gaining excessive weight, they worried how it all impacted his psyche. "He ate junk," said Conley. "Fettuccine Alfredo with crumbled bacon. Chili dogs. Corn dogs. And fried pork chops, and I mean fried hard." Never an imbiber as a player, Payton now drank his fair share of beer. He behaved erratically and was prone to strange and confounding moments. Holmes vividly recalled visiting the office for a meeting. "Walter came in and he was bouncing off the walls," he said. "He was totally incoherent, all hopped up on these painkillers. I remember he turned on his computer and he wanted to show some old porn crap. His eyes were all weird. I said, 'Walter, what the hell?' He drank a couple of beers and I couldn't believe it. Who was this person?"

By this point in his life Payton was convinced that he suffered from attention deficit hyperactivity disorder, and began taking the Ritalin tablets prescribed to a friend's son. Quirk and Tucker encouraged him to resume exercising—*Walter, go to the gym; Walter, take a jog.* Nothing. They took his calls at all hours, wondering what odd or exciting or devastating words would emerge from his lips. Payton berated. Payton praised. Payton laughed. Payton cried. He hated his wife—"Why won't she just fucking leave me?" He hated Gonzalez—"What the fuck is wrong with this bitch?" He wanted Choy back. He wanted Choy dead. What appointments were scheduled for the next day? Cancel them. Don't cancel them. Let's do lunch. No, let's not. I have an amazing idea. I have a terrible idea. Like many Americans, Payton turned especially forlorn during the holiday season. He felt the pressure of having to be everywhere at once—with Lita in New Jersey; with his kids in Arlington Heights; with his mother in Jackson, Mississippi. He said he hoped something bad would happen to him, just so he had an excuse to stay home and hide. "No matter what I do," he said, "I can't win."

Payton made spur-of-the-moment decisions that baffled those around him. He accepted an invitation from the World Wrestling Federation to serve as Razor Ramon's guest manager for something called SummerSlam. Despite being petrified of deep water, he teamed up with Chuck Norris to try and break the Chicago-to-Detroit 605-mile powerboat record (they failed). He became founding director of the First Northwest Bank of Arlington Heights. He hinted at a run for mayor of Chicago (this from a man who often failed to vote). He tested Quirk and Tucker's loyalty with insults and threats and, literally, thirty to fifty phone calls per day. Walter on his cell. Walter from his apartment. Walter in the house. Flowers one minute, taunts the next. "It was like having a husband," said Tucker, "without the intimacy. He was terribly lonely. People loved Walter. People were drawn to him. But he never had the love of a partner who filled him up. It was tragic."

"He was so manic," said Quirk. "The flux in his moods was unlike anything I'd ever seen."

On multiple occasions Payton threatened to commit suicide. Usually following a fight with Connie or Lita. Or after being reminded that, even with such a legendary high-profile career, he still had to worry about finances. Payton looked in the mirror and hated the reflection. He was supposed to be happy and secure, and yet he was anything but. The love he received from fans was wonderful and great, but it wasn't real. The diehard Bear loyalist wearing the No. 34 jersey knew Walter Payton as a halfback, but he didn't *know* Walter Payton. Everything was surface and superficial. What would they think, Walter wondered, if they saw him away from the field, cheating incessantly and failing as a businessman?

Once, during a particularly down period, he entered the house at 34 Mudhank with his gun drawn, telephoned a friend, and crying, uttered, "I'm going to end it now."

"Walter would call me all the time, saying he was about to kill himself," said Holmes. "He was tired. He was angry. Nobody loved him. He wanted to be dead." The first time such a threat was made, Holmes dropped what he was doing and flew from Mississippi to Illinois to console his client. By the time he arrived, Payton's mood had swung positive. Holmes never again took his threats seriously.

Despite the urging of those around him, Payton refused to see a psychologist or social worker. What would that say about his strength and fortitude? He was supposed to be a hero. Heroes didn't do therapy.

On one particularly dark day, Payton wrote a friend a letter, saying that he needed to get his life in order and that he was afraid of doing "something" he'd regret. In the note, Payton admitted that he regularly contemplated committing suicide. Thinking about "the people I put into this fucked-up situation," he wrote, "maybe it would be better if I just disappear." Payton said he imagined picking up his gun, murdering those around him, then turning the weapon on himself. "Every day something like this comes into my head," he wrote. He was distraught over these persistent thoughts about wanting to "hurt so many others" and not thinking "it is wrong." Payton ended the letter by admitting that he needed help—but that he had nowhere to turn.

Payton often called Quirk late at night, his voice soft and emotionless. Quirk could usually tell what was coming. Doom. Gloom. "You won't see me when you get to the office tomorrow," he'd say. "Enjoy life without me."

On one occasion, Quirk picked up the phone and heard this: "I'm ending it. I'm no longer going to exist. And if you think I'm not taking you with me, you're wrong."

"I usually chose to ignore those threats," said Quirk. "I never fully believed him. But it was definitely a cry for help."

Quirk and Tucker often considered leaving. There were certainly other job opportunities out there that didn't involve this sort of drama. But the women found themselves bonded by a confounding sense of loyalty toward Payton. They saw him at his best, and believed his goodness outweighed the negatives.

"When you love someone," said Quirk, "you don't simply throw them away."

. . .

Along with Studebaker's, Payton was an investor/owner in four other establishments. Those who asked were told that Payton relished the business; that there was nothing he'd rather do than show up at the Pacific Club in Lombard or the Acapulco Bar in the Holiday Inn–Elk Grove to shake hands, sign autographs, and mingle with his customers. The claim was nonsense—Payton hated having to worry about money, and resented that so many past investments had fallen flat. Were it not for Payton Power, the profitable power equipment company he owned with Mike Lanigan, Payton's business track record would be uniquely terrible. "It ate him up," said Tucker. "The instability of it all."

In 1993, Payton was in the midst of opening America's Bar, a downtown

Chicago club that would feature Top 40 music and the city's only one-dollar all-you-can-eat smorgasbord. With the establishment set to debut in ten days, three building inspectors stopped in, conducted an evaluation, and told Gary Wallem, the general contractor, that the opening would have to be delayed until a proper permit was acquired. Payton requested a meeting with the men the following day, and showed up carrying a large gym bag. He looked at the first inspector and said, "What's your name?"

John Doe.

"Walter pulled out a football and a pen and wrote, 'To John Doe—your good friend, Walter Payton,'" said Wallem. "Then he did it for the other two inspectors as well."

At the conclusion of the ritual, Payton said, "So, about that permit . . ."

"What permit?" replied the first inspector. "Your permit is fine with us."

The story is funny, and Wallem tells it with gusto. Yet Payton detested this sort of thing. He had always scoffed at celebrities trading in their fame for perks and business favors, and now Payton was trading in his fame for perks and business favors. This wasn't how he had envisioned his life after football. It was beneath him. Beneath his image of Sweetness.

On many nights Payton refused to sleep, instead staying up to drink bottles of Coca-Cola, gorge banana-flavored Laffy Taffys, and watch old movies. He would slump down on his couch, his eyes gazing longingly toward the escape of the large screen before him. When a Roger Ebert–esque thought entered his head, he had to share it.

"Ginny, quick, turn to channel seven. *Scaramouche* is on."

*Walter, it's four thirty* A.M.

On multiple occasions Walter would excitedly call one of the women from a clothing store or jewelry kiosk or shopping mall. "I want to buy something, but I need an opinion first," he'd say. "Drop everything and get over here now."

"We had no choice," said Quirk. "We dropped everything. We were possessions to Walter. People were like puppets on a string to him. He tested you and tested you. Did Kimm and I have healthy relationships with him? No."

The women hated Payton. The women cherished Payton. At his absolute best, when the darkness subsided and the sun shone brightly, Payton could be spectacular. "He was," said Tucker, "addicted to laughter. When he was happy, all he wanted to do was laugh and laugh and laugh. He had many flaws. But Walter had a genuine desire to make people happy." If fans approached him with footballs to sign, Payton first insisted on a quick game of catch. If they wanted him to shake a child's hand, Payton knelt down and engaged the youngster in a conversation about school. When John Gamauf, his friend and business partner, told him about the passing of his father, John, Sr., Payton asked for the phone number of his mother, Irma. "Walter called her regularly for the next six months," Gamauf said. "Just to say hello."

While traveling to Orlando for a vacation, Payton—sitting in first class—was told that a ten-year-old boy named Billy Kohler was on the plane, heading to Disney World courtesy of the Make-A-Wish Foundation. In need of both liver and kidney transplants, Billy's odds of survival were long. "We're on the plane and a stewardess comes up and says, 'There's someone who would like to meet you in first class,'" said Jim Kohler, Billy's father. "We go up front and who's standing there—Walter Payton."

Payton introduced himself and knelt down to Billy's level. "You've been facing a lot of adversity," he told the boy. "You will come through this. No matter what follows, you need to keep your head up, you need to keep fighting forward, and you need to believe. You've gone through more in your short life than most of us have in a lifetime."

Overcome by the moment, Billy began sobbing. Payton tickled him beneath the chin. "You're a hero," he said. "Just know that—you're a hero."*

After retiring from the Bears, Payton traveled most places with a pair of bodyguards, David Robinson and Tony Frencher. They were big men—both in excess of three hundred pounds, with muscles and scowls to match. Payton, however, never wanted them to intimidate or keep people at bay. "We were there mainly to help him out," said Robinson. "Walter was a man of the people." In the early 1990s Frencher coached a Pop Warner team in the Chicago suburb of Bolingbrook. Though loathe to make requests of his employers, Frencher asked Payton to appear at the year-end banquet. "Walter told me he'd try his best and that he'd call to get directions," Frencher said. "Well, he never called, and on the night of the event I was worried he wasn't coming. I'm sitting at the banquet when a kid walks in and says, 'Coach Tony, someone is outside looking for you.'" Frencher exited and was greeted by a breathtaking sight: Walter Payton surrounded by the entire Bolingbrook Police force. "He had called the cops to ask for directions,"

---

* Billy Kohler is now twenty-four and living in Orlando, where he works construction.

said Frencher, "and every officer in the city came to get pictures with him." Payton's talk, Frencher recalled, was "amazing," as was the ensuing hour, during which he posed for individual photographs with every Pop Warner player. "The kids were between nine and eleven," he said. "And their year was made that night."

A part of Payton actually looked forward to giving speeches, for which he earned anywhere from ten thousand to twenty-five thousand dollars a pop. He would pick up the microphone, pace the stage, feed off the energy. It mattered not whether he was addressing a convention of Cub Scouts or American Express executives. He never relied on notes or any sort of script. "Walter would always say, 'If you have to speak, speak from the heart,'" said Conley. "He said that if you speak from the heart, you can't go wrong." Those who expected stories of Mike Singletary and Jim McMahon found themselves surprised, but not disappointed. Payton talked mainly of life—"If you go somewhere, always have pictures of your children on you," he would say. "They're the meaning to it all. The real meaning."

With the message guiding his way, and with nowhere else to turn, Payton seemed to devote more time to his two children with Connie. Though never an overwhelmingly bad father to Jarrett and Brittney, Payton was too often an absentee one. There was always somewhere else to be and someone else to attend to. Football. Racing. Business. Women. "Do you think Walter made any sort of effort to be home for dinner with the kids every night?" said Conley. "Do you think Jarrett and Brittney had a genuinely happy home life with their father? Of course not." Now confronting his own personal struggles, Payton tried harder. He committed himself to teaching his off-spring right from wrong. Especially Jarrett. Having grown up in rural Mississippi, loading mounds of dirt onto a wheelbarrow and spending summers spreading it across his yard, Walter feared his son's corruption via money and celebrity. The boy had enjoyed countless perks because of his father's fame—a weekend at Camp David with President George H. W. Bush, a spot at the impossible-to-get-into Michael Jordan Basketball Camp, appearances in television commercials. Walter often complained to friends about his son's apparent softness ("He didn't understand why Jarrett didn't run more, why he didn't lift more," said Dan Davis, a fellow coach at Hoffman Estates High. "He didn't think he had much desire."), and he wanted him to know grit and grasp dedication and appreciate the virtues of an honest day's work. Throughout the bulk of his teenage years, Jarrett spent summers employed at Payton Power, a company Walter co-owned that supplied heavy equipment. "People might have thought he'd go easy on me," Jarrett said. "No way. I made minimum wage, and I did every hard task there was. I'd cut grass, pick up machines and bring them back to the shop, hose them down, make sure they were OK. I was lunch boy—every day I was the guy sent to get everyone lunch. He didn't have to do that . . . he could have let me stay home and play video games. But my dad felt like something needed to be instilled in me."

When it came to his son, Walter was all about lessons. Right vs. wrong, noble vs. selfish, wise vs. inane. During his eighth-grade year at Barrington Middle School, Jarrett was caught with alcohol on his breath—a byproduct of the screwdrivers he and a friend had shared the night before. When Walter found out, he brought his son downstairs, sat him at the basement bar, poured him a glass of Jack Daniel's and said, "If you wanna drink, Jarrett, drink this."

"No," the boy cried from beneath his hangover. "I don't want to drink. I don't want anything."

"No, no, no," his father replied. "You said you wanted to drink. Drink this."

"Dad, please," Jarrett said. "Please, no."

"Look," Walter said, "you have many decades ahead of you to have drinks whenever you want. Right now is just not the time."

That same year one of Jarrett's fellow students, a girl named Becky Glance, was slapped by a male student. Jarrett challenged the boy to a fight, and wound up breaking his nose and causing a blood clot in his eye. After picking her son up, Connie called Walter to fill him in. He asked to speak to Jarrett. "So you got in a fight, huh?" Walter said.

"Yeah," Jarrett replied.

"Well," said Walter, "I've got something to give you tonight."

Jarrett knew he was in trouble. When Walter entered the house later that evening, though, he removed his wallet from his pocket and handed his son three hundred-dollar bills. "That was the right thing you did," he said. "You stand up for women. I'm proud of you."

Long a lover of video games (he was a master of *Ms. Pac-Man*), Payton delighted in visiting arcades with his son and challenging him to marathon competitions of *Terminator 2* or *Street Fighter*. "People would gather around," Jarrett said, "just to watch my dad." In 1997, Payton purchased a new Porsche

911 Turbo. The car was black, and sleek as a leopard. One night, at two A.M., Walter entered the house on 34 Mudhank, snuck into Jarrett's room, and shook him awake. "Get up, kid!" he said. "Come on . . . get up!" He proceeded to lead Jarrett out of the house and into the Porsche. "We drive out to [Interstate] 90, and there are no cars on the highway," Jarrett said. "He says, 'Get your seat belt on.' I'm like, 'What?'

"I got my seat belt on and he just let that baby loose, man. I still remember my head going back. The speedometer had the little red numbers, and we hit almost one-eighty. How cool was that? How many dads do that type of thing?"

Unlike his father, Jarrett wasn't an otherworldly athlete, destined for unquestionable superstardom. He refused to play football until his junior year at St. Viator High School in Arlington Heights, choosing to make a name for himself as an all-state soccer player (he spent several years as a member of the Chicago Pegasus Soccer Club, one of the top amateur clubs in the country). Though he had little interest in or knowledge of the intricacies of the sport, Walter attended most of Jarrett's soccer games, cheering from the sidelines alongside all the other parents. When, as a junior, Jarrett decided to give football a shot, Walter's emotions were mixed. On the one hand, he could now offer his son valuable advice. On the other, Jarrett Payton would inevitably be compared with Walter Payton—and that wasn't fair. "I call it the gift and the curse," said Jarrett. "It's great having a name, but it can hold you back, too."

Brittney felt no such pressures. As a student at Station Middle School in Barrington, she participated in track and field, standing out as a sprinter and long jumper. Walter made as many of her meets as possible, and quietly applauded when she did well. As demanding as he could be with his son, he was equally docile with his daughter. Payton loved having a girl, but was perplexed by the dresses and flowers and tea-party birthday celebrations. ("I was probably seven or eight for that one," Brittney recalled. "We had someone come in and bring funny hats and boas for everyone to wear, and my mom put out real china. My dad was around, but he wasn't going to sit there with a bunch of little girls drinking tea.") He could wrestle with his son, throw balls with his son, trade barbs with his son. "With me, he did a lot of tickling," Brittney said. "He and my brother would pin me down and tickle me to death. I hated that."

Every so often, Walter would present Connie with an idea for the children. His best one involved money. When Jarrett was fourteen and Brittney ten, he took the kids to the bank and had them open their own checking accounts. The goal was to teach the value of currency—know how much you're spending and grasp the power of the dollar. "It was very wise," Brittney said. "I remember taking home economics in high school, and when it came to money I was way ahead. I learned at a young age to know how much I had in my account at all times.

"Because if you're not careful, it's all gone."

# PART FIVE

# FINAL

## *Jarrett Payton,*
## *Walter Payton's son*

---

*Dad had a sweet tooth for Laffy Taffys. The banana ones. My mom used to go to Sam's Club and buy the big buckets.*

*About two years after my father died, we moved out of our house. We were packing up everything, and one of the things we had was this big vase by the glass in the atrium that had been there for years. It was sitting on top of something, so you never got to see in it because it was high up. When we were moving we picked up this big vase, and it almost tipped over. It made a rustling noise, and I was like, "What's in here?" Well, I dumped it out and hundreds upon hundreds of Laffy Taffy wrappers came pouring out.*

*It was the most beautiful thing in the world.*

CHAPTER 25

SICK

WHEN HE DECIDED TO RACE IN THE TRANS-AM SERIES IN 1990, WALTER Payton was required to undergo a physical as extensive as any he had ever endured as a member of the Chicago Bears.

Weight and height were measured. Blood was taken. He urinated into a small cup, sprinted for forty-five seconds on a treadmill, and jumped straight into the air. When the results were returned Payton was told—as he had always been told before—that he was in good health.

*With one seemingly miniscule blip.*

According to the exam, Payton appeared to have elevated liver enzymes. He underwent further testing with Jay Munsell, a former team physician with the Bears, who confirmed the findings. "But nobody paid it much mind," said Kimm Tucker, the executive director of Payton's charitable foundation. "Walter was so physically above the curve, it just didn't register as a real problem." The indifference was hardly uncommon. Although elevated liver enzymes *can* be a symptom of liver problems, they might also appear because of alcohol consumption, gallstones, or several other minor issues. To Payton, this was the equivalent of testing for slightly elevated blood pressure. No big deal. "It was something nobody even considered a problem," Tucker said. "Walter was invincible."

Three years later, following his near-fatal crash at Elkhart Lake, Wisconsin, Payton underwent a liver biopsy assessment because, as cited in a report issued by the Mayo Clinic, "there was concern of toxic exposure in the cockpit of the car." Again, the test results showed elevated liver enzymes. Again, nobody seemed especially concerned.

In the summer of 1998, Walter Payton was a busy man. In the process of shedding himself of his nightclub holdings, Payton had become one of three owners of Walter Payton's Roundhouse, an enormous brewpub/restaurant in the suburb of Aurora. He also co-owned a CART racing team, and was heavily invested in the future of his son, Jarrett, who by now had emerged as a superstar quarterback/running back at St. Viator High. Rated the nation's number fifty-eighth overall prospect by *The Sporting News*, Jarrett was being recruited by most major Division I colleges. Walter attended nearly all of Jarrett's games, sitting atop the home press box to avoid crowds and commotions. He delighted in seeing his boy follow so ably in his footsteps, and loved speaking to recruiters from Notre Dame and Northwestern, Miami, and Minnesota. The whole experience made Walter Payton feel special again—this time not for something he did, but for someone he created.

Through all the commotion, Payton hardly noticed that his appetite had started to wane. Nothing especially alarming. It was just that, for a man used to eating like a blue whale, food no longer held much interest. "I wasn't as hungry," Payton said. "Things that I ate did not digest as well."

Because he was a football player, and because football players are instructed to ignore pain and irritation, Payton paid the discomfort little mind. He swigged from bottles of Pepto-Bismol and continued with his days. Here was a man who made a living out of running over defensive ends; who had survived a fiery race car crash and who could count on one hand the number of sick days he had ever taken. Upset tummy? Waning appetite? Not a big deal.

"I had been traveling between Chicago and Panama for a potential business venture and I figured I must have caught an intestinal bug from eating some uncooked crab," Payton said. "I had been eating a ton of crab in Panama. I loved it. But the pain and discomfort didn't go away. Each day that summer I felt a gradual progression of fatigue and just an overall sense of feeling lousy."

Because Payton took such pride in his appearance, friends rarely mentioned the physical changes that were beginning to manifest. The bulging white acne puffs along his neck. The yellowish tint to his skin. "Different things started to click in," said John Gamauf, the vice president of Bridgestone/Firestone and a partner with Walter on a racing team. "He was still such a powerful, muscular man that they were less obvious. But they were there." In particular, Gamauf recalled a July trip to the Raceway Laguna Seca in California. Upon spotting Payton for the first time, Gamauf expected the usual sternum-splintering bear hug. "This time he didn't give me one," Gamauf recalled. "He said, 'Man, my back has just been killing me. I don't know what's wrong.'"

On August 25, 1998, Payton showed up at his Roundhouse restaurant in Aurora to serve as a cohost of *The Monsters of the Midday*, a weekly radio show that aired every Tuesday on WSCR. Now in his fifth year with the program, Payton shared the microphone with Dan Jiggetts, the former Bears offensive lineman, and Mike North, a local media personality. Once per month, the eatery played host to the show. Scott Ascher, Payton's partner in the business, always looked forward to the day. "But this time Walter looked different," Ascher said. "His eyes were actually yellow. His skin was actually yellow. His stomach was killing him. He went on the air and did fine, but you could tell he wasn't doing well."

When the program ended, Payton walked to the front of the restaurant and grabbed a handful of the Brach's Star Brites mints he loved so much. He unwrapped one, placed it in his mouth, then spit it out.

He tried another one—same thing.

"Taste one of these," Payton said, handing a red-and-white mint to Mark Alberts, another restaurant partner.

Alberts sucked on the mint. "It seems OK to me, Walter," he said.

Payton shook his head.

At home, he began most days by splashing on aftershave. Now—*sniff* . . . *sniff*—the smell was wrong. Weird. Off.

One day John Skibinski, a former Bears running back, stopped by Payton's office in Hoffman Estates. He was used to Walter the laugher, Walter the kidder. "He was all alone and in a very dark mood," Skibinski said. "He was stuffing these bags, and I asked if he needed help." For the ensuing hour the two men worked side by side, and no more than two or three words were exchanged. Before he left, Skibinski asked his old pal whether everything was OK.

"You know, John," he said, "something just doesn't feel right."

Finally, at the urging of Kimm Tucker and Ginny Quirk, Payton went to a hepatologist. Tests were conducted, a diagnosis was presented: vitamin toxicity.

*Vitamin toxicity?*

Six months earlier, Payton had started working with a pair of Las Vegas–based radiologists who were searching for a celebrity to speak on behalf of their new, self-hyped "revolutionary" antiaging program. To win him over, Payton was provided with monthly shipments of human growth hormone and vitamins, valued at thirty thousand dollars a pop. "Walter was very needle phobic," said Quirk, "but he would inject himself with the HGH and he would gorge on all those vitamins. It was at a point in his life when he was becoming acutely aware of aging. He wanted to stop the process."

Instead of feeling stronger and livelier, Payton began experiencing the stomach pain and sensory malfunctions. He chalked it up to the HGH and vitamins, and suspended the routine. He was convinced the "vitamin toxicity" diagnosis was on the mark. Others, though, weren't so sure. The abdominal pain and acne could *perhaps* be side effects of excessive vitamin intake, but what about the puzzling sensory shifts in smell and taste? "His skin was getting more and more yellowy," said Gamauf. "It wasn't normal."

By early fall Payton was waking up sluggishly and becoming only more tired as the hours passed. The man famously known for his limitless energy suddenly possessed very little. He had no appetite, and whenever he did eat he wound up with gray-tinted diarrhea. Quirk initially chalked the decline up to age and an unrealistic workload—along with the businesses and the radio show, Payton was traveling the country giving motivational speeches, helping Jarrett pick a college, writing a weekly newspaper column for the Copley News Service, working as a color commentator for Bears' preseason games, and serving on the team's board of directors (admittedly, he did very little in this capacity). But as the days passed and Payton's strength and appearance only worsened, Quirk began to believe this was more serious than initially advertised. "His health was [starting to affect] his business schedule," she said. "I had to carve out some time for Walter to get some rest so he could try and shake off what was bothering him."

Finally, with the uncertainty burdening him both mentally and physically, Payton scheduled an appointment at the Mayo Clinic in Rochester, Minnesota. World renowned for treating rare medical conditions, Mayo's services were so in demand that Payton, a man who rarely had to wait for anything, would not be seen until early December. "I was not panic-stricken at this point," he said. "I realized I've got to find a resolution. I've got to find something that's going to make me better."

Payton flew to Rochester on December 17, checked in for a three-day stay, and underwent a bevy of tests. Albert J. Czaja, Mayo's head of gastroenterology and hepatology, filed a detailed assessment of Payton's symptoms:

Mr. Walter Payton, age 45, first developed nausea after eating in mid-August of '98. There was also associated increased fatigue with justified frequent rest periods during the day. Additionally his sleep patterns became reversed and he was awake at night and tired during the day. Diarrhea subsequently developed on a daily basis. The diarrhea would be related to eating and was non-recurrent in the fasting stage. Usually it would develop within ten to fifteen minutes after the completion of a meal. But [it] could occur as early as five minutes after eating. The symptoms would be unrelated to the amount or type of food eaten and there were no specific food intolerances. There would be associated borborygmi, but no abdominal cramping, bloating, distention or urgency. The bowel functions were well controlled and the texture would vary to loose to soft in nature, with colors that were gray and pale brown. There was no evidence of mucus discharge, bleeding, oil or greasy stool. The episodes did not occur at night and there was no fecal incontinence. Concurrent with these symptoms there was a variable appetite. He would be hungry prior to eating, but there would be postprandial nausea that would limit intake. Vomiting was absent. The weight decreased from 221 pounds to 194 pounds over a four-month period. . . . He recognized the development of a generalized itch. . . . The itch could be associated with excoriation and was worse at night. There are no associated rashes. He would also experience intermittent mid-chest discomfort, as though the food lodged. And there would be inability to burp and relieve the pressure. He was seen by his local physician in September of 1998 and liver tests were abnormal but etiologic studies were negative. In October of 1998 he was seen by a hepatologist who identified stabile liver tests abnormalities and suspected possibility of toxic effects related to the use of a vitamin pack since March of 1998 that included Vitamin E and probably Vitamin A. These vitamins were discontinued in September of 1998 but the symptoms and abnormalities have persisted. Currently Mr. Payton feels fatigue. He continues to have postprandial mid-chest lodging of food, although the symptom has improved over the last two weeks since using wheatgrass. His diarrhea has become less severe and his stools are now solid and gray in color. He continues to have postprandial nausea and the itch is less intense, although apparent during quiet periods. His weight has stabilized between 190 and 193 pounds. He denies receipt of blood transfusions, contact with jaundiced individuals, homosexual contact or exposure to hepatotoxic medication or chemicals. He does not consume alcohol. There is no family history of significant liver disease. His past medical history is unremarkable.

The ensuing test results were not good. According to Dr. Greg Gores, a Mayo liver transplant specialist, something was wrong with Payton's liver and bile duct, and it appeared to be primary sclerosing cholangitis (PSC). A rare (three of one hundred thousand people are affected) and mysterious disease, PSC scars the bile ducts, which carry bile from the liver to the small intestine to help digest food. When the ducts get blocked, bile backs up and migrates elsewhere. The body's immune system then mistakenly attacks its own tissues.*

A 10-French 9 cm biliary stent was placed in Payton's body to keep the bile ducts open (the Mayo report: "The procedure was well tolerated and Mr. Payton is well this morning."), though a momentarily optimistic Payton was informed the stent would serve as only a brief remedy. He was also pre-scribed Actigall, a drug normally used to fight gallstone disease, and was told to take 300 mg four times per day.

Wrote Gores in a report filed shortly after first evaluating Payton: "The findings were fully discussed with Mr. Payton and he understands the pre-sumptive diagnosis at this point is primary sclerosing cholangitis. This is a disease which is an unresolving disorder by definition. It has an aggressive nature. The . . . progression varies, but the diagnosis implies a worsening condition with time. He also understands there is no established therapy for primary sclerosing cholangitis, and that the individuals with chronic inflam-mation of the bile ducts are at increased risk for developing cholangiocarci-noma [cancer of the bile duct]." Gores then noted that Payton's CA 19-9 level, a blood test from the tumor marker category, was "abnormally increased" and that cancer of the bile duct might already be present.

"Walter," said Quirk, "wigged out. He was devastated."

On January 1, 1999, Payton, traveling without companionship, checked into St. Mary's Hospital for three and a half days of testing at Mayo. He was terrified and alone, and had no idea what the future held. When Charley Walters, a staff columnist for the *Saint Paul Pioneer Press*, was tipped off about Payton's presence at the clinic, he pursued the story. "I'm here for a physi-cal," Payton told him. "No big deal."

---

* During his time at Mayo, it was also determined that Payton was a carrier of Hepatitis C, a viral disease that leads to swelling of the liver. However, according to Dr. J. Steve Bynon, head of the liver transplant center at the University of Alabama-Birmingham, Hepatitis C and primary sclerosing cholangitis are unrelated. "Hepatitis C can be very serious," Bynon said. "But it has nothing to do with PSC. They are separate entities." During his stint as a patient at Mayo, Payton acknowledged to confidants that he had known of the Hepatitis C for more than a decade, and that he probably contracted it as a result of knee surgery following the 1983 season. The disease, however, is often difficult to detect, and for years Payton refused to tell anyone—even loved ones—that he was a carrier.

Payton returned home on the evening of January 4, convinced that somehow, someway the news would be positive.

It wasn't.

Gores explained to Payton that he was, without question, suffering from PSC. He told him that the disease could be measured in different levels, ranging from hours to live to weeks to live to months to live. "I was at level three," Payton said, "where they figured I probably had a year or two at that point."

"This won't get any better," Gores told him. "There's no medication or anything that we can give you to make this better. It's going to progressively get worse to the point where, in about a year or a year and a half, you're going to need a liver transplant."

The report punched Payton in the ribs. Until now, everything had been hypothetical. *Maybe* liver disease. *Maybe* cancer. "He thought the best," said Quirk. "Until he heard the real diagnosis." It didn't compute. Sure, Payton wasn't feeling like himself. But he was still strong and, at times, energized. There was no way this could be true. Payton knew he would overcome. He didn't hope or guess he'd overcome—he *knew*. The average wait for a liver in Illinois was said to be 127 days. He could handle that. The success rate was 88 percent. He could handle that, too. Payton would inevitably receive the transplant, and that would be that. End of story. "I beat everything mentally," he told Mike Lanigan, his friend and business partner. "I prepared myself for Sunday mornings when people said I couldn't play. I'm gonna do this, too." The next time he spoke with Quirk and Tucker, Payton made an executive decree: No more bad news. From that point on, Quirk would do most of the talking with the Mayo people (Payton made it clear to Mayo that absolutely no information was to be conveyed directly to Connie). If they had positive updates, Payton wanted to hear them. If they had terrible news, well, keep it away from Walter's ears.

Upon returning from Rochester, Payton called Connie and asked that they hold a family meeting at the home at 34 Mudhank. The four Paytons gathered in the basement, and Walter—positive, laughing, upbeat—told his children that he required a liver transplant, and there was nothing to worry about. "I was kind of nervous, but he was Superman to me," said Jarrett. "He didn't say anything about dying. Everything was positive—'When I get this transplant, I'll be fine.' I was numb. I didn't cry, because I didn't think he'd die. I assumed the best."

"I don't think I understood," said Brittney, who was thirteen. "I'd never been to a funeral and I never knew anyone who had been really sick. There were some tears and nervousness, but he assured us he'd be fine. Death wasn't a part of my world."

At the time the Roundhouse was preparing to distribute bottles of its newest beer, Payton Pilsner, to the Dominick's grocery stores scattered throughout Chicago. "The trucks were actually loaded and ready to go," said Ascher, "and Walter called me and said, 'I can't explain, but please don't deliver the beer.'" Ascher and Alberts were livid. Here was an enormous business opportunity. Why would Payton want to ruin things? "We knew Walter was a good man, so we begrudgingly pulled the beers off the trucks," Ascher said. "It turns out he didn't want his name on beer at the same time he was fighting liver disease. We had no idea."

Along with his various endeavors, Payton had been working with Matt Suhey, his old pal and blocking back, to purchase an Arena Football League team for Chicago. The two spoke regularly, and shortly after his return from Mayo Payton met with Suhey and several other potential investors at the Millrose Restaurant in South Barrington. When the meeting ended, Payton pulled Suhey close.

"Matt," he said, "I have a problem."

Throughout their friendship, Suhey had been pranked by Payton hundreds of times. He wasn't falling for this one. "OK, Walter," he said. "What's the punch line here?"

"No," he said. "I've really got a problem."

Payton wasn't giggling. "He got an inch from my nose," Suhey said. "We spent about an hour talking about it right there, and he was extremely positive he'd be getting a transplant."

What Payton didn't know was that he had a zero percent chance of receiving a new liver. Whether he was misinformed by the Mayo Clinic or provided erroneous information via Quirk or merely lying through his teeth to maintain good karma and positively impact organ donations, well, one will never know. What is now known, however, is that by the time Payton had visited Mayo his body was being ravaged by cancer of the bile duct. It was spreading to the lymph nodes and throughout the liver. The jaundice and weight loss, neither of which are direct byproducts of PSC, were damning indicators. "Most people with sclerosing cholangitis look pretty good until they're at the very end," said David Van Thiel, director of the liver transplant program at Loyola University Medical Center in Chicago. "He may well have had sclerosing cholangitis for a long time, even when he was still playing football. It's possible. I don't know that, but it's certainly possible to have mild sclerosing cholangitis that's relatively asymptomatic."

According to one Chicago physician, a liver specialist who, in the late-1990s, worked specifically with transplants, Mayo's doctors were informed that, were he in need, there was a liver available for Payton. "The people at Mayo told us, unambiguously, that he was not on the list," said the physician, who requested anonymity. "Somebody misinformed Walter." Payton was, in a sense, the *Titanic* passenger convinced the RMS *Carpathia* should be arriving in a matter of minutes. Unbeknownst to him, a transplant would never come. Once a person on the list is diagnosed with cancer, he is no longer a candidate for a new organ.

John Brems, the director of intra-abdominal transplantation at Loyola, had the opportunity to view Payton's X-rays. "You never say a condition is one hundred percent hopeless," Brems said, "but he clearly wasn't ever a transplant candidate. That would be impossible."

. . .

On the afternoon of January 29, 1999, Jarrett Payton held a press conference at St. Viator High School to announce that he would be signing a letter of intent to attend the University of Miami on a football scholarship.

It was that time of year in America, when hundreds of high school gridiron stars ritualistically sat alongside their coaches and family members and donned red caps and blue caps and green caps and orange caps as the flashes exploded and local reporters collected uplifting quotes about the future.

Now here was a smiling Jarrett, flanked by Kevin Kelly, head football coach at St. Viator, Connie Payton, and Walter Payton. "Miami is the best fit for me as a student and as an athlete," said Jarrett, a six-foot-two, 210-pound block of granite who had passed for 973 yards and ran for nearly 1,400 yards as a senior. "When I went down there, I fell in love with it. I like the fact that it is a private school and that it has a small-school atmosphere where I can get help and not be just a number. It just felt right."

Jarrett's future was interesting and intriguing, but the elephant in the room was Walter Payton, making his first public appearance since the diagnosis. Beneath a pair of dark sunglasses, Payton looked shrunken. By now he had lost more than fifty pounds. When a reporter asked about his slimmed-down figure, Payton lied. "I'm training to run a marathon in a year," he explained. "I've lost twenty-three pounds."

Payton hoped the discussion was over. It wasn't. That evening Mark Giangreco, the principle sports anchor at Chicago's WLS-TV 7, cracked that Payton appeared "all shriveled up" and that he resembled Mahatma Gandhi. "I think," Giangreco added, "I could take him on."

Watching from his home, Payton was devastated. "That upset me beyond what you can imagine," he said. "I had felt betrayed." So, for that matter, did Quirk. Though Giangreco's barbs were the first public comments Payton had heard of his condition, that was only because he wasn't paying attention. Throughout the Windy City, a vicious rumor had been spreading that Payton was dying of AIDS. "Walter was definitely not gay, though that was being said a lot," said Quirk. "And he definitely didn't have HIV, even though every person I would deal with in Chicago was asking me about Walter and AIDS. I've heard people in hindsight say that wasn't a real rumor. Well, it was real. I was the one being asked—and I was being asked *every single day*."

Moved by Giangreco's words and Quirk's urging, Payton came to the dreaded decision to go public with his condition. He was scheduled to cohost his radio show, *The Monsters of the Midday,* on Tuesday, February 2, at Carlucci's restaurant in Rosemont, Illinois. The scene, Payton concluded, would now double as a press conference.

With as little advance hype as possible, Quirk and Tucker called the various Chicago media outposts and invited them to Carlucci's for a ten A.M. announcement. Over the course of the previous weeks North and Jiggetts could tell something was seriously off. As with most of his acquaintances, however, Payton maintained enough of an emotional distance that neither man felt comfortable pressing the issue. "He looked more and more like Sammy Davis Jr. every week," said North. "I don't say that humorously—he really did. He lost all this weight, and he started wearing sunglasses for every show. One time I was able to see behind them, and his eyes were glowing yellow. I thought, 'Uh-oh. That can't be right.'"

On the morning of the press conference, North received a telephone call from Jeff Schwartz, an executive with WSCR. "We have an issue," Schwartz told him. "Walter has decided he's finally going to talk about what's wrong with him, and he's using the radio show as an outlet to do so."

North, a nonstop gabber, was speechless. "Wow," he said. "This is going to be big."

By the time the show was scheduled to begin, the thirty assembled seats in front of the broadcast table were filled. Payton had asked Tucker to write his speech, and despite having recently been discharged from the hospital with forty stitches caused by a ruptured appendix, she did so.

On most Tuesdays, Payton had looked forward to sitting down with North and Jiggetts for four hours of on-air gabbing. Now, with his arrival at

Carlucci's, he was visibly nervous. Payton had asked his assistants to make certain Jarrett would be there, and he was. What he didn't count on—and what he did *not* want—was the presence of Connie. Armed with her comforting smile and Reagan-esque charisma, Connie approached her husband from behind, patted him on the shoulder, and said, warmly, "I'm here."

Payton couldn't believe it. Despite their on-again, off-again dramas, he and Lita Gonzalez remained a couple. They spoke several times per week, and she even made a few trips to Mayo to accompany Payton. "Walter and Lita were in love," said a mutual acquaintance. "It might have looked like he was with Connie, but that was all a show."

Now, standing on the stage, his wife by his side, Payton reached for Quirk and Tucker and barked, "I need to see both of you in the men's room—now!"

The three retreated to the lavatory, where Payton lit into his assistants. "Why the fuck is Connie here?" he screamed. "Who the fuck told her to come to my press conference? Which one of you fucking did this?"

Tucker was irritated and in pain. She had spent the previous six hours finalizing Walter's speech, and the last thing she needed was a lecture. "You know what, Walter," she shouted. "It'd be much easier to deal with this if you were divorced! If you had done the right thing from the beginning, we wouldn't be having this problem right now, would we?"

There was nothing Payton could say. He marched out of the bathroom and sat down at the middle of a long brown table adorned with a black-and-white radio station banner. Jarrett, wearing a plaid shirt, sat to his right. Connie, dressed in black, sat to his left—and Walter barely looked her way. As always, dark sunglasses guarded Walter's eyes. A black leather jacket hung from his shoulders. He gripped a white microphone with his right hand and, in that familiar high-pitched voice, spoke about contracting a disease that, until recently, he had never heard of. "I can't lay around and mope around and just hope everything is going to be OK," he said. "I'm still moving and grooving."

Asked if he was scared, Payton didn't flinch. "Hell yeah, I'm scared," he said. "Wouldn't you be scared? What can you do? I mean, like I said, it's not in my hands anymore. It's in God's hands, and if it's meant for me to go on and to be around, I'll be around."

Over the course of the decade the media had been presented with a couple of similar situations. In 1991 Magic Johnson held a press conference to announce he had contracted the HIV virus. Four years later Mickey Mantle, his body ravaged by a lifetime of alcoholism, also met with the media to discuss the inoperable liver cancer that facilitated his need for a transplant. Both of those moments were memorable and, in the context of superstar athletes, shocking. Yet Johnson's disease could be chalked up to unprotected sex, and Mantle's to the bottle. Here was Payton, a shell of his former self, seemingly the victim of bad luck. "There was some unspoken comfort level in knowing that [Johnson and Mantle] had brought it on themselves," Bud Shaw wrote in the following day's Cleveland *Plain Dealer*. "Not so with Payton."

Toward the end, Jiggetts asked Payton if there was anything he wanted to tell his fans. Payton's hands began to shake. He put his head on his son's shoulder and began to cry. "To the people that really care about me, just continue to pray," he said. "And for those who are going to say what they want to say, may God be with you also."

. . .

Immediately after the press conference, Payton headed for O'Hare Airport to catch the forty-minute flight back to Rochester for some tests. He called Tucker and asked her to meet him outside the terminal to bring him some material. When she arrived, Tucker was shocked by what she saw: There stood Walter Payton, alongside his curbside car, moving to the music blasting from his speakers. "He looked so peaceful and so happy," she said. "He said he was spending some time with God and he felt like dancing."

. . .

Later that night Larry King, famed host of CNN's *Larry King Live*, left a message at Payton's office. "Walter," he said, "Larry King here. Listen, I'm not calling to get you on the show. I'm calling to give you my home number if you want to talk as friends [the two had never actually met], and just to let you know that I'm thinking about you and I want to make sure you're OK."

When the sentiment was relayed to Payton, he told Tucker, "Call Larry King and tell him I'll do the show." On the afternoon of Wednesday, February 3, Tucker and Payton returned to O'Hare to fly to New York. Payton was dressed normally—jeans, collared shirt, thick jacket, sunglasses. Yet as he strode through the terminal, something staggering took place: Absolutely nothing. Nobody requested an autograph, asked for a picture, brought up that game against the Bucs in '83. Nothing. "Not one person recognized him," said Tucker. "That's the first time I'd ever seen that happen."

When they boarded the plane, Tucker tucked her head into her arms and sobbed. "I knew," she said, "that Walter Payton was done as we knew him."

Payton was the marquee guest on a program that also featured senators

Robert Byrd, Dianne Feinstein, and Jon Kyl discussing the impeachment trial of President Bill Clinton. King introduced him by saying, "In case you are new to the planet, Walter Payton is forty-four years old . . ." and the interview took off. The majority of Americans had not seen Payton's press conference, so this was their first glance at the emaciated star. The man who, only months ago, weighed in at 221 pounds was now hovering around 170. His skin and eyes were yellowish, and he wore the weathered appearance of a man in his seventies. As is the way of many athletes, Payton communicated with King in the lingo he knew best. "It was sort of like when I had Coach Ditka," Payton said. "I said, 'I'm going to believe in his philosophy, and I'm going to do as he tells me, because he's going to take us to the Super Bowl.' And the same way with this doctor. I'm going to use the same philosophy."

Payton told King he was on the waiting list for a liver—not true. He either didn't know or didn't mention that cancer was ravaging his body. Had King done his research, he would have known the visible symptoms Payton was showing had little to do with PCS and everything to do with bile duct cancer.

The show's finest moment came toward the end, when Payton looked at King and, for the first of many times, made an impassioned plea for organ donations. "I've been a donor, you know, ever since I had my Illinois license," he said. "One of the things that I said was that, you know, being a football player for thirteen years, you know, I probably wore out just about everything in my body, but if there's something in there that somebody can use, you know, so well. And Mike Ditka said it—in death you can give life and what better gift is there? And I think that a lot of people should look at that now. I know there are religious reasons and everybody thinks of other reasons, but I think that we all should just stand back and look at it."

After taking a couple of phone calls, King wrapped up what would go down as one of the most moving segments of his fifty-three-year career.

> **Payton:** When I do cry, they're tears of joy.
> **King:** We wish you everything you wish yourself. Godspeed and when you get that transplant, you'll be sitting right here and we'll reminisce about carrying the football.
> **Payton:** OK.
> **King:** Thanks, Walter.
> **Payton:** Thanks, Larry.

**King:** Best of luck.

**Payton:** Oh, God's with me. I'll be OK.

. . .

In the immediate aftermath of his appearance on *Larry King*, Walter Payton's world shook. The calls of support were nonstop—from Mike Singletary and Mike Ditka; from Evel Knievel and Michael Jordan. Jay Leno sent a note that read, "We're all here for you. When you get your new liver, put your old one in a jar and bring it on *The Tonight Show*." Payton was a guest on *Oprah* and *CBS This Morning*. Connie and Brittney accepted an award on his behalf at the ESPYs (Payton watched from home, ordering in P.F. Chang's). Columnists across the nation sang his praises as the new face of American courage. "Cry for him, pray for him," wrote Jay Mariotti of the *Chicago Sun-Times*. "But never lose faith in him."

Most amazing was the impact his condition had on organ donations. In the week following Payton's press conference, the Illinois secretary of state's office averaged 115 donor inquiries per day—compared to roughly twelve per day before the announcement. "Never before have we had anything come close to this happening," said Jan Grines, manager of the secretary of state's organ and tissue donor registry. "Payton has touched the hearts of Illinoisans." The producers of the hit CBS television show, *Touched by an Angel*, asked Payton to film a commercial promoting organ donation that would air during the program. "Along with me, over sixty thousand Americans are awaiting organ transplants," he said in the spot. "Only half of us will receive them unless a real hero steps up."

Payton's press conference was held on a Tuesday. By Friday, his office had been besieged by nearly twenty thousand letters, postcards, and packages (some thirty-odd letters came from people offering their livers). Bundles of flowers lined the doorway. Payton didn't merely look at the piles from afar. He dug in, reading many of the notes, personally responding to some of the people. One letter especially moved him:

> *Dear Mr. Payton:*
>
> *My name is Christopher and I am nine years old . . . I have a [liver ailment] too. My doctors don't know how I got it and they don't know what caused it. They don't even know a name for my sick liver. . . . I've got an enlarged spleen, too. I can't play any sports so my spleen won't bust. I need to help my liver. I'm real popular at the hospital. They keep taking my blood to run tests, but they can't figure out why I have it . . . I'm sorry that you*

*have to go through all of this. I'll pray for you. Mommy said God will take
care of you just like he's going to take care of me. Don't be scared, please.
Maybe you can do tests with me at my hospital. Will you please write back?*
    *Yours truly,*
    *Christopher Cash, Jonesboro, Georgia*

Payton wrote back, and kept the piece of lined notebook paper with
Christopher's words on his desk. When a *Sports Illustrated* writer came to visit
him, he picked the page up and read it aloud. "Christopher says I shouldn't
be scared," Payton said. "God will take care of me." *

In early February a spokeswoman for Payton told the *Associated Press*
that his liver disease was progressing faster than expected, and private planes
had been offered to speed him to Mayo when a transplant became available.
In April Dr. Joe Lagattuta, one of Payton's personal physicians, reportedly
told the Itasca Business Council in a speech that Payton had an excellent
chance of receiving a new liver imminently. Once again, the information was
puzzling. Within weeks of Payton's press conference, his doctors confirmed
the news many had suspected: He had cancer of the bile duct. By now,
Payton—despite his hear-no-evil approach to negative news—was well aware
that a transplant would not be in the cards. Though the word "cancer" was
being avoided at all costs (as far as the general public was concerned, Payton
was only battling a liver ailment), the disease was his greatest enemy.

Payton began making regular trips to Rochester to undergo lengthy,
nightmarish chemotherapy treatments. He often flew on an airplane belong-
ing to Tom Wieringa, a wealthy sponsor of Payton's CART racing team.
One of his regular companions was Suhey, who refused to let his longtime
friend go through this alone. It was during that time, seeing Payton at his
absolute lowest, that Suhey saw Payton at his absolute greatest.

"Walter would get his chemo at Mayo at night," said Suhey. "And typically
he would feel horrible afterward. He'd go back to the hotel and sleep. One
night it was cold, and Walter and I were going upstairs to the room. This family
just drove up from Chicago; they had just gotten there. And the child, who was
probably ten or eleven or twelve, had cancer. He had no hair, he looked weak.
It was not great. And all he wanted to do was meet Walter. I said, 'Walter, do
you really want to?' and he said, 'Absolutely!' He walked outside, and it was

---

* I was the *Sports Illustrated* writer. I've never forgotten sitting across from Payton that day.

really cold out. He met the kid, talked to the kid, and they sat down—just he and the kid went and sat down. And Walter felt just horrible, but he sat there and talked to the kid for half an hour. Right after chemo. God bless him. The family wrote me a letter, I think I still have it. It was written a year or two after Walter passed. I don't think the child lived, but it meant a lot to him. Under very difficult circumstances. That moment really spoke to the kindness—to walk out there and spend the time with the kid. That was Walter."

If people assumed Payton was sitting inside his house, bemoaning his fate, they were mistaken. "I don't feel sorry for myself, because that's the first step toward giving up and I'm not giving up," he said. "I know something good is going to come from this. I just haven't figured out what it is yet." When he wasn't receiving treatment at Mayo, Payton fought to stay active. He took a trip with Mike Lanigan to Las Vegas, where for an hour straight he stood at the roulette table and placed chips on number thirty-four. ("It never came up," said Lanigan. "Not once.") He helped finalize a deal to bring Chicago an Arena Football League team in 2001. He confided regularly in his fellow Roundhouse owners. Years earlier Payton had agreed to make appearances on behalf of Bridgestone/Firestone. Now that Payton was sick Gamauf expected him to remain in Chicago and rest. "I called him once to see how he was doing," Gamauf said. "Walter said to me, 'Gam, I don't want to sit home and look at the walls. I have to stay active and keep my mind fresh. I want to keep doing engagements.'"

Gamauf lined up a series of speaking opportunities. "Walter was 160 pounds when I saw him," he said. "He needed different suits because his shoulders had gotten so small, and there were times when he was doubled over in pain. But he never walked onto the stage showing any weakness. He was the same old Walter Payton, and people loved him."

In particular, Gamauf treasured a trip the two took to New York in April to speak at a dealership, Wholesale Tire, on Long Island. On the night before the event, the men talked for two and a half hours inside Gamauf's hotel room. They laughed and cried and swapped stories. Whether Payton consciously realized it or not, he was preparing to die. "Walter either let you in or he didn't," Gamauf said. "He let me in."

The following morning, Payton gave one of the most moving speeches of his life. "Hell yes, I'm scared," he told the two hundred attendees, "but I'm not going to sit here and worry about it. The Lord's got it in His hands, and I'm going to say all the prayers I can and I appreciate all the prayers everybody else can say.

"Now let's talk about cars."

CHAPTER 26

# THE END

ON THE AFTERNOON OF APRIL 12, 1999, MATT SUHEY PICKED UP HIS OLD teammate in his Mercedes 430 and drove him to Wrigley Field. It was the day of the Chicago Cubs' ninety-seventh home opener, and Walter Payton was scheduled to throw out the first pitch.

En route to the ballpark, an excited Payton turned to Suhey. "Maybe I'll do this again next year," he said, "when I nip this thing."

There was nothing for Suhey to say. When the prognosis was still in doubt, he could laugh as Payton cracked lines like, "This is gonna be another *Brian's Song*—only here the brother dies in the end." By this point, though, Suhey was well aware that, hope and prayer and optimism be damned, his friend was dying. "The cancer was severe," he said. "His odds were not good."

Five months earlier, when he first learned of Payton's illness, Suhey dedicated himself to being by his side as often as possible. Though the two had shared a nice friendship through the years, it was never an overwhelmingly close one. They spoke every so often, partnered in some business dealings, traded holiday cards, hugged when they happened to be at the same place at the same time. That was the extent. When Payton became ill, however, something in Suhey snapped. He had blocked for his friend for eight years, and now he needed to block once again. "Matt was loyal to Walter," said Mike Lanigan, their friend and business partner. "Fiercely loyal." Suhey accompanied Payton on many of his trips to Mayo, consulted with the physicians, served as a buffer between former teammates anxious to visit and a star determined to maintain some semblance of privacy. "Matt," said Ginny Quirk, "was right there when Walter needed him most. What better compliment can you give a person?"

Payton was escorted into Wrigley Field through the media gate, where he was met by a handful of club officials. They presented him with a pin-striped Cubs jersey, which he slipped over his T-shirt, as well as a light blue cap. Before delivering the pitch, Payton ran into Jerry Vainisi, the former Bears general manager, whose law firm owned a box at the stadium. By now Payton's weight had dropped to 170 pounds. His famously chiseled physique was skin dangling off of bone. "I was stunned," said Vainisi. "He was a shadow of the Walter Payton I remembered."

When Payton was introduced by Paul Friedman, the Cubs' public address announcer, he strode to the mound, removed his jacket to reveal the jersey, crossed himself, and spun his hat backward. The 39,092 fans at the sold-out stadium stood and cheered. The sun was bright, the temperature forty-nine degrees. A gentle breeze blew across the field. Sammy Sosa, the team's star right fielder, crouched behind home plate, pounded his mitt, and waited for the pitch. With all the energy he could muster, Payton reached back and threw a looping strike. Sosa jogged to the mound, and the men embraced in a bear hug. "Walter Payton, we're praying for him," Mark Grace, the Cubs first baseman, said afterward. "I hope he treats this disease like an oncoming defensive back."

Walter Payton *wanted* to believe. He was, at his core, a professional athlete, and professional athletes—as Grace's words illustrated—are trained to uncover a way to overcome everything. It was Mike Ditka, the gritty coach, who initially greeted news of Payton's illness by insisting his old halfback would "find a way to beat this"—as if *this* were an opposing linebacker moving in for the tackle.

The harsh truth, however, was now impossible to ignore. On the day after the first pitch, Payton had been scheduled to speak to the Machinery/Materials Conference and Exposition at Chicago's McCormick Place. That morning, he could barely lift himself out of bed. "He was too taxed to make the trip," Quirk told the *Tribune*. "He had a very big day yesterday."

For most Chicagoans, Walter Payton standing atop the Wrigley Field mound would be a final image of the iconic hero. The summer months were harsh ones for Payton. On May 10, when his CA 19-9 levels were frighteningly high, Mayo's doctors performed exploratory surgery. The results were devastating. The cancer had spread to his lymph nodes. "The malignancy was very advanced," Gores later explained, "and progressed very rapidly." Should the chemotherapy and radiation treatments he was receiving at Mayo fail to work, Payton would be dead within a half-year's time. This, there was no debating.

"The lowest moment came after that diagnosis," said Quirk. "Dr. Gores told him there was a three-week protocol where he was supposed to be at Mayo Monday through Friday for different treatments. At the start of the third week Walter called and said, 'Ginny, get me out of here. I'm coming home.' He kind of threw in the towel. It was too much.

"When I spoke with Dr. Gores about Walter's decision, he cried. I'll never forget that."

Payton's final public appearance came on July 25, when he attended a ceremony at the Destiny Church in Hoffman Estates (Walter stayed for fifteen minutes, leaving when the pain became too great). He forced himself to eat, and when his appetite gave out he was fed intravenously. His weight dropped by the day, and his optimism crumbled with it. Payton became increasingly downcast and despondent, and a man known for his moodiness turned even moodier. Not that anyone could blame him. The trips to Mayo for chemotherapy and radiation were excruciating, and Suhey still cringes at the memory of Payton's suffering. "For a guy who could take so much pain on the football field, this was a real test," Suhey said. "I've never seen anything like it. Just nightmarish."

Payton reassured people that he was on the waiting list for a new liver, and he expected the pager to go off "any day now." Truth be told, there was no pager. There never had been a pager. "He didn't want us feeling sorry for him," said Scott Ascher, his restaurant partner. "He wanted everyone to think he would be all right. It wasn't about him. It was about us. Making *us* feel better." One day, while sitting at home, Rick Telander, a noteworthy *Sun-Times* columnist, was surprised to receive a call from Payton. He was hosting a dinner for a handful of former Bear teammates at the Roundhouse, and wanted to know if Telander had an interest in attending. When the guests—Telander, Suhey, Calvin Thomas, and Thomas Sanders—sat down, Payton pulled up a chair next to the writer. Telander was nibbling on a plate of french fries. "Can I just have one fry?" Payton asked. Telander pushed the plate his way. "Walter tasted it, but he couldn't eat it," Telander said. "It was crushing."

Payton held a couple of more dinners for old Bears, and while it was never stated, the purpose was to say good-bye. "I was there with about thirty other guys," said Jimbo Covert, the star offensive lineman. "Walter took time to go around to everybody personally and grab you and say, 'What are you doing?'—just getting the down-low on how you'd been. Can you imagine how strong of a person he had to have been to do that? He knew he was going to die. He absolutely knew . . ."

By late July, Payton's health took a terrible turn. He had been living at his home in West Dundee, but when his kidneys began to fail, Payton moved back into the house at 34 Mudhank, which—even after leaving ten years earlier—remained the most comfortable place he'd ever known. Because of the presence of Jarrett and Brittney, Walter never fully divorced himself from the residence. He came and went as he pleased, still used the fishing pond and the shooting range and a cozy zebra-print chair. In particular, Payton enjoyed the garden room, which was located in the basement and filled with plants. "It was a great place to meditate," said Ken Gallt, the designer of the room. "When Walter died Connie let me know how much he loved it in there."

In the ensuing years Connie has told warm stories about those final months, when the family came together as one. The recollections are, at best, gross exaggerations. Walter had to be convinced to return to 34 Mudhank, and initially did so because he knew Luna Picart, the beloved nanny, would once again be cooking his meals (and if anyone could get Walter to eat, it was Miss Luna). Walter never shared a bed with Connie, instead alternating between the rooms of Jarrett and Brittney. "He would migrate," said Jarrett. "At the time I didn't get it, but now I think it's so cool. He wanted to share himself with us." Walter spent many of his first few full-time weeks back at the house either napping or sitting on the front porch alongside Quirk, his omnipresent assistant. "It was really a strange time," Quirk said. "Walter was in and out. He was coherent, but he wasn't the normal Walter. We'd sit out there in the summer sun. We'd sit in two chairs and he kept saying, 'I don't know what you're so worried about, Ginny. I don't know what you're so worried about.'"

Quirk fought to hold back the tears. Payton's insistence of no negative news had left him in the dark when it came to details—but not to the grand picture. He certainly grasped the bleakness. "Because this is serious, Walter," she would say. "Because . . ."

Payton heard none of it. "Relax," he'd say. "I've got it covered."

Suhey stopped by on most days, and often took Payton on drives around the neighborhood. With the windows rolled down, Payton could lean back and soak in the breeze. Sometimes, they'd sit together in the car and listen to *The Monsters of the Midday*, the show he had cohosted with Dan Jiggetts and Mike North. "He even called in one time," said Jiggetts. "Just to say hello."

On occasion Suhey or Quirk or Mark Alberts, a business partner, or even Connie would take Walter to Dairy Queen or Kentucky Fried Chicken. He liked heading to Michigan Avenue in downtown Chicago and seeing the cow statues. "One time we got stuck in traffic and he started getting pains in his stomach," said Alberts. "Walter would try and rock himself until the pain went away. That time, I had to turn off the expressway and take side streets back to his home."

Every so often, on Payton's good days, a surprise guest was allowed to enter the house. Sometimes it'd be Scott Ascher, one of his co-owners of the Roundhouse. Other times Mike Lanigan, a business partner, might appear. Jay Hilgenberg, a teammate for seven seasons with the Bears, came once. "A bunch of the guys stopped by, and Walter and I talked a little golf," he said. "Walter asked me why I wasn't coaching with the Bears. I said, 'Walter, how about you just get that liver and get healthy, and we'll play some golf together?'"

Payton scowled. "Hey," he snapped, "I'm healthy!"

He wasn't.

"I felt about this big," said Hilgenberg, holding an index finger and thumb less than an inch apart. "That was the last time I ever saw him."

Payton's illness did at least lead to an important reconciliation. Ever since that day in 1985 when he confronted his teammate about his infidelities, Mike Singletary had been persona non grata in Payton's life. Now retired as a player and working as a motivational speaker, Singletary—a devoutly religious man whose father had been a Pentecostal preacher—reached out to Payton, via Suhey, in hopes of easing his burden and reintroducing Jesus Christ into his life. By the beginning of fall Singletary was a regular at 34 Mudhank, often conversing at length with Payton about life and death and football and love and eternal salvation. Mostly, Singletary talked and Payton, lying in bed, quietly listened. "I never heard him say, 'Why me?'" Singletary said. "I want to tell you, I know I would have been saying, 'Why me? Why me? There are other guys out there killing people and doing this—why me?' I never heard Walter say that."

· · ·

"I need to see you."

The words were spoken by Rob Chudzinski, the tight ends coach for the University of Miami football team. On the other end of the telephone line was Jarrett Payton, the Hurricanes' freshman halfback. He was sitting in his dormitory room.

"OK, Coach," Jarrett said. "I'll be right over."

Upon entering Chudzinski's office, Jarrett sat down and heard the words he had hoped would never come. "You have to go home right now to be with your family," Chudzinski said. "Your father wants you there."

That night, October 28, 1999, Jarrett boarded a flight from Miami International to O'Hare. He knew few of the details, only that his father was in Waukegan's Midwestern Regional Medical Center and nearing his last breath.

"I hated hospitals, just like my dad did," said Jarrett. "So instead of immediately going to see him, I went home, got one of my dad's cars, and just drove around. Before I left for college, Dad liked to drive around with me for hours. Just the two of us driving. So that's what I did now. This might sound strange, but driving that day, all alone, I felt like he was hanging with me. It was just the two of us, doing what we loved."

The preceding few weeks had been rough on Walter. There were several emergency trips to the hospital. No longer able to eat, he was receiving nourishment solely via an intravenous tube. The majority of his time was spent in bed atop an enormous heating pad, and he kept his finger permanently affixed to the morphine pump by his side. "In that last week or two he looked awful," said Quirk. "His nails were long and yellow. His beard had grown in. I had never seen him with scruff. Ever. This was a guy who would shave a couple of times per day if it fit the need. I had never seen him with a beard. It had grown in gray. He looked like a street person. He was in a hospital bed at that point. The bed was put in Connie's bedroom, but only because he had no say."

There are people from Payton's life who like Quirk and others who considered her to be pushy and overly eager to please. All seem to agree, however, that during Payton's last stand she had his best interests at heart. Quirk had spent nearly fourteen years glued to Walter's side, and even as he drove her insane with nonstop calls, she continued to love and defend him.

As Quirk watched her boss and friend fade away, she found herself disgusted. Not by his physical appearance, but by the behavior of Connie.

Payton had asked to come home from Midwestern Regional Medical Center to enjoy a last meal of take-out Chinese, and on October 29, 1999, his wish was granted. A handful of media outlets reported that Payton was in a critical state, and two sports talk stations, New York's WFAN and WYSP of

Philadelphia, erroneously told listeners that he had died. "Walter probably weighed a hundred pounds at the end," Quirk said. "You wouldn't have believed it was him. He had more pride than anyone I've ever met, and there's no way he would have wanted people to see him like that. But Connie led a parade past his body. Anybody who wanted to come through there, it was, 'Oh, no problem. Come see him.'"

Added Kimm Tucker: "I'm guessing Connie had nine different preachers come by to see Walter—men he'd never before met. It was as if there was this rush of everyone wanting to say they saved Walter Payton's soul."

According to Quirk, she finally confronted Connie during Walter's last week. Through the years, she had resisted any temptations to get involved in a truly odd relationship. Now, enough was enough. "If he does snap out of this," Quirk told Connie, "he's going to kill you. Because what you're doing to his dignity is atrocious."

. . .

On the night of Sunday, October 31, 1999, Jarrett Payton took another long drive before coming home to bid good night to his father. When the son walked into the bedroom, Walter—dazed, weakened, near death—lifted his head ever so slightly. His brother, Eddie, and sister, Pam, were in the room, as was Alyne, Walter's mother. "Where have you been?" Walter whispered.

"I was out," replied Jarrett, "looking at some motorcycles."

Without uttering another word, Walter gave his son the glare from hell. "I'm joking," Jarrett said. "Dad, I'm joking."

Brittney Payton was at a Halloween party hosted by her friend, Molly. Fourteen years old and a freshman at Barrington High School, Brittney was trying her best to maintain normalcy. "My closest girlfriends were there," Brittney said, "and I just broke down and I was crying to them about my dad and how sick he was. All my friends were lying on the floor with me, in a big group huddle, and they were crying with me."

The following afternoon, around twelve thirty, Brittney was sitting in class when she was summoned to the principal's office. Miss Luna was there, waiting to bring her home. "She didn't say anything," Brittney said. "Just that I needed to go." Upon reaching the house, Brittney found Connie and Jarrett in her bedroom, crying and hugging.

"Do you want to see Dad one last time?" mother asked daughter.

Brittney nodded.

Walter Payton was all alone. His eyes and mouth were closed. His skin was cool to the touch. "I hugged him," Brittney said. "I told him I loved him. I was sad, but a part of me was relieved."

For nearly a year, a man accustomed to pain had endured unspeakable suffering.

"Now," said Brittney, "he was at peace."

Walter Payton, age forty-six, was dead.

CHAPTER 27

LEGACY

ON THE MORNING OF APRIL 5, 2000, CONNIE PAYTON SERVED AS THE KEY-note speaker for the community prayer breakfast at the Glendale Lakes Golf Club in Glendale Heights, Illinois.

Standing before a crowd of approximately a hundred people, Connie spoke of the love she and her husband had shared for twenty-three years of marriage. Through it all, she said, the Lord was present to guide and coax and lead through the highs and lows. "God doesn't give us more than we can handle," she said. "I have no regrets. I can really say I'm at peace with everything, even his passing. Even on the day he died, he was ready. I couldn't be upset."

The words were moving. When she finished, Connie received a standing ovation. "She's one of the most heroic people I've ever heard about," said Mary Jo Sobotka, a spectator who left the event with tears streaming down her cheeks.

Indeed.

Though few question Connie Payton's sincerity when it comes to her faith in God, some of those who knew Walter well—*really well*—remain baffled by the way she handled his illness, and especially the aftermath of his passing. When Walter decided to ask someone to serve as executor of his estate, he first approached Ginny Quirk. When she suggested he turn elsewhere, Payton asked the trustworthy Matt Suhey. Connie, *his wife*, was never considered. "It's sort of like there's the truth," said Linda Conley, a longtime friend of the Paytons, "and then there's Connie's version of the truth. They're pretty wide apart."

Three months before Walter passed, Conley invited Connie her to her house for a conversation. The two had been close for a long time, and Conley felt compelled to finally share an important detail. When Connie arrived, Conley told her about Nigel, the out-of-wedlock son who was now fourteen years old. "I think you deserve the chance to confront Walter about this before he dies," Conley said. "You have that right."

Connie's response stunned Conley. "She told me she'd once asked Walter if he had any other children, and he said no," she recalled. "Connie said she believed him. I don't see how she could have, but she said she believed him. Maybe she just didn't want to believe the entire truth, because it killed her whole narrative."

· · ·

Walter Payton took his final breath right around noon on a Monday afternoon. As is the case with most passings, a prolonged numbness ensued. Family members and friends grieved, former teammates were contacted, the Chicago media was alerted. President Bill Clinton issued a statement, marveling how Payton, "faced his illness with the same grit and determination that he showed every week on the football field." As the news began to make its way across talk radio, one listener after another called in, sharing stories and memories of a man who ranked alongside Ernie Banks as a Windy City icon. Bob Armstrong, an Oswego, Illinois, resident and lifelong Bears fan, was driving past the Roundhouse restaurant when he learned Payton had died. "With tears in my eyes I pulled over to visit the little museum they had inside," Armstrong said. "I knew the hostess, and she said, 'Bob, what brings you here?'"

"I just heard," Armstrong said, "and I wanted to pay my respects."

"Heard what?" she replied.

"Walter," Armstrong said. "He's dead."

Silence.

The *Chicago Daily Herald* asked readers to send in their best Payton anecdotes. A former Burger King drive-thru worker named Phil Lawitz recalled the time he screwed up Payton's order, but still landed an autographed napkin. Sue Matthews told of Payton passing a little boy his Super Bowl ring through a crowd at the Chicago Auto Show. "I had always admired Walter Payton as a role model for children," she wrote, "but from that moment on I also looked at him as a truly gentle man."

Quirk had worked with Payton for fourteen years. She was now five months pregnant and, upon receiving the call from Matt Suhey, in a state of shock. "How could he be dead?" she said later. "Even though we all saw it coming . . . it still didn't seem real. Walter Payton no longer alive?" After collecting herself, Quirk realized there was nobody inside the home at 34 Mudhank who would take the initiative and handle arrangements. She went ahead and called the Davenport Family Funeral Home in Barrington, booked the date and time, even picked out the blue suit Payton would wear for his family's final private viewing. She spent fifteen hundred dollars on flowers and paid a handful of moonlighting police officers thirty-five hundred dollars to provide extra security in the coming days.

When Quirk arrived at the house, she was disheartened to hear Connie and Alyne, Walter's mother, discussing burial options. "Alyne was a devout Baptist, and apparently Baptists don't believe in cremation," said Quirk. "But Walter had told me, in very direct terms, that he was to be cremated, not buried. He even wrote it in his will. The truth was, in fifteen years I never knew Walter as someone who willingly went to church. Ever. He was not a religious man, and he wanted to be cremated."

When Quirk told the family of Walter's wishes, they resisted. There was a lovely cemetery a stone's throw away from South Barrington, and beneath an oak tree Walter could . . .

"Guys, I'll help you with everything, but I'll go to war on this," Quirk said. "He's going to be cremated. He wished it. He wrote it. The least we can do is honor that request."

The family begrudgingly acquiesced, and the funeral parlor agreed to perform the cremation. When it came to the memorial service, however, Connie had her own ideas. Although Payton spent many of his final days staring up from his bed at a vulture-like gaggle of preachers and reverends, he was hardly a man of deep faith. Did he believe in God? Yes. Did he believe that Jesus was Lord? Perhaps. Had he lived what any rational human being would describe as a wholesome, Christ-like existence? Not in years. The young Walter Payton who attended team Bible studies and spoke glowingly of God's magical ways had existed a long time ago. On his deathbed, a medicated Payton listened as Keith Russell Lee, pastor of the Destiny Church and Walter's self-described "spiritual coach," utter the words "Jesus" and "heaven."

Does that make a man a believer? Apparently so.

The funeral was to be held on Friday, November 5, at Connie's place of worship, the Life Changers International Church in Barrington Hills.

Because of Payton's celebrity status, it would be an invitation-only affair. Quirk consulted with Kimm Tucker and Ken Valdiserri, the Bears vice president of marketing and broadcasting, and the three compiled the guest list. Even though Payton disdained politics and barely knew the men, Governor George Ryan and Chicago mayor Richard M. Daley were must-haves. So, Quirk initially thought, was O. J. Simpson, Payton's gridiron rival who, in the years since his retirement, had gone on to fame as an actor, football commentator, and alleged murderer. When Marcus Allen, the legendary Raiders and Chiefs halfback, said he wouldn't attend if Simpson were present, the Juice was left off the list. The most complicated issue had to do with Lita Gonzalez, the girlfriend of nearly eleven years. On the day after Payton's death, Gonzalez called Kimm Tucker to find out when she should fly in for the funeral. Tucker nearly dropped the phone. "Lita, I don't care what relationship you had with Walter," she said. "If you come the world will look at you as the mistress. I don't care that he didn't live with Connie. When the rubber hits the road she'll be the widow and you'll be the mistress, and people despise the mistress."

Translation: You're not invited.

The funeral began at ten A.M., and had Walter Payton been alive he surely would have cringed. The presiding clergyman was Gregory Dickow, the church's thirty-five-year-old founder. Decked out in a snazzy black suit, his dark hair slicked back like a used-car salesman, Dickow paced back and forth, Bible in hand, and spoke loudly and knowingly of a man he hardly knew. "Five years after retiring from the NFL, Walter Payton was voted unanimously into the Hall of *Fame*," Dickow said, placing emphasis on end of his words. "Six years after that Walter Payton was voted unanimously into the hall of *faith*. But the hall of faith he was voted into was not based on your vote, not based on my vote, not based on anybody's vote except three people—the father, the son, and the holy spirit. They voted him in because he had accepted Jesus Christ into his life as his lord and savior."

"It was embarrassing," said Quirk. "Just embarrassing."

The service picked up when Dickow sat down. Quirk had asked Jarrett Payton, Eddie Payton, John Madden, Mike Singletary, and Mike Ditka—men who actually knew and cherished Walter—to speak on his behalf, and they were all spectacular. Jarrett recalled a loving father. Madden and Ditka recalled a warrior-like football player. Singletary recalled a gentle man with a golden heart.

The most memorable words were uttered by Eddie, Walter's older brother, occasional hunting partner, and lifelong rival. Depending on the source, Walter and Eddie were either somewhat close or not close at all. They were, however, brothers who grew up sharing a bedroom; who both knew what it was to be young and black in Columbia, Mississippi, in the 1960s; who both excelled in football at Jackson State and in the NFL. A love existed, and Eddie, now the golf coach at Jackson State, was filled with despair as he stepped to the podium. "A great man once said it's not a celebration unless you have a group of friends," he said. "This truly is a celebration because all of Walter's friends are here. As late as last night I wondered, one, if I'd be able to do this, and two, how long I'd be able to do it before breaking up. I asked Connie, 'What do you think Walter would want me to say?' She said, 'Just wing it.' And five minutes later she came back and said, 'Look, let me explain what 'Just wing it' means. Keep it clean and keep it short.' So I'll try that."

Eddie thanked Walter's family members and friends, spoke passionately about how much Chicago meant to his brother, then offered up a story that, years later, the day's attendees still retell:

[Walter would] probably look at me and say, "Slick, tell me one to make me feel good." And I am probably a jokester, not a prankster. So the one I like best, and I didn't know which it would be until everybody that passed by [today] kept saying, "Man, I looked at you and you looked just like Walter." Or said, "Man, I thought you were Walter. Y'all are the spitting image." Obviously those are people who couldn't tell true beauty when they were looking at it. But that's always had its advantages and disadvantages.

I was driving to south Mississippi, to the rural community to speak at an athletic banquet, and I stopped to get some gas in my car and the attendant came out. As he was pumping gas he was kind of staring at me. I kind of looked at him and smiled. He says, "You're that Payton boy, ain't you?" I said, "Yes, sir, I am." He said—rural Mississippi, now . . . "I followed your career for a long time. I watched you when you ran up and down the field at Columbia, Mississippi, and I was a big fan." I said, "I appreciate that." He said, "You don't understand." He says, "I watched you at Jackson State College and I thought you were the best." I said, "I appreciate it."

And he was about to finish and fill up, and I started walking to him. He said, "You don't understand. I watched you play in that professional league and you was about the best I've ever seen." I said, "Thank you, I appreciate it." He says, "No, you really don't understand, I am your biggest fan." He says, "To show you what a big fan of yours I am, Walter, I'm gonna give you this tank of gas for free." So I did the only thing I could do. As I got in my car, I looked him straight in the eye, and I thanked him, and I told him if he was ever in Chicago, look me up and I'll get him two tickets.

. . .

One day after the funeral, the Chicago Bears hosted a public memorial service at Soldier Field. Between fifteen thousand and twenty thousand spectators showed up, many with signs offering sentiments like THANKS, PAYTON, FOR THE SWEET MEMORIES and YOU'VE TOUCHED SO MANY. The Sweet Holy Spirit Choir sang joyfully, and the thirty-yard line on each side of the stadium was repainted into a 34 in the team colors of orange, blue, and white. The play clock was frozen at Payton's number. "In some respects," wrote J. A. Adande of the *Los Angeles Times*, "this was just like so many other days, when the only reason to go to Soldier Field was Walter Payton."

Family members, former teammates, and the entire 1999 Bears roster entered Soldier Field with roses in hand. "In this stadium where he glowed, we wanted an encore," said Jesse Jackson, who maintained a friendship with Payton. "Walter flew like an eagle, he flew high. We have lost Sweetness, but there is a lot of 'Sweetness' left. The light did not go out. This light called 'Sweetness' belongs to the heavens, belongs to the ages."

"I remember this guy playing on this field and leaving it on this field time after time," added Dan Hampton, the legendary defensive lineman whose voice quivered as he spoke. "I have a little girl (who's) four years old. Ten years from now, when she asks me about the Chicago Bears, I'll tell her about a championship and I'll tell her about great teams, great teammates, and great coaches, and how great it was to be a part of it.

"But the first thing I'll tell her about is Walter Payton."

For Jarrett and Brittney, the event proved much more difficult—and, in the long run, enriching—than the funeral. Emotionally drained from the previous few weeks, Walter's children stepped onto the field, saw the hundreds upon hundreds of No. 34 jerseys, heard the unyielding cheers—and felt whole. The funeral had been more of a show. This was gritty and heart-felt and real. "I just cried and cried," said Brittney. "I couldn't stop crying."

Here, at Soldier Field, Walter Payton had been his absolute happiest. In his uniform, on the green turf, there were no business transactions or marital difficulties or out-of-wedlock children. Here, Peter Payton didn't die in jail and Alyne Payton didn't work three jobs. Here, Walter wasn't ignored by colleges because of the blackness of his skin. There was no racism; no liver disease or bile duct cancer. He didn't have to try and come off as someone he wasn't. He could be himself. He could run free.

Ever since Payton's death, people had been trying their best to define him in *their* terms. The religious leaders who had only recently met him. The wife who didn't live with him. The reporters who were usually kept at bay. Within the confines of a crumbling stadium, however, the real Walter Payton could still be found. Even in his death, it took only a closed pair of eyes and the texture of a brisk Lake Michigan wind to visualize Sweetness rolling around tackle, spinning past the outside linebacker, and slamming his elbow into a defensive back's chin.

The fans are standing, cheering, chanting "Walter! Walter! Walter!" He pops up off the ground and jogs back toward the huddle, a blinding smile peeking out from beneath his face mask.

Walter Payton is home.

CHAPTER 28

# AFTERWORD

THROUGHOUT THE WORLD OF PROFESSIONAL SPORTS, LEGACY IS A TRICKY thing.

For most of the athletes who wear a uniform of some sort, legacy simply does not exist. You're a rookie. Then you're a veteran. Then you retire. Then you vanish. *Poof!* Gone, as if your career never really existed to begin with.

Of the hundreds upon hundreds of players Walter Payton called teammates over his thirteen NFL seasons, how many do we remember? How many would we recognize strolling through an airport or sitting at a table inside Burger King? Truth be told, how many would we recognize if they walked up to our front doors, knocked, and said, "Hello, I'm [FILL IN THE NAME]?"

Walter Payton was different.

*Is* different.

Twenty-four years after his final game and twelve years following his death at age forty-six, Payton has attained an iconic spot atop the sports pantheon. Whose image can be seen in the background whenever one tunes into the NFL Network's studio show? Whose name is attached to the award for the NFL's Man of the Year, as well as the most outstanding offensive player in the Division I Football Championship Subdivision? Who is the namesake behind one of Chicago's top college preparatory high schools? Whose foundation continues to raise funds for abused, neglected, and underprivileged children in the state of Illinois? Whose nickname—*Sweetness*—is, within the context of sports, as identifiable as Toyota or IBM or KFC?

Walter Payton.

Truth be told, Payton probably isn't the greatest pure running back in NFL history. Jim Brown was more skilled. Emmitt Smith gained more yards (he broke Payton's record in 2002). Earl Campbell was stronger, Gale Sayers was faster, Barry Sanders was more elusive. Throughout his career, Payton was routinely overshadowed by his peers in the same position. He never matched the splendor of O. J. Simpson or the grace of Eric Dickerson. Marcus Allen boasted a regalness Payton lacked. Billy Sims entered the league with greater hype.

Payton, however, touched people. They identified with him, related to him, understood him. Coming out of tiny Jackson State, Payton was far from the collegiate golden child, running before seventy thousand fans and national television audiences. Playing for the oft-miserable Bears, he took brutal shots, but refused to stay down for long. He was a workman, lacking only a hard hat and lunch pail. He was never overwhelmingly fast or especially big, but he fought for everything he gained. He was a trooper. A survivor. A dogged workhorse. You loved Walter Payton because you appreciated Walter Payton. Unlike Dickerson, he rarely whined. Unlike Simpson, he never preened. "Do you think they still wear Jim Brown jerseys in Cleveland?" said Mike Ditka. "No. Do they still wear Paul Hornung jerseys in Green Bay? No. Johnny Unitas jerseys in Baltimore? No. You know why, at Bears games, you'll see hundreds of Walter Payton jerseys? Because people know what he was all about. They know that when Walter put on his uniform and the game started, he was going to give everything he had, no matter what. That's awfully powerful."

In the modern history of sports, Payton's smile is rivaled only by the one flashed by Magic Johnson. It seemed to emit its own energy, and the radiance only intensified as children approached for an autograph or a high-five.

Was Walter Payton perfect? Far from it. He was flawed, as all of us are. He was prone to terrible lapses in judgment and often treated women as objects, not people. He ignored his out-of-wedlock son, blew much of his money, struggled with a form of depression that led to suicidal thoughts and threats. The confident swagger with which he walked often served as a front for deep-seated insecurities and a man crying out for help.

In other words, he was human.

As I wrap up work on this book, that's what I love most about Payton. Yes, he was a superstar. And yes, his death—as was the case with celebrities ranging from James Dean and Marilyn Monroe to Jimi Hendricks and Shannon Hoon—served to freeze him in time, forever a Chicago Bear, forever young and strong and vibrant.

What makes a person truly unique, however, is his shortcomings, and how he chooses to deal with them. Through all his highs and all his lows, Walter Payton continued to possess a rare sense of humanity. Having now covered sports for sixteen years, I've seen an endless stream of athletes treat their fans as eczema-like irritations. They walk through the world as if encased in a Plexiglas bubble, immune to the fact that a minute's worth of attention will often never be forgotten.

Until the day he died, Payton refused to lose sight of this.

Had I so desired, I could have written a seven-hundred-page book consisting solely of *You're-not-gonna-believe-this* stories of Payton's goodness. The time he met a University of Central Florida defensive back named Todd Burks on an airplane and hooked him up with a tryout with the Bears. The time he pulled aside a Jackson State running back named William Arnold and offered the pep talk of a lifetime. The times he gave away autographed helmets, autographed footballs, autographed pictures to one charity or another.

Here at the end, however, I want to conclude with my personal favorite.

In 1984, Brandon Peacy was a twelve-year-old student at Jack Benny Middle School in Waukegan, Illinois. One day his father, Bill, surprised him by saying, "Grab some football cards, we're going on a trip." Forty-five minutes later Brandon found himself at the Chicago Bears' training facility in Lake Forest. "My dad knew someone who worked for the Bears," Peacy said. "We were given a tour of the facility—the locker room, the weight room. I was blown away."

Brandon strolled toward the field, where he stood on the sideline, playing with a football. He heard a high-pitched voice—"Hey, buddy! Hey, buddy! Come here, buddy!" It was Walter Payton.

The running back was standing in a circle with Jim McMahon, Steve Fuller, and Matt Suhey. He asked Brandon his name and introduced him to the players. "Brandon, you don't have to be nervous," he said. "I'm just a guy." Before Payton headed off for an adjacent field, he removed the wristbands from his arms and tossed them to Brandon. "Great meeting you!" he said. "Have a great time!"

"Best day of my life," Brandon said. "I was floating on air."

Eleven years later, twenty-three-year-old Brandon Peacy was working as a producer for WKRS, a five-thousand-watt radio station out of Wauke-gan. A couple of days before the October 22, 1995, Oilers–Bears game at Soldier Field, Peacy returned to Lake Forest to pick up press credentials at Halas Hall. While waiting for assistance, he spotted Walter Payton, now forty-two and eight years retired, walking down a hallway.

"Hey, how ya doing?" Payton said.

"Hi, Walter," Peacy replied. "It's good to see you."

The two chatted for a couple of minutes, when Payton said, "I have this thing for faces—something tells me I met you before."

"You did," Peacy said. "But I was just a kid, so you probably don't . . ."

"Try me," he replied.

Peacy told Payton the story, how he was a twelve-year-old boy in 1984, and it was during a practice, and McMahon and Suhey and Fuller and . . .

"Were you with a real tall guy?" Payton asked. "A tall guy wearing a green hat?"

Bill, Brandon's father, is six foot seven. He had, indeed, sported a green baseball cap.

"Uh . . . yeah," Peacy said.

"So you must have been the little kid," Payton said. "The one in the purple shirt."

Peacy was dumbfounded. His jaw dropped. His eyes widened. All he could say was, "Holy shit." Walter Payton broke up laughing, then jabbed Brandon in the arm. "I tell everyone I have a great memory," Payton said, "but nobody believes me.

"I'm glad you know the truth about me."

## WHAT BECAME OF THE MAIN CHARACTERS

**Connie Payton**, Walter's wife of twenty-three years, still lives in Chi-cago, where she heads the Walter and Connie Payton Foundation and speaks glowingly of her late husband. In 2008, she married Michael Strot-ter, a native Chicagoan and the CEO of Advanced Medical Imaging Cen-ters. She is, according to her children, comfortable and happy in her role as gatekeeper of her late husband's legacy.

· · ·

After graduating from the University of Miami in 2004, **Jarrett Payton** went on to play, briefly, with the Tennessee Titans, the Amsterdam Admirals (of NFL Europe), and the Canadian Football League's Montreal Alouettes and Toronto Argonauts. He now hosts a weekly Internet radio show in his native hometown and is working toward becoming a hip-hop artist and comedian. Of the fourteen tattoos that adorn his body, five are depictions of his father. When, in 2009, he married Trisha George, the wedding took place on March 4—3/4, in honor of his dad. The reception was held at Soldier Field. Should he one day be blessed with a son, Jarrett already has a name picked out. "Tres Quatro," he says. "I love that."

When people speak with Jarrett, they often feel as if they are in the presence of his father. The smile is the same, the gregariousness toward others eerily familiar. Just as his hero loved reaching out toward strangers, so does Jarrett. Shortly after Walter died, Jarrett said he was faced with a choice—he could either run away from the comparisons, or embrace them. It was, he says, an easy decision. "I want to hear about my dad every chance I can get," he said. "I know this sounds crazy, but I believe he's watching down on me, guiding me. Whenever I look at the clock, it's 1:34, 2:34, 3:34. The number's everywhere which, to me, means he's everywhere."

. . .

Though softer and less engaging than her older brother, **Brittney Payton** is also a local media personality. A graduate of DePaul University, she now works for WGN as one of the hosts of a TV show, *Chicago's Best*. Like both of her brothers, Brittney looks very much like her father, from the almond-shaped brown eyes to the high cheekbones. "There are a lot of days I'm sad my dad isn't here," she says. "Just because of all the things he's missing. When my brother got married it was such a happy day, but it also hurt, because there was a real void."

. . .

**Eddie Payton** has been the golf coach at Jackson State University since 1986. In his time with the program, he has emerged as one of the nation's top collegiate coaches, leading the Tigers to 22 men's and 14 women's SWAC titles. "There's not a day when I don't think about Walter," he says. "But I'm not sad, because I know he's in a better place."

Sadly, Eddie is largely estranged from Connie, Jarrett, and Brittney. Though they talk every few years, mistrust reigns. Eddie and Connie operate their own Walter Payton–themed charities, and the animosity is palpable. Says Brittney: "I think my uncle and that side of the family all felt as if they were owed something from my dad. Even during his career, I think they felt like they were owed something from him and they didn't get it while he was alive and so they really expected they would get something from him in the end. I think they had a lot of issues with that. I don't think he had the best relationship with them, and I think that filtered over to me and my brother because he never made it a point for us to reach out to them."

· · ·

**Lita Gonzalez**, Walter's longtime girlfriend, still lives on the East Coast, and she continues to work as a flight attendant. She has never married, and has worked hard to put the drama with Walter Payton out of her mind. "It's painful," she says. "Everything that happened, the way his life ended—I don't want to think about it anymore. I've moved on."

· · ·

**Bud Holmes**, Walter's agent for the entirety of his career, still lives in Pedal, Mississippi. He is retired, but stays involved in local high school and college sports. Like Eddie, he is no longer on regular speaking terms with Connie. "I like Connie," says Holmes. "But she's gone out of her way to cut off the people who know the truth about Walter. She's probably smart to do that. There's an image to keep up."

· · ·

**Ginny Quirk**, Walter's coworker for fourteen years, lives in Illinois. She is married to Mark Alberts, Walter's former business partner. The couple has two children. The Payton family has accused Quirk of forging Walter's signature and then selling "autographed" Payton items for large amounts of money. "Completely untrue," she says. "I don't even want to dignify that with any sort of response. It's character assassination."

· · ·

Walter's mother, **Alyne Payton**, lives in a quaint suburban home in Jackson, Mississippi. Now eighty-five years old, she spends her days gardening and hosting random visitors. "I'm happy," she says. "It's been a wonderful life."

· · ·

In the summer of 2008, a handsome twenty-three-year-old biracial man took his first-ever flight from Chicago to Jackson, Mississippi.

Though he knew some about the faraway city in the faraway state, any details had always been in the abstract. "Your father is from down South," he'd been told. "That's where your roots are."

Until now, **Nigel Smythe**, Walter's second son, had never looked especially hard into this part of his life. He understood that his biological father was one of the most famous sports figures in the United States. But he also knew the same man—one adored by millions of people—had made no effort to be a dad. From the day Nigel was born in 1985 until Walter's death in 1999, the two never lived more than thirty miles apart from one another. Despite that, Walter Payton—the onetime Illinois Fatherhood Initiative Chicago Father of the Year—wanted nothing to do with the boy.

Now, however, his father was nine years deceased, and Nigel sought answers. With his grandmother and girlfriend by his side, he flew to Jackson to meet the family he never knew. He was, as they say down South, *nervous as all heck.*

The trepidation vanished, however, as soon as Nigel touched down in the Magnolia State. Alyne Payton, his long-lost grandmother, squeezed him tight and fed him Southern delicacies. His aunt Pamela told stories about her brother that made Nigel laugh. He looked at pictures and asked questions about a father he both loved and resented. Cousins stopped by—Brandi, Pam's daughter; Erica, Eddie's girl. He even met Holmes. "He was a real nice kid, and I think he really appreciated coming to Mississippi and understanding where he comes from," said Holmes. "He looks a whole lot like Walter. Has that same glow."

Wary of the attention that could come should people learn of her son's heritage, Angelina and her husband raised Nigel cautiously. He was homeschooled for much of his youth, then attended a high school for the intellectually gifted. Now twenty-six and living in Illinois, Nigel is completing his college education. He tells precious few people of his lineage and chose not to speak for this book. "He's an incredible person," said Angelina. "Despite it all, he's a man I'm very, very proud of. It wasn't always easy, but it's worked out well."

Though the Mississippi branch of the Payton family has come to embrace Nigel, the same cannot be said for the Illinois faction. Connie has never mentioned his existence in public. When Jarrett and Brittney are asked about their family, they never broach the subject of their half-brother. They know he resides nearby, yet seem to treat him as they would a cardboard cutout—present, but mostly ignored. Perhaps they have good reason; perhaps the embarrassment that would accompany the revelation of a philandering father outweighs the potential positives.

Whatever the case, it is heartbreaking.

# ACKNOWLEDGMENTS

I AM WRITING THESE ACKNOWLEDGMENTS FROM THE BOYHOOD BEDROOM OF Elliot Lieberman, my wife's twenty-eight-year-old cousin and a kid who, judging by the CD rack situated alongside my laptop, once had an inexplicable thing for the pop band B★Witched.

Elliot's room is an ode to the eternalness of youth. There are Little League trophies and academic plaques, a poster of the 1994–95 Luveabulls, a small wooden bat, baseball cards, a pair of weathered KangaROOS sneakers. Over the course of the past two and a half years, I have spent a great amount of time here. Thanks to Elliot's wonderful mother, Cathy Lieberman, I come and go as I please, often flying into Chicago on a second's notice and taking up residence—rent, meals, towels, Internet, Molly the dog, and engrossing conversation included free of charge. As a result, I know the intricacies of this room by heart. The large green pillow at the foot of the bed. The photo montage of various family vacations. The dusty books lining the shelves.

Of the myriad objects, my favorite is a simple one. In the corner of the room, at the base of a hat rack, sits what appears to be a Cincinnati Reds baseball cap. It is red and a bit bulky, and on the back the words CHAMPION COACH MARK are stitched in white capital letters.

Whenever I enter Elliot's room, I inevitably pick up the hat and smooth over the embroidery with my fingers. I think about Mark raising two wonderful kids, Elliot and his sister, Lisa, and how proud he'd be today had he not passed seven years ago. Mark was a passionate Chicago sports fan, and as I lie in bed at night I often imagine him sitting on the edge of the mattress, asking aloud whether I've yet spoken to Mike Ditka; if Jimmy Mac has returned my phone calls; if I'm happy with how things are going thus far.

Like Walter Payton, Mark Lieberman passed from cancer. And while his death was a tragedy the family will never fully recover from, it has allowed me to personalize parental loss; to understand the harrowing void that comes with no longer having a father to turn to. The pain can never be fully healed. The reminders of a lost hero serve to both soothe and bruise the psyche. One wants to move on. One can never fully move on.

I cannot overstate my appreciation and gratitude toward the Lieberman clan. At the start of this project, they were my wife's family. Now I feel as if they are mine, too. So, to Cathy, Lisa, Aaron, Julia, Elliot, Emily, and Bart—huge thanks. This project does not exist without your assistance and compassion.

· · ·

Writing a book is a nightmare.

Those exact words appeared seven years ago in the acknowledgments of my first release, and while I try and wear a happy-happy-joy-joy face whenever possible, the sentiment remains undeniably true. I am, on the one hand, blessed to be able to do what I love. Journalism is my passion, and the long-form journalism that is the 180,000-word biography is my über-passion. Yet this sort of endeavor is also the most anomalous of pursuits. As the great Leigh Montville once told me, "It's an unusual thing. You spend two years in a cave, you pop your head out to see the light for a couple of weeks, then you return to the darkness."

In other words, I am a caveman. But, luckily, I keep great company.

I am continually blessed to work with the A-Team of literary support groups. Casey Angle, my researcher, is the Hannibal Smith of misplaced statistics, and Michael J. Lewis, Queens College's finest, reads through material in the same manner with which B. A. Baracus mourns for fools. My spiritual guru/tax attorney, Stanley Herz, knows absolutely nothing about sports, but his keen eye and instinctive sense of timing remain invaluable. I cannot say enough amazing things about Don Pierson, the former Bears beat writer for the *Chicago Tribune*, who took my calls and e-mails without once cursing me out. If I gained nothing else from this book, combing through years of Don's clips introduced me to one of the true masters of the trade.

David Black, my Brooklyn-based agent, is the king of righteous representation, and David Larabell and Allison Hemphill are dukes of decency. Paul Duer, thirty-feet-from-the-hoop huckster, and Gary Miller of the Raleigh Canine Book Club & Donut Shop, continue to offer sage advice. This was my first book for Gotham, and I'd like to thank the whole crew for a fabulous experience. Patrick Mulligan, the quiet editor who was initially described to me as a "mystery man," was nothing of the sort. His deft touch will forever be appreciated. Equal gratefulness goes to Travers "I'm the Man!" Johnson and Gary Mailman.

From Columbia to Jackson to Chicago and all points in between, I interviewed 678 people for this book. Some were thrilled to talk. Others, *ahem*, not so much. But I am forever indebted to anyone who helped me complete this journey. Early on I was fortunate to have audiences with Charles Boston, Bud Holmes, and Bob Hill, three quirky/unique/big-hearted men who I am better for knowing.

I encountered three cornerstones in Ginny Quirk-Alberts, Kimm Tucker, and Linda Conley—the women who knew and loved Walter most. Ginny and Kimm could, in all seriousness, double as Walter Payton encyclopedias. Linda, meanwhile, is working on her own Sweetness memoir, but was kind enough to step away from her notes and speak freely. I am grateful beyond words to all three.

Forrest Dantin, Walter's former high school teammate, was a marvelous source, and my belated condolences extend to his family for his passing. Vernon Perry and Robert Brazile surrendered precise details on the Jackson State years, and Jack Pardee, Neill Armstrong, Mike Ditka, Bob Thomas, Bob Avellini, Roland Harper, Johnny Roland, Jay Hilgenberg, Jim Covert, Willie Gault, Thomas Sanders, Calvin Thomas, Steve Fuller, and so many others followed suit when it came to the Bears. Matt Suhey, Walter's blocking back and, later, the executor of his estate, walked cautiously throughout, but with genuinely righteous intentions. I had the pleasure of lunching with two of Walter's children, Jarrett and Brittney, as well as with Eddie Payton, his brother. All three should be very proud of the man they represent.

I spent the majority of my time working on *Sweetness* in a cornucopia of Westchester, New York, eateries and coffee shops. The employees became my coworkers, and I theirs. To Cosi's Anthony Bocchino; Donna Massaro of Mahopac's amazing Freight House Cafe; Starbucks' Yvonne Parks, Laurie Belfiore, and Sara La Marca; Panera's Anthony Gibbs, Cynthia

Reeves, and George Kutty; Michelle Thompson of the Mirage Diner (A note to all the drunk Iona students: Tip more than $1. Really.)—huge thanks for the banter and kindness. Oh, and big ups to Mandy, the tattooed, late-night waitress at Howley's in West Palm Beach. Those twenty-three coffee refills kept me sharp.

As a New Yorker, I grew up with a certain perception of Mississippi—and it was not an especially good one. Researching this book, however, introduced me to a state rich with flavor, passion, and, quite often, overflowing goodness. Richard Howarth of Square Books in Oxford (seriously, America's best book shop) was invaluable in pointing me in the right direction. Jesse Bass of the University of Southern Mississippi busted his rear combing through the city of Columbia's vast archives. Laura Love, a senior library assistant at Ole Miss, delivered me from microfilm hell, as did Dorothy Yancy, Lerekka Gorham, and Belva Cauthen at the Eudora Welty Library in Jackson and Kendra Smith at the Columbia-Marion County Public Library. Roy L. Washington and Mildred Matthews were as helpful as could be at the Jackson State University Library. Without Tabatha Allen, Columbia's upbeat city clerk, I'm lost.

In no particular order, I'd also like to cite the contributions of Meghan Scott, my dazzling Web designer; Jerry B. Jenkins, author of another *Sweetness*; Chuck Hathcock of the *Grenada Star*; Joy Birdsong, Susan Szeliga, and Natasha Simon of the *Sports Illustrated* library; Don Yaeger, author of *Never Die Easy*; Aaron (DJ White Owl) Handelman; Brian Allee Walsh; Craig Harvey of the L.A. County Coroner's Office; Ciaran Boyle; Jill Cohen, Debra Mayblum, and Diana Waxler, my chief medical consultants; Caroline Goldmacher Kern; David Pearlman; Jessica Guggenheimer; Norma Shapiro; Leah Guggenheimer; Jordan and Isaiah Williams; Richard Guggenheimer; Laura and Rodney Cole; Dr. Jorge Ortiz of the Albert Einstein Medical Center; Saman Salih; Bianca Webster; Frank Zaccheo; Russ Bengtson; Greg Kuppinger; Jill Murray; Joseph (Cat) Kuppinger; L. Jon Wertheim; B. J. Schecter; Bev Oden; Steve Cannella; Ryan Gavin (the pride of Kansas State); Rob Massimi (Mayor of Starbucks); Judy Wertheim (great pad!); Jonathan Eig; Pat Brown of *The Magee Courier*; David Epstein of *Sports Illustrated*; *ESPN*'s Rob Tobias; Bob Doyle; Ann Goldstein; Abe Pearlman; and Mahopac's own Victoria Rose Omboni—distributor of Quan to the world.

When I was losing my mind one particularly awful night, Peter Richmond, my fellow crazed author, IMed me the following: "Step back. Breathe. Have a glass of wine. Tell yourself that NO ONE could tell this story except you. And, more importantly: that you want to tell this story, even if, at this point, you'd rather not. Just . . . write what you know. You are, at this point, in possession of a PhD in Walter Payton—a degree which no one else possesses. You have surrounded the story. You are the expert. Tell it. Don't worry about profundity, or brilliance of prose, or all the other trappings of this silly business. Just tell the tale. People will read."

Man, did I ever need that.

My folks, Joan and Stan Pearlman, have been my biggest supporters ever since I started forcing them to listen as I read my *Chieftain* articles aloud on their bed. Against all logic, they continue to listen to my blatherings.

This is my fifth book, and never have I devoted more time, energy, and anguish to a project. For every minute I spent thinking about Walter Payton, there was a minute I was either emotionally and/or physically absent from my family. I would like to apologize to my beautiful children, Casey Marta and Emmett Leo, for any of the missed moments that we'll never have back. I love you both more than I've loved anything. Even Hall and Oates.

My wife, *Dr.* Catherine Pearlman, is the gem of my life. I can't imagine what it's like to be married to someone who utters "Walter Payton" every fourth sentence, but you continue to stroll the sandy beaches of Blanes by my side (*mmm—Shrek pops*). To quote someone named G. Moore: "Other men said they have seen angels. But I have seen thee. And thou art enough."

Lastly, a word about Walter Payton. Actually, three words: I love him. I love what he overcame, I love what he accomplished, I love what he symbolized, and I love the nooks and crannies and complexities. Once, not all that long ago, I asked my uncle, Dr. Martin Pearlman, whether he thought much about aging and death. His response has stayed with me. "No," Uncle Marty said, "I try to think about the richness of life. It's more fun that way."

NOTES

## CHAPTER 1

3   *Chip Loftin had a festive party on his fifth birthday*: "Chip Loftin Has Festive Party On Fifth Birthday," *Columbian-Progress*, April 16, 1970.

5   *In 1937 Marion County's Historical Society commissioned*: Marion County Historical Research Project, January 21, 1937, by Maggie Byrd and Gizelle Sylverstein.

5   *"The first meal I ever cooked"*: Janet Harrison English, "Most Valuable Biscuit-Maker," *Jackson Clarion-Ledger*, March 4, 1992.

6   *Columbia was a place where the camellias*: Industrial Survey of Columbia, Miss., by the New Industries Department Mississippi Power Company, 1962.

6   *"Back then we didn't have birth control"*: "Mrs. Alyne Payton: A true definition of the world 'Mother,'" *Jackson State University Athletic Foundation News*, Fall 2001.

7   *When Walter and his Bluff Road pals weren't weaving through dill stacks*: Mark Sufrin, *Payton* (New York: Charles Scribner's Sons, 1988), 38–39.

8   *James Meredith, who in 1962 became the first black*: Paul Hendrickson, *Sons of Mississippi* (New York: Vintage, 2004), 68.

8   *"I told my children I was going to raise them"*: "Mrs. Alyne Payton: A true definition of the world 'Mother,'" *Jackson State University Athletic Foundation News*, Fall 2001.

9   *He also manned a five-acre garden*: Walter Payton with Don Yaeger, *Never Die Easy* (New York: Random House, 2001), 21.

9     *"We didn't have a babysitter"*: "Mrs. Alyne Payton: A true definition of the world 'Mother,'" *Jackson State University Athletic Foundation News*, Fall 2001.

10    *"When* Tarzan *was over"*: Walter Payton with Jerry B. Jenkins, *Sweetness* (New York: Contemporary Books, 1978), 21.

12    *Alyne's goal was to win the* Columbian-Progress' *Yard of the Week*: Rick Telander, "Bears' Unclear Situation Gives Payton Plenty to Worry About," *Chicago Sun-Times*, January 26, 1996.

12    *"It rains like you wouldn't believe during the summer"*: Payton and Yaeger, *Never Die Easy*, 23.

12    *"[My mother is] probably the reason I'm so muscular"*: Bobby Hall, "Payton Finds His Place In College Football's Society," *The Commercial Appeal* (Memphis), November 9, 1974.

13    *Whenever Alyne stumbled upon a vintage*: John Husar, "Mama The Coach," *Chicago Tribune*, September 30, 1977.

14    *"When you have an angry sister chasing you with a broom"*: Tom Fitzgerald, "Sibling rivalry at Payton's place motivated runner," *The Topeka Capital-Journal*, November 30, 1999.

15    *Afterward, everyone would retreat to Cook's Dairy Delight*: Anna Nixon, "Mrs. Cooks: A favorite spot since the 1950's," *Columbian-Progress*, August 6, 1987.

16    *"Eddie loved school and he loved football"*: "Mrs. Alyne Payton: A true definition of the world 'Mother,'" *Jackson State University Athletic Foundation News*, Fall 2001.

17    *"I look back at my style of playing football, and that evolved"*: Payton and Yaeger, *Never Die Easy*, 29.

## CHAPTER 2

24    *"The first time I got the ball in practice"*: Payton and Jenkins, *Sweetness*, 37–38.

25    *On October 30, 1969, the* Columbian-Progress *actually ran*: "Jefferson High," *Columbian-Progress*, October 30, 1969.

# Carson City Library

Phone (775) 887-2244

---

Date: 3/15/2012 Time: 11:52:28 AM

Items checked out this session: 1

---

Title: Sweetness : the enigmatic life of Walter Payto
Barcode: 31472400092957
Due Date: 04/12/2012 23:59:59

---

900 N. Roop St.

Carson City, NV 89701

NEW EXPANDED HOURS

MONDAY - THURSDAY

10:00 AM to 8:00 PM

FRIDAY & SATURDAY

10:00 AM - 6:00 PM

## CHAPTER 3

31   *With its April 10, 1969, staff editorial, titled RACE DIFFERENCES*:
Lester Williams, "Race Differences," *Columbian-Progress*, April 10, 1969.

32   *Thurman Sensing, a columnist for the* Progress *and executive vice president*:
Thurman Sensing, "HEW's Attack on Freedom of Choice,"
*Columbian-Progress*, January 1, 1970.

35   *Eight teenagers, all white, paraded back and forth*: Bill Crider, "Desegregation
Comes Quietly At Columbia High School," *Associated Press*, January 6,
1970.

## CHAPTER 4

39   *On April 27, 1970, Columbia High announced the hiring*: "New Columbia
Wildcats Coach is Announced," *Columbian-Progress*, April 30, 1970.

42   *As is often the case, the game failed to meet*: "Columbia Wildcats Paw
Bulldogs 14–6," *Columbian-Progress*, September 10, 1970.

45   *"It was a long [run], and I was hit"*: Payton and Jenkins, *Sweetness*, 44.

47   *"I began to see that once in a great while you can use"*: Ibid.

## CHAPTER 5

57   *"I didn't let them fight"*: Telander, "He's Aiming to Make History," *Sports
Illustrated*, September 5, 1984.

58   *That spring a portly defensive assistant from Florida State*: Steve Conroy,
"Football Bill misses Payton's place," *Boston Herald*, July 19, 1994.

59   *The school had gained fame for producing Willie Heidelburg*: Rick Cleveland
and Billy Watkins, "It took rare type to integrate college football,"
*Jackson Daily News,* July 1, 1984.

60   *"The campus was as beautiful as I remembered it"*: Payton and Jenkins,
*Sweetness*, 51–52.

61   *Alyne Payton—strong-willed, tough, focused*: Sufrin, *Payton*, 51.

62   *A rugged former lieutenant commander in the navy*: Kansas State University
Library, Exhibit: K-State Presidents & Their First Ladies.

## CHAPTER 6

65 *"Before it's too late, you had better start thinking"*: Jonathan Grant, "Awaken Black Youths," *The Blue and White Flash*, November 1971.

66 *Grant's piece ran alongside another column*: Tommie Steen Calhoun, "A Black Man's Hope," *The Blue and White Flash*, November 1971.

66 *The altercation began when police mistook the sound*: Jesse Crow, "Person of the Day: James Green," *Jackson Free Press*, April 27, 2010.

68 *"I was feeling right at home"*: Payton and Jenkins, *Sweetness*, 56.

76 *The paper finally got around to the Tigers*: Orley Hood, "J-State Seeks Improvement," *Jackson Daily News*, September 5, 1971.

80 *Walter Payton's first collegiate touchdown*: David Boone, "Jackson St. Rattles Bishop," *Jackson Daily News*, October 10, 1971.

## CHAPTER 7

83 *"If you have to come under control to make a cut"*: Don Pierson, "The Last Word," *Chicago Tribune*, November 7, 1999.

86 *"At first I was glad to room with people"*: Payton and Jenkins, *Sweetness*, 61.

88 *The Tigers were returning twenty-three lettermen*: "Frosh Stars, 23 Lettermen Set For Play At Jackson State," *The Clarion-Ledger*, September 3, 1972.

93 *A sellout crowd arrived at Memorial Stadium the following*: Billy Brantley, "Jackson State Rips Kentucky State, 28-14," *The Clarion-Ledger*, October 1, 1972.

## CHAPTER 8

96–97 *She was even a standout dancer*: Payton and Yaeger, *Never Die Easy*, 60.

97 *"I was very surprised to hear Walter's distinctive, high-pitched voice"*: Connie Payton, Jarrett Payton, and Brittney Payton, *Payton* (New York: Rugged Land, 2005), 28.

97 *"We spent that evening just kind of talking about her"*: Payton and Yaeger, *Never Die Easy*, 60–61.

98 *"When it was dinnertime, he wouldn't eat"*: Ibid., 61.

99 *"A greyhound with muscles"*: Red Smith, "Philadelphia Story," *The New York Times*, January 12, 1981.

100 *A mere three months later, Montgomery ran for 146 yards*: "Faces in the Crowd," *Sports Illustrated*, November 12, 1973.

101 *Yet despite the sludge, and despite Omaha stuffing*: "Sloppy Field Didn't Stop JSC's Payton," *The Clarion-Ledger*, September 13, 1973.

102 *In the immediate aftermath of the Omaha victory, Mississippi Governor Bill Waller*: "JSC's Payton Lies In 'SWAC Shadow,'" *The Clarion-Ledger*, October 4, 1973.

102 *They entered the game 1-3*: "Rebounding J-State Welcomes Bishop For First Home Date," *The Clarion-Ledger*, October 5, 1973.

105 *Yet even though Waller officially proclaimed October 20*: Ponto Downing, "J-State, Grambling Head Small College Attractions," *The Clarion-Ledger*, October 20, 1973.

106 *"Payton is fantastic," Robinson said*: Bernard Fernandez, "Payton Marked Man," *Jackson Daily News*, November 20, 1973.

106 *Some of the pain was lessened*: Al Harvin, "Jones Heads Black All-Americans," *The New York Times*, December 20, 1973.

CHAPTER 9

108 *"Most of the time, I thought, 'You can have him'"*: Debra Pickett, "We were opposite, opposite," *Chicago Sun-Times*, May 12, 2002.

110 *"Long range, long-shot prediction"*: Walter Payton, Jackson State running back"*: Dick Young, "Young Ideas," *The Sporting News*, July 6, 1974.

111 *"The Payton-for-the-Heisman drive"*: "Payton a 'Heisman' hopeful," *Pascagoula Press*, September 1, 1974.

111 *"There's no comparison," Payton told*: "Quotable," *The Atlanta Journal-Constitution*, January 14, 1975.

112 *"What Walter really needs is exposure"*: "Flash Talks To Frank Banister," *The Blue and White Flash*, November 21, 1974.

113 *"Lots of newspapers around the nation don't even print"*: Bernard Fernandez, "Payton Finding Place in sun at Jackson State," *The Sporting News*, November 30, 1974.

114 *With his death less than two months before the start*: Carlos Boyd, "Former Wyoming line coach dies," *The Denver Post*, May 6, 2001.

116 *The Tigers won 75–0*: John Stamm, "Tigers Rout Omaha 75-0," *Jackson Daily News*, October 6, 1974.

116 *Four days later, the* Associated Press *named*: "Buckeyes' Griffin Back Of Week," *The Clarion-Ledger*, October 9, 1974.

116 *So lightly regarded was Jackson State*: Husar, "Team Canada stung by 'bugs'?" *Chicago Tribune*, October 10, 1974.

117 *"If they are going to go by ability"*: "Payton All-Time Scoring Champ," *The Blue and White Flash*, November 1, 1974.

119 *The only news outlet to run the photograph*: "You Be The Referee," *The Blue and White Flash*, November 1, 1974.

119 *The Tigers fell again, to Grambling*: Bill Sanders, "Tigers End Home Play," *The Clarion-Ledger*, November 9, 1974.

119 *"I'm telling you, I chugalugged"*: Payton and Jenkins, *Sweetness*, 91.

120 *"Pro scouts, judging from my research"*: Tom Siler, "Griffin Leading Heisman Race," *The Sporting News*, November 9, 1974.

## CHAPTER 10

130 *Three days before the January 11, 1975, contest*: Ponto Downing, "JSU's Payton Comes Close On Prediction," *The Clarion-Ledger*, January 12, 1975.

130 *In a dull 17–17 tie, Payton*: "Mike-Mayer's FG Earns South 17-17 Senior Tie," *Associated Press*, January 12, 1975.

131 *"I am strictly a thrower"*: Will Grimsley, "Bartkowski Wants To Play," *Associated Press*, January 29, 1975.

131 *"I remember the debate"*: CNN, Mike Ditka interview with Lou Waters. November 1, 1999.

132 *"Without question, the best offensive lineman"*: "NFL Kicks Off Clouded Draft," *Associated Press*, January 29, 1975.

133 *When Ponto Downing of the* Clarion-Ledger *arrived*: Ponto Downing, "J-State Pair 'Buzzing' After Hearing Draft News," *The Clarion-Ledger*, January 29, 1974.

133 *More than two hours after he was selected, Tom Siler*: Tom Siler, "Walter Payton—Gifted Runner," *The Sporting News*, February 15, 1975.

133 *"We've been sweating it out"*: Robert Markus, "Bears go after 'little big man' in first draft pick," *Chicago Tribune*, January 29, 1975.

134 *"He was easy to find on film"*: Pierson, " 'If the people of Chicago give me some time and be patient, I'll give them a new Gale Sayers,' " *Chicago Tribune*, November 7, 1999.

134 *Bud Holmes, however, wasn't sold*: Downing, "J-State Pair 'Buzzing' After Hearing Draft News," *The Clarion-Ledger*, January 29, 1974.

136 *"There are other leagues"*: Pierson, "Elusive Payton talks," *Chicago Tribune*, January 30, 1975.

138 *"Walter, they ain't got no grits"*: Bill McGrane, *Sweetness*, (Los Angeles: National Football League Book, 1988), 8.

139 *"The major deciding factor was that it has been his life's"*: Ed Stone, "Bears sign Payton for big bucks," *Chicago Tribune*, June 4, 1975.

## CHAPTER 11

140 *"Gale Sayers has been my idol"*: Pierson, "Payton shows up . . . with his agent," *Chicago Tribune*, February 4, 1975.

141 *It was once said that if Helen of Troy*: Jack Schnelder, "Gibron Brings New Image to NFL—300 Pounds," *The Sporting News*, September 14, 1972.

142 *Halas was born on February 2, 1895*: Eugene Carlson, "George Halas Put Pro Football in Big Leagues," *Wall Street Journal*, June 20, 1989.

142 *In helping the Illini capture the 1918*: Arthur Daley, "Story of the Papa Bear," *The New York Times*, December 7, 1951.

143  *The Staleys finished 10-1-2*: Frank Graham, "Keeper of the Bears," *New York Journal-American*, March 5, 1947.

143  *"I'm afraid we can't make a go of it"*: Ibid.

143  *It came on the morning of January 30, 1922:* Jerry Liska, "Halas: Last of a Series," *Associated Press*, December 12, 1962.

144  *As Frank Graham wrote*: Frank Graham, "Keeper of the Bears," *New York Journal-American*, March 5, 1947.

144  *In 1933, Halas, along with Redskins owner:* Jerry Liska, "Halas: Last of a Series," *Associated Press*, December 12, 1962.

144  *He also added—among other things*: Frank Deford, "'I Don't Date any Woman Under 48,'" *Sports Illustrated*, December 5, 1977.

144  *"Our game has assumed many of the characteristics"*: Cooper Rollow, "Papa Bear," *The Sporting News*, November 14, 1983.

145  *"The juices of humanity seem to have been squeezed"*: Bill Furlong, "George Halas: Saint or Sinner?" *The Sporting News*, December 15, 1962.

145  *"[Halas]," wrote Furlong*: Richard W. Johnston, "Chicago: The Once and Future Bears," *Sports Illustrated*, December 9, 1974.

145  *The Bears, wrote Jerry Green of* The Sporting News: Jerry Green, "New Era for Bears With Finks," *The Sporting News,* September 28, 1974.

146  *"I have the authority to hire or fire"*: Ibid.

146  *A quarterback with the Steelers from*: William N. Wallace, "Ex-Quarterback Behind Surging Vikings," *The New York Times*, December 11, 1969.

146  *"He has the temperament and disposition"*: "Bears Hire Pardee as Head Coach," *The New York Times*, January 1, 1975.

147  *On June 1, 1975, two days before Payton signed*: Roy Damer, "McKay selects 54 College All-Stars," *Chicago Tribune*, June 1, 1975.

152  *At one point Payton was sent to Illinois Masonic*: Stone, "Payton is hospitalized; Bears sell Pagac, Barnes," *Chicago Tribune*, August 6, 1975.

152 *He was milking cows on the family's farm*: Tony Kornheiser, "Pardee!" *The Washington Post*, September 17, 1979.

152 *Told he could either die or*: Sam Smith, "This time, Pardee will stay a while," *Chicago Tribune*, September 13, 1987.

152 *"I didn't think I'd die"*: Kornheiser, "Pardee!" *The Washington Post*, September 17, 1979.

153 *"It was more of a gut feeling"*: Phil Elderkin, " 'Sleeper' coach shakes Bears from hibernation," *The Christian Science Monitor*, November 2, 1976.

156 *While booting balls during a practice*: Pierson, "Bears' Coady waived," *Chicago Tribune*, August 29, 1975.

157 *As Don Pierson noted in that day's* Chicago Tribune: Pierson, "Bears vs. Dolphins tonight; Payton to make debut," *Chicago Tribune*, September 6, 1975.

## CHAPTER 12

158 *In a piece titled "Bears are putting"*: Pierson "Bears are putting it all together," *Chicago Tribune*, September 14, 1975.

158 *In the lead-up to the game*: Stone, "Payton: 'Give me time, I'll give 'em a new Sayers,' " *Chicago Tribune*, September 14, 1975.

159 *The Bears lost 35–7*: Pierson, "Unbearably Colt (35-7) NFL debut," *Chicago Tribune*, September 22, 1975.

160 *"Zero yards for the number one pick?"*: Payton and Yaeger, *Never Die Easy*, 77.

161 *"He ran for zero yards, but it was"*: Pierson, "1975: 'I just like to do whatever it takes to win. And if it takes that much I'll do it,' " *Chicago Tribune*, November 7, 1999.

162 *Payton, in the words of*: Pierson, "Bears prevail 15-13 with :08 left," *Chicago Tribune*, September 29, 1975.

163 *"They weren't as good as I expected"*: Pierson, "Tarkenton, Vikes stifle Bears 28-3," *Chicago Tribune*, October 6, 1975.

163 *"That's the first time I've ever seen an opponent laugh"*: Pierson, "Lions ax Bears in 'laugher' 27-7," *Chicago Tribune*, October 13, 1975.

163 *"He played a good game"*: Pierson, "Bear offensive line criticized by Pardee," *Chicago Tribune*, October 14, 1975.

167 *That Sunday, Payton stood on the sideline*: Stone, "Bears battle Steelers in 'morbid' mismatch," *Chicago Tribune*, October 19, 1975.

169 *"I can't believed it's the Mike Adamle"*: Neil Milbert, "Cosell crew kind to Bears over TV," *Chicago Tribune*, October 28, 1975.

169 *Payton was a backup for the first*: Pierson, "Vikes turn back stubborn Bears 13-9," *Chicago Tribune*, October 28, 1975.

169 *"If they want me to run, I'll run"*: Joe Mooshil, No headline, *Associated Press*, November 18, 1975.

171 *Five months later, when he prepared to return to Chicago*: Payton, Payton, and Payton, *Payton*, 179–181.

## CHAPTER 13

172 *On July 14, the third straight day*: Pierson, "Bears run 'best practice' despite heat,' *Chicago Tribune*, July 15, 1976.

174 *Fed up, Pardee announced after*: Pierson, "Musso moves us after Bear win," *Chicago Tribune*, August 9, 1976.

174 *When Finks slyly told the* Tribune: Pierson, "Payton ready to carry big load, shed pressure," *Chicago Tribune*, August 12, 1976.

177 *The lineman began the process of bringing the back*: Pierson, "Bears top 49ers but lose Buffone," *Chicago Tribune*, September 20, 1976.

180 *The story was published in the November 22, 1976*: Dennis Breo, "Since Walter Joined the Football Bears, Chicago Has Turned Into Payton's Place," *People*, November 22, 1976.

181 *He craved the bright lights and glitter*: Rollow, "Beating Payton no special kick for Simpson," *Chicago Tribune*, March 13, 1977.

182 *By the time the half ended, Payton had run*: Pierson, "Payton has his best day," *Chicago Tribune*, December 6, 1976.

183 *With Soldier Field's scoreboard*: Pierson, "Payton vs. O. J. to take back seat to Bears win," *Chicago Tribune*, December 10, 1976.

183  *Among those in attendance were*: David Condon, "Celebration turns into anxiety for Payton's mom," *Chicago Tribune*, December 14, 1976.

184  *Late into the third quarter*: Pierson, "Broncos ruin finale for Bears, Payton," *Chicago Tribune*, December 13, 1976.

185  *"It was, I guess, the low point of"*: Rollow, "Loss to O. J. 'low point' of life: Payton," *Chicago Tribune*, February 17, 1977.

## CHAPTER 14

186  *"Walter Payton is concerned enough about"*: Stone, "Payton's goal: quit in 1 piece," *Chicago Tribune*, November 1, 1977.

188  *Five months later, in another*: Pierson, "Bears, Phipps flop in Cleveland," *Chicago Tribune*, August 26, 1977.

189  *Later on, following a third-quarter sweep*: Pierson, "Robertson backs down—sort of," *Chicago Tribune*, October 12, 1977.

190  *"Wally Chambers is the poorest excuse"*: Rollow, "Rams rage over Bear 'cheap hits,'" *Chicago Tribune*, October 11, 1977.

191  *The Bears were coming off a 47–0*: Pierson, "Bears take early hibernation, fall 47–0," *Chicago Tribune*, November 7, 1977.

193  *"It was the first time I saw him," recalled Brown*: Interview with NFL Network for 100 Greatest Players program, 2010.

194  *Asked now to assess the Bears*: Pierson, "It's high noon of Bears' season," *Chicago Tribune*, November 20, 1977.

194  *He had prayed throughout the week for health*: "Payton Breaks Record, Rushing for 275 Yards," *The New York Times*, November 21, 1977.

196  *"It never came up"*: John Underwood, "Payton Runs All Over The Place," *Sports Illustrated*, November 28, 1977.

197  *"Nobody would ever confuse running back Walter Payton"*: Phil Elderkin, "Wonderful Walter makes end zone 'Payton Place,'" *The Christian Science Monitor*, December 13, 1977.

198  *"Payton's record rushing brought out"*: Pierson, "World runs to Payton," *Chicago Tribune*, November 22, 1977.

198  *The one Bear who seemed most irked by Payton*: Joe Lapointe, "Memories Of a Stadium, Served Cold," *The New York Times*, December 27, 2009.

199  *"I think we'll be the Beehive"*: Pierson, "Payton enjoys day of slipping past cameras," *Chicago Tribune*, December 14, 1977.

199  *The red-hot Bears traveled to Detroit*: Richard L. Shook, "Payton Leads Bears' Lion-Tamers," *The Sporting News*, December 10, 1977.

200  *"If I don't catch any passes I feel worthless"*: Stone, "Bears want rushing record for Payton, but . . . ," *Chicago Tribune*, December 18, 1977.

201  *As soon as he spotted the rain*: Sufrin, *Payton*, 98–99.

203  *"I was getting worried there"*: Pierson, "Bears reach playoffs—miraculously," *Chicago Tribune*, December 19, 1977.

204  *Just in case the sentiment didn't resonate*: Lapointe, "Memories Of a Stadium, Served Cold," *The New York Times*, December 27, 2009.

204  *What if Thomas had shanked*: Pierson, "Bears reach playoffs—miraculously," *Chicago Tribune*, December 19, 1977.

## CHAPTER 15

207  *On the evening of Monday, December 11, 1978*: "Payton's father dies in jail," *New York Post*, December 13, 1978.

209  *According to Gonzalez's report*: "Payton autopsy," *Chicago Tribune*, December 16, 1978.

210  *Jack Pardee, the only professional coach*: Wallace, "Pardee Quits as Bears' Coach; Will Apply for Redskins' Post," *The New York Times*, January 20, 1978.

211  *"No one cares that he's leaving"*: Pierson, "Bears were losing respect for Pardee," *Chicago Tribune*, January 20, 1978.

211  *"I hate to see the guy leave"*: Pierson, "Add Marchibroda to Bear stew," *Chicago Tribune*, January 22, 1978.

212  *"I don't know what people consider dull"*: Pierson, "Bears End Long Snooze, Name Armstrong," *The Sporting News*, March 4, 1978.

212 *On the final day of taping, Payton*: Markus, " 'New' Payton keeps audience, himself in stitches," *Chicago Tribune*, February 9, 1978.

213 *A couple of weeks after Armstrong*: Pierson, "Bears hire ex-coach of 49ers," *Chicago Tribune*, March 21, 1978.

214 *Were that not bad enough*: Pierson, "Bears land 'safe pick' in Texas star Shearer," *Chicago Tribune*, May 3, 1978.

214 *According to a scathing March 13* Tribune *article*: Pierson, "How Bear salaries rate," *Chicago Tribune*, March 13, 1978.

214 *"I wish Walter were a free agent"*: Pierson, "Agent's goal: satisfy Payton on his worth," *Chicago Tribune*, July 2, 1978.

214 *Holmes assumed Chicago's fans*: Bill Jauss, "Even lawyer pulls for Payton to sign," *Chicago Tribune*, July 18, 1978.

214 *On July 19, Finks offered Payton*: Pierson, "Payton weighs $375,000-a-year offer," *Chicago Tribune*, July 20, 1978.

215 *In 1997, years after both men had retired*: Caulton Tudor, "Dickerson gets Sayers' nod as best," *The News & Observer* (Raleigh), January 31, 1997.

216 *"Walter's not running as well as he had"*: Jauss, "Dispute hurting Walter, team—Noah," *Chicago Tribune*, August 9, 1978.

216 *Finally, one day before the Bears'*: Pierson, "Payton agrees to sign for $400,000," *Chicago Tribune*, September 3, 1978.

216 *The call came to the Chicago Bears*: "In brief," *The New York Times*, September 5, 1978.

217 *The Bears won 17–10, and Payton played*: Davis Israel, "Payton's spark electrifies Bears," *Chicago Tribune*, September 4, 1978.

218 *"Payton is acting like a very hollow person"*: Pierson, "Payton figures to rebound," *Chicago Tribune*, September 29, 1978.

219 *In the days leading up to a matchup at Green Bay*: Rollow, "Packer pride is avenged, Luke crows," *Chicago Tribune*, October 9, 1978,

219 *On October 10, two days after*: Byron Rosen, "H-e-e-e-r-e Come the Women," *The Washington Post*, October 12, 1978.

220  *"I kind of liked Jack Pardee's philosophy"*: "Payton said he 'kind of liked Jack Pardee's philosophy,'" *Chicago Tribune*, October 18, 1978.

221  *Through the first eight games, the Bears had opened with*: Pierson, "It's predictable—Bears will run," *Chicago Tribune*, October 27, 1978.


## CHAPTER 16

230  *When asked to name his extravagances*: Pierson, "Payton," *Chicago Tribune*, December 14, 1979.

230  *"[It] just seemed like this cold, faraway"*: Pickett, "'We were opposite, opposite,'" *Chicago Sun-Times*, May 12, 2002.

232  *"Even that great year he had [1977]"*: Pierson, "Payton: Doing it all, and doing it better," *Chicago Tribune*, September 23, 1979.

232  *The Bears beat two two-win clubs*: Pierson, "Bears' streak doesn't mean they're a good team yet," *Chicago Tribune*, November 22, 1979.

233  *When the Raiders offered Ken Stabler*: "Bears Nixed Stabler," *The Sporting News*, November 10, 1979.

234  *When asked about Harold Carmichael*: Pierson, "Bears on Eagles: who you don't know can't hurt you," *Chicago Tribune*, December 19, 1979.

234  *Seconds before the ball was snapped*: Bob Verdi, "Payton's pride hurt more than shoulder," *Chicago Tribune*, December 24, 1979.

235  *Payton spoke optimistically of better days*: Ibid.

235  *In the summer of 1980 the team moved*: Bob Logan, "Title thoughts dominate Bear camp opening," *Chicago Tribune*, July 26, 1980.

237  *"If I never face another defense like them"*: Verdi, "Bears seem to be in prevent offense," *Chicago Tribune*, November 4, 1980.

237  *"A resoundingly innovative"*: Ibid.

238  *He was named after a character*: Bob Herguth, "Off and running with Payton," *Chicago Sun-Times*, August 11, 1996.

238  *"My son brought me tremendous joy"*: Payton and Yaeger, *Never Die Easy*, 198.

240 *"I talked to a lot of clubs, just social"*: George Vecsey, "Walter Payton Fits in Chicago," *The New York Times*, July 28, 1981.

240 *When Holmes told the* Tribune *Payton would*: Pierson, "Payton won't get $1 million: Halas," *Chicago Tribune*, February 3, 1981.

240 *Under the new ownership of a*: Pierson, "I've made offer to Payton— Montreal owner," *Chicago Tribune*, May 1, 1981.

242 *"Pay me eight hundred thousand dollars"*: Pierson, "Too often, Payton finds Bear linemen blocking his way," *Chicago Tribune*, September 27, 1981.

242 *The following week, after gaining forty-five yards*: Paul Zimmerman, "He Can Run, But He Can't Hide," *Sports Illustrated*, August 16, 1982.

242 *Jerry Kirshenbaum, the editor of* Sports Illustrated*'s Scorecard section*: Jerry Kirshenbaum, "Mush!" *Sports Illustrated*, December 28, 1981.

242 *After paying $58.40 for two tickets*: Laura Garraway, "Fan can't 'Bear' Chicago's charade," *New York Post*, October 13, 1981.

243 *"Maybe Walter's best years are behind him"*: Pierson, "If new Payton plan catches on, he'll run less, enjoy it more," *Chicago Tribune*, October 11, 1981.

## CHAPTER 17

244 *So it was that one day*: Mike Ditka with Don Pierson, *Ditka: An Autobiography* (Chicago: Bonus Books, 1986), 156.

245 *Once asked by* Sports Illustrated*'s Curry Kirkpatrick*: Curry Kirkpatrick, "Once a Bear, Always a Bear," *Sports Illustrated*, December 16, 1985.

245 *He was born on October 18, 1939*: Ibid.

245 *"We played sports day and night"*: Ditka and Pierson, *Ditka*, 47.

246 *"My whole life was based on beating"*: Pierson, "Ditka: The coach who hates to lose," *Chicago Tribune*, November 17, 1985.

246 *"Pound for pound, Mike was as tough"*: Pat Livingston, "Mike Ditka, His Career at Pitt," *Sports Illustrated*, October 31, 1985.

246 *In 1962, the editors of* Look *magazine*: Tim Cohane, "Pain can't stop a pro," *Look*, December 4, 1962.

247  *"Are you a member of the Fellowship"*: Kirkpatrick, "Once a Bear, Always a Bear," *Sports Illustrated*, December 16, 1985.

247  *On January 20, 1982, two weeks after*: Husar, "Ditka may bring in Dallas offensive aides," *Chicago Tribune*, January 21, 1982.

248  *In a blistering piece titled "Hiring Ditka Would Be Madness"*: John Schulian, "Hiring Ditka Would be Madness," *The Sporting News*, January 30, 1982.

248  *"It's been a tough year physically"*: Sharon Stangenes, "Good intentions," *Chicago Tribune*, January 4, 1982.

249  *According to the* Tribune, *the team was strongly*: Pierson, "Another Walter tempts Bears as No. 1 pick," *Chicago Tribune*, April 11, 1982.

250  *"I don't know where he is"*: Pierson, "Ditka unloads on AWOL Watts," *Chicago Tribune*, May 28, 1982.

251  *Noah Jackson, the overweight*: Zimmerman, "He Can Run, But He Can't Hide," *Sports Illustrated*, August 16, 1982.

251  *"I don't know how long I can play"*: Pierson, "'Same old story' has Payton upset," *Chicago Tribune*, December 5, 1982.

252  *"I feel like I've been on a free ride"*: Ibid.

253  *Payton addressed the media, accusing*: Pierson, "Bears star at private party," *Chicago Tribune*, December 6, 1982.

253  *"I'm happy we won," he said*: Steve Daley, "Walter's 'problem' has Bears on run," *Chicago Tribune*, December 6, 1982.

254  *"It's unfortunate"*: Pierson, "Bears' pass-run rift hasn't healed yet," *Chicago Tribune*, December 7, 1982.

254  *"There's no problem at all"*: "Ditka, Payton talk it over," *Chicago Tribune*, December 10, 1982.

## CHAPTER 18

258  *Oftentimes, Payton merely covered his head*: McGrane, *Sweetness*, 10.

258  *"Dad messed up a couple of couches"*: Jarret Payton, *The Jarrett Payton Show*, Chicagoland Sports Radio, November 1, 2010.

263   *"I took a lot of pride in my cars"*: Payton and Yaeger, *Never Die Easy*, 161.

263   *His CB handle was Mississippi Maniac*: Pierson, "The Reason Sports Provide Such Dramatic Material is That The Climax Comes So Early in a Man's Life, the Decline So Swiftly," *Chicago Tribune*, November 7, 1999.

266   *When a reader wrote the* Tribune: Pierson, "Jim Brown the reason Payton ran," *Chicago Tribune*, October 7, 1983.

266   *"I'd rather turn back the eleven thousand"*: Pierson, "Bears mistakes pile up," *Chicago Tribune*, November 7, 1983.

57–268   *Which was why, on January 10, 1984*: Pierson, "Blitz offers Payton $6 million," *Chicago Tribune*, January 11, 1984.

268   *Michael McCaskey, the Bears' new president*: Robert McG. Thomas Jr., "Payton Weighs $6 Million Offer," *The New York Times*, January 12, 1984.

270   *Impeccably dressed and mildly tempered*: Pierson, "Payton keeps 'em guessing," *Chicago Tribune*, February 7, 1984.

270   *"I have a great deal of respect for Franco"*: Pierson, "Walter will pass Franco quietly," *Chicago Tribune*, September 20, 1984.

270   *"Gaining a thousand yards in a fourteen-game season"*: Bob Greene, "For the record: Go, Jim Brown, go!" *Chicago Tribune*, November 23, 1983.

271   *Now being held at the University of Wisconsin–Platteville*: " 'Nobody Awes this Football Team,' " *Chicago Tribune*, January 4, 1985.

271   *In the lead-up to 1984, however, Payton*: Pierson, "Payton," *Chicago Tribune*, September 2, 1984.

272   *"Sometimes a seed has to be planted"*: Kevin Lamb, "Bears Try to Avoid Another Slow Start," *The Sporting News*, September 10, 1984.

273   *"They're a bullshit team"*: Telander, "On Top of The Pack," *Sports Illustrated*, September 24, 1984.

273   *Harris led Payton by thirty-four yards*: Pierson, "Walter will pass Franco quietly," *Chicago Tribune*, September 20, 1984.

274   *"As far as I'm concerned"*: Bernie Lincicome, "Payton has only Brown left to chase," *Chicago Tribune*, September 24, 1984.

274   *The Seahawks released Harris*: Pat Mealey, "Franco Harris Mum On Release By NFL Seahawks," *Jet*, November 26, 1984.

274   *In fact, Payton never even viewed footage of Brown*: Telander, "On Top of The Pack," *Sports Illustrated*, September 24, 1984.

275   *"There were a lot of people that hated Ali"*: Mike Freeman, *Jim Brown: The Fierce Life of an American Hero* (New York: Harper, 2006), 175.

275   *"My feeling is you're a sportsman"*: Smith, "Only his record will fall," *Chicago Tribune*, October 7, 1984.

276   *When asked by Michael Janofsky of*: Michael Janofsky, "Payton: Team Player On the Move," *The New York Times*, October 7, 1984.

276   *His game pants, meanwhile, were nothing*: McGrane, *Sweetness*, 13.

279   *Moments later, Payton accepted a call*: Janofsky, "Call From Reagan Caps Payton's Day," *The New York Times*, October 9, 1984.


CHAPTER 19

280–81  *"It's like a boxer"*: Steve Delsohn, *Da Bears!* (New York: Crown Archetype, 2010), 1.

281   *Shelby Jordan, the Raiders' offensive tackle*: Rollow, "Raiders snarl back from locker room," *Chicago Tribune*, November 5, 1984.

282   *As he walked off the Metrodome turf*: Pierson, "A 1st for Bears," *Chicago Tribune*, November 26, 1984.

282   *The lifespan of an NFL running back*: John DeShazier, "New Orleans Saints backup running backs hurt Pierre Thomas' chances of getting paid," *The Times-Picayune* (New Orleans), August 24, 2010.

283   *"I asked Ed [Hughes, the offensive coordinator]"*: Pierson, "Fresh out of Luckmans," *Chicago Tribune*, February 16, 1997.

283   *"If Rusty Lisch were the little Dutch boy"*: Lincicome, "Lisch second best in battle of third stringers," *Chicago Tribune*, December 10, 1984.

284  *The Bears were listed as*: Verdi, "It's a Tale of Two Cities," *Chicago Tribune*, January 6, 1985.

284  *"We're not going to lose the game"*: Pierson, "'We're Not Going to Lose,'" *Chicago Tribune*, January 6, 1985.

284  *"We know what we have to do to win"*: "Payton Might Be Punter Against San Francisco," *The Washington Post*, January 1, 1985.

285  *"What stood out," wrote Christine Brennan*: Christine Brennan, "Bears Are Sacked Nine Times en Route To a 23–0 Defeat," *The Washington Post*, January 7, 1985.

285  *San Francisco coach Bill Walsh termed it*: Rich Roberts, "For Once, Two Favorites in Super Bowl," *Los Angeles Times*, January 7, 1985.

285  *"When you wait ten years"*: Verdi, "Payton is Brought Down—Hard," *Chicago Tribune*, January 7, 1985.

285  *On the morning of February 25, 1985*: Della L. Palmer, "NFL Star Walter Payton Wins Black Athlete Award," *Jet*, February 25, 1985.

288  *"This is my eleventh year, and nobody"*: Robert W. Creamer, "Payton's Place," *Sports Illustrated*, September 9, 1985.

289  *What irked Payton most was the emergence*: Mike Berardino, "Refrigerator Chilling Out in Aiken," *The Augusta Chronicle*, January 28, 1996.

289  *He had a twenty-two-inch neck*: Delsohn, *Da Bears!*, 18.

290  *"Unfortunately, when the 49ers beat us"*: William D. Murray, "Sports News," *United Press International*, October 14, 1985.

290  *Here was a coach who, two years earlier*: Gary Pomerantz, "Bears Have Found the Right Mix," *The Washington Post*, October 15, 1985.

291  *He inserted Perry, thus far*: Pierson, "Look Out! Bears May Run Perry Again," *Chicago Tribune*, October 15, 1985.

291  *Chris Cobbs of the* Los Angeles Times: Chris Cobbs, "'The Refrigerator' Falls on Packers, 23–7," *Los Angeles Times*, October 22, 1985.

291  *"Can McPerry be far behind?"*: "Executives Going After Bears for Endorsements," *Los Angeles Times*, December 15, 1985.

291 *Far from trying to make a fashion*: Kevin Cook, "Playboy Interview: Jim McMahon," *Playboy*, October 1, 1986.

294 *"This team has not reached"*: "Bears Roll On, 36-0, Over Falcons," *The Washington Post*, November 25, 1985.

294 *"We aren't satisfied yet"*: Verdi, " 'We Aren't Satisfied Yet,' " *Chicago Tribune*, November 25, 1985.

294 *"We are going to kick the Bears' butts"*: Delsohn, *Da Bears!*, 162.

295 *"Every time we had a game in Florida"*: Steve McMichael with Phil Arvia, *Steve McMichael's Tales from the Chicago Bears Sideline* (Champaign, Illinois: Sports Publishing LLC, 2004), 98.

295 *A Miami radio station came up*: John Mullin, *The Rise and Self-Destruction of the Greatest Football Team in History* (Chicago, Triumph Books, 2005), 104–105.

295 *"Reporters fell from the sky like a seven-inch snow"*: Mike Singletary with Armen Keteyian, *Calling the Shots* (Chicago: Contemporary Books, 1986), 175.

295 *"It was like they were trying to put the voodoo on us"*: Delsohn, *Da Bears!*, 165.

295 *Back at the University of Pittsburgh, Marino had roomed*: Ibid., 169–171.

296 *Early in the fourth quarter, with the score 38–24*: Ibid., 172–173.

298 *"Willie Gault? When he was traded"*: Fred Mitchell, "Bears Forget Gault Already," *Chicago Tribune*, September 14, 1988.

298 *"We told them we weren't coming"*: Jon Greenberg, "Shuffling down memory lane," ESPN.com, January 15, 2010.

299 *The "Shuffle" went on to become a smash hit*: Delsohn, *Da Bears!*, 180.

299 *"The guy had the balls to come back"*: Ibid., 181.

300 *"Dealing with the media has been"*: Pierson, "AP Honors Singletary," *Chicago Tribune*, January 1, 1986.

301 *Payton desired more acclaim*: Ken McKee, "Bears' Walter Payton admits he needs acclaim," *Toronto Sun*, January 5, 1986.

302 *"For me, the Super Bowl would"*: Ed Sherman, "Payton Running Out of Time," *Chicago Tribune*, January 9, 1986.

303 *As was tradition, the Bears spent*: Sherman, "Payton's Day Finally Arrives," *Chicago Tribune*, January 13, 1986.

303 *With 4:26 remaining in the* first quarter: Pierson, "Superb Bears in Super Bowl," *Chicago Tribune*, January 13, 1986.

303 *Over the past decade, he had attended*: Jim Proudfoot, "Only Super Bowls for Payton were as a spectator," *The Toronto Star*, January 24, 1986.

## CHAPTER 20

305 *Weeks before kickoff, NFL Films*: Roberts, "Bears Favored to Shuffle Past Patriots Today," *Los Angeles Times*, January 26, 1986.

305 *Some 175 journalists from across*: Ira Berkow, "Secrecy at Bears' Workout," *The New York Times*, January 17, 1986.

306 *"We got on the buses from the airport"*: Delsohn, *Da Bears!*, 201.

313 *"I ain't no damned monkey on a string"*: McGrane, *Sweetness*, 12.

315 *"When they called the play for Perry"*: Verdi, "No-TD Payton Admits he was 'Upset,'" *Chicago Tribune*, January 30, 1986.

## CHAPTER 21

316 *He was asked to attend*: Larry Black, "Reagan joshes 'Kid' Mulroney at dazzling White House bash," *The Canadian Press*, March 19, 1986.

316 *As always, he appeared at the annual*: John Holland, "There'll be Enough Bears to Field a Team, and Others," *Chicago Tribune*, February 9, 1986.

316 *Both the Cubs and White Sox*: Skip Myslenski and Linda Kay, "Popular Guy," *Chicago Tribune*, March 21, 1986.

316 *He participated in Hands Across America*: Charles Krauthammer, "Celebrities in Politics," *Time*, April 21, 1986.

316 *And was saluted by Jackson, Mississippi*: David Beard, "Walter Payton Day," *Associated Press*, May 12, 1986.

316–17   *Bob Richards, Brice Jenner, Mary Lou Retton and Pete Rose*: "Wheaties puts Payton on cover," *USA Today*, May 6, 1986.

317   *"To be on the box"*: William C. Trott, "Wheaties Cover Boy,"*United Press International*, May 7, 1986.

317   *Take two football stars*: "News," *PR Newswire*, February 7, 1986.

318   *"He's a scholar"*: Pierson, "Bears Tab Anderson of Florida," *Chicago Tribune*, April 30, 1986.

318   *When he finally signed*: Pierson, "It's sign-up day in the NFL," *Chicago Tribune*, August 14, 1986.

318   *Throughout the season stories were*: Ron Borges, "Anderson Surviving in Payton Place," *The Boston Globe*, November 9, 1988.

319   *Even Ditka, Payton's biggest*: Pierson, "Ditka May Slow Payton," *Chicago Tribune*, September 4, 1986.

319   *Unlike Anderson, whose absence*: Pierson, "Payton lands with Class at Bears Camp," *Chicago Tribune*, July 18, 1986.

319   *From the commercialism*: Sally Jenkins, "With the Chicago Bears, Things Never Are Boring," *The Washington Post*, January 1, 1987.

320   *"My arm was coming out of the socket"*: Pierson, "Bringing in Flutie Helped Bring Down Club," *Chicago Tribune*, August 16, 1995.

321   *On the day after the trade*: Pomerantz, "As Flutie May Learn, Bears Are a Team of Rugged Individualists," *The Washington Post*, October 19, 1986.

322   *With the Redskins leading*: Pierson, "Bears' Super Rule Ends at XX," *Chicago Tribune*, January 7, 1987.

323   *"Instead of appearing like the old"*: Pomerantz, "Time Could Be Running Out for a Finally Run-Down Payton," *The Washington Post*, January 7, 1987.

323   *"My goal is sixteen hundred"*: Pierson, "'I'm Going for 18,000. Life Changes Every Day. Maybe Next Week It might Be 20,000,'" *Chicago Tribune*, November 7, 1999.

323  *Why, in the February 1 Pro Bowl*: Brennan, "NFC Mistake-Prone in 10-6 Loss," *The Washington Post*, February 2, 1987.

324  *Thanks to the efforts of Jesse*: Frank Dexter Brown, "Jesse Vs. The Big Leagues," *Black Enterprise*, July 1987.

326  *"Nothing is final"*: Pierson, "'The Best Way to Go Out,'" *Chicago Tribune*, July 29, 1987.

328  *Much was made of the Herculean matchup*: Pierson, "And Now, the Game," *Chicago Tribune*, September 14, 1987.

328  *The next day's* St. Petersburg Times: Bruce Lowitt, "End Near for Payton?" *St. Petersburg Times*, September 15, 1987.

328  *"The Bears were so good in every way"*: Michael Wilbon, "Bears' Defenders Sack Giants, 34–19," *Chicago Tribune*, September 15, 1987.

328  *Neither did the following week's triumph*: Mooshil, "Bears 20, Buccaneers 3," *Associated Press*, September 20, 1987.

329  *"They're keying on Walter"*: Lincicome, "The Game Should Matter, But . . . ," *Chicago Tribune*, September 21, 1987.

329  *"You can tell he's upset"*: Mike Kiley, "Anderson Answers Call of Duty," *Chicago Tribune*, September 21, 1987.

329  *"Like the way John Havlicek did it"*: Mike Conklin and Rich Lorenz, "Dr. J has Some Advice for Payton: Say Farewell," *Chicago Tribune*, January 22, 1987.

329  *On the day after the Tampa game*: James Warren, "NFL Clock Runs Out," *Chicago Tribune*, September 23, 1987.

330  *Meanwhile, three games were played*: Pierson, "Bears Forge on with New Faces," *Chicago Tribune*, September 23, 1987.

330  *"I had little to gain out of this strike"*: David Steele, "Payton's Place," *St. Petersburg Times*, October 22, 1987.

330  *Before the game Payton agreed to meet*: "Angry teen says there's more to story of fairy-tale Bear meeting," *St. Petersburg Times*, October 30, 1987.

331 *"I know what's going on"*: Jay Lawrence, "Little sweetness for Payton,"
*Orange County Register*, November 1, 1987.

331 *"There are ample examples of all-time great professional"*: Randy Minkoff,
"Payton's numbers drop in 13th season," *United Press International*,
November 14, 1987.

331 *The Bears were scheduled to play at San Francisco on*: Wilbon, "49ers Pelt
Bears with Rice, 41–0," *The Washington Post*, December 15, 1987.

332 *Mayor Eugene Sawyer presented*: Kiley, "Walter's Time, Win or Lose,"
*Chicago Tribune*, December 21, 1987.

333 *Throughout the season*: Linda Kay and Mike Conklin, "Year-end
report," *Chicago Tribune*, December 29, 1987.

333 *"Three seconds left"*: Clark Judge, "49ers not yet legend, says a critical
Ditka," *The San Diego Union-Tribune*, January 8, 1988.

334 *"We haven't played [the 46 Defense]"*: Ralph Wiley, "Hats off to the
Redskins," *Sports Illustrated*, January 18, 1988.

334 *"I think we'll win it all"*: Pierson, "Ditka Defiant: 'We'll Win it All,'"
*Chicago Tribune*, January 5, 1988.

334–35 *"Sometimes I feel I'm the problem"*: Tom Friend, "Payton: The Hard Way
Out," *The Washington Post*, January 10, 1988.

335–36 *"All my life, I've wanted to be on the same field"*: Wiley, "Hats off to the
Redskins," *Sports Illustrated*, January 18, 1988.

336 *"One more year, Walter!"*: Dave Anderson, "Walter Payton's Last
Time," *The New York Times*, January 11, 1988.

336 *"I was just recapping some of the great moments"*: *Pure Payton*, VHS
(PolyGram USA Video, 1997).

337 *"One by one, he tugged at the fingers"*: Anderson, "Walter Payton's Last
Time," *The New York Times*, January 11, 1988.


CHAPTER 22

355 *The first time Payton drove at famed Lime Rock Park*: Bruce Newman,
"Walter Payton," *Sports Illustrated*, August 2, 1993.

CHAPTER 23

358 *Best known as Craig*: Scott Fowler, "Miami Loses CB Judson, Four Others," *The Miami Herald*, March 30, 1990.

359 *Among the first to be auditioned*: Greg Cote, "Dolphins Likely to Sign RB Today," *The Miami Herald*, October 25, 1989.

360 *"I always felt that Walter was one"*: Jim Thomas, "4-Wheel Drive: Unusual Quartet Homes in on Paydirt," *St. Louis Post-Dispatch*, January 20, 1993.

361 *Raised in a housing project on the south*: Tim Poor, "Fumbled Away; Behind-the-Scenes Turmoil Doomed NFL Hopes," *St. Louis Post-Dispatch*, December 5, 1993.

361–62 *Growing up in Philly, he sold sodas*: Jerry Clinton with Rob Rains. *Accept the Challenge* (St. Louis: Reedy Press, 2007), 89.

362 *"He had on a blue pinstripe suit"*: Poor, "Fumbled Away; Behind-the-Scenes Turmoil Doomed NFL Hopes," *St. Louis Post-Dispatch*, December 5, 1993.

362 *Payton had first outwardly expressed*: "Payton Considers Buying NFL Team," *The Washington Post*, August 7, 1986.

363 *Payton and Clinton were first introduced*: Thomas, "4-Wheel Drive: Unusual Quartet Homes in on Paydirt," *St. Louis Post-Dispatch*, January 20, 1993.

363 *"This is a difficult track"*: Clinton and Rains. *Accept the Challenge*, 57.

363 *"Jerry was just kind of an ego guy"*: Payton and Yaeger, *Never Die Easy*, 144.

364 *Despite mounting hostilities between*: Poor, "Fumbled Away; Behind-the-Scenes Turmoil Doomed NFL Hopes," *St. Louis Post-Dispatch*, December 5, 1993.

364 *Shortly thereafter, bonds to*: Thomas, "4-Wheel Drive: Unusual Quartet Homes in on Paydirt," *St. Louis Post-Dispatch*, January 20, 1993.

365 *"The demographics are there"*: Mitchell, "St. Louis could become Payton's place," *Chicago Tribune*, March 11, 1990.

366  *"You know what?"*: Payton and Yaeger, *Never Die Easy*, 145.

366  *On September 9, 1993, the partnership*: Poor, "Fumbled Away; Behind-the-Scenes Turmoil Doomed NFL Hopes," *St. Louis Post-Dispatch*, December 5, 1993.

368  *Although Walter Payton would never*: Brian Hewitt, "Payton High-steps Into the Hall," *Chicago Sun-Times*, January 31, 1993.

368  *"I have mixed emotions"*: Jay Mariotti, "Was Vote Unanimous? It Doesn't Matter, Walter," *Chicago Sun-Times*, January 31, 1993.

368  *One week later Payton, citing*: Pierson, "Payton misses his Hall induction," *Chicago Tribune*, February 7, 1993.

369  *Around this same time, Payton also turned*: Ivan Maisel, "Historical Perspective," *The Dallas Morning News*, February 21, 1993.

369  *A couple of days later, Payton groused*: Pierson, "Ex-teammates' snub hurts: Payton," *Chicago Tribune*, February 14, 1993.

369  *The first person to come to mind was Jim Finks*: "Finks Was to Present Payton," *The Times-Picayune*, August 1, 1993.

373  *He missed an important Thursday*: Mariotti, "Honors Day Tugs, Tears At Payton," *Chicago Sun-Times*, August 1, 1993.

374  *"This is an historic event that my dad"*: Steve Springer, "Younger Payton steals show," *Houston Chronicle*, August 1, 1993.


## CHAPTER 24

382  *"He ate junk"*: Mark Konkol, "Restaurant employee turned into good friend," *Chicago Sun-Times*, November 1, 2009.

389  *He spent several years as a member of the Chicago*: "Presenters named for 1993 Pro Football Hall of Fame enshrinement," *Business Wire*, July 15, 1993.


## CHAPTER 25

393  *He underwent further testing*: Payton and Yaeger, *Never Die Easy*, 202.

394  *He delighted in seeing his boy*: Charley Walters, "What? Moss Wants to Play Pro Basketball, Too," *Saint Paul Pioneer Press*, June 2, 1998.

394  *"I wasn't as hungry"*: Walter Payton, interview by Larry King, *Larry King Live*, February 3, 1999.

394  *He swigged from bottles of Pepto-Bismol*: Payton, Payton, and Payton, *Payton*, 145.

394  *"I had been traveling between Chicago"*: Payton and Yaeger, *Never Die Easy*, 203.

395  *Tests were conducted*: Payton, Payton, and Payton. *Payton*, 145.

396  *"His health was [starting to affect] his business"*: Payton and Yaeger, *Never Die Easy*, 204.

396  *"I was not panic-stricken at this point"*: Ibid.

398  *When Charley Walters, a staff columnist*: Walters, "Hall of Famer Payton at Mayo Clinic," *Saint Paul Pioneer Press*, January 3, 1999.

399  *Gores explained to Payton*: Don Babwin, "Doctors Discuss Payton's Condition," *Associated Press*, November 1, 1999.

399  *"I was at level three"*: Payton and Yaeger, *Never Die Easy*, 206.

399  *"This won't get any better"*: Walter Payton, interview by Larry King, *Larry King Live*, February 3, 1999.

399  *The average wait for a liver in Illinois*: Joe Gergen, "Description Irked Payton," *Newsday*, February 4, 1999.

399  *The success rate was 88 percent*: Bud Shaw, "Payton Puts Sports, Life In Perspective," *The Plain Dealer*, February 4, 1999.

401  *On the afternoon of January 29, 1999*: Steve Tucker, "Miami a sweet choice for Payton's son," *Chicago Sun-Times*, January 30, 1999.

401  *"Miami is the best fit for me as a student"*: D. L. Cummings, "UM Feels Chipper Over Blue-Chippers," *The Miami Herald*, February 1, 1999.

401  *That evening Mark Giangreco*: Robert Feder, "Giangreco offers apology for jokes about Payton," *Chicago Sun-Times*, February 3, 1999.

402 *"That upset me beyond what you can"*: Payton and Yaeger, *Never Die Easy*, 212.

403 *He gripped a white microphone*: Cote, "Day of Irony for Payton Family," *The Miami Herald*, February 3, 1999.

404 *"There was some unspoken comfort level"*: Shaw, "Payton Puts Sports, Life In Perspective," *The Plain Dealer*, February 4, 1999.

404 *Toward the end, Jiggets asked Payton*: Mike Lupica, "Sweetness Needs Liver: Explains, Doesn't Complain," *New York Daily News*, February 3, 1999.

404 *Payton was the marquee guest*: *Larry King Live*, February 3, 1999.

406 *Jay Leno sent a note that read*: Steve Schoenfeld, "Greene Lays Down The Law," *The Arizona Republic*, February 14, 1999.

406 *"Cry for him, pray for him"*: Mariotti, "Payton's dignity shines through life's dim reality," *Chicago Sun-Times*, February 4, 1999.

406 *"Never before have we had anything"*: Erica Key, "Payton sparks rise in organ donations," *The Bloomington (Indiana) Pentagraph*, February 5, 1999.

406 *Some thirty-odd letters came from people*: Don Yaeger, "One of a Kind," *Sports Illustrated*, November 8, 1999.

407 *Payton wrote back, and kept*: Jeff Pearlman, "A Hard Burden to Bear," *Sports Illustrated*, February 22, 1999.

407 *In early February a spokeswoman for Payton*: "Payton's Disease Progressing," *Associated Press*, February 12, 1999.

407 *In April Dr. Joe Lagattuta, one of Payton's*: Leslie Cummings, "Payton's doctor says hero has good chance," *Chicago Daily Herald*, April 16, 1999.

408 *"I don't feel sorry for myself"*: Payton and Yaeger, *Never Die Easy*, 225.

## CHAPTER 26

410 *When Payton was introduced*: Rick Gano, "Payton makes first pitch for Cubs," *Associated Press*, April 12, 1999.

410 *On the day after the first pitch*: "Payton Fatigued After His Appearance at Cubs Opener," *Chicago Tribune*, April 13, 1999.

411   *Payton's final public appearance came*: Teresa Mask, "Faith gave Payton strength in last days, pastor says," *Chicago Daily Herald*, November 4, 1999.

413   *"One time we got stuck in traffic"*: Payton and Yaeger, *Never Die Easy*, 235.

413   *"I never heard him say, 'Why me?'"*: Ibid., 248.

414   *That night, October 28, 1999*: Stephen Nidetz, "Payton's Son Called Home," *Chicago Tribune*, October 29, 1999.


CHAPTER 27

417   *On the morning of April 5, 2000*: Judith Cookis, "Payton's widow shares family memories," *Chicago Daily Herald*, April 6, 2000.

418   *President Bill Clinton issued a statement*: No byline, "Clinton Statement on Payton," *Associated Press*, November 1, 1999.

418   *A former Burger King drive-thru worker*: "Remembering Walter," *Chicago Daily Herald*, November 7, 1999.

422   *Between fifteen thousand and twenty thousand spectators*: Mask, "A most sweet sendoff," *Chicago Daily Herald*, November 7, 1999.

422   *The Sweet Holy Spirit Gospel Choir sang*: "Payton's Soldier Field 'encore,'" *The Star-Ledger* (Newark), November 7, 1999.

422   *"In some respects"*: J. A. Adande, "Memories of Payton Raise Cheers During Service at Soldier Field," *Los Angeles Times*, November 7, 1999.

422   *"I remember this guy playing on this field"*: John Mullin, "Inspirational Leader Recalled," *Chicago Tribune*, November 7, 1999.

# BIBLIOGRAPHY

*75 Seasons: The Complete Story of the National Football League, 1920–1995.* Atlanta, Ga.: Turner Publishing, 1994.

*The '85 Bears: Still Chicago's Team.* Chicago: Triumph Books, 2005.

Anderson, Lars. *The First Star: Red Grange and the Barnstorming Tour That Launched the NFL.* New York: Random House, 2009.

Berghaus, Bob. *Black & Blue: A Smash-Mouth History of the NFL's Roughest Division.* Cincinnati, Oh.: Clerisy Press, 2007.

Clinton, Jerry, with Rob Rains. *Accept The Challenge.* St. Louis, Miss.: Reedy Press, 2007.

Conrad, Dick. *Walter Payton: The Running Machine.* Chicago: Childrens Press, 1979.

Cramer, Richard Ben. *Joe DiMaggio: The Hero's Life.* New York: Simon & Schuster, 2000.

D'Amato, Gary, and Cliff Christi. *Mudbaths & Bloodbaths.* Black Earth, Wisc.: Prairie Oak Press, 1997.

Davies, David R. *The Press and Race: Mississippi Journalists Confront the Movement.* Jackson, Mississippi: University Press of Mississippi, 2001.

Davis, Jeff. *Papa Bear: The Life and Legacy of George Halas.* New York: McGraw-Hill, 2005.

Delsohn, Steve. *Da Bears!* New York: Crown Archetype, 2010.

Dittmer, John. *Local People: The Struggle for Civil Rights in Mississippi.* Champaign, Ill.: University of Illinois Press, 1995.

Ditka, Mike, with Don Pierson. *Ditka: An Autobiography.* Chicago: Bonus Books, 1986.

Ditka, Mike, with Rick Telander. *In Life, First You Kick Ass.* Champaign, Ill.: Sports Publishing LLC, 2005.

Ditka, Mike, with Rick Telander. *The '85 Bears: We Were the Greatest.* Chicago: Triumph Books, 2010.

Eagles, Charles W. *The Price of Defiance.* Chapel Hill, N.C.: The University of North Carolina Press, 2009.

Ford, Liam T. A. *Soldier Field: A Stadium and Its City.* Chicago: The University of Chicago Press, 2009.

Freeman, Mike. *Jim Brown: The Fierce Life of an American Hero.* New York: HarperCollins, 2006.

Graziano, A. J. *Racing with the Stars: A Memoir.* Cleveland, Oh.: Felsen Press, 2010.

Halas, George, with Gwen Morgan and Arthur Veysey. *Halas by Halas.* New York: McGraw-Hill, 1979.

Hamilton-Smith, Katherine, and Rebecca Elliot. *A Picture Is Worth 1000 Yards: Sports Photography of Walter Payton.* Lake County, Ill.: Friends of the Lake County Discovery Museum, 2004.

Harkey, Ira. *The Smell of Burning Crosses.* Bloomington, Ind.: Xlibris, 2006.

Hendrickson, Paul. *Sons of Mississippi.* New York: Vintage Books, 2004.

Jiggets, Dan, with Fred Mitchell. *"Then Ditka Said to Payton . . ."* Chicago: Triumph, 2008.

Lamb, Kevin, *Portrait of Victory: Chicago Bears 1985.* Provo, Utah: Final Four Publications, 1986.

Leavy, Jane. *The Last Boy: Mickey Mantle and the End of America's Childhood.* New York: Harper, 2010.

MacCambridge, Michael. *America's Game.* New York: Anchor Books, 2004.

MacLean, Harry N. *The Past Is Never Dead: The Trial of James Ford Seale and Mississippi's Struggle for Redemption.* New York: BasicCivitas, 2009.

McCaskey, Patrick, with Mike Sandrolini. *Bear With Me*. Chicago: Triumph, 2009.

McGrane, Bill. *Sweetness: A Celebration of Walter Payton's 13 Seasons With the Chicago Bears*. Los Angeles: National Football League, 1988.

McGrath, John, and Ryan Ver Berkmoes. *The Official Chicago Bar Guide*. Chicago: Buckingham Books, 1994.

McMahon, Jim, with Bob Verdi. *McMahon!* New York: Warner Books, 1986.

McMichael, Steve, with Phil Arvia. *Steve McMichael's Tales from the Chicago Bears Sideline*. Champaign, Ill.: Sports Publishing LLC, 2004.

Moody, Anne. *Coming of Age in Mississippi*. New York: Dell, 1968.

Morris, Willie. *The Courting of Marcus DuPree*. Jackson, Miss.: University of Mississippi Press, 1983.

Mullin, John. *The Rise and Self-Destruction of the Greatest Football Team in History*. Chicago: Triumph Books, 2005.

Norris, Chuck, with Ken Abraham. *Against All Odds: My Story*. Nashville, Tenn.: B&H Publishing, 2006.

Payton, Connie. *Stronger Than Cancer*. Lynwood, Wash.: Compendium Publishing, 2002.

Payton, Connie, Jarrett Payton, and Brittney Payton. *Payton*. New York: Rugged Land, 2005.

Payton, Walter, with Jerry B. Jenkins. *Sweetness*. Chicago: Contemporary Books, 1978.

Payton, Walter, with Don Yaeger. *Never Die Easy: The Autobiography of Walter Payton*. New York: Random House, 2000.

Peoples, John A. *To Survive and Thrive: A Quest for a True University*. Jackson, Miss.: Town Square Books, 1995.

Reamon, Tommy, with Ron Whitenack. *Rough Diamonds: A Coach's Journey*. Chicago: Triumph Books, 2001.

Rollow, Cooper. *Cooper Rollow's Chiago Bears Football Book*. Ottawa, Ill.: Jameson Books, 1986.

Rollow, Cooper. *Cooper Rollow's Bears 1978 Football Book*. Ottawa, Ill.: Caroline House, 1978.

Sayers, Gale, with Al Silverman. *I Am Third*. New York: Viking, 1970.

Sayers, Gale, with Fred Mitchell. *Sayers: My Life and Times*. Chicago: Triumph 2007.

Singletary, Mike, with Armen Keteyian. *Calling the Shots*. Chicago: Contemporary Books, 1986.

Singletary, Mike, with Jerry Jenkins. *Singletary on Singletary*. Nashville, Tenn.: Thomas Nelson, Inc., 1991.

Spinney, Robert G. *City of Big Shoulders*. DeKalb, Ill.: Northern Illinois University Press, 2000.

Sufrin, Mark. *Payton*. New York: Charles Scribner's Sons, 1988.

Sutherland, Elizabeth. *Letters from Mississippi*. New York: Signet Books, 1965.

*Sweetness: The Courage and Heart of Walter Payton*. Chicago: Triumph, 1999.

Taylor, Roy. *Chicago Bears History*. Charleston, S.C.: Arcadia Publishing, 2004.

Thompson, Barbara R. *Just Plain Bill*. Decatur, Ga.: Pathway Communications Group, 1996.

Towle, Mike. *I Remember Walter Payton*. Nashville, Tenn.: Cumberland House, 2000.

Vass, George. *George Halas and the Chicago Bears*. Chicago: Henry Regnery Company, 1971.

Welty, Eudora. *The Collected Stories of Eudora Welty*. Orlando, Fl.: Harcourt Brace Jovanovich Publishers, 1980.

Whittingham, Richard. *What Bears They Were*. Chicago: Triumph, 2002.

Woog, Adam. *Walter Payton*. New York: Chelsea House, 2008.

# INDEX

Page numbers followed by an *n* refer to notes at the bottom of the page.

Abercrombie, Walter, 249
Adamle, Mike, 157, 166, 168, 169, 174
affairs. *See under* women
agent. *See* Holmes, Paul H. "Bud"
Alberts, Mark, 275, 395, 400, 413, 429
Albrecht, Ted, 192, 198, 201, 218, 248
Allen, Egypt, 326–27
All-Star football team, 147–51
Anderson, Neal:
  drafted, 317
  injury, 334
  1986 season, 322
  Payton's blocks for, 331
  as Payton's replacement, 317–19, 323
  as starting fullback, 327, 328
  success of, 328, 329
Andrews, Tom, 306
Armstrong, Neill:
  background, 212
  on Baschnagel, 235
  coaching style, 212, 219, 220, 222, 248
  death threat, 217
  drive of, 232
  hired as coach, 211–12
  initial meeting with Payton, 213
  moodiness of Payton, 218–19
  1978 season, 215, 217–22
  1979 season, 232, 234, 235
  1980 season, 238
  1981 season, 241, 243
  replaced by Ditka, 247
Ascher, Scott, 395, 400, 411, 413
athleticism of Payton:
  balance, 195–96
  in college career, 74–75, 134, 148
  in professional career, 153–54, 155–56
  spatting technique, 231–32
  stiff-arm tactic, 17, 47, 91, 95, 101, 148, 178

  training regime, 99–100, 129, 148–49, 173, 195–96, 199, 271
  in youth, 12, 14, 16–17, 23–25, 40–41, 53
Atlanta Falcons, 120, 130–31, 179
Atlas, Ron, 210, 221*n*, 229, 238–39, 344
attention deficit hyperactivity disorder (ADHD), 225, 382
auto racing of Payton, 351–57
Avellini, Bob:
  on Armstrong, 222
  and Finks, 232
  on Gault, 297–98
  irritation with Payton, 198
  limitations of, 165, 184, 217, 233
  linemen's regard for, 198
  1976 season, 174–75, 184
  1977 season, 191–92, 195, 196, 197, 202–4
  1978 season, 222
  1979 season, 233, 234
  1982 season, 252
  on personality of Payton, 164, 172, 178, 273
  release of, 283
  on tackling Payton, 192

Baker, T. J., 287
Baltimore Colts, 120, 132, 133, 159–61, 174
Bannister, Frank, Jr., 112
Barbaro, Gary, 193
Barnhardt, Tommy, 333–34
Bartkowski, Steve, 127, 130–31, 147, 148, 150
Baschnagel, Brian:
  on Gillman, 189, 191
  1976 season, 175
  1977 season, 194
  1979 season, 234–35
  1985 season, 289
  Super Bowl XX, 312
Becker, Kurt, 227, 265

Beckman, Witt, 151
Bell, Todd, 278, 285, 327
Berry, Raymond, 306, 308–9
Black College All-American Football Team (1971), 106
Blackmon, Don, 309, 312
Bleier, Rocky, 131–32, 166–67
Bortz, Mark, 278
Boston, Charles:
  background, 20–22
  and college-bound seniors, 54
  and college recruiters, 57–58
  as Columbia High's receivers' coach, 40, 44
  and Eddie Payton, 22–23
  Hall of Fame induction, 374
  initial interaction with Payton, 19, 20
  and integration, 51–52
  as Jefferson High's coach, 24–25, 26–28, 39
  and jersey number, 75
  plays designed for Payton, 46
  and running style of Payton, 78
bowl games:
  college bowls, 128–29, 134
  Pro Bowls, 224, 232, 243, 282, 292, 323, 342
  *See also* Super Bowl XX
Brandt, Gil, 131
Brazile, Robert:
  on athleticism of Payton, 99, 104
  on attire of Payton, 108
  College All-Star football team, 147, 148
  on Connie Norwood, 107
  East-West Shrine Game, 127, 128, 130
  on future of Payton, 81
  on Heisman campaign, 110
  and Holmes, 123, 124
  Mavericks game, 115
  NFL draft (1975), 131, 132
  relationship with Payton, 87
  talent of, 77

Brewer, Jill, 48
Brockington, John, 270
Brown, Jim:
  all-purpose yards record, 273
  all-time rushing record, 264–65,
    266, 267, 269–71, 277–79,
    305
  on athleticism of Payton, 193,
    271
  background, 274
  Payton-Harris showdown,
    269–71
  Payton's regard for, 271, 276
  skills of, 274, 425
  social and political activism,
    274–75
Brupbacher, Ross, 153
Bryant, Bear, 141, 152, 167
Bryant, Waymond, 157, 175, 189,
    201
Buffalo Bills, 180–81
Buffone, Doug, 203, 232
Buford, Maury, 306, 315
Buick events, 229, 231, 259–60
Bunting, John, 162
business dealings of Payton. See
    investments and business
    dealings
Butkus, Dick, 140, 145, 246
Butler, Kevin, 287, 289, 292,
    295, 307

Cabral, Brian, 242, 243
Caito, Fred:
  on endurance of Payton, 242
  injuries of Payton, 150, 165,
    184, 322–23
  on missed game, 168
  on moodiness of Payton, 218
  pain management of Payton,
    187–88
  on post-Super Bowl team, 320
  on Sayers, 215
  on Scott, 249
  on state of Payton's body, 331
  on steroid use, 285, 324
  on training regime of Payton,
    326
  on Watts, 250
Callahan, Ray, 160
Campbell, Earl, 222, 282, 292,
    296, 425
Canadian Football League, 136,
    240–41
cancer of Payton, 393–408
  announcement of, 402–4
  cancer diagnosis, 398–401, 404,
    405, 407
  cancer's spread, 410–11
  chemotherapy treatments,
    407–8, 411

death of Payton, 415–16, 418
decline of Payton, 401–2,
    409–15
early warning signs, 393–94
final months of Payton's life,
    412–13
impact on organ donations,
    405, 406
and potential liver transplant,
    399–401, 405, 407, 411
primary sclerosing cholangitis
    diagnosis, 398–400, 405
public appearances, 404–6, 408,
    409–10, 411
public response to, 406–7
symptoms, 394–95, 396–97
vitamin toxicity diagnosis,
    395–96
Carmichael, Harold, 234
Carter, Virg, 161
Chambers, Wally, 167, 175, 187, 190
Cherry, Deron, 367–68
Chicago Bears:
  Chicago Blitz's pursuit of
    Payton, 268–69
  coaches (see Armstrong, Neill;
    Ditka, Mike;
    Pardee, Jack)
  contracts with Payton, 136,
    138–39, 214–16, 239–41,
    259, 269
  death threats, 216–17, 219
  defensive line, 237, 272, 281, 320
  Ditka–Ryan divide, 272, 289,
    295–96
  drafts, 132–33, 134, 232, 235–36,
    271, 317–18
  drug use, 176–77
  economy of, 247, 268, 269
  end-of-career negotiations,
    324–26
  equipment of Payton, 276–77
  facilities, 145, 166, 205, 213, 235
  greatest run of Payton's career,
    191–93
  inconsistency of, 177
  irritation with Payton, 163–64,
    179, 198, 227–28
  jersey number of Payton retired,
    325, 333
  last game of Payton, 333–38
  memorial service for Payton, 422
  1975 season, 147, 151–57,
    158–63, 166–69, 170–71
  1976 season, 172–79, 181–85
  1977 season, 188–97, 199–206
  1978 season, 214, 216–17, 219,
    220, 221–22
  1979 season, 232–35
  1980 season, 235–38, 239
  1981 season, 239, 241–43

1982 season, 248–54, 265
1983 season, 264–67, 272
1984 season, 271–74, 276–79,
    280–83, 284–85
1985 season, 289–91, 293–97,
    299–300, 302–3 (see also
    Super Bowl XX)
1986 season, 319–20
1987 season, 326–36
origins and early years of, 143–45
phasing out of Payton, 323–25
player strikes, 251, 329–30
quarterbacking of Payton, 283
quarterback issue, 211, 212,
    233, 250, 252
racial divide in, 154–55
rookie period of Payton, 160,
    161–68, 172
salaries, 214, 288
scouting Payton, 120
second-tier status of, 140–41,
    145
social awkwardness of Payton,
    162, 164 (see also persona of
    Payton)
successor of Payton, 317–18,
    323
telegraphing of Payton, 179
Walter Payton Day, 332–33
See also injuries and physical toll
    of football
offensive line of the Chicago
    Bears
rushing competitions and
    records
Chicago Blitz, 268–69
Chicago Cubs, 316, 409–10
Childers, Jack, 250
Cleveland Browns, 188, 237
Clifford, Tim, 233, 241, 263
Clinton, Jerry, 357, 361–67
Coady, Rich, 141, 146
college scouting and recruitment,
    43–44, 54–62. See also
    Jackson State College
Columbia, Mississippi, 3–6, 8–9,
    30–35, 207–10
Columbia High School:
  football in, 1, 38–47, 51–52,
    54–55
  integration of, 32–37, 41, 42,
    44–45
  and Jefferson High, 20, 22, 24,
    26
  Payton's number retired, 342
  race relations in, 47–48
  Super Bowl XX, 310
commodities broker internship,
    225
Conley, Linda, 262, 370–71, 380,
    381, 387, 417–18

Coryell, Don, 211, 212
Cosby, Bill, 331
Cosell, Howard, 168–69
Covert, Jimbo:
  cancer diagnosis of Payton, 412
  1983 season, 265
  1984 season, 278, 285
  1985 season, 289, 295, 297
  1986 season, 322
  on personality of Payton, 226
  on replacement of Payton, 327
  "Super Bowl Shuffle," 293
  Super Bowl XX, 306, 312, 315
Crawley, Colleen, 49–51, 108
Cuie, Ron, 176
Cumby, George, 291

Dallas Cowboys, 120, 131–32,
  204–5, 277
Davis, Brian, 335–36
Davis, Tommy:
  and black players, 44
  and college-bound seniors, 54
  as Columbia High's coach,
    39–40, 42
  and integration, 39–40, 51–52
  motivating Payton, 1
  plays designed for Payton, 46
DeBerg, Steve, 233
Deloplaine, Jack, 242
Denver Broncos, 183–84, 273
Detroit Lions, 163, 175–76, 199–200
Dickerson, Eric, 215, 302–3, 425
Dickey, Lynn, 283
Ditka, Mike:
  and Anderson, 318, 327
  attitude of Payton, 254, 265–66
  background, 245–46
  book deal, 319
  cancer diagnosis of Payton, 406,
    410
  celebrity, 292
  coaching style, 248
  on Cowboys draft picks (1975),
    131
  drive of, 245–46
  on fans' love of Payton, 425
  funeral of Payton, 420
  on loyalty in sports, 323
  1982 season, 251
  1984 season, 272, 284–85
  1985 season, 289, 290–91,
    295–97, 299–300
  1986 season, 322
  1987 season, 327, 328,
    329, 334
  on organ donation, 405
  phasing out of Payton, 323
  as player for the Bears, 244, 245,
    246–47, 248
  players' reactions to, 249–51

pursuit of coaching position,
  244–45, 247
on the Raiders, 280–81
and rushing record, 296–97
and Ryan, 272, 289, 295–96
on Super Bowl potential, 249,
  285, 334
Super Bowl XX, 304, 305, 312,
  313–14, 315, 316
on Walsh, 211*n*
Donchez, Tom, 153
Douglass, Bobby, 141, 165, 175
Douthitt, Earl, 165, 176, 177
Downing, Ken, 174
Dukes, Delores, 30–31
Dunsmore, Pat, 278, 284

Earl, Robin, 192, 195, 198
Earley, Ray, 201, 251, 276
Eason, Tony, 309
Ecklund, Brad, 189
Edwards, Cid, 166
Ehlebracht, Tim, 255–56, 339
Ehrmann, Joe, 159, 161
Ellis, Allan, 234
Ely, Larry, 121, 154
Emrich, Clyde, 145, 188
Erving, Julius, 329
Evans, Vince:
  and Chicago Blitz, 268
  as confidant of Payton, 327
  on facilities, 145
  and Finks, 232
  1979 season, 233
  1980 season, 236–37
  1981 season, 243
  1982 season, 252
  on retirement, 381–82

Falks, Frank, 55–56
fans of Payton, 229, 286, 383, 425,
  426
Fencik, Gary, 289, 299, 310
Fergerson, Duke, 227
Fichtner, Ross, 274
finances of Payton:
  and birth of son, 240
  in retirement, 360–61, 383
  salary and bonuses, 214, 238,
    269, 288, 361
  *See also* investments and
    business dealings
Finks, Jim:
  and Armstrong, 212
  background, 146
  contract negotiations, 138,
    214–16
  death threat, 216–17
  drafts, 132, 134, 232, 235–36
  on durability of athletes, 174
  Hall of Fame induction, 369

  hired by the Bears, 146
  introductory press conference,
    135
  lung cancer diagnosis, 369
  and Pardee, 153
  on performance of Payton, 243
  quarterbacks, 233, 250
  resignation, 247, 269
  rookie of the year award, 172
  Vikings-Bears game, 194
Fisher, Bob, 248
Fisher, Jeff, 263, 276–77
Flutie, Doug, 321–22
Flynn, Tom, 283
Frederick, Andy, 290
Fuller, Steve:
  1984 season, 282, 283, 285
  1985 season, 295, 296
  1986 season, 320
  on Simpson, 200
  Super Bowl XX, 304

Gallagher, Dave, 154
Gamauf, John, 381, 386, 394, 396,
  408
Garrett, Carl, 155, 157
Gault, Willie:
  endorsements, 319
  and McMahon's hair style, 291
  1985 season, 289
  1986 season, 321
  1987 season, 335
  "Super Bowl Shuffle," 293,
    297–98, 299
  Super Bowl XX, 309, 310, 311
Gayle, Shaun, 257, 289, 298, 310,
  322
Gentry, Dennis, 301, 311
Gerhart, Doug, 235
Gershuny, Greg, 291, 298–99
Gibbs, Phillip, 66
Gibron, Abe, 133, 141–42, 153,
  159, 167
Gibson, Vince, 55, 56, 60, 146
Gillman, Sid, 188–89, 191, 195, 196
Gonzalez, Lita:
  cancer diagnosis of Payton, 403
  current status, 429
  divorce paperwork of Payton,
    380
  early relationship with Payton,
    350–51, 356
  emotional instability of Payton,
    382
  funeral of Payton, 420
  Hall of Fame induction, 370–75
Gorden, W. C., 63
Grandberry, Ken, 155, 157
Grant, Bud, 194
Gravelle, Gordon, 202
Green, James, 66

Green Bay Packers, 219, 273, 282–83
Griffin, Archie, 111–12, 116, 117, 120

Halas, George:
  on Antoine, 160
  background, 142–44
  contract negotiations, 240
  death, 265n
  defensive unit, 272
  and Ditka, 244, 246–47
  economy of, 247, 269
  and Gibron, 141, 142
  introductory press conference, 135
  management of the Bears, 144–46
  reserved persona of, 363
Hall of Fame induction, 368–75
Hampton, Dan, 235, 290, 296, 320, 330
Harper, Roland:
  on activity level of Payton, 225–26
  on Armstrong, 222
  as confidant of Payton, 169–70, 177, 327
  cut from team, 265n
  hunting trips, 264
  injuries, 232, 236, 243
  on moodiness of Payton, 218
  on motivating Payton, 182
  1975 season, 168
  1977 season, 189
  1978 season, 222, 231
  1979 season, 232–35, 236
  1980 season, 236
  1981 season, 243
  religious faith, 170, 231, 257
  replacement of, 236, 265n, 327
  and Robertson incident, 190
  rookie of the year award, 172
Harrah, Dennis, 132, 147, 189
Harrell, Willard, 258
Harris, Al, 235, 243, 254, 265n, 272, 331
Harris, Franco, 267, 269–71, 273–74
Harris, Frank, 326
Harris, Richard, 163, 182
Hart, Tommy, 177
Hartenstine, Mike, 289
Harvey, Paul, 209
Haupt, Dale, 287
health issues:
  AIDS rumor, 402
  Epstein-Barr diagnosis, 308n
  Hepatitis C diagnosis, 398n
  herpes diagnosis, 307–8
  See also cancer of Payton;

injuries and physical toll of football
Heinold Commodities, Inc., 225
Hickey, Mike, 128
Hicks, Tom, 187
Hilgenberg, Jay:
  on Anderson, 318
  on blocking for Payton, 292
  final months of Payton's life, 413
  1983 season, 265
  1984 season, 283
  1986 season, 320, 322
  1987 season, 334
  on quarterbacking of Payton, 283
  on rushing yardage, 251
  "Super Bowl Shuffle," 297
  Super Bowl XX, 315
Hill, Bob:
  background, 68–73
  coaching Payton, 90, 101
  coaching style, 58, 68, 73–74, 77, 78–79, 93
  and dancing of Payton, 83
  expectation management strategy, 178
  Hall of Fame induction, 374
  Heisman Trophy campaign, 109, 111, 115–16
  and Holmes, 123–24, 127
  and Montgomery, 99, 100
  New Orleans Saints, 277
  NFL draft, 130, 133
  1971 football season, 75–77, 80, 81
  1972 football season, 89, 90–94
  1973 football season, 95, 100–106
  1974 football season, 113–14, 115–16, 118
  Payton's romantic life, 96, 97–99, 107
  recruitment of Payton, 56–57, 58, 59–61
  relationship with Payton, 92–93
  rushing title competition of 1976, 183
  scouting Jefferson High, 43–44
  superstitious nature, 92–93
  SWAC Coach of the Year award, 81
Hilton, John, 196
Hoffman, James, 268
Holmes, Paul H. "Bud":
  background, 125–26
  Blitz's pursuit of Payton, 268–69
  business dealings of Payton, 346
  Canadian league, 240
  on celebrity of Payton, 381
  as confidant of Payton, 381

contract negotiations, 136, 138–39, 214–16, 240–41, 259, 269
current status, 429
death of Peter Payton, 207–9
on drug use, 187, 345, 382
early relationship with Payton, 134–35
end-of-career negotiations, 324–25
on fatherhood of Payton, 262
Hall of Fame induction, 369, 373, 375
and Hill, 123–24, 127
on image of Payton, 286, 293, 313, 371–72, 429
initial meeting with Payton, 123–25
on marriage of Payton, 351
media coverage of Payton, 179
on Miami Dolphins game (1985), 296
Musburger interview, 136–38
NFL draft, 133, 134
NFL franchise bid, 324, 325, 326, 341
on Nigel Smythe, 430
on personality of Payton, 223–24, 287, 288, 301
on potential return from retirement, 359–60
public relations efforts of, 286–87, 293
on retirement years of Payton, 382
rookie season of Payton, 161, 165–66, 168
rushing title competition of 1976, 183
on suicide threats of Payton, 383
Super Bowl XX, 304, 311n, 313–14, 316
on winning, 238
on women in Payton's life, 229–30, 258, 370, 375
hometown. See Columbia, Mississippi
honors:
  All-Time Black College Football Team, 369
  ESPYs award, 406
  Father of the Year, 261
  first pitches for the Chicago Cubs, 316, 409–10
  Gordon Gin Black Athlete of the Year award, 285–86, 287
  Hall of Fame induction, 368–75
  NFC Player of the Year award, 187
  NFL Most Valuable Player, 211
  NFL's Player of the Month, 282

Payton's numbers retired, 325, 333, 342
post-Super Bowl XX, 316
Pro Bowls, 224, 232, 243, 282, 292, 323, 342
and retirement, 342
Walter Payton Day, 332
Wheaties cereal box, 316–17
World Book James Arneberg Award, 342
Hood, Estus, 238
Houston Oilers, 191
Hrivnak, Gary, 141, 154
Huff, Gary, 175
Huff, Ken, 132, 133, 165, 169, 284
Hughes, Ed, 252, 283, 285
Humphrey, Claude, 234
Hutson, Elmer "J. R.," 348–49

image of Payton:
disparity in, 254
as family man, 293, 344, 371–72, 380
Holmes on, 286, 293, 313, 371–72, 429
idealization of Payton, 293
importance of, 257–58
teammates' reinforcement of, 301
injuries and physical toll of football:
and All-Star team, 149–50
declining physicality of Payton, 282, 328, 331
in later career, 322–23
1975 season, 151–52, 156, 163, 164, 166–68
1976 season, 172–74, 184–85
1981 season, 242
1982 season, 253
1983 season, 266
1984 season, 271
1986 season, 322–23
and pain management, 187–88, 324, 382
Payton's concerns about, 186–87
from Superstars competition, 212–13
investments and business dealings:
franchise bid of Payton, 324, 325, 326, 341, 342, 360–68
nightclubs and lounges, 346–49, 361, 384–85
Payton Power, 381, 384, 388

Jackson, Henry, 319
Jackson, Jesse, 239, 324, 369, 422
Jackson, Noah:
criticisms of Payton, 216, 242
on Ditka, 251
1975 season, 160
1976 season, 187

1977 season, 192
1978 season, 216
1980 season, 238
perceptions of, 192
on rushing title, 238
Jackson, Rickey, 277
Jackson State College:
campus, 67
and Connie Norwood, 98–99, 107
graduate degree from, 173
Heisman Trophy campaign, 102, 107, 109–13, 116, 117, 119, 120
and Montgomery, 99–100
and NFL scouting, 92–93, 100, 119–20, 124, 127–28
1971 football season, 73–81
1972 football season, 88–92, 93–94
1973 football season, 95, 100–106
1974 football season, 109–10, 113–16, 117–19
recruitment of Payton, 55, 56–57, 58, 59–62
scouting Jefferson High, 43–44
social climate at, 65–67, 107–8
social life of Payton, 82–88, 107–8
state police shooting at, 66
See also Hill, Bob
Jefferson, Sam, 101, 102, 111, 113
Jenkins, Jerry B., 225, 230
John J. Jefferson High School, 4, 14–17, 19–28, 32
Jones, Lorna, 87–88, 95–96, 97, 98
Jones, Mary "Bullet," 82–83, 85–86, 108
Jordan, Michael, 339, 406, 422

Kansas City Chiefs, 191–93
Kansas State University, 55–56, 58–59, 61–62, 67
King, Lee, 84–85
Koch, Greg, 273
Kovach, Jim, 278
Kraker, Pete, 228
Kuhlman, Hank, 222, 243

Landry, Greg, 282
Landry, Tom, 131, 244, 247
Lanigan, Mike, 381, 399, 408, 409, 413
Larry King Live show, 404–6
Latta, Greg, 175, 203
legacy of Payton, 424–25
legal representation Payton, 123–25. See also Holmes, Paul H. "Bud"
Leno, Jay, 406
Levy, Marv, 268

Lick, Dennis, 175
Lisch, Rusty, 282, 283
Lister, Adrian, 205–6
Lohmeyer, John, 193
Long, Kevin, 269
Los Angeles Rams, 178, 189–91, 302–3
Los Angles Raiders, 120, 280–81
loyalty in sports, 99, 210, 272, 273, 323
Luke, Steve, 219

MacLeod, Tom, 159, 160
Madden, John, 420
Malham, Mickey, 228
Marcantonio, Steve, 155–56
Marchibroda, Ted, 241
Margerum, Ken, 253
Marino, Dan, 294, 295, 305
Marshall, George Preston, 144
Marshall, Wilber, 289, 303, 311, 320
Martin, Charles, 45
McCaskey, Michael, 268, 278, 323, 324–26
McClanahan, Brent, 196
McClendon, Willie, 227, 232, 243
McElroy, Vann, 280, 281
McGrane, Bill, 138
McGrew, Larry, 310, 312
McInally, Pat, 148, 150–51
McIntyre, Guy, 285, 291
McKay, John, 147, 148, 149
McKinnon, Dennis, 297, 309
McMahon, Jim:
book deal, 319
celebrity, 291, 292
drafted, 250, 272
endorsements, 319
injuries, 281, 320
1982 season, 252, 253, 254
1984 season, 278, 281, 282, 283
1985 season, 289, 295, 296–97
1986 season, 320, 321, 322
1987 season, 335
salary, 288
"Super Bowl Shuffle," 293, 298
Super Bowl XX, 304, 306–7, 309–13, 311n, 315
McMichael, Steve, 295, 305–6
media coverage of Payton:
complaints addressed to media, 253–54, 300–301
on early retirement plans of Payton, 186
enigmatic nature of Payton, 179–80, 226
moodiness of Payton, 197–98, 218, 329
promised press conference (1982), 251–52, 252n, 253
Simpson's reaction to, 181

Meredith, James, 8, 34
Meyer, Ken, 213–14, 237
Miami Dolphins, 120, 294–97, 305, 358–60
Mike-Mayer, Steve, 177
Mills, Dale, 116–17
Minnesota Vikings, 163, 168–69, 178, 193–97
*Monday Night Football*, 168–69
*Monsters of the Midday* radio show, 395, 402–3, 413
Montana, Joe, 232, 290
Montgomery, Wilbert, 99–100, 282
Montreal Alouettes, 240–41
Moorehead, Emery, 278, 309
Morris, Jon, 227–28, 335
Moss, Rick, 262–63
Muckensturm, Jerry, 177, 267
Mullaney, Mark, 129–30
Murray, Eddie, 290
Murray, Francis W., 361–66
Musburger, Brent, 136–37, 279
Musso, Johnny, 174

Namath, Joe, 167, 189
National Football League:
    early years of, 143–44
    franchise bid of Payton, 324, 325, 326, 341, 342, 360–68
    scouting of Payton, 92–93, 100, 119–20
Neal, Dan, 204
New England Patriots, 128, 305, 306, 309
Newman, Paul, 354
New Orleans Saints, 170–71, 277–79
New York Giants, 200–204, 222, 328
Noll, Chuck, 150
Nordquist, Mark, 156, 160, 187

O'Connor, Fred:
    athleticism of Payton, 150, 153
    injuries of Payton, 166–67
    1975 season, 159, 160–61
    1976 season, 175, 184
    1977 season, 195
    praise for Payton, 181
offensive line of the Chicago Bears:
    celebrity, 292
    inadequacy of, 160, 163, 177, 187, 237, 241–42
    lack of camaraderie between, 192
    1976 season, 187
    1977 season, 188–89, 192
    1980 season, 236, 237
    1981 season, 241–42
    1982 season, 252, 253
    1983 season, 265

1984 season, 272
    relationship with Payton, 199
    and single-season rushing record, 201
    Super Bowl XX, 306
Orthwein, James Busch, 365–66
Osborne, Jim, 153, 164, 272
out-of-bounds, crossing into, 101, 203, 266

Page, Alan, 272
pain management, 187–88, 324, 382
Parcells, Bill, 58
Pardee, Jack:
    background, 152–53
    coaching style, 173, 220, 248
    concerns about Payton, 172–73
    drive of, 232
    game theory, 175
    hired as coach, 146
    injuries of Payton, 152, 153, 156, 167, 168, 174
    introductory press conference, 135
    NFL draft, 133–34
    1975 season, 157, 163, 166, 170
    1976 season, 184
    1977 season, 188–89, 191, 192, 194–96, 201
    offensive line, 188–89
    resignation, 210–11
    rookie of the year award, 172
    on rushing title, 182
Parsons, Bob, 153, 156, 204, 220–21
pastimes and passions of Payton:
    dancing, 83–86, 154
    hunting, 263–64, 346
    music, 12, 17–18, 23, 25, 293, 317, 330
    racing, 351–57
    in retirement, 346
    vehicles, 262–63, 351–52, 388–89
    in youth, 7–8, 11–13, 17, 51
Paul, Whitney, 278
Payton, Alyne Sibley:
    background, 5
    and Boston, 23
    in Chicago, 161
    children, 6–7
    college recruiters, 56, 60, 61
    college years, 67–68
    current status, 429
    death of Peter Payton, 209
    desegregation, 32, 36
    final hours of Payton's life, 415
    funeral of Payton, 419
    Hall of Fame induction, 373, 375
    musicianship of Payton, 17
    NFL draft, 133

and Nigel Smythe, 430
    rushing title competition of 1976, 183
    youth of Payton, 8–10, 11, 12, 13–14
Payton, Brittney:
    birth, 261, 292
    cancer diagnosis of Payton, 399–400
    current status, 428
    death of Payton, 415–16
    on fashionability of Payton, 258
    final months of Payton's life, 412
    Hall of Fame induction, 373, 374
    memorial service for Payton, 422–23
    and Nigel Smythe, 430
    parents' marriage, 344
    racing career of Payton, 356, 357
    relationship with Payton, 389
    retirement of Payton, 342, 351
    values of Payton, 387, 389–90
Payton, Connie Norwood:
    cancer diagnosis of Payton, 399–400, 403, 417–18
    in Chicago, 176, 230–31
    children, 238, 261
    as confidant of Payton, 381
    current status, 427
    death of Payton, 415
    divorce proposed by Payton, 380
    final months of Payton's life, 412, 414–15
    funeral of Payton, 419
    Hall of Fame induction, 371–75
    home, 271, 342–43
    infidelities of Payton, 231, 259, 372–75, 418
    at Jackson State, 96–99, 107–8, 109, 154, 161
    married life, 230–31, 257, 262, 343–44, 351, 380
    and Nigel Smythe, 418, 430
    perceptions of, 417–18
    salary of Payton, 269
    Super Bowl XX ring, 379
    wedding, 171
Payton, Edward Charles "Eddie" (brother):
    athleticism, 15–16, 19–20, 22–23
    current status, 428–29
    final hours of Payton's life, 415
    funeral of Payton, 420, 421–22
    Hall of Fame induction, 373
    and Holmes, 127
    at Jackson State, 57, 66, 67, 74, 80, 81, 83, 86
    in Memphis, 161
    professional football career, 83, 188, 240

relationship with brother, 57, 67, 343, 421, 428–29
scouting of, 72
youth, 6–14, 18, 19–20
Payton, Edward Charles "Peter" (father):
and Boston, 23
children, 6–7
and college recruiters, 56, 60
death, 207–10, 221, 342
desegregation, 32
infidelity of, 231
musicianship of Payton, 17
on nicknames, 5
and youth of Payton, 8–11, 13–14
Payton, Jarrett Walter (son):
birth, 238, 240, 287
cancer diagnosis of Payton, 399, 403
childhood, 259
college career, 401
current status, 427–28
death of Payton, 413–14, 415
final months of Payton's life, 412
Hall of Fame induction, 369, 371, 373–74
on Jheri curl of Payton, 258
and Nigel Smythe, 430
parents' marriage, 344
racing career of Payton, 356
relationship with Payton, 388–89
retirement of Payton, 351
services for Payton, 420, 422–23
on sweet tooth of Payton, 391
values of Payton, 387–88, 389–90
Payton, Pamela, 7, 9, 12–14, 373, 415, 430
Payton, Walter Jerry:
age discrepancy, 110
appearance, 108, 258
birth, 7
celebrity, 229, 231, 286–87, 381
character, 52–53, 111, 205–6
childhood (see youth of Payton)
children (see Payton, Brittney; Payton, Jarrett Walter; Smythe, Nigel)
confidants, 169–70, 177, 301, 327, 344–45, 381
death, 415–16, 418, 419 (see also cancer of Payton)
depression, 425
drug use, 187–88, 324, 345, 382
education (see Columbia High School; Jackson State College; John J. Jefferson High School)
fatherhood, 238–39, 260–61, 262, 292, 351, 387–90, 429–30

finances (see finances of Payton)
football career (see Chicago Bears; retirement of Payton)
funeral and memorial service, 419–20, 422–23
home, 263, 271, 342–43
humanity of, 425–26
memory, 426–27
nicknames, 7, 26, 74, 149, 424
parents (see Payton, Alyne Sibley; Payton, Edward Charles "Peter")
personality (see persona of Payton)
recreation (see pastimes and passions of Payton)
sexuality, 227 (see also women)
siblings (see Payton, Edward Charles "Eddie"; Payton, Pamela)
skills on the field (see athleticism of Payton)
social and political interests, 274, 274n, 316
wife (see Payton, Connie Norwood)
See also retirement of Payton
Payton Power, 381, 384, 388
Peacy, Brandon, 426–27
Pear, Dave, 128–29
Pearson, Drew, 131
Peiffer, Dan, 160, 162, 192, 199, 201, 202
Peoples, John, 61–62, 66, 73, 98
Perry, William "Refrigerator":
celebrity, 291, 292
drafted, 289–90
endorsements, 319
Miami Dolphins game, 295, 296
"Rappin' Together," 317
reactions to, 289–90
"Super Bowl Shuffle," 293
Super Bowl XX, 306–7, 312, 313, 315
persona of Payton:
anxiety, 162
charisma, 223–25
compassion, 228–29, 257, 286–88, 386, 407–8
"complicated" nature, 225–26, 227–28
desire for attention, 130, 164, 277, 292, 300, 301
enigmatic nature, 226, 286
immaturity, 173, 190, 198, 260
insecurity, 129, 174, 254, 288, 289, 300, 301, 425
mischievous nature, 27–28, 51, 108–9, 136–38, 164, 173–74, 355–56

moodiness, 88, 108, 218, 224, 230, 254, 292, 382, 411
perfectionism, 231–32, 326
reticence, 16, 154, 186
self-effacement, 178
selfishness, 251, 266, 313, 315
Philadelphia Eagles, 222, 234–35
Phillips, Bum, 278
Phillips, Reggie, 330
Phipps, Mike, 214, 222, 232, 233, 234
Pierson, Don:
on attitude of Payton, 218
on debut of Payton, 157
on drafting Payton, 147
on growing maturity of Payton, 198
on Halas, 145
on honesty of Payton, 300
on McClendon, 243
on 1975 season, 158, 159, 162, 170
on 1977 season, 198
on 1978 season, 221
on 1979 season, 232
on 1981 season, 243
on 1983 season, 266
on 1985 season, 300
on painkillers, 188
on quarterback issue, 232
on rushing record, 198, 266
on salaries of Bears, 214
Pifferini, Bob, 190
Pinckney, Mike, 255–57
Pittsburgh Steelers, 147, 150–51, 166–68
Pitzele, Lewis, 314–15
Plank, Doug, 154, 198, 203, 217, 237, 263
Playboy Club luncheons, 213n
Plumb, Ted, 252, 271, 299
Poole, Barney, 43–44
Potocnik, Ron, Jr., 268
Powers, Clyde, 202
Pullano, Eugene, 138–39

Quirk, Ginny:
cancer diagnosis of Payton, 395, 396, 400, 402, 403, 410, 411
as confidant of Payton, 381
current status, 429
death of Payton, 418–19
on death of Peter Payton, 209
on drive of Payton, 96
on Eddie Payton, 343
emotional instability of Payton, 383, 384
executor of Payton's will, 417
final months of Payton's life, 412, 413, 414–15
funeral of Payton, 419–20

Quirk, Ginny *(cont.)*
  Hall of Fame induction,
    372–73, 375
  on marriage of Payton, 380
  moodiness of Payton, 382
  on NFL franchise bid, 363
  on Nigel Smythe, 261
  on relationships of Payton,
    350–51, 370, 371, 380
  relationship with Payton,
    385–86
  responsibilities, 341, 344–45
  on Studebaker's, 347
  on Suhey, 410

race issues:
  black pride, 107–8
  and Brown, 275
  death threats, 216–17
  desegregation, 29–37, 41, 42,
    44–45, 126–27
  in high-school football, 51–52
  Holmes on, 126–27
  at Jackson State, 65–67
  in Mississippi, 3–5, 8, 11, 19,
    29–30, 53
  in professional sports, 154–55
Raines, Mike, 216
Ralston, John, 211
"Rappin' Together," 317
Rather, Bo, 141, 154, 162, 173, 183
Reagan, Ronald, 279, 316
Reamon, Tommy, 228
Reed, Frank, 178
Reel, Deana, 330–31
religious faith of Payton:
  in college, 93
  in early adulthood, 162, 217,
    231, 257
  and infidelities, 308
  in later life, 419
  in youth, 9–10
retirement of Payton, 341–90
  adjusting to, 341–43, 345–46,
    359, 381–82
  bodyguards, 386
  community service, 376–78
  confidants of Payton, 381
  drug use, 345, 382
  eating habits, 343, 382
  emotional instability during,
    382–84
  extramarital relationships
    during, 343–44, 349–51,
    356, 370–71, 380
  family life, 343–44, 351
  Hall of Fame induction, 368–75
  investments and business
    dealings, 346–49, 384–85,
    394
  loss of Super Bowl ring, 376–79

  and NFL team ownership bid,
    324, 325, 326, 341, 342,
    360–68
  potential return from, 358–60
  racing career, 351–57
  shooting incident, 348–49
  speaking engagements, 344,
    387, 408
  staff, 344–45
  suicide threats, 383, 384
Rhodes, Wayne, 173
Richards, Golden, 233
Riebandt, Jim, 278
Rives, Don, 153–54, 155, 164,
    197, 204
Robertson, Isiah, 190–91
Rogers, Jimmy, 279
Roland, Johnny:
  1983 season, 265
  1984 season, 282
  1987 season, 329
  and Payton's bid for St. Louis
    team, 364
  on rushing record, 266
  on Suhey, 327
  on telegraphing of Payton, 179
Roller, Dave, 191
Rothschild, Doug, 327
Rozelle, Pete, 144, 324–25, 342,
    360, 362
Runck, Dennis, 227
rushing competitions and records:
  Brown's all-purpose yards
    record, 273
  Brown's all-time rushing
    record, 264–65, 266, 267,
    269–71, 277–79, 305
  consecutive hundred-yard
    games, 292, 294, 296–97
  and drive of Payton, 277
  Harris–Payton competition,
    267, 273–74
  rushing title of 1979, 233
  rushing title of 1980, 238
  Simpson–Payton competition,
    181–85
  single-game rushing record,
    196–97
  single-season rushing record,
    200–204
  tracking of yardage, 251
Rust, Rod, 309
Ryan, Buddy:
  departure, 320
  and Ditka, 272, 289, 295–96
  on importance of Payton, 237
  Los Angeles Rams game, 303
  Miami Dolphins game,
    295–96
  on Perry, 289, 290
Ryan, Tim, 278

Saldi, Jay, 285
Sanders, Thomas, 299, 301, 326, 411
San Francisco 49ers, 177–78,
    233–34, 284–85, 290, 331–32
Sayers, Gale:
  criticisms of Payton, 215–16, 373
  and Ditka, 244, 246, 252
  and Halas, 145
  Payton compared to, 215, 327,
    425
  Payton's regard for, 140, 374
  retirement, 133
  rushing yards, 171, 184
Schembechler, Bo, 128
Schletzer, Jim, 228–29
Schmidt, Terry, 196
Schons, Ronald, 219
Schubert, Steve, 162, 164, 179,
    180–81, 197
Scott, James, 200, 248–49, 327
Seattle Seahawks, 273–74
Selmon, Dewey, 221
shooting incident at Studebaker's,
    348–49
Siemon, Jeff, 186–87
Simmons, Berl, 153
Simms, Phil, 328
Simpson, Bill, 189, 190
Simpson, O. J.:
  consecutive hundred-yard
    games, 296
  Ditka on '75 draft, 131–32
  funeral of Payton, 420
  Payton compared to, 187, 200,
    425
  rushing title competition of
    1976, 180–85
  salary, 214–16
  single-game rushing record,
    196
  single-season rushing record,
    200, 201
Sims, Billy, 238, 271*n*, 282, 288,
    425
Singletary, Mike:
  book deal, 319
  cancer diagnosis of Payton, 406
  as confidant of Payton, 301
  final months of Payton's life,
    413
  funeral of Payton, 420
  1985 season, 289, 294, 295, 297
  1986 season, 320
  1987 season, 330
  and Ryan, 272
  "Super Bowl Shuffle," 293, 299
  Super Bowl XX, 305, 310, 311
  on womanizing of Payton, 308,
    413
Sipe, Brian, 237
Skalbania, Nelson, 240–41

Skibinski, John, 188, 218, 237–38, 263, 264, 395
Slocum, R. C., 58, 59
Smythe, Angelina, 260–62, 430
Smythe, Nigel, 261–62, 292, 418, 425, 429–30
Sorey, Revie, 187, 192, 195, 199
*Soul Train* National Championship Dance-Off, 85–86
South's emphasis on football, 38
Southwestern Athletic Conference (SWAC), 55
spatting technique of Payton, 231–32
Spencer, Ollie, 211
*Sports Illustrated*:
    on Bears' 1984 season, 272
    on Brown, 270
    cancer diagnosis of Payton, 407
    College Football Preview issue, 112
    complaints addressed to, 288
    Payton on cover of, 179
    on racing career of Payton, 355
    on speed of Payton, 181
Staley, A. E., 143
Staubach, Roger, 131
Stevenson, Mark, 227
St. Louis Cardinals, 174, 216–17, 360
St. Louis NFL franchise bid, 360–68
Studebaker's, 346–49, 350, 361, 370, 384
Suhey, Matt:
    cancer diagnosis of Payton, 400, 407–8, 409–10, 411
    on celebrity of Payton, 257
    as confidant of Payton, 301, 327–28, 381
    death of Payton, 418–19
    as executor of Payton's will, 417, 433
    final months of Payton's life, 412–13
    1980 season, 236
    1984 season, 277, 278, 283
    1985 season, 303
    1987 season, 327, 330
    on pride of Payton, 277
    as replacement of Harper, 236
    Super Bowl XX, 310, 311
    "Super Bowl Shuffle," 280, 293, 294, 297, 298–99
Super Bowl XX, 304–15
    game, 310–12
    party preceding, 306–7
    Payton's participation, 309, 310–11
    postgame reaction of Payton, 304, 312–15, 316
    pregame attitude of Payton, 302, 305
    preparations for, 305–6, 309–10

ring, 376–79, 418
subsequent honors and endeavors, 316–17
*Superstars* competition, 197, 212–13
Sweetness (dog), 220–21, 221*n*
Sweetness (nickname), 149, 424

Tagge, Jerry, 151
Tampa Bay Buccaneers, 174, 221, 273, 328–29
Taylor, Ken, 295
Telander, Rick, 411
Thomas, Bob, 196, 203–4, 287–88, 289
Thomas, Calvin, 301, 306, 311, 322, 336, 411
Thompson, Arland, 227
Thompson, Bill, 184
Thrift, Cliff, 303, 305
Till, Emmett, 11, 43
Tobin, Bill, 134, 271–72
Tobin, Duke, 286
Tobin, Vince, 320
Tomczak, Mike, 319, 321, 328
Traficant, Jim, 246
Tucker, Kimm:
    cancer diagnosis of Payton, 393, 395, 402, 403, 404
    as confidant of Payton, 381
    on eating habits of Payton, 343
    emotional instability of Payton, 383, 384
    final months of Payton's life, 415
    funeral of Payton, 420
    Hall of Fame induction, 371
    on marriage of Payton, 344
    moodiness of Payton, 382
    on Nigel Smythe, 261–62
    relationship with Payton, 385–86
    responsibilities of, 341
*24 Karat Black Gold*, 84–86, 87, 259, 293

United States Football League (USFL), 267–69

Vainisi, Jerry, 269, 312, 318, 410
Valdiserri, Ken, 153, 226, 312, 313, 420
Vanderventer, Donna, 259
Van Horne, Keith, 265, 282, 328

Wagner, Bryan, 333
Walker, Herschel, 267
Waller, Bill, 102
Walsh, Bill, 211, 212, 233–34, 285, 290
Walter Payton Foundation, 341, 381
Walterscheid, Len, 198, 263
Washington Redskins, 178, 221–22, 284, 322, 333–36

Waters, Charlie, 224–25
Wattelet, Frank, 277
Watts, Rickey, 250
Wedge, Don, 178
Weishuhn, Clayton, 253
Wheaties cereal box, 316–17
White, Randy, 127, 131–32, 147, 148
White, Steve, 161
wife. *See* Payton, Connie Norwood
Williams, Dave, 236
Williams, Delvin, 178
Williams, Oliver, 228
Wilson, Otis, 236, 289, 297, 311, 321
Winston, Dennis "Dirt," 278
Winter, William, 102
women:
    attention from, 107, 255–57, 258–60
    college relationships, 87–88, 95–99, 107–8, 109
    disposability of, 262
    extramarital relationships with, 231, 258–62, 307–8, 343–44, 349–51, 356, 370–71, 380
    herpes diagnosis of Payton, 307–8
    high-school romantic interests, 48–51
    objectification of, 425
    Payton's preferences in, 108, 229–30, 307
    *See also* Gonzalez, Lita
World Football League, 131, 138–39, 152–53

Young, Rickey:
    and Holmes, 123, 124
    Mavericks game, 115
    on-field defense of Payton, 102, 106
    as Payton's roommate, 86
    professional career of, 161
    talent of, 89, 91
    and World Football League, 139
youth of Payton, 7–18
    athleticism, 12, 14, 16–17, 23–25, 40–41, 53
    and black community, 8–9, 10
    church attendance, 9–10
    discipline, 11, 12, 13–14
    home, 8
    musicianship, 17–18, 23, 25
    nicknames, 7
    pastimes, 7–8, 11–13, 17
    and racial climate, 8, 11, 15, 29–37
    *See also* Columbia High School; John J. Jefferson High School

In the final months of his life, Walter Payton received remarkable care from the Mayo Clinic, the worldwide leader in medical treatment, research, and education.

If, in the aftermath of completing this book, you find yourself inspired by Walter's life and are interested in making a contribution in his name, Mayo is a wonderful option—one Walter Payton surely would have appreciated.

Donations can be sent to:
Mayo Clinic: Department of Development
200 First Street SW
Rochester, MN 55905